CANADA AND THE AGE OF CONFLICT

C.P. STACEY

CANADA AND THE AGE OF CONFLICT
A History of Canadian
External Policies

VOLUME 2: 1921-1948
THE MACKENZIE KING ERA

UNIVERSITY OF TORONTO PRESS
TORONTO BUFFALO LONDON

© University of Toronto Press 1981
Toronto   Buffalo   London
Printed in Canada

ISBN 0-8020-2397-5 (cloth)
ISBN 0-8020-6420-5 (paper)

Canadian Cataloguing in Publication Data

Stacey, C.P. (Charles Perry), 1906-
Canada and the age of conflict

Vol. 2 published by University of Toronto Press.
Includes bibliographies and index.
Contents: v. 1. 1867-1921 – v. 2. 1921-1948.
ISBN 0-7705-1428-6 (v. 1). – ISBN 0-8020-2397-5 (v. 2
bound). – ISBN 0-8020-6420-5 (v. 2 pbk.)
1. Canada – Foreign relations. I. Title.
FC242.S73   327.71   C77-001317-1 rev
F1029.S73

This book has been published with the help of a grant from the Social Science
Federation of Canada, using funds provided by the Social Sciences and Humani-
ties Research Council of Canada. Publication also has been assisted by the Canada
Council and the Ontario Arts Council under their block grant programmes.

CONTENTS

Illustrations vii

Preface ix

1 Mackenzie King and the Reversal of Policy 3

2 The Reversal Completed, 1922-25 35

3 The Later Twenties: Prosperity and Problems 73

4 Depression Diplomacy 122

5 Turning-Points in North America and Africa 164

6 Towards a New Catastrophe 194

7 1939: The Outbreak 237

8 The Second World War: 1939-41 270

9 The Second World War: 1942-45 324

10 Facing a New Era, 1945-48 374

Epilogue 427

APPENDIX A Canadian External Trade:
Statistics of Imports and Exports, 1921-48 431

APPENDIX B Exports from Canada to the United Kingdom and the
United States: Selected Important Commodities, 1928-48 437

Abbreviations 439

References 441

Index 485

ILLUSTRATIONS

Mackenzie King at his Country Retreat (PAC, C-16768) 11

Knee Breeches and Equal Status (PAC, C-964) 84

Mackenzie King at the League of Nations, 1928 (PAC, C-9055) 101

Hopeful Arrivals at the Imperial Economic Conference, Ottawa, 1932
(PAC, C-81448) 141

Signing the Canadian-American Trade Agreement,
Washington, 1935 (PAC, C-31017) 175

Franklin and Mackenzie on a Gala Day (PAC, C-26031) 225

'The People of the United States Will Not Stand Idly By'
(PAC, PA-52568) 227

Arcadian Interlude, 1939 (PAC, PA-76381) 247

Conference of the Powers, 1941 (PAC, PA-119399) 290

Marshalling Lancasters Against Stuttgart
(Canadian War Museum, 11836) 297

First Meeting of the Canadian-American Permanent Joint Board
on Defence, Ottawa, August 1940 (PAC, C-5767) 313

A Host and Two Guests, Quebec, 1943 (PAC, C-14170) 335

Canadian Soldiers and Sailors Together on D Day
(PAC, CM-2176) 346

'The Speech Would Have Been More Successful Had It Been Shorter'
(PAC, C-13194) 368

Canada at San Francisco (PAC, C-18352) 383

'The Conference was Largely an Exercise in Frustration'
(PAC, C-31312) 388

Malcolm MacDonald Signing the Anglo-Canadian Financial Agreement,
1946 (PAC, PA-112297) 401

PREFACE

This second and final volume of *Canada and the Age of Conflict* deals with the years 1921-48. Except for Arthur Meighen's brief moment of office in 1926 and the Depression regime of R.B. Bennett, William Lyon Mackenzie King was Prime Minister of Canada for this whole period, and it has seemed suitable to give the volume the sub-title *The Mackenzie King Era*.

Some readers may feel that the book concentrates too much upon the men who held the office of Prime Minister during these twenty-seven momentous years, but I do not feel disposed to apologize for this emphasis. Quite apart from the fact that for almost the whole period the Prime Minister was also Secretary of State for External Affairs, nothing has impressed me more in the course of this study than the overmastering importance of the office of Prime Minister. To a remarkable extent the policies of the government of Canada were essentially the personal policies of the man who held that office, and nowhere was this more clearly the case than in the field of external affairs. It is fortunate for the historian that the man who presided in the East Block in Ottawa for twenty-one years was a notable preserver of paper and kept one of the most remarkable diaries in human annals. The diary helps us find our way through the grim inter-war period, the grimmer times of the Second World War, and the onset of the new and complex problems that confront the historian after 1945; though there are times, the reader will discover, when even this extraordinary document lets us down.

This book is comparatively short, and it deals with a long and crowded era. I have had to omit many things, and to deal with others very briefly. I have tried to concentrate upon the topics that seem to me important, and to avoid side-alleys. Many readers, I am sure, will disagree with my choices.

The kindness of many people has helped me in my enterprise. At the Public Archives of Canada, where a great deal of the work was done, I have special debts to J.W. O'Brien, Mrs J.M. White, Peter Robertson, and particularly Barbara Wilson. The Historical Division of the Department of External Affairs in Ottawa was most helpful, particularly by making available to me the documents collected for future but as yet unpublished volumes of the invaluable series *Documents on Canadian External Relations*; I am especially grateful to Donald M. Page and J.F. Hilliker. Hugh Halliday of the Canadian War Museum kindly found an illustration I needed. My former student and officer Jack Granatstein, with great generosity, allowed me to use his large collection of photocopies of documents in the Public Record Office, London, chiefly of the years 1938-48; these papers have made an important contribution to the book. Douglas LePan, Robert Bothwell, and Norman Hillmer have helped with advice at various points. Patricia Kennedy of Massey College, who among her other distinctions is the best typist in North America, kindly typed the manuscript. Some other debts, particularly those to helpful former students, are acknowledged in detail in the text or the references.

In the first volume I acknowledged generous grants from the University of Toronto and the Canada Council. I am happy to say that the writing (as distinct from the publication) of the present volume has been carried out without the aid of any grant from anybody.

C.P.S.

Massey College in the University of Toronto

CANADA AND THE AGE OF CONFLICT

CHAPTER ONE

MACKENZIE KING
AND THE REVERSAL OF POLICY

NEW MAN, NEW POLITICS

On December 29, 1921, William Lyon Mackenzie King was sworn in as Prime Minister of Canada, realizing an ambition he had nourished for at least two decades.[1] The Mackenzie King era of Canadian history was beginning.

In retrospect the general election of December 6, 1921 is an important turning-point in the history of Canadian external policies, yet those policies were not an issue in the election; they were never placed before the voters. The Liberals, it is true, had a platform, approved at the same convention of 1919 that selected King as leader.[2] We have already seen that it contained a plank on 'Canadian Autonomy' which demanded that any change in Canada's relation to the Empire should, after passage by Parliament, be submitted to the people in a referendum. This curious constitutional suggestion has remained a dead letter; there has never been a referendum on Canada's relations with the Commonwealth or the rest of the world, though those relations have been transformed since 1919, largely under Liberal auspices. King, breaking with tradition, issued no election manifesto (his early mentor, Sir William Mulock, had warned him against such things);[3] he did publish a statement just before the election which did nothing much but promise 'a government of the country's ablest men.'[4] Meighen issued a manifesto, the last of its species; it declared that Canada's destiny was 'nationhood within the British Empire' combined with 'the fullest autonomy,' and went on at much greater length to glorify the protective tariff.[5] During the campaign the contending leaders, it has been said, talked on every subject under the sun except Canada's status in the Empire.[6]

The election, we have already seen, was a Conservative disaster; Meighen's party took only 50 seats. It was still short of being a total Liberal victory. King's party got 117 seats (if one includes the lone Independent Liberal); but the Progressive party (primarily an organization of Western farmers) took 64. The Liberals were just short of an absolute majority in a house of 235 seats.[7] It was a notable fact that they had taken every riding in Quebec, Nova Scotia, and Prince Edward Island.

In spite of the absence of discussion of external affairs in the campaign, no one could doubt the significance of the election in this respect. 'Quebec dominates the situation in the House of Commons'; so King had written early in 1919 (Volume I, page 285). It was even truer now. And the solid bloc of 65 seats that Quebec had given the Liberals was unquestionably a manifestation of French-Canadian isolationism, a protest against the war and above all against the war's most hated by-product: conscription. Furthermore, the Progressives, whose support King needed and whom it was his object to absorb into his own party, were in general scarcely less isolationist in their views than the French. It should be noted, however, that the Farmers' Platform of 1918, the nearest thing to a national programme which the various Progressive groups had available in the election, did approve 'a League of Nations';[8] whereas the Liberal convention the next year, meeting in the midst of the League controversy in the United States, carefully avoided the whole question.

We said with respect to the events of 1911 that in that year the citadel of government was transferred from Quebec to Ontario, and that the result in terms of Canadian external policies was easily predictable (Volume I, page 150). In 1921 the balance of political power shifted again. The new government, with its 65 seats in Quebec, had been able to get only 21 in Ontario; the Conservatives, in spite of Progressive inroads, still held 37 there. Given this situation, and given also the general disillusionment with overseas adventures and commitments that we have noted, it was to be expected that Mackenzie King's government would swing back towards the policies pursued by its Liberal predecessor before 1911. It was symbolic that King's first important act as Secretary of State for External Affairs was to rush to the defence of Sir Wilfrid Laurier's Naval Defence Act of 1910 (Volume I, page 354).

King's domestic party connection certainly affected his relations with British governments. Canadian Liberals and Conservatives had always tended to identify their parties with those in the United Kingdom bearing the same names. King's intense dislike for Tories in Canada extended to the British variety; and his almost superstitious regard for the mere word Liberal led him to give the British party of that name the same respect that he gave his own. This feeling was reinforced by personal relationships. He received much courtesy from members of H.H. Asquith's Liberal cabinet when in England in 1908; in particular, a visit to Fallodon left him a lifetime admirer of Sir Edward Grey. In 1914 the fact that the British government was Liberal reconciled him to the Empire's involvement in the European war. He felt at first that Asquith, Grey, and Haldane would prevent Britain's going to war with Germany, whereas 'If the other party were in power war with Germany wd. be a certainty.' Later, Grey's speech in Parliament on August 3, 'a noble, dignified & righteous utterance,' left King feeling that this Liberal war had to be accepted.

In these circumstances it may be thought unfortunate that the war extinguished the British Liberal party as a powerful factor in national affairs. Had that party governed between the two World Wars, political relations between Canada and Britain would have been somewhat different. King would certainly have been more favourably disposed towards Liberal governments than he was towards the Conservative ones with which he actually had to deal; and while the ultimate result, in terms of the constitution of the Commonwealth, would probably have been much the same, it might have been arrived at considerably more smoothly.[9]

King did not like the Lloyd George coalition which was in power in Britain when he himself became Prime Minister of Canada. He clearly regarded it, not without reason, as Tory in all but name. His own loyalty was to Asquith and his associates who had been pushed out by Lloyd George in 1916. Writing favourably of the Asquith cabinet in his diary in 1914, he never mentions Lloyd George, and incidentally calls Winston Churchill 'the one dangerous factor.' It is likely that the manner in which Lloyd George became Prime Minister repelled him, and it may be that he was further alienated by Lloyd George's later association with the Canadian Conservatives in the Imperial War Cabinet.

It is not irrelevant to say a word here about King's personal life. In spite of the conviction he had recorded in his diary in 1919, that he could not live the 'cruel life' of politics 'without a home & someone to love & to be loved by,'[10] and in spite of many more or less promising attachments, he was still a bachelor, as indeed he was to remain throughout his life. But beginning in 1918 he had formed a close friendship with Mrs Godfroy B. Patteson of Ottawa, and Joan Patteson in effect was now providing for him (with her husband's apparently rather grumpy acquiescence) the home he had so felt the need of since his mother's death in 1917. This platonic friendship afforded him a much appreciated refuge and base during the campaign of 1921, as it did for the rest of his career. It is arguable that without it that career might have been considerably less successful.[11]

The government changed at the end of 1921, abruptly. The government's advisers on external policy also changed, but this change was more gradual. At the cost of some violence to precise chronology, it may be described here.

For the moment, it is true, the official advisers who had served Borden and Meighen remained; but they were not listened to and indeed were almost never consulted. The permanent head of the tiny Department of External Affairs was still Sir Joseph Pope; but apart from the fact that, as we have seen, Sir Joseph had no aspiration to be a maker of policy (and he was a thorough-going colonial with no use for 'equality of status and suchlike nonsense'), his health had failed in October 1921 and the department saw little of him thereafter.[12] For years before that the active element in the department had been the Legal Adviser, Loring Christie, whom we have noted functioning as the real source of policy under Meighen. At the moment when King came to power, Christie was absent from Ottawa, assisting Sir Robert Borden at the Washington Conference; but it is evident that even had he been available King would not have been disposed to consult him. It tells a good deal about King and his views that at this point he turned for advice to the author of *The Kingdom Papers* and *The Independence Papers*, John S. Ewart (Volume I, pages 299, 354).

The Christie story is distressing. Christie, as a good civil servant, remained at his post after the change of government, presumably prepared to serve King as he had served Borden and Meighen. It appeared for a moment that a satisfactory relationship might develop. King wrote in his diary on February 14, 1922, after one of those great Ottawa observances, a Canadian Club luncheon: 'Christie of the External affairs branch turned up at the luncheon and we had a talk together after. It went off better than I had anticipated, as I feared the effect of changed administration upon him after his close association with Sir Robert Borden & Meighen. We had a good talk together ...' This was a false dawn. There is no evidence that King ever gave Christie a chance to show that he was ready to give him loyal service. Christie simply found that he was not consulted; and it appears that beginning in March 1923 (when he was, in fact, about to resign) he was denied access to cables from the British Foreign Office.[13] In these circumstances Christie developed a healthy hatred for King; we find him gleefully repeating another man's assessment of the Prime Minister: 'He is such a pompous ass that an orang-outang that would flatter him could choose its own reward.'[14] Christie discussed his situation with his old chief, Sir Robert Borden, who recorded it in his diary: 'Mackenzie King and [W.S.] Fielding have treated him abominably. Fielding, who is essentially small and jealous, was petty enough to resent the printing of my report on the Washington Conference, for which he blamed Christie. King is deliberately driving him out of the service and will hypocritically feign regret when Christie retires.'[15]

This seems to have been an unpleasantly accurate prophecy. Christie did not go without representations being made on his behalf. In February 1923 the Progressive, T.A. Crerar, whom King had tried to inveigle into his cabinet in 1921, wrote King saying that he had heard a rumour that Christie proposed to leave the Department of External Affairs and that he considered this would be unfortunate: 'I venture to say, that if Mr. Christie goes there is no one with the knowledge in the Department to properly secure and analyze the information that is necessary for a wise and prudent conduct of policy.' He recommended that Christie should succeed Pope as deputy head of the department. King wrote back asserting that he had 'a very high opinion of Mr. Christie's character and ability' and promising to keep Crerar's suggestion in mind.[16] This had no, or very little, effect. (Crerar was no longer a party leader and had resigned from the House of Commons.) In an interview with the Prime Minister on March 10, 1923, Christie, who had lately suffered the loss of both his parents, told him he proposed to take some leave in England and offered to resign at once. 'He was good enough,' Christie wrote to Borden, 'to express regret on behalf of himself and his colleagues at the situation, and he himself suggested at once that I should rather take my regular leave of absence now and leave the other question until my return.'[17] But in the following May Christie resigned, to go into a financial house in London. He wrote to N.W. Rowell: 'I am sorry to leave the work I have been on during the past eight or nine years but in reality the work has left me, and I see nothing else for it but to take the step I have taken.'[18]

This is not the last of the story. Christie's views changed, as we shall see (below, page 82), and in 1935, in the last days of the Bennett administration, he returned to the Department of External Affairs. In 1939 King appointed him Minister to Washington. Before his departure the two men had another conversation. King had now convinced himself that he had in fact offered Christie the under-secretaryship in 1923. The Prime Minister wrote in his diary: 'I said to him it was a double pleasure to me [to see him going to Washington] as he would recall I had, at one time, offered him the position which Dr. S.[kelton] now holds ... I said to him that some people, at the time, had tried to create the impression that I was responsible for his leaving the service instead of being the one that really wished to retain him for the highest position in External Affairs.'[19] One wonders what Christie's thoughts were.

In the end the person who succeeded both to Sir Joseph Pope's appointment and to the influence which Christie had enjoyed under Borden and Meighen was Oscar Douglas Skelton.

Skelton, a native Canadian of Irish extraction, had had a distinguished academic career. At the time when he forsook university life for Ottawa, he was head of the Department of Political and Economic Science and Dean of Arts at Queen's University, Kingston, Ontario. He was the author of a considerable list of political and historical works; very notably, he wrote the authorized biography of Sir Wilfrid Laurier, published in 1921. He had been on friendly terms with Laurier and was a strong Liberal partisan.[20] He was also an old acquaintance of King's. In 1911 he prepared a report on prices for King's department – Labour – and after King's and the government's defeat in the election of that year Skelton wrote him a letter of encouragement concluding, 'I know that whether you take another seat in Parliament or decide to enter other work for a few years the country will receive from you the same progressive and effective service given in the precedent-setting years of the Ministry of Labour. And ahead – no limit.'[21] When King's tedious *Industry and Humanity* was published, Skelton welcomed it with a review which, though not fulsome, seems warmer than it really deserves.[22] If we are not to write him off as a sycophant, he must be accounted a genuine admirer of King's.

On January 21, 1922 – three weeks before King's interview with Christie on a similar occasion – Skelton addressed the Ottawa Canadian Club on 'Canada and Foreign Policy.' The speech was a vigorous attack on the concept of a unified foreign policy formulated by consultation between Commonwealth governments and executed through the British Foreign Office. This, he said, was 'a reversal of the lines upon which we have been developing for the past two generations.' He argued persuasively that 'each part of the Empire has its own foreign affairs and must substantially have its own foreign policy in dealing with those affairs.'[23] It has been suggested that Skelton may possibly have been 'preaching for a call.'[24] If so, he succeeded. Mackenzie King heard him speak, and wrote in his diary afterwards: 'Skelton's address would make an excellent foundation for Canadian policy on External Affairs, and Skelton himself would make an excellent man for that department. At the luncheon I told him that he might be wanted there one day. He might make a very good Under-Secretary of State in succession to Sir Joseph Pope. He certainly has the knowledge & the right point of view. The department as at present constituted is a Tory hive [?].' Christie was the chief inhabitant of the hive. It is a fair assumption that King's mind was essentially made up before he talked to Christie on February 14, and that Crerar's letter was a waste of ink.

There was, however, some delay before Skelton was brought in, and his absorption into the Department of External Affairs was a gradual process. He was first employed in 1923 as an adviser to King before and during the Imperial Conference of that year (below, page 66). (The telegram King sent him offering this temporary assignment remarked: 'Colleagues in Council agree with me that this opportunity might have far-reaching consequences of first importance to yourself.') In 1924 he became a Counsellor in the department, on leave from Queen's University. That year he went to Geneva to attend the Assembly of the League of Nations.[25] Only in 1925 did he finally change careers, when Sir Joseph Pope at last retired and Skelton succeeded him. On March 31 Sir Joseph wrote in his diary: 'Went to my old office for the last time. Met Dr. Skelton. Introduced him to Mr. Walker and Baker,* and put him in possession of the Department.'[27] Skelton remained in firm possession of the department until his death in 1941.

While the nature of Mackenzie King's relationship with O.D. Skelton will emerge increasingly as we proceed, some general remarks may here be made about it. There is no doubt that King, a notoriously difficult man to serve, gave Skelton more of his confidence than he ever gave to any other civil servant. Another close associate of King's has described Skelton as his 'closest adviser on all public affairs, domestic as well as external.'[28]

---

* W.H. Walker, a university graduate, was Assistant Under Secretary of State for External Affairs from 1909 to 1933. Frederick M. Baker, also a veteran of the very early days of the department, was at this time Accountant and Chief Clerk. Essentially, this was the department. There was no replacement of Christie as Legal Adviser. Temporarily, the Chief Electoral Officer, O.M. Biggar, was designated early in 1924 to prepare legal opinions required on external matters. The office of Legal Adviser was abolished by order-in-council PC 79/1394, August 22, 1925, but was revived in 1929 when John E. Read was appointed.[26] The salary of the Legal Adviser ($5,000) was applied in 1924 to the office of Counsellor set up for Skelton; see King's statement in House of Commons, June 9, 1924.

Because the Prime Minister was also Secretary of State for External Affairs, he was Skelton's own Minister, and Skelton had an access to him that no other civil servant enjoyed. The deputy heads of other departments, however important the department or trusted the individual, had to *get* in to see King. Skelton *was* in. This, combined with his own distinguished abilities and King's confidence, made him the most powerful civil servant in Canadian history.

From the moment when Skelton first began to work in External Affairs, King was delighted with him.[29] Skelton possessed an industry and a capacity for detailed work that matched King's own; he was a practised and pungent writer; and (though King would certainly not have admitted it) he had a stronger and sharper intellect than the Prime Minister's. Inevitably in these circumstances the question arises, Was Skelton the originator of the King system of foreign policy? Did King get his ideas from Skelton? The answer appears to have been given in the previous volume. Those who examine King's statements in Parliament in 1920, on the Bulgarian treaty and on Canadian representation in Washington, will find in them the essence of his later policies and, one may say, the essence of Skelton's Canadian Club speech too. The most striking thing about King's ideas is how very little they changed during his long career. In Skelton's speech he recognized his own ideas, or ideas similar to his own, put forward with a force and skill that he himself would have found difficult to match; and he seems to have felt at once that here was one who might be an ideal associate and assistant in his task at External Affairs.

It should be remembered that in spite of this it was a year and a half before King first had the benefit of Skelton's help. During this period, declining to make use of Christie, he operated essentially without advice. On this basis, he negotiated the Chanak crisis in the autumn of 1922 (below, pages 18-27); and Skelton, from his academic fastness at Queen's, applauded him in terms that this time did approach the fulsome:[30] 'You have made history. Never again will a Canadian Government be stampeded against its better judgment into giving blank cheques to British diplomacy, now that your Government has set this example of firm and self-respecting deliberation.' When in the following year Skelton joined King for the Imperial Conference, he was hitching his wagon to the star of a statesman who had identified himself with a definite concept of imperial relations, a concept to which Skelton had declared his allegiance. He clearly did not go to Ottawa in the hope of introducing a totally new set of ideas into the Department of External Affairs; he went there to

MACKENZIE KING AT HIS COUNTRY RETREAT

The Prime Minister sitting on the steps of his original Kingsmere cottage. With him are his sister Jennie (Mrs H.M. Lay) and his closest official adviser, O.D. Skelton, the Under Secretary of State for External Affairs.

assist in putting into practice ideas which King had already proclaimed publicly and which Skelton thoroughly approved.

It does not follow by any means that King and Skelton were pursuing the same goals or harbouring the same basic assumptions. British politicians, who in general disliked and distrusted them about equally, and who did not trouble themselves to be students of Canadian affairs or personalities, would have been impatient of such distinctions, arguing that differences in ultimate goals meant little; in immediate practice, King and Skelton were united in pursuing policies that slackened Canada's ties to the Empire and therefore weakened the Empire itself. Differences however there were, and they were important.

At bottom, Mackenzie King thought of himself as British. He attached enormous importance to his heritage from his grandfather, the rebel of 1837 (Volume I, page 298); he considered himself a man of destiny entrusted by God with the mission of carrying on William Lyon Mackenzie's work.[31] But he did not think of Mackenzie as a foe of the British connection; on the contrary, he contrived to regard him as a worker for union between Canada and Britain.[32] The Tory 'centralizers' were, in King's book, the real enemies of the Commonwealth idea; in 1944 he spoke of himself as taking up the 'perpetual struggle to save the Empire despite all that Tories' policies will do.'[33] A couple of years earlier he wrote, concerning his apprehension that American military activity in Canada might bring the country into the United States' 'orbit': 'I am strongly opposed to anything of the kind. I want to see Canada continue to develop as a nation, to be, in time, as our country certainly will, the greatest of nations of the British Commonwealth.'[34] Many people in London, and many in Canada too, measuring these opinions against King's actions, would have accounted them hypocritical; but the careful reader of his diary will be convinced that they were sincerely held.

No such sentiments are recorded of Skelton. Like King, he can be tagged a 'Canadian nationalist' (how many eminent Canadians cannot?) and an 'isolationist' – a term less universally deserved. But he was something more. The influences that formed his ideas and prejudices remain rather obscure. The Irish nationalist opinions attributed to his father may be significant. One should also note an incident of his early career, when he applied for admission to the Indian Civil Service. Contrary to some reports, he passed the examination – no small achievement for a young Canadian, whose academic training and background were unlikely to impress an English board in 1901; but he then withdrew, possibly because a medical examination had disclosed weak eyesight.[35] The whole episode is enigmatic and in the absence of any account from Skelton himself one can only speculate as to whether it left him with a sense of grievance against Britain or the British governing class. But a letter[36] he wrote the following year from the United States, where he was in temporary employment, tells much about his views. It is concerned with the preferential trade agitation and the 'imperialist flood' then 'running high':

Every time I pick up a Canadian paper now and read the enthusiastically Britisher speeches or editorials or Board of Trade debates I wonder where I'm at and faint-hearted fears trouble me that perhaps after all the ideal I've always cherished, Canadian independence, is fated to be only an ideal. However, it's some consolation that it can't be any more impracticable than the policy of those who believe they can afford to neglect the U.S. as a factor in Canada's future, pile up tariff barriers & deepen national prejudices in a vain attempt to deflect the current of destiny, and who believe there can be any real or lasting community of interest between Canada and Australia or Timbuctoo, or whatever other part of the map a Jingoistic spree may chance to paint red ...

The tone of Skelton's memoranda reminds one of Dafoe's criticism of John S. Ewart (Volume I, page 300). Skelton, addressing his audience of one, the Prime Minister, speaks in much the same terms of consistent hostility to British policy that Ewart used in addressing everybody who would listen. Vincent Massey bluntly called Skelton anti-British.[37] Massey was too determinedly British himself to be an impartial witness. But King, normally prejudiced in Skelton's favour, said something very similar at least once. Less than a year before the outbreak of the Second World War, when Skelton was giving freer rein than usual to his views, King wrote in his diary:[38] '... I felt more and more – the materialistic "scientific" point of view which Skelton had in all things – a critical frame of mind, also a "republican" attitude. I felt his negative viewpoint and inferiority complex in so many things – a real antagonism towards monarchical institutions, and Britain, a sort of communist sympathy – lack of larger view in reference to world affairs – an isolated Canada – which I cannot accept. It ... raised a sort of wall of separation between us. He seeks to dominate one's thought, is intellectually arrogant in some respects ... I can see I must control policy ... lead and not be controlled, while in many ways he is the best of Counsellors and guides ...'

An entry in King's diary for 1924 leaves one wondering whether perhaps he had not toyed with the idea of offering the under-secretaryship to Ewart. It also gives us an illuminating glimpse of King's own views. On January 18 Ewart and Skelton were both guests of King at dinner. He wrote later: 'Ewart is very able & better informed than any one in Canada on foreign affairs, but too extreme. Is for separation. I am not, I believe in the Br. Empire as a "Cooperative Commonwealth." Skelton, I think, has modified his [own] views somewhat ...' Certainly the appointment of Ewart would have raised a storm. And it seems evident that King harboured some apprehensions about Skelton's opinions, and was seeking to reassure himself. It may be seriously doubted whether the Doctor had in fact modified his own views in any important particular.

In the early days of King's first administration another eminent Canadian offered him free public advice on foreign policy in an address delivered at (where else?) the Ottawa Canadian Club. This was Sir Clifford Sifton, who spoke, with the Prime Minister as one of his auditors, on 'The Political Status of Canada.' He dwelt, in a style not unlike Ewart's, on the surviving formal limitations on Canadian sovereignty and the desirability of Parliament's acting to remove them. But like Skelton he assailed particularly the idea of a common Empire foreign policy, which Lloyd George had, rather unwisely, advertised in a recent speech; decisions involving participation in war, he said, should be made in Ottawa and not elsewhere. 'I think the people of Canada will demand that responsibility for contributing to any war shall rest exclusively with the Parliament of Canada.' King wrote in his diary that it was a 'splendid address.' That evening he called on Sifton and they had 'a good talk over Canada's status matters.'[39]

THE POST-WAR ECONOMY

The Canada that emerged from the First World War was a different country from the one that had gone into the conflict so light-heartedly in 1914. It had been through an appalling experience. The losses and the victories alike had no parallel in the Dominion's history. The political consequences would appear fully only with the passage of years. The economic results seemed evident almost at once. Unlike many countries, Canada was richer at the end of the war than at the beginning. A friendly English historian wrote with a touch of envy: 'She earned what she reaped, but she reaped much. She gave greatly to the war and in turn the war gave much to her.'[40]

The industrial revolution that took place in Canada during the war is demonstrated (and exaggerated) by some dramatic statistics. In the fiscal year 1913-14 the Dominion exported to the United Kingdom only $8,583,540 worth of manufactured goods. In 1916-17 the amount rose to

$339,013,448.[41] The goods exported were largely shells. The gross value of production of manufactured goods rose from $1,151,722,000 in 1910 to $3,165,139,000 in 1918,[42] the increase being partly due to the contemporary inflation of prices. The wartime production was large in quantity but limited in variety: shells (primarily), ships, and aircraft. Inevitably it caused an expansion of the steel industry; and even when the demand for these very specialized commodities collapsed at the peace, the industry did not fall back to its old status. Urbanization went hand in hand with industrialization; though in 1911 only 3,147,000 Canadians are reckoned to have been town-dwellers as compared with 4,059,000 countrymen, by 1921 the urban population was not much more than 250,000 below the rural one, and in 1931 the urban figure was up to 5,574,000 as compared to 4,802,000 for the country.[43]

These developments must not be over-emphasized, particularly in terms of foreign trade. After the First World War Canada was on the way to becoming an industrial nation. But even after the further industrial growth accompanying the Second War, industry 'modified and supplemented' rather than supplanted the older national economic patterns. Canadian industry found its markets largely within Canada; 'the older staples, such as wheat, fish, and lumber, continue to provide a livelihood for millions of Canadians and the bulk of Canada's earnings in international trade.'[44] The wheat market is still a matter of primary importance to the Canadian economy, as it has been since the wheat boom began about the turn of the century. The expansion of the pulp and paper industry, which continued to find its market mainly in the United States, was a striking feature of the immediate post-war years.

Britain had given greatly to the war, but the war gave nothing to her except a barren victory. The debilitating effort of four years of conflict left a legacy of economic distress whose effect is still felt. The United States, in contrast, had exerted in proportion a much smaller war effort, and its resources were vastly greater. It came out of the war wealthier and more powerful than ever, well able to disregard 'the envy of less happier lands.' These new circumstances were reflected in the two countries' post-war economic relations with Canada.

In 1914 the United States' capital investment in Canada was only about one-third that of the United Kingdom. During the war it very nearly doubled, while Britain's remained roughly constant. After the war American capital continued to pour into Canada. Britain had less capital available for investment; and British investors may have been repelled by the aftermath in 1921 of the nationalization of the Grand Trunk Railway, when an arbitration board decided that the holders of the railway's preference and common shares – most of whom lived in the United Kingdom – deserved no compensation.[45] In 1922 American investment in Canada surpassed British for the first time, and it galloped ahead thereafter. The United States had plenty of money to invest, and there was money to be made in Canada. Moreover, the Canadian tariff encouraged American corporations to open branch plants in Canada, in order to reach the protected Canadian market. A key manufacturing industry of the new age, the motor-car industry, had been passing through a process of concentration and at the same time coming under U.S. control. The greatest landmark here was the acquisition of the McLaughlin Motor Car Co Ltd by General Motors late in 1918.[46]

In July 1923 President Harding, returning from Alaska, stopped off very briefly at Vancouver (it was the first time an American President had visited Canada while in office). Presumably wishing to say what was agreeable to his hosts, he commented: 'Since the Armistice, I am informed, approximately $2,500,000,000 has found its way from the United States into Canada for investment. That is a huge sum of money and I have no doubt is employed safely for us and helpfully for you.' It appears that the audience saw nothing in this remark to dispute.[47] The time was still distant when Canadians in any numbers would talk of the need for 'buying back Canada' from the United States.

The general pattern of Canadian external trade after the war was not greatly different from what it had been before. As at the beginning of the century, Canada continued to sell more to the United Kingdom than she bought from it, and to buy more from the United States than she sold to it.[48] The tariff policies of the two other countries of the Triangle varied the pattern without fundamentally disturbing it. The conservative postwar reaction in the United States produced a return to high tariffs which inevitably meant difficulties for and with Canada (below, page 45). Britain's economic troubles led to demands for a return to protection there. The tariffs introduced on a narrow range of commodities during and immediately after the war included provision for imperial preference; this incidentally was an additional argument for the establishment of American branch plants in Canada, since their products could enter the United Kingdom at preferential rates. But the British public was not ready for any general abandonment of the hallowed policy of free trade, and certainly not for taxes on food products, which were Canada's chief exports to Britain. In 1923 the Baldwin government espoused protection (though not food taxes) and was beaten in a general election.[49] The restoration of protection would have to await another great economic crisis.

STILL LESS DEFENCE

Mackenzie King had never had any connection with the armed forces. He was unmilitary and anti-military; in this as in many other respects not an untypical Canadian. Visiting Victoria, BC, in 1920 he went over the dockyard and the Naval College and was unfavourably impressed; he wrote in his diary: 'The whole institution with the "Rainbow" at the wharf seemed a great waste of public money. Idle officers, 15 mounted police etc. It is shameful the waste on these military & naval fads ...'[50] By the time King took office the Conservatives had established the country's defences on an extremely modest basis (Volume I, pages 321-6); but King was determined to make further cuts, and did. On February 13, 1922, he recorded that a cabinet meeting had got 'a good deal straightened out on consolidation of defence forces.' With respect to the Navy, the government told the sailors to cut their estimates from $2,500,000 to $1,500,000; they in turn decided that the best way to use this paltry sum was to set up a naval reserve force with units across Canada which might foster popular interest in naval affairs and provide a basis for mobilization in time of war. Apart from some minesweepers, all the ships were disposed of except the two destroyers. These, manned by a tiny professional force, would serve for training the volunteer reserve.[51] Thus the Navy was reduced to the barest minimum. Nevertheless, the remark made with respect to Conservative policy (Volume I, page 324) may be repeated here: the essential nucleus of a national naval force continued to exist.

The 'consolidation' which King had referred to was effected by the National Defence Act which became law in June 1922.[52] By it one minister became responsible for all three defence forces, those formerly governed under the Militia Act, the Naval Service Act, and the Air Board Act of 1919. Under the new regime defence expenditure as a whole declined until in the fiscal year 1924-5 it was a little less than $13,500,000.[53] Inevitably, the forces maintained were quite negligible as an element in the international balance of power; they were at best a support to civil authority at home and a foundation upon which larger forces could, after considerable passage of time, be raised in case of war.

CHANAK

Some of the people who heard Clifford Sifton's speech to the Ottawa Canadian Club in April 1922 (above, page 14) may have wondered five months later if Sifton had some kind of second sight. 'According to Mr.

Lloyd George,' he had said, 'we have agreed to become jointly responsible for everything they [the British government] do, and, consequently, if they get into a war over oil concessions in Mesopotamia or Persia and get an army massacred or captured, as has happened before, our Government is liable to get a cable calling on it to implement its responsibility and send an army to take part in the war.'[54] In September a British army was suddenly in jeopardy on the shores of the Dardanelles; and the cable duly arrived.

A good deal has been written about the 'Chanak affair';[55] but it is too important to pass over briefly. In 1921-2 Turkish nationalism, directed by the genius of Mustapha Kemal Pasha, upset the Treaty of Sèvres, which Canada had gone through the motions of signing (Volume I, page 257). That treaty had partitioned Turkish Asia Minor and in particular had handed over a large slice of territory centring on Smyrna to Greece. In the summer of 1922 Kemal's army inflicted a shattering defeat on the Greeks. On September 9 it occupied and sacked Smyrna (now Izmir).[56] Immediately it was threatening the few battalions of British troops which, backed by the Mediterranean Fleet, were holding Constantinople and a 'neutral zone' around the Straits; the outpost at Chanak on the Asiatic shore of the Dardanelles was particularly exposed.

Although the French and the Italians, both of whom had been awarded spheres of influence in Anatolia under the Treaty of Sèvres, were now showing signs of making terms with the resurgent Turk, the Lloyd George coalition government decided to stand firm. For the moment, discussion of its motives can wait; let us describe what it did. In the afternoon of Friday, September 15, the cabinet met and resolved to reinforce Chanak with what forces were available in the Mediterranean; to ask help from France, Italy, and the Allied Balkan nations; and to invite the Dominions to contribute contingents. Winston Churchill, the Colonial Secretary, seems to have been first to suggest that 'the Empire' might 'put up some force to preserve Gallipoli.' The Chief Secretary for Ireland, Sir Hamar Greenwood (a Canadian by origin and a classmate of Mackenzie King's at the University of Toronto), suggested that the invitation should go to Australia and New Zealand. The idea of distinguishing between the Dominions on the basis of their differing interests was unusual, but the cabinet accepted it. The recorded 'conclusion' on this matter read:[57]

(k) That the Secretary of State for the Colonies should draft for the Prime Minister, a telegram to be sent by the latter to the Prime Ministers of the Dominions, informing them of the general policy proposed in regard to this question and inviting their co-operation and particularly that of Australia and New Zealand in the despatch of military reinforcements.

This would presumably have involved a message to Australia and New Zealand, repeated to Canada and South Africa for information and for action if they chose. But the conclusion was not carried out.* The message went out to all the Dominions without any distinction being made between the addressees.

It was sent as from the Prime Minister to Canada, Australia, New Zealand, and South Africa at five minutes before midnight London time:[58]

Cabinet to-day decided to resist Turkish aggression upon Europe and to make exertions to prevent Allies being driven out of Constantinople by Mustafa Kemal and in particular and above all to maintain freedom of Straits by securing firmly the Gallipoli Peninsula. The French Government have notified us that they are in agreement with us in informing Mustafa Kemal that he must not violate neutral zone by which Straits and Constantinople are protected ... and the Italians are also in general accord with us. We are addressing ourselves to Roumania, Serbia and Greece with a view to securing their military participation in defence of deep water line between Europe and Asia. We are ... placing a British division under orders to reinforce Sir Charles Harington, the Allied Commander-in-Chief at Constantinople. The British Navy will co-operate to the fullest extent necessary. These arrangements are intended to cover period which must elapse before a stable peace with Turkey can be secured. For this purpose a conference is being proposed, probably at Venice, possibly at Paris, and it is essential that we should be strong enough to maintain our position at Constantinople and round the Straits until this peace has been achieved. We do not think it likely that forces of Mustafa Kemal will attack if a firm front is shown by a large number of Powers acting together ... But it is imperative we should take timely precautions. A defeat or a humiliating exodus of the Allies from Constantinople might produce very grave consequences in India and among other Mohammedan populations for

* Since Churchill drafted the message, and it was sent out through his department, he must be considered responsible. King wrote in his diary for October 18, 1926 (during the Imperial Conference of that year) that Churchill in conversation with him said that the message 'was to be sent to Australia and New Zealand and not Canada ... What should have been done was to have sent us a copy of the cable sent to Australia and New Zealand.' King does not record that Churchill admitted any responsibility in the matter.

which we are responsible. I should be glad to know whether Dominion Government wish to associate themselves with the action we are taking and whether they would desire to be represented by a contingent. Apart altogether from the vital Imperial and world wide interests involved in freedom of Straits for which such immense sacrifices were made in the war, we cannot forget that Gallipoli Peninsula contains over Twenty thousand British and Anzac graves and that these should fall into the ruthless hands of Kemalists would be an abiding source of grief to the Empire. The announcement that all or any of the Dominions were prepared to send contingents even of moderate size would undoubtedly in itself exercise a most favourable influence on situation and might conceivably be a potent factor in preventing actual hostilities ...

So far no damage had been done. This telegram was marked 'Secret' and sent in cipher; and it had been duly approved by the full cabinet. Something quite different ensued. On the following morning (September 16) Churchill, he said later, was asked by Lloyd George to draft a statement for publication. 'As I felt strongly,' wrote Churchill, 'that the public had a right to be informed about the situation and ought not to be carried forward further in ignorance of its gravity, I consented to do so. I sent my draft to Mr. Lloyd George, who consulted with such of his colleagues as were accessible, made certain alterations, and authorized its publication.'[59] This statement, variously called a 'semi-official statement,' a 'communiqué,' and a 'manifesto,' was given to the British press 'sometime after 3.0 p.m.' on Saturday the sixteenth.[60]

This document[61] was very similar to the telegram sent to the Dominions. It was emotional in tone. It asserted that Britain's views were shared by France and Italy, added that an approach was being made to Yugo-Slavia, Romania, and Greece, and proceeded: 'His Majesty's Government have also communicated with the Dominions, placing them in possession of the facts and inviting them to be represented by contingents in the defence of interests for which they have already made enormous sacrifices and of soil which is hallowed by immortal memories of the Anzacs.'

Just who Lloyd George's 'accessible' colleagues were who joined with him in approving the issuance of this manifesto has never been fully established. One thing is clear: the Foreign Secretary, Lord Curzon, who might have expected to be consulted before so fundamental a statement of foreign policy was given to the world, was not among them. He was out of London. Subsequently there was an unseemly (and rather comic) exchange between him and Churchill about the incident.[62] There seems to be little doubt that at this period the inner cabinet – the real makers of policy – consisted of Lloyd George, Churchill, and Lord Birkenhead.[63] In 1944 – twenty-two years later – Lord Greenwood, as he then was, gave his classmate King his memories of how things were done. Here, for what it is worth, is his account as recorded by King:[64]

He said he was in the cabinet at the time and the debate they had had was a very hot one. That, as a matter of fact, Churchill, Lord Birkenhead and Lloyd George had all been out dining pretty well that evening and that the decision to fight the Turks and to send out the appeal to the Dominions to aid in preventing the advance of the Turks was made under those conditions. Greenwood said he was speaking to me of course as a Privy Councillor and was deploring the effect that alcohol had on men who have to deal with national affairs and how whole nations may be brought into the peril of their lives through this painful influence.

This seems hardly likely to be an accurate picture of the cabinet of September 15, which began at 4 p.m. Greenwood was present, but not Birkenhead. Nor does it seem probable that Greenwood was remembering the gathering of the sixteenth which supposedly authorized the 'manifesto.' Even though an official statement given to the press on September 19 averred that it was issued 'with the approval of all the Ministers present in London,' it is more than doubtful whether there was a gathering. According to Maurice Hankey, he himself lunched with Lloyd George that day. He heard later that Churchill came round to Downing Street after lunch and 'he and Lloyd George had between them settled the matter.' The Cabinet Secretary knew nothing of the manifesto until he read it, with astonishment, in the evening paper. The cabinet records contain notes of various 'conferences of ministers' (as distinct from full cabinets) during this crisis, but of none on September 16.[65] There does not seem to be much evidence to support Greenwood's alcoholic interpretation of history. But that there was some extraordinary procedure cannot be doubted.

There have been widely varying interpretations of the British government's policy in this crisis. It has been argued that it was a 'reckless and triumphant gesture,' which saved Britain from humiliation by Kemal; the last time before 1939 when she stood up boldly to an aggressor.[66] At the other extreme, at least one member of Lloyd George's cabinet – Stanley Baldwin, the President of the Board of Trade – was convinced that Lloyd George and his closest associates were engaged in a disgraceful conspiracy to bring on war with Turkey and thereby enable the tottering coalition government to win an election. Outside the government Lord Beaverbrook was of the same opinion. A year later Baldwin, by then Prime Minister, gave Mackenzie King privately his interpretation of the affair. This is King's record of the conversation:[67]

... Roughly what Mr. Baldwin said was as follows:

England and the Empire were in the hands of three dangerous men, all intoxicated with their own cleverness and love of power, and prepared to sacrifice everything to it; foolish and blind even to the point of believing that they could win an election by bringing on another war. They were determined to have war with Turkey and were doing everything in their power to bring it about; they felt that if they could once launch war they could then appeal to the people and come back as a government triumvirate (Mr. Baldwin did not use this expression but it was what was implied). It was pure madness and we were within an ace of a conflict.

The message which had been sent to the Dominions had never been shown to the Cabinet. Lloyd George pretended that he had not seen it, but there was no doubt he had. Churchill had drafted it, but Birkenhead and Lloyd George were equally responsible for it; it was part of the campaign of war and the election manœuvre which they had planned ...

Mr. Baldwin said that he was going to resign from the Ministry when he learned of the message to the Dominions; it was only through the persuasion of Bonar Law and other of his colleagues that he determined to stay ...

There are obvious errors here. Either King's memory of the conversation with Baldwin, or (more probably) Baldwin's memory of the events of 1922, was at fault. As we have seen, the cabinet did approve the message to the Dominions. What it did not see or approve was the manifesto announcing that message to the world. It seems evident that what Baldwin was speaking of, and what he so desperately resented, was the action taken on September 16 and the war policy which he believed it represented.

It is time to look at the reaction which these remarkable proceedings produced in Canada.

Casualness and bad luck in Ottawa reinforced irresponsibility in London to produce a disaster. As we have seen, the message to the Canadian government, having been enciphered, was sent off just before midnight, September 15-16. In Ottawa at this time the only cipher facilities were at the Governor General's Office. Deciphering this rather long message took time – possibly more time than usual because it was a week-end. The message was delivered at Government House between 10 and 11 p.m. on

Friday night. Presumably there was no cipher officer on duty, and it was 'dealt with the first thing Saturday morning.' One of King's secretaries reported that the deciphered version did not reach the Prime Minister's Office until three that afternoon; the Governor General's Office believed that it left Government House at 1:30 and was delivered 'about 2 p.m.' At King's office, being addressed to his secretary, F.A. McGregor, who was absent, it was locked up until his arrival the next morning.[68]

The newspapers' facilities were more efficient than the government's. The manifesto did not have to be enciphered. It sped across the world. London time was five hours ahead of Ottawa's. Mackenzie King was not in the capital that Saturday afternoon; he was visiting his constituency north of Toronto. He recorded how he first heard about it all: 'I was about to go into the temple of Peace at Sharon, when the Toronto Star reporter, about 2.45 handed me a despatch to the effect that Britain had invited Canada to participate in an attack against the Turks, & in the maintenance of the Dardanelles. I replied I had nothing to say, other than that there was a meeting of the Cabinet on Monday when any representations of the kind would be considered by my colleagues & myself in Council.' When King returned to Ottawa early on Sunday morning the seventeenth he finally received Lloyd George's message.[69]

Overnight King had had some advice from political friends. Old Sir William Mulock, while speaking of the 'impertinence' of the British government's making its request public, was 'non-committal,' 'cautioned delay, consideration in Council.' Joseph E. Atkinson, proprietor of the Toronto *Star*, 'thought it would be well to give a contingent & then have it out with Britain that never again would we go into anything on which we had not been consulted.' King made up his own mind. His reaction to Lloyd George's message was not surprising. 'I confess it annoyed me,' he wrote. 'It is drafted designedly to play the imperial game, to test out centralization vs. autonomy as regards european wars.'[70] His first act was to send a cable complaining of the news being released to the press before the official message had reached him, a 'most embarrassing situation.' He inquired whether he was at liberty to disclose the contents of the message.[71] He also cabled his colleagues Fielding and Lapointe at Geneva asking them to sound out the British and Dominion representatives there. In his diary[72] he set down his intentions and calculations:

I have thought out my plans as regards the near Eastern problem. No contingent will go without parliament being summoned in first instance. I am inclined to cable Lloyd George, mentioning that it will be necessary to take this step & inquiring whether the situation seems to render it necessary. I shall not commit myself one way or the other, but keep the responsibility for prlt. – the executive regarding itself as the committee of prlt. – I do not believe prlt. would sanction the sending of a contingent. The French Canadians will be opposed. I believe most if not all our [Liberal] members in Ont. & the maritime provinces will be opposed. I am not so sure of B.C. – I feel confident the Progressives will be opposed almost to a man – It is the time now to bring them into the Government. My thought is to send for [T.A.] Crerar and [A.B.] Hudson at once & point out to them the issue is Canada vs. Imperialism, the people vs. the jingoes & have them come into the Government on that ground to strengthen us in our attitude of refusing to send a contingent without sanction of prlt. ... New Zealand has offered a contingent ... Australia will probably follow her example. I doubt if S. Africa will. I feel sure she won't. I am sure the people of Canada are against participation in this european war. However the issue is serious it will arouse jingoism & with jingoism passion, which combined with the prejudice against me on account of conscription & war feeling still lingering, will mean a heavy & difficult role for me. It might mean anything, attempts at my life etc. I shall be firm & stand by the people. I am convinced it is not right to take this country into another european war, & I shall resist to the uttermost. It means a difficult and trying time ahead, but I have a feeling the Turks will climb down before we get very far & that the whole business is mostly a Lloyd George election manœuvre ...

In 1922 the daily press was still the public's only source of news. The crisis burst on the Canadian people in the evening papers of Saturday, September 16. Monday morning's papers were full of 'another war emergency.' The Toronto *Globe* appeared with the streamer headline, 'British Lion Calls Cubs to Face the Beast of Asia.' Numerous offers of service were reported. In this atmosphere of excitement King's Cabinet met at eleven in the morning to decide what answer should go to London. With two adjournments the meeting went on until 11:15 that night.

King recorded that he found 'all present' strongly against sending a contingent; there was a 'feeling of exasperation' over the manifesto. D.D. McKenzie 'was for recognition of principle that when Britain is at war we are at war, – which others agreed to, with premise that it is for us to determine our part in the conflict.' Charles Stewart of Alberta was for some expression of approval of the British attitude. All agreed that a contingent could not be sent without summoning parliament, and that parliament should not be summoned unless the government were prepared to recommend intervention. King 'kept out for an open mind, pending events, – we are a minority govt.' A telegram from Fielding, while approving the British attitude, opposed sending troops without parliament's consent.[73]

In the evening two telegrams came from London.[74] One was a message for publication, in place of the original request for aid which was 'not suitable for textual publication.' The other was an explanation from Churchill. The British government, he said, had communicated with Australia and New Zealand because of their associations with Gallipoli 'and we felt bound to make the message common to all the Dominions' (had the Colonial Office officials, one wonders, urged this?). There was 'no probability of a serious war'; but anything Canada could contribute 'towards sense of empire solidarity' would be most valuable. A statement that Canada associated itself in insisting on the freedom of the Straits 'and would be represented by a contingent if the need arose' would be 'quite sufficient at this time.' Churchill concluded, 'I am sure you will handle the matter in such a way as to give utmost moral support at this stage.' It is evident that this nearly tipped the balance in the Canadian cabinet, and one cannot help asking what would have happened if Churchill had had the good sense to omit the mention of a contingent at this point. King wrote: 'We debated long over question of giving 'moral support' & approving attitude. I felt that involved whole question of participation, in European wars & held back on it. Cabinet agreed in this. We all were inclined to feel whole business an 'election scheme' of Lloyd George & Co. – influence public mind with the "unspeakable Turk."'[75]

The formal Canadian reply that went to London that night was brief:[76]

Following from Prime Minister for your Prime Minister, begins:
The Cabinet has had under consideration the representations contained in your telegram of the fifteenth instant. It is the view of the Government that public opinion in Canada would demand authorization on the part of Parliament as a necessary preliminary to the despatch of a contingent to participate in the conflict of the Near East.
We will welcome the fullest possible information in order to decide upon the advisability of summoning Parliament.

From this ground King's cabinet refused to budge, although London continued to beg for some commitment. On September 19 Lloyd George cabled that a definite statement that 'Canada will stand by the Empire in the event of terms of Armistice being broken' would do much to ensure the maintenance of peace. The reply the following day was, 'We have not thought it necessary to reassert the loyalty of Canada to the British Empire.'[77] With this the men in London had to be content. New Zealand had offered a contingent on the instant; Australia also offered one, but only after lengthy complaints about the absence of consultation; in South

Africa, Smuts was absent at the critical moment and no real answer was ever given. Sir Richard Squires, Prime Minister of Newfoundland, was in London. When approached by *The Times*, he said: 'Newfoundland does not want the British Empire to get into another row, but if there is one she wants to be in it.' Newfoundland, unlike Canada, had graves at Gallipoli.[78]

The crisis passed; the Turks did not attack at Chanak; Lieutenant-General Sir Charles Harington, in command on the spot, did not carry out an order he was sent to present them with an ultimatum which might well have led to war;[79] and on October 11 an armistice was signed at Mudania which provided a basis for peace in the area of the Straits pending the meeting of a definitive peace conference.[80] On October 19, in a famous meeting at the Carlton Club in London at which Stanley Baldwin, while making no direct reference to the Turkish situation, made a strong attack on Lloyd George, the Conservative party decided to withdraw from the Coalition. Lloyd George at once resigned, and Bonar Law became Prime Minister. In the election that followed Churchill lost his seat.[81]

So far as the Dominions were concerned, Churchill's administration of the Colonial Office had been disastrous, particularly for the cause of those who believed in the possibility of a common Empire foreign policy based on consultation. As we have seen, the Imperial Conference of 1921 had approved this general idea, but had entirely failed to produce the arrangements for continuous consultation that alone could make it effective. Whatever else Churchill did during the year that followed, he did nothing to repair this omission. (The fact is, as his official biography amply shows, he was too busy with Mesopotamia, Palestine, and Ireland to spare a thought for the Dominions, which do not figure in the story at all.) And in the Chanak affair his action, from the imperial point of view at least, was thoroughly deplorable. The flamboyant gesture of approaching the Dominions was a mistake, and the way it was done made it very much worse. It was not only the ineffable performance of the 'manifesto' reaching the Prime Minister of Canada before the British government's official cable; it was the utter failure during the preceding days and weeks to keep the Dominions informed of the development of the crisis and of British policy. In his cable of September 18 Churchill said to King, 'I very much regret that it was not possible to give you longer notice but the crisis developed very suddenly.' This was not wholly true. On September 7 – eight days before the sudden approach to the Dominions – the British cabinet fully discussed the Graeco-Turkish situation. The minutes record the Prime Minister as saying, 'It was inconceivable that we should allow the Turks to gain possession of the Gallipoli Peninsula and we should fight to prevent them doing so.' The meeting decided that 'maintenance of the control of the deep sea water separating Asia and Europe was a cardinal British interest, and any attempt by the Kemalists to occupy the Gallipoli Peninsula should be resisted by force.'[82] If consultation meant anything, here surely was the moment when the Dominions should have been informed. Surely also the person who should have made it his business to see that they were informed was the Colonial Secretary; but he did nothing. Maurice Hankey's biographer has suggested that the blunder of not consulting the Dominions might have been avoided had Hankey been at his usual post. Unfortunately, the Cabinet Secretary was on holiday, and did not return to London until September 15.[83]

Certainly at this moment there was not a conspiracy against Dominion autonomy; nobody was doing what King's suspicious mind projected, testing out 'centralization vs. autonomy.' What was in evidence was a rather appalling casualness. Nobody thought of the Dominions at all, it seems, until the idea of getting them to throw their strength into the scales came up on September 15. Above all, nobody in authority in London thought of the fact that in Ottawa there was a new Prime Minister, apprehensive of imperial schemes, who needed to be handled with gloves. On the contrary, everything was done in the manner best calculated to confirm his suspicions, and to enable him to convince his colleagues of the soundness of his own ideas. King wrote in his diary on September 19: 'It is perhaps no[t] unfortunate this case has presented itself. It is the best that could have come up.'

As we have already suggested, King's policy in this affair, like the London pavement-artist's pictures, was all his own work. He had no assistance except clerical help and the advice of his political colleagues. There was no expert civil servant to advise him and to draft dispatches for him. He recorded that during the crisis he consulted Pope and Christie about the Rush-Bagot Agreement concerning naval craft on the Lakes (below, page 33);[84] but there is no indication that he made any use of these two suspected Tories in the negotiation with Whitehall. And it is a notable fact that the policies of the government were those he had formulated in his diary on September 17 (above, page 23). The untried Prime Minister had carried his colleagues with him.

It is interesting too that in 1922 one individual could still handle the foreign business of the Canadian government. King that year was essentially a one-man Department of External Affairs. After that year this situation never fully recurred.

What was the source of the ideas that King applied to the Chanak crisis? The diary doesn't say, but the convenient formula of remitting the decision to Parliament (and thereby avoiding having to make any decision at the moment) had been familiar in the mouths of Liberal statesmen for many years. It had been used by Sir Frederick Borden during the Imperial Defence Conference of 1909; Sir Wilfrid Laurier had had recourse to it in his famous statement on the Naval Service bill the following year; and Sir Clifford Sifton had affirmed it in his Canadian Club speech only a few months before. Sifton, never a modest man, told Dafoe, 'I accept full responsibility for furnishing Mackenzie King with a ready-made policy.'[85] It is not impossible that King did remember in the crisis that speech and his subsequent discussion with Sifton.

Did he remember historical precedents on September 17? He was certainly consulting them nine days later:[86] '... Read Sir Jno [Macdonald]'s letter to Tupper in the 80's regarding sending troops to the Soudan.* The situation is almost a complete parallel, only it is the Straits of the Dardanelles instead of the Suez. – Read next Laurier's life by Skelton re S.[outh] A.[frica] here the parallel is even more marked.* Much is to be feared once war is declared with "The Globe" "Citizen" [Ottawa] and other papers already committed. Fortunately the *Free Press* Winnipeg & *Gazette* [Montreal] are not ...' King had been reading Skelton's *Laurier* at the beginning of the year.[87] His reference to the South African crisis suggests that even if war had broken out with Turkey he would have emulated Laurier and tried to prevent Canada becoming involved. It may be doubted whether he would have succeeded. It is quite possible that an actual attack on the British force standing at bay at Chanak would have produced the sort of outburst in English Canada that led to the sending of a contingent in 1899.

In 1922, as in 1899, Canadian opinion was divided. French Canada seems to have been as solidly hostile to involvement in Turkey as it had been to involvement in South Africa. The Saint-Jean Baptiste Society demanded that 'Canada, a North American country, shall refuse all participation in the present crisis in the Near East.' Henri Bourassa, the veteran of 1899, inevitably took the same line in *Le Devoir*. In Ottawa *Le Droit* said, 'It is time that those who govern us should let the masters of the British Empire know once and for all that Canada is not a colony ...' English Canada, after four years of world war, was clearly less unitedly in favour of intervention than on the earlier occasion; nevertheless, there

* On these episodes, see Volume I, pages 43, 58-68.

was a perhaps rather surprising warmth of feeling. The *Canadian Annual Review* asserted, 'In many large centres and small places throughout the Dominion the pulpits on the 17th [September] rang with an appeal for support to Britain.'[88] King wrote in his diary on the nineteenth: 'The most distressing as well as amazing factor is the way the "Christian" churches – Methodist in particular – calls [sic] for war "to kill" the Turk.' There was a long background of clerical horror of Turkish persecution of Christians, and newspaper reports of atrocities in Smyrna had certainly had their due effect. And in 1922 the pulpit possessed an influence which it no longer has today. The voice of the English-language press was divided, and King did not get unanimous support from Liberal papers. Notably, the Toronto *Globe* favoured intervention (King's private explanation was, 'the Armenians are being persecuted, & [W.G.] Jaffray is a fanatic on some of these matters').[89] However, the Toronto *Star*, also Liberal, carried a strong campaign on the opposite side.[90] As one would expect, Clifford Sifton issued firm orders to his employee John Dafoe at the *Manitoba Free Press*: 'the policy of the Free Press must be one of opposition to sending troops ... In my judgment the whole question of autonomy vs entanglement in European & Asiatic wars must be fought out now.' Dafoe was nothing loath, and Sifton was delighted with the result. 'You have done your work,' he wrote the editor on October 4, 'more effectually than you have any idea of. The whole press of Canada was on the verge of an hysterical shriek for war. Your first article steadied them. I think the danger is over. Your articles have been the admiration of the whole country & have made thousands of converts.' He now advised Dafoe not to overdo it.[91] It was presumably the 'first article' that T.A. Crerar read to King when they met on September 22. The Prime Minister too was delighted ('our position to the letter').[92]

That the cabinet was not wholly united we have already seen. The two ministers at Geneva, Fielding and Lapointe, represented the opposite points of view.[93] They managed to agree in the message sent to King on September 18, which began by approving the British attitude, and proceeded: 'Would willingly have some statement made on behalf of our government indicating readiness to participate if necessary, but send troops abroad at present without parliamentary authority very undesirable. Cannot something be said that will serve the purpose without actual sending of contingent?' Next day Lapointe sent a personal cable: '... Imperial authorities should not have made such request ... Would advise delaying answer and being non-committal ...' And on September 26 Fielding gave his own view: 'Lapointe concurs entirely in your action. In the main

I concur, but if I had been with you I would have advised the making of a more emphatic statement of our willingness to co-operate in case of actual war.'

As King had expected, the Progressive leadership supported his stand, though he did not succeed at this moment in bringing them into the government as he had hoped to do. It is evident that Dafoe, Crerar, and King saw eye to eye. After his interview with King on September 22, Crerar announced that what he had heard in Ottawa had not altered his opinion 'that no Canadian troops should be sent or promised until the people's representatives have had an opportunity of considering the matter in Parliament.'[94] It appeared that King's minority government was now assured of a safe majority on this issue if it came to a vote. (Nevertheless, it is possible that both Liberal and Progressive members might have had second thoughts, in case of actual war, under pressure from their constituents.)

With the Conservatives, the official parliamentary Opposition,* the case was different. Their leader, Arthur Meighen, declared himself on September 22 to the Conservative Business Men's Association of Toronto in the most famous (and perhaps the most fatal) speech of his life.[95] 'When Britain's message came,' he told them, 'then Canada should have said: "Ready, aye ready; we stand by you."' The words were those of Sir Wilfrid Laurier in 1914 (Volume I, page 176). Meighen's argument was that a declaration of solidarity was 'the best step in our power to ensure that war shall not come.' His Toronto audience applauded loudly, but in French Canada the speech was used against him for many years afterwards.[96] The weakest point in his case was the suggestion that Canada had obligations resulting from signing the Treaty of Sèvres. He was hampered by not having seen the British communications (even the 'manifesto' of September 16 does not seem to have been fully published in Canada). The British government had not in fact taken the ground of maintaining the treaty; they had argued merely that it was necessary to maintain the situation at the Straits pending a new conference to make a stable peace. King pounced on this point and issued a statement on September 23 pointing out that the treaty had never become operative† and was in fact a dead letter.[98]

* Although the Progressives had more seats in the Commons than the Conservatives, they declined, chiefly because of divisions among themselves, the status of official Opposition.

† As recently as June 1922 the Canadian Parliament had passed virtually without debate 'An Act for carrying into effect the Treaties of Peace between His

As an episode in Commonwealth history the Chanak story is sad. Even if one discounts Greenwood's story of the three boozy ministers; even if one disallows Baldwin's belief that there was a plot to make war – and this is harder to do – the affair still reeks of irresponsibility. The business of the 'manifesto' is close to being incredible, but it happened. The only hope for an acceptable common foreign policy for the Commonwealth lay in the readiness of British statesmen to keep the Commonwealth constantly before them and ensure that their Dominion counterparts, if not actually 'consulted,' were at least provided with up-to-date confidential information. The Chanak episode suggests that this was in fact too much to hope for. British statesmen were simply not sufficiently interested in relations with the Dominions to provide a basis for the co-operative diplomacy that people like Sir Robert Borden had looked forward to.

The rather lengthy and complicated sequel to Chanak – the making of peace with Turkey, and Canada's relation to it – may best be left to be summarized in another chapter (below, page 35).

A GESTURE TO WASHINGTON

Before Chanak came to shake the Empire, Mackenzie King had inaugurated his administration's relations with the American corner of the North Atlantic Triangle with something of a flourish. The episode has escaped the historians, chiefly because King, surprisingly enough, allowed his famous diary to lapse at this point. As a result of this, his trip to Washington in July 1922 got left out of his authorized biography.

King had spent much time in the United States, as a student at Chicago and Harvard and as an industrial consultant. He had numbers of American friends, and many of them – notably the Rockefellers – were wealthy and eminent. He undoubtedly considered himself exceptionally qualified to conduct Canada's relations with the United States, and he was a fervent believer, like Sir Robert Borden and so many other Canadians, in the 'linch-pin' theory – the destined role of Canada as the interpreter between the United States and Britain.[99] Undoubtedly also Washington had an important place in his long-range plans for the country's external policy. If Canada was to have a policy independent of Great Britain's, Washing-

Majesty and Hungary and Turkey.'[97] This could in other circumstances have been construed as approval (cf the action of the British Parliament in connection with the Treaty of Versailles, Volume I, page 275); but King preferred to emphasize the point, which indeed was vital, that the King had never ratified the treaty. The Hungarian treaty had been ratified.

ton was one of the chief places where it would appear in practice, and a gesture there was a natural way of initiating it. One might have expected King to press on with the plan for distinctive Canadian representation in the American capital; however – perhaps because of division in his cabinet – he did not. What he did do was to journey there himself as soon as his first parliamentary session as Prime Minister was over.

One misses the diary, which might tell us his private thoughts; but it is fair to assume that he considered this an important diplomatic mission, a vital move in his new game. A diplomatic mission must have a subject. The great issue between Canada and the United States is always trade; but with the Republicans now in control of the executive and legislature in Washington there was no point in trying to talk trade. The St Lawrence Seaway had not yet reached the stage of being practical politics. King apparently looked about him for an issue and hit upon one as unobjectionable as motherhood – the Rush-Bagot Agreement of 1817 limiting naval armaments on the Great Lakes.

The original exchange of notes was still in effect, but improvements in naval technology had rendered its details wholly obsolete. The Canadian naval service had at various times expressed a degree of concern over the fact that the Americans were maintaining more and larger armed vessels on the lakes than the letter of the agreement allowed. (Canada had none at all.) Sir Joseph Pope had called Meighen's attention to the subject in September 1920. King himself seems to have felt that the agreement's worst deficiency was the fact that it was subject to cancellation on six months' notice by either party; he is on record as saying that it lacked 'that element of certainty and permanence which is all-important with respect to matters pertaining to defence.'[100] It is worth remembering that the agreement had been a subject of sentimental pride on both sides of the border, but particularly probably in Canada; a natural centre of interest to a politician who had been prominently involved in the movement for celebrating the centenary of Anglo-American peace in 1914. An issue less immediately important it would have been hard to find, but it provided an excuse for the mission to Washington.

Since defence was in question, King was accompanied on his trip by the Minister of National Defence, George P. Graham. On July 12 they called on the Secretary of State, Charles Evans Hughes, and 'Proposed that the ideals of the Rush-Bagot agreement ... be perpetuated in a new treaty.' Hughes was stated to be 'highly sympathetic and interested.' King is reported as saying to the press, 'We feel that here is an opportunity for Canada and America to give a lesson in international good-will and friendly dealings'; and he called the agreement 'an object lesson to the continents of Europe and Asia of New World methods in the mainte-nance of international peace.'[101] That afternoon King and Graham called at the White House to pay their respects to President Harding. Next day they went to the Senate, and King's old friend Senator Gerry, whom the Prime Minister had tutored back in 1899, entertained them at dinner.

Canadian newspapers of different political stripes gave their readers rather different accounts of these events. In Toronto the Liberal *Globe* gave the impression that the British Embassy played little part; but the Conservative *Mail and Empire* emphasized that King and Graham were accompanied to the State Department by 'Henry G. Chilton, counsellor of the British Embassy and Chargé d'Affaires in the absence of Ambassa-dor Geddes, who had arranged for the conference.' Chilton, it also pointed out, went with them to the White House, and gave a dinner for them that evening, Secretary Hughes being among the guests. The *Mail and Empire* mildly satirized the whole operation, observing that the United States had not yet officially shown any consciousness of the change in the British Dominions' status, and remarking further, 'There is no occasion for Mr. King thrusting himself into this international busi-ness.'[102]

Nevertheless, King probably returned to Ottawa with a sense of satis-faction. He had given a demonstration – cautious and limited, it is true – of Canada's new and more independent status, and had made a successful foray into personal diplomacy. He had in fact demonstrated the way he thought important issues between Canada and the United States ought to be handled; his trip of July 1922 prefigures the procedures of the Franklin D. Roosevelt administration, when King would be a fairly frequent visi-tor to the White House. He was far from being the first Canadian Prime Minister to visit Washington – one remembers particularly Borden's very fruitful trip at a moment of crisis in 1918 – but such visits now seemed likely to become more ordinary occurrences. And the enterprise may pos-sibly have made official Washington a little more aware that there had been constitutional progress north of the border.[103]

So far as the Rush-Bagot Agreement was concerned, the ultimate result of the enterprise was precisely nil. But the negotiations are interesting for one detail. Secretary Hughes had asked for a draft treaty. The Canadian naval staff quickly prepared one in consultation with Loring Christie. (It proposed that armed vessels on the lakes should be limited to those required for 'revenue and police duties' as might be from time to time agreed between the Canadian and American governments, and – in spite of King's earlier view – that the treaty should remain in force until two years after one of the parties had given notice to terminate it.) King sent the treaty off to London for the British government's comments. His cable to Lloyd George explained the background and described his visit to Washington. King wrote that the Canadian government entertained no thought that the existing American armed vessels might indicate any unfriendly intention towards Canada: 'Their presence, however, if it became realized might arouse unfortunate recriminations and misunderstandings in the minds of the Canadian people who have valued so highly the arrangement of 1817, and it would be deplorable if the situation were allowed to precipitate demands for counter-arming on our part.' However, the most interesting paragraph of the message was this: 'As for the method of signature of the proposed Treaty our view is that, having regard to the character and implications of the document, it would be appropriate that the full powers should be issued to Canadian subjects of His Majesty. When the time comes therefore we propose to pass an Order in Council authorizing the issue of full powers to myself as Prime Minister and Secretary of State for External Affairs and to my colleague, the Minister of National Defence, to sign on behalf of His Majesty.'

This proposed a considerable constitutional innovation. As the reader knows, the existing practice in such cases was that treaties on behalf of Canada with the United States or other foreign countries were in practice negotiated by a Canadian representative or representatives, but were signed on behalf of the King not only by the Canadian or Canadians but also by the British Ambassador; thus the formal 'diplomatic unity of the Empire' was maintained. The Colonial Office in London duly called attention to the implications of King's proposal: 'The constitutional point arising is whether the Treaty should be signed, on the British side, *only* by Canadian plenipotentiaries.' The British government might have been expected to argue against the plan. But apparently no policy on the matter was arrived at before the Chanak crisis exploded, and in the debris of Chanak the constitutional point got lost. When Lloyd George finally replied to King his cable made no reference to the method of signing.[104] It appears in fact that King never got an answer to his constitutional suggestion, and this should be borne in mind when assessing his performance in the matter of the Halibut Treaty the following year.

As for the draft treaty to replace the Rush-Bagot Agreement, in due time it simply withered on the vine; and it was the Canadians, who had initiated the whole business, who were responsible for allowing it to die.[105]

CHAPTER TWO

THE REVERSAL COMPLETED, 1922-25

MAKING PEACE WITH TURKEY

By the end of 1922 it was beginning to be evident that the new Canadian government, now one year old, was steering a different course from its predecessors in matters of external policy. Another year made the differences much more evident. The King ministry's actions concerning the settlement with Turkey and the signature of treaties were unmistakable signposts; and the Prime Minister's views on the constitution and operation of the Commonwealth were made crystal-clear in an Imperial Conference in London.

Even before the Chanak crisis was over, the question arose, What was to be Canada's relationship to the conference to make a new peace with Turkey, which was to meet at Lausanne in November 1922? Mackenzie King thought of this betimes. He wrote in his diary on September 27, 'I think we should not participate at Peace Conference, having had nothing to do with note of Allies sent Mustapha Kemal Pasha' – meaning presumably an Anglo-French-Italian invitation to a conference sent on the twenty-third.[1] But as it turned out none of the British Dominions was invited to Lausanne. British relations with France were at a very low ebb, largely as a result of the Chanak 'manifesto,' and when Lord Curzon raised the question of the Dominions with M. Poincaré, the French President of the Council, there was a rather comic interlude. Poincaré snapped that if the Dominions and India were represented at the conference, France would insist that her protectorates of Morocco and Tunis should get the same treatment. Curzon recalled the status of the Dominions and India as established at the Paris Peace Conference and in the League of Nations, and pointed out that the protectorates had no such position. He added that, pending consultation with the Dominion and Indian governments, 'I am not sure that they will desire to participate in the preparation of the new Peace Treaty or the Straits Convention although they will necessarily have to sign these instruments as they signed the Treaty of Sèvres.' In a second letter Curzon formally reserved the right of the Dominions and India to be represented 'in the British delegation' and said that he did not object to Moroccan and Tunisian representatives being attached to the French delegation. We now know, however, that the British Foreign Office was itself determined that the Dominions would not be at Lausanne. The Permanent Under-Secretary, Sir Eyre Crowe, wrote that it would be 'deplorable' to repeat the Paris arrangement by which Dominion delegates represented the Empire on 'highly technical committees'; and Curzon said loftily that he would have 'no time for daily or frequent conferences with a British Empire Delegation.' What is more, extraordinary as it may seem, in the cabinet meeting of September 15 – the one that decided to ask the Dominions for help – Curzon remarked that to the conference already planned only those 'specially concerned' should be invited; to invite all the signatories of the Treaty of Sèvres would make things 'very difficult.'[2]

Presumably as the result of a decision made in informal conferences between ministers – because of the general election, there was no meeting of the British cabinet between October 10 and November 1[3] – the new Colonial Secretary, the Duke of Devonshire,* cabled the Dominions on October 27[4] informing them that invitations to the conference had gone to various governments and adding: 'Dominion Governments will be kept informed from time to time of the general lines of policy on which British plenipotentiaries propose to proceed and of course of negotiations and in case of other Treaties arising out of the peace will of course be invited to sign new Treaty and any separate instrument regulating the status of the Straits. His Majesty's Government trusts that this procedure will be in accordance with the wishes of your Government ...' Mackenzie King's feelings were mixed. He noted the absence of any consultation and observed that this made Australia and New Zealand, who had offered contingents, look rather silly. He added, 'I had expected an invitation & was dreading the refusal it might be necessary to send.'[5]

On the twenty-ninth King – working, it appears, entirely on his own – set about drafting a reply, making no complaint but 'pointing out that we would take no responsibility or assume no obligation [sic] because of what is being done.' He added to his record, 'This will prove an historic despatch. It is making history, breaking new ground in inter-imperial &

---

* He had been Governor General of Canada, 1916-21.

international relations.'[6] The cabinet accepted the draft, with some 'modification' of a passage which might have implied regret at not having been invited. 'Motherwell* said "Thank God we weren't" which seemed the sentiments of all present.' There was some slight merriment over 'Tunis & Morocco,' Devonshire having reported the exchange with France in a dispatch which took credit for having maintained the rights of the Dominions.[7] The Canadian telegram went off on October 31.[8] It ran in part:

As ... it is proposed to keep our Government informed from time to time of the general lines of policy on which British plenipotentiaries propose to proceed and of the course of negotiations and to invite us to sign a new Treaty and any separate instrument regulating the Status of the straits, we deem it advisable to avail ourselves of the earliest opportunity to inform His Majesty's Government that in our opinion the extent to which Canada may be held to be bound by the proceedings of the Conference or by the provisions of any Treaty or other instrument arising out of the same, is necessarily a matter for the Parliament of Canada to decide and that the rights and powers of our Parliament in these particulars must not be held to be affected by implication or otherwise in virtue of the information with which our Government may be supplied.

King's shortcomings as a diplomatic draftsman are evident here. It is hardly surprising that London had difficulty in interpreting this interminable sentence. It said nothing as to whether or not Canada would accept the proposed invitation to sign the new treaty. And the passage concerning the rights of Parliament was anything but clear. On November 16 Bonar Law's cabinet in London – confirmed in power by the general election held the previous day – approved telegrams to the Dominions about the impending conference. That to Canada said, 'We fully understand that it is desire of Canadian Government that any treaty with Turkey which may result from Conference should be submitted to Canadian Parliament for approval before His Majesty is advised to ratify it.'[9] This was not what King had meant. On the twenty-fourth he drafted another 'important despatch' in reply and his colleagues approved it. It explained that the Canadian government did not wish to be understood as requesting approval of the treaty by Parliament. Just what it did want the message still did not succeed in making particularly clear: 'In our opinion Parliament will desire, as respects the Treaty with Turkey and any other instruments arising out of the Lausanne Conference to reserve

* W.R. Motherwell (Saskatchewan), Minister of Agriculture.

to itself the right to decide upon the merits of the case what action on the part of the people of Canada is right and proper.'[10] 'Upon the merits of the case': one suspects that what King meant was that Parliament would decide, not what should be done about any treaty signed at Lausanne, but what should be done in a future crisis to which the treaty was relevant – in other words, another Chanak. He did not say so, and evidently found it embarrassing to be frank on the subject; but this would seem to be what he had in mind.

London tried again early in December, in a cable to King from Devonshire:[11]

May I ... set out the position as it appears to us. It is this. Any Treaty resulting from the Lausanne Conference will of course replace the Treaty of Sevres and until it comes into force, a state of war between the British Empire and Turkey will technically continue. Treaty must therefore be binding on the whole Empire when ratified. It remains to be seen whether there will be a successful issue to the Lausanne Conference, but if there is, we should much prefer that any new Treaty should follow Paris precedent, and include signatures on behalf of all the Dominions. Do I gather from your telegram that the Canadian Government are not averse to the procedure proposed as regards the signature of the new Treaty and of any separate instrument regarding the Straits but wish to make it clear that should anything in the Treaty or instrument be held to impose any serious international obligation on Canada, as part of the British Empire, it cannot be considered binding on Canada until approved by Parliament?

On December 30 King drafted a reply to this ('what I think will be a state paper of importance') which he sent off after reading it to two of his colleagues.[12]

In this cable[13] the Prime Minister recalled the procedures followed, so far as Canada was concerned, in connection with the treaties with Germany, Austria, and Bulgaria and those resulting from the Washington Conference. There were, he said, 'four separate, distinct and essential stages': first, direct representation of Canada and participation by the Canadian representatives in the conference drafting the treaty; second, formal signing of the treaties on behalf of Canada; third, approval of the treaties by the Parliament of Canada; and, fourth, assent by the government of Canada to ratification of the treaties by the King. The Canadian government would certainly desire to follow this procedure; but only, King said, 'as regards treaties in which Canada is supposed to have a direct or immediate interest.' The fact that Canada had not been invited to Lausanne had been regarded by the Canadian government as indicating that in the opinion of the inviting countries Canada did not have in this case the sort of interest she had had in the conferences at Versailles and Washington. King repeated that Canada did not complain of this; but his telegram concluded: 'Canada has not been invited to send representatives to the Lausanne Conference and has not participated in the proceedings of the Conference either directly or indirectly. Under the circumstances, we do not see how, as respects signing on behalf of Canada we can be expected ... to follow the procedure adopted in the case of the treaties with Germany, Austria and Bulgaria.' King made no reference whatever to the Treaty of Sèvres; but it is evident that he was, by implication, rejecting the possibility of following the procedure then used, by which a Canadian representative signed the treaty without taking any actual part in drafting or negotiating it.

At this time the Governor General, Lord Byng, was on the friendliest of terms with Mackenzie King, as the Prime Minister's diary shows, and was doing his utmost to assist him. He had undoubtedly observed with embarrassment how far London was from understanding his Prime Minister's position, and feared that King's new message would not improve matters. He therefore accompanied it with a 'private and personal' telegram to the Colonial Secretary which King did not see:[14] 'I understand Prime Minister is afraid that representative of Canada may be asked to sign Treaty and does not want to be put in position of refusing request. He holds that as Canada is not represented at Conference Canada cannot sign Treaty. He is quite agreeable that Lord Curzon should sign for Empire and that Treaty should be presented to Canadian Parliament for ratification in usual way.' The first two sentences were a useful clarification. The third sentence, while undoubtedly representing Byng's understanding of King's views, was to have mildly disastrous consequences. For the moment, however, the air was cleared. The Colonial Secretary cabled that the British government was willing to fall in with King's suggestion that any treaties resulting from the conference should be signed only by the British representatives who negotiated them, and was inquiring whether this would be agreeable to Australia and New Zealand.[15] In fact, this was the procedure followed when the Lausanne treaty 'and 17 other instruments' were finally signed on July 24, 1923.[16]

The ground was covered again, not without acrimony, in the spring of 1924, when the treaty, having been delayed by British 'Parliamentary exigencies,' belatedly came up for ratification. It was now that Lord Byng's well-meant telegram blew up in the British government's face. Ramsay MacDonald was Prime Minister in London. When the British government expressed the hope that the Canadian ministers would shortly be able to concur in ratification, King drafted (March 24) a reply which repeated much of the language of his earlier cables: Canada had not been invited to Lausanne, had not participated in the conference, and had not signed the treaty; therefore the cabinet felt they could not recommend to Parliament approval of the treaty and the other instruments. 'Without the approval of Parliament they feel they are not warranted in signifying concurrence in ratification of the Treaty and Conventions. With respect to ratification, however, they will not take exception to such course as His Majesty's Government may deem it advisable to recommend.' After the cabinet had approved this, King 'had it submitted' to John S. Ewart, who suggested adding words pointing out that the position being taken was in accord with the formula on ratification of treaties adopted by the Imperial Conference of 1923 (below, page 69). King was delighted. He felt that Canada was protected against commitments, while at the same time escaping from any suggestion that because she had not signed or approved the Lausanne treaty as she had signed and approved that of Sèvres she was still in a state of war with Turkey: 'So much for "our war" with Turkey. Ewart's words secure us against any obligation. The ratification by the King secures us peace along with the rest.'[17]

Shortly, however, the Prime Minister was again disturbed. On April 1, during the debate on second reading of the Treaty of Peace (Turkey) bill,* Ramsay MacDonald, under questioning about the position of the Dominions, said that the Dominions had been asked 'whether Lord Curzon and Sir Horace Rumbold should be their representatives, as Imperial representatives, as well as British representatives,' and that they had accepted this. Canada had raised 'one or two constitutional points' which MacDonald suggested were not very seriously meant. When pressed as to whether Canada had accepted obligations under the treaty, MacDonald said 'Canada, I am perfectly certain, accepts the obligation, having been represented by Lord Curzon at Lausanne, with her full knowledge and consent.'[18] King, not surprisingly, boiled over. He sent off a very long telegram quoting the earlier correspondence at length and complaining that he had been wholly misunderstood. The Colonial Secretary now cabled privately to Lord Byng inquiring whether King had known of his personal cable of December 31, 1922 (above, page 39). Byng replied that

---

* During this debate the Parliamentary Under Secretary of State for Foreign Affairs, Arthur Ponsonby, stated that it was Labour party policy that all treaties without exception should be approved by Parliament before ratification.

King had not: 'I sent that telegram because I considered Prime Minister's telegram of same date not at all clear. I had previously talked the matter over with him and understood his views were as outlined in my telegram.'[19] King probably never knew that Byng had made this unfortunate intervention and that it was in great part responsible for his misunderstanding with MacDonald. No other communication from Ottawa had suggested that Canada recognized Curzon as having a right to speak for her.

A tortuous and unsatisfactory exchange of cables[20] followed. MacDonald was unwilling to make an outright statement that he had been mistaken, as King requested. There was prolonged controversy over the publication of the correspondence, ending, after King had obtained the rather unenthusiastic assent of the other Dominions, in the release of a selection ending with King's cable of March 24 (above, page 40).[21] The French argument concerning Tunis and Morocco was suppressed. On June 9 the Lausanne affair was discussed in the Canadian House of Commons, and the Prime Minister made himself at least a little clearer than he had in his telegrams:

... So far as the British Empire is concerned, internationally in relation to Turkey and other countries, the action of the king in signing this treaty binds to my mind the whole Empire.

As to the extent of obligation arising between different parts of the Empire, in other words, considered intra-imperially, in the carrying out of its provisions, the government takes the position that it will be for this parliament to decide what, should occasion arise, in the light of all the circumstances, and in the light of the manner in which this treaty was negotiated, and the discussion we are having at the present time, its obligation may be under the terms of the treaty.*

One might say that we have here a parallel to Laurier's famous statement of Canada's position in case of war; Canada was bound by the treaty, but the extent of the action she might take to fulfill that obligation in any future crisis was for Parliament to decide.

In this debate the Conservative Opposition maintained the position of Sir Robert Borden: that is, it supported a common imperial foreign policy,

* This is the version of the revised Hansard. Mr Neatby in his biography of King gives the rather different unrevised version including the words, 'Legally and technically Canada will be bound,' which King evidently decided to remove from the record.

but a policy arrived at by consultation between the United Kingdom and the Dominions. Arthur Meighen argued that Canada should have been at Lausanne: 'if we could not be at the conference table – wehat reason was there why we could not have been in closest touch with the British representatives from the beginning? What reason was there why we should not have been there to advise the British representatives of the view point of Canada?' The King government, he said, had 'acquiesced, apparently cheerfully, in the old colonial situation.' Asked what could have been done if the treaty developed along lines unsatisfactory to Canada, he replied: 'we might have had a clause inserted, which frequently was inserted in treaties before, that it did not bind any dominion unless that dominion expressly ratified it.'

During this controversy King clearly felt the need of the sort of expert advice that he had received from O.D. Skelton in connection with the Imperial Conference the year before (above, page 9, and below, page 66). His application to Ewart suggests this. He also applied to Skelton, who was back at Queen's University, and on April 14, 1924, Skelton provided him with a memorandum.[22] This succinctly pointed out that in the existing dilemma concerning Canada's state of war with Turkey there were four possible courses: remain at war with Turkey; negotiate a separate treaty to end the state of war; approve ratification of the Lausanne treaty; or admit that ratification by the King on advice of the British government was binding on Canada. King was unwilling to accept any of these courses; but in practice, as we have seen, he did accept the last one, with the proviso that the treaty was binding towards the outside world but not in terms of obligations within the Empire. Many people in England and in Canada were certainly repelled by his stand, either by its apparently separatist tendency or by the obscure language in which it was expressed, or both. The obscurity was due, we have suggested, partly to King's unwillingness to call an unpleasant spade a spade, partly to his congenital incapacity for lucid exposition. But in the atmosphere of 1924 King was in little danger of a damaging crisis. Not many Canadians were in a mood to object to a policy that limited the country's commitments abroad.

The Lausanne episode of 1922-4 was undignified and in fact rather absurd. Nevertheless it was important. Effectively it marked the end of the experiment in associating the British Dominions with British foreign policy that had been undertaken in 1918-19. The responsibility for this result is shared between the governments of Britain and Canada.

The deplorable fiasco of Chanak had prepared the way, poisoning the relationship between Whitehall and the new Canadian Liberal administration. Mackenzie King and a good many other Canadians were left feeling that Churchill and his colleagues in the Lloyd George ministry had – to borrow a much later phrase of Churchill's own – used the Empire as a public convenience. A good many Britons were undoubtedly left feeling that Canada had failed the Empire in an hour of need. Friendly co-operation was rendered more difficult in the next phase, the making of peace with Turkey.

The deterioration of British relations with France, which the famous Chanak 'manifesto' accelerated, led to the French objection to the presence of the Dominions at Lausanne. It seems that in spite of Curzon's firm line with Poincaré (above, page 35) these objections were used within the British government as a partial justification for the decision not to invite the Dominions to Lausanne, though the precedent of the Treaty of Sèvres was put in the forefront. The minutes of the British cabinet for November 1, 1922 (by which date the Dominions had already been abruptly told that they were not to be invited), record Lord Curzon as saying:

As regards the representation of the Dominions and India at the Conference, he thought the Government should largely be guided by the course adopted in negotiating the Treaty of Sèvres. Although the Dominions and India had not taken part in the Conference, the Treaty had been signed by their representatives. What he desired was that the Dominions and India would allow him to represent them, and he could assure them that he would keep their interests constantly to the fore. Their presence in the Council Chamber was extremely difficult to arrange, and when he had proposed it to M. Poincaré the latter had insisted that in that event, Tunis, Algeria and Morocco would also have to be represented.

These considerations had force, and it could be contended that the Dominions would have little direct contribution to make at Lausanne. Nevertheless, it was only a few weeks since they had been asked for military aid in the area concerned. If a common imperial policy was considered an aim worth pursuing, then the British government would have been wise to permit and to insist upon a British Empire Delegation at Lausanne, and to invite the Dominions and India to take part. Lloyd George was not being foolish when he told the British House of Commons on April 9, 1924, that the failure to invite the Dominions was 'a very grave departure from a precedent set after the Great War' and likely to have an adverse effect upon the unity of the Empire. In retrospect, it seems clear that what was done made it easier for Mackenzie King to pursue his isolationist course, and in fact went far to ensure that no British

Empire Delegation of the type seen at Paris in 1919 and at Washington in 1921 would ever again appear at an international conference. This, we have seen, was perfectly agreeable to Lord Curzon and the Foreign Office. In the final controversy over ratification, King was prickly and MacDonald obtuse and tactless. It was again made to appear that London's attitude to Dominion problems was careless and casual.

ISSUES WITH THE UNITED STATES

We have noticed Mackenzie King's visit to Washington in July 1922, and mentioned in that connection that while he clearly attached importance to demonstrating that his administration was on good terms with the United States government, he was in no hurry to inaugurate the direct Canadian representation in Washington which had long been discussed and which the Borden government had in fact arranged for (Volume I, pages 311-17). The fact is that he found the issue thorny in more ways than one.

In October 1922 Sir Auckland Geddes, the British Ambassador in Washington, visited Ottawa and King discussed the matter with him at length. Geddes favoured a Canadian representative with an office outside the British Embassy, but opposed a minister with diplomatic status; the other Dominions would inevitably follow suit, and the British Ambassador would be embarrassed by having five Dominion diplomatic representatives around him. King made it clear that no final decision had been taken, and wrote in his diary:[23] 'I shld not like Canada to take a step which might produce difficulties in a frgn. ctry. or Br. Empire. I am inclined to feel that a step in the right direction, not going the length of "diplomatic" representat'n at the start, but reserving this right as conceded, might be best for the start ...' King clearly thought that the ideal representative would be Sir Arthur Currie, who had commanded the Canadian Corps in France and was now Principal of McGill University. He sounded Currie out a few weeks later, and Sir Arthur replied that 'the expense' would be too much for him.[24] Nevertheless, in the spring of 1923 King raised the question of Currie's appointment in the cabinet; the term 'Minister Plenipotentiary' was now used. On April 10 King recorded that he got his colleagues' consent to the appointment; but three days later old Mr Fielding, the Minister of Finance, offered very strong opposition:[25] 'Fielding trembled like a leaf as he spoke of his ideals being different from [Raoul] Dandurand's etc., in not wanting any of this Washington business. He first said he wd not oppose his colleagues if they were favorable & later asked that the matter be held over for a time. I understand he has since intimated possible resignation – His is the old Colonial viewpoint. It was a trying situation.' Next day King had another interview with Currie, who was 'non-committal as to what he might be willing to do' and again spoke of his relative lack of means.[26] What finally happened is not clear from King's diary, but the matter lapsed. No Canadian Minister to Washington was appointed until 1926, by which time Fielding had left the government.

As we have said more than once, the most fundamental question between Canada and the United States in modern times has always been commercial policy: more briefly, the tariff. And we have also mentioned that an important part of the conservative reaction in the United States after the First World War was the return to a high tariff. An 'emergency' tariff, representing in the words of the Canadian Prime Minister, Arthur Meighen, 'the most prohibitive level in force for many years,'[27] was enacted by Congress in the spring of 1921. It was largely inspired by the American farmers' demand for protection, and it provided 'high duties on wheat, corn, meat, wool, sugar.' In 1922 it was replaced by what became famous if not notorious as the Fordney-McCumber Tariff. 'The special conditions of 1921-22,' wrote Frank W. Taussig, 'led to an extreme of protection which few had thought possible.'[28] Canadian producers suffered in consequence. Some particular examples may be given. In the 1921 fiscal year Canada sold to the United States wheat worth more than $91,000,000; in 1925 (wheat prices, it must be noted, having fallen), sales were down to about $6,000,000. In the same period sales of wheat flour fell from about $12,000,000 to under $300,000. Barley sales were $472,000 in 1921; they fell to about $8,000 in 1925. Sales of cattle fell from over $600,000 in 1921 to $125,000 in 1925. Overall, the fiscal year 1921 set a record for Canadian exports to the United States: $542,322,967. By 1925 (when the economy had recovered from the 1922 post-war depression), the figure was $417,417,144; that was 39 per cent of Canada's total exports, whereas in 1921 the United States had taken 45.6 per cent of them.[29] Such were the consequences of Fordney-McCumber. It should be added, however, that in one respect the liberal principles of the Underwood Tariff survived: newsprint remained on the free list. A tariff on this item would have been a real disaster for the Canadian economy; but it would also have been a disaster for the powerful and influential American press.

The Meighen government that met defeat in December 1921 was unabashedly protectionist. The tariff, Meighen said, was the 'very root' of Canada's prosperity;[30] and his devotion to it undoubtedly cost him vast numbers of votes in the West, where the Progressives were bitterly hostile to protection. The Farmers' Platform of 1918 demanded 'complete Free Trade between Britain and Canada in five years.'[31] The victorious Liberals' policy was cautious. Their platform of 1919 pledged them to 'substantial reductions' in the tariff, but they were as much aware of the industrial East as they were of the agricultural West. Reciprocity had cost the new Prime Minister his own seat in 1911; and the revival of protectionism in the United States was a convenient and powerful excuse for going slow. The fact is that there were just too many protectionists in King's cabinet and party to make genuine tariff reform practicable. The government attempted no retaliation against the Fordney-McCumber Tariff; on the other hand, it made no very important reduction in the Canadian Tariff until the budget of 1924, which effected some cuts, particularly with respect to agricultural implements.[32]

Prohibition, introduced as a war measure in both Canada and the United States, caused trouble along the border for half a generation. The 18th Amendment to the Constitution of the United States (1918) forbade the 'manufacture, sale or transportation of intoxicating liquors,' but Canadian provincial prohibition laws in general did not go so far; the Ontario Temperance Act of 1916 merely forbade sale.[33] Partly as a result of this, liquor smuggling from Canada to the United States soon became big business.

A wave of distasteful alcoholic problems now broke over the British Embassy in Washington (whose staff, one suspects, were probably not very sympathetic to prohibition anyway). Honest British and Canadian rum-runners who claimed that their vessels had been illegally arrested outside the three-mile limit demanded countenance and aid. On the other side, the United States government considered that Britain and Canada should help *it* in its high-minded attempt to improve the behaviour of its citizens, in particular by preventing vessels from clearing their ports with cargoes of liquor intended for the United States. Such clearances were entirely legal in Canada as things stood. An additional complication was the refusal of the United States to allow liquor to be transported across the Alaska panhandle to the Yukon Territory, whose inhabitants were thus threatened with the advantages of prohibition whatever the territory's laws might say.[34]

The first British and Canadian reaction to the American requests for co-operation tended to be adverse (the Colonial Office remarked that under international law a state is responsible for enforcing only its own laws);[35] but as always there were many reasons for being complaisant to the United States, and as time passed both governments made large concessions. The first was a treaty extending the right of search beyond the three-mile limit and making the limit for such purposes one hour's steaming, in effect twelve miles; this was signed by the British Ambassador on January 23, 1924. Canada had accepted the treaty, on condition that it should be subject to approval by the Canadian Parliament before ratification; no Canadian representative signed it.[36] In November 1923 a conference of Canadian and American officials met in Ottawa to discuss the problems arising from liquor smuggling. The Americans asked that Canadian officials should furnish American officials along the border with information concerning cargoes or loads of liquor destined for the United States, American officials reciprocally informing their Canadian opposite numbers of shipments of dutiable articles intended for Canada which might be smuggled. The Canadian representatives made no objection to this. When the Americans asked that clearance be denied to cargoes of liquor intended for the United States, the reply was that existing Canadian law gave no authority for this. The Canadians were doubtful of proposals for extending extradition arrangements to cover violations of liquor laws, and for allowing prisoners in custody for breaches of liquor legislation to be conveyed by officers of one country through the territory of the other; and they would have nothing to do with an American suggestion that revenue cutters should be permitted to pursue suspected vessels across the international boundary on the Great Lakes, and search and seize vessels hovering along the line with the purpose of smuggling. Both parties agreed that there should be a treaty permitting the Canadian authorities to move liquor across Alaska to the Yukon under proper safeguards.[37] In June 1924 Ernest Lapointe, now the Canadian Minister of Justice, signed in Washington a treaty embodying the common ground established at the Ottawa meeting, including the matter of transit through Alaska.[38]

The United States government continued to press for the denial of liquor clearances (and for the desired change in the existing extradition treaty). Force was lent to the former request when the Canadian Royal Commission on Customs and Excise reported in 1927 that putting a stop to liquor clearances would have an important effect in reducing smuggling into Canada. When in that year the Canadian Legation finally opened in Washington the British Embassy must have handed over its Canadian prohibition business with a deep sigh of relief. Mackenzie King, however, was still slow to act on clearances. While anxious to appear in Washington as the friend of the United States, he was also afraid of being accused in Canada of truckling to that country. But he had strong views on the liquor question (he is on record to the effect that drink is 'the devil's principal agent'); and in 1929 he brought in legislation outlawing clearances on liquor shipments to the United States and pushed it through Parliament.[39] By that time the steam had long gone out of the prohibition movement in both countries. Too much crime had come in prohibition's wake; too many Canadians and Americans disliked this sumptuary law. The Canadian provinces were discovering that there was money to be made by making the sale of liquor a government monopoly; and in 1933 the United States finally repealed the 18th Amendment. Peace returned to the unfortified frontier.*

Water as well as alcohol caused international problems. What Canadian newspapers regularly called the 'Chicago water steal' – the large diversions of water from Lake Michigan for the sewage disposal system of Chicago – was still in progress, and from time to time it was reported that the diversions were increasing. It may be recalled that this problem already existed when the Boundary Waters Treaty was signed in 1909, and that it was excluded from the jurisdiction of the International Joint Commission by the treaty's provision concerning issues already under discussion (Volume I, page 152). The authority controlling diversions on the American shores of the Great Lakes was the United States War Department, and if it was alleged that the Chicago Sanitary District (a municipality in itself, separate from the city of Chicago) was diverting larger quantities of water than it had a permit for, the United States government could only appeal to the courts, a process which was always very protracted. It was perhaps fortunate for Canada that many American communities on the Lakes suffered by Chicago's action just as she did; even so, obtaining justice from Chicago was a very difficult business.

The Canadian government explained the problem in a telegram to the British Ambassador in Washington in 1921:[40]

Existing diversion, which has never been acquiesced in by Canada and which is in fact greatly in excess even of amount authorized by Secretary of War on December 5th, 1901, has done serious injury to navigation and water power interests throughout all of the Great Lakes and St. Lawrence System from Lake Huron to tidewater, and Canadian Government look upon whole position with apprehension. In their view no solution of such cases can be permanently sound and satisfactory unless it is based upon a recognition of the principle of international practice that no permanent diversion should be permitted to another watershed from any watershed naturally tributary to the waters forming the boundary between two countries.

* On the celebrated *I'm Alone* case, see below, pages 104-7.

This telegram referred to correspondence on the question going back to 1912. Further correspondence with the American State Department followed. The federal government at Washington clearly found the authorities of Illinois and Chicago obstructive and difficult to deal with; the Canadian government found the whole business very frustrating. In March 1925 the Secretary of War issued a new permit to the Chicago Sanitary District allowing a diversion of an annual average of not more than 8,500 cubic feet per second; this was hedged about with conditions including a requirement for the initiation of a sewage treatment programme which would ultimately permit of greatly reducing the diversion. This proviso held out hope for the future; but what troubled the Canadian government at the moment was that the new permit authorized a diversion 'in amount over twice that stipulated in any previous permits.'[41]

It may be well to summarize the later developments here. The controversy and the correspondence dragged on. Fortunately the American lake states (particularly Ohio, Wisconsin, Michigan, and Minnesota) kept up the pressure. The United States Supreme Court appointed a 'special master' to report on the matter; and in December 1929 he reported that Chicago's sewage treatment plants should be required to be completed by 1938, and that in the meantime the water diversion should be progressively reduced until in 1939 it should be limited to 1500 feet per second (excluding Chicago's normal water supply) unless Congress authorized more for navigation purposes. (Canada and the lake states had been alarmed by a project for diverting water for an 'Illinois-Mississippi Waterway.') In April 1930 the Supreme Court issued a decree embodying these recommendations. Progress, however, continued to be slow. In 1933 the Supreme Court delivered an opinion requiring the state of Illinois to take all necessary steps to meet the 1938 deadline. The Canadian Legation in Washington (which had been handling the question on behalf of Canada since it was set up in 1927) reported that this caused an outcry in Illinois; from the Canadian point of view, however, 'the decision seems to be wholly satisfactory.'[42] In due course the sewage treatment plants were finished, and this malodorous issue became less troublesome, though it was not finally disposed of until 1966.

'BADGES OF COLONIALISM': THE HALIBUT TREATY

The curious and rather celebrated episode of the Halibut Treaty belongs, formally speaking, to the history of Canada's relations with the United States; but its historical significance arises mainly from its place in the constitutional development of the British Commonwealth.

The fisheries are a never-ending continued story. In 1919 Sir Douglas Hazen, Chief Justice of New Brunswick and formerly Borden's Minister of Marine and Fisheries, negotiated two fishery treaties in Washington on behalf of Canada. One dealt with the protection and preservation of the sockeye salmon fishery on the Canadian and American Pacific coasts; the other with various fishery matters, including reciprocal port privileges for Canadian and American fishermen on the Pacific coast, and with the preservation of the Pacific halibut fishery in both countries' waters and the adjacent high seas. There was a momentary diplomatic flurry when Hazen (apparently without specific instructions from Ottawa) proposed to sign one or both of these treaties alone, taking the view that the full powers issued to him by the Crown authorized this. It appears that Lord Grey of Fallodon, then British Ambassador, saw nothing wrong with this. He wrote to the Governor General, 'Sir Douglas Hazen has full power to make and sign on behalf of the King, and he is anxious to sign at once. I have told him, therefore, that I see no objection to treaty being signed by him at once. Treaty does not affect any other Imperial interest ...' It transpired, however, that the Foreign Office had specified when forwarding Hazen's full powers that he was to sign 'in conjunction with His Majesty's Ambassador at Washington'; and this was done. Clearly the idea of an independent Canadian signature on treaties was in the air, and not only in Liberal circles.[43]

Neither of the two treaties of 1919 was accepted by the American Senate. The salmon treaty was withdrawn and renegotiated in 1920; but again it failed of ratification by the Senate and for the moment the matter languished. In 1922 Canada proposed that since the two countries seemed to be in accord on the protection of the halibut fishery, a separate treaty should be made on this matter alone. Accordingly the article (Article VII) of the second treaty dealing with the halibut question was made the basis of a new treaty. Early in 1923 this was ready for signature.[44]

It seems evident that Mackenzie King saw this as an opportunity to put into effect the plan for independent diplomatic action that he had proposed to the British Prime Minister after his Washington trip in July (above, page 31). The Halibut Treaty was an even better vehicle for the purpose than a re-negotiated Rush-Bagot Agreement. That would have been based on a purely British instrument, and even in 1922 the defence of Canada against the United States was still a matter of British interest. But the halibut fisheries of the Pacific coast seemed to affect Canada and the United States alone, and if the Canadian government wished to assert an independent diplomatic position and insist on signing treaties without the participation of any agent of the British government, no better occasion than this was likely to arise.

King's precise motives remain speculative, for he seems to have put no statement of them on record. It was possible to argue that Canada already had all the practical powers she needed in diplomatic negotiations; her agents had long carried on all international discussion on her behalf, and it was only at the stage of signing a formal instrument that custom required a British diplomatist to join with them, thus affirming the unity of the Empire before the world. Clearly, however, King desired the form as well as the substance. And in dealings with the United States, at least, it is arguable that a practical consideration was involved; it is more than doubtful whether Americans, and particularly the American Congress, could ever have been convinced that Canada was diplomatically a free agent as long as a British diplomatist was involved in signing treaties with her.

On January 11, 1923 King briefly noted in his diary a discussion in cabinet: 'Took up many miscellaneous matters including Treaty Canada & U.S. re Halibut Fisheries, decided to have it signed only by Lapointe [Minister of Marine and Fisheries] not by Br. Ambassador at Washington.' On February 17 the Prime Minister recorded that the Governor General (Lord Byng) said in a lunchtime conversation that 'he thought we were quite right.' King continued, probably referring to January 11, 'At Council all were agreed save Fielding who thought the Br. Ambassador should be included as in France but "wd not object" – if we wished to raise a question.' The reference to France is to a commercial treaty lately signed between that country and Canada, with British participation in the traditional manner; another commercial convention, with Italy, had been signed in the same way.[45] On February 20 King's diary records a more detailed discussion with Byng:

His Ex., at Sladen's* instance seemed anxious to know if the matter had been fully thought out, also why the Br. ambassador shld have signed in Europe and not in US. I explained that Fielding was all for the 'colonial status' & glad to have it so recognized, that the same attitude that made us desire separate representation at the League of Nations made us also desire direct representation in matter of signing treaties affecting only ourselves & our neighbors. I told him we were decided & agreed, Fielding having acquiesced. Also that if we cld not sign direct we wd at once go in for direct representation by Minister at Washington. So long as one Minister cld. go to Washington for the purpose there was less need for a Minister there. His Ex. was quite agreeable. I later had a despatch prepared for him to send to Sir Auc[k]land ...

* A.F. Sladen, Secretary to the Governor General. King had a tendency to blame Sladen for any difficulties he encountered at Government House.

The dispatch went to Geddes the following day. The last sentence read: 'My Ministers are of the opinion that as respects Canada, signature of the treaty by Mr. Lapointe alone will be sufficient and that it will not be necessary for you to sign as well.'[46]

The British Ambassador in Washington was thus told of King's plan, some six weeks after the Canadian cabinet had made its decision. King had still not informed the British government. On January 16 a telegram had gone to the Colonial Secretary asking him to arrange for full powers to be issued to the Hon. Ernest Lapointe to 'enable him to sign the Treaty ... on behalf of the Dominion at an early date.' This would have been the natural point at which to mention the Canadian government's desire that Lapointe alone should sign, but this was not done. However, Ottawa did indicate the direction of its thinking in one of the 'modifications' to the draft treaty which it proposed simultaneously: that the words 'The Dominion of Canada' should be substituted for 'Great Britain' in the title. The British authorities managed to side-step this; Geddes informed the Governor General that since the treaty as signed would 'bear no title,' the British Government had instructed him to omit this particular modification from his communication on the subject to Secretary Hughes.[47]

On receiving Byng's telegram of February 21, Geddes replied, 'I have been instructed by His Majesty's Government to sign Treaty in association with Mr. Lapointe.'[48] King now perforce had to raise the question openly with London, which he did in a telegram of February 28 from the Governor General to the Duke of Devonshire: 'My Ministers are of opinion that, as respects Canada, signature of the Treaty by Mr. Lapointe alone should be sufficient. They proceeded on this assumption in asking for full powers for Mr. Lapointe ... The view of my Ministers ... is that the Treaty being one of concern solely to Canada and the United States, and not affecting in any particular any imperial interest, the signature of the Canadian Minister should be sufficient, and they would respectfully request that His Majesty's Ambassador at Washington be instructed accordingly.' The telegram went on to ask for immediate action, to enable the United States Senate to ratify the treaty before it rose on March 4. The reply from London was prompt and terse: 'The wishes of your Ministers are being telegraphed to His Majesty's Ambassador at Washington by the Secretary of State for Foreign Affairs.' Devonshire accompanied this with a purely private note to Byng explaining that he had discussed the matter with Curzon. The message was not a definite instruction to the Ambassador because 'he might possibly feel difficulty on account of his own position.' 'I think however that result should be that Lapointe will sign alone. I should be glad if you would explain privately to Mr. Mackenzie King.'[49]

On March 2 the treaty was duly signed in Washington, Lapointe (alone) signing on behalf of Canada, and Secretary Hughes signing on behalf of the United States. Mackenzie King's authorized biographer is responsible for the story* that the British Embassy, resenting the Canadian action, omitted the customary courtesies to the Canadian minister: 'No one met Lapointe; no one communicated with him; and ... he telephoned to the American Secretary of State, and he himself made the necessary arrangements.'[50] It is pleasant to be able to report that this tale is untrue. The Toronto *Globe*'s man in Washington informed his paper on March 1, 'Mr. Lapointe was met at the train by the Secretary of the British Legation [sic], and drove to the Embassy before visiting the State Department.'[51]

In fact, London had heard of King's intentions over a week before he sent his belated cable.[52] Lord Byng, immediately after talking with King on February 20, telegraphed the Colonial Office reporting King's threat to proceed with opening a Canadian legation in Washington. He said that King had intimated that if Lapointe signed alone it would make his own position 'much easier as regards the proposal to appoint a Canadian Plenipotentiary to Washington, though he did not say that the matter would be dropped.' It was this that did the trick, for the British Foreign Office regarded a Canadian legation as a much greater evil than an independent signature on a treaty. The Ambassador was told that the signature by Lapointe alone would avoid this greater misfortune which 'you agree with us in desiring to escape.'[53] It is possible that King assumed that Byng would inform London of his remark about the legation. It is equally possible that King – still comparatively new in the office of Prime Minister – had not suspected that his good friend Byng was corresponding with the British government without informing him. It was, of course, perfectly legitimate for Byng to do this; for in 1923 the Governor General was still the agent of the British government as well as the representative of the Sovereign.

In Ottawa on March 2 Mackenzie King dined at Government House. 'His Ex. spoke of the Treaty, said it had given him pleasure to see it accomplished. He had written the Duke [of Devonshire] he thought the right thing had been done 1. because the Govt. wanted it, set great store on it, 2nd, it couldn't do any harm, & 3rd if it was to be done better do it with good grace ... He told me too last night he put his foot into it, by

* MacGregor Dawson's source was Alex Johnston, Lapointe's Deputy Minister, who must have talked to Dawson some thirty years later. Incidentally, Johnston did not arrive in Washington with Lapointe, but joined him there.

saying to Mr. Fielding he was glad it had been done. Mr. F. had warmed up & said he could not see why, – adding he expected His Ex. wd be glad. I told His Ex. I was sure it was right to remove any badge of "colonialism."'[54] If King had not realized before that Byng was corresponding with the Colonial Secretary, he knew it now.*

King's biographer Dawson comments that the Prime Minister appears to have deliberately kept the British government in the dark about his intentions until the very last moment in order to give it as little opportunity as possible for dissent. The official correspondence fully supports this interpretation. If one takes the view that King considered informal talks with the Governor General equivalent to informing the British authorities, his action perhaps looks somewhat better, but he does not seem to have mentioned the matter to Byng until over a month after the cabinet decision. It must be said in his favour that he had set his ideas on the signature of treaties before the government in London quite fully in August 1922, in connection with the proposal concerning the Rush-Bagot Agreement (above, page 34). There was ample opportunity then for discussion of the issue, but the British simply did not choose to discuss it. Their defence must consist in the fact that the Chanak crisis broke a month after King's telegram was sent, and at the end of that crisis the Lloyd George government fell. That intervening month, however, afforded plenty of time to pursue the question had they wished to do so. The British government had no right to feel surprised by King's proposal about the Halibut Treaty. Nevertheless the affair undoubtedly left the offices in London liking King even less than before. Chanak had made it clear that he was from their point of view a prickly customer and certainly no imperialist; now he had been made to look a bit 'sharp.'

This impression was doubtless heightened by a sequel. Meighen in the House of Commons pressed King for the correspondence about the signing of the treaty, and made a reference to 'secret diplomacy.' King sought, through the Governor General, permission from London and the Washington Embassy to bring down the papers (most of which were labelled 'Secret'). But before any reply arrived the Prime Minister gave the papers

---

* On November 10, 1924, King recorded in his diary that Byng had told him that 'he wd. & had refused to write any *private* letters, without letting me [know] of them or showing them to me, otherwise he could not expect to share my complete confidence.' Reading John Buchan's *Minto* had convinced him of the desirability of this. This was probably a new resolution; we know that Byng had sent a telegram without informing King in December 1922 (above, page 39), with unfortunate consequences.

to Parliament.[55] The Colonial Office, the Embassy and, above all, the Foreign Office were scandalized. King defended himself by citing the political pressure to which he had been subjected, and said that he had assumed that obtaining permission was a mere formality. Byng explained privately that he had found King 'extremely ignorant of the amenities that are always observed between Governments, as well as individuals, in connection with secret and confidential correspondence.'[56] There is no doubt that King resented the need for seeking British permission to publish, thinking this another 'badge of colonialism,' and gave no thought to the fact that even between fully independent countries the convention is observed of not publishing correspondence without the concurrence of the other party. At Byng's tactfully-phrased request King wrote him what amounted to an apology. Even then the Foreign Office insisted on pursuing the matter until King also produced an apology to the authorities of the United States.[57] For him the affair was painful but doubtless also instructive.

The Halibut Treaty did not pass into history without producing a revealing if transitory difficulty with the United States Senate.

The Senate duly considered the treaty on March 4, 1923, and passed a resolution of ratification (apparently sponsored by Senator Wesley Jones of Washington State) which, however, amounted to an amendment. It stipulated 'that none of the nationals and inhabitants and vessels and boats of any other part of Great Britain [sic] shall engage in halibut fishing contrary to any of the provisions of this treaty.' The British Ambassador obtained through the Secretary of State confirmation that by this the Senate intended to extend the treaty to cover any part of the British Empire. (One should not blame the Senate too much for the curious phrasing, for President Harding's message transmitting the treaty for its consideration described it as 'a convention between the United States and Great Britain.') This was clearly a modification which the government of Canada had no inclination, and the Parliament of Canada no power, to concur in. When therefore the Prime Minister presented the treaty to the House of Commons for approval on June 27, it was made clear (though with extreme tact) that it was the treaty as signed and not the treaty as amended by the American Senate. The Foreign Office in London, with a quite extraordinary display of bad temper, at first refused to allow the Washington Embassy to raise with the State Department the possibility of moving the Senate to reconsider; but under heavy pressure from the Colonial Office this was finally done in September. On May 31, 1924, the Senate quietly ratified the Halibut Treaty without reservations. It thus, by implication, accepted Canada as a power independently capable of making treaties with the United States: a minor landmark in the country's development as an 'international person.' Whether the Senate realized this, however, may be doubted; for there seems to have been no discussion of the treaty on the Senate floor either in 1923 or in 1924.[58]

The debate on the treaty in the House of Commons revealed once more the variety of Canadian attitudes on the country's external relations. Arthur Meighen for the Conservatives poked fun at the little drama that had been played at Washington: 'I wonder how much better off we are. Is our autonomy in the slightest degree enlarged? Does anyone understand just how we are advantaged by the supreme glory of having the Minister of Marine and Fisheries execute this treaty alone, having, figuratively speaking, kicked the British Ambassador out of the door in the execution of a treaty with a foreign power?' He went on to call the government's action 'unnecessary and, to my mind, indelicate.' Mackenzie King was not put down. A Conservative ex-minister had said that it was not necessary for Canada to exercise actively all the rights that she possessed. King retaliated: 'Mr. Speaker, we have passed that stage. We want not only the right, we want also to exercise our rights. We believe that in the exercise of all our rights we will gain more of strength and of influence as a nation; and, so far as the British Empire is concerned, we believe that its greatness will be proportionately greater as our strength and influence as a country increases.' Old Mr. Fielding said nothing.[59] But he had already made his views clear to the House during the discussion of his Italian treaty some weeks before: 'Whatever others may have said, it appeared to me that the name of the distinguished Principal Secretary of State for Foreign Affairs, Lord Curzon of Kedleston, rather added to the weight of this document, and I was glad to have it there.'[60]

GENEVA: THE FIRE-PROOF HOUSE

In Volume I we explored Canada's early contacts with the League of Nations, and noted that the representatives sent to Geneva by the Meighen government carried on a tradition established by Sir Robert Borden and his colleagues at Paris when the League Covenant was under discussion in 1919: they continued the attack on Article 10 of the Covenant. This article, it will be remembered, bound the members of the League to 'respect and preserve as against external aggression the territorial integrity and existing political independence of all Members of the League.' Many Canadians thought the burden of obligation thus laid upon their country excessive and unfair. In this matter Mackenzie King's new Liberal administration followed precisely in the footsteps of Borden and Meighen.

The delegates whom King's government sent to the League's Third Assembly (September 1922) were eminent: Fielding, the Minister of Finance; Lapointe, the Minister of Marine and Fisheries; and Peter Larkin, merchant prince and friend and benefactor of King, whom the Prime Minister had appointed to succeed the Conservative Sir George Perley as High Commissioner in London. Note the careful balance: Fielding, English-speaking and a conservative in his views on external policy; Lapointe, French-speaking and an autonomist. The mix bears what was to be the characteristic mark of King.

In advance of the Assembly meeting Loring Christie (who was still in the Department of External Affairs) prepared, presumably on King's instructions, a memorandum on the question of Article 10. He suggested that, in the light of the controversy about it since 1919, the article might in practice never have the effects its opponents feared. If, however, it was considered necessary to proceed with the campaign against it, Christie advised that it would be better to seek to amend it rather than to continue to urge that it be eliminated altogether.[61] This was what the Canadian delegation did, though it did not adopt the precise formula Christie provided; one may recall Fielding's hostility to Christie, lately reported by Sir Robert Borden (above, page 7). The delegates decided to move an amendment ending with the words, 'but no Member shall be under the obligation to engage in any act of war without the consent of its Parliament, legislature, or other representative body.' What might have been expected happened. Joseph Barthélemy, on behalf of France, made a strong speech in the Assembly opposing any interference with Article 10; and the matter was held over to the Fourth Assembly 'in order that the subject may be considered in all its bearings.'[62]

At the Fourth Assembly (September 1923) the Canadian representatives were Sir Lomer Gouin (Minister of Justice) and George P. Graham (Minister of Railways and Canals). Larkin was also appointed but could not attend. In the interim the Council of the League had polled all members inviting them to express their views on the Canadian proposal. The replies 'clearly showed that a large majority of the States were absolutely opposed to any change in the Article.' Gouin and Graham accordingly abandoned the plan of amendment and decided instead to ask for an Assembly resolution interpreting Article 10 in the sense desired by Canada. This plan had rather more success. A sub-committee of the Assembly's First Committee drafted a resolution. When this was discussed in the First Committee the British representative proposed a change of wording giving more emphasis to the obligation to preserve the independence and territorial integrity of all League members; and on this basis France was prepared to support the resolution. Gouin announced that Canada would be satisfied with a majority vote in the Assembly in favour of it, though unanimity was required, under the Covenant, to make resolutions effective.

The amended resolution as it went before the Assembly read as follows:

It is in conformity with the spirit of Article 10 that, in the event of the Council considering it to be its duty to recommend the application of military measures in consequence of an aggression or danger or threat of aggression, the Council shall be bound to take account, more particularly, of the geographical situation and of the special conditions of each State.

It is for the constitutional authorities of each Member to decide, in reference to the obligation of preserving the independence and the integrity of the territory of Members, in what degree the Member is bound to assure the execution of this obligation by employment of its military forces.

The recommendation made by the Council shall be regarded as being of the highest importance and shall be taken into consideration by all the members of the League with the desire to execute their engagements in good faith.

In the event, the resolution failed of unanimous support by one vote – that of Persia. Twenty-nine members voted for it, among them the 'British Empire' (the United Kingdom), all the other Dominions and India, and France. There were twenty-two abstentions or absences. The President of the Assembly declared the resolution 'not adopted,' for want of unanimity.[63]

It is pretty clear that the Canadian campaign against Article 10 had not been popular with some small countries which saw the article as a safeguard against aggression; though only one, Persia, pushed the matter to the point of actually voting against the resolution. It has been suggested that 'a certain irritation' provoked by Canada's tendency to take lofty moral positions and specifically by her attack on Article 10 was responsible for the apparent readiness of several small states to give some countenance to the – ultimately unsuccessful – attempt of a representative of the hereditary council of the chiefs of the Six Nations Indians to gain a hearing from the League for their grievances against Canada in this same year. At one stage the delegates of four states wrote the President of the Assembly suggesting that his appeal be communicated to the Assembly; they were the Irish Free State – newly admitted to the League – Panama, Estonia, and, again, Persia.[64]

The Canadian delegates, not unnaturally, chose to interpret the all-but-unanimous vote on the Article 10 resolution as a victory. 'While it is true that unanimity is necessary under the constitution of the League to give legal effect to a declaration of this nature, it nevertheless remains that should occasion arise the Council would be expected to give to Article 10 the interpretation which by its vote the Assembly has expressed ... Your delegates feel that, under the circumstances, a satisfactory answer has been given to the question ...'[65] At any rate, the long campaign could now be called off.

Looking at the resolution that ended it, one has a feeling that one has been here before. 'It is for the constitutional authorities of each Member to decide ...' One recalls again Sir Wilfrid Laurier in 1910: 'If England is at war we are at war and liable to attack. I do not say ... that we would take part in all the wars of England. That is a matter that must be determined by circumstances, upon which the Canadian parliament will have to pronounce ...' The same defences which Canadian politicians had set up against automatic active involvement in the wars of Britain they were now seeking to set up against the possible wars of the League. Any international company which Canada joined was going to be a strictly limited company if she could make it so. So far as her campaign against Article 10 had had any success, it had weakened the League as it pursued the quest for international security; and many of her partners in the League, great and small, were clearly well aware of it.

That the limitation of obligations was Canada's prime concern in her dealings with the League appears in other episodes of these years; notably in the matters of the draft Treaty of Mutual Guarantee and the Geneva Protocol.

The Treaty of Mutual Guarantee (later called the Treaty of Mutual Assistance) grew primarily out of the search for 'security' on the part of France and other neighbours of Germany. Disarmament was a great ostensible object of the League; but these countries claimed they could not disarm until they had firm guarantees of assistance in case of German attack. The Tripartite Pact of 1919, providing such guarantees, had foundered on the opposition of the United States Senate (Volume I, pages 256-7). The draft Treaty of Mutual Assistance which emerged from the League's Fourth Assembly of 1923 was an attempt at a substitute. All members of the League were asked their views on it. The treaty would have 'involved for every signatory State the obligation to give military support to any other signatory which was the victim of aggression,' though no state was to be obliged to take part in military operations outside its own continent.[66] Canada had already replied to a League inquiry at an earlier stage* that it seemed unlikely that the Canadian people would consent to such an agreement; now the government told the Secretary General that the proposed treaty created 'an obligation wider in its extent and more precise in its implications' than Article 10, about which Canada had had such grave doubts; 'it would be hopeless to expect the people of Canada to accept it.' Britain and the other Commonwealth countries also opposed the scheme, as did many other states; and it collapsed.[68]

It was shortly revived in another form. The Protocol for the Pacific Settlement of International Disputes, usually called the Geneva Protocol, was recommended to the members of the League by the Fifth Assembly (1924). It was 'a highly ingenious, and, as many thought, a highly successful attempt to translate into a formal system the formula, Arbitration, Security, Disarmament.' It required every signatory to adhere to the so-called Optional Clause of the Statute of the Permanent Court of International Justice, accepting compulsory arbitration in all cases of a judicial character; there were other provisions for arbitration in cases not coming before the Court. Again there were stringent provisions for sanctions against states resorting to war. Signatories of the protocol were bound to come to the aid of a victim of aggression, though (a reminiscence of the not-quite-successful resolution interpreting Article 10) their obligations were to be limited by their geographical positions and the state of their armaments. Finally, signatories were to agree to take part in a general disarmament conference to meet in June 1925.[69]

Canada's delegates to the Fifth Assembly were Senator Raoul Dandurand, Government Leader in the Senate, and E.M. Macdonald, a comparative nonentity who was Minister of National Defence. Dandurand now made his first appearance at Geneva, where he was to become a familiar figure, regularly representing Canada under Liberal administrations until the eve of the Second World War. One of his earliest tasks was to explain the Dominion's position on the Protocol. He did so in a speech containing a phrase that was to have a dubious fame.[70] He began with a characteristi-

---

* In the first instance Sir Joseph Pope, who was as we have seen in poor health, sent off, evidently without consulting anybody, a one-sentence reply indicating that Canada had 'every sympathy with the object sought to be obtained.' Sir Herbert Ames, a Canadian official of the League, delicately called attention to the desirability of a fuller reply. Sir Joseph shortly dispatched the letter summarized in the text, the substance of which had been suggested to Mackenzie King by Ernest Lapointe.[67]

cally Canadian boast about peaceful North America: 'Not only have we had a hundred years of peace on our borders, but we think in terms of peace, while Europe, an armed camp, thinks in terms of war.' As to arbitration, Dandurand said: 'It is my firm conviction that Canada, faithful to her past, will be prepared to accept compulsory arbitration and the compulsory jurisdiction of the Permanent Court of International Justice.' Disarmament? Canada had already disarmed. But he warned his hearers that there were elements in Canada's situation that might make her doubtful about accepting heavy obligations: 'May I be permitted to add that in this association of mutual insurance against fire the risks assumed by the different states are not equal? We live in a fire-proof house, far from inflammable materials. A vast ocean separates us from Europe. Canada therefore believed it to be her duty to seek a precise interpretation of what appeared to her to be the indefinite obligations included in Article 10 of the Covenant.' He promised that the Protocol would be studied 'with the fullest sympathy.'

Canadians who went through the fiery trial of the Second World War would remember with wry humour that remark of Dandurand's about the fire-proof house.

The Protocol was, indeed, carefully studied in Ottawa; though the result of the study could have easily foretold. On February 2, 1925 Mackenzie King gave a dinner party at Laurier House. The guests included six cabinet ministers (both Dandurand and Macdonald among them, as well as Lapointe), two senators, two members of his staff, including Skelton, and one private citizen – John S. Ewart. King recorded that they 'spent the evening discussing the Geneva Protocol. Decided not to approve on ground U.S. not being in League it placed us at disadvantage, also re questions of domestic significance it raises an embarrassing situation. Decided Canada to take her own stand as a member of League of Nations.' The domestic question was presumably the unpopularity, actual or apprehended, of the Protocol in French Canada. Dandurand asserted in later years that he defended the Protocol at Laurier House, but was overborne by the majority; he said he found it hard to believe that Canada would refuse to accept compulsory arbitration, and suggested that the reply should make it clear that Canada supported the basic principles of the Protocol. To this small gesture all agreed.[71]

It is fair to assume that the fundamental Canadian decision was taken in that irregular gathering at Laurier House. However, King went through the motions of appointing an 'informal interdepartmental committee' of civil servants including Skelton, which held five meetings and came to essentially the same conclusions as the dinner party. Skelton himself had previously prepared a long analysis of the Protocol, listing, in a manner that was to be characteristic of him, the arguments for and against it and, predictably, coming down strongly against. Among other things he remarked, 'Article VIII of the Protocol is more vague and dangerous than Article 10 of the Covenant to which Canadian governments of all parties have stood opposed.'[72]

Commonwealth relations became involved in the Protocol controversy. There had been discussion of the Treaty of Mutual Assistance between King's administration and the Labour government of Ramsay MacDonald in Britain, and King had sent the latter the text of the rejection which he proposed to send to Geneva, remarking however that he would not dispatch it until the British had concurred.[73] Stanley Baldwin returned to power after MacDonald's defeat late in 1924, with Leo Amery as Colonial Secretary. Amery was one of the few British politicians of cabinet rank who took an active interest in the overseas Empire. To King this was no recommendation; he saw Amery as a centralizing schemer.[74] In December Baldwin sent King a cable about the Protocol, writing: 'We conceive it to be essential in regard to a problem of this magnitude the Empire should have a single policy and we are equally convinced that such a policy can only be determined as a result of personal consultation between Ministers.' He went on to propose 'a special meeting of the Imperial Conference.' The Canadian Prime Minister had no use for this suggestion. His reply, however, was conciliatory: 'We agree it is highly desirable that similar attitudes should be adopted towards the Protocol by the countries of the British Empire which are members of the League of Nations.' (Professor Glazebrook has pointed out that 'a single policy' and 'similar attitudes' are rather different things.)[75] King went on to say that the Canadian parliamentary schedule seemed to make a conference impracticable; he suggested 'an interchange of opinion by cable and post,' with the understanding that if this proved inadequate a conference could again be considered. (He took a similar line, on occasion, during the Second World War.) Other Dominions were also unenthusiastic about a conference and the idea was abandoned.[76]

An exchange of messages early in March 1925 made it evident that all the Commonwealth governments found the Protocol unacceptable. The British government now inquired whether there was any objection to the Foreign Secretary (Austen Chamberlain) announcing this at a coming meeting of the Council of the League. This message was evidently discussed at a meeting of the Canadian cabinet on March 7. King wrote in his diary that day: 'All were agreed on our keeping our separate identity in the League to the fore. The Eng. Tory game is to have a common foreign Policy voiced by Chamberlain. Aust. & N.Z. will join in that & doubtless Newfoundland. S. Africa & Canada will not. – Our relations with U.S. puts [sic] us in a position where we can render Br. Empire greater service by being an interpreter of each to other –' A rather stiff cable went to London on March 8:

Your telegram 7th March. My Ministers see no objection to Mr. Chamberlain making general statement to Council of League of Nations to effect Dominions mentioned and India are not prepared to accept Protocol.

Statement of Foreign Secretary at December meeting of Council to effect that he spoke there for all Governments of Empire has been commented upon as indicating change from original understanding upon which Dominions received distinct representation in Assembly, and if so interpreted is likely to prejudice position of Dominions in League.

My Ministers of course believe this is not intention of Foreign Secretary but to avoid any misunderstanding in present instance suggest that Foreign Secretary might state that he has been authorized by Dominions concerned to make this statement on their behalf ...[77]

On March 9 Mackenzie King sent to the Secretary General of the League Canada's formal rejection of the Geneva Protocol. After careful consideration, he said, the government had come to four conclusions. First, Canada should 'continue to give whole-hearted support to the League of Nations and particularly to its work of conciliation, co-operation, and publicity.' Note the last ten words; they define the limited role which the government thought proper for the League. King continued:

(2) That we do not consider it in the interests of Canada, of the British Empire, or of the League itself to recommend to Parliament adherence to the Protocol and particularly to its rigid provisions for application of economic and military sanctions in practically every future war. Among the grounds for this conclusion is the consideration of the effect of the non-participation of the United States upon attempts to enforce the sanctions and particularly so in the case of a contiguous country like Canada.

The sugar on the pill followed. We hear the voice of the author of *Industry and Humanity*, but also that of the cautious politician. Canada believed firmly in the submission of international disputes to joint inquiry or arbitration; therefore 'we would be prepared to consider acceptance of the compulsory jurisdiction of the Permanent Court in justiciable disputes with certain reservations, and to consider methods of supplementing the provisions of the Covenant for settlement of non-justiciable issues, including method of joint investigation, reserving ultimate decision in domestic issues and without undertaking further obligations to enforce decisions in case of other states.' Finally, Canada would be prepared to take part in any general disarmament conference 'which did not involve prior acceptance of Protocol.'[78]

Canada's arrow was only one of many; the Protocol was dead.

It seems likely that King had consented to include the reference to accepting the compulsory jurisdiction of the Permanent Court as a concession to Dandurand. Incidentally, as drafted the document said that the government would be 'prepared to recommend' such action; at the last moment the phrase was weakened to 'prepared to consider.'[79] The consideration turned out to be a long process. The matter was discussed at the Imperial Conference of 1926. In January 1929 the Canadian government informed London that they had concluded it would be desirable for Canada to accept the Optional Clause. This was announced in the Canadian Parliament in February. The second Labour government of Ramsay MacDonald, which took office in Britain in the following June, felt that the time had come for a move, and tried to organize united Commonwealth action, suggesting a meeting of representatives – not an Imperial Conference, presumably a High Commissioners' meeting – in London. This was duly held in August – without any representative from Canada. Mackenzie King's diary, often so useful on motives, is silent here; but he had shown himself very hostile to meetings of High Commissioners with the Colonial Secretary.[80] However, there was essential unity on the main issue, and early in September MacDonald announced at Geneva that Britain and the Dominions were going to sign the Optional Clause. Canada gave a grumpy assent to this: 'We should have preferred MacDonald restricting his statement to announcement of intention of his own Government to sign,' the Canadian office at Geneva was told. Canada actually signed the clause on September 20, 1929, the most important reservation being that her acceptance did not extend to disputes between members of the British Commonwealth of Nations.[81]

In 1925 Senator Dandurand was elected President of the League Assembly. Skelton noted that there had been 'some intimation from official quarters that if Canada were to send for two consecutive years a delegate proficient in the two official languages, there would be a strong possibility of his being chosen as President with the support of the British and French delegations.' The Under Secretary asked Dr W.A. Riddell, who at the beginning of 1925 became Canadian 'Advisory Officer' at Geneva – an addition to the Canadian diplomatic service – to discuss the matter with the Secretary General, Sir Eric Drummond. Contrary to a story that has been told, there is no evidence that Mackenzie King opposed the idea.[82] Dandurand met the specifications, and before long King was cabling Stanley Baldwin thanking him for the British government's support and its good offices with the French. In September Dandurand was duly chosen by the Sixth Assembly, according to Riddell 'amid great enthusiasm.'[83] The courtly old senator, a good Canadian and a good French Canadian, fluently bilingual and proud of it (he wrote in his memoirs, 'Je crois que mon bilinguisme me donne la physionomie d'un Canadien intégral, supérieur à l'unilingue, malgré ce qu'en pense l'abbé Lionel Groulx'), seems indeed to have been a great success.

In 1926 the possibility presented itself of Canada's being elected to a non-permanent seat on the Council of the League. In September of that year Germany was admitted to the League and given permanent membership on the Council, and the number of non-permanent seats was increased from six to nine. There was now some chance of one of the British Dominions being elected, and Riddell reported that he had been told that Sir Austen Chamberlain (as he had now become) would be prepared to support Canada. In July 1927 Ernest Lapointe cabled Skelton from Geneva urging that Canada should be a candidate, to 'advertise Dominion status to international world.' Skelton passed this message to the Prime Minister, covered by a cautious memorandum recommending on balance that Lapointe's advice should be taken.[84]

King did not agree. This was a different matter from the presidency of the Assembly, which was largely an honorific affair. On the Council Canada would be for three years a member of the organ of the League that carried the main weight of its activity, and would be involved in the business of settling international disputes, obliged to take sides. King was particularly perturbed by the thought of having to take sides as between Britain and France.[85] He wrote in his diary on June 8: 'At luncheon with Dandurand yesterday, I opposed the idea of his or rather Canada taking a seat on the Council of the League of Nations. We are just as wise not to get too far into European politics (& entanglements). It wd mean French Can. representation & Canada's siding on the League against England, possibly, which wd raise a major political issue here. If not likely to differ with Eng. then no need for separate representation. Better avoid mistakes.' Again the cautious politician, intent on avoiding unnecessary domestic complications, intent above all on not awakening the sleeping 'race question.' But Lapointe returned to the charge in a cable in which he said, 'Let Canada again lead Dominions,' and subsequently in conversation on September 4. King, unlike Borden, was not interested in leading;

but he yielded to his valued lieutenant. Lapointe, King wrote in his diary that day, 'Said it was the only time or thing on which we had differed. I sd I wd not differ with him & he was free to cable ...'[86] The Canadians at Geneva now plunged into electioneering. Skelton reported from there: 'Our dual language situation gives us double means of contact; the independent position Canada has taken in the League and her pioneering in the Empire, all helped. No other Dominion could have secured half our support. Senator Dandurand's personal popularity, the quiet, but effective, canvassing of Mr. [Philippe] Roy and Dr. Riddell, the vigorous support of the Irish Free State, made the most of the situation.' Even so, the result was scarcely brilliant. Canada got one of the three vacant Council seats, but she ran third to Cuba and Finland, getting 26 votes against their 40 and 33 respectively. Skelton wrote: 'We had the solid vote of the British Empire delegations, Northern and Central Europe, and other scattering votes; we do not know whether France voted for us or not.'[87] With Canada sitting on the Council of the League, another national milestone had been passed.

THE IMPERIAL CONFERENCE OF 1923

Because of its central importance for Mackenzie King's policies, it has seemed best to leave to the end of this chapter the Imperial Conference that took place in London in October and November 1923.

King, within himself a very insecure man, approached his first Empire conference with trepidation: 'It is much worse than a general election.'[88] But he had one great resource and comfort: O.D. Skelton, who now joined him for the first time. As has already been mentioned (above, page 9), Skelton came to him from Queen's University, on a temporary basis, to accompany him to the conference and to prepare studies of the topics to be considered there. Of these the most important was a paper entitled 'Canada and the Control of Foreign Policy.'[89] King read it on September 11 and called it in his diary 'a splendidly prepared brief ... with every line of which I am in hearty and entire accord.' The paper may be said to have been a revised and extended version of Skelton's Canadian Club address which had so impressed King in January 1922 (above, page 8). It was basically an attack on the idea of a common foreign policy for the Empire founded on consultation between Britain and the Dominions. Skelton wrote at one point: 'It is claimed that this course of action, this endeavour to change the trend of past development and to set up a common foreign policy for the whole Empire means an extension of influence and power for the Dominions. Exactly the contrary is the case. It offers a maximum of responsibility and a minimum of control. It commits a Dominion in advance to an endorsement of courses of action of which it knows little and of which it may not approve, or in which it may have little direct concern.'

This was an able and in many ways an impressive paper, but it was an extraordinarily partisan production. Its most curious feature is the fact that it represents the plan for a unified foreign policy as entirely a British scheme – a British plot, though it does not use that word – and says no word of the Canadian share in it. There is absolutely no reference to Sir Robert Borden's long campaign for a 'voice' for Canada in the formation of Imperial policy. Nothing is said even of Resolution IX of the Imperial War Conference, 1917, which Borden originated and moved, with its proclamation of the right of the Dominions 'to an adequate voice in foreign policy' and of the desirability of 'effective arrangements for continuous consultation in all important matters of common Imperial concern.' A whole decade of determined Canadian effort in the field of external policy is wiped from the record. Skelton represents the common-foreign-policy idea as 'a direct reversal of the whole trend of Dominion development in the past half-century,' and nowhere recognizes the fact that he is urging King to reverse a policy developed by Canadian governments to meet the challenges of the most eventful years in the Dominion's history.

There is no evidence as to Skelton's motives. Even if he did little research in the External Affairs records, the main facts were public property. One wonders whether he can have refrained from describing Borden's policies from apprehension that King, if fully informed of the extent to which the country had been committed to them over many years, might have taken alarm and hesitated to commit himself to the very different policies that Skelton favoured. Skelton's paper may have been good politics, but it was very bad history. In effect, if not in intent, it was mendacious.[90]

At any rate, King swallowed it whole, and regurgitated great parts of it for the benefit of his colleagues at the conference table. The Conference's treatment of foreign policy began on October 5 with a review by the Foreign Secretary, Lord Curzon (who had sufficiently recovered from the bitter blow of having Baldwin preferred over him for the office of Prime Minister to consent to remain at the Foreign Office). Skelton's word for the presentation was reported by King as 'olympic' (perhaps he actually said 'Olympian'). King himself was sufficiently impressed to engage in a flight of British sentimentality in his diary: 'If one's regard is for humanity, rather than for any other "anity," whether empire, country, or local community, one cannot but feel that to the British family of nations at the moment comes the call to stand firmly and strongly together, and in their own unity and sense of security help to restore confidence to a much distracted world.' This would certainly have surprised the people who listened to King's own presentation three days later.[91]

That presentation, he thought, was indeed 'in the nature of a surprise to those present.'[92] He made a survey of Canada's foreign relations, just as Curzon had surveyed those of Britain, remarking in the beginning that Canada's direct international relations were 'preponderatingly, though not wholly,' with a single country. He proceeded to describe Canada's dealings with the United States at some length: the International Joint Commission, the Chicago water diversion, the proposed St Lawrence Waterway, the Halibut Treaty (perhaps some of his auditors woke up at this point), the Rush-Bagot Agreement, the liquor problem, etc., etc. Then he passed on to 'Relations of various parts of the Empire in foreign policy,' and gave the conference Skelton's brief. The British Empire, he said, was 'a league of peoples plus an Empire'; its diversity was endless; and 'it is inevitable that each of these communities should seek to control those foreign affairs which concern it primarily.' 'If it is not possible or desirable that Great Britain or other Dominions should control those foreign affairs which are distinctly of primary concern to one Dominion, so it is equally impossible and undesirable for the Dominions to seek to control those foreign affairs which primarily affect Great Britain.' Nevertheless, 'There are issues which are of fundamental concern to all parts of the Empire; and with these all parts of the Empire must deal; the Governments of the Empire must confer; the Parliaments of the Empire, if need be, must decide.' The issue is clearly stated as between a common policy for the Empire and an independent policy for each empire country; and King leaves no doubt that he is insisting on the latter.

There was clearly considerable astonishment and some dismay among his hearers; Australia and New Zealand dissociated themselves from his views, and at a later stage Maurice Hankey is reported to have said to Skelton that the British 'could not find out where Canada stood. Borden some years ago had asked for a share in foreign policy and last Conference Canada had agreed to uniform policy and common responsibility. Now Canada repudiated this policy.' Skelton, forced to be a little more open than in his brief for King, 'said the position of the present Government was that the decision of two years ago was a reversal of the policy which had been developing for fifty years and its intention was to see that the effects of this aberration were removed.'[93] It would have been more accurate to say that King himself was reversing a policy which had been pursued, not merely in the Conference of 1921, but since 1911. That, however, might have seemed a little strange.

The specific point on which King made most difficulty at the conference concerned, not surprisingly, the portion of the final report dealing with foreign relations. Curzon submitted a draft on November 5. King saw it as 'an effort to commit the conference to a common foreign policy'; he recorded, 'I had a most difficult and unpleasant hour or two strongly opposing many of the paragraphs that were inserted.' He spent November 7 in discussions with Hankey and Smuts attempting to reach an accommodation. Finally Smuts inquired whether King would accept reducing his reservations to a brief concluding paragraph indicating that the conference proceedings were all subject to the approval of the participating countries' parliaments, plus the elimination from the draft of passages concerning Turkey and Egypt; and King agreed. The report as published ended with this statement: 'This Conference is a conference of representatives of the several Governments of the Empire; its views and conclusions on Foreign Policy, as recorded above, are necessarily subject to the action of the Governments and Parliaments of the various portions of the Empire, and it trusts that the results of its deliberations will meet with their approval.' The references to Egypt and Turkey were not omitted, but both were considerably shortened. Future policy concerning Turkey was not referred to, and a specific remark about the importance of the Suez Canal was cut out.[94] The exercise had clearly earned King a good deal of illwill, and the dividend had been hardly worth it.

On another matter King had a pleasant surprise. The conference considered the question of procedure on the signing of treaties. This was consigned to a committee of Prime Ministers, King being one. When the committee met on October 25 Lord Curzon put before it a draft proposal which led the Canadian Prime Minister to write in his diary: 'Had I drafted the memorandum, I could not have better expressed the views which were in my own mind.' Essentially, King's Halibut Treaty procedure now appeared in a British official document. The proposal met with no opposition except from Massey of New Zealand (King 'asked him whether New Zealand was a Crown Colony or a self-governing Dominion').[95] It was written into the conclusions of the conference, the kernel of the matter being thus expressed:

(a) Bilateral treaties imposing obligations on one part of the Empire only, should be signed by a representative of the government of that part. The Full Power issued to such representative should indicate the part of the Empire in respect of which the obligations are to be undertaken, and the preamble and text of the Treaty should be so worded as to make its scope clear.*

(b) Where a bilateral treaty imposes obligations on more than one part of the Empire, the treaty should be signed by one or more plenipotentiaries on behalf of all governments concerned.

At international conferences, the 'existing practice' of signature by plenipotentiaries on behalf of all the governments of the Empire represented at the conference should be followed.[97]

King wrote, 'I am more than delighted with the result which I think marks a distinct triumph and will prove a mile-stone in the constitutional evolution and development of the Empire.'[98] His delight might have been tempered had he been acquainted with the background of the British action, which has only recently been brought to light. We have seen the attitude of the Foreign Office on the Halibut Treaty; they accepted the independent Canadian signature because it was a lesser evil than a Canadian legation in Washington. And we have witnessed at Lausanne their determination not to have a repetition of Paris; clearly they wanted no more British Empire delegations – the instrument which Sir Robert Borden had seen as almost certainly the answer to the problem of reconciling imperial diplomatic unity with Dominion autonomy (Volume I, page 355). Curzon and his staff approached the 1923 conference convinced that the Dominions should be given the right to negotiate and sign, quite freely and independently, their own treaties; they told the Colonial Office: 'Both the rights and the liabilities of such treaties will be confined to that Dominion and the Government of the Dominion concerned will be responsible for seeing that the treaty is observed.' Consultation had become a dirty word at the Foreign Office; in the midst of the conference, when it appeared that Australia might press for some new consultative machinery, Curzon obtained from the British cabinet a decision that there would be no British initiative in suggesting 'any alteration in the present association of the Dominions with foreign affairs,' and no Dominion initiative would be accepted without further cabinet consideration. Consulting the Dominions was seen as merely complicating the Foreign Office's task; Eyre Crowe observed (truly enough, it must be said) that it was not

---

* This represented a battle lost by the Colonial Office, which beginning in 1919, when the Full Powers given to Dominion ministers were issued 'in respect of' their own countries, had consistently resisted this practice, as likely to be fatal to the diplomatic unity of the Empire.[96]

practicable in diplomacy to delay all action until the Dominions had been consulted and agreed. In a crisis this certainly could rarely be done.[99]

To put it very bluntly, the Foreign Office was in favour of a common Empire foreign policy only so far as it was a policy both decided on and administered in Whitehall. If it involved consultation with the Dominions, the Office greatly preferred a system under which Britain would pursue her own foreign policy, and the Dominions would pursue theirs; in fact, the system advocated by King and Skelton. Since in 1923 the Dominions, with the exception of New Zealand, were very unlikely to accept a plan which gave them no 'voice,' the days of the common policy were over. Stanley Bruce of Australia was in a sense the heir of Borden when he argued in the conference for a widening of consultation; but with both King and Curzon against him his chances of success were nil. The Colonial Office continued to argue for a system of consultation, but its influence was small compared to that of the Foreign Office. As Philip Wigley has pointed out, in spite of the rude things they said about each other privately, in this conference King and Curzon were essentially at one. King went home feeling he had won a great victory; he did not realize that he had had an ally much more influential in Whitehall than he was.[100]

Here then is the end of a noble experiment: the attempt to put into practice what Loring Christie called the 'project of co-operative unified diplomacy' associated with the name of Borden. It could only have succeeded if a great deal of care, goodwill, and determination had been devoted to it in both Britain and the Dominions. The reverse was the case; Mackenzie King hated it, so did Lord Curzon. King hated it because he thought it a menace to Canadian autonomy, Curzon hated it because it was a trammel on the freedom of action of the Foreign Office. But it may be doubted whether the great idea was ever really practicable. Given more goodwill on both sides it might have been made to succeed for a time. But those who examine the confrontation between Meighen and Hughes over the Anglo-Japanese Alliance in 1921, or the extraordinary performance of British statesmanship in the Chanak affair the following year, will realize just how difficult the system would have been to work in practice. And any success the plan of unified policy based on continuous consultation attained could hardly have been more than transitory; it would have been overthrown, sooner rather than later, by the rising tide of Dominion nationalism.

Other aspects of the 1923 conference we can pass over. Quite inevitably, King refused to have anything to do with commitments on imperial defence; he and Skelton were deeply suspicious of the Admiralty. He brought up the question of publication of correspondence (a consequence of the controversy following the Halibut Treaty), and the conference agreed that any communication not marked 'confidential' or 'secret' or not clearly intended to be treated as such might be regarded as available for publication without reference to any other government.[101] An Imperial Economic Conference met coincidentally with the main conference, Canada being represented in it by Graham and Gouin. It accomplished little of importance; King's government was in no position to make important commitments on the tariff.[102] When the President of the British Board of Trade (Sir Philip Lloyd-Greame) approached King privately, told him that Baldwin was planning to adopt protection and suggested that Canada give 'a straight fifty percent preference on everything' in exchange for similar action by Britain, King told him instantly that any such thing was impossible.[103] A group of British financiers discussed with King the idea of floating a loan for Canada in London on favourable terms. King liked it, thinking it might 'mean much for the credit of Canada in England'; but it was vetoed by his Minister of Finance, Fielding, who preferred to borrow on the domestic market.[104]

Before taking final leave of the conference of 1923, we might note one small item in the record. In the course of his statement on foreign policy on October 8, King referred to United States influence on Canada, suggesting that if the Americans persisted in their policy of isolation, and Canada went to the other extreme, assuming 'daily responsibility' for settling the affairs of Europe, the result might be a growth of 'Continental sentiment' which would be a danger to the Empire. King proceeded: 'That is a consideration which may be overruled. If a great and clear call of duty comes, Canada will respond, whether or no the United States responds, as she did in 1914, but it is a most important consideration against intervention in lesser issues.' Few people perhaps took note of this remark, but it was important. What the Prime Minister was saying was that Canada had no intention of getting involved in Chanaks; but a world crisis, with Britain and the Empire in danger, would be a different matter. King clearly believed that in such a crisis Canada would instantly and inevitably be involved. There is no reason to think that he ever changed that view.

CHAPTER THREE

THE LATER TWENTIES:
PROSPERITY AND PROBLEMS

THE SHAPE OF POLITICS, 1925-6

The years 1925 and 1926 witnessed in Canada a prolonged political crisis. Its final result was to place Mackenzie King more firmly in power than before; and he controlled the government until after the onset of the Great Depression in 1929.

King's ministry, nearly four years old now, 'went to the country' in October 1925. In this campaign, just as in that of 1921, external policies were hardly mentioned at all. At first glance this might seem surprising; for there had been important developments since the last general election, and King was certainly proud of his record in this field. The refusal to co-operate at Chanak; the Halibut Treaty, and the vindication of the policy it represented by the Imperial Conference; in general, the reversal of the Borden-Meighen approach to relations with Britain – all these things might have been made issues, but were not. Arthur Meighen and his Conservatives did not choose to attack King on these questions. The fact is that such matters were politically dangerous, and they were dangerous mainly because of Quebec. It was still true, as King had written in 1919, that Quebec dominated the House of Commons. The solid Quebec bloc provided the foundation of King's power. In contrast, Meighen, unless he could gain at least a few more seats in Quebec, could scarcely hope to obtain a solid parliamentary majority. If King boasted of his anti-imperial exploits, it would be popular with most Quebec voters, but he already had virtually all the seats from that province; and he might lose seats in Ontario and perhaps in other provinces as well. If Meighen attacked King's policies as anti-British, it would be on the whole popular in Ontario, where he was already strong, and to some extent elsewhere, but would make it very difficult for him to get those additional Quebec seats that he so badly needed. It was far better for both sides to say nothing.

The one question that could be called external that was well ventilated during the campaign was the tariff. Meighen continued to be obsessed with it; and with what a better party tactician might have thought unfortunate directness he made it the main point of his appeal: 'a sound and strong and definite protective policy is the only means by which we can live and prosper.' King on the other hand contrived to come close to being on both sides of the issue. In his opening speech he declared, 'The policy of the Liberal party is a tariff primarily for revenue,' but went on to say, 'We cannot have either high tariff or absolutely free trade in Canada ... Our tariff must have regard for all parts of the country in its present state of development.'[1]

Meighen's war record, particularly his identification with the policy of conscription, made him a liability to his party in French Canada. It was impossible to find a French leader who would carry his standard. E.L. Patenaude, who had (belatedly) resigned from Borden's government on the conscription issue, now (belatedly) consented to lead the party in Quebec; but he at once announced that he was 'free from Mr. Meighen, even as I am free from Mr. King.' The Liberal campaign against Meighen in Quebec was, in Mr Neatby's words, 'characterized by exaggeration, distortions, and outright falsehoods.'[2] In the end, the Conservatives got only 4 of Quebec's 65 seats. Seven more, there or elsewhere, would have made Meighen Prime Minister again. Quebec's continued loyalty (60 Liberal seats) saved King from disaster. As it was, the Conservatives got the largest group in the House of Commons: 116 seats. The Progressives, with a much diminished group of 24, still held the balance of power.[3]

Mackenzie King, with his strength in the Commons reduced from 116 before the election to 101 (including two Independent Liberals), was in a quandary. The Governor General, Lord Byng, who had continued to be on consistently friendly and indeed intimate terms with him, advised him to resign. King's first decision seems to have been to do so; but his cabinet colleagues, loath to abandon power, convinced him that he should hold on, meet Parliament, and hope for enough Progressive support to enable the government to survive. And this support proved in fact to be forthcoming, at least for the moment.[4]

Before Parliament met, Meighen made a desperate attempt to overcome Quebec's implacable isolationist hostility towards himself and his party. In a speech at Hamilton, Ontario, on November 16 he proclaimed the doctrine that no government would 'so much as dream of sending troops beyond our shores unless the authority of Parliament was first obtained.' He went further. If war again threatened, he said, 'I believe it would be best, not only that Parliament should be called, but that the decision of the Government, which, of course, would have to be given promptly, should be submitted to the judgement of the people at a general election before troops should leave our shores.'[5] Meighen said later that he had consulted various Conservatives, including Sir Robert Borden, and that the only one who dissented from his proposal to make the speech was G. Howard Ferguson, the Premier of Ontario. Nevertheless, widespread criticism of the speech was at once heard in the party. The man who had cried 'Ready, Aye Ready' at the time of Chanak had now, it seemed, fully accepted King's Parliament-will-decide policy; indeed, he had gone far beyond King. The idea of holding a general election before sending troops abroad in an emergency seemed to many absurd and impracticable. And while the Hamilton speech created dissension among Conservatives, it seemed to make no impression on Quebec. In a by-election in Bagot County, Quebec, in December Meighen campaigned actively for the Conservative candidate, developing his Hamilton theme; but the Conservative still lost, though the Liberal majority of the previous election was somewhat reduced. Meighen now quietly abandoned the policy of the Hamilton speech; though he wrote long afterwards that he thought this abandonment the greatest mistake of his public life.[6] Many would have said that that mistake was the speech itself.

However, a more powerful weapon soon came to the Opposition's hands. Serious abuses came to light in the Customs Department, affecting the incumbent Minister and an ex-Minister. Progressive confidence in the government was shaken. By June 26, 1926, after a great deal of parliamentary manoeuvring, Mackenzie King found himself faced with the imminent possibility of the House of Commons passing what amounted to a vote of censure on the ministry. He decided that the best way to avoid this was to ask the Governor General to dissolve Parliament; and to his considerable surprise his friend Lord Byng refused. Men who have commanded army corps and armies are not likely to be frightened of responsibility. And Byng was not afraid of anybody. In 1924, when the Prince of Wales misbehaved while on a visit to Ottawa, Byng told him that he was never to return to Canada as long as Byng was Governor General.[7] Constitutional authorities, inclined at the time to side against him, now tend to consider that Byng was quite within his rights in refusing King a dissolution; though King's biographer has argued cogently that he was right for the wrong reason. He would have been on stronger constitutional ground had he based the refusal on King's attempt to use dissolution to escape parliamentary censure, instead of contending that

Meighen, having won the largest group in the 1925 election, was entitled to a chance to form a government.[8]

The 'King-Byng affair' was not really an episode in the history of Canadian external relations. It would have been such had the Governor General accepted the surprising advice which the autonomist King tendered him on June 26 and again later – to consult the Secretary of State for the Dominions.* Byng declined to do any such thing. The former Corps Commander took the view that after five years in Canada he knew the conditions there better than anybody in London. He played, in fact, the part of a Canadian constitutional monarch, acting as the Sovereign would have acted in a similar crisis in Britain. In a private letter to Byng, Leo Amery called King's advice a 'preposterous suggestion'; in a more official communication he wrote: 'Clearly the matter is one concerning Canadian internal affairs in which Ministers here could not take it upon themselves to intervene. I may say that had you referred to me I could only have replied on similar lines to the statements with regard to the political situation in New South Wales which I made in the House of Commons on 25th March – viz, that in my view it would not be proper for the Secretary of State to issue instructions with regard to the exercise of his constitutional duties to a Governor.'[9] As it was, King resigned on June 28, leaving the country without a government. Byng sent for Meighen, who accepted office. Under the law as it then stood, a member of Parliament accepting an office of profit was obliged to resign his seat and stand for re-election. But if all the members of a prospective cabinet left the House, in the then state of parties, there would be no hope of the government having a majority. Meighen's solution was to take office himself as Prime Minister, resigning his seat, and to appoint a small group of acting ministers who could administer the various departments legally while remaining in the Commons. This arrangement was at once attacked by the Liberals as unconstitutional, and enough Progressives accepted this view to defeat the government in the House on July 2.

Byng now granted Meighen the dissolution he had refused to King, and the country was plunged into another general election campaign. Meighen emphasized the Customs scandal. King emphasized the 'constitutional issue,' centring in the refusal of a dissolution, which proved to be a splendid red herring to divert attention from the Customs scandal. The Liberals, Ernest Lapointe said, were waging a fight for 'Canadian auto-

* The Dominions Office had been formed (from the Dominions Department of the Colonial Office) in July 1925; but for the time being Leopold Amery continued as Secretary of State for both the Colonies and the Dominions.

nomy and self-government.' It is a safe bet that not many of the voters fully understood what had happened, but it seems fairly evident that a large number had a general idea that an appointee of Downing Street had been guilty of unwarrantable interference in Canadian politics. At any rate, when the votes were counted on September 14, 1926, Mackenzie King and the Liberals had won. They did not achieve a formal overall majority, but they got 116 seats and could count in addition on ten Liberal-Progressives led by Robert Forke, who joined King's new cabinet. The post-war Progressive movement was now essentially at an end, and King had largely succeeded in his long-term aim of absorbing the Progressives into the Liberal party.[10]

Ontario gave Meighen 53 seats as compared with 68 in 1925; perhaps the Hamilton speech had been something of a liability here. Quebec remained solidly Liberal; again the Conservatives got only 4 seats there, again not a single French-Canadian Conservative was elected. The 'constitutional' issue, with its anti-imperial overtones, was good fighting ground for the Liberals in French Canada. King did well in the West, taking many former Progressive votes in addition to absorbing Forke and his group. He was doubtless helped by the budget which his new Minister of Finance, James A. Robb – ill health had finally forced Fielding to retire – had presented in April 1926. It contained one major tariff reduction – relating to automobiles – and a material cut in the income tax. 'Don't be robbed of the Robb budget' was a Liberal slogan in the election. The Liberals also gained a few seats in the Maritime provinces, which had been strongly Conservative in 1925.[11]

Arthur Meighen lost his own seat in Portage la Prairie, Manitoba. He never sat again in the House of Commons, of which he had been so distinguished an ornament. The Conservative group in the new House was reduced to 91 members, although it should be added that Conservatives had received almost the same proportion of the popular vote as in 1925. As for Mackenzie King, he was on top of the world. He was solidly in power for the duration of another Parliament. He had humiliated Byng and Meighen. And his position in his own party had been greatly strengthened. He had, or so it seemed, turned impending defeat into victory. From now on he was the indispensable leader.

THE LOCARNO TREATIES

During the period between the two Canadian general elections of 1925 and 1926, King's shaky minority government had to deal with a ticklish international question – that of the Locarno Treaties.

We have seen the abortive attempts of the League of Nations to solve the problem of European security by means of the Treaty of Mutual Guarantee and the Geneva Protocol, and have noted the unwillingness of Canada (as of many other countries) to undertake the obligations which those instruments involved. Though arranged outside the League, the Locarno Treaties were a further episode in the same sequence of effort, which may be said to have produced a temporary success. They were in great part the work of Sir Austen Chamberlain. Initialled at Locarno in Switzerland in October 1925, they centred in a new Treaty of Mutual Guarantee under which France, Belgium, and Germany accepted and agreed to maintain their existing boundaries (including the demilitarized zone in the German Rhineland set up by the Treaty of Versailles) and Great Britain and Italy guaranteed these undertakings. 'Locarno' was hailed as the beginning of a new era in Europe, and one of its hopeful consequences was the belated appearance of Germany at Geneva as a member of the League of Nations (above, page 65). On the day the treaties were formally signed in London (December 1, 1925) King George V wrote in his diary: 'I pray this may mean peace for many years. Why not for ever?' He reckoned without Adolf Hitler.[12]

Like Europeans, Canadians welcomed Locarno. Anything that rendered less probable another European war that might involve Canada was an occasion for satisfaction. But whether Canada wished to join in guaranteeing the new settlement was quite another thing. The Dominions had had no part in the negotiations that produced it. They had been kept fully informed of progress, and Canada could have offered comment or advice had the government chosen to do so, but it did not. Amery at the Colonial Office was doubtful of driving on into European commitments that the Dominions might not associate themselves with, but as one might have expected Sir Eyre Crowe, Chamberlain's chief adviser, was scornful of this attitude. Following Crowe's line, Chamberlain explained to the British House of Commons that it was impossible for him to say to international statesmen in conference: 'We have not yet been able to meet all the governments of the Empire, and [therefore] we can do nothing.'[13] What he did do was to follow the precedent of the stillborn treaty of guarantee of 1919 (Volume I, page 257) and insert in the Locarno guarantee treaty an Article 9 which read: 'The present treaty shall impose no obligations upon any of the British Dominions or upon India, unless the government of such Dominion or of India signifies its acceptance thereof.'

At the turn of the year King and his cabinet were faced with the question of whether or not to accept the treaty. The British government had proposed that before any Dominion made a decision in this matter it should be discussed in an Imperial Conference.[14] Reviewing the records, one is struck by the difference between the treatment of this question and the performance when the Lausanne treaty was under discussion in 1922. The Canadian attitudes were completely parallel, but whereas in 1922 the government's view was expressed in tortured papers drafted by King himself, now he had O.D. Skelton at his elbow. The British government might not like the dispatches Skelton wrote for King, but at least it was unlikely to misunderstand them.

The cabinet discussed the problem on January 6, 1926, on the basis of what the Prime Minister called 'an excellent brief' by Skelton. If there was any opposition to Skelton's views King did not record it.[15] The brief was one of those papers in which Skelton considered the arguments for and against and (quite inevitably) decided against commitments.[16] He referred once more to the 'Imperialist theories' which had long been 'trying to foist upon us a doctrine of diplomatic unity,' and pointed out, truly enough, that this time it was the British government that had 'declared against diplomatic unity,' signing the treaties without consultation with the Dominions. 'If a case can be made out for a guarantee by Britain it by no means follows that Canada has a similar interest or similar duty. Britain is part of Europe, Canada separated by three thousand miles of sea and incalculable differences in culture, in problems, in outlook. We are British North America; Britain is British West Europe.' Another remark had unquestionable force: 'Canada must decide on her course in the full light of te facts and situation of the time. We cannot give a blank cheque to whatever statesmen will be in power in London in 1940: their course will be more circumspect if they know they cannot count upon our aid automatically, but must prove a good case, a real emergency, a real interest.' Skelton had got the date just one year wrong.

The dispatch that went to the British Prime Minister on January 8 was formally polite; it remarked, 'We have noted with particular pride the unceasing striving for peace and reconciliation and the skill and patience displayed by British statesmen in recent years.' It took no exception to 'the decision of the British Government ... to determine its policy without consulting the Dominions in an Imperial Conference or otherwise.' Nevertheless, the dispatch held out no hope that Canada would adhere to the guarantee:

As regards Canada, the Canadian Government has not been able to conclude that it would be warranted in recommending Parliament to guarantee this European settlement. Considerations similar to those which have led the British Government to decide not to increase its obligations in the case of the eastern boundary of Germany appear to make it inadvisable for Canada to increase its obligations on either boundary ... Instead of undertaking in advance to fight either on the side of France against Germany or on the side of Germany against France, as the case may be, in any future Rhine war, it appears advisable to leave the question of participation for determination at the time in the light both of the situation abroad and the situation at home.

There was irony here. It appeared again in connection with the question of whether the matter should be discussed in an Imperial Conference. Canada agreed that it might profitably be considered 'in personal conference when occasion permits.' 'It is not apparent, however, that such a conference is more essential to enable a Dominion Government to determine its policy after the signature of the treaty than it was for the British Government before signature.' Yet the cable ended with something like a *non-sequitur*: while King could not undertake 'to postpone discussion or expression of opinion' in Parliament until after the Conference, he was 'quite prepared to maintain an open mind upon the question.'[17] The immediate British request had been complied with.

King's essential resolution not to adhere to Locarno was strengthened by conference with his favourite unofficial isolationist advisers. John S. Ewart called and offered help. King's private comment was: 'His point of view while extreme is in the right direction, and many are coming his way. – A staunch Canadianism will gain ground with the years.' (It must be admitted that as a piece of historical interpretation this is perfectly sound.) A dinner party including Sir Clifford Sifton, John W. Dafoe, and James A. Robb were all 'against Canada agreeing to Lacarno [sic] pact.'[18]

There was another adviser. King's diary recorded on March 9 that Henri Bourassa came to dinner: 'He suggested a motion re Lacarno [sic] to effect that agreement should not be signed without approval of prlt. thereby leaving door open to meeting of imperial conference for discussion and preventing signature of pact secretly before prlt. advised, in case there shld be change of Govt meanwhile ... He was most agreeable & far from anti-british. He said he had declared a truce on independence so long as the imperialists kept the truce on avoiding their extreme measures.' King took this advice, though he did not make the motion specifically one on Locarno. On June 21 (only a few days before his crisis with Byng) he introduced in the House of Commons a resolution reciting the recommendation of the 1923 conference on the signing of international agreements, and proceeding: 'This House approves of the procedure proposed for the negotiation, signature and ratification of treaties and conventions, and considers further that before His Majesty's Canadian ministers advise ratification of a treaty or convention affecting Canada, or signify acceptance of any treaty convention or agreement involving military or economic sanctions, the approval of the parliament of Canada should be secured.' The motion was agreed to without a vote. In the course of the debate King said with respect to Locarno, 'the government does not propose to reach a final decision in the matter until after the Imperial conference which will be held this fall.' The affair is interesting as suggesting how genuine King's fears of Canadian Tory imperialism were; though readers of this book are aware that there is nothing in the Conservatives' record when in power to indicate that Canadian autonomy was less safe in their hands than in the Liberals'. Needless to say, he did not mention in the debate his apprehensions of possible action by a Conservative government.

At the Imperial Conference Canada, speaking through the mouth of Ernest Lapointe (it is significant that King should delegate this task to his French-Canadian lieutenant), made a firm statement along the lines which Skelton had laid down: 'The Treaty involves additional obligations in a European field which, while of interest to us as to all the world, is not our primary concern.' Lapointe admitted that the Canadian attitude involved the possibility that one part of the Empire might be at war and others not, but said (paraphrasing Skelton) that this was not a new difficulty. 'If we do not sign, the question remains as it was, to be settled as occasion arises in the light of the conditions and needs of that day, and in full regard of our obligations as a member of the British Commonwealth and of the League of Nations.' In the subsequent discussion King quoted his favourite British Liberal statesman* and dropped a passing but enormously pregnant comment similar to the one he had made at the conference of 1923 (above, page 72): 'After some discussion as to the possible wording of a resolution, MR. MACKENZIE KING said that he was much impressed by Lord Grey's recent statement that it was a mistake for the Dominions to go in for anything half-heartedly. Canada was satisfied with the Treaty and with all its terms; there was no question at all of that; *and if the situation arose Canada would do her part.* But was it wise to open up in the Canadian Parliament a debate as to whether Canada had approved or not?' The italics are mine.[19]

This was all severely private. The conference's final public word on Locarno committed nobody to anything.[20] It was drafted by Mackenzie

* A few days after this meeting King consulted Viscount and Lady Grey on a matter of spiritualism. See my book *A Very Double Life: The Private World of Mackenzie King* (Toronto 1976), pp. 164-5.

King: 'The Conference has heard with satisfaction the statement of the Secretary of State for Foreign Affairs with regard to the efforts made to ensure peace in Europe, culminating in the agreements of Locarno; and congratulates His Majesty's Government in Great Britain on its share in this successful contribution towards the promotion of the peace of the world.' This was the sole action of the Dominions on Locarno. Australia and New Zealand would have been prepared to adhere formally to the Treaty of Mutual Guarantee, but in the light of the conference statement they refrained from doing so. Imperial unity, of a sort, had been preserved.

Two footnotes may be added to the Canadian aspect of the Locarno story. Both relate to personalities of the Borden era.

One concerns Sir George Foster, Conservative, elder statesman, imperialist, and League of Nations enthusiast, and near-signatory of the Treaty of Versailles (Volume I, page 255). In the summer of 1926 it fell to Arthur Meighen's short-lived administration of that year to appoint the Canadian delegates to the Seventh Assembly of the League. It appointed Sir George Foster, Sir Herbert Ames (lately retired from the League Secretariat), and Philippe Roy, the Canadian *commissaire général* in Paris. They were given instruction concerning their actions at Geneva;[21] comparison with the situation concerning the delegates to the First Assembly (Volume I, page 326) indicates how the day-to-day operation of the Department of External Affairs had improved under Skelton. But Foster's big moment had nothing to do with those instructions. On September 10, 1926, when for the first time German delegates appeared at Geneva, and Gustav Stresemann and Aristide Briand made speeches declaring that henceforth their countries' rivalry would not be on the battlefield but in the arts of peace, it was old Sir George who led the cheering with 'the British *Hip-Hip Hurray*,' giving emphasis to his enthusiasm and effect to his leadership by waving a large red handkerchief.[22]

The other footnote is rather more important. It relates to Loring Christie, sometime right-hand-man to Sir Robert Borden and one of the architects of the project of a unified imperial foreign policy worked out in consultation between Britain and the Dominions. When Mackenzie King froze him out of the Department of External Affairs, Christie went to England and worked for some years in London. He remained devoted to the concept of a united Empire based on 'co-ordinate autonomy' and was an active member of the Round Table. But Locarno changed all that. Just how far Christie realized what had been going on in the Foreign Office under Crowe, Curzon, and Chamberlain is not clear. He had had doubts for some time, but the failure to bring the Dominions into the Locarno negotiations convinced him that the great imperial experiment initiated in 1917-19 had been betrayed. He wrote to Borden: 'It seems to me it was a valiant idea that you and the others – Botha, Smuts and so on – conceived; but the nerve to carry it along seems to have gone out everywhere.' Christie resigned from the Round Table and shortly returned to Canada. Almost overnight the liberal imperialist who believed that Canada could realize her full potential only within the Commonwealth pattern became a bitterly anti-imperial isolationist.[23] On September 24, 1926, Mackenzie King wrote in his diary: 'Dr. Skelton ... tells me that Loring Christie has returned to Canada a Canadian nationalist stronger than Dafoe and myself; that his time in London has made him anti-Round Table and all its point of view; he is really very strong in his present Canadian attitude; he told Skelton he had regretted we had not had a chance of a closer association together.' It would seem that at this time Christie would have been glad to come back to the Department of External Affairs to work under King, whom three years before he had so deeply hated. In fact his return was long deferred, but when it took place Christie was indeed to show himself a stronger nationalist than the Prime Minister.

Christie's reaction was so strong that one wonders whether it did not reflect some inborn instability. But he was not the only actor in the drama of 1917-19 who was deeply disturbed by the implications of Locarno. From South Africa, Jan Smuts, now in opposition, also wrote to Borden; from the Empire point of view, he said, 'a very evil precedent' has been set: 'The British Empire Delegation for which you and other Imperial statesmen were responsible seems to have disappeared and the united front broken. Will it ever be restored again?' Borden himself was moved to write a private protest to Sir Austen Chamberlain against the abandonment of the principles of Resolution IX. 'I am wholly confident,' he wrote, 'that in the Resolution of 1917 the true basis and sure hope of Imperial unity are to be found.'[24] But his was a voice from the past. Neither the British Foreign Office nor the leadership of the Liberal Party of Canada had any use for the consultation recommended in Resolution IX.

THE IMPERIAL CONFERENCE OF 1926

Two weeks after the election of 1926 that restored him to power, Mackenzie King embarked for England to take part in his second Imperial Conference. He was accompanied by Ernest Lapointe, and, of course, O.D. Skelton; also by Vincent Massey, lately for a brief space a member of his

KNEE BREECHES AND EQUAL STATUS

King George V and the Commonwealth Prime Ministers during the Imperial Conference of 1926. On the King's right, Stanley Baldwin (UK); on his left, Mackenzie King (Canada). Second row, left to right: W.S. Monroe, Newfoundland; J.G. Coates, New Zealand; Stanley Bruce, Australia; General J.B.M. Hertzog, South Africa; W.T. Cosgrave, Irish Free State government, and now designated as the first Canadian Minister to Washington.

Fresh from his great political victory, the Prime Minister approached this meeting in a relatively mellow mood. In contrast with his position in 1923, he was now an experienced and successful leader. And Canada came to the conference, as Massey put it, 'conciliatory and contented,'[25] with no demands to make. King, indeed, thought that the only constitutional matter requiring attention from the delegates was the status of the Governors General of the Dominions[26] – certainly a consequence of his recent encounter with Lord Byng. He was in an admirable position to play a moderating and mediating role, and this in general was to be his part in the conference.

The people who made the running in 1926 were the South Africans and the Irish. Here we must look back into imperial constitutional history. Resolution IX of the Imperial War Conference of 1917 had deferred detailed consideration of the constitution of the Empire pending a special conference on the subject to be held after the war. At the conference of 1921 General Smuts had desired that the constitutional question be faced and the new status of the Dominions defined; but Australia and New Zealand were opposed and Canada indifferent, so the question was dropped. Now in 1926 it was brought up again by General J.B.M. Hertzog, the nationalist Prime Minister of South Africa, in a form that demanded action. In his opening speech[27] he made it clear that South Africa was not satisfied with the present state of things. Her goodwill towards the Empire-Commonwealth, he said, 'can be assured for the future only if she can be made to feel implicit faith in her full and free nationhood upon the basis of equality with every other member of the Commonwealth. That implicit faith she does not possess to-day, but she will possess it the moment her independent national status has ceased to be a matter in dispute and has become internationally recognised.' The clear implication was that if South Africa did not obtain satisfactory clarification of her status she would secede.

Definition of the nature of the imperial tie thus became the conference's most urgent task. The eighth meeting of the conference, on the motion of Stanley Baldwin, the Prime Minister of Great Britain, referred this question to a Prime Ministers' Committee, the 'Committee on Inter-Imperial Relations,' to be presided over by Lord Balfour, a former Prime Minister, as Baldwin's deputy. In this committee the most important work of the conference was done. (Among other things, it dealt with the Locarno Treaties in the manner already noticed.) After long labour, it produced its famous definition of the 'position and mutual relation' of

Great Britain and the Dominions: 'They are autonomous Communities within the British Empire, equal in status, in no way subordinate one to another in any aspect of their domestic or external affairs, though united by a common allegiance to the Crown, and freely associated as members of the British Commonwealth of Nations.' It is worth noting that a draft declaration put before the committee at the beginning of its work by General Hertzog[28] contained the phrases 'equal in status' and 'united by the common bond of allegiance to the Crown and freely associated as members of the British Commonwealth of Nations.' Hertzog may therefore be considered as one of the chief authors of the definition. However, his draft also referred to the communities constituting the Commonwealth as 'independent states ... with Governments and Parliaments independent of one another.' The word 'independent' did not survive. Mackenzie King recorded an interview with Hertzog in which 'Hertzog stressed very strongly the need for a declaration of the independence of the several Dominions. I told him I did not like the word "independent," and anything like a declaration of independence would not be understood in Canada in the sense in which he meant it; it would be looked upon as a parallel to that of 1776 of the United States. I suggested that the emphasis be put on equality of status, and adhering to that all along the line as the fundamental principle.'[29] This well symbolizes King's contribution to the conference.

The definition of status was certainly the main achievement. The Irish brought up a number of constitutional 'anomalies.' One of these was the matter of reservation or disallowance of Dominion legislation; the conference decided that this and a number of other legal matters should be examined by a future expert committee to be set up by the Commonwealth countries. This committee turned out to have the task of recommending legislation to turn the Balfour Committee's definition of status into practical measures. Another matter was appeals to the Judicial Committee of the Privy Council; the Irish decided not to press this for the moment, reserving the right to proceed with it on another occasion. The question of procedure in the signing of treaties, dealt with in 1923, was now again examined by a sub-committee of the conference, presided over by Ernest Lapointe.

The nub of the problem here was what was termed the 'central panel': the convention by which, while the Dominions signed treaties for themselves individually, Great Britain signed for the British Empire on the basis of 'full powers' which were geographically unlimited. Readers will remember that Sir Robert Borden raised this question at Paris, suggesting that the British delegates should sign for 'Great Britain' alone; he also brought it up in connection with the listing of the Commonwealth countries in the League Covenant. He was unsuccessful in both cases (Volume I, pages 254-5, 269). Although before the 1926 conference the Dominions Office, in a very stiff interdepartmental tussle, overcame the opposition of the Foreign Office to abandoning the central panel idea,[30] the Foreign Office, in the person of Sir Cecil Hurst, insisted on fighting the battle all over again in Lapointe's committee. Almost inevitably, it was again lost.

There was no great difficulty about Mackenzie King's chief personal interest – the position of the Governors General. The issue here really had no direct connection with King's controversy with Byng – if the Prime Minister had tried to obtain a decision from the conference depriving Governors General of the right to refuse a dissolution he would certainly have met the strongest kind of opposition. What King wanted was to end the situation which made the Governor General an agent of the British government, and ensure that henceforth he would be exclusively the representative of the Sovereign. This again was an old issue; it had been discussed in the Imperial War Cabinet in 1918, notably by N.W. Rowell (Volume I, page 226). The conference recommended that the Governor General should no longer be the channel of communication between the government in London and the Dominion governments; the channel should be 'between Government and Government direct.' The position of the Governal General was protected: 'it was recognised by the [Balfour] Committee, as an essential feature of any change or development in the channels of communication, that a Governor-General should be supplied with copies of all documents of importance and in general should be kept as fully informed as is His Majesty the King in Great Britain of Cabinet business and public affairs.' (Without these advantages, a Governor General would not be able to perform his constitutional functions – such as deciding when it might or might not be in order to grant a Prime Minister's request for a dissolution!)

On the whole, the Imperial Conference of 1926 must be accounted a striking success. A *Manitoba Free Press* correspondent wrote to John Dafoe, 'Hertzog is well pleased, according to Skelton, and the Irish are going home happy.'[31] That in itself was no small achievement. The conference began in an atmosphere of doubt and apprehension; it ended with many difficulties resolved and the Commonwealth on a sounder footing than before. It is hard to read the records of the meeting without being impressed by the good will and good temper with which difficult questions were discussed. Lord Cave, the Lord Chancellor, who was reported to have stamped out 'saying he was not going to be a party to the breaking up of the British Empire,'[32] was only the exception that proved the rule.

The *Commonwealth*. The word had made its appearance in 1917-18, but in Imperial Conferences and elsewhere *Empire* continued to be normal usage. From 1926, however, *Commonwealth* (formally, *British Commonwealth of Nations*) began to replace it. Some people of course disliked the innovation. One of them was Sir Austen Chamberlain, who wrote to Maurice Hankey urging him to use 'British Empire' as much as possible and 'get rid of "British Commonwealth of Nations" which is not a term of art.'[33] Whether it was a 'term of art' or not, it was henceforth increasingly accepted as the symbol of a new era.

In Canada public opinion received the results of the conference with satisfaction. Equality of status was a concept which most Canadians, including French Canadians, found agreeable in 1926. If the word *independence* had been used it would have provoked explosive criticism in many quarters. Mackenzie King's advice to Hertzog was a good example of his shrewd assessment of his own countrymen. A few months after the conference Sir George Foster, a believer in the old imperial order whom we have called the Conservative equivalent of W.S. Fielding, wrote to Balfour: 'We are discussing in Canada the results of the Imperial Conference, and have come, I think generally, to the conclusion that nothing new has taken place, but are confirmed in the view that special efforts must hereafter be made to link together in sentiment and co-operation the various parts of the Empire, clustering around and converging towards the greatest possible imperial unity.'[34]

In 1928 Chamberlain was in Ottawa. In his speech at a dinner for the visitor Mackenzie King made free use of the word Commonwealth. Sir George Foster (now 82) took some exception to this, saying: 'Empire is the thing. Empire has been a strong word to me.' Chamberlain now spoke in terms quite different from his letter to Hankey: 'I venture at this point to break a lance [King's version was 'to break alliance'] with Sir George Foster, and I hope Sir George will forgive me if in the matter of the word "Commonwealth" I range myself on the side of the Prime Minister of Canada ... I like the term "Commonwealth of Nations," because it indicates that each of us exists not only to pursue his own interests, but exists for the common weal ...'[35] Had Chamberlain changed his views, or was he merely being a good politician? To complete a rather curious picture, we may recall that King himself had preferred 'Empire' to 'Commonwealth' five years before (Volume I, page 213).

'Nothing new has taken place.' Perhaps it was true that in Canada (unlike South Africa) freedom had broadened down so slowly that the movement was almost imperceptible. But if Sir George Foster had thought back to 1914 he would have realized that in fact a good deal had changed. The tragedies and sacrifices of the war were beginning to pass from men's minds, yet their seismic effect was still being felt. Thanks to them, things that were vague aspirations in 1914 were becoming realities in 1926. Nor was the process yet quite complete.

MORE REPRESENTATIVES ABROAD

Mackenzie King's aggressively autonomist policies after he came to power in 1921 did not result, as might have been expected, in a rapid proliferation of Canadian diplomatic posts in other countries or in an increase in the staff of the Department of External Affairs. Skelton replaced Pope and fell heir to the role that had been played by Christie; but there was little change in the tiny department. In 1925 it still possessed only three administrative officers (Skelton, W.H. Walker, and Jean Désy, appointed that year). At the end of the year Skelton reported to King, 'it is absolutely impossible, even with 7-day weeks and 16 hour days to secure the independent and exact knowledge of external affairs which has now become desirable.' The cautious Prime Minister, careful of public money and always fearful of criticism, was in no hurry. But things began to change in 1926. The Imperial Conference, while recognizing that in the sphere of foreign affairs, as in the sphere of defence, 'the major share of responsibility rests now, and must for some time continue to rest, with His Majesty's Government in Great Britain,' accepted the principle of direct Dominion representation in foreign capitals (it could not do much else, for as we know agreement had been reached in 1920 on Canadian representation in Washington, and while that agreement was not immediately implemented the Irish Free State had used it to justify opening a legation in the United States in 1924).[36] Moreover, after the political troubles of 1925-6 King was now firmly established in power; and growing prosperity made larger expenditures less likely to excite adverse comment. Finally, the departure of Fielding had removed from King's cabinet and party the most determined opponent of an independent Canadian diplomatic service.

In the spring of 1926 King offered Vincent Massey the appointment of Canadian Minister to Washington, and after some hesitation Massey accepted. By the time of the election which returned King to power after the Meighen interlude it was being publicly reported that he intended to open a legation in the United States and to appoint Massey. When King visited Byng to receive and accept his invitation to form a new government, the Governor General had on his desk a cable from Leo Amery noting these press reports and expressing the hope that King would remember that he had promised not to take action in the matter of a Washington legation without notice to the British government. The new Prime Minister authorized Byng to tell Amery 'what I purposed doing, intimating in general terms that it was the intention to appoint Massey to Washington, but that no official announcement would be made until after I had taken the matter up while in England at the Imperial Conference.' At a press conference later that day King, as he put it, 'announced in general terms the opening of parliament and the appointment of Massey to Washington.'[37] No doubt some rather acid things were said in London. King made, however, the gesture of refraining from formal action – asking the King to issue Massey's letter of credence – until he had consulted with British ministers during the conference. Massey presented the letter to President Calvin Coolidge on February 18, 1927.[38]

Charles Vincent Massey was a member of a Toronto family that had made a great deal of money by manufacturing farm implements. He was a person of high education and broad culture, a product of the University of Toronto and Balliol College, Oxford, who had for a time taught history at Toronto. In 1925 he had entered King's cabinet as a minster without portfolio, but had been defeated in the general election of that year. Failing to find a seat in the new parliament, he was finally glad to take the Washington post. He remained in it until 1930.[39]

Only two other Canadian legations were established at this period. Paris was an obvious place for one. France had much less economic importance for Canada than the United States had, but its political importance was considerable. A legation in Paris would presumably be popular in Quebec, and as we know there had in fact been a Canadian *commissaire général* in the French capital since 1882. In November 1927 the Canadian government opened the question with London, and the Foreign Office arranged for Senator Dandurand, on the way to Geneva to represent Canada on the League of Nations Council, to discuss the matter with the French Foreign Minister. The intention of the French and Canadian governments to exchange legations was announced on January 10, 1928. Philippe Roy, who had been *commissaire général* since 1911, was appointed the first Canadian Minister to Paris.[40]

The third legation was in Tokyo. There were fewer traditional pressures indicating the desirability of representation in Japan, but trade considerations and problems of immigration (with which King himself had been closely connected of old) seem to have been the most important. A new immigration agreement was being discussed with the Japanese Consul General in Ottawa. In January 1928 the Japanese Foreign Minister informed the British Ambassador in Tokyo that the government of Japan would be happy to receive a Canadian Minister in Japan and to send a Minister to Canada. The first Canadian Minister to Tokyo was Herbert M. Marler, appointed in June 1929. Like Massey, he was a former member of King's cabinet who had lost his seat in Parliament. If the impressions of a member of his staff in a later appointment are to be relied on, he had few other qualifications. Massey (urged perhaps by his staff?) had suggested appointing a 'career' diplomat, but this was not done.[41]

One consequence of these developments was the beginning of a diplomatic corps in Ottawa. The arrangement with the United States had not been reciprocal; but in December 1926 the United States government proposed to the British Foreign Office that it should send ministers to both Ottawa and Dublin; and in June 1927 William Phillips, formerly U.S. Ambassador in Belgium, arrived in Ottawa as the first United States Minister and presented his letter of credence to the Governor General, Lord Willingdon, who transmitted it to the King. The event occasioned some scurrying around to establish the proper ceremonial procedure. The first French Minister was G.J.H.M. Knight, a former commercial attaché in China; the first Japanese Minister was Iyemasa Tokugawa.[42]

The Canadian Conservative party, cheerfully discounting the fact that a Conservative Prime Minister had made the original arrangement for a legation in Washington, chose to attack the new developments on the ground that they were damaging to the unity of the Empire. On April 13, 1927 the Opposition assailed the Washington project in the House of Commons. The immediate complaint was cost – $500,000 for a legation building – but R.B. Bennett, the new Conservative leader, raised the question of fundamental policy: 'I am wholly opposed to the establishment of this embassy at Washington. It is but the doctrine of separation, it is but the evidence in many minds of the end of our connection with the empire. For that is what it means. It means nothing else ultimately, because if we are a sovereign state we cannot belong to the British Empire ...' The only proper function of a Canadian office in Washington was the encouragement of trade: 'What we ought to establish is a trade commissioner's office, a high commissioner's office if you will.' In retrospect these views have an archaic look, but in 1927 they certainly still struck a responsive chord in many Canadians.

The new diplomatic arrangements with foreign powers produced a curious controversy with the British Foreign Office. The letter (November 19, 1926) in which the *chargé d'affaires* at the British Embassy in Washington proposed to the State Department the establishment of the Canadian Legation contained the following paragraph:[43]

The arrangements proposed by His Majesty's Government would not denote any departure from the principle of the diplomatic unity of the Empire. The Canadian Minister would be at all times in the closest touch with His Majesty's Ambassador and any question which may arise as to whether a matter comes within the category of those to be handled by the Canadian Minister or not would be settled by consultation between them. The Canadian Minister being responsible to the Canadian Government would not be subject to the control of His Majesty's Ambassador nor would His Majesty's Ambassador be responsible for the Canadian Minister's actions.

It will be noted that the plan adopted in 1920, under which the Canadian Minister would be a member of the British Embassy staff and would be in charge in the absence of the Ambassador, had been quietly dropped. It had been anathema to King from the beginning, and had been specifically repudiated in the Canadian order-in-council asking that the King be moved to appoint Massey. But aspects of this letter, which was presumably phrased in accordance with instructions from the Foreign Office and on which Canada had not been consulted, disturbed the Department of External Affairs. When the time came to accredit Mr Roy in Paris, the department cabled London suggesting that it did not 'appear necessary' to make 'any specific affirmation' about the diplomatic unity of the Empire. It also suggested that another sentence of the letter had given the mistaken impression that the Canadian Minister 'would be excluded from dealing individually or jointly with any question affecting other parts of the Empire as well.' A different form of words was suggested.[44]

This cable involved Mackenzie King in an unpleasant personal altercation. When it was sent (August 16, 1928) he was about to sail for France to sign the 'Kellogg Pact' for the renunciation of war. At Plymouth he received the 'full powers' from the King authorizing the signing. In Paris three days later he met Lord Cushendun, Acting Foreign Secretary while Chamberlain was ill, and discussed Roy's appointment with him. It seems clear that the politely-expressed Canadian doubt about the necessity of using the phrase 'diplomatic unity of the Empire' had aroused hostility in the Foreign Office, and that Cushendun's behaviour was, to say the least, undiplomatic. King wrote in his diary that his attitude 'was that of a bully and a brutal bully ... I shall never feel the same again towards Great Britain.' Next day (August 27), in connection with the signing of the Pact, King recorded, first that Cushendun was 'somewhat apologetic' and later that he was 'most apologetic.'[45]

Nevertheless the 'bully' got what he wanted, at least for the moment. He had told King that if the wording used in the case of the Washington appointment were followed, it would be possible to arrange for the immediate issue of Roy's letter of credence; if the form were modified, this could not be done in time for King to preside at the opening of the Legation in October, as he wished to do. On the 27th King wrote to him accepting the use of the Washington wording, 'leaving to a more convenient season' the consideration of modification.[46] The Foreign Office had traded on the fact that it was still in a position to obstruct the issuance of letters of credence – and had certainly ensured that King would do his utmost to change the position shortly. There are some occasions when one sympathizes with the British in their controversies with King; but this is not one of them.

Before the end of 1928 the discussion of modification of the form of words began. It consumed a great deal of time and paper, and we shall describe it as briefly as possible. The occasion for launching it was a proposal by the Irish Free State to appoint ministers to Paris and Berlin. King opened the ball with (significantly) a Prime-Minister-to-Prime-Minister cable. It should be noted that, whereas this would formerly have gone through the Governor General and the Dominions Secretary, it now went from the Under-Secretary of State for External Affairs to the Canadian High Commissioner in London.[47] It took exception to the ambassadorial letter raising the question of a Canadian Minister in France, which followed as we have seen the same form as the letter about a Minister in Washington; the points complained of were the sentence (already mentioned) which said that matters 'which are of Imperial concern or which affect other Dominions ... in common with Canada' would continue to be handled by the British Embassy, and the paragraph (three) quoted on page 92 above. It suggested three possible versions, 'in all cases allowing first sentence of paragraph three regarding diplomatic unity to remain, but avoiding any use of term "joint action"' (this term had not in fact been used in the British letter). It is possible that his experience in Paris had convinced King that any questioning of the phrase 'diplomatic unity of the Empire' would be a red rag to the bulls of the Foreign Office.

In the multilateral discussion that followed, South Africa and the Irish Free State were again the radicals; clearly they would have preferred to have all reference to 'diplomatic unity of the Empire' eliminated. Australia and New Zealand had no quarrel with 'diplomatic unity' or with the Foreign Office formula generally. Canada stood in between, unenthusiastic for 'diplomatic unity' but prepared to accept it to keep peace in the family. It seems evident that King and Skelton differed on this point; if Skelton had had his own way completely, Canada would have stood with the South Africans and the Irish, continuing to take the line indicated in the dispatch that had aroused Cushendun's ire, but King was less intransigent. He had discussed the matter with Chamberlain when Sir Austen was in Ottawa in November 1928, and when the Foreign Secretary asked him to 'meet him' on the diplomatic unity question King made no difficulty, saying that Canada was more concerned about the matter of the handling of questions affecting more than one Commonwealth country. King complained in his diary at one point in 1929 of Skelton's 'putting one over' on him in connection with a cable to Ireland and South Africa on the subject, but it appears that in fact King had approved the message.[48] In the end what emerged, after a certain amount of brokering by Canada, was the following agreed formula:

> The arrangements proposed would not denote any departure from the principle of diplomatic unity of the Empire, that is to say, the principle of consultative co-operation among all His Majesty's representatives as among His Majesty's Governments themselves in matters of common concern. The method of dealing with matters which may arise concerning more than one of His Majesty's Governments would therefore be settled by consultation between representatives of His Majesty's Governments concerned.

Somewhat strangely, the Department of External Affairs two years later decided to communicate the revised formula to the American State Department, setting the record of 1926 right in 1931.[49]

The new arrangements of 1926-8 brought another representative from abroad to reside in Ottawa: a High Commissioner for the United Kingdom.

King and other people had felt that such an appointment was a necessary consequence of the altered status of the Governor General. If he was no longer to be a channel of communication with the British government, then some other channel had to be provided. N.W. Rowell had urged this on King early in 1926 – Britain, he said, should have a High Commissioner or Minister in Ottawa.[50] King argued along these lines at the conference that year, and the Balfour Committee referred to the 'desirability of developing a system of personal contact, both in London and in the Dominion capitals, to supplement the present system of inter-communication ...' But when the British government came to consider the matter of representation in Ottawa in 1927, internal differences of opinion appeared. The Dominions Office wanted an important establishment under its own control; the Foreign Office wanted the representative to be a diplomat; the Treasury was afraid of expense; and the cabinet parsimoniously decided that 'the British representative in Ottawa should not be regarded as being there to balance the representative of the United States of America.'

Mackenzie King (who, of course, did not have to find the money) had no sympathy with this cheese-paring attitude. His innate British feelings presumably asserted themselves. He thought that Britain's man in Ottawa should be, and appear, more important than any foreign representative. Stanley Baldwin visited Canada for the Diamond Jubilee of Confederation in 1927 (the first British Prime Minister to visit the country while in office); and it is possible that the matter was discussed while King and Baldwin rambled around Kingsmere on August 4, though King's diary does not mention it. At any rate, Baldwin had a good look at the prosperous Canada of 1927, and may have been impressed. And when Leo Amery came visiting in January 1928 King made it clear to him that Canada wanted a man who could 'hold his own with the American Minister.' On his return to England, Amery was supported by Baldwin when he argued for a respectable British establishment in Ottawa. Baldwin wrote to the King's private secretary: 'For us to appoint any British Government representative in Canada who could not hold his own with Mr. Phillips either personally or in the general status and importance assigned to his office would not only be seriously detrimental to Imperial policy generally, but would be from the very outset construed by Canadian public opinion as implying that we did not take as great an interest in Canada as the Americans do.'

Thanks to Baldwin, Amery won the day. In April 1928 Sir William Clark, recently comptroller general of the Department of Overseas Trade, was appointed the first British High Commissioner to Canada; he was to report to, and receive his instructions from, the Dominions Office. The importance of the new British post was agreeably underlined in 1930, when the High Commissioner established himself in 'Earnscliffe,' splendidly situated on the bank of the Ottawa, once the home of Sir John A. Macdonald. The appointment was, of course, not officially considered a diplomatic one; but from the beginning there was no doubt of the position the High Commissioner held in the official and social life of the capital.[51]

The developments we have been describing demanded an increase in the staff of the Department of External Affairs – the first major increase since the department was organized in 1909. In the years 1927-9 men were appointed who would play leading parts in shaping Canadian policy in time to come, and the pattern of the department for the next generation was firmly established. Like George Foster when improving the Trade Commissioner Service in pre-war days, O.D. Skelton turned to the universities for bright young men.*

When the Washington Legation was set up in 1927, Vincent Massey was given 'a fairly free hand' in choosing a staff.[52] He inherited one officer who had actually been in Washington since the days of the Canadian War Mission – Merchant Mahoney, who had borne the imposing if vague title of 'Canadian Agent' and had been attached to the British Embassy as an assistant mainly in Canadian commercial matters. As First Secretary, Massey appointed Humphrey Hume Wrong, a member of the history department at the University of Toronto, where Massey himself had once taught and of which Wrong's father was head. Hume Wrong was one of the ablest of an able family. Some thought him a snob, and there was an acidulous strain in him which did not endear him to everybody; but his competence was undoubted, and Canadian diplomatic dispatches become better reading after he joins the service. The balance between French and English had of course to be maintained, and Laurent Beaudry from Quebec was given the same rank as Wrong in the new Legation. It is interesting to note that Ernest Lapointe, King's senior French-Canadian cabinet minister, was clearly (at a later stage, at any rate) kept informed of appointments and promotions in the Department of External Affairs, and watched over the fortunes of the French Canadians.[53]

In 1928 another member of the Toronto history department, Lester Bowles Pearson, followed his more senior colleague Wrong into the Department of External Affairs. Few of his students (of whom the present writer was one) would have tapped Pearson as a future Prime Minster of Canada; but they knew him as an interesting if hardly scholarly lecturer with an agreeable personality and the cheerful adolescent charm that he never lost. He was recommended to External Affairs not by anybody in his own department but by a professor of law, W.P.M. Kennedy, author of *The Constitution of Canada*, a very famous book in its day. He passed first in the stiff competitive examination for First Secretary, and reported for duty in Ottawa, being appointed officially on August 13, 1928.[54] Another important appointment was made on May 13, 1929: that of Norman Alexander Robertson, a graduate of the University of British Columbia and of Oxford, who is remembered by those who knew him best as a quiet man of no pretensions but of vast knowledge and abilities.

* One of Foster's young men, Dana Wilgress, in due course came over to External and held senior posts abroad.

In Pearson's opinion, Skelton, Wrong, and Robertson were 'the main architects of our foreign service.'[55]

It is unnecessary to introduce here all the individuals who were recruited at this stage. More of them will appear in due course. It is fitting, however, to mention John E. Read, sometime dean of Dalhousie University's law school, who was appointed to External in June 1928. Next year he was appointed Legal Adviser, when that post, which had been created for Loring Christie and abolished in order to provide a salary for Skelton as Counsellor, was again set up.[56] In the new and larger department his services, unlike Christie's, were largely limited to legal business; but he certainly wielded considerable influence.

The men whom Skelton recruited for External in the later twenties, if not the near-demigods that legend tends to make them, were a very able group, and in the Canadian civil service of that day they stood out. Mackenzie King in his capacity as Secretary of State for External Affairs does not seem to have concerned himself very much with the recruiting; he left that to his Under-Secretary. But he was clearly happy about the result, and about the new position of the department generally. Complacently totting up the achievements of his ten years as Liberal leader in August 1929, he listed among them 'A department of External Affairs expanded into the most conspicuous & in some respects the most important department of government.'[57]

MR KELLOGG'S PACT

The so-called Pact of Paris or Kellogg Peace Pact signed in August 1928 deserves at least passing notice in a history of Canadian policy.

The origins of it need not delay us. It began in a French suggestion for a bilateral renunciation of war as between France and the United States. President Coolidge's Secretary of State, Frank B. Kellogg, converted the idea into a plan for a renunciation of war as an instrument of policy to be subscribed to by all the nations of the world. The essential paragraphs of the treaty as signed are so brief that they can be quoted here:[58]

ART. 1. The high contracting parties solemnly declare in the names of their respective peoples that they condemn recourse to war for the solution of international controversies, and renounce it as an instrument of national policy in their relations with one another.

2. The high contracting parties agree that the settlement or solution of all disputes or conflicts of whatever nature or of whatever origin they may be, which may arise among them, shall never be sought except by pacific means.

Undoubtedly a good many international statesmen were doubtful of the practical value of such a declaration, but nobody is against motherhood; and nobody wanted to discourage the United States from making a move towards international co-operation in the maintenance of peace, even though this move involved no commitment of any kind to collective security. So a first group of nations signed the Pact with ceremony at the Quai d'Orsay on August 27, 1928; and within a short time almost every country in the world* had adhered to it.[59]

The author of this book, a student visiting from Oxford, was in Paris on that now remote day when the Pact was signed. My exiguous diary took no note of it, and I cannot now remember whether, craning our necks in the street, my friends and I succeeded in seeing any of the great men who came to affix their names. What I do remember is that, while the diplomats were at work inside, a frowsy troop of French cavalry, moving from somewhere to somewhere else, came clattering past the Foreign Office; and people wondered whether this portent symbolized the intrusion of reality upon idealism. In the light of later history, Kellogg's Pact recalls the policies of King Edward VII as described in an English classic of those days: 'King Edward's new policy of peace was very successful and culminated in the Great War to End War.'[60]

The Canadian connection remains to be narrated. After preliminary discussion with France, Kellogg had opened his plan to Germany, Britain, Italy, and Japan on April 13, 1928. The British government had some doubts and thought of discussion; but Kellogg (Stanley Baldwin told King) was 'opposed to any meeting, either of jurists or of Ministers, and ... his view is that there should be no difficulty in way of direct acceptance as proposed treaty is so simple.' London accordingly felt that it was best to accept the draft as it stood, simultaneously, however, setting forth certain British reservations stemming from 'special responsibilities and commitments analogous to those of Monroe Doctrine which draft treaty presumably covers.' The British Prime Minister went on:

His Majesty's Government in Great Britain, I would add, feel that question is of such a character that it would be essential that acceptance of United States proposal, if given, should be expressed by formula which would make it clear that acceptance is with concurrence of all His Majesty's Governments, and implies their readiness to subsequently participate in treaty. To this aspect of matter I would ask that urgent consideration may be given. Of course, we

* In 1936 it was recorded that the only countries not adhering were Argentina, Bolivia, El Salvador, Uruguay, and Yemen.

contemplate that treaty should be concluded in name of all His Majesty's Governments in accordance with procedure agreed to, for treaties of this nature, at the Imperial Conference.[61]

Mackenzie King's reaction to this cable was predictable: 'I suggested [to Skelton] we should ask to be specifically invited by U.S. to become a party, not merely to "concur" with Eng. I see danger in that word. The Foreign Office won't like [it], & [still] less the Dominions Office. Baldwin will see the other side, but it is important we should hold out as a country with equality of status, not come in as falling in line when told to by Grt. Br. Then, too, care has to be taken not to be put in position of endorsing Br. view as expressed in despatch re Egypt, etc.'[62] The formal reply recognized that Kellogg's proposal 'may involve for signatories with previous commitments [such as Egypt] difficulties of varying degree,' but also observed that it was 'of first importance to secure so striking and definite a renunciation of war ...' Therefore Canada was glad to hear of the British decision to accept. However, if it were the intention, as it seemed to be, that the Dominion governments should sign the treaty simultaneously with the British government, 'It appears to us ... to be essential that an explicit invitation covering Dominions should be extended by United States Government.' 'Unofficial statements' led the Canadians to believe that the U.S., 'upon intimation of a desire,' would be pleased to produce the invitation.[63] Five days later information arrived that the Foreign Secretary proposed to inform the American Ambassador accordingly.[64]

King and Skelton, however, made assurance doubly sure. On May 18 a question was asked in Parliament, and on this peg Skelton hung a letter to the United States Minister mentioning the action about an invitation taken through London. If such an invitation were extended, he wrote, 'we assume that it would be transmitted through the United States Legation in Ottawa, in harmony with the method followed in transmitting the original invitation to His Majesty's Government in Great Britain.' He added that there was no basis for press reports that Canada considered it should have been included in that original invitation: the Canadian government fully realized that, 'in view of the tentative character of the proposals and of the emphasis laid upon the desirability of securing the assent of the leading countries first, the procedure adopted by the United States Government in first discussing the matter with His Majesty's Government in Great Britain was wholly appropriate.'[65] Three days later the desired result eventuated. King wrote in his diary: 'Today's event of real historic interest was a presentation by the U.S. Minister in person to me at my office of the invitation of the U.S. to Canada to become a party to the multi-lateral peace pact. This marks the high water mark of achievement & recognition thus far of Canadian nationality. Events have moved rapidly, & in the course of a natural & inevitable evolution peacefully & constitutionally achieved.'[66] Personal and national egos alike were flattered.

During the weeks that followed there was considerable discussion, domestic and international, of the proposed Pact and the difficulties which it seemed to present. Kellogg had tried to meet some of the objections in a speech to the American Society of International Law.[67] At this date and in our present context it is unnecessary to go into all this. It is enough to quote two letters sent to Ottawa by Hume Wrong, then acting as *chargé d'affaires* at the Washington Legation in Massey's absence. On July 12 he wrote:

The root of the difficulty in securing any modification of the text is that Mr. Kellogg regards the treaty as being of much greater importance than the League, while most League powers regard it as a possible buttress to the League which may or may not be of serious value. When, therefore, difficulties connected with League obligations are pointed out to Mr. Kellogg, he is inclined to be impervious, and his receptivity has not been improved by the torrid weather from which we have been suffering. The insistence by the British Government especially, on the necessity of safeguarding the complete integrity of the Covenant seems to have served only to strengthen Mr. Kellogg's determination not to alter his text by one iota.

A fortnight later Wrong produced a somewhat ingenious opinion as to the treaty's importance to Canada. 'Insofar as it may serve to prevent the outbreak of war anywhere,' he wrote, 'it has general utility. There is, however, a special value in its effect on relations between Canada and the United States since it constitutes a real guarantee against war ... the Kellogg Treaty gives an inclusive undertaking that, even if all means of conciliation fail, war shall not ensue. Whatever may be the chances of the treaty being faithfully observed and generously interpreted by other powers, the United States, as author of the treaty, is bound more strongly than any other signatory to observe both letter and spirit ... I feel that the treaty is a real fortification of our undefended frontier.' Skelton agreed that the treaty was good business for Canada: 'There is practically nothing, so far as Canada is concerned, on the debit side of the sheet.'[68]

Mackenzie King decided to go to Paris to sign the treaty in person, killing two birds by also representing Canada at the Ninth Assembly (and the Council) of the League of Nations at Geneva. Full of the usual

MACKENZIE KING AT THE LEAGUE OF NATIONS, 1928
Left to right, O.D. Skelton, Philippe Roy, Raoul Dandurand, King, C.A.
Dunning, W.A. Riddell

thoughts of his mother and father, he affixed his signature with the others in the Salle de l'Horloge on August 27.[69] The forms of signature reflected the changes made by the Imperial Conference. Below the King's name, Lord Cushendun signed, no longer for the Empire as a whole without limitation, but in much the manner Sir Robert Borden had recommended in 1919: for 'Great Britain and Northern Ireland and all parts of the British Empire which are not separate Members of the League of Nations.' Mackenzie King signed next, for Canada; then came the other Dominions* in order.[70]

Readers who remember those events of 1919 will have realized that for Canada the Kellogg Pact was a sort of little Versailles. Just as had happened nine years earlier, Canada's government had contrived to use an international treaty-making event to enhance her status in the world. The Dominion had been separately and individually invited by the United States to an international gathering. The contrast with the procedure before the Washington Conference in 1921 was marked. The country's status as an international person in the eyes of the world was clearer than before. It is true that this was not an absolute 'first'; for Italy had invited Canada individually to the Genoa Economic and Financial Conference of 1922. In Canadian eyes, however, acceptance by the United States was much more important. Perhaps a little gilt was taken off the gingerbread by the fact that Canada had had to nudge the Americans so strongly to get the invitation; but progress is seldom made in international affairs by merely waiting and hoping. There can be little doubt that the presence now of a Canadian Legation in Washington made it easier to attain the desired end. The friendly co-operation of the British government, and the innovations made by the Imperial Conference of 1926, had been important. But it does no harm to recall once more that the whole achievement had its origin on the battlefields of France and Flanders.

Enough has been said to make it evident that King thought the treaty's main advantage the enhancement of national status. Indeed, in retrospect,

---

* Newfoundland, not a member of the League, did not sign. Vincent Massey in Washington was asked whether Newfoundland should be included. His answer to the State Department was No. 'Question: "But isn't Newfoundland a self-governing dominion?" Answer: "Yes, but not a signatory of the Covenant of the League." Question: "Is India a self-governing dominion?" Answer: "No." Question: "Is she a signatory of the Covenant?" Answer: "Yes." Comment: "What a funny empire you've got!"' (Vincent Massey, *What's Past is Prologue: The Memoirs of the Right Honourable Vincent Massey, C.H.* (Toronto 1963), p. 163).

it had no other. But it is interesting that when he laid the Pact before the House of Commons for approval in February 1929, the Prime Minister said no word about status and very little about his own part. Clearly he thought it would have been impolitic to mention these things.[71] The House talked about what the Pact meant to the prospects for peace, and about other countries' reservations; the Left, including notably J.S. Woodsworth and the pacifist Agnes Macphail, who would have liked to abolish the Canadian Department of National Defence, were much to the fore. One gets the impression that the Canadian Parliament very much wanted to believe that the Kellogg Pact had some practical value. Tommy Church, the ex-mayor of Toronto and an unregenerate old-fashioned imperialist, was the only audible strong dissenter. 'In my opinion,' he said, 'the League of Nations is comic opera at its worst and the Kellogg note [sic] is burlesque at its worst.'

THE VIEW FROM THE WASHINGTON LEGATION

When Vincent and Alice Massey opened the Canadian Legation in Washington in 1927 – one should mention Alice, for his wife was very important to Massey – both Canada and the United States were wallowing in prosperity. Canada was doing well in spite of the disadvantages imposed by the Fordney-McCumber Tariff; in the fiscal year 1927 the national revenue touched $400 million.[72] Both countries were under essentially isolationist governments, anxious to avoid external complications; but day-to-day relations along their long and active common frontier ensured that there would be no shortage of routine diplomatic business. And the King government, like all Canadian governments, was anxious to make the United States aware of Canada. It particularly desired that Americans should understand the Dominion's new national status.

One piece of national advertising which Massey was able to arrange was a state visit to Washington by the Governor General and Lady Willingdon in December 1927. This set a precedent and occasioned some dubitation in London. The Governor General was not really a 'head of state'; the Canadian head of state was the King, and the Governor General was his representative. Could Lord Willingdon, visiting on behalf of the Canadian nation, be treated in practice as a head of state in Washington and be received by the President as an equal? It was finally decided that he could, though it is clear that King George V had grave doubts. The Americans received the Willingdons with royal honours – cavalry escorts and 21-gun salutes. On December 6 Lord Willingdon called on

President Coolidge, and the President immediately returned the call to the Canadian Legation. Lady Willingdon is reported to have succeeded in making that rather difficult man laugh! That night the Willingdons were guests of honour at a glittering state dinner at the White House. The visit was a great social success. Washington society was undoubtedly aware of it. The advertising aspect was perhaps not quite so successful with respect to the American nation as a whole. The *New York Times*, which reports everything, reported the affair quite fully, but the main story was on page 23.[73] Apart from this, the only sour note was struck by Massey's particular friends at the British Embassy. At the dinner which they gave, Massey was 'much surprised' to find that the Secretary of State and Mrs Kellogg had been placed above the Willingdons. He recalled that on October 28 the Ambassador, Sir Esmé Howard, had shown him a Foreign Office cable to the effect that the King 'had given consent to the Willingdons' visit but wished it to be understood that H.M. had only one personal rep. in U.S.A. i.e. Brit Amb.' The arrangement of seating, he thought, might be 'a quiet demonstration of conformity – with H.M's views.' At Massey's dinner the previous night the Willingdons, surely quite properly in the circumstances, had been placed above the Howards. It is just possible that this had had its own influence.[74]

The sequel was less satisfactory. The Canadians assumed, a bit simple-mindedly perhaps, that the President would return the Governor General's compliment, by making a state visit to Ottawa. In January 1928 we find Mackenzie King (who had himself had a satisfactory reception at the White House in the previous November)[75] cabling to London about the project. The following month he discussed it with Willingdon: 'He asked if he or I shld write. I sd for him to extend the invitation & I wd write & say the Govt. supported it & hoped Coolidge wd come. The King has cabled his approval.' But the President answered Willingdon regretting that it was not possible for him to accept.[76] Coolidge never returned the Governor General's courtesy, nor did his successor President Hoover. The first American President to make a state visit to Canada was to be Franklin D. Roosevelt.

On March 23, 1929, careful readers of the *New York Times* noted the following item on page 2:

New Orleans, March 22 (AP). – The British auxiliary schooner Imalone of Belize, suspected of being a contraband carrier, was sunk off the Louisiana coast today in a battle with a Coast Guard craft.

One member of its crew, a negro seaman, was killed or drowned.

Next day the story was promoted to page 1, and it stayed there for some time. The British Ambassador had called at the State Department to inquire about a case reported to be 'without precedent' in the history of Prohibition violence. It emerged that the schooner's name was actually *I'm Alone*. She had been unarmed, and the 'battle' had consisted in her being sunk by Coast Guard gunfire some 200 miles from the American coast. It further came to light that she was of Canadian registry, and the Canadian Legation then took over the case from the British Embassy; Sir Esmé Howard handed the file over to Mr Massey with undisguised relief.[77]

Some further facts may be stated at once. The schooner's captain was John T. Randell, a Newfoundlander domiciled in Liverpool, NS. He was a veteran of the South African War and had won the Distinguished Service Cross with the Grand Fleet in 1915. No one, least of all Randell, denied that the *I'm Alone* was a rum-runner. She had been approached by the Coast Guard cutter *Wolcott* while at anchor (according to Randell) some fourteen miles off the U.S. coast. Since Randell claimed that his ship's speed was not much more than nine knots, he was outside the zone of legitimate search (one hour's sailing) prescribed by the liquor treaty of 1924 (above, page 47). He therefore refused to allow the cutter to search the schooner, and turned to sea with the cutter in pursuit. Another cutter, the *Dexter*, was called up by radio and intercepted the *I'm Alone* on March 22. Randell still refusing to stop, the *Dexter* fired on the schooner with guns, machine-guns, and rifles; Randell stated that she clearly tried to avoid hitting any members of the crew. Ultimately the *I'm Alone* was sunk by shells fired into her hull; the crew, struggling in the water, were picked up by the Americans. One man, the boatswain, Leon Mainguy, was apparently dead when taken on board (Randell testified that a coast guards-man risked his life by diving into the sea to rescue him). On the cutters the captain and crew were placed in irons. They were taken into New Orleans, where after a time Randell was allowed to see the British consul.* He was shortly released.[78]

The nature of the *I'm Alone*'s business quite aside, it was clearly very doubtful whether the violent action of the Coast Guard cutters could be justified. Massey proceeded to discuss the matter in correspondence with Henry L. Stimson, Secretary of State in the new Hoover administration. It is evident that the negotiations were closely watched and supervised by

---

* It may be noted here that, since a Canadian consular service came into existence only gradually, Canada continued to avail herself of the services of British consuls.

the Department of External Affairs in Ottawa, though the almost total absence of references in Mackenzie King's diary suggests that the Prime Minister took comparatively little personal interest in it. The issues were thus stated by Massey in a letter to the department in the beginning:[79]

The main questions which are raised appear at present to be as follows: (1) The exercise of the right of pursuit against a foreign vessel which has never come within the territorial jurisdiction of the United States; previous decisions appear to indicate that a United States court would uphold the exercise of this right, if the pursuit began within twelve miles of the coast. (2) Whether a pursuit which was carried on for two days and was ended by a vessel different from the vessel which began it can legitimately be considered as hot and continuous in international law. (3) Whether, even if the position of the United States Coast Guard is admitted on the first two points, the sinking of the vessel with loss of life was justified by her conduct.

The correspondence with Stimson was amicable, but the parties completely failed to agree; and in April 1929 the United States proposed, and Canada accepted, the submission of the question to arbitration under the terms of the 'liquor treaty' of 1924, which provided for joint report by two persons, one to be nominated by each country.[80]

The procedural discussions that followed need not be summarized.[81] The two arbitrators who finally considered the question were Mr Justice Willis Van Devanter for the United States, and Mr Justice Lyman Poore Duff (a puisne judge of the Supreme Court of Canada, who became Chief Justice in 1933) for Canada.* In 1933 they made an interim report which did not agree on the question of the right of hot pursuit but which did conclude that 'the admittedly intentional sinking of the suspected vessel was not justified by anything in the [1924] Convention.' Their final report, dated January 5, 1935, added that the sinking of the vessel 'would not be justified by any principle of international law.' It found that the *I'm Alone*, though 'a British ship of Canadian registry,' was owned by persons who were 'entirely, or nearly so,' United States citizens; in these circumstances, the commissioners considered that no compensation should be paid for the loss of the ship or cargo.

The act of sinking the ship, however, by officers of the United States Coast Guard, was, as we have already indicated, an unlawful act; and the Commis-

---

* The first Canadian appointee was Eugene Lafleur, KC, who died before proceedings commenced. The 'Canadian Agent' to prepare the case was John Read, Legal Adviser in the Department of External Affairs.

sioners consider that the United States ought formally to acknowledge its ille-
gality, and to apologize to His Majesty's Canadian Government therefor; and,
further, that as a material amend in respect of the wrong the United States
should pay the sum of $25,000 to His Majesty's Canadian Government; and
they recommend accordingly.

The commissioners recommended compensation for the captain and
crew, 'none of whom was a party to the illegal conspiracy to smuggle
liquor into the United States and sell the same there': $7,906 to the cap-
tain, $10,185 to the family of the boatswain who had lost his life, and
smaller sums to other members of the crew or their heirs.[82]

Two weeks after the final report was rendered, Cordell Hull, Secretary
of State in the Roosevelt administration, wrote the Canadian Minister in
Washington informing him that he was taking steps 'to obtain an appropriation for $50,666.50' to cover the payments to be made under the
award. He added: 'Although the Commissioners find that the mission and
use of the vessel at the time of its sinking were unlawful, nevertheless
they also find that its sinking by the United States officers was unlawful.
The government of the United States, therefore, tenders to His Majesty's
Canadian Government an apology for the sinking of the vessel.'[83] By this
time Prohibition was a thing of the past, and any repetition of the *I'm
Alone* affair was happily improbable.

Both countries could regard with satisfaction the civilized manner in
which this rather unpleasant incident, the worst of many international
difficulties arising out of Prohibition, had been liquidated. Of course, the
importance of the achievement was reduced by the fact that the case was
not one calculated to inflame national passions on either side. The nature
of the *I'm Alone*'s business militated against Canadians becoming violently
excited over her fate; while on their side Americans were unlikely to be
roused to chauvinistic fervour in support of Coast Guardsmen enforcing
the Volstead Act. But an achievement there was, and one that gave some
colour to boastings about the North American Idea.

When the St Lawrence Seaway was finally opened in 1959, it was the
realization of a dream that North Americans, and particularly Canadians,
had cherished since the seventeenth century.

The St Lawrence River and the Great Lakes present on the map the
picture of a tremendous water highway, ready to carry the commerce of
the world into the heart of North America, and the products of the North
American heartland out to the world. From the Strait of Belle Isle to the
head of Lake Superior it stretches more than two thousand miles. The
map, however, is deceptive. Formidable obstacles obstructed the passage.

The first of these was the Lachine Rapids at Montreal. Not many miles above, there was another range of rapids (Cascades, Cedars, and Coteau). In the vicinity of Cornwall the international boundary strikes the river and from there to Lake Ontario the St Lawrence forms the border. In this reach between Cornwall and Prescott there were further dangerous rapids. Between Lakes Ontario and Erie interposes the great barrier of the Niagara Escarpment and Niagara Falls. Finally, the entrance to Lake Superior from Lake Huron is blocked by the rapids of the St Mary's River at Sault Ste Marie.

The process of improving the St Lawrence artery seems to have begun 'before 1689,' when the Sulpician François Dollier de Casson set men to work digging a canal at Lachine.[84] Through the two hundred and seventy years that followed, the progress of the great idea was marked by a variety of conflicts of interests such as few projects have had to contend with. The fact that the boundary settlement at the end of the American Revolution made the St Lawrence an international river and the Great Lakes an international boundary rendered canalization a matter of foreign policy. But it was not just a question of reconciling two national points of view. On each side of the border, with the passage of time, regional and local and special interests might take sides for or against the plan. Many communities in the American Middle West were strongly for it; but inevitably New York and other Atlantic ports saw it as a menace. In both countries the railways disliked it, seeing it as a potential dangerous competitor. Local governments, state and provincial, had strong views that had to be taken into account. And the project had great possibilities for the generation of electric power as well as for the improvement of navigation, and the interests of power and navigation were not the same. And all these rivalries affected the political balance in both countries.

Dollier's plan at Lachine proved abortive. The first effective improvement was during the War of the American Revolution, when the Royal Engineers built short canals to enable batteaus to by-pass the Cascades, Cedars, and Coteau rapids. In 1821-4 the first real Lachine Canal was built by Lower Canada, and in 1824-9 the first Welland Canal was built by a private company with (ultimately) a great deal of public support, to circumvent Niagara Falls. Sanguine Canadians had hoped that the products of the American lake states might take an improved St Lawrence route to the ocean, but New York State, by building the Erie Canal (1817-25) connecting Buffalo on Lake Erie with the Hudson River, ensured that most of them would go out through New York port. After 1841 the legislature of the united Province of Canada undertook a large programme of improvements on the St Lawrence, and by 1848 there was an uninterrupted channel for vessels of not more than nine feet draught of water from Montreal to the head of Lake Huron. Gradual improvements increased the permissible draught to fourteen feet throughout this route by early in the twentieth century. The United States built a canal at Sault Ste Marie beginning in 1853, and a Canadian canal was constructed there in 1887-95.[85] But the era of the First World War found the idea of a waterway that would enable ocean shipping to sail the inland seas clear to the head of Lake Superior still only a dream.

The Seaway story is far too complicated to be told in detail here.[86] As early as 1914 pressure for a deep waterway was sufficient to prompt the United States government to inquire whether Canada would approve of the International Joint Commission investigating the best procedure for developing the waters of the Great Lakes-St Lawrence basin for navigation and power purposes. Within a few months Canada was at war, and the Borden government never replied to the inquiry. When the war was over agitation revived, and in 1919 pressure-groups were organized in both countries to work for the project: the Great Lakes-St Lawrence Tidewater Association in the United States and (rather less active and shorter-lived) the Canadian Deep Waterways and Power Association in Canada. In the same year Washington renewed its inquiry about a reference to the IJC, and this time Sir Robert Borden and his colleagues agreed to the idea. The commission held public hearings on both sides of the border. Most of the Americans who appeared favoured the scheme; fourteen states sent representatives to support it, and only one – New York – formally opposed it. In Canada support was much less general. The commission noted that it centred in Ontario. The Ontario Hydro-Electric Power Commission (whose head was Sir Adam Beck, who was also a leading figure in the Canadian Deep Waterways and Power Association) had strongly supported the waterway, but insisted that the commission itself, and not the national government, should control the development of power from the St Lawrence. Among the bodies opposing were the Montreal Board of Trade, the Chambre de Commerce de Montréal, and the Montreal Harbour Commission. In December 1921 the International Joint Commission recommended that the United States and Canada should enter into a treaty for improving the St Lawrence River.[87]

The following spring the United States proposed going ahead on this basis. Secretary of State Hughes informed the British Ambassador that he was authorized by President Harding to state that he favoured the negotiation of a treaty based on the IJC report 'or such modifications as might be agreed upon.' Alternatively, if a definitive treaty was considered undesirable, Hughes suggested that it might be practicable to conclude one 'pledging the two Governments to undertake the execution of the project ... and making provision for a joint commission charged with the duty of formulating ... a complete plan, which should be subject to the approval of the two Governments prior to the beginning of the work of construction.' In Canada Mackenzie King's new government shot this project down without even the courteous pretence of careful consideration. The Governor General wrote to the Ambassador: 'Minute of Council approved May 29th setting forth that my Ministers have not thus far had opportunity to give report of International Joint Commission and accompanying report of Board of Engineers careful consideration, and having regard to magnitude of project and very large outlay of public money involved, they are of opinion that it would not appear to be expedient to deal with matter at present time.'[88]

The motives of King and his colleagues remain conjectural. (King's diary for 1922 contains large gaps, and unfortunately one of them falls at this point.) Perhaps the fact that the reference to the IJC had been authorized by the Borden government had its influence. Perhaps the current depression had something to do with it. And it would be strange if the cabinet had not taken note of the fact that the waterway scheme was popular in the predominantly Conservative province of Ontario, and unpopular in the almost unanimously Liberal province of Quebec. At any rate, King met the American approach with an appearance of discourtesy that was to be rare in his diplomacy, and particularly in his dealings with the United States; and for the moment the plan languished.

Continued urgings from the American Middle West, however, kept it alive; and in Canada the Ontario Hydro-Electric Power Commission began to press for power development in the International Rapids section of the St Lawrence. The King government now found it expedient to exhume and reply to the U.S. proposal of nearly two years before. They carefully refrained from committing themselves to any treaty, but suggested further investigation of the project by an enlarged joint board of engineers such as had advised the IJC, and indicated that they proposed to appoint a committee to look into the whole matter 'from a national standpoint.' The U.S. government expressed gratification and proceeded to appoint a similar committee of its own. Its suggestion that the two committees should consult together from time to time did not however find favour in Ottawa. The American committee, called the St Lawrence Commission and presided over by Herbert Hoover, President Coolidge's Secretary of Commerce, reported late in 1926, strongly supporting the seaway plan and wholly discountenancing a rival scheme advanced in New York for an internal deep waterway across that state to the Hudson.

The Canadian National Advisory Committee, headed by George P. Graham, did not report until January 1928. It recommended that the United States should finance the improvement of the international section of the St Lawrence, and that the first development should be in the purely Canadian section.[89] Thereafter the Canadian government, through its Minister in Washington, laid before the Americans a detailed statement of its position on the seaway project.[90] It boiled down to an assertion that the scheme was considerably more important to the United States than it was to Canada. It expressed agreement with the propositions of the National Advisory Committee, and invited American comment upon them. It pointed out that railway rates were in general lower in Canada than in the U.S., and remarked that since the greater part of Canadian railway mileage was owned by the state, any proposal that might affect the revenue of the railways had a rather different aspect in Canada from that across the border. It mentioned the heavy financial burden resulting from the war, and remarked, 'it is considered that it would not be sound policy to assume heavy public obligations for the St. Lawrence project.' And it observed that 'public opinion in Canada has not so clearly crystallized in favour of the waterway project as appears to be the case in the United States.'

Washington refused to be discouraged by this rather frosty document. Within three months it came back with a note[91] accepting as a basis for negotiation the National Advisory Committee's suggestion that the U.S. should undertake the deepening of the various interconnecting channels of the Great Lakes and the improvement of the international section of the St Lawrence both for navigation and for power, while Canada should undertake construction in the wholly Canadian sections – the Welland Canal and the parts of the St Lawrence below the international boundary. The note, however, did not agree as to postponing the work in the international sector. It did accept a Canadian suggestion that all channels provided should have a minimum depth of twenty-seven feet, the permanent structures having a thirty-foot depth with a view to future expansion. It ended by suggesting the appointment of commissioners to discuss the problem jointly 'with a view to the formulation of a convention appropriate to the subject' – that is, a treaty. The Canadian government's response was to mention the constitutional difficulties resulting from the interest of the provinces of Ontario and Quebec in the matter. It now proposed to discuss the problem with those provinces, after which it would be in a position to engage in further discussion with the United States.[92]

It is amply evident that at this period the United States wanted a St Lawrence Seaway and wanted it as soon as possible, and was correspond-

ingly anxious for an early treaty with Canada. There was no such enthusiasm in Ottawa. The government was prepared to discuss the matter, to
such an extent as to mollify the Americans and the Canadian supporters
of the project, but clearly would not have complained if construction had
been postponed to the Greek Kalends. Mackenzie King's attitude was
reflected in a note in his diary (March 12, 1926) of an interview with
Francis H. Clergue, the millionaire promoter from Sault Ste Marie. Clergue,
it would seem, had been put up by important friends in Washington to try
to convert the Prime Minister. King recorded that he presented the plan
as a sort of cure-all, that might solve the problem of the Chicago water
diversion, satisfy Ontario and Quebec on the power question, 'and all at
little or no cost to Canada': 'It would appear he was speaking for Mellon*
& Hoover & Coolidge of U.S. the latter with Taft as an adviser & outlining
a scheme which would help the American Govt. solve many problems. I
confess the size of the project alarms me, & its problematical character.'
'Thinking big' was not one of King's characteristics, and at the time of
this conversation, with his government very shaky indeed, he was particularly unlikely to embark on ambitious and expensive schemes.

While he was in Washington in November 1927 King had brief talks
on the Seaway with Secretary Kellogg and President Coolidge. To both of
them he put forward a reminiscence of Reciprocity in 1911: every evidence of eagerness on the American side would make the path in Canada
more difficult, as had happened then. King also pointed out to Kellogg
'how all propaganda in Canada had been largely from power interests
there that wished to prevent Canal construction.'[93]

During the remainder of the life of King's second ministry the situation
did not change very materially. Arrangements were made for deepening
the channel of the St Lawrence above the rapids, between Lake Ontario
and Prescott. The Canadian government in 1929 approved a proposal by
a private firm, the Beauharnois Light, Heat and Power Company, to build
south of the St Lawrence, in the Canadian section west of Montreal, a
power canal that could also be used for navigation. King held discussions
with Premier G. Howard Ferguson of Ontario and Premier L.A. Taschereau of Quebec (both of whom favoured Beauharnois) without
succeeding in resolving the constitutional difficulties about power development. All this took time, and this did not seem to be at all disagreeable
to the Canadian government. Reports of an impending upward revision
of the American tariff troubled the waters. In November 1928, in conver-

---

* Andrew W. Mellon, Secretary of the Treasury under Harding, Coolidge, and
  Hoover.

sation with the American Minister, King referred to these reports and the Seaway scheme together. His memorandum of the conversation remarked: 'I mentioned ... that while I did not think – and it was not intended – that the two matters should in any way join together, Mr. Hoover's pronouncements [on the tariff] had made it very difficult for them to be considered apart.' Phillips told his government that a judicious handling of the tariff question might improve the Seaway's chances. King had not seemed to be impressed by a hint that the U.S. might turn to an all-American route. On April 4, 1929, James Malcolm, the Minister of Trade and Commerce, told King of an interview he had had with President Hoover during which Hoover 'spoke of the possibility of changes in U.S. tariff being held over pending St. Lawrence Waterways development'; King's private comment was that this was 'something that could not be thought of for a moment.' Next day he said the same thing in the House of Commons. Since King's remark to Phillips was certainly at the bottom of Hoover's observation, the President may have been surprised.[94]

In any case, musings about connections between the Seaway and the American tariff did not serve to deflect Congress and the Hoover administration from their courses. In the summer of 1930 the President signed the bill enacting the Hawley-Smoot Tariff. A few weeks later Mackenzie King's government went down to electoral defeat without any agreement having been made to build the St Lawrence Seaway.

SLACKENING THE FORMAL BONDS

The Imperial Conference of 1926 had recommended (above, page 86) that an 'expert committee' should be convened to consider the technical aspects of the task of converting the general principle of equality of status into actual legislation. This committee finally met in London in the autumn of 1929 under the appellation of Conference on the Operation of Dominion Legislation and Merchant Shipping Legislation.

This was not a session of the Imperial Conference, nor technically even a sub-conference similar to that of 1909 on defence. It was primarily a meeting for lawyers, and Canada's chief delegate was the Minister of Justice, Ernest Lapointe, KC, an experienced negotiator who was quite as capable as King of combining urbanity with firmness. He was accompanied by O.D. Skelton and other civil servants, one of whom was John Read, now installed at External Affairs as Legal Adviser. A year before the conference actually met, Skelton summarized the Canadian government's position for Lapointe: 'As I understand it, the purpose of our investigation should be to consider how far it is possible to remove every vestige of

Imperial legislative supremacy, save for the present the power of the British Parliament to amend the Canadian Constitution.'[95] It is a fair assumption that this summary was the outcome of discussion with Mackenzie King.

The Labour party was now again in power in the United Kingdom, but there is no indication that this affected the British attitude in the conference. The fact is that the British representatives tried hard to interpret the decisions of 1926 in a centralist sense. Skelton remarked that their opening brief was 'pervaded by the assumption that something short of equality was adequate, and that it was necessary to retain the supremacy of the British parliament for many purposes.' They argued against total and violent breaks with past practice. The chairman of the conference, the Secretary of State for the Dominions, Lord Passfield (better known as Sidney Webb), quoted in his introductory remarks his own most famous phrase, 'the inevitability of gradualness.'[96] The general course of the meeting might have been fairly accurately forecast by anyone familiar with the conference of 1926. Again it was the Irish Free State delegation that demanded quick and radical action. It was led by Patrick McGilligan, Minister for External Affairs. McGilligan had no time for gradualness. He disturbed the tranquillity of the opening plenary session by saying that pace mattered as well as direction, and adding: 'There are certain old survivals which are in the circumstances definitely anomalous, quite anachronistic, and only to be described as a continuance of usurpation.'[97] Skelton said of the Irish: 'A successful outcome of the Conference, they held, was absolutely essential to prevent the republican movement in Ireland getting the upper hand.' Nevertheless, McGilligan was not the worst problem for the British. At the crisis of the meeting, Skelton remarked: 'The British stood at one pole, the South Africans at the other.' He described F.W. Beyers, the leader of the South Africans and a former member of the Hertzog government, as 'about the most obstinate Dutchman in history'; the Irish and the Canadians both found themselves acting as moderators. Australia and New Zealand, as in 1926, were on the conservative side; but they were not represented by cabinet ministers, and their voices were correspondingly less forceful.

Lapointe was invariably polite, but he hewed pretty close to the line Skelton had indicated the year before, which certainly accorded with his own inclinations. The discussion on merchant shipping legislation exemplified the situation. Although no British shipping legislation had applied to the Dominions since 1910, some earlier acts, notably that of 1894, did; and Canadian admiralty courts were still governed by the Colonial Courts of Admiralty Act of 1890. These survivals clearly had to go, but Sir William Jowitt, Attorney General of the United Kingdom, the most active member of the British delegation and its effective leader, was anxious that the conference should preserve the character of the 'British ship' on a basis of uniformity throughout the Commonwealth:

At the present moment the term 'British ship' has a precise legal meaning, which is an element in the high commercial value which British ships possess among the mercantile marines of the world ... It is not a thing to be altered lightly or except by common consent of all those concerned, and if this Conference is successful in finding some agreed method by which certain fundamental principles are to prevail throughout the whole Empire and not be alterable at the will of any single part it is the definite view of His Majesty's Government in the United Kingdom that the definition of 'British ship' should be one of the points to be dealt with by that method.[98]

Lapointe was prepared to go along with this to a considerable extent, but suggested that it was desirable to have a designation indicating the country of registration, such as 'British ship, United Kingdom,' 'British ship, Canada,' etc. McGilligan, however, suggested that it might be better to give up the use of the term 'British ship' and simply use 'United Kingdom ship,' 'Canadian ship,' and the like. Passfield remarked that there was nothing to prevent the Irish Free State using the term 'Irish ship' if they wanted to; and in the end the final report of the conference made no attempt to define a 'British ship.' It did, however, make rather elaborate recommendations for maintaining uniform standards throughout the Commonwealth, and concluded that 'the different parts of the Commonwealth should continue not to differentiate between their own ocean-going ships and similar ships belonging to other parts of the Commonwealth.'[99]

At one point Skelton made a rather characteristic intervention. The conference looked at 'the existing provisions under which the Admiralty have certain powers in regard to the flag to be flown on a British ship which is not a United Kingdom ship.' Incautiously, if not tactlessly, Jowitt 'said that the matter was really one of contract, that in return for the protection of the Navy, the Admiralty claimed the right to impose conditions.'

Dr. SKELTON stated that it was impossible to include in any free agreement a provision enabling the naval or other authorities of one part of the Commonwealth to determine the flag of any other part, and that Canada wanted to be at liberty to change the details of the Red Ensign, such as by putting the

Maple Leaf in the flag. This Ensign, which was granted to Canada by warrant under Section 73(1) [of the Merchant Shipping Act, 1894], should now come under the exclusive authority of the Dominion. He said that he was opposed to the bringing into the idea of agreement that of a pre-eminent power.

Mr. LAPOINTE said that anything which admitted the right of the Admiralty to decide what should be the flag of Canada would be objectionable.

It is to be feared that to Skelton the mere word 'Admiralty' was something of a red rag. Jowitt dropped the question of flags.[100]

Apart from its recommendations on uniformity for Commonwealth ocean shipping, the conference's report advised British legislation providing that Dominions in which the Colonial Courts of Admiralty Act was in force should have power to repeal that act as relating to them, and that certain sections of that act and of the Merchant Shipping Act, 1894, should respectively cease to have effect in any Dominion and be construed as though reference in them to the legislature of a British possession did not include reference to the parliament of a Dominion.

The other matters with which the conference was required to deal were the disallowance or reservation of Dominion legislation, the extra-territorial operation of Dominion legislation, and (the most contentious) the Colonial Laws Validity Act of 1865.

Disallowance meant the right of the Crown, on the advice of ministers in the United Kingdom, to annul acts passed by a Dominion or colonial legislature. These powers had not been exercised with respect to Dominion acts for many years, and it was clear to the conference that they could no longer be so exercised. Therefore, it concluded, Dominions possessing the power to amend their constitutions could abolish the legal power of disallowance if they so desired. Those (such as Canada) which did not possess this power could request the government of the United Kingdom to ask Parliament to pass legislation abolishing the power, and it would be 'in accordance with constitutional practice' for that government to take such action. As for *reservation*, this meant the withholding of assent by a governor or governor general to a bill passed by a legislature so that 'His Majesty's pleasure' (meaning in practice the pleasure of the British government) might be taken upon it. On this the conference reported:

Applying the principles laid down in the Imperial Conference Report of 1926, it is established first that the power of discretionary reservation if exercised at all can only be exercised in accordance with the constitutional practice in the Dominion governing the exercise of the powers of the Governor-General; secondly, that His Majesty's Government in the United King-

dom will not advise His Majesty the King to give the Governor-General any
instructions to reserve Bills presented to him for assent, and thirdly, as regards
the signification of the King's pleasure concerning a reserved Bill, that it
would not be in accordance with constitutional practice for advice to be
tendered to His Majesty by His Majesty's Government in the United Kingdom against the views of the Government of the Dominion concerned ...

Thus so far as Canada was concerned both reservation and disallowance,
as practised by the British government against Canadian legislation, were
declared unacceptable in theory, as they had been almost universally in
practice for many years.

As for the extra-territorial operation of Dominion legislation, there
were certainly constitutional limitations on British colonies in such matters as the control of their citizens and ships abroad. (As an extreme case,
it had even been suggested, in the earliest days of Canadian naval effort,
that the new Royal Canadian Navy would have no authority to operate
outside the three-mile limit.) Whether such limitations were still in effect
against the modern Dominions was a moot point. The Canadian lawyers
at the conference argued that Canada did in fact possess the right to pass
legislation having extra-territorial effect. The conference report sagely
observed, 'The subject is full of obscurity,' and it was agreed by all that
'the most suitable method of placing the matter beyond possibility of
doubt' would be a declaratory enactment passed with the consent of the
Dominions by the British Parliament.[101]

Concerning the Colonial Laws Validity Act, it was pointed out that in
its time this statute actually enlarged the legislative competence of the
British colonies; but it also provided that colonial statutes 'repugnant' to
legislation passed by the Imperial Parliament were void. The United
Kingdom representatives showed themselves very reluctant in the beginning simply to sweep the Act away so far as it affected the Dominions;
they desired to ensure the maintenance of a uniform body of legislation
on certain matters throughout the Commonwealth. Jowitt 'suggested that
the United Kingdom and the Dominions should give up some of their
independent powers by mutual agreement' where matters of 'fundamental importance to the structure of the British Commonwealth' were concerned. 'He urged that some common nucleus of legislation should be
retained.' And Lord Passfield made the rather doubtful point that 'the
Report of 1926 assumed as one of the principles that there should be one
organ capable of legislating for the whole British Commonwealth after
consultation and with the consent of its constituent members, and [he]
said that this possibility should not be ruled out altogether.'[102] Canada,

Ireland, and South Africa showed no sympathy whatever for this point of view, in effect refusing to compromise on the principle of legislative independence; and although Australia and New Zealand were more disposed to accept the British position, in the end the conference report simply recommended that 'legislation be enacted declaring in terms that the [Colonial Laws Validity] Act should no longer apply to the laws passed by any Dominion.'[103] The British rear-guard action had failed, and total legislative decentralization, qualified only by voluntary co-operation, had been accepted.

Lord Passfield had the gravest doubts about the conference report, and only signed it after a final unrecorded heads-of-delegations meeting at which, in Skelton's words, 'Mr. Lapointe, who had been very pacific hitherto, put the fear of the Lord into' the British representatives. The British government was much troubled; fearing trouble in Parliament, it consulted the opposition (Baldwin, Amery, and Lloyd George) and got consent from the two Conservatives but not from Lloyd George. It instructed Passfield and Jowitt to sign, but to make no promises beyond undertaking to use their good offices to obtain government adoption of the report. Jowitt, Skelton reported, 'said that in signing he could not pledge his government, but he did commit himself to resign if his government did not support it.' The Australian and New Zealand representatives in signing the report stipulated that this did not preclude further free discussion of the issues at a later time.[104]

The conference's basic conclusion was that those of its recommendations requiring legislative action should be incorporated in a statute which, after approval by another Imperial Conference and by the Dominions individually, might be passed by the Parliament of the United Kingdom. This statute duly materialized in 1931 as the Statute of Westminster.

To judge by his diary, Mackenzie King took little personal interest in the lawyers' conference of 1929. However, he had every reason to be pleased with its report; and he clearly decided that it should be placed before the House of Commons for formal approval. On May 26, 1930 Ernest Lapointe moved in the House that the recommendations of the conference be approved; the motion concluded, 'and [the House] considers that steps should be taken at the forthcoming Imperial conference to ensure their being given effect at an early date.'

The brief end-of-session debate is interesting chiefly for the attitude of the Conservative Opposition. King summed it up in his diary by saying, 'Cahan was very extreme, & Bennett jingoistic & contradictory.' King

had a vocabulary all his own. R.B. Bennett's contribution was not jingoistic in the usual sense of the word, but his tone was certainly sentimental:
'What resentment did they [the Liberals] harbour against the little islands
in the North sea? ... Why should we endeavour to have the people of this
country believe that we are suffering untold wrongs which we in some
way must rise up and redress?' This was exaggerating the Liberal arguments. C.H. Cahan stated the real issue much more clearly and precisely:
'Briefly, I am persuaded that it is in the best interests of Canada that the
British commonwealth of nations, which is commonly known as the British Empire, should remain a subsisting political unit, and not merely a
free association of independent states.' This was an accurate statement of
what was happening. The Borden policy, accepting the idea of an agreed
Commonwealth foreign policy, had assumed that the Commonwealth
would continue a political unit. The King policy assumed the other thing.
Lapointe, indeed, had said so at the conference, when during the discussion on merchant shipping legislation he dropped the remark: 'The British Commonwealth of Nations is an association, not a federation, nor a
political unit.'[105]

No doubt there were many other Conservative members who agreed
with Cahan; undoubtedly also his ideas had many supporters in the country at large. It must be assumed, however, that the party's assessment of
the situation was that the majority of Canadians thought otherwise; for it
did not choose to divide the House. No amendment was proposed, and
Lapointe's motion was agreed to on May 27 without a vote. One must as
always, of course, remember Quebec. To oppose the conference recommendations would have confirmed Quebec's image of the Conservatives
as the party of imperialism, and would have been an additional obstacle in
the way of re-establishing the political fortunes of the party in that all-
important province.

Politics were important at that moment, for three days after the motion
passed Parliament was dissolved. In the general election campaign that
followed imperial relations cannot be said to have been an important
issue. It is true that in his 'keynote' speech of June 16 King boasted of the
government's record on 'the right to make our own treaties' and 'the
establishment of Canadian legations in other lands,' recalled Conservative
carping at these measures, and in effect challenged Bennett to say where
he stood on these questions. Bennett's own programme, presented in
Winnipeg on June 9, had nothing to say about such things. His references
to the Empire were strictly economic.[106]

Faced with the American tariff wall, the King ministry had sought new
markets within the Commonwealth. A trade agreement was made with

Australia in 1924. It was not immediately implemented, for King was shocked when, belatedly, he realized that it involved some tariff increases as well as decreases. A revised arrangement was made and approved by the Canadian Parliament in the summer of 1925.[107] It provided for Canadian newsprint, linotype machinery, and cash registers entering Australia free; while on the other side Australian eggs and cheese and some other items had free entry to Canada, and Australian butter paid a duty of only one cent per pound. The act authorized the Governor in Council by order-in-council to 'extend the said advantages to goods the produce or manufacture of any British country.' These advantages were shortly extended to New Zealand. New Zealand butter became prominent in the campaign.*

It was at once amply evident that Bennett's sentimental 'imperialism' did not extend to the field of economics. And he was, if possible, a more convinced devotee of the protective tariff than Meighen. In his opening address he spoke of King 'introducing measures under the pious cloak of Empire trade':

What do they mean by that? ... If it means we should admit free into our markets Empire goods in competition with our own, without securing a real benefit for ourselves, and without obtaining a preferred place in their markets for our products, then I oppose it, as did Sir John A. Macdonald.

For it is not good for Canada. I give place to no man in my love for our Empire, but there is a greater love in my life and that is my love for Canada. Judge me by that ...

Listen, you agriculturist from the West, and all the other parts of Canada. You have been taught to applaud free trade. Tell me where did free trade ever fight for you? You say our tariffs are only for the manufacturers. I will make them fight for you as well. I will use them to blast a way into the markets that have been closed to you.[108]

People were prepared to listen to this sort of talk, for there had been a catastrophic change in the economic climate. The boom had burst. In 1928 there had been newspaper headlines like, 'Wild Speculative Orgy Hits New York Market, Creating New Record.'[109] In October 1929 the bottom suddenly fell out of the stock market. This signalled the onset of the Great Depression. The Canadian economy, particularly vulnerable

* In 1925 Canada also made a comprehensive trade agreement with the British West Indies, Bermuda, British Guiana, and British Honduras, which was approved by Parliament by the West Indies Trade Agreement Act, 1926.

because of its dependence on exports, was hard hit almost at once. The situation was made worse by the failure of the western grain harvest. Already by the end of the year many men were out of work; unemployment in Canadian trade unions rose from 3.7 per cent in September 1929 to 11.4 per cent in December; by June 1930 it was 10.6 per cent as compared with only 2.9 per cent a year earlier. In these early months of the crisis Quebec and the western provinces suffered most heavily.[110]

It was this situation that ruined the Liberals. In the voting on July 28, 1930 they suffered a great defeat, electing only 91 members against 137 for the Conservatives. For the first time since 1911 the Conservatives obtained a substantial representation in Quebec. The Liberals still held 40 seats there, but the Conservatives got 24, and actually polled over 44 per cent of the popular vote. New Zealand butter had given them a powerful weapon in the dairy-farming areas of the province.[111] Mackenzie King went into opposition, and on August 7 Richard Bedford Bennett became Prime Minister of Canada.

NOTE: In 1927 the Judicial Committee of the Privy Council in London ruled on Canada's last major boundary dispute – an intra-Commonwealth one, concerning the border between Newfoundland's territory of Labrador and the province of Quebec. Lawyers for Canada argued that the line should run just one mile from high-water mark along the whole coast, a boundary which the Judicial Committee not surprisingly described as 'fantastic.' The committee awarded to Newfoundland a large territory embracing particularly the whole drainage area of the Hamilton River, including Grand (now Churchill) Falls.[112] The award has continued to be a source of grievance in Quebec.

CHAPTER FOUR

DEPRESSION DIPLOMACY

A DIFFERENT PRIME MINISTER

The Prime Ministers of Canada between the two World Wars were not a notably attractive group. We have already remarked that neither Meighen nor King enjoyed the warmly personal esteem that had been felt for some of their predecessors. And R.B. Bennett, who had the misfortune to govern through the depths of the Great Depression, came to be probably the most unpopular chief executive the country has ever had.

He was not helped by being a millionaire, nor by the fact that his physical appearance was that of the cartoonists' traditional capitalist, lacking for completeness only the dollar signs on the waistcoat. Nor has his historical image in Canada been improved by the further fact that after he retired he abandoned the country he had tried to rule, moved to England, and became a Viscount. It is perhaps not accidental that, although his friend Lord Beaverbrook is understood to have made active efforts to find a distinguished biographer, no full-dress life of Bennett has yet appeared.[1] The fact would seem to be that he has not been found an inviting subject.

Nevertheless, this lonely man – he was, like King, a bachelor – was a far from uninteresting personality. In spite of his rather forbidding reputation, he was a man of generous impulses, as his responses to the innumerable tragic requests for help that poured in upon him show.[2] The Governor General's secretary, Alan Lascelles, described him to Stanley Baldwin: 'One who has known Bennett for many years is reported to have said of him, "R.B. is partially educated, but wholly uncivilised." With this somewhat primitive habit of mind go several other primitive characteristics; an almost savage sensitiveness to ridicule, small vanities, a child-like impatience of obstacles, an equally child-like appreciation of sympathy & small acts of friendliness – traits that are, perhaps, not ... infrequently found with first-rate intellectual capacity, which he certainly has.'³ Some of these characteristics he shared with King. Like King also he had a great capacity for work, which during his administration he put unstintingly at the disposal of his country. He carried an enormous burden. He was accused, not without reason, of running a one-man government. He gave colour to the charge, and added to the burden, by carrying for the first year and a half of his administration the responsibilities of the office of Minister of Finance in addition to those of Prime Minister and Secretary of State for External Affairs.

The whole of Bennett's period in power was overlain by the dark cloud of the Depression. The misery seemed the worse because of the febrile prosperity that had preceded it. When the present writer returned to his native town in 1929 after two years abroad, parts of Toronto seemed hardly recognizable. The pleasantly domestic old Queen's Hotel, with its wide veranda where one could imagine Union agents sitting as they watched the Confederates who made the place their headquarters during the American Civil War, had been replaced by a towering and obviously enormously expensive structure called the Royal York. The skyscrapers at the corner of King and Yonge Streets, so impressive to my boyhood, had been dwarfed by a new Bank of Commerce Building ('the tallest building in the British Commonwealth'). This sort of conspicuous construction was about to end. The symbol of the next era in Toronto would be the gaunt and ugly skeleton of the unfinished Park Plaza Hotel, looming year after year over the prominent intersection of Avenue Road and Bloor Street like a monument on the grave of dead hopes.

The desperate problem of the economy pervaded every area of Canadian policy, and certainly that of external affairs. Particularly in the early years of Bennett's administration, relations with the Empire and with foreign states were wholly subordinated to the struggle against the Depression. If a measure in any field offered the hope of creating a few more jobs, of doing something to restore some part of the prosperity that had fled, it needed no further recommendation.

Inevitably, with a different party in power, there were changes in the officials around the Prime Minister. Many people must have wondered what would happen to O.D. Skelton, King's indispensable Man Friday, when Bennett sat in King's chair. We cannot reconstruct what took place, for Bennett, unlike King, kept no diary, and Skelton's private papers long since perished in a fire. It would have been extraordinary if Bennett had not been suspicious of Skelton. An attitude of doubt, to say the least, is suggested by the fact that when Bennett left for an Imperial Conference in London only a few weeks after coming to power, he did not take Skelton with him. Long afterwards John Read asserted that Bennett told Skelton that Imperial Conferences were the business of the Prime Minister, not of the Department of External Affairs. The story is plausible – more so, perhaps, than Read's other report that Bennett considered abolishing the department altogether.[4] King had thought of the department he inherited as a 'Tory hive' (above, page 9); Bennett could perhaps be forgiven if he looked on it as a nest of Grits. When Bennett made his first trip to Washington (below, page 146), Skelton was again left at home. In Bennett's first months in office, it would seem, the Under-Secretary was given little to do. Nevertheless, he survived; he was not frozen out, as Loring Christie had been frozen out by King. Everything suggests that in due course Skelton became almost as useful to Bennett as he had been to King. When he died, Bennett, then long retired, wrote of him:[5]

It is difficult to imagine a better public servant than Skelton, but sometimes I wonder whether or not I was right in leaving him where he could continue his Isolationist activities. During the five years I was there there were no difficulties for I explained to him my position at the start and he loyally gave effect to my views, but he never disguised the fact that he did not think Canada was wise in accepting certain responsibilities which flowed from our being part of the empire.

I was very fond of him and only once did we differ on our views on a matter of foreign policy and in which [sic] I had to take a firm stand.*

By the time he wrote this, Bennett was probably inclined to exaggerate the extent to which he himself had accepted imperial responsibilities. Skelton's survival is a tribute to his ability to subdue his personal opinions to his duty as a civil servant, and also to his commanding capacities. It is clear, however, that he never became as intimate with Bennett as he had been with King.

One of King's associates in External Affairs did not survive. Only a few days before the 1930 election King appointed Vincent Massey, whom we have seen as Canadian Minister to Washington, to the High Commissionership in London, which had been vacant since the death the previous year of that stalwart Liberal, Peter Larkin. Massey seems to have regarded himself as a member of the professional diplomatic service, and instead of resigning after the change of government he asked Bennett for instructions. Massey, however, was clearly highly objectionable to Bennett

* This was presumably the question of sanctions against Italy during the Ethiopian War; see below, page 182.

because of the part he had played in the election campaign of 1925, when he deserted the protectionist cause (as Bennett at least saw it) and entered King's cabinet. Perhaps personality had something to do with it too. Prim, precise, over-educated, and very, very English, Massey got under a certain number of skins. Using the argument that the High Commissionership was different from a diplomatic appointment and should be held by an individual closely in sympathy with the government of the day, Bennett in effect asked for Massey's resignation. The High Commissionership went to G. Howard Ferguson, the Conservative Premier of Ontario, whom no one could call over-educated. Before leaving for London Ferguson made an extraordinary speech in which he announced that he was going to make it his business to revive the British people's 'old spirit of pride and self-respect' – an utterance which certainly did not make for a successful mission.[6]

The 'Adviser' who accompanied Bennett to the Imperial Conference in Skelton's place was a newcomer on the official scene, his 'personal assistant,' William Duncan Herridge. He was a son of the Very Reverend W.T. Herridge, the minister of St Andrew's Presbyterian Church in Ottawa. Mackenzie King in his salad days had been involved for many years in a curious triangular relationship with the elder Herridge and his wife, and young Bill would seem to have been in a degree a protégé of King's. He became a lawyer and later served with distinction in the First World War, emerging as a major with the DSO and the MC. Like so many Canadian soldiers, he had a warm regard for Lord Byng, and appears in King's diary as an 'habitué' of Government House in Byng's time.[7] His intimacy with King was terminated by the King-Byng crisis of 1926. Having formed a friendship with Bennett, apparently as the result of an accidental meeting, Herridge was prominent in the new Prime Minister's entourage. In 1931 he was appointed Minister to Washington (the post having been vacant since Massey's withdrawal) and about the same time married Bennett's sister Mildred. He formed many useful friendships in Washington and was an effective Minister. At the same time he continued to bombard the Prime Minister with political advice, sometimes in personal letters, often through Bennett's private secretary, Rod Finlayson. (There were times, apparently, when the two brothers-in-law were barely on speaking terms.) Herridge was the son of brilliant but erratic parents; perhaps – not least in the light of his adventure as leader of the 'New Democracy' party in 1939-40 – the same adjectives might be applied to him.[8]

One other King diplomatic appointee survived – Herbert Marler, Minister to Japan. He too had been, briefly, a member of King's cabinet, but evidently not so personally obnoxious to Bennett as Massey was. Moreover, there was no doubt of the appointment being a diplomatic one, so Bennett could not use the argument he had used with Massey to get rid of him, even had he wished to. Marler became *persona grata* with the new Prime Minister, for in due course he profited by Bennett's revival of the practice of recommending Canadians for knighthoods; in 1935 he became Sir Herbert.[9] This put him one up on poor Massey, who would certainly have loved to be a knight. But Massey had attached himself to a party, and a leader, who sternly reprobated such undemocratic fripperies.

OFF TO THE TARIFF WARS

The United States' Hawley-Smoot Tariff was not a Depression measure; it was before Congress a long time, and its character was well established before the Wall Street crash. In his presidential campaign of 1928 Herbert Hoover undertook to call a special session of Congress to make 'limited changes' in the tariff and provide 'farm relief' – a euphemism for (mainly) higher protection for agriculture. As had happened before, Congress made more than limited changes. 'In the end the bill made 1125 changes in the existing revenue law, of which 890 were upward, ranging on the average from thirty-one to thirty-four per cent.'[10] In his statement issued when signing the bill Hoover remarked, 'The increases in tariff are largely directed to the interest of the farmer.' The Canadian farmer suffered in proportion. Dairy farmers were particularly hard hit: the rate on skim milk was raised from 2½ cents to 6½ cents a gallon, that on cream from 30 cents to 56.6 cents, that on butter from 12 cents a pound to 14 cents.* The rates on beef and veal were doubled, from 3 to 6 cents a pound. Tomatoes in the natural state went up from half a cent a pound to 3 cents, canned tomatoes from 15 per cent to 50 per cent.[11]

While this unpleasant enactment was taking shape there was considerable discussion in Ottawa on the question of whether or not Canada should make a formal protest. In February 1929 an exhaustive study of the matter was made by J.S. Macdonald, who had joined the External Affairs Department the year before. He elicited the fact that in 1921, in parallel circumstances, the British Ambassador in Washington had inquired whether the Meighen government would consider making representations against proposed tariff increases. The reply discouraged the idea; the Governor General wrote, 'Indeed very doubtful if representa-

---

* The rate on butter had previously been raised by presidential proclamation in 1926 from 8 cents to 12, that on cream in June 1929 from 20 cents to 30.

tions urged from Canadian standpoint by Canadian Government would not have undesirable effect.'[12] Macdonald's conclusion was that this had been a sound decision: 'A diplomatic protest might serve merely to prove to United States legislators that in raising certain duties they are on the right track.' His paper, written before the advent of the Depression, is complacent in tone; Canada, it remarks, is no longer so dependent on United States markets as she has been. The matter was subsequently discussed between Skelton and Massey. Massey was in favour of making representations, but Skelton told him that Mackenzie King preferred to wait: 'He had a long conference yesterday with Phillips [the American Minister] who leaves for Washington tomorrow and will see President elect.' When Massey raised the question again, Skelton, after further discussion with the Prime Minister, wrote to him: 'The Canadian viewpoint has, I think, been amply brought to the attention of the President and Congress informally and through the press. I am inclined to think that for the present it would be best to lay off.'[13]

It seems likely that on this matter King and Skelton were right and Massey wrong. The fact is that the American Legation staff in Ottawa (having of course been informally briefed by various Canadians) themselves made representations to their superiors in Washington against the tariff proposals. Both William Phillips and Lynn Meekins, the chief agent of the US Department of Commerce in the Legation, argued against a tariff which would damage the Canadian economy without conferring much benefit on the United States. Such a measure, Phillips said, would drive Canada back on her British connections and make her abandon any idea of continental partnership. These arguments (surely more likely than any Canadian diplomatic protest to carry weight in Washington) were in fact disregarded there.[14] On June 17, 1930, President Hoover, disregarding also the protest of over a thousand American economists, signed the Hawley-Smoot bill into law.

Even if Mackenzie King had won the election the following month, he would probably have felt forced to raise the Canadian tariff in retaliation. The budget his Minister of Finance brought down while the Hawley-Smoot measure was still under discussion provided for 'countervailing duties' – that is, raising the Canadian tariff on certain items important both in import and export trade to the same level a foreign state might impose on the same goods coming from Canada. Simultaneously the British preference was somewhat widened.[15] This was clearly intended as a polite warning to the United States of the consequences that might be expected if their tariff were raised. From R.B. Bennett, who was just as convinced a protectionist as Representative Hawley or Senator Smoot, and who had promised to use the tariff to blast a way into foreign markets, dramatic action was to be expected. The blasting operation began in September 1930, when a short special session of the Canadian Parliament passed an amendment to the customs tariff[16] which raised the rates on a wide range of commodities, particularly iron and steel, many machines, and textiles. Increases were made in the British preference rates as well as in the intermediate tariff (applying to countries with which Canada had trade agreements) and the general tariff (applying to other countries, including the United States). To cite one example, woollen fabrics and clothing, previously paying respectively 27½ per cent, 35 per cent, and 35 per cent under the three tariffs mentioned, would now pay 30 per cent, 40 per cent, and 40 per cent. At the same time 'special or dumping' duties were provided where the price charged to an importer in Canada was less than the price when sold for consumption in the exporting country; and the law was altered to permit the government to fix by order-in-council arbitrary values for duty purposes on imported goods.

In 1931 there was further blasting. The act of 1930 had made no reference to automobiles; now[17] the General tariff on passenger cars worth between $1200 and $2100 was raised from 20 per cent to 30 per cent; on other motor vehicles it was raised from 27½ to 40 per cent. The British Preference rate in both cases remained at 15 per cent. Parts and accessories to be used in the manufacture or assembling of cars in Canada remained free under all three tariffs. The rates were raised on a wide variety of other items.

All this legislative activity had no useful result. The Depression merely deepened. The markets of the world did not open to Canadian exports; on the contrary, the statistics of exports plummeted disastrously. The total to all countries fell from $1,120,000,000 in the fiscal year 1929-30 to $528,000,000 in 1932-3. The effect of the American tariff appeared in the fact that the percentage of Canadian exports going to the United States fell during the same period from 46 per cent to 37.4 per cent. Although the percentage going to the United Kingdom rose from 25.1 to 34.9, the absolute volume of trade declined steeply. Unemployment in Canada grew more and more tragic. A contemporary official account says: 'The low point of the depression was reached in 1933, when it was estimated that, on the average, there were 265 unemployed men and women in each thousand wage-earners.'[18] Recent statisticians do not put the figures so high, but the situation was appalling. South of the border conditions were generally similar. The 1028 economists who had begged President Hoover to veto the Hawley-Smoot bill had written, 'We cannot increase employment by restricting trade.'[19] The truth of this was now painfully clear. By

1933, as we shall see, R.B. Bennett was anxious for a trade agreement with the United States. Tariff war had been an unprofitable policy. But at least it could not be said that Canada had started the war.

BENNETT AT WESTMINSTER

Immediately after the special parliamentary session of September 1930, Bennett, still flushed with electoral victory and unchastened by adversity, set off for London and the Imperial Conference. He was accompanied by an imposing retinue, including three of his cabinet colleagues (who, however, played comparatively little part in the proceedings). Sir Robert Borden, the retired Conservative Prime Minister, made a ceremonial appearance. There were no fewer than fourteen senior officials and officers, including Major-General A.G.L. McNaughton, the Chief of the General Staff, and two people involved in the selling of wheat. The most notable absentee, as we have already remarked, was O.D. Skelton. At the head of the list, where Skelton's name might have stood, was that of the Prime Minister's Personal Assistant, W.D. Herridge.[20]

It was now a year since the collapse of the American stock market, and the shadow of the Depression was heavy over the conference. The possibility of action to improve the state of the economy was clearly the delegates' overmastering interest; most certainly this was the case with the Canadian representatives. But the conference had other business to do; notably, it had to deal with the legacy of the conference of 1926, consider the report of the 1929 Conference on the Operation of Dominion Legislation and, presumably, set the wheels in motion for the enactment of the proposed Statute of Westminster. These important constitutional matters it is best to look at first.

The reader may recall that at the Conference on the Operation of Dominion Legislation (the ODL Conference, the British tended to call it) the British government had showed itself concerned to reduce within as narrow bounds as possible the impact of the 'equality of status' agreed upon in 1926, and to retain something of the apparatus of central legislation represented in the Colonial Laws Validity Act. This attempt had been largely defeated. The election in Canada of a Conservative government headed by a man who spoke the language of old-fashioned imperialism encouraged some people in London to hope for a better result at the coming conference. If Canada were to change sides and take the same attitude as Australia and New Zealand, it might be possible to reject the ODL report or at any rate to modify it in important particulars. The British cabinet – still the Labour cabinet of Ramsay MacDonald – considered the matter on the eve of the conference, went on record with a rather adverse view of the report, and decided that it was desirable 'to proceed somewhat slowly in giving effect to the Report ... and to concentrate on those portions of the Report which were of real urgency.' Sir William Jowitt, the Attorney General, who had played such an important part in the 1929 conference, was asked to prepare a paper indicating what might be done along these lines. He concluded that if Canada would raise objections to the report, then the situation could be reconsidered, and such areas as the Crown and prize law could remain as preserves of the Imperial Parliament. With Canadian support, the Irish and South Africans might be pressured into making concessions. It is clear, however, that Jowitt was not really optimistic about the likelihood of such developments.[21] Well-informed people could hardly expect them. The British High Commissioner's office in Ottawa had pointed out in the spring that nationalism 'exists in the ranks of all Canadian parties today.'[22]

It will be remembered that before the general election the Canadian Parliament had approved the report of the Conference on the Operation of Dominion Legislation and had specifically expressed the opinion that the forthcoming Imperial Conference should ensure its recommendations being put into effect 'at an early date'; and that Bennett and his party, while making what may be called vaguely imperialistic noises about the report, refrained from dividing the House of Commons on the question (above, page 119). In these circumstances it would have been both difficult and politically inexpedient for Bennett to oppose the report now, even if he really felt strongly on the subject, which there is no evidence he did. In fact, in the conference in London he made it clear that Canada would take no action inconsistent with the Canadian Parliament's resolution.[23] With that announcement the British hope of nullifying or modifying the ODL report went glimmering.

Bennett actually took little part in the constitutional discussions.[24] The most contentious item was the abolition of appeals to the Judicial Committee of the Privy Council, on which a long battle raged between the British and the Irish, the former arguing that for the Irish Free State to abolish appeals would be a breach of the Anglo-Irish Treaty of 1921. Bennett showed no deep interest in this matter; he did remark that 'every person in the Commonwealth had an inherent right to appeal to the King,' but he also observed, not once but twice, that after the Statute of Westminster was passed every Dominion – including, of course, the Irish Free State – would be able to abolish the right of appeal if it chose.[25]

Bennett's main constitutional concern was the position of the Canadian provinces under the Statute of Westminster. This had been forced upon his attention by an eminent member of his own party, the Premier of Ontario, Howard Ferguson. Before departing for London he received from Ferguson a strong letter accompanied by a memorandum on the amendment of the Canadian constitution which objected to the proposals of the Conference on the Operation of Dominion Legislation. Ferguson argued that Canadian Confederation was the result of a compact between the provinces and that the British North America Act (a British statute) could not properly be amended without consultation with the provinces.[26] Subsequently Premier Taschereau of Quebec sent Bennett a rather similar communication. Bennett explained to the conference the necessity of allaying the provincial apprehensions; and the conference report accordingly recognized the need for providing for consultation between the government of Canada and the provinces, and for such limitations in the application of the proposed Statute of Westminster to Canada as might be indicated as a result. The conference recommended the passage of a statute incorporating the recommendations of the ODL report, and added the advice 'that the Statute should contain such further provisions as to its application to any particular Dominion as are requested by that Dominion.'[27] In the end, as is well known, the Statute of Westminster provided: 'Nothing in this Act shall be deemed to apply to the repeal, amendment or alteration of the British North America Acts, 1867 to 1930, or any order, rule or regulation made thereunder.' It went on to state that its provisions that the Colonial Laws Validity Act should no longer apply to laws made by the Parliament of a Dominion, and that no law made by a Dominion Parliament should any longer be void because it was 'repugnant' to an English law, extended to laws made by the legislatures of the Canadian provinces; and it provided further, 'The powers conferred by this Act upon the Parliament of Canada or upon the legislatures of the Provinces shall be restricted to the enactment of laws in relation to matters within the competence of the Parliament of Canada or of any of the legislatures of the Provinces respectively.'[28] These formulas had been agreed by a Dominion-Provincial conference assembled by Bennett in April 1931, and incorporated in the address to the Crown requesting the enactment of the Statute of Westminster, passed by both houses of the Canadian Parliament in June-July 1931.[29] The provinces were thus fully protected against the remote possibility of the Statute of Westminster being used as justification for the Parliament of Canada altering unilaterally the distribution of powers between the federal government and the provinces as established by the British North America Act. On the insistence of the provinces, one great exception remained to the legislative independence conceded to Canada by the new Statute: the central document of the Canadian constitution could still be amended only by the Parliament in London.

During this conference Bennett attended a meeting of the Committee of Imperial Defence. The question of Canada's relationship to this famous committee in the inter-war years may as well be treated here.

Readers of Volume I of this book may recall that in the days before 1914 the opportunity of attending meetings of this committee was held out to the Dominions as a means by which they could be admitted to 'knowledge of the policy and proceedings of the Imperial Government in foreign and other affairs' (Volume I, page 163). Sir Robert Borden received the offer with modified enthusiasm, and Canadian ministers attended meetings of the CID on various occasions. During the war the Committee was in a state of suspended animation, and when sittings were resumed in 1920 Dominion representatives were not invited. During the Imperial Conference of 1926, however, the British Prime Minister, Stanley Baldwin, took occasion to describe the work of the committee and to invite the Dominions to resume their connection with it.[30] On November 11, 1926, a meeting of the committee was held for the visiting Prime Ministers' benefit. Mackenzie King attended it, accompanied by Ernest Lapointe and the Chiefs of the Canadian General and Naval Staffs, and made several contributions to the discussion (on the Geneva Gas Protocol he remarked, 'in no circumstances ought we to deprive ourselves of the means of making use of gas should the necessity arise'). Canada, however, did not avail herself thereafter of the opportunity to send a representative to the committee. From May 1928 Australia, South Africa, and New Zealand frequently sent observers (often, their High Commissioners in London); though meetings continued to be held at which no Dominion representatives were present. Canada – and the Irish Free State – held aloof. O.D. Skelton intensely disliked the CID; he was fond of pointing out, quite truly, that it was a British government committee, not a genuinely imperial body like the Imperial Conference. It was undoubtedly felt in Ottawa that attendance at the CID might have implied some general commitment to British military arrangements and some limitation on Canadian freedom of action.

As the Imperial Conference of 1930 approached, the CID decided that this time there would be no special meeting during the conference unless the Dominion Prime Ministers requested it. Nevertheless, a meeting took place on November 28. Bennett, and W.D. Herridge with him, attended; the only other Prime Minister present, apart from Ramsay MacDonald who presided, was Forbes of New Zealand. The New Zealand and South African High Commissioners attended, as did an Australian general described as the Australian representative on the Imperial General Staff, a label which to Canadians by that date would have seemed a bit anachronistic. Bennett spoke more than once. When the question was raised of Dominions perhaps 'making themselves responsible for the immediate reinforcement on the outbreak of war of particular areas outside their own territory in which they had special interest,' he said that this raised the question of political control: 'For example, no Prime Minister of Canada could ask for expenditure on the defence of the West Indies without political control ...' No doubt the British had hopes that this Conservative Prime Minister would reverse the King policy and bring Canada back into the committee. If so, they were disappointed. On December 2, having received the minutes of the meeting, Bennett wrote a letter to Sir Maurice Hankey:

As you are aware, Canada has never accepted membership on the Committee of Imperial Defence and the question of the position she should now take in respect thereto is one requiring careful consideration by my Government. From a literal reading of the first page of the Minutes it must be taken that I am now one of the Committee. As this is, of course, contrary to the facts, I would suggest, as the readiest means of correction, that my name and that of Mr. Herridge, together with the remarks I made, be deleted from the Minutes.

I attended the Meeting on your invitation as an unofficial observer and, as such, I greatly appreciated the opportunity of securing information on matters naturally of great interest to me.[31]

The status of this letter is uncertain. The copy in the Bennett Papers is a signed original, not a carbon copy. And the minutes of the committee were not amended as suggested. The probability seems to be that Bennett on further thought decided against sending the letter. Yet it may perhaps be taken as expressing his views; for Canada continued to refrain from sending a representative to the committee. On this matter the Bennett administration followed the same line as King's.[32]

When King George V assented to the Statute of Westminster on December 11, 1931, a century of constitutional evolution, extending back to Lord Durham and beyond, came to a logical conclusion. Six 'Dominions' – Canada, Australia, New Zealand, South Africa, the Irish Free

State, and Newfoundland* – received, in effect, complete legislative in-dependence so far as they desired it. The Statute provided that its central provisions should not apply to three conservative Dominions, Australia, New Zealand, and Newfoundland, 'as part of the law of' those countries unless their Parliaments adopted them. Australia and New Zealand adopted the Statute only in 1942 and 1947, respectively. Newfoundland lost its Dominion status in 1933 when bankruptcy compelled it to ask the United Kingdom to assume responsibility for Newfoundland's finances.[34]

In the final stage of this long constitutional evolution, that is to say in the years 1926-30, Canada had not been a prime mover. South Africa and the Irish Free State had been the radicals in the conferences, demanding a definition of the Commonwealth relationship in terms of complete equality of status with Great Britain. Australia and New Zealand had hung back; well content with things as they were, they saw no virtue in trying to reduce the Commonwealth mystique, as they might have called it, to writing. Canada had favoured the forward movement but had not led it. Her representatives had stood between the extremes and had often played a moderating part. But there was no doubt whatever that they were among those who wished to push autonomy to its logical end; and if they had not been the result would have been different.

It was by no means unsuitable that in Canada a Conservative Prime Minister presided over the final stage. W.P.M. Kennedy wrote in 1937: 'It is well to remember that all political parties in Canada have contri-buted to the long processes which issued in the Statute of Westminster, and the leaders of all parties now speak unequivocally of nationhood, of equality. I believe this all reflects the great middle body of Canadian opinion.'[35] The Liberals under King thought of themselves, and repre-sented themselves, as the party of autonomy, and the Conservatives made it easy for them by their tendency to talk in terms of outmoded sentimental imperialism; but no one who knew the facts was likely to forget that the longest strides towards nationhood had been taken under the leadership of the Unionist government of Sir Robert Borden, con-solidating in the council chamber the victories won by Canadian soldiers in France and Flanders.

---

* Newfoundland was represented at the Imperial Conference of 1930 by its Prime Minister, Sir Richard Squires, who however played virtually no part in the proceedings. He had done the same at the ODL Conference the year before, when Skelton reported to King that he 'did not even turn up for the official photograph'; 'Care was taken to exclude any reference to Newfoundland in the Report.'[33]

The word 'independence' is not found in the Statute of Westminster; Australia, New Zealand, and Newfoundland would not have dreamed of countenancing it, and we have seen Mackenzie King in 1926 explaining to General Hertzog that the Canadian people would not have it. Nevertheless there is no doubt that the Canadian people came to think of themselves, if not in 1931 then not long afterwards, as independent. The present writer (who was not perhaps altogether a bad sample of 'the great middle body of Canadian opinion') recalls that in 1939, groping for a phrase to describe the contemporary position of his country, he came up with 'an independent British state in North America.'[36] The word 'British' now has an archaic look; Canada remains a member of the Commonwealth, but the Commonwealth no longer calls itself British. But it may have a degree of significance that a fairly young Canadian of mildly conservative tendencies thought of Canada on the eve of the Second World War as independent. And if one seeks for a date on which Canada became independent, there is no other to be had than December 11, 1931.

The day after the Statute of Westminster became law, R.B. Bennett, returning from a trip to England, landed at Halifax. He made a statement that was widely reported: 'With the adoption of the Statute of Westminster the old political Empire disappears.'[37] These were words that might have been spoken by Ernest Lapointe, though hardly perhaps by Bennett's cabinet colleague C.H. Cahan (above, page 119). But Bennett went on to say that everywhere 'in the Old Land' he found people looking forward to a new Imperial Conference at Ottawa in the belief that it would lay 'the foundations of a new economic Empire.' It is time to turn to the economic aspects of the Imperial Conference of 1930.

THE COMMONWEALTH AND THE SLUMP

We have already said that the Depression dominated the 1930 conference. To most of the delegates the economic troubles of the moment were far more important than constitutional questions. This was certainly true of R.B. Bennett.

Here we must look for a moment at remote backgrounds. The reader will recall that Britain, urged on by the radicals of the Manchester School, had adopted free trade in the 1840s, and that free trade thereafter was regarded as an almost sacred doctrine, particularly in the Liberal party of W.E. Gladstone. The memory of the 'hungry forties' and the Corn Laws (finally repealed in 1846) was strong, and ordinary Englishmen were conditioned to reject automatically any idea of returning to the days when imported food was taxed for the protection of British farmers, and colonial produce enjoyed preferential rates. Colonials, on the other hand, took precisely the opposite view. Their economic ideal was a protected British market which Canadian wheat, and other colonial products, could enter either free or at low rates, while foreign competitors were compelled to pay high tariffs. Canada's British Preferential Tariff of 1897 was intended to nudge British policy in this direction. A majority of the colonies had advocated imperial preference in the Ottawa conference of 1894, and thereby incurred the wrath of orthodox free traders in Whitehall. At the Colonial Conference of 1902 Laurier and Fielding in particular continued the fight for preference, hoping to see Canadian wheat given an advantage in the English market. Joseph Chamberlain's 'tariff reform' campaign gave the colonial protectionists hope; but the Liberal victory in the British general election of 1906 made it quite clear that free trade was to remain in the saddle.

Britain's difficulties after the First World War led, we have seen (above, page 16), to protectionist agitation and to some limited protectionist measures (notably, a tariff on motor cars); but when Stanley Baldwin went to the country in 1923 on a protectionist platform (not, however, extending to food taxes), the voters again stood by free trade. Another great crisis, we remarked, would have to supervene before protection returned to Britain. This crisis arrived in 1930 in the shape of the Great Depression.

The Labour party was committed to free trade; and Ramsay MacDonald's Chancellor of the Exchequer was Philip Snowden, dedicated socialist, veteran of the Independent Labour party, but fiscally speaking as much a member of the Manchester School as Richard Cobden. The demand for protection, however, was being loudly voiced in the British press; in 1929 the Canadian-born press magnate Lord Beaverbrook had launched his crusade for Empire Free Trade – total free trade within the Empire and protection against all outsiders.[38] Had Beaverbrook known more about his native country, he would have realized that no Canadian government could consider this for a moment. W.S. Fielding had explained the matter, once and for all, at the Colonial Conference of 1902: 'We do not profess that we want to introduce British goods to displace the goods made by the manufacturers of Canada. That is a point upon which we must speak with great frankness. Whether or not it was a wise policy for Canada to foster her manufacturers by high duties is a point hardly worth discussion now; we must deal with things as we find them' (Volume I, page 77). But not all British protectionists were as naïve as Beaverbrook. It was clear in 1930 that there was some possibility of realizing the old

Canadian dream of achieving a preferential status for Canadian produce in the British market.

R.B. Bennett's approach to the question, however, was scarcely less naïve than Beaverbrook's. On October 8, quite early in the Imperial Conference, he made his proposition with characteristic pomposity.[39] The policy of his administration, he said, was protection of the home producer, but not the exclusion of foreign goods, 'so long as their importation does not threaten a reduction in the high standard of living which our citizens enjoy.' It was a policy of 'Canada first,' and 'In approaching the economic problems of our Empire I stand four-square behind that policy.' He went on to sing the praises of imperial preference, and gave one concrete example: 'The primary concern of Canada to-day is profitably to sell its wheat. We believe that we shall be reaching towards a solution of that problem if we can establish a better market in Great Britain. This market we want, and for it we are willing to pay, by giving in the Canadian market a preference for British goods.' After proclaiming that 'the day is now at hand when the people of the Empire must decide, once and for all, whether our welfare lies in closer economic union or whether it does not,' Bennett made his pitch:

I offer to the Mother country, and to all the other parts of [the] Empire, a preference in the Canadian market in exchange for a like preference in theirs, based upon the addition of a ten percentum increase in prevailing general tariffs, or upon tariffs yet to be created. In the universal acceptance of this offer, and in like proposals and acceptances by all the other parts of Empire, we attain to the ideal of Empire preference.

Empire free trade, he remarked parenthetically, was 'neither desirable nor possible.' He proceeded to suggest that after discussion of his plan and the making of arrangements for preparing reports upon it in the various countries represented, the conference should adjourn 'to meet at Ottawa early next year, as the guests of the Canadian people' to consider those reports and take action.

The reaction of the MacDonald government, and particularly of the Chancellor of the Exchequer, to this proposal might have been foreseen. Snowden came to the conference the following day and confronted Bennett. The clash between the frail but passionate little socialist and the burly Canadian millionaire was one of the more dramatic moments in the history of the Imperial Conference. Snowden lost no time in putting his finger on the essential objection to Bennett's plan:

His understanding of Mr. Bennett's proposal was that Canada contemplated no reductions in the Canadian preferential and general tariffs, but that, in consideration of the United Kingdom granting a preference to Canadian goods, Mr. Bennett would be prepared to raise the Canadian general tariff rates by some 10 per cent. This would mean no general reduction in the present preferential rates of duty fixed to protect Canadian industry.

Canada wanted a market for her wheat and the other Dominions for their raw materials. The suggestion, as he understood it, was that the United Kingdom should place a tariff on foreign goods and a lower preferential or no duty on goods from the rest of the Empire.

The position of the United Kingdom was different from that of the Dominions. The United Kingdom's existence depended on her external trade, and it could be no part of United Kingdom policy to make a change which would jeopardise a large part of that trade.

Snowden went on to observe that the Australian and Canadian tariffs on woollen and worsted goods had had 'disastrous effects' in Britain. 'Mr. Bennett proposed no reduction in any of the existing tariffs, although these were designed to keep out British goods.' Snowden 'could hold out no hope of any departure from the established fiscal policy of the United Kingdom, especially in respect of taxes on foodstuffs and raw materials.'[40]

The discussion continued on later days without Snowden budging an inch. The British opinion of Bennett's 'offer' perhaps received its most accurate as well as its frankest expression in the British House of Commons on November 27, after the conference was over, when J.H. Thomas, the Secretary of State for the Dominions, remarked, 'there never was such humbug as this proposal';* nevertheless, it could not be just dismissed and forgotten. Britain and all the other countries represented at the meeting were in dire economic straits, and much was hoped of imperial co-operation. (It is interesting that the Manchester Chamber of Commerce, while remarking in a letter to Ramsay MacDonald that the Canadian proposal seemed 'to call for sacrifices by Great Britain out of all proportion to the contributions proposed by Canada,' nevertheless expressed the hope that the conference would 'investigate thoroughly' the Bennett scheme, and went on to say that it considered there would be support for 'variations in Great Britain's Fiscal Policy as part of an Empire-wide plan designed to ensure an all-round encouragement of

---

* The text of his remarks is to be found in the Canadian as well as the British Hansard, for Mackenzie King gleefully read them into the record on March 16, 1931.

inter-Empire trade.')[41] While refusing to embrace protection, Snowden and his colleagues were prepared to consider other expedients for ensuring the Dominions shares of the British market. The most hopeful seemed to be some form of quota system, and a committee of the conference explored this possibility. Much time and effort were devoted to the consideration of quotas during the next two years, but since these discussions ultimately came to nothing there is no point in describing them here.[42] And Bennett's invitation to hold a further meeting in Ottawa was repeated and accepted. At the final plenary session of the conference he moved that the 'Economic Section of this Conference' adjourn to Ottawa to meet at a date within the next twelve months to be agreed upon, and promised a most hearty welcome from the Canadian people.[43] In economic matters the Imperial Conference of 1930 had failed to achieve anything; the hopes of the Commonwealth would now centre – to an almost embarrassing extent – upon the meeting to be held in Ottawa.

Considerably more than twelve months passed before the Ottawa conference could be held. Political events supervened: Australia and New Zealand both had general elections. And economic crisis produced in August 1931 a new government in Britain: a 'National' government, still headed by MacDonald, but including Conservatives and Liberals as well as Labour men. Snowden remained Chancellor of the Exchequer. In October this government went to the country. On the question of the tariff, MacDonald asked for a free hand – 'a doctor's mandate.' He got it. The Labour party had been disrupted, most of its MPs regarding MacDonald's decision to form a coalition as desertion of the cause. The government got a great majority, but it was a Conservative majority. The government was reconstructed, likewise with a Conservative majority. Philip Snowden went to the Lords, remaining in the cabinet as Lord Privy Seal. Neville Chamberlain, Joe's son, with an hereditary interest in imperial preference, became Chancellor of the Exchequer. In February 1932 he introduced an Import Duties bill, an interim measure providing for a 10 per cent general tariff from which Empire goods and most foodstuffs were for the present exempted. With the passage of this measure Britain ceased to be a free-trade country, and her representatives could go to Ottawa with the means of bargaining with Dominion protectionists.[44]

The preparations for Ottawa were inadequate. The British, it is true, hoped that schedules of items on which tariff concessions would be practicable could be exchanged with the Dominions, and the essence of agreements arrived at before the conference met. This did not happen; in the case of Canada, a British schedule reached the Canadian government in February 1932, but thanks to various causes including the slowness of the

Canadian Manufacturers' Association no Canadian schedule came to the British officially until after the conference had opened. In May the Dominions Office sent what Sir William Clark called a 'drastically businesslike' circular dispatch to the Dominions complaining of the slowness of progress and asking for early information on the concessions they would be prepared to make – concessions, it indicated, which would have to be substantial. The chief result was to annoy the Dominions. The British government was divided within itself, the Liberal element clinging stubbornly to free trade principles (stretching constitutional conventions to the breaking point, it had been agreed that the Liberals in the cabinet might openly oppose the cabinet's Import Duties bill). The United Kingdom delegation left for Ottawa with a completely free hand from the full cabinet, and no certainty about the agreements it was to advocate or accept.[45]

The delegation included no fewer than seven cabinet ministers. When Howard Ferguson in London heard that the leader was to be J.H. Thomas, he thought this most unfortunate. Thomas, he reported to Bennett, 'goes about everywhere spreading reports that the Canadians are out to get every thing they can regardless of the interests of Great Britain' (doubtless Ferguson also remembered 'humbug'). Ferguson himself had had an unpleasant row with Thomas after a private dinner at the House of Commons. Thereafter he 'quietly set a movement on foot' to have Neville Chamberlain lead the party. When he was told that the leader might in fact be Stanley Baldwin, Lord President of the Council and Conservative leader, he 'did not relish this idea as much of an improvement.'[46] Nevertheless it was Baldwin who got the job. He was accompanied by Chamberlain, Thomas, Lord Hailsham, Sir Philip Cunliffe-Lister, Walter Runciman, and Sir John Gilmour.

Canadians, suffering the miseries of the Depression, saw in the Imperial Economic Conference a chance of salvation. The press gave it tremendous coverage.[47] A National Day of Prayer was held for its success; in the words of a writer for the Toronto *Globe*, 'The people of a whole Dominion knelt in supplication.'[48] Ottawa was not used to international conferences in those days. The citizens gawked at the famous visitors as they entered or left the Buicks which the host government provided for them, and speculated about the unfamiliar flags flying in a row on the Post Office. (There were familiar flags in the middle of the row; two Union Jacks, one for the United Kingdom and one for Canada, which had no national emblem of its own.) The troubles of the time made themselves evident in the appearance of a 'Workers' Economic Conference,' assumed to be Communist-inspired, which organized a demonstration on August 2

HOPEFUL ARRIVALS AT THE IMPERIAL ECONOMIC CONFERENCE,
OTTAWA, 1932
The Canadian Prime Minister meets the United Kingdom delegation.
Centre, left to right, Stanley Baldwin, R.B. Bennett, Neville Chamberlain

that led to conflict with the police. I remember seeing the members of this body marching rapidly past the Parliament Buildings in a sort of mild running fight with the Mounted Police guarding the gates.[49]

The conference was opened by the Governor General, Lord Bessborough, with due ceremony, on July 21, 1932. Apart from Canada and the United Kingdom, the countries represented were Australia, New Zealand, South Africa, the Irish Free State, Newfoundland, India, and the colony of Southern Rhodesia. This was the worst-recorded of all the Imperial Conferences. Maurice Hankey was not present; his place as Secretary of the conference was taken by O.D. Skelton, assisted by various members of the Canadian External Affairs staff, notably Head, Pearson, and Wrong. Canadian politicians had never shared Hankey's love of precise recording; but it was not primarily their prejudice that made the Ottawa record so inadequate. At a quite early stage it became evident that no general Commonwealth agreement or treaty was to be expected; what had to be contemplated was a series of bilateral agreements between the nine countries represented. Accordingly the essential business of the conference was done in private conversations between negotiating teams designated by the various delegations, of which the conference secretariat could have no cognizance and of which few if any formal records were kept. The official records of the conference, in these circumstances, are extremely uninformative.[50] At the closing session twelve bilateral agreements were signed; others were reported to be in prospect. Canada was a party to four of the completed agreements, with the United Kingdom, the Irish Free State, South Africa, and Southern Rhodesia.[51]

For us, as for Canadians at the time, the interest focusses chiefly in the negotiations between Canada and Great Britain. These, it must be said, were very unpleasant indeed. In them the Canadian Prime Minister appeared at his 'uncivilized' worst. When it was over, Neville Chamberlain wrote in his diary: 'Most of our difficulties centred round the personality of Bennett. Full of high Imperial sentiments, he has done little to put them into practice. Instead of guiding the conference in his capacity as chairman, he has acted merely as the leader of the Canadian delegation. In that capacity he has strained our patience to the limit.'[52] Early in August he presented the British delegates with the Canadian offer, and got their backs up completely. Chamberlain recorded that he 'adopted a very aggressive tone' and declared that the British had among their official advisers 'persons who were interested in the import of Russian fish and lumber.' Runciman speaks of Bennett's 'bullying manner' and his 'insulting references to U.K. businessmen and their "lack of enterprise."'[53] Runciman had a long private talk with Bennett on August 5 and remonstrated with him. His memorandum of the conversation ends by saying that he left Bennett carrying with him 'a very indefinite impression of what his views were on individual problems or what was to be the real tendency and final decision that would spring from this shallow restless mind.'[54] Unfortunately, no one has ever found any account of these exchanges by Bennett himself.

The British found the Canadian negotiators not only rude (at least in the case of Bennett) but also indisposed to make concessions. This was due in some, probably slight, degree to the fact that Bennett had put the detailed discussions in the hands of R.W. Breadner, the Commissioner of Tariff, a 'sincere protectionist' and a former employee of the Canadian Manufacturers' Association. In his conversation with Runciman Bennett was inclined to blame 'old man Breadner' for the difficulties that had arisen, and he did in fact substitute for Breadner the Commissioner of Customs, Hector McKinnon, who was at least a little more accommodating.[55] The British attached what seems exaggerated importance to obtaining assurances on certain general principles, notably 'the principle that duties against British goods in Dominions should not be at a higher rate than is necessary to put the United Kingdom manufacturer in the position of a domestic competitor in the Dominion market, and that Tariff Boards in Dominions should be instructed to review duties in accordance with this principle and that British Industries should have right of audience.' Bennett was obsessed with alleged Russian dumping of wheat and timber on the British market and demanded action to end it.[56] All this was in addition to contention over actual tariff schedules. The negotiation came close to breakdown, and probably would have broken down had it not been for the exaggerated hopes that were riding on the conference, and the political necessity for both governments – but particularly perhaps for the British – to produce an appearance of success. Only on August 19, after a 'long and angry meeting' (the phrase is Ian Drummond's) in which Bennett accepted the British 'domestic competition' principle, was agreement reached.[57]

The Anglo-Canadian agreement signed at the conference's final session on August 20[58] incorporated Canada's acceptance of the principles that 'protection by tariffs shall be afforded against United Kingdom products only to those industries which are reasonably assured of sound opportunities for success,' and that 'protective duties shall not exceed such a level as will give competition on the basis of the relative cost of economical and efficient production'; while Canada undertook to constitute forthwith the Tariff Board provided for in a Canadian Act of 1931[59] which had not yet become effective, and further agreed that no existing duty on United

Kingdom goods should be increased without a report from the Tariff Board, and that United Kingdom producers should be entitled to 'full rights of audience' before the Board. The tariff schedules attached to the agreement reflected the hard bargaining that had gone on. The Canadian preferential tariff was altered on over 200 items, but it is difficult to find among them one that was likely to have a fundamental effect upon the British economy. Window glass, which had paid from 1¼ to 3¼ cents per pound, would now come in free. Motor vehicles (not including buses), which had been rated at 15 per cent, were also free. But concessions on iron, steel, and textiles were in general limited to types not made in Canada, or intended for further manufacture in Canada.

Canada on her side achieved the end she had worked for since 1902; the British agreed to place a duty of two shillings per quarter (eight bushels) on foreign wheat. The delegates explained to their colleagues remaining in London that they had had great difficulty in accepting this, but they had been helped by Bennett's agreeing that the United Kingdom would be at liberty to remove the duty at any time if the price asked for Dominion wheat in the United Kingdom rose above the world price.[60] The British likewise agreed to continue the free entry for Dominion goods specified in the Import Duties Act during the life of the agreement (at least five years). As for the Russian problem, to which Bennett attached so much importance, the British refused the complete embargo on Russian timber imports which he had asked for, but Article 21 of the Anglo-Canadian agreement provided that either government would impose a temporary embargo if the preferences provided in the agreement were in danger of being frustrated by the manipulation of prices 'through state action on the part of any foreign country.'*

The Ottawa agreements were bound to be regarded with doubt and hostility in the United States and other foreign countries outside the Commonwealth system; their trade, it seemed, was likely to suffer as the result of artificial measures taken to increase that between British countries. It is true that the conference before dispersing passed a resolution recording its conviction 'that by the lowering or removal of barriers among themselves provided for in these agreements, the flow of trade between the various countries of the Empire will be facilitated, and that by the consequent increase of purchasing power of their peoples, the trade of the world will also be stimulated and increased.'[61] There had in

* A much fuller account of the conference than could be given here will be found in Ian M. Drummond's excellent *Imperial Economic Policy, 1917-1939: Studies in Expansion and Protection* (Toronto 1974).

fact been a good many increases in tariffs on foreign goods, and the agreements were an exercise in the spread of protectionism rather than a movement towards freeing the channels of trade.

Although political motives led the participants to represent the conference as a success, neither Canada nor Britain had achieved a great deal. Those who had seen in the conference the remedy for the Depression were wholly disappointed. And when in the fulness of time the trade statistics for the post-conference years became available, they revealed that Canadian exports to the United Kingdom had increased far more than *vice versa*: rising from $174,043,725 in 1932 to $290,885,237 in 1935, while Canada's imports from Britain rose only from $106,371,779 to $111,682,490. *The Economist* remarked grimly, 'Clearly ... the British-Canadian tariff agreement has operated greatly to the benefit of Canada, and in a much smaller degree to the benefit of Great Britain.' It is evident, however, that at least part of the disparity was due to the fact that the United Kingdom was recovering from the Depression considerably more rapidly than Canada.[62] Such were the fruits of R.B. Bennett's close-fisted bargaining. The harvest also included a good deal of illwill. When Bennett went to England a few months after the conference, the Governor General's secretary thought it necessary to write a letter to Stanley Baldwin saying that if Bennett was not 'welcomed as a friend' in London the results might be disastrous to the relations of Canada and Britain.[63]

NAVIGATING THE RAPIDS

The year 1930, which witnessed the passage of the Hawley-Smoot tariff and the Bennett government's retaliation, marked a low point in Canadian-American relations. The first landmark in the gradual improvement that followed was the St Lawrence Waterway treaty of 1932.

In the general election campaign of 1930 both Canadian parties committed themselves to the waterway project. Bennett's platform promised 'the development of the St Lawrence waterways,' and in a speech near the end of the campaign King said that if his party was returned 'one of the first measures we will proceed with is the construction of the St Lawrence Waterway.'[64] It seemed that the Hoover administration in Washington was assured of realizing one of its policy objectives (above, page 113); and the new administration was hardly installed in Ottawa before the American Minister was inquiring whether Canada was now in a position to negotiate a Seaway treaty. Bennett's reply was that, with Parliament in session and the Imperial Conference in immediate prospect, the moment was not suitable. He promised, however, 'to go into the matter immediately upon my return from the Conference in November.'[65]

Late in January 1931 Bennett went to Washington, accompanied by W.D. Herridge. This was the first of the two visits he made to the American capital as Prime Minister. He dined with President Hoover at the White House, and afterwards the two men were reported to have talked informally. 'No statement bearing upon the conference was issued by the White House.' The Prime Minister said nothing to the press about the discussions, and even declined to be photographed. 'Bennett Departs, Silent As To Trip' was the New York Times headline on February 2. Four days later, however, a front-page story in the same paper declared that as a result of Bennett's visit steps were at last to be taken towards construction of the St Lawrence Waterway. No source was given; it may have been a White House leak. It has been asserted that Hoover had tried hard to get Bennett to commit himself to some form of immediate action, but in vain.[66]

Canadian documentation on the Seaway negotiations of 1931-2 is extraordinarily slight.[67] The implication seems to be that at this early stage in his administration Bennett, mistrusting Skelton and the Department of External Affairs, was conducting the whole business himself, assisted no doubt by Herridge, and was keeping the record in his head. The parallel with King at the beginning of his first ministry is evident.* It is clear that Hoover continued to press, and that Bennett, unpleasantly aware of the opposition to the project in Quebec, continued to procrastinate.[69] Finally, however, he consented to write to the American Minister (Hanford MacNider) a note, dated September 12, 1931, which was a formal continuation of the exchange before the Imperial Conference a year before. He observed that he had discussed 'certain points involved in the general proposal' informally with the President during 'the month of March.' He concluded, 'It is my belief that in the near future the Government will be in a position to discuss concrete proposals with your Government for the completion of the St. Lawrence Waterways project. Steps have already been taken to reconstitute the Canadian section of the Joint Board of Engineers.' The Minister reported that the Prime Minister had consented to write this 'only on the condition that its contents should be considered

---

* A précis of the External files on the matter, prepared in 1933[68] indicates that between September 1930 and December 1931 there was nothing in them except Bennett's letter to MacNider of September 12, 1931. Bennett's talk with Hoover is misdated as it is in that letter, suggesting that External had no contemporary information about that conversation.

strictly confidential and that neither the text nor the substance of it should be given out or published without the consent of the Canadian Government.'[70] Bennett presumably was remembering the *New York Times* story. It is interesting that he misdated his visit to Hoover by two months.

Things now began to move. Press releases issued in Washington and Ottawa on October 7 announced that negotiations would begin at once, and on November 14 Herridge (now Canadian Minister in Washington) had an 'exchange of views' with Secretary of State Stimson.[71] The Joint Board of Engineers was authorized to go to work. Its report, dated April 9, 1932, formed a basis for a treaty.[72] On July 11 an agreement was signed between the government of Canada and that of Ontario by which the federal government made over to the province for the generation of power the Canadian share of the flow of water in the international section of the St Lawrence, and the division of costs between the two governments was settled.[73] Finally, on July 18, 1932 (three days before the opening of the Ottawa conference), Stimson and Herridge signed at Washington a treaty providing for the construction of the St Lawrence Deep Waterway.[74]

The treaty provided, in the words of its preamble, for 'a deep waterway, not less than twenty-seven feet in depth, for navigation from the interior of the Continent of North America through the Great Lakes and the St. Lawrence River to the sea, with the development of the water-power incidental thereto.' It took note of Canada's declaration of its intention to provide for the completion of the New Welland Ship Canal between Lakes Erie and Ontario and of canals in the Soulanges and Lachine areas of the Canadian section of the St Lawrence, and of the parallel United States declaration concerning works in the Great Lakes system above Lake Erie. The treaty had direct reference to construction only in the international section of the St Lawrence. Here a two-stage plan was proposed, with dams at Crysler Island and Barnhart Island, each with two power houses, one on each side of the international boundary. Construction was to be shared between the two countries, both in the Thousand Islands and in the International Rapids sectors; in the latter Canada would undertake the work in the Crysler Island area and the United States that at Barnhart Island. Irrespective of any other treaties, both parties were guaranteed rights of navigation in the St Lawrence, the Great Lakes system, and canals existing or to be constructed; this involved giving the United States rights of passage in the Welland Canal and Canada the free navigation of Lake Michigan. And Article VIII of the treaty provided that the diversion of water through the Chicago Drainage Canal should be 'reduced by December 31st, 1938, to the quantity permitted as of that date by the decree of the Supreme Court of the United States of April 21st, 1930' (above, page 49); it also provided that no diversion 'from the Great Lakes System or from the International Section [of the St Lawrence] to another watershed shall hereafter be made except by authorization of the International Joint Commission.'

The treaty itself made no reference to costs; but the Joint Board of Engineers had made estimates which were publicized when the treaty was signed.[75] The entire cost of the project was calculated as $543,429,000; of this the U.S. share was $272,453,000, and Canada's $270,976,000. Canada, however, was credited with the cost of the Welland Ship Canal, whose locks had a 30-foot depth over the sills and which was formally opened the month after the treaty was signed;[76] this was $128,000,000. Ontario was to pay $67,000,000 for the power works on the river; and Bennett estimated that new expenditure by the federal government of Canada would thus be reduced to below $40,000,000.[77]

It may as well be said at once that this treaty, signed with much fanfare, never went into effect. Like several others of earlier years,* it was rejected by the United States Senate. Congress had risen when it was signed, and Hoover did not transmit it to the Senate until January 1933. By that time he was a lame-duck President. The Depression had ruined him; he was defeated in the election of November 1932 by the Democratic candidate, Governor Franklin D. Roosevelt of New York. Many people in that state had always doubted the Seaway project. As Governor, Roosevelt had clashed with Hoover over the power aspects of the scheme, and had even shown some interest in the still-extant idea of an all-American canal through his state. (When asked which of the two navigation schemes he favoured, the accomplished politician replied, 'I am in favour of both'.)[78] As President, he supported the treaty, but certainly less strongly than he would have supported one negotiated by his own administration. This perhaps was the greatest single reason for its failure. And the special and sectional interests that had opposed the Seaway from the beginning brought their influence to bear. Predictably, the Chicago Sanitary District was squealing like a stuck pig before the ink was dry on the document.[79] And the railways and the eastern ports were certainly not idle, nor were the people interested in a Great Lakes-Mississippi navigation system.

---

* Three Canadian treaties lay unapproved before the Senate at this time: two concerned with preservation of the fisheries (one on sockeye salmon, and a new halibut treaty) and one dealing with power and scenic conservation at Niagara Falls.

There were complaints about the 'internationalization' of Lake Michigan; Senator J. Hamilton Lewis of Illinois, who apparently had not heard of the abrogation of the Anglo-Japanese Alliance, suggested during the Senate debate that in case of war between the United States and Japan British cruisers might enter the lake on an ostensibly peaceful mission and 'decimate' the unsuspecting American communities along its shores.[80]

In January 1934 the President sent a message to the Senate urging it to approve the treaty. There was talk of approval with reservations, but as the final crisis approached the hostile senators felt confident enough to go for outright rejection. By March 12 the supporters of the treaty felt that their cause was lost unless the President issued a strong statement attacking the opposition. This did not happen, and in the vote on March 14 the treaty failed to get the required two-thirds majority, the vote being 46 for to 42 against. The *New York Times* observed that it showed 'both parties cut in two': 'the opposition was more regional than political.'[81]

The Seaway project moved no further during Bennett's administration. In October 1934 the new Premier of Ontario, a Liberal, Mitchell Hepburn, repudiated his Conservative predecessor's unratified agreement with the federal government on costs. The Canadian Legation had discussions with the State Department as to possible alterations in the treaty; in one in which Skelton took part it was suggested (apparently on behalf of Roosevelt) that its chances might be better if it were re-written 'so as to retain the same meaning but in another form of words' – to make it in fact 'a Roosevelt rather than a Hoover Treaty.'[82] But no action was taken.[83]

In Bennett's time, as at all times, there were Canadian-American discussions on a variety of miscellaneous problems, major and minor. Some of the major ones may be briefly mentioned here.

Prohibition continued to make business for the diplomats. We have already noted that the *I'm Alone* case of 1929 was finally disposed of by the arbitrators towards the end of the Bennett administration (above, pages 104-7). Another unpleasant affair was that of the *Josephine K.*, a Canadian rum-runner which was apprehended by the U.S. Coast Guard off the New Jersey coast in January 1931 only after she was fired on and her master, William P. Cluett, mortally wounded. The Canadian authorities took the matter up; but it was a different case from that of the *I'm Alone* in that (in the words of the Department of External Affairs Legal Adviser) 'the ship was caught *in flagrante delicto*, at a point that was at any rate very close to the hour's sailing distance.' The United States government 'refused to consider any settlement based upon negotiation' and it was doubtful whether commissioners appointed as in the *I'm Alone* case would agree. In the end, it appears, the heirs of the unfortunate Captain Cluett got no compensation.[84]

The Department of External Affairs was anxious to know precisely when Prohibition in the United States came to an end. This, for the record, was on December 5, 1933. Legitimate imports resumed at once. On that same date, it is pleasant to report, the Canadian Minister in Washington wrote: 'I understand that, after a brief delay, the issue of import permits was resumed yesterday, and that a privileged status was given to applicants who wish to import American type whiskey from Canada. Yesterday permits were issued for between 3,000,000 and 5,000,000 gallons of this type of liquor, and as much again may be authorized today.'[85] Depression or no Depression, in one line of trade business was good.

The state of the economy is constantly reflected in the diplomatic correspondence of the day. Immigration policies caused friction. When jobs are scarce foreign competition for them is resented. We find the Canadian Legation asking the State Department to intervene on behalf of Canadian commuters crossing the border daily to work in the Detroit area; the number of these was reported to have fallen from 15,600 in 1927 to 3,600 in December 1930, but they were meeting obstacles placed in their way by the American immigration authorities. The Legation claimed that along the whole border the daily movement of commuters from the United States to Canada then 'approximately balanced' that in the opposite direction, and pointed out that in spite of the current unemployment problem the Canadian government had 'not departed in any way from the policy of permitting United States citizens to enter daily to work in Canadian establishments.'[86]

In western Canada the Bennett administration witnessed the climax of the curious affair of the Trail Smelter. Here we must try to condense into a few paragraphs a business that covered many years and occasioned reams of diplomatic correspondence.

In Trail, British Columbia, only a few miles from the boundary of the State of Washington, the Consolidated Mining and Smelting Company operated a large smelter. It emitted sulphur dioxide fumes which did not stay on the Canadian side of the border. Farmers in Washington complained of damage. The complaints became serious in 1927 and the company, though prepared to pay reasonable compensation, was unable to resolve them. Settlements were made with some individual farmers, but there were none of these after 1928, when a Citizens' Protective Associa-

tion was formed whose members were required to undertake not to negotiate separately. The national governments were drawn in. The difficulty
of the question is indicated in a report O.D. Skelton made to Mackenzie
King in 1928:

> The farmers in the State of Washington picture the position as being that of
> honest and struggling, home-loving, peaceful farmers in Washington being
> driven from their happy homes by a greedy and arrogant alien corporation.
> The Company views the case as an attempt at holdup by farmers in a nearly
> hopeless section who have come to think that they can get much more out of
> farming this rich corporation across the boundary than from farming their
> farms, and who are endeavouring to use the Governments at Washington and
> Ottawa to threaten a complete cessation of operations and thus force extrava-
> gant indemnity. There may be some truth in both views, but from what I
> have been able to see of the situation I think the Company's case is much the
> stronger.[87]

Later events suggest that this assessment was accurate.

Although the International Joint Commission had never had to deal
with any question not concerned with waterways, this seemed an emi-
nently suitable matter for it, and in 1928 the two governments referred
the Trail Smelter controversy to the Commission for report. After investigation, the IJC reported in February 1931. It unanimously recommended
that the Consolidated Mining and Smelting Company should pay the
United States Treasury the rather modest sum of $350,000 for distribu-
tion to the aggrieved farmers. It stated that the company, at a cost of
$10,000,000 was effecting improvements in its plant which would elimi-
nate the trouble in the future. In the event of future damage, however,
the extent of it should be determined by the two governments and the
company required to pay compensation. Secretary Stimson expressed satisfaction with the manner in which the Commission had dealt with the
problem and remarked that every such decision 'should conduce strongly
to the good relations of the two countries.'[88]

This was very far from ending the matter. In 1933, in the dying days of
the Hoover administration, the United States alleged that in spite of the
belief of the IJC that the smelter would practically cease to cause damage
by the end of 1931, 'extensive damage' in the State of Washington was
still continuing; the State Department proposed that the two countries
should make an agreement providing for the payment of $350,000 to
cover damage before January 1, 1932, and the appointment of a 'board or
commission' to assess damages after that date. There was disagreement,

however, over the precise conditions which the agreement might impose upon Consolidated Mining and Smelting, and the definition of 'damage.'[89]

In January 1934 the respected Secretary of State in the new Roosevelt administration, Cordell Hull, signed an extremely long and heated dispatch to the United States Minister in Ottawa which was passed on to the Canadian government as a note.[90] It referred to the alleged continuing damage from the smelter and demanded quick action. It was notable for its depreciatory references to the International Joint Commission, recalling that the treaty of 1909 setting it up stated that its reports should 'in no way have the character of an arbitral award' and describing the smelter report as 'merely an advisory expression of that body.' This somewhat shocked the Canadians; Hume Wrong remarked: 'The United States is, of course, repudiating its own members of the International Joint Commission, and the prestige of the Commission is bound to suffer. It already had very little prestige in Washington and this will reduce it to the vanishing point.'[91] There may have been a whiff of party politics here; the reference to the IJC had been initiated by the Republican administration of President Coolidge. Politics certainly affected the issue in another way; the United States Minister, Warren D. Robbins, when delivering the note to Mr Bennett (who was, of course, Secretary of State for External Affairs as well as Prime Minister), remarked that the people in the State of Washington had persuaded the redoubtable Republican Senator William E. Borah of neighbouring Idaho to bring up the question in the Senate, and this was the reason for the haste and the truculent tone.[92]

Bennett replied with a long rebuttal in the course of which he dwelt on the IJC report, writing: 'I am sure your Government will agree that it would be calamitous to weaken the position of the Commission and imperil the future of this North American experiment by rejecting outright, save upon grave and plainly evident grounds, its unanimous recommendation upon any question.'[93] But he showed readiness to effect an early settlement. An exchange of visits followed, John Read going to Washington (where a draft convention was drawn up during his visit) and a State Department lawyer going to Ottawa. In October 1934 President Roosevelt sent William Phillips (now Under Secretary of State) to see Bennett; they discussed both the Smelter question and the St Lawrence Seaway. In December Skelton and Read both went to Washington.[94] Agreement was now in sight; but would it be accepted by the complainants in Washington – and would the senators from that state not prevail on the Senate to reject it? In March 1935 Phillips reported to Roosevelt that a representative of the State Department had gone to Washington to confer with the leaders of the Citizens' Protective Association. He presumably told them that the proposed agreement was the best they could hope to get; and the association's board 'adopted a resolution approving the proposed Convention and requesting that steps be taken to conclude it and to put it into effect.' The senators' opposition now evaporated.[95]

The officers of Consolidated Mining and Smelting having apparently assured Bennett that they would recommend to their directors that the company pay the indemnity that was involved, the agreement that had been so long in the making was signed in Ottawa on April 15, 1935, and was ratified shortly.[96] It incorporated a good part of the IJC report. Canada agreed to pay the United States $350,000 in payment of all damage the smelter had caused in the United States before January 1, 1932. The two countries agreed to set up an *ad hoc* tribunal to adjudicate other aspects of the matter. It would decide whether there had been damage after the beginning of 1932, and if so what indemnity should be paid for it; also, if damage had occurred, whether the smelter should be required to refrain from causing damage in Washington in future, 'and, if so, to what extent?' It should also decide what 'measures or regime,' if any, the smelter should adopt, and what further compensation, if any, should be paid. The tribunal was to be composed of three jurists, one from Canada and one from the United States, with a neutral chairman.

The chairman agreed upon was a Belgian, Jan Frans Hostie. The Canadian was R.A.E. Greenshields, Chief Justice of the Quebec Superior Court; the American, Charles Warren, a former Assistant Attorney General of the United States. In 1938 the tribunal made a unanimous interim award accepting the fact that there was damage after January 1, 1932, but fixing the indemnity for it at the comparatively trifling sum of $78,000 (the United States had asked for more than $2,000,000, including interest). In 1941, when all eyes were on greater matters, the final decision was made, likewise unanimously. The *New York Times* reported, 'Canada has won what is regarded by lawyers as a sweeping victory over the United States.' It was decided that the United States had proved no damage since the interim decision, although some $35,000 was claimed, and that if damage should be done in future it would be a matter for negotiation between the two governments. A U.S. claim for the costs of investigation was not allowed.[97]

The indemnity that Consolidated Mining and Smelting paid – an overall total of $428,000 – was probably smaller than the expense of the long investigation to the two governments. The implication seems to be that the actual amount of damage done by the Trail Smelter south of the border was comparatively small in proportion to the noise that was made about it. But it had again been demonstrated that the disparity in power between the two countries did not prevent Canada from obtaining just settlements from the United States.

It was perhaps a reflection of the deteriorating international situation abroad that some military or quasi-military questions arose between Canada and the United States in Bennett's time.

One such subject was 'overflights' of military aircraft. In 1932 permission was requested for U.S. military planes flying between Selfridge Field, Michigan, and Cleveland or Buffalo to take the short route across the Ontario peninsula. This was granted, the United States undertaking to afford similar privileges to Canadian military aircraft flying across Maine between Quebec and New Brunswick. The agreement was for one year only but was regularly renewed.[98]

In the spring of 1935 some 'secret' testimony before the Military Affairs Committee of the House of Representatives in Washington reached the newspapers, and it was revealed that Brigadier-General Frank M. Andrews, commanding the General Headquarters Air Force, had declared that in case of war the United States should be prepared to seize British and French islands (including Newfoundland) adjacent to North America. He also referred to the possibility of Canada being 'involved on the side of a hostile coalition,' though he admitted this was unlikely. Reference was also made to a 'camouflaged air base' being developed near the Canadian border. The committee's chairman, Representative McSwain, hastened to explain that this was analogous to French fortifications along the Belgian border, maintained 'not against Belgium, but against what might come over or through Belgium.' President Roosevelt at once wrote publicly to the chairman repudiating the statements of Andrews and other officers, and observing, 'This Government does not in any of its plans or policies envisage the possibility of a change in the friendly relationship between the United States and any foreign country.' (In that case, Hume Wrong observed acidly to Skelton, why does it need an army and navy?) The President further remarked: 'I call your special attention to the fact that this Government not only accepts as an accomplished fact the permanent peace conditions cemented by many generations of friendship between the Canadian and American peoples, but expects to live up to not only the letter but the spirit of our treaties relating to the permanent disarmament of our three thousand miles of common boundary.' This was highly satisfactory, even if a bit fuzzy. As Wrong noted, the only such 'treaty' was the Rush-Bagot Agreement concerning the Great Lakes, which certainly did not disarm the three thousand miles of border.[99]

During these years the project of a highway from the United States to Alaska across Canadian territory began to be discussed. The arguments advanced for it in the United States were strategic, but many western Canadians, including Premier T.D. Pattullo of British Columbia, favoured it for economic reasons. In 1935 the American Congress passed a law requesting the President to negotiate an agreement with Canada for the construction of the highway, and in 1938 Roosevelt appointed a commission to investigate the question. Under pressure from Pattullo, Mackenzie King appointed a parallel commission, which did not report until 1941.[100] The highway was finally constructed as a war measure (below, pages 361-2). Under the conditions of 1935-9, however, the project for it impressed some Canadians as dubious. One of these was Major-General E.C. Ashton, the new Chief of the General Staff. He wrote to O.D. Skelton pointing out that in case of a war between Japan and the United States in which Canada was neutral the existence of such a road might be a serious embarrassment: 'a strong military inducement to the U.S.A. to ignore our neutral rights.' The Under Secretary, apart from being less disposed to fear menaces to Canada's autonomy from Washington than from London, had a decided disinclination to take advice from the military. He brushed Ashton off: the project, he said, seemed 'to represent a perfectly intelligible aspiration on the part of the Pacific Coast people, and if the Province should want it and it should turn out to be feasible, I should think any military objections would have to be very carefully and firmly established before they could be allowed to overcome such a project.' Ashton's reply was to send some press clippings indicating that 'the other side of the case' was now receiving attention. Doubts continued to be expressed in Canada until Pearl Harbor.[101]

This is a good point at which to mention a matter that has lately received more attention than it deserves: the obscure existence on both sides of the border of 'war plans' implying the possibility of hostilities between the United States and Canada.

When the present writer became Director of the Historical Section of the Canadian General Staff after the Second World War, he inherited, along with some other curious objects, a large, ugly, awkward looseleaf book which turned out to be labelled *Defence Scheme Number 1. (The United States)*. In the official history of the army in the Second World War which was later produced, I wrote: '... in an earlier day the defence of Canada had meant defence against the United States, pure and simple; but steady improvement in Anglo-American and Canadian-American relations had relegated conflict with that country to the realm of the highly improbable. Nevertheless, some people felt that this contingency could not be entirely overlooked; and a plan of defence against the United States, known as 'Defence Scheme No 1,' was prepared and circulated to Military Districts under 'Very Secret' cover, beginning in April 1921. Work on it continued in a somewhat desultory fashion until 1926. After that year no attempt was made to keep it up to date, and in fact it was never reduced to final form.'[102] This, I thought, was about all the subject was worth; but other people became interested in it and pursued it to such a degree that a considerable literature now exists about it.[103] I had better mention the main points that have been thus elicited.

Defence Scheme No 1 was almost entirely the brainchild of one officer, Colonel James Sutherland Brown, who was Director of Military Operations and Intelligence at National Defence Headquarters, Ottawa, from 1920 until 1927. It clearly derived from British plans of the nineteenth century, and indeed has affinities with the concept followed with success by Sir Isaac Brock in his defence of Upper Canada in 1812. The aspect of it that has amused poor 'Buster' Brown's critics most is the fact that it called for offensive movements into American territory, directed against certain points (Fargo, North Dakota, is an example) which would be important in any American plan of attack upon Canada.[104] Brown's conception, it is evident, was basically defensive; his offensive enterprises were to be limited 'spoiling attacks' intended to disrupt an American invasion and to provide a protective zone covering the frontier. Brown must be accounted one of the great optimists of Canadian history. But that there were limits to his optimism is indicated by a passage in Chapter VI of the scheme. The 'ultimate defence of Canada,' it says, revolves around three 'strategical centres' – Edmonton, Quebec, and Halifax. These, it is clear, were to be centres for a final defence. 'If the initial action of the Canadian Forces is unsuccessful in holding in general the tactical positions it reaches in the first effort, after deployment, and is forced back and is unable to hold the frontier line or a reasonable corresponding line before the forces of the Empire can come to our aid, the retirement will be directed so that various bodies acting originally in separate roles, will converge on the strategical centres above mentioned. The retirement should be carried out as slowly and stubbornly as possible ...'

The military weakness of Brown's plan (if it is worth while to examine it for just one moment) was that the forces to carry it out simply did not exist. In 1812 Canada, as a British dependency, had been better prepared for war than the United States. The latter, potentially infinitely stronger than the British provinces, was overmatched in quality in the beginning by the regular regiments and professional leadership of the British garrison. Brown, when he began preparing his plan, may perhaps have been slightly hypnotized by the memory (then very recent) of the powerful fighting force that Canada had maintained in France and Flanders in 1915-18. But that force was already history and no more. The United States, on the contrary, had continued to maintain a relatively large regular army in addition to its very powerful navy. In more ways than one Brown was living in the past.

It would have been strange if the United States had not had in its files paper plans for military action against Canada (and against many other countries). Planning of this sort did in fact go on throughout the period between the two World Wars. Before the first war, U.S. planning had been carried on entirely in the Army and Navy War Colleges, but in 1921 the General Staff acquired a War Plans Division, and this and the parallel navy organization were the chief planning agencies thereafter, though the colleges continued to play a part. Up to twenty 'colour' plans existed for war with various countries: Black was Germany, but it got little attention; Red was Britain (usually including Canada); Crimson was Canada itself; Orange was Japan (always the one that got most emphasis). It was always assumed that the Red and Crimson contingencies were improbable, but planning was carried on nevertheless. There is no point in going into details; but it is amusing to note that an Appendix to Army Strategic Plan Red (1924) described policy after Canada was occupied: 'Blue [US] intentions are to hold in perpetuity all Crimson and Red territory gained. The policy will be to prepare the provinces and territories of Crimson and Red to become states and territories of the Blue Union upon the declaration of peace. The Dominion government will be abolished ...' Thus a group of obscure and anonymous American officers disposed (on paper) of the destinies of millions of people – matters that were not their province as soldiers at all. But no doubt it gave them pleasure, and lying hidden in the files it did no harm. This particular plan seems to have been declared obsolete and ordered burned in 1937; but even then planning for war with Red and Crimson (as with all the rest) did not end.[105] It is well to emphasize that all this activity was highly theoretical and almost completely divorced from American national policy; the plans have been called 'abstract exercises in the technical process of detailed military planning, providing useful training for the officers who drew them up.'[106]

The end of Canada's Defence Scheme No 1 should be noticed. Brown ceased to be Director of Military Operations and Intelligence in 1927; he was promoted and sent to the Imperial Defence College in London. On January 1, 1929, Major-General A.G.L. McNaughton became Chief of the General Staff. It would seem that some people at the Department of

National Defence, while not taking Brown's anti-American performances too seriously, had tolerated them as harmless. McNaughton, a man of high intelligence (and incidentally no sense of humour), evidently decided that it was time for this nonsense to cease. The new atmosphere was somewhat comically reflected in the proceedings of the Joint Staff Committee (later the Chiefs of Staff Committee) which was set up at Ottawa in 1927. The committee held one meeting that year and one in 1928; at both there was brief consideration of defence measures against the United States, originating doubtless with Brown. (It may be pointed out that if there had been any serious apprehension of war with the U.S. the heads of the Canadian armed forces would certainly have found it desirable to meet more than once a year.) In 1929 there was again one meeting. This time the Commander-in-Chief of the Royal Navy's America and West Indies Station was present as a guest. He was told that Canada was 'on the most friendly terms with the United States, with whom the possibility of war is not seriously considered in any Defence Plans.'[107] This was not technically true, since Defence Scheme No 1 was still slumbering peacefully in various safes; but it certainly represented the practical truth.

In an appreciation written in January 1931 McNaughton wrote: 'the direct defence of Canada against invasion by the United States is a problem which in the last ten years has become increasingly susceptible to political solution but quite incapable of being satisfactorily answered by Empire military action.'[108] That year a committee composed of the Chiefs of the Naval and General Staffs and the Under Secretary of State for External Affairs was convened to consider Canada's defence requirements in connection with the coming Geneva Disarmament Conference. This was presumably the first time O.D. Skelton heard of Defence Scheme No 1. (It seems likely that no Prime Minister had ever heard of it.) In May of that year orders were sent to Military Districts cancelling the scheme. Two years later it was ordered destroyed by fire.[109] One copy survived for the historical record.

THE GATHERING STORM

The Great Depression, whose baneful effects in North America and the British Commonwealth we have been examining, had disastrous consequences also in the countries of Europe and in Asia, and contributed to putting in train the events that ultimately produced the Second World War. Empty bellies make for desperate measures. The Bennett administration in Canada had to cope with the shock waves produced by Japanese aggression against China and by the breakdown of the expedients which a generation of European statesmen had devised in the hope of producing a durable peace. Canadians watched in fascinated apprehension as Adolf Hitler seized power in Germany and began to reconstruct the military machine that had held half a world at bay in 1914-18. In the Bennett government's last weeks in office Italian aggression against Ethiopia raised the spectre of immediate European war and gave the death-blow to the League of Nations, upon which men of goodwill had founded so many hopes.

In her dealings with the other members of the British Commonwealth and with the United States, Canada was a principal actor. She was always painfully conscious of her weakness relative to the United States, but thanks to the great neighbour's civilized attitude it was possible to carry on bilateral negotiation without serious embarrassment. On the larger stage of the world, and specifically at the League of Nations, it was different. Canada had made good her claim to be treated as an international person; but considered apart from her British connections she was a comparatively small international person, with a population a little less than Siam's and somewhat larger than those of the Netherlands or Portugal. She was no longer a member of the Council of the League after 1930, and the fact had to be faced that her influence on the deteriorating international situation was bound to be slight.

It is interesting that R.B. Bennett's reaction to the advent of Hitler should have been to counsel his countrymen to support the League of Nations. The Nazi leader became Chancellor of Germany in January 1933. In December of that year Bennett made a speech in London, Ontario, in which he said: 'Today the transcendent duty of every lover of peace – and that means every Canadian – is to support the League of Nations in its struggle for the maintenance of peace, for the obligations of the Treaty of Versailles are being flouted, and millions in pounds and dollars are being expended by the world in a new armament race.'[110] 'Support the League.' What did that mean for the average Canadian? If it came to that, what did it mean for the Canadian Prime Minister? The speech moved an eminent Toronto clergyman, the Reverend Richard Roberts, to write to Bennett. He had been appalled by the developing prospect of the bombing of civilian populations from the air. Would it not be possible, he asked, for Canada to move at the next League assembly 'for the appointment of a committee, constituted very much like the Disarmament Conference, *for the single purpose of getting the nations to look frankly at the actual facts bearing upon the production and development of arms and materials for aerial warfare, and in that light to endeavour to envisage the situation both psychological and material which would immediately be created in the event of an outbreak of war'?*

Bennett replied at length, marking his letter 'confidential.' It was difficult, he said, to determine what part Canada could play in the maintenance of peace. She had 'promoted' the League and the Kellogg Pact and every other such measure. The League's usefulness had been rendered questionable by the failure of the United States to join. 'I still believe, however,' wrote Bennett, 'that it has played a great part in forming a public opinion that is so rapidly developing that I am not without hope that it will control the attitude of European governments.' The Prime Minister proceeded:

> I think I should frankly say that, despite all that you have read and the somewhat loose talk that you have heard, Canada is not an important member of the League except insofar as we are an active member from the North American Continent. Our military prowess in the next war is regarded as of little concern, in view of the chemical [sic] character of the campaign that will be waged. At times I have thought of going to an assembly of the League and saying in effect what you have said although in somewhat stronger terms; but, after noting the fate of those who have endeavoured to take just such action, I ask: What can one man do who represents only ten and a half millions of people?[111]

It was an unusually realistic assessment of the Canadian situation.

Bennett's general attitude towards the League would seem to have been materially warmer than Mackenzie King's (so far as I know, King never made an appeal for support of the League such as Bennett made in his London speech, and in later years, as is well known, he actually blamed the League for the Second World War).[112] But as we have just seen, Bennett had reservations. His close associate Finlayson wrote retrospectively, 'He hadn't much faith in the League ... but he wanted to see Canada stand up and play her part together with the other powers.'[113] Conscious as he was of the futility of trying to take an independent line at Geneva, he was content to give general support to the British delegation.[114] It is worth noting here that, continuing the practice followed from the beginning, the Dominion delegations (Senator Dandurand called them the 'Cubs') met regularly with the United Kingdom representatives for discussion.[115] This had the advantage of keeping the Dominions informed of what was going on among the great powers.

The most prominent League development in Bennett's time was the long-prepared general Disarmament Conference which opened at Geneva in February 1932. Canada, though coming close to being a totally disarmed state already, sent a delegation, as she had also to the London Naval Conference of 1930 which extended the system of battleship quotas adopted in the Washington Treaty of 1922 (Volume I, pages 351-2) to other types of warship.[116] The Canadian group at Geneva was led by Sir George Perley, Minister without Portfolio in the Bennett government, who had served Canada abroad with such distinction in the days of the First World War. His greatest achievement perhaps was to make an opening speech that avoided the traditional Canadian *clichés*. Lester Pearson wrote: 'We have been congratulated by all and sundry in Geneva on the fact that it is the first Canadian deliverance for some years which has not mentioned one or all of "the hundred years," "the three thousand miles" or "the International Joint Commission."'[117] Lecturing the backward Europeans on the superiority of the North American Idea had been a notable Canadian failing. Though the Disarmament Conference bulks large in the diplomatic documents of the day, it need not detain us long, for it was a total failure. In May 1932 Perley cabled Bennett: 'I need not tell you that the crucial problem is to find some formula of [sic] reconciling views of France and Germany. One demands security and the other equality.'[118] The formula was not found. The prospects of success were never bright. Eleven months after the conference began Hitler came to power, and from that moment, we can now see, it was doomed. In October 1933 he withdrew Germany from the conference – and from the League of Nations. The conference died gradually away, coming to a final end in 1935. In March of that year Hitler denounced the disarmament clauses of the Treaty of Versailles and stated that conscription was to be reintroduced in Germany and the peace establishment of the German Army increased to 36 divisions.[119]

To Canadians – except perhaps to those living in British Columbia – the Far East was much less important than Europe. It was a European quarrel that had dragged Canada into the bloodbath of 1914-18. Japan, however, broke the peace before Germany. In September 1931 an incident near Mukden was followed, with what seemed suspicious speed, by the Japanese Army's occupation of large portions of the Chinese province of Manchuria, which had long been in contention between Japanese, Russian, and Chinese interests. In February 1932 the Japanese set up in Manchuria an 'independent' republic known as Manchukuo, which was quite clearly a puppet state. These actions appeared to contravene, not only the League Covenant, but also the nine-power treaty signed at Washington in 1922, to which Canada had been a party (Volume I, page 351). China appealed to the League of Nations immediately after the Mukden incident; and the League dispatched to the Far East a commission of inquiry headed by the Earl of Lytton. The commission's report in effect accused Japan of aggression; it recommended the establishment in Manchuria of a regime which, while recoognizing Japanese economic interests, should have a large degree of autonomy under Chinese sovereignty. The matter came before a special meeting of the League Assembly in December 1932, and Canada had to take a stand. C.H. Cahan, Secretary of State in the Bennett government, who had led the Canadian delegation at the regular assembly session that autumn and was still abroad, was asked to represent Canada at this assembly, with W.A. Riddell, who was still Advisory Officer at Geneva, as substitute delegate. Cahan's cautious instructions from Bennett, based on a memorandum written by Skelton, noted that the Lytton recommendations appeared 'useful and reasonable,' but added that for the present it was desirable to strive for a conciliatory settlement and avoid any discussion of sanctions.[120]

Cahan felt moved to speak in the assembly on December 8 and made something of a sensation. He had shown the speech in advance to Sir John Simon, the chief British delegate (who had urged him to speak), but had let his civil-service colleague Riddell see it only just before it was delivered, and had disregarded his attempts at protest. The speech incorporated Cahan's instructions, but unfortunately prefaced them with what he called 'more or less personal' opinions in which, however, he said he thought his government would concur. These included reflections on the weakness of China's central government and even questioned her qualifications to be a member of the League; Cahan also said that the Assembly could not 'wholly disregard' the Japanese representative's assertion that his government had no connection with the independence movement in Manchuria. As Riddell reported, the speech was considered 'highly pro-Japanese.' Skelton was 'warmly thanked' (to his considerable embarrassment) by the Japanese Minister in Ottawa, and received almost tearful protest from the Chinese Consul General. The Canadian Minister in Tokyo (Herbert Marler) was delighted; the State Department in Washington (to which Herridge had incautiously communicated a copy of Cahan's instructions) was astonished. Skelton told Riddell that the Prime Minister was 'much disturbed by Mr. Cahan's action'; but he was probably considerably less disturbed than Skelton, and seems to have made no attempt to discipline his colleague.[121]

An embarrassing aspect of the matter was that there was a difference in attitude between the two great English-speaking powers on the question at issue. The United States, though not a member of the League, had taken the lead in condemning Japan and encouraging the League to condemn her; the American Secretary of State had produced what was at once labelled the 'Stimson Doctrine' – the principle of refusing to recognize any situation brought about by means contrary to the Kellogg Pact of 1928. Simon, the British Foreign Secretary, approached the question more cautiously, seeking to effect some reconciliation between Japan and China. Cahan's speech had seemed to reject the American position, and was assailed by those, in Canada and elsewhere, who wanted the League to convict Japan of aggression and take action against her. One of these was John Dafoe of the *Winnipeg Free Press*. Shortly, however, Canada was able to regain safe middle ground. A Committee of Nineteen, not including Canada, which had been struggling with the problem on behalf of the League, completely failed to achieve reconciliation, and Japanese military action in China continued. The Committee had no choice but to bring in a report based on that of the Lytton commission. On February 24, the League Assembly, unanimously, except for the opposition of Japan and the abstention of Siam, adopted the report. That afternoon in Ottawa the Prime Minister read in the House of Commons the solemn message which had gone to Riddell (now the sole Canadian representative at Geneva) instructing him to vote for the report. Mackenzie King and J.S. Woodsworth hastened to approve it. Canada was safely lodged in the anonymity of a large League majority, and the embarrassing moment of notoriety was over. The League itself, however, suffered a severe setback. Condemned by the League, Japan announced her intention of withdrawing from it. She was the first great power to do so. The League of Nations, and the world, were now running downhill.[122]

CHAPTER FIVE

TURNING-POINTS IN NORTH AMERICA AND AFRICA

ANXIETIES AND QUESTIONINGS

The middle thirties were years of growing popular anxiety. In Canada as elsewhere Japan's successful defiance of the League of Nations over Manchuria troubled some people; the advent of Hitler and the prospect of a rearmed and aggressive Germany were much more disturbing. What could or should Canada do in the face of such menaces? What should she do if another war broke out? Even the continuing Depression did not wholly mute these concerns. A confused debate began which ended only with the outbreak in 1939.

The current anxieties were reflected in a discussion in the Canadian Senate in the spring of 1934. Brigadier-General A.D. McRae, an overseas veteran of 1914-18 and a Conservative party stalwart whom Bennett had made a senator, moved a resolution: 'That this House is of opinion that Canada should withdraw from membership in the League of Nations, and that no further money should be voted to the League.' McRae's speech amounted to a statement that events had made him an isolationist. He may have embarrassed Arthur Meighen, the former Prime Minister who was now government leader in the Senate, by saying that, when it was made, he had not agreed with Meighen's Hamilton speech of 1925, calling for an election before troops were sent overseas, but he agreed with it now. He considered that Canadians did not understand how heavy were their responsibilities under Article 10 of the League Covenant. 'Call me an international pacifist if you will,' he said, 'for I would have Canadian boys fight no more in foreign wars.' The Conservative ex-general's views were a curious echo of those of the Liberal ex-major C.G. Power expressed in the debate on the Versailles treaty in the House of Commons in 1919 (Volume I, pages 292-4).

The Senate debate maundered on for weeks, the general tone being one of mild approval for the League. Nobody fully supported McRae, and in the end his motion was negatived without a recorded vote. Perhaps the most important aspect of the affair was that both Meighen and the Opposition leader, the Geneva veteran Raoul Dandurand, made firm statements supporting the League. Bennett in the House of Commons had already disavowed McRae. But the fact that McRae made the motion at all was evidence of the disquiet that was beginning to be abroad in the country.[1]

'Intellectuals' inevitably played an active part in the developing national discussion, and they made themselves heard in great part through two organizations that had been set up in the 1920s – the League of Nations Society and the Canadian Institute of International Affairs (Volume I, pages 301-2). The Institute in particular came to serve as a sounding-board for various people of nationalist and isolationist views, and conservatives looked askance at it accordingly. Sir Maurice Hankey, visiting Canada in December 1934 to spy out the land on behalf of his chiefs in the British government, spoke of the Society and the Institute with the cheerful freedom of an outsider recording hasty impressions quite confidentially.

my own belief, is that these bodies represent public opinion as much as, but no more than, the corresponding bodies at home. They draw to their ranks extremists of all kinds – 'highbrows', isolationists, French Canadians, Irish disloyalists, with a sprinkling of sound people who for one reason or another – sometimes because they know too much – take no leading part ... In my tour of the Dominions [Dominion?] the only real 'defeatists' I met were leading members of these bodies, and I felt the utmost sympathy with Mr. Bennett in a tirade he delivered to me against the Institute of International Affairs as a body that did nothing but harm and ought to be abolished.

Since Hankey was chiefly interested in discovering the answer to 'the brutal question of whether Canada would come to our assistance in another war,' his 'defeatists' were presumably people who openly opposed such assistance.[2] Perhaps it is well to quote his conclusions: 'Both Mr. Meighen and General McNaughton, in each case after reflection, expressed a deliberated, considered view that, if our cause was just, if every effort to maintain peace had been exhausted, and it was clear to the world that war had been forced upon us, Canada would come along ... For my part, I am convinced that Mr. Meighen and General McNaughton are right, and that in the only circumstances in which this country could be caught into a war Canada would respond exactly as she did in 1914.' Hankey was justified by the event, but there was to be five years of painful soul-searching before the moment of decision came.

Bennett seems to have made a distinction between the CIIA and the League of Nations Society; both he and Mackenzie King gave a degree of patronage to the Society, which had always received a small government subsidy. (As we have seen, Ernest Lapointe was for a time its national president; this lent it current political respectability.) In his diary for May 25, 1934, King describes attending a luncheon meeting of the Society. He writes, 'Escot Smith spoke on foreign policy – a very good address but revealing a want of understanding of the magnitude of the forces to which he was referring as in the following sentence as to what the League's members in Canada should do, 'bring pressure to bear on the Government to adopt perilous policies for peace' – That is the kind of thing for which Massey is responsible – 'live dangerously' etc. Why the need of this when the end to be achieved can better be achieved by the opposite course, taking safe and sane policies.' Bennett spoke on this occasion; Lapointe, who presided, invited King to speak also, but he refrained.*

Bennett's government continued to give cautious support to the League. R.J. Manion, one of Bennett's ministers, was sent to the Assembly meeting in 1933 (it is a rather notable fact that Cahan was never given a chance to repeat his performance of 1932). Skelton sent Manion for his guidance a memorandum written by L.B. Pearson defining Canadian policy. The core of it was found in the sentences, 'We should continue ... our policy of co-operation through the League, while remaining true to our constructive position, that the League must remain consultative and not executive. The teeth must be kept out of Articles X and XVI ..."[4] It was the traditional stance, going back to 1919. Bennett himself went to the Assembly in 1934, accompanied by Skelton. He voted, with some reluctance, for the admission of Soviet Russia to the League.[5]

Always there, in the background, was the brooding presence of French Canada – a little further in the background under Bennett than under King. Bennett clearly had less awareness of the French fact; after all, he had only 24 seats in Quebec, not 60, and there was no Lapointe in the Bennett cabinet. And his eye was always much more on the economy than on external affairs as such. It is strange how little aware of French Canada many of the leading English-speaking nationalists were. Sir Clifford Sifton and John S. Ewart (who died in 1929 and 1933, respectively)

---

* The speaker was in fact Escott Reid, national secretary of the Canadian Institute of International Affairs.

had little to say about it; John Dafoe was more hostile than friendly when he thought about it; O.D. Skelton, whose views were calculated to win much applause in Quebec, had Quebeckers known about them, showed little interest. (It is curious that Hankey made no mention of Skelton; he would probably have classified him as an Irish disloyalist.) But nobody could seek to chart Canada's course in the troubled world of the thirties without thinking of Quebec. And there was no evidence that Quebec's views had changed. The province was still as hostile as ever to entanglements abroad, and it is clear that the League of Nations was no more popular there in 1935 than it had been in 1919, when so many MPs from Quebec expressed grave doubts about it in the debate on the Treaty of Versailles.

This may be a convenient place to note that on October 14, 1935, in the midst of chains of international events which we have yet to describe, a general election in Canada removed R.B. Bennett from power and restored Mackenzie King. Even though it took place in the midst of the crisis caused by Benito Mussolini's Ethiopian war, the political campaign and its result were little affected by foreign affairs. The Depression beat Bennett, as it had beaten King five years before. Any ministry governing under very adverse economic conditions becomes unpopular, and Bennett's, we have already said, was probably the most unpopular in the country's history. In January 1935, urged on by W.D. Herridge and R.K. Finlayson, Bennett attempted to reverse his government's fortunes by proclaiming a reform programme clearly reflecting the influence of Franklin D. Roosevelt's 'New Deal' in the United States, which Canadians had watched with deep interest and some envy. The attempt was a total failure. The night before the election King and his friend Mrs Patteson sought information about the outcome from the spirit world. Sir Wilfrid Laurier announced that King would 'win handsomely': 'He thinks that you will carry the country from East to West.' All the detail Laurier went on to give was wrong, but on the main point he was right. The Conservatives suffered a worse disaster than that of 1921, taking only 39 seats in the House of Commons (40, if one counts an Independent Conservative elected in Quebec). Mackenzie King won the largest majority accorded any Canadian political leader to that time: the Liberals took, at the lowest computation, 171 seats. The new socialist party, the Co-operative Commonwealth Federation or CCF, a protest movement spawned by the Depression, got only seven seats, all in the West. Notable was the complete return of Quebec to what was now its traditional allegiance; the Liberals obtained 55 of its 65 seats.[6]

Things rapidly returned to what Liberals considered normal. King wrote: 'It was a great delight to me to be again in association with Skelton, and he spoke of our relationship in similar terms.'[7] There was, however, one slight difficulty. Some months before the election, Ernest Lapointe, King's faithful and indispensable Quebec lieutenant, had said he would like the External Affairs portfolio. King had no intention of giving it to him. On October 17, six days before the new government was sworn in, King broke the bad news to him:

... I said to Lapointe I thought I had better take on External Affairs for a time at least, because of the [Ethiopian] war situation in Europe ... I could see that Lapointe was disappointed ... I realize, however, that English speaking Canada would not welcome his having control of External Affairs while war is on; also, he, himself, has not stood up for the League of Nations as I think he should have, having been President of the Ottawa Society,* and having been its strongest advocate in Canada; also, that Dandurand, who was President of the Assembly, would be ready to forsake their [sic] obligations to the League. On matters of this sort, a feeling is immediately aroused, and judgment no longer plays its part.[8]

It is perhaps a fair assumption that King was thinking not so much of the interests of the League and the League of Nations Society as he was of the embarrassment to himself that might result if the League's supporters in Canada chose to criticize him for appointing a person who might be considered an apostate. King clearly intended to keep External Affairs in his own hands. He did not separate the External Affairs portfolio from the office of Prime Minister until 1946.

Herridge in Washington and Ferguson in London resigned immediately after the Liberal victory. As we have already seen, King had now begun to have doubts about Vincent Massey; but he appointed him without hesitation to the High Commissionership, of which he had been robbed by the accession of Bennett in 1930 (above, pages 124-5). It is interesting that during the process of cabinet-making King offered John W. Dafoe two possible appointments – the post of Minister to Washington and a seat in the cabinet. The veteran newspaperman declined both.[9] It is to be suspected that King's regard for Dafoe stemmed not so much from the ardent support of the *Winnipeg Free Press* for the League of Nations as from its peculiarly virulent criticism of the Bennett government.

* Actually, as we have seen, he was national president.

THE RETURN OF RECIPROCITY

In its last months of power Bennett's administration was trying hard to reach a trade agreement with the United States. As things turned out, however, the agreement was not achieved until after the change of government, and the credit for it went to Mackenzie King.

By the spring of 1933 Bennett was strongly convinced that Canada badly needed increased access to the American market. He said so in conversations with the American *chargé d'affaires* in Ottawa, holding out as one quid pro quo the prospect of changes in customs administration that would do away with the system of arbitrary valuation, introduced at the outset of his ministry, which had been a particular cause of complaint among traders seeking to do business in Canada.[10] At this point, of course, the advent in Washington of the new Democratic administration offered good hope of more liberal commercial policies.

Late in April 1933 Bennett made, by invitation, his second and last visit to Washington during his tenure of power. He went rather reluctantly, noting that many other foreign leaders had been invited before him.[11] Nevertheless, he received more courtesies from President Roosevelt than he had from Hoover, spending a night at the White House and being tendered a state dinner. Bennett himself was much more forthcoming than on his previous visit, holding a press conference in which he voiced Canada's desire for increased trade with the United States within the terms of the Ottawa agreements, and making two radio addresses. Before he left Washington on April 29, he and Roosevelt issued a joint statement. It dealt chiefly with the coming World Economic and Monetary Conference in London,* but the two leaders said further: 'We have also discussed the problems peculiar to the United States and Canada. We have agreed to begin a search for means to increase the exchange of commodities between our two countries and thereby promote not only economic betterment on the North American continent, but also the general improvement of world conditions.'[12]

The most important word in this statement was 'begin'; for the search proved to be very long. It turned out that no business could be done until Congress passed the Reciprocal Trade Agreements Act which Roosevelt had requested. This measure authorized the President, within certain

---

* This conference, of which much was hoped, was held in June and July 1933. It proved a fiasco. It was generally considered that the unpredictable Roosevelt 'torpedoed' it by sending a message peremptorily rejecting plans for currency stabilization which were under discussion.

limitations, to negotiate with foreign states, without the consent of the Senate, agreements conceding tariff reductions up to 50 per cent of the prevailing rates. It was signed into law only on June 12, 1934. Even now the American administration showed no urgent desire to get on with a Canadian negotiation. Apparently there were some people in the State Department who thought Bennett did not really want an agreement and was indisposed to make genuine concessions.[13] Herridge advised Bennett to 'jump in ... with a good bold note,' in the hope of getting either action or decisive rejection. On November 14, accordingly, Herridge presented to Secretary Hull a long formal communication recalling (perhaps not altogether tactfully) his administration's public commitments to the reduction of international trade barriers generally and those between Canada and the United States in particular. It proposed that the two countries should make a joint declaration 'that their common objective is the attainment of the freest possible exchange of natural products' between them. It urged 'the immediate initiation of negotiations and their speedy conclusion'; it offered on behalf of Canada to extend to the United States the country's intermediate tariff, in addition to other concessions; and it suggested that the U.S. rates of duty be reduced by 50 per cent, as permitted by the new law, 'on a specified number of natural products, including, *inter alia*, lumber, fish, potatoes, milk and cream and live cattle; a number of other agricultural products, and several minerals both metallic and non-metallic.'[14]

This diplomatic *démarche* had no great result. The wiseacres in the State Department felt that it was directed primarily to the Canadian voter; Bennett would publish it when it suited his purposes. It would be too dangerous to accept the Canadian suggestion concerning a declaration on natural products; the American farmer would howl. After many drafts had been considered, Hull sent a cautious reply on December 27. He believed that the point had been reached where an 'exchange of views' should be undertaken. There could be no commitment as to particular products in advance of negotiations. He suggested that 'the question of methods of determining the value of merchandise for duty purposes' should be included among those to be discussed. On this basis, 'this Government holds itself in readiness to begin immediate preparations for trade agreement negotiations.'[15] 'Begin immediate preparations': it was an echo of the joint statement of April 1933. It appeared that the Americans were in no hurry; and the sequel showed that appearances were not deceptive.

Part, at least, of the reason for the further delay, however, was the cumbersomeness of American procedure. A Committee for Reciprocity

Information created after the passage of the Trade Agreements Act had to hold public hearings, which began in March 1935.[16] Late in May Herridge informed Ottawa that a trade agreement between the United States and Sweden was about to be signed: 'With this out of the way State Department may be ready to begin Canadian negotiations next week.' This was too hopeful. On June 22 the Minister told Skelton that his belief was that the Americans were going to offer 'wholly unimportant concessions.' Herridge, who knew everybody, went on to give the Under-Secretary a glimpse of one of the men closest to Roosevelt:

Believe me, it is all baby stuff. Harry Hopkins told me that when Beatty [President of the Canadian Pacific Railway] gave him a lunch in Montreal, he was amused at Beatty's references to the impending trade agreement. According to Beatty, the big idea was to have the P.M. come down here a few days before the general election and sign a resounding pact. To all of which Hopkins replied: 'Say, how do you get that way?' And added: 'You may be taking a lot of interest in this trading proposition up here in Canada, but I can assure you that there is absolutely no interest being taken in it at Washington.'[17]

Early in July J.D. Hickerson of the State Department's Division of European Affairs, an officer who was long to be prominent in negotiations with Canada, told Hume Wrong that the department had been 'working day and night' to complete preparations for negotiation, and that a memorandum of recommended concessions was virtually ready for submission to the President. Herridge reported: 'Hickerson says that they are anxious to push on with the negotiations as rapidly as they possibly can once they are in a position to begin. He talks about signing an agreement within a month and having it in effect by September. This impresses me as being an optimistic view of the situation.'[18]

After pressure by Bennett on Norman Armour, the American Minister in Ottawa, actual negotiations began, at last, in Washington on August 26. Herridge was assisted by a team of experts from Ottawa: Norman Robertson of External Affairs, Dana Wilgress (now Director of the Commercial Intelligence Service in the Department of Trade and Commerce), and Hector McKinnon (above, page 143). In his exiguous memoirs long afterwards Wilgress recalled how they were received by Hickerson, heading the American negotiators: 'We were handed a sheet of paper listing an offer of trade concessions. We said, not very hopefully, that we would study it and return to Washington in two weeks' time.' Herridge was 'very disappointed' with the American offer, though as we have seen he can hardly have been surprised. Wilgress writes: 'Obviously, the conclusion of a trade agreement with the United States was not going to be one of the means by which the Bennett government could cling to office.'[19]

Early in September a letter from Bennett to Herridge emphasized the importance of concessions by the Americans on 'fish of the cod family, cream and potatoes.'[20] The American experts, after consideration, were inclined to give way to some extent on these items, except cod, and also on cattle and lumber. It was President Roosevelt himself who prevented progress at this point. In a conference on September 26 with Phillips, Armour, and two of the American negotiators he 'stood firm against giving any substantial concessions on meats, potatoes and cream.'[21] He must have realized that he was making an agreement before the Canadian election impossible. The two negotiating teams met again in Washington on October 2 and 3, with the election less than a fortnight away. Herridge, the Canadian record states, 'emphasized our disappointment at the inadequate concession which had been offered on cattle and the inability of the United States to grant any concessions on cream, codfish or potatoes.' The Canadians 'indicated how difficult it would be to extend most-favoured-nation treatment to United States products unless we secured concessions on at least three of the five important products mentioned in the Note of November 14, 1934' – that is, 'lumber, fish, potatoes, milk and cream and live cattle.' Hickerson said that concessions on cream and codfish were out of the question 'owing to the effect this might have on the domestic price level.'

During these sessions it was made fully clear, if it had not been before, that a pre-election agreement could not be hoped for. Hickerson explained 'that it would be physically impossible to conclude an agreement in less than two weeks. It normally took this amount of time for their Customs Department to check the schedule, while the State Department also required two weeks to prepare Press releases and to attend to other technical details following the conclusion of the actual negotiations.' He nevertheless 'expressed the desire of the United States Government that the negotiations should be continued.' Again Herridge cannot have been surprised. He had written to Skelton on September 21, 'I never dreamt for a moment that there was the remotest possibility of signing a deal before the fourteenth of October.'[22] On that October 14 the Canadian election came and went, and the Bennett government passed into history; and the trade negotiation with the United States remained incomplete.

It has been generally assumed that the Roosevelt administration welcomed the return of Mackenzie King and the Liberals to power in Canada. Did the American negotiators deliberately drag their feet to avoid giving Bennett an agreement that might have improved his position with the voters? No one has ever discovered any direct evidence to this effect (but it must be remembered that such matters might not be committed to paper). If there was deliberate delay the responsibility was President Roosevelt's, for he kept all the important decisions on the negotiation in his own hands. We shall see that there is evidence (admittedly second-hand) that Roosevelt was convinced that it would be easier to get an agreement (meaning, presumably, an agreement satisfactory to the United States) with King than with Bennett (below). It seems quite likely that he stalled the negotiation in order to avoid helping Bennett and to contribute to the election of a government who might be less tough bargainers and more generally co-operative.

Mackenzie King's new government was sworn in on October 23, 1935. The next day was Thanksgiving Day, but for King it was a working day. He devoted it to new initiatives in the field of foreign relations.

He began with a visit to the new Japanese Minister, clearly intended to begin the resolution of a serious trade crisis which had arisen with Japan (below, page 191). He went on to the residence of the United States Minister, with the object of launching an offensive intended to produce a trade agreement at the earliest possible moment. After reminding Armour of his own numerous American connections, he plunged into this subject. Armour suggested that it might be a good idea if King wrote to the President about it. King, however, had a still better idea:

As I was leaving, I said to Mr. Armour that, instead of writing, it might be better for me to go down to Washington and see the President and have a talk with him. I asked him what he thought of that. He said that would be infinitely better; indeed, nothing would be better than that. He said: 'I will tell you in confidence that, as long ago as last June, the President had said that if he had you to negotiate with he believed it would have been possible for the two countries to reach an agreement.' I said I believed there was nothing as true as that ...[23]

Reporting this conversation to Washington, Armour wrote: 'In concluding, Mr. King stressed the great importance of a successful trade agreement at this time on the relations between our two countries. He made it plain, as Dr. Skelton had done, that there were two roads open to Canada, but that he wanted to choose 'the American road' if we made it possible for him to do so. From every point of view it was important that our attachments should be strengthened and our relations brought closer in every way, politically as well as economically ...' As to King's suggestion of a visit to Washington, Armour refrained from reporting the warm welcome which King claimed he had given the idea. He wrote, indeed, 'I take it for granted that his suggestion of the possibility of his proceeding to Washington for a talk with the President was merely a friendly gesture as showing the lengths to which he would be willing to go to accomplish his purpose.' A week later the Counsellor of the Legation called on Skelton at Armour's request, and emphasized the fact that the trade negotiations were still 'exactly in the *status quo* existing before the elections.' If King went to Washington, and an agreement was not 'provided for him to bring back with him,' would he perhaps 'feel he had been put in an awkward position'?[24]

The Legation seems to have under-estimated King's determination to get an agreement, and it may also have under-estimated the President's readiness to meet him halfway. The Canadian experts went back to Washington, reopening negotiations there on November 4. On November 7 King himself arrived in Washington; that day William Phillips told the President that the negotiators had drafted an agreement, 'a far more favorable set-up than with the Bennett government.'[25] On November 8 King dined and slept at the White House and discussed the agreement with the President. Roosevelt recalled that he had met King before, when Harvard gave the Canadian an honorary degree. At dinner the President talked about old days at the Roosevelt summer home in New Brunswick, and King and Mrs Roosevelt found a common interest in Jane Addams and the Hull House settlement at Chicago. 'In saying goodnight, the President said it was great just to be able to pick up the telephone and talk to each other in just a few minutes. We must do that whenever occasion arises. I will always be glad to hear from you.'[26] It was the beginning of a new and auspicious relationship. Next day King and Secretary of State Hull initialled the draft trade agreement. The Prime Minister went back to Ottawa to get the approval of his cabinet colleagues. On November 11 Roosevelt announced the agreement at Arlington Cemetery: 'It is fitting that on this Armistice Day, I am privileged to tell you that, between us and a great neighbor, another act of cementing our historic friendship has been agreed upon and is being consummated.' On November 15 King and Hull signed the agreement formally in the President's executive office at the White House.[27]

We must look at the agreement. By it Canada and the United States agreed to give each other most-favoured-nation treatment – that is, duties on any article were not to be higher than those allowed to any third party. It was recognized that Canada's British preferences, including those established by the Ottawa agreements, should be an exception to this rule.

SIGNING THE CANADIAN-AMERICAN TRADE AGREEMENT,
WASHINGTON, 1935

President Roosevelt watches as Secretary of State Cordell Hull (left) and
Mackenzie King affix their signatures. In the background, second from
left, O.D. Skelton; third from left, Henry Morgenthau, Jr, U.S. Secretary of
the Treasury; fourth from right, Henry Wallace, U.S. Secretary of Agriculture; extreme right, Dana Wilgress

Canada extended to United States goods the rates in her intermediate tariff, which had existed since 1907 for the benefit of countries with which she had special trading arrangements (Volume I, page 79). The United States gave Canada special rates on a wide range of items. Of the 'five important products' so important during the negotiation, 'fish of the cod family' was the only one on which Roosevelt made no concession at all (he was too frightened of New England). On the other four there were concessions, but they were severely limited by quota arrangements. On potatoes (another matter of great interest to New England) there was no concession on food potatoes, but certified seed potatoes would come in at special rates according to the time of year – but only up to 750,000 bushels annually.* Cream, fresh or sour, would pay 35 cents a gallon – but this special rate would apply on not more than 1,500,000 gallons a year. There were somewhat similar provisions about cattle and lumber. Since there was still a whisky famine in the United States, Canadian whisky was to be admitted at $2.50 a gallon – but only if aged in the wood for four years. Newsprint and wood pulp remained on the free list, as they had since 1913.[29]

King had noted in his diary on November 8 that in his conversation with Roosevelt he did not touch codfish, 'as I had been told it would only upset the President for me to mention cod.' He did speak of seed potatoes, cream, and cattle, in addition to lumber; on this last point the President did not seem to be fully informed about the state of the negotiation. King records Roosevelt as saying: 'Mr. King, all these three, cattle, cream and potatoes are political. If the campaign [of 1936] were over, I would feel we would have no difficulty with regard to them' (or, King added, words to that effect). Whatever its shortcomings, in the conditions of 1935 the agreement was certainly generally welcomed in Canada. The *New York Times* reported from Ottawa that 'the two great disappointments' for Canadian producers were the failure 'to lower the duties on cod or on potatoes for food.'[30] King had got his quick agreement, but he had paid a price. That cautious man Dana Wilgress was still cautious when he wrote his memoirs, but reading between the lines one sees what he thought of the agreement he had helped to draft: 'The extension of the Intermediate Tariff to imports from the United States was indeed revolutionary and many people, though not the public generally, thought the 1935 trade agreement conferred more benefits on the United States than on Canada.'

* Skelton had mentioned seed potatoes to Armour on September 21, evidently suggesting that something might be done for them even if the Americans could not see their way to concessions on potatoes for food.[28]

Bennett had offered the intermediate tariff to the United States in November 1934, apparently on Wilgress's own urging.[31] But he had asked in return much larger concessions than King had now obtained. By way of assessing the agreement, we should look at the Canadian trade figures for the next few years:[32]

	Exports to United States	Imports from United States
1935	$304,721,354	$303,639,972
1936	$360,302,426	$319,479,594
1937	$435,014,544	$393,720,662
1938	$423,131,091	$487,279,507

These are crude figures and were recorded at a time when both countries were gradually recovering from the Depression, and trade was naturally expanding; not too much, therefore, should be read into them. But so far as they go they seem to support Wilgress's implication: the agreement King rushed into was rather more favourable to the United States than it was to Canada. To people at the time, however, the most important thing was that trade was reviving; and to this, it cannot be doubted, the agreement made at least a modest contribution.

In 1935 a general agreement between Canada and the United States came into existence for the first time since Lord Elgin's treaty lapsed in 1866. In retrospect it is evident that 1935 was a very important date in the relations of the two countries. The trade agreement marked the beginning of a *rapprochement* which was to go on for many years and to effect a drastic alteration in Canada's traditional international position. To put it briefly and bluntly, from 1935 onwards Canada's relationship to Britain became less important and her relationship to the United States much more important in her scheme of things. We have clearly reached a vital turning-point in our story.

Canadians who experience a certain emotional rebellion against this development (and the present writer, a member of the Georgian generation, may as well admit that he is one of them) frequently tend to blame the whole thing on the Liberal party, and, more specifically, on Mackenzie King. And it must be said that in 1935 King gave these critics a lot of ammunition to use against him. In that interview with Armour on Thanksgiving Day he talked as though his American connections – which were undoubtedly very important to him – had been the mainspring of his life. He said that people called him 'the American.' We have seen him saying that he wanted to choose 'the American road' for his country if the

United States would make it possible for him; he wanted the United States and Canada brought closer together 'in every way, politically as well as economically.' This is what Armour tells us; King's own private record is not quite as explicit. O.D. Skelton had talked much the same way to Armour the day after the election. It would all have made a wonderful text for Donald Creighton's idiosyncratic book *The Forked Road*, and it really seems a pity that Creighton apparently never read King's diary or Armour's reports.

When Skelton, under the euphoric influence of the Liberal victory at the polls (and the figures of the majority were undoubtedly music in his ears), let down his hair and told Armour that Canada was faced with two alternatives, agreement with the United States or closer union with the Empire, and that, for both political and economic reasons, he preferred the former,[33] he undoubtedly meant precisely what he said; it accords with everything we know about him (above, pages 8-14). With King it is somewhat different. King was a politician pursuing political ends, and his great end at the moment was an immediate trade agreement with the United States. He knew that most Canadians would welcome this; he knew also that Roosevelt was already much admired in Canada, and he certainly perceived that it would be a political asset to him to demonstrate that he had a close association with this commanding personality whose charisma had been purveyed by the Canadian media* for two-and-a-half years past. The trade agreement would be the means of doing this. King undoubtedly told the Americans what he thought they would like to hear. It was an art he thoroughly understood.

One can, I think, assert with considerable confidence that King did not really want to cultivate the American tie to the exclusion, or even to the disadvantage, of that with the Commonwealth. There is other evidence besides the frequent asseverations in his diary that he wanted Canada to be a growing power within the Commonwealth, not a country within the American orbit. It consists in the written records of his numerous *séances* with Mrs Patteson over the 'little table' which they used as a means of communicating (so they believed) with the spirit world. These curious documents in King's handwriting are, if the present writer is not deceiving himself, an index to his mind and ideas, for it can hardly be doubted

---

* The plural is now suitable, for radio broadcasting (which first played an important part in a political campaign in 1930) had become one of the great facts of life. It was radio, very largely, that enabled Roosevelt's powerful charm to overleap international boundaries and that gave him his influence in Canada.

that these 'experiences' came out of his own head. And they reveal a man who was certainly not an American at heart. The mind reflected in them is a product of the late-Victorian Ontario in which King grew up. He reveres the Crown, has deep respect for British statesmen (though only for Liberals), and is anxious for British approval. On his sixtieth birthday (December 17, 1934) King received good wishes (his word was 'love') from a galaxy of dead British Liberal politicians, from Gladstone to the lately-deceased Sir Donald Maclean. Canadian Liberal leaders also came. But it is surely a notable fact that no Americans came to this anniversary observance (of course, there is no Liberal party in the United States). Theodore Roosevelt, whom King had known in life, did not come; nor did Lincoln, whom he much admired, though Lincoln did speak to King (along with Gladstone) on another occasion. There are parallels at other important junctures in King's life.[34]

Forty-odd years later, 1935 is visible as one of those moments when the course of history began to change. But it is not evident that in that year Canadians were presented with any real choice. And the theory of a Liberal conspiracy will not hold water, in spite of King's and Skelton's talk about the 'American road.' The country's course was set by economic facts and public opinion. If the Bennett government had been returned to power, it would certainly have made a trade agreement with the United States within months if not weeks, and the Canadian public would have been delighted, as it was delighted by King's. And the move towards freer trade was only the simplest common sense; economic nationalism had done the world, and Canada, great harm. Four years after the agreement of 1935, the Second World War broke out. It was not planned by the Canadian Liberal party; but it moved Canada far down the American road. The arrangement made by King and Roosevelt at Ogdensburg in the desperate crisis of 1940 was clearly fateful for the country's future; but given the circumstances of the time any other Canadian government would have made much the same arrangement if it could, and almost all Canadians applauded. The fact is that Canada was being borne along, willy nilly, by what Churchill might have called the great movement of events; though the direction of the movement was one which Churchill himself found regrettable. These things we must deal with in due time.

THE ETHIOPIAN CRISIS

In 1935 the Italian Fascist dictator Benito Mussolini attempted to gain cheap military glory by the conquest of the one surviving ancient independent state in Africa, the landlocked Empire of Ethiopia. He thus set off a crisis which brought Europe to the brink of war, shook and finally discredited the League of Nations, and incidentally embarrassed two Canadian governments.

Much has been written about the Canadian relationship to this humiliating affair,[35] and we shall therefore seek to avoid describing it in great detail. The Canadian embarrassment stemmed largely from the fact that the election and the change of government took place in the midst of it. It was clear from the beginning of 1935 that Mussolini was contemplating an attack, though it did not actually start until October 3, ten days before the Canadian election. The critical phase began in August. Clearly, if the League of Nations invoked sanctions against Italy, and Britain stood by the League, Italy might attack her. On August 22 the British cabinet ordered precautions, and ships, troops, and air units began to move. Inevitably, therefore, the threat of war hung over the Canadian political campaign. Both Bennett and King avoided the issue as far as they could, but neither could avoid it entirely; and they both dealt with it in isolationist terms. Bennett said on September 6: 'In peace, the Conservative party stands for Canadian rights, and stands against the economic aggression of any foreign country. So also in war. We will not be embroiled in any foreign quarrel where the rights of Canadians are not involved.' The following day Ernest Lapointe said: 'in my opinion no interest in Ethiopia, of any nature whatever, is worth the life of a single Canadian citizen.' King, at the same meeting, said: 'You can trust the Liberal party to see to it that, as regards the great questions which involve the lives of men and women, any Liberal Government will see to it that not a single life is unnecessarily sacrificed in regard to any matter beyond what affects the safeguarding and rights of our own country.' His Quebec City audience applauded when he recalled the Chanak affair of 1922 and his attitude that no military action would be taken without Parliament being consulted.[36]

On September 9 the Assembly of the League of Nations met, faced with the task of trying to prevent Italian aggression against Ethiopia. The election prevented any Canadian cabinet minister from attending. The country's chief representative was Howard Ferguson, the High Commissioner in London, who was assisted by W.A. Riddell, the 'Advisory Officer' at Geneva, where he had been serving for ten years; L.B. Pearson, of the High Commissioner's staff, was also present. There were other delegates, including Miss Winnifred Kydd, the president of the National Council of Women, but they did not play important parts.[37] At the outset the British and French representatives (Sir Samuel Hoare and Pierre Laval) made strong statements in favour of enforcing the League Covenant.* The Canadians asked Ottawa whether they should support this stand. The first reply, inspired by Skelton and approved by the cabinet, was that no statement should be made at this point. Immediately, however, Bennett, having read the Hoare and Laval speeches, 'switched' and decided that the British and French should be supported. The Prime Minister had sharp exchanges with Skelton and Loring Christie (the erstwhile imperial federationist had lately returned to External Affairs and was now Skelton's close associate and supporter); Bennett accused the two officials of 'welshing' on Canada's obligations to the League. New instructions were sent authorizing a statement to the effect that if the worst happened Canada would 'join with the other members of the League in considering how by unanimous action peace can be maintained.' This was on September 13. Ferguson made the statement in the Assembly the following day.[38] It seemed that Canada, represented by the Bennett government, might be adopting the policy of running risks for peace which Mackenzie King had so strongly reprobated, in the privacy of his diary, not so long before (above, page 166); and King was likely to be Prime Minister again in a month.

After the actual invasion of Ethiopia, the League Council promptly declared that Italy had resorted to war in defiance of the League Covenant, and the question of sanctions immediately arose. The Canadian delegation at Geneva asked for instructions, and following a consultation between Skelton and Bennett it was told on October 9 'to refrain from voting at the present juncture.' The telegram went on: 'In view of fact that the Canadian Parliament has been dissolved and that a new Parliament is to be elected next Monday, it is not considered advisable to anticipate in any way the action of that new Parliament.' The Canadian delegation was thrown into consternation. The question immediately to be voted on was merely that of the fact of aggression, and the prospect of Canada abstaining (along with Italy and countries that sympathized with or feared her) was unpleasant. A strong protest went by cable, and Ferguson followed it up by a trans-Atlantic telephone call to Bennett arguing that the impending vote implied no commitment to sanctions. Bennett agreed that Ferguson might use his own judgment. Canada accordingly went with the majority; Italy, Austria, and Hungary alone opposed.[39]

* It should be remembered that in Britain the results of the 'peace ballot' organized by the League of Nations Union had been published late in June. Nearly twelve million people voted, and the great majority expressed strong support for the League of Nations.

Bennett's decision produced another verbal scuffle between him and Skelton; the Under Secretary was undoubtedly encouraged by the imminent prospect of a change of government. Over the telephone (for Bennett was off campaigning) Skelton argued that to declare Italy's guilt without qualification implied consent to sanctions. Canada had always opposed sanctions, and should not change her position 'merely because Britain has changed.' Bennett denied any commitment, and added that even if there was one it could not be evaded. 'We went into League, took benefits, must assume responsibilities or get out, not try to hornswoggle ourselves out.' The conversation ended with the Prime Minister saying: 'No one in Canada is going to deny Italy guilty or object to our saying so. If they did, not going to wriggle out if it meant I didn't get one vote. Have made my position about war clear.'[40] That day (October 10) the Assembly set up a committee representing all the member nations to consider necessary measures. Instructions from Ottawa authorized the Canadians to accept membership but added, 'no definite attitude should be taken until further communication is sent.' Ferguson nevertheless accepted membership, not only in the large committee but also in a smaller one (ultimately of eighteen members) intended to recommend specific sanctions; Ottawa was informed afterwards. In the Committee of Eighteen on both October 11 and October 14 he made speeches urging the League on to firm action against Italy. A Canadian observer wrote: 'Ferguson ... has twice cut across rambling apologies and withdrawings and has made it clear that the Canadians are determined to see the collective system put in motion in this case.'[41] Geneva was not accustomed to hearing such sentiments from Canadian representatives. But on October 15 news came of Mackenzie King's great electoral victory. Ferguson returned to London and shortly resigned. The Assembly having closed, Canadian representation was left to Riddell.

As soon as the election results were known, a message went to Riddell from Ottawa telling him that since the new government could not take office for some days, 'it will not be possible for you to take position on any further proposals in the meantime.' It would have been only prudent to act on this warning; but Riddell had the bit in his teeth. In his later book he refers to this message as 'the usual cablegram' sent at a change of government. He recalled to Skelton certain instructions sent to him in July when the possibility of sanctions being invoked was under discussion, and the Bennett government had shown a distinct disposition to co-operate in them. Skelton did not attempt to cancel these now, though he did remind Riddell of the order of October 10 against taking a definite attitude. Riddell continued to follow the Ferguson line, taking an active part in the discussion of economic measures against Italy; and he was encouraged when the King government, after taking office on October 23, agreed to co-operate in the first economic sanctions proposed by the League. The government did cautiously affirm that this was not a precedent for future action, and it also declared that no commitment to military sanctions could be made without the prior approval of Parliament.[42]

The crisis in Riddell's career was now at hand. On November 1 Skelton wrote him a letter commenting very sharply on the fact that in spite of the instruction of October 10 'the Canadian Delegation actually took the initiative in making the first proposal for the application of sanctions.' Skelton no doubt thought that a personal rebuke of this sort went best in a personal letter. But he should have cabled. Long before the letter could reach him Riddell had got himself into much worse trouble. The Committee of Eighteen was now discussing the widening of sanctions; in particular, the question of whether goods including copper, iron, steel, and petroleum should be placed on the list of items forbidden for export to Italy. Oil was vital to the Italian war effort; and there was at least the possibility that if it were embargoed Italy would make a 'mad dog' attack on the countries – primarily the paramount naval power, Britain – that were denying it to her. On the morning of November 2, when it was apparent that the matter would be discussed in the committee that afternoon, Riddell cabled Ottawa asking for instructions: 'Reply urgently requested immediately as discussion continued [?continues] this afternoon and I shall be expected to express our attitude.' He must have known that there was little chance of receiving a reply before the meeting. In fact, when the cable was received in Ottawa, 'Within an hour an "immediate" telegram was sent'[43] which told Riddell, 'As to inclusion petroleum and copper not desirable to make statement but you may support majority view.' It proceeded: 'Regarding press despatches reporting your taking prominent part in committee discussions yesterday, no position should be taken on any question of importance in committee without definite instructions.' It was too late. Later that day Riddell cabled: 'After consultation with main delegation[?s]* this morning moved in Committee of Eighteen that petroleum, coal, iron and steel be added to list in Proposal No. 4.'[44]

Riddell later explained that he had taken this initiative because other countries, including France, were considering proposing longer lists including copper, which he thought the Canadian government would not want included. He had consulted Robert Coulondre of France and

* The reference is presumably to his conversations with the British and French.

Anthony Eden of Britain, 'and secured their support, although Coulondre felt that copper at least should be included.' Eden had encouraged him to proceed. The Committee of Eighteen shortly approved the proposal, which provided that the new sanctions should be formally proposed to governments 'As soon as it appears that the acceptance of this principle is sufficiently general to ensure the efficacy of the measures thus contemplated.'[45]

Inevitably there was a strong reaction from Ottawa to Riddell's performance of November 2. When he attempted to defend himself, the Secretary of State for External Affairs (that is, King) replied: 'I have noted your explanation but must insist that position which you took was not in my judgment in conformity with important factors in Canadian situation and not within the scope of your authority. As I have already indicated no position on any question of importance should be taken without positive and definite instructions.'[46] Riddell now fell silent in the Committee of Eighteen, as he would have been wise to do earlier.

Here the matter might have rested; but the King ministry continued to be troubled by the repercussions of Riddell's initiative at home and abroad. It became particularly sensitive to the fact that the oil sanction was regularly referred to as 'the Canadian proposal.' The government had been prepared to go along with this measure if it could do so merely as an anonymous member of a League majority; to find itself ticketed as the leader it found acutely embarrassing. The situation is described in a memorandum of the whole affair prepared by Skelton for King: 'The press, particularly in England, referred to the proposal as Canada's proposal. Increasing reference was made to the alleged initiation of the proposal by the Canadian Government, and its insistence upon the enforcement of further sanctions. The British Government was criticised for holding back.'[47] After the signing of the American trade agreement, King, accompanied by Skelton, had gone to Sea Island, Georgia, for a holiday. He read the English press reports with perturbation.[48] On November 28 the Acting Under Secretary (Laurent Beaudry) telegraphed Skelton, 'Mr. Lapointe [Acting Prime Minister] is disturbed by headlines in Press emphasizing initiative taken by Canada and is wondering whether some course of action would be adopted to counteract this effect!'[49] King's diary notes on November 29: 'I took very strongly, with Skelton, the view that we should not delay in making it known, through an interview with the press by Lapointe, that the resolution was not one of which our Government had any knowledge, nor with respect to which Riddell had authority from the Government ... If not for Dr. Skelton's desire to protect Riddell as much as possible, I would have gone the length of making a complete statement as to his unauthorized action. Skelton feels that he should be dismissed from the service, but is anxious, meanwhile, to avoid weakening the hands of Britain, France, and the other countries, in the League, against Italy ...' King discountenanced Ottawa's suggestion that Senator Dandurand should go to Geneva, because 'With the European situation what it is, it is better for our French Canadian members to appear in it as little as possible.' King thought that Massey in London should be instructed to tell the British government that Riddell's action had been unauthorized.[50]

On December 1, accordingly, Lapointe issued a statement for publication in the next day's papers.[51] It pointed out that Canada was enforcing the sanctions against Italy that had been requested by the League of Nations, but that Canadian action 'has been and will be limited to co-operation in purely financial and economic measures of a pacific character which are accepted by substantially all of the participating countries.' It went on:

The suggestion which has appeared in the press from time to time that the Canadian Government has taken the initiative in the extension of the embargo upon exportation of key commodities to Italy, and particularly in the placing of a ban upon shipments of coal, oil, iron and steel, is due to a misunderstanding. The Canadian Government has not and does not propose to take the initiative in any such action; and the opinion which was expressed by the Canadian member of the Committee – and which has led to the reference to the proposal as a Canadian proposal – represented only his own personal opinion, and his views as a member of the Committee – and not the views of the Canadian Government.

This statement inevitably caused a sensation in Canada and elsewhere. It could have been better phrased, and King shortly found himself explaining that Canada was not actually opposing the oil sanction.[52] The reaction within the country reflected those 'important factors in Canadian situation' of which he had reminded Riddell. There was great division of opinion. Idealistic supporters of the League, like N.W. Rowell and Sir Robert Falconer (a former President of the University of Toronto), criticized the government. The *New York Times* described the symbolic division of press comment:[53]

The French-Canadian press, without exception, approved the government's move, L'Action Catholique declaring that it had 'set an example of national pride which should be pursued in the future.'

The English-language newspapers ranged from qualified approval to emphatic disapproval. The Toronto Telegram's views were represented by a front-page streamer reading, 'Britain Stands Firm for Sanctions, but Canada Lies Down.'

The *Telegram*'s coarsest comment was provided by a cartoon entitled 'His Master's Voice,' which represented Lapointe restraining Riddell on the whispered instructions of a priest. Needless to say, this was duly reported in French Canada.[54] At the opposite pole was the reported remark of Camillien Houde, the mayor of Montreal, that in the event of war between Britain and Fascist Italy, French-Canadian sympathies would be with Italy.[55] The simple explanation is that Catholic Quebec tended to identify Italy with the Papacy. It is not surprising that a government as dependent on Quebec as King's should shy away from the bold sanction-ist policies of Ferguson and Riddell. The threat to the country's unity was only too evident. So, of course, was the threat to the power of the Liberal party.

It was probably fortunate for King that a week after Lapointe's state-ment a much greater sensation broke. Baldwin's National government in Britain had just won a general election on a platform of support for the League. Now it leaked out that Hoare and Laval had agreed on a plan that would have given the greater part of Ethiopia to Italy (the Emperor would have been assured of the remnant, and would have been given a corridor to the sea).* A wave of public indignation swept Hoare from the Foreign Office, where he was succeeded by Eden. The plan was aban-doned, but Ethiopia was conquered and the League of Nations had suffered a mortal blow. The oil sanction was never approved, and the sanctions that had begen adopted were withdrawn in the course of 1936. That year King himself led the Canadian delegation to the League Assembly. In a careful speech he defined Canadian policy towards the League in the old terms, repudiating the idea of collective security. He piously reaffirmed Canada's devotion to League principles, but asserted that the League should 'emphasize the task of mediation and conciliation rather than punishment'; 'automatic commitments to the application of force is not a practical policy.' John W. Dafoe later made the oft-quoted comment: 'the League of Nations, with assurances of the most distin-guished consideration, was ushered out into the darkness by Mr. Macken-

---

* In justice to the British government, it must be said that the French had made it clear that they would not support Britain in a war against Italy brought on by sanctions.

zie King.'[56] The whole affair left King with a decided dislike of the League. He took a poor view of the international ragtag and bobtail gathered in the Assembly hall: 'Countries named by the dozens of which one has seldom or never heard.' Next year, after another trip to Europe, he wrote: 'I wish the League of Nations could be gotten out of the way altogether. Every feeling I had had about the mischief being wrought through the intrigues of that institution has been intensified by what I have seen and heard while abroad.'[57]

The attitudes of the two successive Canadian prime ministers to the Ethiopian crisis present a piquant contrast. King's was perfectly predictable. He followed the line that he and Skelton had long laid down – and which, it should be added, had been foreshadowed in the actions of Canadian administrations going back to Borden's first attack on Article 10 in 1919. It was anything but heroic; but Canada's circumstances did not encourage heroism. With French Canada – roughly one-third of the country's population – apparently strongly opposed to any commitments to the League of Nations, there was ample reason for caution. The attitude of the King government – that it would go along with collective economic action supported by a majority of the members of the League, but would not take the lead – had a good deal to commend it. It was the great powers that would have to bear the chief burden of action against Italy in peace or, if it came to that, in war. It was arguably better that the great powers should be allowed to make the basic decisions. But if there is much to be said for King's policy, there is little to be said for his style. To refrain from leading a crusade for the League was one thing; to perform a private dance on its grave, as he did in his diary and letters, was quite another. The League and its friends had embarrassed King, and he would not forgive them. He was a small-spirited man.

Bennett's attitude is more complicated. We have seen that he clearly had at least a little more regard for the League than King; and he had a realistic view of the limited influence that Canada could wield in the League or in the international field at large. We have also seen that he had a sentimental regard for the British Empire, and in the Ethiopian crisis this played its part, in Bennett's mind and in those of other Canadians. For a few weeks Britain seemed to be standing forth as the champion of the League and of collective security; British loyalty and League idealism pushed English-speaking Canadians in the same direction. This is why in the controversy over the repudiation of Riddell such a curiously-assorted body of critics confronted the King government: Rowell and Falconer and labour leaders and the socialist mayor of Toronto, Jimmie Simpson, stood shoulder to shoulder with the imperialist ex-mayor Tommy Church and the *Telegram* and the chiefs of the Orange Order.[58] There was a potentially powerful combination of the visceral and the idealistic. A similar combination was to be quite irresistible in different circumstances in September 1939.

What is one to say about Walter Riddell? It is pretty apparent that he acted from the highest motives. Of the situation just before he proposed the oil sanction he wrote in his book: 'By this time I had become thoroughly convinced that this was the last and the best chance that the Member States would have of preventing a European collapse and another world war.'[59] He may well have been right. Certainly the League of Nations was having its last chance at that moment. Its failure to deal with Italy finally discredited it, and from 1935 Europe was on the road towards war. Riddell had been at Geneva for ten years and had become devoted to the League and the "Geneva spirit.' Encouraged no doubt by the obvious rebuffs that Skelton had received from Bennett, he chose to look only at those instructions from Ottawa which fell in with his views. When on October 29 he received the cable informing him that the government had decided to accept the League's first sanctions, he 'at once concluded,' he says, 'that it was intended to govern my actions in the Committee.'[60] The two messages cautioning him against taking initiatives he passed over. Unfortunately he was taking decisions that were not his to take. He was a servant of the government of Canada, and it was his business to carry out its orders. If he had done so, indeed, the country would have been spared the considerable humiliation incurred when he was disavowed. Administratively speaking, it would seem that Riddell had been left too long in the Geneva post.

Perhaps the verdict of history on Riddell will be that his heart was a little better than his head. It is not the worst form of weakness. At a crisis in human affairs he did what he thought the interests of mankind required. It is interesting that although Mackenzie King was clearly extremely angry with him he did not venture to take action against him.* Riddell was left at Geneva for two more years, and he ended his diplomatic career as High Commissioner to New Zealand.[61]

King's record of the reactions of his new cabinet to the Ethiopian crisis which it inherited makes fascinating reading. On October 19, before the government was formed, the Prime-Minister-elect had an interview with

---

* Describing an interview with Riddell in Ottawa in his diary for January 30, 1936, King wrote, 'He really should be summarily dismissed and would be but for his years of service there.'

two men who would be prominent in it, Ernest Lapointe and J.G. Gardiner, the Premier of Saskatchewan. King wrote: 'I came back each time in my thoughts to the condition of Canada and the world at the present time. Europe may be in a state of war very soon; Britain may be drawn in; we may have very big problems on our hands here – the country itself divided. Lapointe immediately said there would be no going into war by Canada. I replied that was well enough to say, but we had in this room itself a divided view on that point; that Gardiner himself thought we ought to go into war, so that was what we may expect – a division of opinion, over which the party may be split wide open ...' On October 25 the 'first regular meeting' of the new cabinet confronted the question of sanctions. King read a brief by Skelton. His record proceeds:

It was interesting to see how clearly the division of feeling disclosed itself. Ilsley [Minister of National Revenue, from Nova Scotia] could scarcely wait to say how emphatic he thought we should be in the matter of declaring for sanctions. Rogers [Minister of Labour, from Ontario], and some of the others, were also quite strong on backing the League. Lapointe, Power and Cardin [all from Quebec] were all in the other direction. They felt the necessity of standing by the League, in view of our platform, from which there was no escape, but were anxious to say and do as little as possible. The entire council was against anything in the nature of military sanctions. Ilsley and some others were not appearing to hesitate [sic] in the reservations we might be making. I pointed out that from the days of Sir John Macdonald and Sir Wilfrid Laurier the aim of British statesmen had been to involve Canada in the whole question of Empire defence, and we had to keep this background in mind, and be careful to leave no doubt about our unwillingness to commit ourselves to a course which would involve military action.

This cabinet meeting made the decision to accept the initial League sanctions which Riddell found so encouraging.[62]

On October 29 King discussed with Skelton and Lapointe statements on these sanctions to be given to the press and sent to Geneva. Lapointe said 'he would resign at once' if the government were to decide on military sanctions. 'Ilsley and one or two others' might resign on the other side. 'In other words,' wrote King, 'if the question of military sanctions comes, we shall have the old war situation over again, with the party divided as it was at the time of conscription.' His conclusion was: 'Our own domestic situation must be considered first, and what will serve to keep Canada united.'[63]

There were to be many changes in the personnel of King's cabinet before the coming war was over; but this pattern of disagreement established in the government's first days would persist, with the representatives of Quebec always on the side of holding back and an English-speaking group – invariably including Ilsley – always on the side of greater activity and effort. On the eve of war, one group would favour commitment and the other delay. During the conflict the same division constantly recurred, particularly with respect to the question of compulsory service. In the autumn of 1944 the total disruption of the government was only very narrowly avoided. And the division within the government and the government party mirrored the dangerous division in the country as a whole, of which the Prime Minister was always so painfully aware.

It was not only the Liberals who brooded on the problem of war and national unity and what it meant for political parties. The restless mind of Bill Herridge, canvassing the situation as he saw it from Washington the week before the election, produced a formula which he put before Rod Finlayson in a letter prefaced with the not uncharacteristic remark, 'This is possibly the most important letter you will ever receive.'[64] (Skelton later explained to Mackenzie King that when he found himself dealing with the 'temperamental' Bennett on these questions, Herridge had 'been of very great help in preventing Bennett from going too far'; he was 'absolutely opposed to another war.'[65] Skelton in fact thought he had found in Herridge a fellow neutralist.) Now, with the League considering sanctions against Italy, Herridge told Bennett, through Finlayson, that sanctions meant war. He explained that he had sent his brother-in-law a cipher message urging him to take the position that 'the Parliament of Canada alone is empowered to make the decision [on accepting sanctions] now required of us.' In his letter he begged him to make a statement 'that hereafter, no compulsion will be put upon any Canadian to leave the shores of Canada to engage in a war in Europe or elsewhere.' Herridge disclaimed any intention of playing politics with a matter so vital to the national life; but he did say that if Bennett took his advice 'he will succeed in obtaining the support of sober and decent people, French and English, from one end of the country to the other.'

What Herridge was doing was reviving, in a more extreme form, the doctrine of Meighen's Hamilton speech of 1925 (above, page 74), which was an unsuccessful attempt to gain Quebec support for the Conservative party. Bennett did not take his advice. There is no reason to believe that if he had the result would have been any different from that of 1925. But the idea Herridge had produced may have lived on in Conservative circles; for in March 1939 another Conservative leader, R.J. Manion, proclaimed it as party policy, with important results (below, page 242).

TRADE WAR WITH JAPAN

In 1935 the Bennett government became involved in what can only be called a trade war with Japan. The trouble was adjusted after the change of government.

The episode offers a good opportunity for examining the general picture of Canadian trade. In these years before the Second World War the Dominion still traded, basically, with only two countries: Britain and the United States. All else was minor. Combining the figures of the dollar value of Canadian imports and exports from and to each country in 1934, we find that the United States was still Canada's chief 'trading partner,' the total coming and going being in round figures $458 million. For the United Kingdom the equivalent figure was $394 million. A very wide gap separated these giants from those who came next, half a dozen countries with roughly similar amounts of trade with Canada. In 1934 the third partner happened to be the Netherlands, with $23 million. Next came Germany, $20.5 million, and France, $19 million. Japan was sixth, with $17 million, a little ahead of Belgium whose total was $16 million.[66]

Japan and Canada had had a special trading relationship since 1907, when the provisions of a British trade agreement with Japan were extended to Canada. In 1913 Canada adhered to a new Anglo-Japanese agreement, which had the effect of giving Japan most-favoured-nation treatment. This arrangement still stood in 1935.[67] In that year Japan took the initiative in severing commercial relations. The diplomatic correspondence is in print,[68] and there is no point in rehearsing all the details. The Japanese considered that they had grievances against Canada, and it is evident that these centred in the imbalance of the two countries' trade* (in 1934 Canada sold $13.8 million in goods to Japan, and bought from her only $3.3 million), and in the Bennett government's emergency administrative trade regulations, which both Britain and the United States had complained of. Japan claimed in particular that she was discriminated against in the application of Canada's 'exchange dumping duty' directed against countries with seriously depreciated currencies – a breach, she asserted, of the most-favoured-nation principle. Canada denied any discrimination and pointed out that Depression conditions had aggravated the imbalance, since Canadian exports to Japan were mainly raw materials and Japanese exports to Canada mainly luxury products such as silk. 'Very strong anti-Canadian feeling' was reported to exist in Japan,[69] and effective July 20, 1935, Tokyo imposed a 50 per cent

* Canada had a 'favourable' balance of trade with almost every country except the United States.

surtax on Canadian imports. Bennett immediately retaliated by imposing on Japanese goods the 33⅓ per cent surtax provided in the customs tariff for use against countries discriminating against Canada.[70]

Although the Japanese let it be known that they wished to continue negotiations, a pause now took place. Skelton wrote to Marler, the Minister in Tokyo, that the government thought the Japanese action was 'simply an endeavour to apply the 'big stick' to a country they considered in a particularly vulnerable position in order to facilitate similar demands in other directions.'[71] But when King returned to power in October, he at once took steps, as we have already seen, to get relations back on to a normal footing. His visit to the Japanese Minister on October 24 (above, page 173) ended with him suggesting to Kato that it would be helpful if, 'as a method of approach,' both countries removed the surtax, pending further negotiations.[72] King was playing two roles which were certainly very agreeable to him: the conciliator, and the leader of the party of freer trade. Tokyo did not accept his suggestion; but on November 6 King signed a note to the Japanese Minister which recalled the satisfactory trade relations with Japan during his earlier period of power and went on, 'It is the policy of the present Administration to restore as speedily as possible the flow of trade between Canada and all other countries and not least Japan.'[73] Passing on to specifics, the Prime Minister mentioned various changes the government proposed to make in administrative practices, including those relating to depreciated currencies. He felt sure enough of a successful issue that on November 14 he announced that a settlement with Japan would soon follow the American trade agreement, then in the final stage of negotiation.[74] At the middle of December a precise proposition was made to Japan, including the provision that on goods of types not made in Canada the current exchange value of the yen should be used for the calculation of duty, while on other goods the rate should be the average value of the past five years. The 1930 provisions of the Customs Act relating to arbitrary valuations on imports would be greatly modified, provision being made for appeal to the Tariff Board, which could make binding decisions. On this basis the trade war ended, both countries cancelling their surtaxes effective January 1, 1936.[75]

The concessions made to Japan were not in fact special to that country, but were part of a general liberalization of trade practices which applied to all countries. To a large extent, indeed, they were by-products of the trade agreement with the United States, in which a majority of them were substantially incorporated. The exchange provisions applied, *mutatis mutandis*, to all nations. The new arrangements were reflected in changes in the Customs Act and the customs tariff enacted in the summer of 1936.[76]

Mackenzie King in 1937 was able to boast that his administration had ended another trade war which had been in progress longer. We have had glimpses of R.B. Bennett's deep dislike and suspicion of Soviet Russia's trade practices (above, page 143). It was argued that Soviet goods produced by forced labour were being dumped in Canada and other western countries. After receiving various strong representations (many of them from Quebec), the Bennett government in February 1931 imposed an embargo on the importation of Russian coal, wood pulp, pulpwood, lumber and timber, asbestos and furs. The Soviet government shortly retaliated with a prohibition of purchases of all goods of Canadian origin. This situation endured until 1936, when King's Minister of Trade and Commerce, W.D. Euler, visited Russia and negotiated a reciprocal end to the embargoes. Discussions then began looking to a Canadian-Soviet trade agreement. The basis arrived at was that Canada would grant most-favoured-nation treatment to Soviet goods, while the USSR agreed to purchase not less than $5 million worth of Canadian goods during the coming year. The arrangement was to be for one year only but might be extended for a second year by mutual agreement. The Russians announced their readiness to sign in August 1939. That, however, was the month in which they made another treaty – the non-aggression pact with Nazi Germany which cleared the way for Hitler's war. No Canadian-Soviet trade agreement was signed until 1956.[77]

Reading Mackenzie King's letters to the Japanese Minister in 1935, one might have thought that the world was on the eve of a golden age such as mid-nineteenth-century idealists had dreamed of, with all nations trading freely with one another and friendly competition in the arts of peace replacing the bloody and wasteful arbitrament of war. This vision would certainly have had a powerful appeal for the author of *Industry and Humanity*. King, however, was enough of a realist to know that the millennium was not just around the corner when he formed his new ministry. What was around that corner was the descent into the unparalleled horrors of the Second World War.

CHAPTER SIX

TOWARDS A NEW CATASTROPHE

PARLIAMENT WILL DECIDE

Those who lived through them sometimes remember the years immediately before the Second World War as in some ways almost worse than the war itself. The war was of course a dreadful experience; one was exposed to the chance of being killed or maimed (although Canadians who stayed out of the armed forces were not subject to these disagreeable possibilities); even the homestayers, even in Canada, encountered a degree of disturbance and deprivation. But (the elderly will tell you), you knew where you stood; you were irrevocably at war with a formidable and ruthless enemy whose policies were an outrage against human decency; your only aim was victory, your only salvation, resolution.

The pre-war years were different. The ruthless enemy was there in plain view, pursuing his steady course of tyranny and aggression; but everyone kept hoping that it would not be necessary to fight him. Everyone remembered the bloodbath of 1914-18, everyone hoped that somehow the common sense of mankind would prevent a repetition of it, everyone was frightened to death. The nations threatened by Hitler needed to be firm, strong, and united; they were scared, weak, and divided. Canadians, whose fate was essentially being decided on the other side of the Atlantic, were in the main mere spectators. What they could do was talk; and that they did, endlessly. We lived for years under Damocles' sword. Perhaps one's memory is deceptive; but it persists in asserting that there was actually something resembling relief when at last Britain and France decided that enough was enough and we found ourselves at war.

The springs of the policies Mackenzie King pursued during these unpleasant years we have already observed at the very outset of his new administration. Faced with only too evident divisions even in his cabinet and his party, to say nothing of the country at large, he laid down his formula at once: 'Our own domestic situation must be considered first, and what will serve to keep Canada united' (above, page 189). He made no secret of this, but declared it shortly in the House of Commons: 'I believe that Canada's first duty to the league and to the British empire, with respect to all the great issues that come up, is, if possible, to keep this country united' (March 23, 1936). He used his speech at Geneva in September 1936 to declare the principles on which he was acting: 'The nations of the British commonwealth are held together by ties of friendship, by similar political institutions, and by common attachment to democratic ideals, rather than by commitments to join together in war. The Canadian parliament reserves to itself the right to declare, in the light of the circumstances existing at the time, to what extent, if at all, Canada will participate in conflicts in which other members of the commonwealth may be engaged.'[1]

King enlarged on this in the Commons on January 25, 1937, in what may be called the first full-dress debate on external policy since he returned to power (neither King nor Bennett, now leading the Opposition, had encouraged extended discussion of the subject in 1936, though there was a considerable debate on sanctions on June 18). J.S. Woodsworth, the leader of the Co-Operative Commonwealth Federation, and a dedicated pacifist, brought it on by moving a resolution which proposed among other things that under existing conditions, 'in the event of war, Canada should remain strictly neutral regardless of who the belligerents may be.' King objected to this as tying Parliament's hands: 'This is something I could not accept for a moment. Parliament must be free to decide its attitude in the light of the circumstances as they may exist at the time. Parliament acting for the people is the supreme authority in the state with respect to all matters, and certainly with respect to what is most vital to the nation, namely, the question of whether or not it shall be involved in war. The policy of the present administration is that, in deciding matters of this kind, as the representatives of the people parliament shall be the voice of the nation; parliament shall decide.' When Woodsworth pressed him on circumstances in which Canada might be 'committed to war,' King said something more: 'Our policy is that parliament alone can commit Canada. I cannot make that too clear. At the present time there are no commitments, so far as Canada is concerned, to participate in any war. Equally, there are no commitments of which I am aware, or of which any one else is aware, whereby we agree to remain neutral under all circumstances. The policy of the government with respect to participation and neutrality is that parliament will decide what is to be done.'

Here were the formulas on which the government took its stand until the outbreak of war: 'Parliament will decide' and 'No commitments.' The former of course was not new; it had been used in Laurier's time, notably by Sir Frederick Borden in the Imperial Defence Conference of 1909 (Volume I, page 133). It was a convenient device for putting off decisions that might divide the country, and not much was said of the fact that it would be up to the Prime Minister and the cabinet (as leaders of the majority party) to tell Parliament *how* to decide. As for 'No commitments,' there were to be a fair number of cases during the next couple of years where King would refuse to take action which he felt might be interpreted as tying the hands of Parliament in advance of the ultimate crisis.

Meanwhile, the situation in Europe continued to deteriorate. Hitler, having begun to rearm Germany in defiance of the Versailles Treaty in 1935, went a step further in 1936. In March he ordered his army into the demilitarized zone of the Rhineland, thus not only breaking the Treaty of Versailles again but, more alarmingly, tearing up the Locarno agreements which had seemed such a victory for peace eleven years before (above, page 78). This, it has often been said, was the moment when Hitler could have been stopped, for his military preparations were still in a very early stage; but nothing was done. For this there were several reasons, but one was adequate in itself: the British public, full of guilt-feelings about Versailles, would not have supported military or perhaps even economic action against Germany: 'After all, they are only going into their own back-garden.'[2] In Canada it was at this point that Bennett and King agreed that a debate in Parliament would not be helpful.[3]

In July 1936 civil war broke out in Spain, adding new dangers to the European situation. Germany and Italy intervened actively on behalf of the insurgents led by General Francisco Franco; Soviet Russia sent aid in various forms to the republican government. The war thus assumed something of the aspect of a conflict between fascism and communism. Britain and France attempted to promote a policy of non-intervention by outsiders, with very little success. Volunteers rallied to the republicans from western countries. Many young Britons, particularly from the left, became deeply involved emotionally with the fortunes of the Spanish republic; their feelings are reflected in Pamela Hansford Johnson's novel *The Survival of the Fittest*. Feeling in Canada did not run so deep; yet over 1200 Canadians, many but by no means all of them Communists, went to fight in Spain, and hundreds died there. The Mackenzie-Papineau Battalion was a curious parallel to the Pontifical Zouaves whom French Canada (and French Canada alone) had sent to fight for the temporal power of the Pope in 1868 (Volume I, page 7); but the two cases remind one yet once more of the fundamental division in the country. The men who went to Spain, their history tells us, 'represented almost every ethnic group in Canada, apart from the notable absence of French Canadians.'[4] French Canada had no interest in saving the Spanish republic; almost universally, its sympathies were with Franco.

In a rather ineffective attempt to maintain an appearance of non-intervention and hold the balance even, the King government put through Parliament in 1937 a new Foreign Enlistment Act to replace the imperial statute of 1870; an order-in-council issued under it applied it to the civil war in Spain and made it an offence to accept service in, or recruit for, any of the forces contending against each other there.[5] The war dragged bloodily on until Franco's final victory early in 1939. Various nasty incidents in the course of it – notably the bombing of Guernica by German aircraft and the bombardment of Almeria by the German Navy – combined with the cynical disregard by the Germans and Italians of the principle of non-intervention which they had undertaken to respect, certainly contributed to a growing sense throughout the west of the essential brutality of the fascist powers.

Fascist brutality confronted Canadians directly with another problem: the admission of refugees. Hitler's persecution of the Jews drove many of these wretched people to seek asylum in more liberal countries. Canadian Jews, and Canadian humanitarians, pressed for opening the country's gates to them, in spite of the fact that Depression conditions had caused restriction of immigration. There was, however, opposition, most notably in Quebec, where anti-semitism, present everywhere, was at its strongest. Within a few months of Hitler's seizure of power, the Ligue d'Action Nationale was urging the federal government: 'That the frontier of Canada should be completely closed *sine die* in this time of general unemployment which weighs so heavily on the national budget; that the Government of Canada should remain completely inflexible in the face of whatever Jewish pressure, national or worldwide, may be brought to bear, to ensure that no consideration be shown to a group which is accused by Germany of Marxism and communism, and which in itself moreover could not be a useful element for Canada, being on account of its faith, its customs and its unassimilable character a source of division and dispute, and hence of weakness for the Canadian people.'[6]

Economic pressures were probably more effective than that from the anti-semites of Quebec, but in any case Canada did comparatively little for the refugee Jews. The total number of Jews entering the country was well below 1000 in every year from 1933 to 1938, both inclusive; a considerable proportion of these were admitted as refugees under special orders-in-council.[7] But the refugee problem only grew as Hitler overran more territory, and in 1938 Mackenzie King told his cabinet that the demands of conscience overrode political expediency. The result was predictable: the Quebeckers Lapointe and Cardin 'looked glum.' The demands of conscience were fairly easily satisfied: it was decided to ask the provinces how many refugees they cared to admit, thus placing Quebec in a position to influence the flow. It was also decided that the existing immigration regulations would continue to govern, though the responsible minister promised a generous interpretation.[8] It was not only Liberals who compromised with their consciences. The new Conservative leader, Dr R.J. Manion, who considered it his special task to recover a position in French Canada for his party, journeyed to Quebec City and made a speech opposing *all* immigration as long as there was serious unemployment. He seems to have made no specific reference to Jews, but everyone knew what he was talking about, especially as he recalled that when at Geneva in 1933 (above, page 166) he was 'pressed to permit refugees from Germany to come here,' but would have nothing to do with the idea. Indeed, the Toronto *Globe and Mail* headline frankly credited him with opposing admitting 'Jewish Refugees.'[9]

In this same year, 1938, an intergovernmental committee on political refugees was set up in Europe on the motion of the United States. The Canadian government took part in its work, though clearly without any great enthusiasm. Nevertheless, the Dominion was now doing a little more to alleviate the problem than it had done before; whereas only 748 Jews came to Canada in 1938, in 1939 admissions totalled 1763.[10] It was still only a drop in the bucket.

A MEASURE OF REARMAMENT

With the situation across the English Channel becoming increasingly menacing, Britain was driven to look to her neglected defences. Baldwin's government took this action reluctantly, in view of the economic situation, the pacifism of the public, and the determined hostility of the Labour party to military expenditure. But in 1934 steps were taken to strengthen the Royal Air Force, and in March 1936 (a few days before Hitler marched into the Rhineland) a White Paper on defence announced that the government was proposing a comprehensive rearmament programme.[11] In due course Mackenzie King in Canada felt obliged to take parallel action, at least in a small way.

As the reader knows, the Canadian forces had been at a very low level since the First World War. The Depression brought them still lower, for they were a special target of R.B. Bennett's retrenchment scheme. The Air Force was particularly hard hit, many officers and men whom the country had trained at great expense being discharged in 1932-3. In that fiscal year the total expenditure of the Department of National Defence was only about $14 million. In Bennett's last years there was some recovery, various construction projects of military importance being carried out as unemployment relief measures. Nevertheless, the country's defences when King returned to power were almost non-existent. The new government was told that the country did not possess a single modern anti-aircraft gun or a single tank; it had only twenty-five aircraft of service type, and they were obsolescent; there was not one service air bomb; there were no facilities in Canada for the production of rifles, machine guns, or artillery weapons. The Navy 'possessed two effective torpedo-boat destroyers, two torpedo-boat destroyers due for retirement, and one inefficient minesweeper.'[12]

King approached the problem of rearmament with due caution. Well he might, for here again we confront the special views of French Canada, upon which he was politically so dependent. All modern Canadian history proclaimed the sensitiveness of Quebec on such questions. Any measure to strengthen the country's forces was certain to be represented by some people there as indicating an intention to become involved in military enterprises abroad, in imperialistic adventures. Only after the Rhineland crisis and the British White Paper did the Prime Minister begin seriously to grapple with defence matters. O.D. Skelton pointed out to him that it was desirable to consider policy 'before the discussion is complicated by developments in Europe or proposals from London.'[13] In August 1936 a Canadian Defence Committee was set up, composed of the Prime Minister and the Ministers of Finance (C.A. Dunning), Justice (Lapointe), and National Defence (Ian A. Mackenzie). The creation of such a body had long been advocated by people interested in defence matters; Canada, they thought, needed some equivalent to the United Kingdom's Committee of Imperial Defence. The new committee was really not that, if only because it lacked the permanent secretariat which was a chief source of the CID's strength; it merely provided a venue for occasional meetings of leading ministers with the chiefs of the country's armed forces. The first such meeting was on August 26, 1936. The situation was surveyed, and King recorded: 'The impression left on my mind was one of the complete inadequacy of everything in the way of defence.'[14]

King, the complete civilian, clearly felt the need of guidance. Bennett would have turned to General McNaughton, who was now President of the National Research Council; but the very fact of the general's intimacy with Bennett ruled him out, it is fair to assume, as an adviser to King at this point. King, though such a convinced spiritualist, rarely consulted the spirits on matters of public policy; it is perhaps the measure of his trouble that he did so now. In a series of *séances* a few days before the meeting with the service chiefs he raised the question. His father reported a discussion with King's grandfather in terms which, one suspects, reflected a conflict going on in King's own mind: '... I have been telling Mackenzie I thought we ought to let Europe look after himself –, and our country take care of itself – and for us to keep out of their claws – he thinks we can't keep out – I would let them fight among themselves. He claims we ought to be prepared ...' When the Prime Minister asked the spirit of his old friend Larkin, the sometime High Commissioner in London, for advice on the international situation, Larkin replied in one word: 'Preparedness.'[15]

Nevertheless, what was probably the most influential advice King received came from a living and very practical politician, his old friend Stanley Baldwin, still at this time Prime Minister of the United Kingdom. King had a confidential talk with Baldwin in England in October 1936, and Baldwin (quite casually, it would seem) made suggestions that almost certainly left their mark on Canadian policy:[16] 'He thought that we should give attention mostly to air force; while Canada might be the last country to be attacked, the air force would be the most helpful of any in case of attack, and training of men for the air and plenty of equipment was the essential of modern warfare. He did not seem to think the navy was the thing to be concerned about, nor did he speak at all of the army.' The more King thought about this, the more the idea must have appealed to him. The Army called up memories of the divisive days of 1914-18, and above all of conscription; the Navy recalled the political crisis of 1909-13; but the Air Force had no such associations. It would be easier, it appeared, to represent a programme centring on the Air Force as a programme of home defence. At the same time, there was a sound military case for giving the air a high priority. Baldwin's advice is the likely origin of the King government's general scheme of defence, which in due course the Minister of National Defence revealed to the House of Commons: 'A certain amount of priority has been established after deliberation: first for the air services; secondly, for naval defence; and thirdly, in regard to the repairing of deficiencies in equipment of militia services, permanent and non-permanent.'[17]

In September 1936 the Joint Staff Committee (not yet called the Chiefs of Staff Committee) produced a specific programme of rearmament. It proposed a five-year plan to cost approximately $200 million, of which the Militia would get roughly $99 million, the Navy, $26 million, and the Air Force, $75 million. The first year, it was estimated, would cost roughly $65 million. These figures, modest as they now appear, appalled the government, for the current national defence expenditures, disregarding those for unemployment relief projects, were running at only about $23 million a year. In December, after some tough work in cabinet, the government accepted for 1937-8 a defence budget of about $35 million. It was absurdly small by comparison with the scale of the emergency which we now know was coming; but it was something. It is a notable fact that C.G. Power, who at first thought that this scheme might cost the Liberals 'the entire province' of Quebec, was won over by King's argument based on a programme centring on the Air Force to the view that the thing might be done. And the whole plan was represented to Parliament as 'a Canadian defence policy for the direct defence of our Canadian shores and our Canadian homes.'[18]

The government-imposed priority for the Air Force became more in evidence as the programme proceeded. In the greatly increased appropriations provided in the spring of 1939 (below, page 219), the air got about 49 per cent of the overall total. Of course, the theory that the programme was strictly one of home defence was largely political; precisely the same forces that defended the soil of Canada could be used for expeditionary purposes if policy made this desirable. This applied to air units as much as to the ground forces or the Navy; a squadron of fighter aircraft could defend Halifax, but it could equally well be sent abroad to defend London. Almost the only element in the scheme which was purely and necessarily domestic was the fixed coast defences, to which a good deal of attention was given. Here it is interesting that those on the Pacific were given complete priority over those on the Atlantic.[19] The main weight of British naval power was in the Atlantic area, between Canada and any European aggressor; and the British Admiralty favoured this priority.[20] It may be however that political motives were influential here too – Canadian isolationists were more sensitive about Europe than about Asia.

Parliament's reception of the increased defence estimates early in 1937 is interesting. The Conservatives in the House of Commons, who might have been expected to congratulate the government, said absolutely nothing, a tactic undoubtedly intended to be embarrassing. The CCF took the same line as Labour in the United Kingdom – blank opposition; they also voiced suspicions that the government had made secret commitments to Britain. King, of course, had problems in his own party. He attempted to meet them by a careful presentation in caucus:

> You read what Meighen said in the Senate yesterday, that the amount in the estimates was not enough, that we were concerned with the defence of the Empire as a whole; that the first line of our defence was the Empire's boundaries. We cannot accept that. But we can put our own house in order [so] that we shall not be a burden on anyone else – neither a burden on the States nor a burden on England. Meighen would do so much more – at least so he says – and Woodsworth would do nothing at all. The safe policy is the middle course between these two views – the safe policy is a rational policy of domestic defence.[21]

This did not entirely succeed in defusing the Liberal opposition. In February the CCF brought on a full-dress debate on the defence estimates by moving a resolution that the House viewed the increase with 'grave concern' in view of Canada's inadequate provision for social security. The motion was lost by 17 to 191, but the debate produced a portent. Normally few members of the solid phalanx of French-Canadian Liberals spoke in the House; they left speeches to their leaders. But in this debate no fewer than sixteen French-Canadian back-benchers spoke. Several spoke in French (at the cost certainly of not being understood by a majority of members);* more than one described himself as the humble representative of a rural constituency. They were against the CCF amendment; in many cases they declared their confidence in the King government; but with remarkable unanimity they expressed their dislike of the increased estimates. Most indicated that they accepted them because of the assurance that they were for home defence; but four declared their intention of voting against them.[22]

THE IMPERIAL CONFERENCE OF 1937

The latter part of 1936 brought the Commonwealth a searing internal crisis: the abdication of King Edward VIII. (Stanley Baldwin had adum-

---

* Mackenzie King's diary, February 18, 1937: 'As the speakers for the evening were, for the most part, from Quebec and likely to speak in French, I did not go back to the House ...'

brated the possibility of trouble with Edward in conversation with Mackenzie King nine years before.)[23] The united action of the Commonwealth governments (apart from Ireland) in this affair suggested that the Commonwealth could still act effectively together when occasion required.

Economic co-operation was also in evidence. Through the second half of 1936 negotiations for a new Anglo-Canadian trade agreement to replace that made in Ottawa in 1932 were taking place in London. There were a good many points of difficulty, but it is evident that the atmosphere was easier than in 1932. The agreement was finally signed in Ottawa in February 1937. It was a more liberal document than its predecessor, conceding reductions in duty on British goods under 179 headings; there were some material concessions on textiles. Norman Robertson, who was one of the negotiators, was pleased, feeling that the poor deal given the British in 1932 had now been set right.[24] On another Commonwealth trade front, negotiations with Australia were protracted and difficult, but modifications of the existing agreement were arranged in 1937, involving considerable concessions to Australian goods entering Canada.[25]

King George VI was crowned in May 1937, and the royal festival was made the occasion of another Imperial Conference. Mackenzie King, usually so insecure, set off for England in a mood of comparative confidence very different from that in which he had approached his first conference in 1923. He knew he would have difficulties, but the policy he had to pursue was clear to him and he was not sorry to escape for a time from the worries of domestic politics.[26] He took with him four of his cabinet colleagues, Skelton, Christie, and the senior service officers.*

The composition of this conference was rather markedly different from earlier ones. We have seen among the Dominions in 1926, 1929, and 1930 in effect a conservative group, consisting of Australia, New Zealand, and (when it chose to appear) Newfoundland, and a radical group, consisting of the Irish Free State and South Africa. Canada, though closer to the radicals than to the conservatives, was sometimes found playing a mediating part. Now the balance had changed. The Irish Free State in 1937 was under a republican government and did not attend the conference; it was moving into the neutral position which it formally adopted in September

---

* L.B. Pearson of Canada House acted as secretary of the Canadian delegation, but the minutes show that he attended only five of the twenty meetings of the Principal Delegates. Skelton was virtually always there, Christie usually, and Norman Robertson occasionally.

1939. Newfoundland had gone bankrupt and reverted to colonial status. South Africa's position was peculiar. The leader of its delegation, General Hertzog, had, one speculates, already formulated in his mind the policy of neutrality into which he attempted (unsuccessfully) to carry his country in 1939. He was curiously aloof from the main controversies of the conference. On military matters, his delegation was content to talk briefly about South Africa's measures of strictly local defence. He showed a rather marked sympathy with Germany and no particular distaste for Hitler; he argued that Germany should be given back some of her colonies (though certainly not South-West Africa, which Hertzog's country had and proposed to hold).[27] The British Prime Minister, as usual, was chairman of the conference and played the role of moderator. For the only time in history, the office changed hands during the course of the conference; at the end of May, Neville Chamberlain succeeded Stanley Baldwin as Prime Minister and as chairman. The other British ministers who reported at length on various aspects of policy had ample opportunity to influence the conference.[28]

In these circumstances, Mackenzie King found himself, willy-nilly, in a confrontation with J.A. Lyons of Australia and M.J. Savage of New Zealand. These two Dominions, as we know, had not yet formally accepted the Statute of Westminster and had no great enthusiasm for the constitutional innovations of which it was the capstone. Both were still prepared to accept the idea of a unified Commonwealth foreign policy which Canada, since 1921, had rejected. Both felt menaced by Japan and in need of British protection. Both had relatively homogeneous populations of predominantly British origin, and found it difficult to understand the problems of a country having a very large minority of non-British origin which was exceptionally sensitive to the possibility of being dragged into the 'vortex of European militarism.' In the case of New Zealand there was a special aspect. Alone among the Commonwealth countries, New Zealand had decided to found its policy firmly on collective security and the League of Nations. While Mackenzie King, for the hundredth time, declared that the League should be limited to the functions of conciliation and mediation, Savage was prepared to commit his country to 'the automatic employment of sanctions (including military sanctions) against an aggressor.'[29]

On May 21 King gave the conference the message that was already familiar to Canadians.[30] He spoke of the diverse character of Canada which made it such a difficult country to govern. He asserted that majority Canadian opinion was 'emphatically against' automatic sanctions, and he proceeded:

It is when we pass from the question of League to Empire war relations that we touch a really vital issue and face the possibility of definite cleavage. It is an issue on which there has been wide and serious discussion, particularly since the intensification of European unrest and the fading of the hope that the League might solve the problem of Commonwealth war-time relations. There are many forces which would make for Canadian participation in a conflict in which Britain's interests were seriously at stake. There would be the strong pull of kinship, the pride in common traditions, the desire to save democratic institutions, the admiration for the stability, the fairness, the independence that characterize English public life, the feeling that a world in which Britain was weakened would be a more chaotic and more dangerous world to live in. The influence of trade interests, of campaigns by a part of the press, the legal anomalies of abstention, the appeal of war to adventurous spirits, would make in the same direction.

On the other hand, opposition to participation in war, any war, is growing. It is not believed that Canada itself is in any serious danger. It is felt that the burdens left by our participation in the last war are largely responsible for present financial difficulties. There is wide impatience, doubtless often based upon inadequate information, with the inability of Continental Europe to settle its own disputes. The isolationist swing in the United States, its renunciation of war profits and neutral rights in order to keep out of war,* have made a strong impression on Canadian opinion. In some sections of the country opinion is virtually unanimous against any participation in either a League or a Commonwealth war. There is outspoken rejection of the theory that whenever and wherever conflict arises in Europe, Canada can be expected to send armed forces overseas to help solve the quarrels of continental countries about which Canadians know little, and which, they feel, know and care less about Canada's difficulties, and particularly so if a powerful country like the United States assumes no similar obligations. No policy in Canada is more generally accepted than that commitments of any kind, involving possible participation in war, must have prior and specific approval by parliament.

King proceeded: 'Certain it is that any attempt to reach a decision, or take steps involving a decision, in advance, would precipitate a controversy that might destroy national unity without serving any Commonwealth interest, and that the decision given on an abstract issue in advance might be quite different from the decision taken in a concrete situation if war

* The reference is to the Neutrality Act passed by the United States Congress in May 1937, which went further in this respect than the acts passed in the two previous years.

arose.' He recalled that the increased Canadian military preparations had been stated to be for the defence of Canada, and that 'even so they met with wide opposition, and ... no party in the House proposed preparations for operations overseas.' And King concluded: 'I shall not attempt to forecast what the decision would be in the event of other parts of the Commonwealth actually being at war. Much would depend upon the circumstances of the hour, both abroad and at home – upon the measure of conviction as to the unavoidability of the struggle and the seriousness of the outlook, and upon the measure of unity that had been attained in Canada. That is not the least of the reasons why we consider peace so vital for the preservation of the unity of the Commonwealth as much as the unity of Canada.'

At the end of this speech nobody said a word of comment, but no doubt there was some hard thinking. During the rest of the conference King did not stir from the position he had taken: there would be no commitments. The result was that the conference took no action on foreign affairs and defence beyond laying down a few very general and innocuous principles. Lyons asked for a public declaration 'that the whole Empire stood firmly with Britain and believed implicitly in her policies'; to which King rejoined 'that he yielded to nobody in the importance he attached to maintaining a united front. If, however, some resolution were to be passed at the Imperial Conference which would afterwards become the subject of heated debate in the Dominion Parliaments, that would be the course of events most likely of all to impair that united front.'[31] Australia also wanted a resolution under which the members of the Commonwealth would 'prepare plans for their common defence.' Inevitably, King would have nothing to do with this.* The British government was anxious for the development of arrangements for munition production overseas, and looked particularly to Canada. King was as anxious to avoid the appearance of commitments here as anywhere else, and the report of the conference's committee on munitions and food supplies was reviewed by him with special care.[33] It was not published, but the paragraph on this matter in the published proceedings of the conference, and the succeed-

---

* The King Papers contain Loring Christie's characteristically acid comments on the Australian project.[32] On the suggestion that it might be optional with each Dominion whether to take part in the planning, he says: 'There is also the calculated impertinence of this suggestion. Those who need General Staff plans can get their Staffs to work without resolutions.' It was just as well that these remarks were strictly confidential.

ing paragraph on defence matters generally, may be quoted as illustrating the caution which King's attitude imposed:

> The Conference gave careful attention to the question of munitions and supplies required for defence both by the United Kingdom and other parts of the Commonwealth, and also to the question of the supply of food and feeding stuffs in time of emergency. The Conference was impressed with the value of the free interchange of detailed technical information and recommended that it should be continued between the technical officers of the Governments concerned, it being understood that any questions of policy arising ... would be submitted to the respective Governments concerned and that each Government reserved to itself complete freedom of decision and action.
>
> In the course of the discussions, the Conference found general agreement among its members that the security of each of their countries can be increased by co-operation in such matters as the free interchange of information concerning the state of their naval, military and air forces, the continuance of the arrangements already initiated by some of them for concerting the scale of the defences of ports, and measures for co-operation in the defence of communications and other common interests. At the same time the Conference recognized that it is the sole responsibility of the several Parliaments of the British Commonwealth to decide the nature and scope of their own defence policy.[34]

That final anodyne paragraph was the product of literally hours of private wrangling between the Principal Delegates, in which Mackenzie King, dissecting the British draft word by word, insisted on eliminating every phrase that might suggest a commitment. Notably, the original document spoke of 'measures for co-operation, if and when the Governments of the British Commonwealth may so decide, between the forces of the several members of the Commonwealth in defence of communications and other common interests.' King's insistence on eliminating the reference to 'the forces' resulted in the formula just quoted.[35] The British, Australians, and New Zealanders undoubtedly found his editing tiresome and picayune; but it can hardly be doubted that those representatives of Quebec constituencies who had expressed anxiety in the Canadian Parliament in February would have seen in the original words the confirmation of their worst fears.

Although the members of Canada's Joint Staff Committee, and their secretary, Colonel H.D.G. Crerar, had come to London with the delegation, they were given (by Dr Skelton) strict instructions to avoid, in discussions with British officers, involving Canada in anything that might suggest a commitment. These instructions went so far as to forbid the officers to discuss with the British authorities what measures the latter might contemplate for the defence of the British colony of Newfoundland – though that island's importance to the domestic security of Canada was painfully obvious.[36] Sensitiveness to 'commitments' could not have gone much further.

That King was able to bend the conference to his will as he did was not due merely to the fact that he was Prime Minister of the senior and most powerful Dominion. It was due also to the support of the chairmen, and particularly of Chamberlain, who took the attitude (traditional in Imperial Conference chairmen) that minority views should not be overridden: he 'was clear,' he said on one occasion,[37] 'that no useful purpose would be served by publishing anything on which Delegations disagreed.'* The sessions left King with a deep regard for Chamberlain. Remembering his father, the great centralizer, he had viewed his accession with some apprehension; but Chamberlain's performance at the conference entirely dispelled this. King was particularly pleased with his reception of King's suggestion in his opening speech to the conference: 'enduring peace cannot be achieved without economic appeasement ... political tension will not lessen without abatement of the policies of economic nationalism and economic imperialism.' This was King's chief (and very modest) initiative at the conference. He did not venture to suggest publicly that it was time for an Anglo-American trade agreement; but he was undoubtedly delighted to hear Chamberlain say on May 27, 'The moral and psychological effect of such an agreement throughout the world would be tremendous.'[38] When Chamberlain told his cabinet colleagues at the end of the conference that 'the personal relations established should prove of incalculable value in the future,'[39] he was talking perhaps more prophetically than he knew.

It has been argued by an English writer that the British representatives in 1937 were stupid in permitting Mackenzie King to take charge of the conference as he did, with the result that 'Not one of the English [sic]

---

* Both H.B. Neatby and Correlli Barnett publish a remark made by Chamberlain in the meeting of June 7: 'Everyone must recognize the force of what Mr. Mackenzie King had said. There was no use making agreements here in London, if they are to cause difficulties in other parts of the Empire. He felt that the Conference would have to be guided by Mr. Mackenzie King on the Canadian aspect.' This passage was edited out of the 'final copy' of the minutes, presumably by Chamberlain.

objectives in promoting a co-ordinated imperial alliance – in strategy, military and naval organisation, industrial development or diplomatic effort – had been achieved.'[40] It was, of course, a little late to set back the clock, and to substitute a centralized empire for the league of British nations that had long been in existence. If King had been overridden, and the conference had produced resolutions from which Canada publicly dissented – and this could not have been avoided – the results for imperial unity, and within Canada, would have been quite incalculable. As it was, there is no reason to represent the 1937 conference as a stage in the decline of British power. It is possible that Neville Chamberlain, who as it chanced was presiding when King made his statement on May 21, was astute enough to take note of the Canadian Prime Minister's remark that a decision given on an abstract issue in advance might be quite different from one taken in the event of actual war (above, page 205). What King was saying was, if the British pressed Canada for a decision now it might turn out to be one they didn't like; they would be wiser to wait until the guns were firing, if they were going to fire. There is a striking parallel with the evidence of Sir John A. Macdonald before the royal commission on the defence of British possessions abroad in 1880: do not ask Canada for military contributions when there is no enemy in the field.[41] To take this advice was the statesmanlike course, and it can be forcefully argued, looking at the matter strictly from the limited viewpoint of the United Kingdom, that in 1939-45 Chamberlain's action paid enormous dividends – in the form of the First Canadian Army, the British Commonwealth Air Training Plan and its product, the contribution of the Royal Canadian Navy to winning the Battle of the Atlantic, and very large economic assistance. Weighed against these considerations, the advantages that would have been obtained from pre-war joint Anglo-Canadian military planning are comparatively slight. It should be noted that there was nothing whatever to keep Australia and New Zealand from making any military arrangements with Britain they might choose – provided they did not insist on passing public resolutions about it in the Imperial Conference. No doubt a more resounding declaration of solidarity from the conference would have had some diplomatic value for the United Kingdom; but the value would have been marginal.

TRYING A HAND AT PEACEMAKING

The night before the election of 1935 a distinguished group of the spirits of the departed, talking to Mackenzie King over the 'little table,' agreed that it was his mission to restore peace to the world. Lord Grey of Fallo-

don, whom King had loved on this side idolatry, said that though Grey
had failed to end war, King would succeed: 'God has chosen you for that
purpose.' On the assumption that the messages received over the table
originated in King's own mind, it is hardly too much to assume that this
represented a private aspiration of King's. After all, he had an impressive
record as an industrial conciliator, and it was an article of belief with him
that the problems of industrial and international peace were very much
the same. Had not the other Lord Grey introduced him to Violet Markham back in 1905 with the words, 'We call him the Peace Maker'?[42] In
fact, he made little effort, after his restoration to power in 1935, to play
the international peacemaker; he certainly knew that Canada afforded far
too small a power base to make such operations effective. In 1937, however, he made one striking attempt: he visited Adolf Hitler and tried to
influence him.

It was not a wholly new idea. When in England in 1936 King had
urged Stanley Baldwin to visit Hitler, and Baldwin did not altogether
reject the idea. King had already discussed with Eden the possibility that
he, King, might go himself, and Eden had urged him to do so. O.D. Skelton, however, discouraged the idea: King wrote: 'he still feels very
strongly that it would be resented in Canada; that it would only be flattering Hitler by having him feel that some more persons were coming to
him; that he was so much of an anglo-maniac, that nothing could influence him. That his speech three months ago that he was following his star
of destiny just as a somnambulist walks in his sleep, shewed how completely mystical he was, and unwilling to view [sic] anything to influence
him in any way from [a] different side.' How much, one is left wondering,
did Skelton know about King's spiritualism? It would seem, very little.
For the moment, King accepted his adviser's views; but the possibility of
visiting a fellow mystic sitting in the highest seats of power was certainly
one to attract rather than repel him.[43]

Now in 1937, in London for the Imperial Conference, he met the German Ambassador, Joachim von Ribbentrop (once, for a time, a resident of
Ottawa), who invited him to visit Germany and undertook to arrange a
meeting with the Führer. King talked to Neville Chamberlain and Eden,
who encouraged him to go. After the conference was over he left for
Berlin. Before departing he wrote to Joan Patteson, his partner in the
'sittings' at the little table: 'All is part of a great plan. The forces that are at
work for international good-will and peace are going to triumph in the
end.'[44] This is clearly one point at which King's private spiritualistic life
impinged upon his political one.

To Chamberlain and Eden he had confided something which he had not said to the full conference and which he had never told the Canadian people: if Britain found herself at war with a European aggressor, Canada would certainly come to her assistance. Apparently he had expressed himself with some vigour; Malcolm MacDonald, the Secretary of State for the Dominions, reported to the British cabinet:[45] 'Mr. Mackenzie King was about to visit Germany, where he would see Herr Hitler. After expressing sympathy with Hitler's constructive work and telling him of the sympathy which was felt with Germany in England, he intended to add that if Germany should ever turn her mind from constructive to destructive efforts against the United Kingdom all the Dominions would come to her aid and that there would be great numbers of Canadians anxious to swim the Atlantic!' In Berlin, King called first on the British Ambassador, Sir Neville Henderson, who gave him a not unfavourable account of Hitler: the dictator was an idealist, and 'there is a lot England can learn from Germany in the treatment of masses of the people.'[46] The Prime Minister also saw Hermann Göring, the Reichsmarshal, and Baron von Neurath, the Foreign Minister; the venerable baron seems to have reminded him of his old patron, Sir William Mulock.[47] But the great experience, of course, was the interview with Adolf Hitler on June 29.

That wise woman, Violet Markham, who knew King well, had warned him against being overborne by the dictator's personality. This, she said, apparently made a considerable impression on those who saw him: 'All the same don't let him hypnotize you! ... He is the head of a detestable system of force and persecution and real horrors go on in Germany today for which he is responsible.'[48] The warning went unheeded; King allowed himself to be hypnotized by Hitler.

King wrote two long accounts of the interview: one in his diary, and the other a memorandum of which he sent copies to Chamberlain and Eden.[49] The former contains some personal description not found in the memorandum. Hitler flattered King, not only by receiving him in a markedly friendly manner but by extending an interview which was supposed to last half an hour or perhaps somewhat longer to nearly an hour and a half. King praised what he had seen and heard of his host's 'effort to improve the conditions of the working classes and those in humble circumstances,' and, inevitably, spoke of his own work in the Department of Labour in Canada. Passing on to the European situation, he spoke of how his government had felt obliged to bring in larger estimates for defence, the result of fear aroused 'by what was taking place in Germany in the way of increased outlays for war purposes.' He went on (his memorandum relates) to remark 'That I thought it was only right to say that if the time ever came when any part of the Empire felt that the freedom which we all enjoyed was being impaired through any act of aggression on the part of a foreign country, it would be seen that all would join together to protect the freedom which we were determined should not be imperilled.' (He did not speak of Canadians swimming the Atlantic, though he did say that far more would have attended the recent Coronation if ship and hotel accommodation had been available.) He mentioned Canada's purely voluntary effort during the Great War. It would seem that his customary weakness of wrapping his ideas in a mist of words affected him at this moment, and one wonders whether the vital point he sought to make penetrated Hitler's consciousness.

Hitler on his side said 'in a most positive and emphatic way that there would be no war so far as Germany was concerned.' Another war 'would mean the decimation of Europe.' He and all the members of his government had been through the late war: 'They knew what war meant, and they did not want others to go through a like experience.' He spoke, King reported, 'with great calmness, moderation, and logically and in a convincing manner.' This was King's summary for the benefit of the British statesmen:

I confess that the impression gained by this interview was a very favourable one. As I told Herr Hitler in the course of the interview, what he said was a relief to my mind because of the very positive manner in which he spoke of the determination of himself and his colleagues not to permit any resort to war. I did feel very strongly that he had big problems within the country which he had to meet. He impressed me as a man of deep sincerity and a genuine patriot. I felt increasingly in the course of my stay that there were conditions in Germany itself which accounted for much that had been done there which it was difficult to understand beyond its borders.

In the diary King described the dictator as he saw him. His face, he said, was 'much more prepossessing' than pictures showed. 'It is not that of a fiery, over-strained nature, but of a calm, passive man, deeply and thoughtfully in earnest. His skin was smooth; his face did not present lines of fatigue or weariness; his eyes impressed me most of all. There was a liquid quality about them which indicates keen perception and profound sympathy.' When King praised 'the constructive side of his work,' Hitler 'smiled very pleasantly and indeed had a sort of appealing and affectionate look in his eyes.' The smile particularly struck the visitor: 'He has a very nice, sweet smile, and one could see how particularly humble folk would come to have a profound love for the man.' Clearly, King was bowled over. Perhaps his most revealing remark about the interview is, 'As I talked with him I could not but think of Joan of Arc. He is distinctly a mystic.'*

Whatever Chamberlain and Eden may have thought when they received King's memorandum of the conversation, the professionals in the British Foreign Office had no difficulty in restraining their enthusiasm. Sir Orme Sargent, an assistant under secretary of state, wrote, 'It is curious how easily impressed & reassured Hitler's visitors are when Hitler tells them that Germany needs to expand at somebody else's expense but of course does not want war!'[51] King, however, remained under Hitler's spell. His private survey at the end of 1937 said: 'clearly the purpose of God is related to my securing the good will of [between?] Germany & the Brit. Empire, working with Hitler towards this end, and saving France thereby & much else.'[52] As the months passed and evidence accumulated of the dictator's aggressive intentions, the evident facts contended in King's mind with his unwillingness to believe ill of the man who had so impressed him. In March 1938, after Hitler's seizure of Austria, King could still write: 'I am convinced he is a spiritualist – that he has a vision to which he is being true ... his devotion to his mother – that Mother's spirit is I am certain his guide ... I believe the world will yet come to see a very great man – mystic, in Hitler ... much I cannot abide in Nazism – the regimentation – cruelty – oppression of Jews ... but Hitler him[self], the peasant – will rank some day with Joan of Arc among the deliverers of his people, & if he is only careful may yet be the deliverer of Europe ...'[53] Only with the outbreak of war did disillusionment finally come to King. On January 23, 1940, he noted in his diary, with respect to General Hertzog's continued refusal to believe that Hitler's aim was world domination: 'I shared that view myself at the time but I have changed it in the light of what has developed since this war began. Germany could not have developed the military machine she has nor proceeded in any way she did unless she were bent on world domination by terror and violence.'[54]

AGGRESSION AND APPEASEMENT: MUNICH

The British response to the threat of Nazi aggression was the policy known as appeasement: a word which, as a result of the policy's disastrous

---

* The comparison with Joan of Arc was not original with King. In 1936 Walter Riddell had told King that Sir John Simon had made it after returning from Germany. Simon too did not think that Hitler 'had any warlike intentions.'[50]

failure, fell in time into disrepute and derision. In its day, however, it was a very respectable word, and not least in Canada, for it stood for the attempt to avert another world war.

The roots of appeasement we have already noticed: the determined pacifism of the British public, and their belief that Germany had been ill-treated in 1919. This was a fund upon which Hitler was able to draw, and it was long before the account was exhausted. The first great landmark of appeasement was the British refusal to take action when Hitler remilitarized the Rhineland in 1936. The year 1937 (when Mackenzie King visited Hitler) was comparatively quiet. Lord Halifax, Lord President of the Council, followed in King's footsteps later in the year, but had a less pleasant interview with Hitler. Early in 1938 Anthony Eden, a less committed appeaser than Chamberlain, resigned as Foreign Secretary and Halifax succeeded him. In March came the *Anschluss*: Hitler's forcible and brutal absorption of Austria. Chamberlain was shocked and shaken, but there was no action he could take. In the House of Commons next day Winston Churchill said the obvious thing: 'Europe is confronted with a programme of aggression, nicely calculated and timed, unfolding stage by stage.'[55] But it was still possible to argue that Austria was, after all, a German-speaking state, and if Germany took it over it was none of Great Britain's business.

Czechoslovakia was next, and Hitler's tempo was quickening. In Czechoslovakia too there were Germans – those of the Sudetenland, occupying the areas which conveniently contained Czechoslovakia's border fortifications covering Prague. The welfare of these people gave Hitler the pretext for his crisis. It burst on September 12, 1938, with Hitler's demand for self-determination for the Sudeten Germans, and it brought the world to the brink of war.[56] On September 15 Neville Chamberlain (who had never flown before) made the first of three flights to Germany to see Hitler. Britain and France brought pressure on Czechoslovakia to surrender the Sudeten areas to Germany. Chamberlain again flew to Germany on September 22, met Hitler at Godesberg, and found to his dismay that he had increased his demands. He now threatened to march into Czechoslovakia within a week. The British Prime Minister returned home and it seemed that war was now unavoidable. On September 27 shelter-trenches were being dug in the London parks and gas-masks were being distributed; on the 28th the British fleet was mobilized. That day, however, Hitler invited Britain, France, and Italy to a conference at Munich. The invitation was accepted with intense relief, Chamberlain made his third flight, and in the early hours of September 30 the four powers made an agreement allowing Germany to occupy the Sudeten areas over a ten-day period beginning October 1. The republic of Czechoslovakia was dismembered. Hitler had won a great victory without fighting. His only concession was to take his loot by courtesy of a conference of the powers instead of by mere seizure. Chamberlain, returning to London flourishing a paper by which he and Hitler agreed that it was the desire of their peoples 'never to go to war with one another again,' said, 'I believe it is peace for our time.' He qualified this a few days later. That was wise.[57]

In Canada the impact of the 'Munich crisis' was only less than in Britain. The present writer was in Toronto that week. I remember the atmosphere vividly. Walking down Bay Street one actually sensed the fear of war in the air; certainly it was on the set faces of the passers-by. I have never had such another experience, before or since. And when the crisis was resolved – even though it was by the sacrifice of a weak and helpless democratic state – the sense of relief, and of momentary gratitude to the peacemaker Chamberlain, was equally overwhelming. A few days later in New Jersey I was genuinely shocked when a newsreel of Munich was introduced with the title 'First Films of Chamberlain's Surrender.' The Americans had a more detached attitude to the episode than we Canadians.

Mackenzie King was a thoroughgoing adherent of appeasement. He – and certainly the vast majority of his countrymen – was for any policy that seemed likely to stave off war. And he had special personal reasons – the confidence both in Adolf Hitler and in the chief appeaser, Chamberlain, which had been implanted in him by his contacts with them in the summer of 1937. It has been pointed out that here we have an exception to King's lifelong opposition to the idea of a common Empire foreign policy: he consistently placed the support of the Canadian government behind Whitehall's policy of appeasing Germany.[58] His contribution to the solution of the Czech crisis was to send a message to Chamberlain on September 14 expressing 'profound admiration' for his decision to visit Hitler, and giving the text of a statement issued to the Canadian press applauding Chamberlain's 'striking and noble action'; and another message to the British Ambassador in Berlin requesting him, if he thought it would be helpful, to transmit a message from King to von Ribbentrop saying: 'Should opportunity permit, I should be deeply grateful if you could let Herr Hitler know how thankful I am that he and Mr. Chamberlain are to meet each other tomorrow and have a conference together, and how sincerely I hope and believe that their joint efforts may serve to preserve and further the peace of the world and the wellbeing of mankind.' A few days later King received an acknowledgement from Ribbentrop through the Acting German Consul General in Ottawa, assuring him that his message would be sent to the Führer.[59] Hitler himself does not seem to have acknowledged it.

At the first news of the Munich agreement, King sent off, and at once published, a message to Chamberlain:

> The heart of Canada is rejoicing tonight at the success which has crowned your unremitting efforts for peace. May I convey to you the warm congratulations of the Canadian people and with them, an expression of their gratitude, which is felt from one end of the Dominion to the other.
>
> My colleagues in the Government join with me in unbounded admiration at the service you have rendered mankind. Your achievements in the past month alone will ensure you an abiding and illustrious place among the great conciliators whom the United Kingdom, the British Commonwealth of Nations and the whole world will continue to honour ...

There is little doubt that King did speak for Canada at that moment. His countrymen may not have been quite so fully with him in the equally fulsome message of thanks which he felt moved to send to President Roosevelt, whose contribution to the settlement had consisted merely of sending telegrams exhorting the powers to keep the peace.

In London the voices of the Dominions were virtually unanimous in the crisis in urging the British government to put pressure on the Czechs to surrender to Hitler. Though Vincent Massey had been told not to attend the High Commissioners' collective meetings with the Secretary of State for the Dominion, at this moment he informed Ottawa that he proposed to do so, and was not forbidden. He had no instructions, and spoke 'as an individual,' but he supported Bruce of Australia, who was particularly voluble in favour of putting the screws on Czechoslovakia. Only one Dominion did not take this line. The New Zealand High Commissioner was absent, and his representative remained silent.[60]

Thanks to King's diary, we can reconstruct in some detail the reactions of his cabinet to the crisis. On September 23 it discussed whether a statement should be issued defining Canada's position. Two senior French Canadians, Lapointe and Cardin, were absent, as was Rinfret; Lapointe was representing Canada at Geneva. King polled the members. There were differences of opinion, but they were not violent. C.G. Power reported that he found opinion in Quebec 'much less antagonistic' to supporting Britain than he had expected. 'Ilsley was strong for immediate promise of co-operation and an immediate public statement.' Mackenzie agreed. W.D. Euler, from the German area of south-western Ontario, and J.-E. Michaud, an Acadian from New Brunswick, were notable among those who hung back. It was decided to issue no statement at present. King cabled Lapointe asking his opinion (he would certainly have done nothing drastic without his advice). The reply showed that Lapointe was deeply troubled:[61]

Cannot see that any statement should be made, prior to an outbreak of war. Situation in important parts of Canada extremely delicate and requires most careful handling. Public opinion will have to be prepared, not aroused by irrevocable steps ... Submit that Parliament should be summoned, if war declared, and no definite commitment made meanwhile ...

I do not see how I could advise any course of action that would not only be opposed to personal convictions and sacred pledges to my own people but would destroy all their confidence and prevent me from carrying weight and influence with them for what might be essential future actions. Please consider these views and submit them to colleagues before reaching final decision. God help you. I still strongly feel that conflagration shall be avoided.

On September 27 the cabinet met again, under the shadow of immediate war. Chamberlain had just made a broadcast in which he called it 'horrible, fantastic, incredible' that Britain should be preparing for war 'because of a quarrel in a far-away country between people of whom we know nothing.' His critics have not allowed these words to be forgotten. But he also said: 'I would not hesitate to pay even a third visit to Germany, if I thought it would do any good ... I am myself a man of peace to the depths of my soul. Armed conflict between nations is a nightmare to me; but if I were convinced that any nation had made up its mind to dominate the world by fear of its force, I should feel that it must be resisted. Under such a domination, life for people who believe in liberty would not be worth living; but war is a fearful thing, and we must be very clear, before we embark on it, that it is really the great issues that are at stake.'[62] With these words in their ears, the Canadian ministers began their discussion. Cardin was now present. He said little, but one gathers that his silence was eloquent. Dandurand pressed the 'complete isolationist point of view,' King says, but neither he nor Cardin actually opposed the majority decision, which was to issue a statement, though not a statement committing the country to fight. It said that the government was keeping in touch with the grave situation abroad and making preparations 'for any contingency and for the immediate summoning of Parliament if the efforts which are still being made to preserve the peace of Europe should fail.' It continued:

For our country to keep united is all-important. To this end, in whatever we say or do, we must seek to avoid creating controversies and divisions that might seriously impair effective and concerted action when Parliament meets.

The Government is in complete accord with the statement Mr. Chamberlain has made to the world today.

No actual commitment had been made, but it was pretty clear that the government had accepted the Chamberlain policy, wherever it might lead. King recorded that Cardin and Dandurand felt that 'going as far as Council had decided, would probably cost us many seats in Quebec.'[63]

A year later, when war was almost certain, the Prime Minister told Lord Tweedsmuir that if it had come in September 1938: 'I wd. not have had a united Cabinet, that Lapointe Cardin & Power (I might have added Rinfret)* wd. probably have resigned, & there wd. have been difficulty besides in fighting for Czecho-Slovakia.'[64] In the light of what he wrote in 1938, he probably exaggerated somewhat. It is hard to believe that Lapointe would have deserted King, and there is really no suggestion of it in the telegram he sent him. Nevertheless, in the following January he did mention the possibility of resigning (below, page 238); and this perhaps was what King remembered. King, it may be noted, had followed Lapointe's advice in maintaining the formula that Parliament would decide. Nor does Power seem to have given any indication of resignation; he was not present on September 27. Cardin, perhaps, might have gone; one remembers his resignation in 1942. Of the general proposition, that unity was less complete in 1938 than it was in 1939, there seems no doubt. King's own attitude is quite clear, though he seems to have refrained from pressing his views at the cabinet table; it is what we would have expected from what we know of him (above, pages 72, 81). He explained himself privately to two of his colleagues as the crisis came on:

I made it clear to both Mackenzie and Power that I would stand for Canada doing all she possibly could to destroy those Powers which are basing their action on *might* and not on *right*, and that I would not consider being neutral in this situation for a moment. They both agreed that this would be the Cabinet's view, Power saying that a coalition might be necessary, with some of the Quebec men leaving the party. I told him that the Cabinet Ministers should realize that it would be the end of Quebec if any attitude of that kind were adopted by the French Canadians in a world conflict such as this one would be. They, as members of the Government, ought to lead the Province in see-

* Fernand Rinfret, Secretary of State. He died in July 1939.

ing its obligation to participate, and making clear the real issue and what it involves ...[65]

As the situation developed, King's confidence in Hitler's good intentions seems to have weakened. Recording Lapointe's hope that war might yet be averted, he wrote: 'That is our natural instinct but it looks to me as though Hitler was determined to challenge, if need be, the world, probably with the understanding that he has with his allies, Italy and Japan.'[66]

THE ACCELERATION OF REARMAMENT

The changes that the September crisis of 1938 had brought to the world and to Canada were strikingly mirrored in the tempo of the country's military preparations. When the crisis broke the scheme, adopted with so many worries and misgivings, was proceeding in a relatively leisurely manner. The total expenditure of the Department of National Defence for the fiscal year 1937-8, the first year of the new programme, was $32,835,000; for 1938-9 it was $34,799,000.[67] It was clear to Mackenzie King and his colleagues that something much larger was now required. On November 14 the Cabinet Defence Committee met the Chiefs of Staff, who presented recommendations (too modest, they seem today) for increasing the estimates for 1939-40 by about $37 million, to a grand total of approximately $73 million.[68]

King wrote in his diary that day: 'In my own mind, what was proposed seemed reasonable and almost necessary in world situation such as we know exists today.' On December 16 the cabinet discussed the estimates. King wrote: 'Spent the afternoon in Council discussing Defence. All were agreed the World situation extremely dangerous. Even Quebec Members felt that considerable increase in estimates were [sic] necessary and would be approved. I proposed by way of a basis of discussion our doubling estimates in the fiscal year which would come to 70 millions, on condition that 36 millions went to Air Defence. After discussion, this was brought down to 54 millions, plus an additional 6 millions for training pilots. There was virtual agreement on these figures. All were in favour of keeping militia estimates to narrowest bound, increases to go to naval services and mostly to air.'[69] As a result of this fixing of an arbitrary figure, the total of the main defence estimates for 1939-40 was exactly $60,000,000.42. In addition, some $3,500,000 was provided for the retirement of borrowing for capital expenditure. Including supplementary items, the ultimate grand total of the estimates was $64,666,000. Small as it seems today, it was enormous by the low standards of the time and place. No remotely comparable defence spending had ever been proposed to the Canadian Parliament in time of peace. As a result of King's determined opposition to the Militia, it got only $21,397,000 in the estimates, though the Chief of the General Staff had asked for $28,657,000. The Air Force got $29,733,000, more than twice what it had received the previous year.[70]

Thanks to the larger appropriations of 1937-9, by the outbreak of war a good deal had been done towards remedying the consequences of decades of neglect. The Canadian forces were in healthier condition, though they were by no means ready for war. The supply situation was the main problem; Canada had only the smallest nucleus of a munition industry, and British industry, her traditional source of supply, was fully occupied in meeting the needs of Britain's own rearmament programme. By September 1939 the RCAF had acquired a few dozen modern aircraft, an organization of twenty-three squadrons (eleven of them regular) was being built up, and new air stations had been established and old ones improved. The Royal Canadian Navy possessed six modern destroyers (including four lately purchased from the Royal Navy) and was about to acquire a seventh. The Canadian Militia, though its training and organization had been somewhat improved, was armed with the weapons of 1918, and the Permanent Force (the professional army) was still only some 4000 strong. The west coast defences had been materially improved. The post-Munich estimates contained belated provision for beginning work on those on the Atlantic.[71]

As the ministers had anticipated, the increased estimates of 1939 had a comparatively easy passage through the House of Commons. There were still doubtful or hostile comments from French-speaking Liberal backbenchers; there was still opposition from the Co-operative Commonwealth Federation; the Conservatives, while not opposing rearmament in principle, attacked various details; but there was no amendment and no vote.[72] The point in the defence programme that attracted most attention was the one major move in the direction of rearming the Militia, the award of a contract for the manufacture of Bren guns in Canada for both Canada and Britain. The procedure followed on this was blown up into the proportions of a scandal and can hardly have failed to discourage the government from undertaking any further manufacturing projects of the same type.[73]

THE AIR TRAINING CONTROVERSY

It is a rather curious fact that this period when Mackenzie King was clearly moving towards closer co-operation with Britain witnessed one of the sharpest of those conflicts that led people in Whitehall to regard him as a prickly, difficult, unpleasant character: the controversy over British air training in Canada. This is already a twice-told tale,[74] so we can deal with it briefly.

The reader may recall that in the later stages of the First World War the Royal Flying Corps and afterwards the Royal Air Force operated in Canada a large air-training scheme. Great numbers of Canadians were recruited and trained for the British flying services, and the whole organization was controlled by United Kingdom authorities; it was, we said, 'a sort of state within a state' (Volume I, page 199). It is evident that these arrangements of 1917-18 were remembered in the Air Ministry in London, and that a version of them was important in its planning for expansion of the Royal Air Force and for another war.

The first tentative British approaches concerning Canadian assistance in carrying out the enlargement of the RAF which had been authorized came in 1936. They were made through both Air Force and ministerial channels. That summer the Minister of National Defence, Ian Mackenzie, was in London and was asked by Lord Swinton, the British Air Minister, what the Canadian government would think of 'the British Government having a Training School for airmen on Canadian territory.' After his return to Ottawa the suggestion was put before the Canadian cabinet and was negatived. 'The view of Council was to the effect that it would be inadvisable to have Canadian territory used by the British Government for training-school purposes for airmen. It is the intention of the Canadian Government to establish training schools of its own. The situation might give rise to competition between governments in the matter of fields, pilots, equipment and the like.' Doubtless there was also an undeclared motive: the desire to avoid any appearance of a commitment.[75] During the Imperial Conference of 1937 the Canadian Joint Staff Committee, meeting in London, recommended 'from a purely Service point of view ... that a Training Station under the control of the Royal Canadian Air Force, but financed by U.K., be developed in Canada and manned by the Royal Air Force for the training of R.A.F. pilots on the understanding that it become available to the Canadian Government in the event of Canadian mobilization.' Mackenzie King rejected this, as he rejected all the other suggestions of the Canadian service chiefs for co-operation with the United Kingdom.[76]

In the spring of 1938 there was another approach. A mission headed by J.G. Weir came to Canada to investigate the country's potential for aircraft production and, on the side, to discuss air training. On the former matter, King took the position that there was no objection to the mission having discussions with Canadian aircraft manufacturers, but the Canadian government would decline to give any advice or to act as an agent for the British authorities; indeed, he told the visitors he didn't want them to meet the manufacturers in Ottawa – some other city would be better. In the end, the British government placed considerable orders for aircraft in Canada. On the matter of training, there was trouble. Weir managed to make a bad impression on King, and unfortunately matters were made worse subsequently by a misunderstanding. In the discussions with King the British High Commissioner, Sir Francis Floud, twice mentioned that the RAF was anxious to enlist Canadians as pilots, and to have them receive their initial training in Canada. King's own record proves this, but later he forgot it, and both he and Skelton (who had read King's notes, but too carelessly) denied that Floud had said it. Shortly, information leaked out that training was being discussed. When the government leader in the Senate (Dandurand) said that there had been no request from the British government, the High Commissioner protested to King; he certainly thought, he said, that he had made a request. King then communicated with Neville Chamberlain, who, doubtless anxious to keep the Canadian Prime Minister sweet, agreed that the approach had been merely 'exploratory and confidential.'[77] The whole affair left a bad taste.

Here it should be explained that under arrangements that had gradually grown up a considerable number of Canadians were actually going to England to join the RAF.* For some years two graduates of Canadian universities or of the Royal Military College of Canada had been recommended annually for permanent commissions in the RAF. In 1937 an arrangement was approved by which each year fifteen candidates for short-service RAF commissions would be selected, medically examined, and given initial training in Canada. On completing their service with the RAF these officers would return to Canada and perform their reserve service with the RCAF, thus providing Canada with a reserve of trained pilots. Furthermore, as a result of the fact that considerable numbers of young Canadians were making their way to England in the hope of joining the expanding RAF, the British authorities asked the Canadian government, beginning in 1935, to arrange for medical examination of such men, and, later, to undertake to 'screen' them and recommend those found suitable for short-service commissions. At first this was done for only twenty-five men a year, but in 1938 Canada, with evident reluctance, agreed to increase the number to 120. These men were dispatched to England untrained.[78]

* None of these arrangements is referred to in any British official history that the writer has seen.

The Opposition having raised the question of British air training in the House of Commons, King made a statement there on July 1. Loring Christie (who had written a little earlier, 'My own working rule is that anything coming out of the Air Ministry is *prima facie* wrong or at least suspect') had produced a paper, which Skelton passed to the Prime Minister, asserting that the British plan for a flying school in Canada 'cannot be defended on grounds of constitutional principle, of history, of patriotism, or of morality.'[79] King knew better than to quote that, but he did borrow from Christie the statement that 'long ago' the Canadian government had established the principle that there should be no military establishments in Canada except those owned and controlled by the Canadian government. Neither King nor Christie took note of the RFC establishment in Canada in 1917-18. But the Prime Minister, under attack for having failed to co-operate with the mother country, made an offer: 'We ourselves are prepared to have our own establishments here and to give in those establishments facilities to British pilots to come and train here.'

Here politics raised its unprepossessing head. The Conservative party was holding a convention to choose a new leader (it turned out to be Manion), and Senator Arthur Meighen attacked the government before the convention for its attitude on air training. The same day King suggested to the cabinet that the British government should be told that Canada was ready to have British airmen come to Canada for training. 'I said I thought we should be prepared to go a considerable way in establishing satisfactory schools of our own. That flying was bound to be all important through years to come, and that the real defence of Canada would be from the air. That everything was to be said for our limiting expenditures on land forces, reserving naval services to the protection of coasts, but strengthening in every possible way the air branch of the Defence forces.' The cabinet agreed; Sir Francis Floud was immediately called to the meeting and asked to inform his government of the offer; and with equal haste the press was called in and told about it. Thus King adroitly pulled the rug from under the Conservatives.[80]

Implementing the offer turned out to be a little difficult. The Air Ministry in London might not be as bad as Christie thought it, but it appeared to be incapable of understanding that the Canadian government did not want Canadians recruited and trained by the RAF in Canada because this was inconsistent with its policy of no commitments. Within limits one can sympathize with the British airmen, for it did seem a little strange that 120 Canadians should annually be sent to England untrained, while Englishmen should be brought to Canada for training. Nevertheless, they would have been wise to accept the situation. The RCAF liaison officer in London undoubtedly put his finger on the nub of the matter when he wrote: 'I knew what the R.A.F. was after was really Canadian man power.'[81] When a visiting RAF officer submitted a plan in August 1938 it turned out to be a plan for training 300 *Canadians*. (It was at this point that Floud was infuriated by being told that the plan had been changed since the suggestions made by the Weir mission.) The Canadian cabinet was not prepared to proceed on this basis.* A revised plan, amounting to training in Canada the 120 Canadians annually sent to England, was also rejected. Finally, early in 1939, an arrangement was agreed by which the RCAF would give intermediate and advanced training to only fifty pupils a year from Britain; the existing schemes, including that under which the 120 Canadians went to England untrained, were maintained. The new scheme was to commence in September 1939; but the outbreak of war put a stop to it.[82] It was nevertheless the progenitor of the great British Commonwealth Air Training Plan then about to be proposed.

FRANKLIN AND MACKENZIE

For the historian it is pleasant, as it was for contemporaries, to turn from the anxieties and terrors of Europe to what seemed by contrast the irenic simplicities of international affairs in North America.

Mackenzie King took a proprietorial view of the state of Canadian-American relations under his government. It was all, he liked to think, the outcome of that call he paid on Norman Armour on Thanksgiving Day 1935 (above, page 173).[83] He indulged in this reflection during President Roosevelt's state visit to Lord Tweedsmuir, the Governor General, at the Quebec Citadel on July 31, 1936. And that visit might well serve as a symbol of an improved condition of things. Lord Willingdon, the reader will recall, had made a state visit to Washington in 1927, but neither President Coolidge nor President Hoover had seen fit to return it. Now, nine years later, another president at long last returned it. It was a striking occasion, a lovely summer day with military pageantry and the old city *en fête* for the President. Wrote King, 'It was friendship – good-will – peace – the blessing of all.' As Roosevelt departed he urged King to come

---

* In the cabinet meeting of August 10 the familiar division appeared. King recorded: 'I could see quite a division of feeling ... Rogers, Ilsley and Power and Howe taking a less critical view of the whole business than Lapointe and Cardin, though all saw the political implications and the danger that this step might seem a commitment of war [sic].' All, however, agreed that 'we should be in a position to co-operate in the event of Parliament deciding we should do so' – in other words, in case of war.

FRANKLIN AND MACKENZIE ON A GALA DAY

Mackenzie King and President Roosevelt on the occasion of the first state visit of a President of the United States to Canada, Quebec City, July 31, 1936. Lord Tweedsmuir, the Governor General, is seen in the background.

and see him: 'wanted to have a talk – perhaps I could slip down to Hyde Park.' And the Tweedsmuirs were invited to Washington. On March 30, 1937, they visited the Roosevelts at the White House.[84]

As the clouds gathered over Europe an almost completely new idea began to take shape in Canadian minds: the possibility that some day Canada and the United States might find themselves co-operating against a menace from abroad. Nobody thought of the republic as a 'hereditary enemy' any longer, but nobody had thought of military co-operation either. There had been a Canadian Legation in Washington since 1927, but when Vincent Massey had suggested that it might be well to have military attachés there and in London, Mackenzie King's comment was unusually vehement: 'damn nonsense.'[85] But now? A fortnight after his visit to Quebec, Roosevelt dropped a remark in a speech at Chautauqua, New York, just across Lake Erie from Canada: 'Our closest neighbors are good neighbors. If there are remoter nations that wish us not good but ill, they know that we are strong; they know that we can and will defend ourselves and defend our neighborhood.' When King was a guest at the White House in March 1937, there was a little – a very little – talk about defence co-operation. The situation abroad grew worse; and in January 1938, on the initiative of Roosevelt, exercised through Norman Armour, the Chief of the Canadian General Staff and the Chief of the Naval Staff, travelling in severe incognito, went to Washington and met their United States opposite numbers. The American officers, who clearly did not know that the President had engineered the meeting, were quite surprised about the whole thing; but some information was exchanged.[86]

On August 18, 1938, with the Czech crisis already making headlines, Roosevelt made another visit to Canada, to take part in opening the Thousand Islands Bridge and receive an honorary degree from Queen's University at Kingston. The latter occasion gave him an opportunity for a speech more outspoken than the one at Chautauqua: 'The Dominion of Canada is part of the sisterhood of the British Empire. I give to you assurance that the people of the United States will not stand idly by if domination of Canadian soil is threatened by any other empire.' This assurance was certainly welcome; listeners to the broadcast of the speech, I remember, heard the piercing whistle with which some youthful member of the audience greeted it. King himself welcomed it publicly two days later, remarking that Canada too had her responsibilities for defence, one of them being to ensure that 'enemy forces should not be able to pursue their way either by land, sea or air to the United States across Canadian territory.' He remarked in his diary that day: 'I think at last we have got our defence programme in good shape. Good neighbour on one side; partners

'THE PEOPLE OF THE UNITED STATES WILL NOT STAND IDLY BY'
President Franklin D. Roosevelt making his famous declaration at Queen's
University, Kingston, 1938. Principal R.C. Wallace of Queen's is visible in
the background.

within the Empire on the other. Obligations to both in return for their assistance. Readiness to meet all joint emergencies.'[87] This seems extraordinarily complacent. No joint planning had been done with the United States, and Canada had refused joint planning with Britain. The Canadian forces were far from ready to meet all emergencies. It might also be remarked that 'domination of Canadian soil' by some hostile empire was not an immediate threat. The threat was the imminent danger of war in Europe; and political conditions in the United States made it quite impossible for Roosevelt to intervene there with any effect.

The dangerous European situation undoubtedly exercised a degree of influence on economic relationships at this period, and specifically had something to do with the conclusion of a trade agreement between the United States and Britain in November 1938, and the simultaneous signing of a new agreement between the United States and Canada.

This is an extremely complicated matter, and the reader would not thank us for attempting to describe it in all its detail.[88] He may remember that at the Imperial Conference of 1937 Mackenzie King attempted to give some encouragement to the idea of an Anglo-American trade treaty, and that Neville Chamberlain went on record to the effect that such an agreement would have enormous 'moral and psychological effect' (above, page 208). That belief doubtless goes far to explain why the agreement was made; and yet nearly eighteen months were to pass after the British Prime Minister made that remark before the day for signing came. The explanation lies largely in the difficulty of reconciling an Anglo-American agreement with the Ottawa agreements of 1932. American politicians generally, and Cordell Hull more than most, intensely disliked the whole imperial preference system; while Britain and the Dominions were very loath to surrender such advantages as they had gained by Ottawa. In the particular case of Canada, it was soon clear that the United Kingdom could give the Americans the concessions they considered essential only if Canada gave up some of her preferences in the British market; an Anglo-American agreement could hardly be achieved unless the United States was prepared to give Canada some compensation for these sacrifices. The Americans on their side explained to the British that they would be 'blown higher than a kite' politically if they made concessions to an agricultural country – Canada – before being assured of an agreement with an industrial country – Britain – which could buy American farm products.[89] These problems were worked out only slowly and with much hard bargaining between the three parties.

The business began in July 1937 in uncertainty and some acrimony. Mackenzie King felt that the two other parties were waiting for initiative from Canada, whereas his view was that the initiative should come from one of them. In a rather unpleasant interview with Sir Francis Floud on July 29, King told him that he had seen a letter to Lord Tweedsmuir from the British Ambassador in Washington which contained the statement 'that Canada would have to be pilloried in order to secure the Agreement.' King said, 'the position was we would make no sacrifice without knowing what others were also doing, and without getting some compensation.' Subject to this, Canada was quite prepared 'to help the general situation.'[90] Perhaps this cleared the air a bit. The detailed negotiations that followed were carried on for Canada by the seasoned three-department team of Robertson, McKinnon, and Wilgress, who made a trip to Washington as early as October 1937,[91] and spent a great deal of time there from March 1938 onward. Wilgress later recalled that the American negotiators divided their time between his group and a British team, meeting the British in the mornings and the Canadians in the afternoons. Sometimes all three groups met together.[92] Early in November the American administration, though not entirely satisfied with the concessions the British had made, decided to accept the situation. On November 17 the two agreements were signed at the White House with much *éclat*, Hull signing for the United States, King for Canada, and Sir Ronald Lindsay for Britain.[93]

Britain had abandoned her tariff on wheat (the preference here had been of doubtful value to Canada in any case). Lumber and apples had been of primary importance to Canada in the negotiation; the preference on Canadian lumber in the British market was reduced, but this was compensated for by concessions by the United States, while Canadian apples continued to enjoy a substantial, though reduced, advantage in Britain. Canada obtained other advantages under the agreement with the United States; both codfish and food potatoes, on which no concession could be obtained in 1935, were now admitted at reduced rates on a quota basis. (The agreement, accordingly, was applauded in the Maritime provinces, but drew some boos from New England.) The principal concession made by Canada to the United States was the exemption of American goods from a special 3 per cent excise tax which had borne heavily upon them. Wilgress, in retrospect, remarked, 'for the first time Canada had succeeded in breaking down the more formidable barriers to trade with the United States.' The agreement brought material benefits to Canadian trade.[94]

In spite of the opposition of special interests, opinion in the three countries concerned seems to have been predominantly favourable to the agreements.[95] Much of the explanation for this is to be found in political considerations: there was satisfaction in the spectacle of democratic countries drawing together at a moment when the world was threatened by the advance of totalitarianism. As the *New York Times* put it, the Anglo-American agreement 'increases the hope of more effective cooperation among all the democracies in defense of peace and order.'[96] Secretary Hull had always believed that his programme of freeing the channels of international trade was in itself the solution to the problems of the modern world. This, unfortunately, was wishful thinking. Something much more concrete was required to stem the totalitarian tide.

The signing of the agreements brought Mackenzie King to the White House as a guest once more: another chapter in the developing story of his relations with President Roosevelt. As always, the President received him with flattering attention. At their first meeting in 1935 Roosevelt had addressed him as 'Prime Minister' or as 'Mr. King'; now King recorded, 'He shook hands very warmly, greeting me as he always does by calling me "Mackenzie."' It is interesting that the only people who ever called King by this name were Roosevelt and Winston Churchill. That they did so is surely evidence that their relationship with him was not particularly intimate. King never ventured to tell these two great men – as he did lesser dignitaries such as Mary Pickford – that his friends called him 'Rex.' And – as he confessed to Roosevelt in 1942 – he was diffident about calling the President 'Franklin,' though he did it.[97]

This is as good a place as any to look at the peculiar relationship of Franklin D. Roosevelt to Canada. John MacCormac wrote in 1936 that Roosevelt was 'more widely known to Canadians – even if only as a golden voice over the radio – than anyone who has ever held his position.' The present writer went further about three years later: 'Mr. Roosevelt is perhaps the first American President of whom it could be said that he was genuinely popular in Canada.' I went on to say that among the reasons for this, 'not least is the simple fact that he has contrived to make Canadians feel that he is interested in and friendly to their country.'[98] He had done this by a series of very simple acts – his unprecedented visits to Canada, the letter to Representative McSwain (above, page 154), the speech at Kingston; these strengthened the effect of the admiration generated earlier by his leadership in the days of the New Deal.

Turning the question the other way round, how is one to explain Roosevelt's evident special interest in Canada? He was certainly not obsessed with the country, but he seems to have had a more genuine interest in relations with Canada than any other President has ever had. The most striking evidence of this is his initiatives in developing common defence. We have seen the steps he took to bring the Canadian Chiefs of Staff to Washington in January 1938, when the American service chiefs had no interest in the matter whatever. (They were much more interested in Brazil; General George C. Marshall made a visit to that country in 1939, just before taking office as Chief of Staff of the U.S. Army.)[99] Even more striking, we shall see, is the fact that it was Roosevelt who brought about the Ogdensburg *rapprochement* with Canada in 1940, when there is still no evidence of interest on the part of the American Chiefs of Staff (below, page 311). No one seems to have attempted to discover the source of Roosevelt's interest by exploring his papers; perhaps, in the absence of a diary, such an inquiry would be fruitless. He is nothing if not enigmatic. Possibly as good an explanation as any is the one he himself gave during his visit to Quebec City in 1936: 'since the age of 2 I have spent the majority of my Summers in the Province of New Brunswick.'[100] Perhaps the Roosevelt summer home on Campobello Island held the secret.

Mackenzie King would certainly have claimed a large share of the credit for Roosevelt's interest in Canada; but one should be backward in attributing too much to his influence. It is true that it is only after the change of government in 1935 that the interest seems to kindle actively; but it can hardly be doubted that this is because the President thought Liberal tariff policies more favourable to U.S. purposes than those associated with Bennett. It is also possible, however, that he didn't like Bennett; and it must be remembered that, for all his awkwardness and insecurity, King when he chose was capable of exerting a great deal of charm, as his innumerable friendships with women testify. And cultivating good relations with wealthy Americans was a pursuit to which he was no stranger.

THE DEBATE GOES ON

We have noted above (pages 164-7) that the middle thirties witnessed the beginning in Canada of anxious public debate on the country's external policy in the light of the threat of war. The discussion continued and grew more heated as the European situation became increasingly threatening.

We have seen French-Canadian suspicion of foreign entanglements finding expression in Parliament, particularly in connection with the increased defence estimates. In English-speaking Canada a new generation of acerbic nationalist critics carried on the tradition of Clifford Sifton and John S. Ewart. They were based chiefly in the universities (where conservative governing boards often regarded them as objectionable) and found outlets for their opinions in the Canadian Institute of International Affairs (above, page 165) and in the *Canadian Forum*, an ably-conducted Toronto monthly of leftist views and small circulation. Notable among them were F.R. Scott, a professor of law at McGill, and F.H. Underhill, a professor of history at the University of Toronto. Underhill, a graduate of Toronto and of Oxford who had served in the British Army in the Great War, took particular pleasure in shocking the Toronto bourgeoisie:

> We must ... make it clear to the world, and especially to Great Britain, that the poppies blooming in Flanders fields have no further interest for us. We must fortify ourselves against the allurements of a British war for democracy and freedom and parliamentary institutions, and against the allurements of a League war for peace and international order ... As the late John S. Ewart remarked, we should close our ears to these European blandishments and, like Ulysses and his men, sail past the European siren, our ears stuffed with tax-bills. All these European troubles are not worth the bones of a Toronto grenadier.[101]

These extremely articulate academic isolationists, though they maintained what would be called today a high profile, probably had little general influence. Nor had the people who still upheld the standard of the now moribund League of Nations and collective security. The veteran John W. Dafoe, an ardent nationalist but no isolationist, continued to carry on the fight for League principles in the *Winnipeg Free Press*, while admitting that for the moment the League was powerless.[102]

One comment may be made about the isolationist critics.[103] In general they avoided what may be called the moral questions raised by the rise of Hitler. They passed over the suppression of liberty in Germany, the progressive extinction of liberty in the countries which Hitler overran, the campaign against religion, the all-pervading cruelty and violence of the regime, the obscene and murderous persecution of the Jews. These horrors, which aroused anger and disgust throughout the free countries of the West, were not good fighting ground for the isolationist professors, and they chose to treat them as irrelevant. But these things certainly played their part, and that no small one, in the gradual process by which the Canadian people reached a state of mind in which a war against Hitler became conceivable. Undoubtedly a good many Canadians who joined the forces in 1939 and later were moved by loathing for a regime to which one might apply the phrase coined by the young Gladstone for a less revolting tyranny long ago: the negation of God erected into a system of government.

Dafoe, speaking in 1937 at one of those academic conferences that provided forums for discussing 'the situation,' produced a classic summary of the divisions of Canadian opinion as he saw them at that moment. There were, he said,

1. The isolationists, mostly pacifists, who want Canada to do nothing at all, relying upon fate, luck, providence, Great Britain and the United States.

2. The isolationists who, while determined that Canada shall take no part in war, no matter how it comes about, admit that a country might properly provide herself with means for self-defence.

3. Those who hold that Canada should avoid all commitments in advance, but should not exclude the possibility of participation in war for adequate cause; and to this end should provide herself with armaments.

4. Collectivists, who are pleased that Canada is arming in the hope that this rearmament, as well as that of Great Britain, will mean a reinforcement of the League if there should be developments bringing it again into play.

5. Imperialists, who think Canada should merge her foreign policy and her defence policy with that of Great Britain; and are in favour of rearmament on the largest possible scale.

Group 3's ideas, Dafoe pointed out, were those of the King government.[104]

Dafoe's classification was, as he himself said, rough, and like all such things is open to criticism. It seems to me that his Group 5 reflects the conditions of a day somewhat earlier than 1937. There were certainly imperialists of the type he describes extant in 1937, but they were not very numerous. There were, however, a great many people in English-speaking Canada who, without holding opinions as extreme as those of Dafoe's Group 5, could not envisage the possibility of Great Britain's being involved in a war for survival and Canada's standing aside. These were the people whose opinions were decisive in 1939; and incidentally Mackenzie King was one of them. It is interesting also that Dafoe, throughout this speech, had nothing to say about the influence of French Canada. This, we have said (above, page 166), is not uncharacteristic of English-speaking nationalists. The great majority of French Canadians would have been found in Dafoe's Groups 1 and 2.

Dafoe went on to suggest what might happen if war came, in which case the policy of 'preserving national unity by postponing decisions' would no longer serve.

The classification of parties which I have submitted to you will be wiped out; and the people of Canada will begin to get on one side or another of a line which will run through every province, every township and through a good many homes as well. On one side will be the isolationists who will demand that whatever the issues and whatever the consequences to the outside world Canada shall withdraw herself from participation in the conflict. Some will support this policy from abstract principles of pacifism, some from fear, some from irrational prejudices, while many will rationalize their attitude and make out a case not without plausibility and strength.

On the other side, there will be all those who are not prepared to see Canada pull out, at the first threat of trouble, from the British Commonwealth, which, of course, would be the immediate and inevitable consequence of a formal declaration of neutrality; those who have not lost the vision of a world freed from war by the co-operation of nations of good intent who, I am very sure, are far more numerous than the politicians think; and those who hold that when Great Britain is in peril the right attitude for Canada is one of 'Ready, aye ready.' The issue upon which the war might come, the form it might take, the shadow it might cast of inevitable consequence if the free nations of Europe were left to their fate, might easily weld these divergent elements into unity upon a defined programme. In spite of much that I hear to the contrary, I think they would together constitute a great multitude.

It is clear that Dafoe considered that the forces in favour of intervention were going to be strong enough to carry the day. In this he proved a true prophet. In another respect, happily, he turned out to be mistaken. The grim picture he painted of Canadians in the crisis getting 'on one side or another of a line' never became reality. He envisaged 'profound disunion and national disintegration over an issue that perhaps cannot be settled by counting heads': phrases that suggest actual civil war. Nothing like that happened in September 1939.

Dafoe was speaking in 1937, three weeks or so after Mackenzie King, that acute assessor of Canadian opinion, had told the Imperial Conference, confidentially, that in Canada 'opposition to participation in war, any war, is growing' (above, page 205). During the next two years many things changed, and Canadian opinion moved on. The contrast between the storm that greeted the modest defence programme of 1937, and the relatively calm acceptance of the much larger estimates of 1939, reflects the movement.

The clash of opinions in the country at large had its reflection in the East Block of the Parliament Buildings at Ottawa. There Mackenzie King found himself increasingly in disagreement with his staff, and particularly with the Under Secretary of State for External Affairs, Dr Skelton.

We pointed out in the beginning (above, pages 12-14) that there were fundamental differences of view between King and Skelton. In spite of all that has been said about him by his innumerable ill-wishers, King's deepest predilections and prejudices were British, and we have seen that there is every reason to believe that he held from the beginning, and never changed, the opinion that Canada could not possibly hold aloof from a great war in which Britain was engaged. Skelton's views and prejudices were quite different, and King of course knew it. In 1929 he wrote, 'Skelton is at heart against the Br[itish] Empire, which I am not.'[105] As war drew closer in 1938-9, these differences came more and more into the open, and the reader of King's diary becomes aware of tension between the two associates. King is increasingly convinced that in this crisis unity with Britain is vital, and increasingly disposed to say so openly. Skelton, the neutralist,* is more and more disturbed by this tendency in his chief.[106]

The tension is very evident at the time of Munich. As the crisis begins, Skelton puts before King a forceful and bitter memorandum on the European situation, the main point of which is that every European state is considering it 'emphatically from the standpoint of its own interest and safety.' Canadians, writes Skelton, are coming to realize that they must approach such questions from a similar standpoint. 'Whatever our sympathies with Germany's victims may be, it is incredible that we would tamely accept the role cast for us by some overseas directors, namely, that every twenty years Canada should take part in a Central European [sic] war, sacrificing the lives of tens of thousands of her young men, bringing herself to the verge of bankruptcy, risking internal splits and disturbances.'[107] King's reaction to the paper was adverse: 'Excellently done, but ... I believe myself that whilst care has to be taken as to determining the part Canada may be called upon to play, and the steps toward that end, that [sic] our real self-interest lies in the strength of the British Empire as a whole, not in our geographical position and resources. That not to recognize this would be to ultimately destroy the only great factor for world peace, to lose the association of the United States and the British Empire and all that it would mean for world peace. That it would place Canada in an ignominious position.'[108] King used Skelton's 'every twenty years' gambit in a speech in Parliament the following year (March 30, 1939) by way of a sop to Skelton and other isolationists. It did not, how-

---

* I have never found a paper in which Skelton specifically recommends neutrality in 1939; but King was well acquainted with his views.

ever, express his inner views. Of a conversation with Norman Rogers, the member of his cabinet who was probably closest to him, King wrote in his diary on September 13, 1938: 'We both agreed that it was a self-evident national duty, if Britain entered the war, that Canada should regard herself as part of the British Empire, one of the nations of the sisterhood of nations, which should cooperate lending every assistance possible, in no way asserting neutrality, but carefully defining in what ways and how far she would participate.'

Whether King's views, progressing steadily towards open co-operation with Britain, reflected his reading of changing opinion in the country, or whether they were the result of the same circumstances that brought about the change in public opinion, would be hard to say. If public opinion influenced the Prime Minister, it had no visible effect upon his staff in the East Block. The little world of External Affairs and the Privy Council Office lived to itself, surprisingly oblivious, it would seem, to the greater world outside. The tone, clearly, was set by the admired Doctor, and of course it was isolationist. This seems to have applied also to the posts abroad, except where some senior and independent officer, like Massey in London, was in charge. In general the younger diplomats whom Skelton had recruited and trained tended to follow the Skelton line. At a moment of strain in January 1939 King felt very much alone, as he told his cabinet colleagues: 'I said I ought to tell Council quite frankly that I thought almost my entire staff was against me. That the intelligent[s]ia held a different view; that one of my staff [J.W. Pickersgill] had said to me that I had made an appalling statement in setting forth what I had,* and I thought it represented the views of practically all of them ... That I knew what the intelligent[s]ia view would be, and that I knew what a handful they were compared with the country as a whole, and that my business was to tell Canada of her dangers. Not of theories that could not save the lives of the people.'[109] To King the 'intelligentsia' was, evidently, primarily Skelton and the other members of his own staff, and, secondarily, the Underhills and Scotts who were addressing themselves to the public at large. As 1939 dawned the debate was still in progress; though in retrospect it seems that Munich had been a considerable turning-point in the evolution of public opinion, and that after the shock of September 1938 most Canadians had accepted the fact that if war came Canada would be in it.

* The speech in Parliament (January 16, 1939) in which King had quoted Laurier's famous remark that when Britain was at war Canada was at war and liable to attack.

CHAPTER SEVEN

1939: THE OUTBREAK

'IF ENGLAND IS AT WAR ...'

When Parliament met in January 1939, Mackenzie King lost no time in giving the House of Commons some indication of the nature of his growing convictions on Canada's position. On January 16, in the debate on the Address, he quoted Sir Wilfrid Laurier's famous dictum, 'If England is at war, we are at war and liable to attack,' and his further remark that it did not follow that Canada would always be attacked or would take part in all British wars, and that it would be for the Canadian Parliament to decide the extent of participation. This, he said, was Liberal policy in 1910, and it was Liberal policy 'as it is to-day and as it will continue to be under the present Liberal administration.'[1]

King's chief concern, it seems, was to make the point that Canada would inevitably be involved in a British war, because an enemy would make no distinction between the different parts of the Commonwealth. But many Liberals were shocked. What of the constitutional progress since 1910? What of the Statute of Westminster? His followers from Quebec were particularly troubled, and King ultimately felt obliged to try to back-pedal in a speech on March 30.[2] This was the pattern of the session. King was torn between his feeling that he must 'tell Canada of her dangers' and prepare people for the worst, and the contrary advice of his isolationist staff and his French-Canadian colleagues. After war broke out he reviewed these speeches and regretted he had not gone further in 'stating [the] probability of war and of Canada's probable part in any conflict that related to aggression.' The best parts of them, he decided, were those he had put in in the face of protests from 'S[kelton] and others at the office.'[3]

On January 26 King received a long Most Secret cable from the Dominions Office in London which amounted to a summary of the intelligence available to the British government concerning Hitler's intentions.[4] It implied that London now considered Hitler capable of almost anything. While stating that there was 'as yet no reason to suppose that Hitler has made up his mind on any particular plan,' it added that reports suggested several very alarming possibilities, one being that he might 'Make a sudden air attack without pretext on England and follow up this initial surprise by land and sea operations against Western powers. We have received definite information from a highly placed German that preparations for such a *coup* are now being made.* This person has, however, no information to show that Hitler has yet made up his mind to execute this plan.' King passed this frightening document (which had gone to all the Dominions and the United States) to the Defence Minister, and on January 27 he read it to the cabinet. From it he moved on to discuss his 'If England is at war' speech, and it became clear that some of his colleagues were more than doubtful about it. When King suggested that the cabinet had discussed the matter some time before and he had thought everyone had agreed, Ernest Lapointe said he must have been asleep at the time. Lapointe argued for continuing the policy of making no commitment until an actual crisis arose, and while agreeing that if Britain were attacked by Germany 'without question ... this country would be at war and into the war,' he went on to say that 'it might be necessary for some of them to consider whether they could do better in the way of steadying the people in their own parts, by being out of the Cabinet rather than in it – helping to explain the situation, etc.'

Faced with this suggestion of resignation, King replied that 'the greatest service we all could render this country in a crisis such as seemed probable, was that the Cabinet should be kept intact.' Everyone realized 'the very difficult situation that our French Canadian colleagues faced,' but if they were to go it would mean 'terrible danger' for their own people. 'I pointed out that a break in the Cabinet would mean an inevitable demand for National Government. That National Government might lead to anything, conscription and all the rest.' The way to avoid such a situation was 'for us all to stay together and not let the control of Government in a crisis of the kind, pass into the hands of jingos [sic] and

---

* See Lord Halifax's memoirs, *Fulness of Days* (London 1957), for the story of how a German staff officer gave this information to a member of the British Embassy staff in Berlin in a nocturnal interview in the Tiergarten.

Tories.' 'This,' King recorded, 'seemed to make an impression.' At the end of his description of the meeting he wrote: 'I confess I felt proud of the Cabinet ... There was not an acrimonious word in the discussion but a keen sense of profound responsibility. As the members left, Dunning turned to me, and said I had done a great day's work today, and had got things along a long way.'[5] Indeed, it seems probable that this false alarm (as it turned out to be) in January 1939 was a stage of some importance in the process that produced an essentially united cabinet in the following September.

THE IDES OF MARCH

A speech by Hitler on January 30, which London had feared might be the beginning of a new crisis, was in fact relatively moderate;[6] but the explosion was only postponed. On March 7 the British government hopefully told the Dominions that they were now inclined to think that Hitler had for the time being abandoned the idea of precipitating an immediate crisis.[7] A week later the crisis came. The attenuated Czechoslovakia that existed after Munich came apart under German pressure, and on March 15 Hitler's troops marched into Prague. The German dictator had torn up the Munich agreement, repudiated all his talk of having no further territorial demands and wanting no non-Germans within his borders, and made a fool of Neville Chamberlain. It was no longer a question of 'righting the wrongs of Versailles'; his plan of action was now revealed as one of naked aggression.[8]

After a brief moment of uncertainty, the British government adopted a new policy.[9] Appeasement had failed; containment was now to be attempted. The countries apparently marked as Hitler's future victims were to be promised support; an anti-Hitler front was to be created capable of meeting force with force. In association with France, Britain proceeded to offer guarantees to Poland, Romania, Greece, and Turkey. On March 31 Chamberlain in Parliament formally declared that in case of a threat to Poland's independence the British government would lend it 'all the support in their power.' It was painfully clear that whether or not Poland would survive if attacked by Germany would depend on Soviet Russia; Britain and France could not protect her. Accordingly, the two allies approached Russia in an attempt to negotiate some sort of defensive arrangement. The negotiations dragged on into the summer. In the meantime, late in April the British government, by way of indicating that it meant business, introduced conscription, which it had never before adopted in a time of peace.[10]

These measures were intended to deter Hitler from further aggression. Historians had frequently said that Britain could have prevented war in 1914 had it been possible for her to declare her intentions at an earlier stage. Now she was making her intentions fully clear. But it was also recognized within the government that the new policy involved a very definite probability of war. Lord Halifax, the Foreign Secretary, said in the cabinet's Foreign Policy Committee on March 27 that Britain was 'faced with the dilemma of doing nothing, or entering into a devastating war.' Doing nothing while Poland and Romania were overrun 'would mean a great accession to Germany's strength and a great loss to ourselves of sympathy and support in the United States, in the Balkan countries, and in other parts of the world. In those circumstances if we had to choose between two great evils he favoured our going to war.'[11]

For the new policy with all its possible consequences the British government took entire responsibility. The Dominion governments were kept fully informed, but they were not consulted before the measures were taken. If they had been consulted the measures could not have been taken, for in the light of the attitudes that had been made manifest in the Imperial Conference two years before it would have been quite impossible to achieve a consensus. The King-Skelton policy had always been to prefer not to be consulted, though this did not prevent people in that circle from complaining (though not to London) when consultation did not happen. In an acrid paper written in the final crisis Skelton said that Canada was threatened with war 'as the consequence of commitments made by the Government of Great Britain, about which we were not in one iota consulted, and about which we were given not the slightest inkling of information in advance.'[12] Loring Christie drew up a long list of the actions on which there had been no consultation and on which information had been sent only after the fact. In many cases he complained in effect, a trifle oddly, that Canada had not been informed of decisions before they were taken.[13]

The person whose attitude was most important was Mackenzie King. The new British policy troubled him in many ways; but he made no protest against it and no complaint of not having been consulted. His first public reaction was to make a prepared speech in the House of Commons on March 20 which contained the most outspoken statement he had yet made looking to support for Britain: 'If there were a prospect of an aggressor launching an attack on Britain, with bombers raining death on London, I have no doubt what the decision of the Canadian people and parliament would be. We would regard it as an act of aggression, menacing freedom in all parts of the British Commonwealth.' He had taken the precaution of having this speech approved by the cabinet, writing in his diary, 'I was determined to put myself side by side with Chamberlain in his statement* as to being prepared to sacrifice nearly everything for peace but not liberty.'[14]

Nevertheless, King was much disturbed by the British commitments in eastern Europe, and most of all by the approach to Russia. As soon as a Russian alliance was mentioned in the press his friend Julia Grant, the Princess Cantacuzene (the author of a book called *The Red Network*), telephoned him to say that she was 'most fearful of any association with Russia.'[15] It is doubtful whether this particularly influenced him; it was his natural bent to mistrust the Soviets, and the deep-rooted hostility of the people of Quebec to communism certainly had its due effect. 'Personally,' he wrote privately, 'I think it terrible that Britain has committed herself to fight for Poland, Rumania and Greece, and to ally herself with Russia ... She has had almost to barter her way into an alliance which would mean she would be drawn into European wars through the action of others with which she should have nothing to do.'[16] He did not communicate these views formally to the British government, but he did not conceal them from the British High Commissioner.

In March Sir Gerald Campbell, the High Commissioner, called on King to discuss the question of consultation. He stated, King recorded, 'that the British Govt. regarded the method we had been following as the one we would [? should] continue, namely, messages from P.M. to P.M. giving information. If we wished to comment on the same, we were free to do so, or if we wished to consult in any way, we were to be at liberty to do so.' King took the opportunity to tell Campbell that in his view all communications 'for which the Government was to be responsible' should pass directly between the two governments and not through the High Commissioners. This would apply to cases where the British government desired 'to consult us specifically.' King clearly wanted any important messages delivered formally on paper. He added, however, that Canada would be glad to have advance notice through Campbell of communications which London thought might be embarrassing, 'so that we could advise in advance whether it would be well to send them, or whether they would raise controversy or require a possible refusal': 'I said, for example, the question of becoming a party to a military alliance. He would see how embarrassing to the Canadian Govt. it would be to ask [? be asked] to become a party to an alliance to which Russia was a partner, or to any

---

* In his Birmingham speech of March 17 in which he first announced the new policy; King had listened to it being broadcast.

military alliance in Europe. Sir Gerald said he saw this quite clearly, and in fact they had spoken of that very matter; they had communicated to him about that very point. He did not say what the question was, and I did not press him.'[17] King thus made it quite clear to the British government that his administration would not associate Canada with any military alliance which Britain entered into, and came close to saying that it would prefer not to be consulted in such matters.

A month later Campbell came to King with a surprising request from London (which was not committed to paper). The British government were greatly concerned, he said, about the impression being created in Germany 'that the British would not fight, and in particular, that the Dominions would not support them in a fight': 'He asked point blank if I would make a statement in the House tomorrow to the effect that Canada was behind Britain's efforts and would support her in whatever course she took.' Campbell must have known that there was no chance whatever of King doing any such thing. King recorded that he told him: 'To take such a course would be to join with Jingos [sic] of Toronto in the very attitude on which we had had publicly to oppose them. Were I to make such a statement, I would immediately create no end of discussion both in Parliament and in the country, which would play right into the hands of the enemy. I told him how Lapointe and I had worked together to keep the Party united in Parliament and in the country by building a bridge that would unite the different parts; that this would be undoing all the good work we had done.' King was angry enough to go on and tell Campbell what he thought of recent British policy, and particularly of the approach to Russia: 'certainly our people would not want to fight to help Russia.' 'I also said that military alliance with Rumania and Poland would make it difficult to have our country go in[to] war on their account.'[18]

By this time there had been further developments in Parliament. As early as January King had made up his mind to make a commitment against conscription for overseas service in case of war. He noted this in his diary account of the cabinet meeting of January 27, though he does not seem to have actually spoken of it at that time. Conscription, he writes, might be necessary if an enemy landed in Canada – 'There will be no conscription, however, for men to go abroad.' This policy came into the open after the extinction of Czechoslovakia. Like other Conservative leaders before and since, the new leader of the Opposition, R.J. Manion, was, as we have already seen, making it his chief concern to re-establish his party in Quebec. He now had recourse to the device that W.D. Herridge had pressed upon R.B. Bennett in 1935 (above, page 190). Hearing that King proposed to make a commitment against overseas conscription, he sought to anticipate him. In an interview with the Toronto *Telegram* on March 27[19] he stated his policy in two propositions: no neutrality in a war in which Britain was engaged, and no conscription of Canadians 'to fight outside the borders of Canada.'

On March 30 there was an important debate in the House of Commons. Mackenzie King made an enormously long and involved statement on foreign policy, in which, as J.S. Woodsworth said later, every school of thought, from the isolationist to the 'belligerent militarist,' could find 'some crumbs of comfort.' He threw to the isolationists a paraphrase of Skelton, rejecting the idea that 'every twenty years ... a country which has all it can do to run itself should feel called upon to save ... a continent that cannot run itself'; and he duly committed the government to a policy of no conscription for overseas service. This gave satisfaction in Quebec.[20] It was Ernest Lapointe the following day who spoke to his French-Canadian compatriots with forthright courage. He, too, rejected overseas conscription; he bluntly said that, in such a conflict as was threatened, neutrality for Canada would be impossible: it would mean civil war. Manion repeated, in effect, what he had said three days before.

It was clear that something important had happened. With spokesmen for the two major parties alike rejecting both neutrality and overseas conscription, a formula existed on which Parliament and the country might find unity when the ultimate crisis came; and no one had much doubt now that it could not be far off. King recorded his regret that he himself should have given 'an impression of aloofness' towards Britain and left it to Lapointe to play the bold part. But he wrote: 'If I had made the speech Lapointe made, the party might have held its own with the Jingos [sic] in Ontario, but would have lost Quebec more or less entirely. If he had made the speech I did, he might have held Quebec, but the party would have lost heavily in Ontario and perhaps some other parts on the score that Quebec was neutral in its loyalty. Together, our speeches constituted a sort of trestle sustaining the structure which would serve to unite divergent parts of Canada, thereby making for a united country.'[21]

ARCADIAN INTERLUDE

Before the long darkness of the Second World War closed in, there was a sunny Arcadian interlude: the visit of King George VI and Queen Elizabeth to Canada in the early summer of 1939. A reigning sovereign had never visited the country before.

If it had not been planned far in advance, the visit would not have happened; for no one would have ventured to propose it under the conditions of 1939. As it was, Mackenzie King had suggested it when he was in London for the Coronation and the Imperial Conference two years before (Lord Tweedsmuir may have been the first to mention it); and the project was well advanced when the situation became really threatening. The Governor-General later recalled that the King confirmed his intention to make the visit on the day the Munich agreement was signed (Tweedsmuir being then in England). The dangers of the moment quite apart, to the shy and tongue-tied King a journey of thousands of miles in strange countries must have presented itself as an ordeal comparable with the Battle of Jutland in which he had fought in 1916; but like most members of his family he had a powerful sense of duty. Lord Tweedsmuir quoted him as saying, 'We must all be Romans in this day.'[22] The tour might well have been cancelled at the last moment; but the only important change made was the substitution of a Canadian Pacific liner for the battle cruiser *Repulse* which had been slated to bring the royal party to Canada. The Royal Navy could not well spare a capital ship from European waters in the spring of 1939; but the change was the King's own suggestion. The *Repulse* nevertheless escorted the liner partway across the ocean; the reason was apprehension that the German pocket battleship *Deutschland* might intercept her and hold the King and Queen to ransom! So low had British opinion of Hitler now sunk.[23]

Mackenzie King, who was deeply devoted to the monarchy, interested himself in even minor details of the planning for the visit. Some aspects of it involved controversies relevant to our subject. The tour was to include a short side-trip to the United States. (As soon as President Roosevelt heard from Mackenzie King that the tour might take place, he wrote personally to the King inviting him.) When in Washington in November 1938, King discussed this with the President, who seems to have been only less interested in the business than he was. The President remarked that the weather was 'pretty warm in June in Washington,' and clearly wished to suggest that the King and Queen should come there at the beginning of the tour. King discouraged this; 'the purpose being to enable them to see the peoples of their own Dominion, there would be considerable disappointment and the possibility of great resentment in Canada if they did not visit the greater part of the Dominion before going to the United States.'[24] He won his point, and the royal visitors saw central and western Canada before crossing the border. After the American episode they went on to the Maritime provinces.

King's personal relationship to the royal tour was the subject of vast discussion and filled many pages of his diary. His never very latent paranoia asserted itself, and he was convinced that he was the victim of a plot on the part of the King's secretaries. One of these, Alan Lascelles (above, page 122), visited Ottawa, and King had a long discussion with him. King explained to his diary that the secretaries' motives were partisan:

Tories like [Sir Alexander] Hardinge, Lascelles and the Tory Court do not wish any Liberal Administration to figure prominently with the King and Queen. Lascelles has been loaded up against me during the time Bennett was in office here; Hardinge knows that I dislike him. They both made up their minds to reduce my part to as small a one as possible:
1. Did not want me to be the first to meet the King and Queen at Quebec;
2. Did not wish me to accompany them through my own country;
3. Did not wish me to appear with the King and Queen in the United States. They will be beaten in all three, much to the advantage of the King and Queen and British connections, as has been the case in every other move that has ever helped to strengthen the relations of the Empire. The Tory mind has been absolutely wrong; the Liberals have once more saved the situation.[25]

Needless to say, King did win in all these matters. Lord Tweedsmuir was not allowed to greet the King at Quebec, as had been proposed; a message[26] from Hardinge told him that the King had accepted the advice of the Prime Minister that he should meet Their Majesties at Quebec 'while Your Excellencies remain in Ottawa.'* Mackenzie King accompanied the royal visitors on their tour across Canada; and what is more he, and not anybody from the United Kingdom, went with them to the United States as minister in attendance. This last victory was won only after King sent Neville Chamberlain what the Canadian Prime Minister called 'I imagine, about as strong a despatch [as has been sent] from any Dominion at any time.' The British had thought of sending Lord Halifax, the Foreign Secretary, as minister in attendance, but had decided against this, lest it appear to be a political ploy. They then thought of sending no minister. But nobody could suspect Mackenzie King of trying to involve the simple republicans in the dangerous intrigues of Europe.[27] King maintained throughout that no element of personal vanity or self-interest on his own part was involved; his concern was to maintain the constitutional

* H. Blair Neatby, *William Lyon Mackenzie King*, Vol. 3: *The Prism of Unity, 1932-39* (Toronto 1976), is uncharacteristically mistaken in saying that the Governor General boarded the ship before it docked, greeted the King and Queen, and remained on board while they landed. King strongly rejected this plan when Lascelles proposed it to him on February 28.

position of Canada as established by the Statute of Westminster.[28] Of this the candid reader may perhaps be left to judge.

None of these exchanges on the backstairs affected the success of the royal tour, which was complete, and not least in Quebec. On May 17 the Sovereign landed at Quebec City with his consort. On May 19, in the Canadian Parliament at Ottawa, he personally gave assent to a number of bills, including that approving the American trade agreement. While in Ottawa he also received the credentials of the new American Minister, Daniel Roper. After travelling to the Pacific coast and back by train, the King and Queen entered the United States on June 7, visited Washington and New York (where they saw the World's Fair) and were entertained by the President at Hyde Park, where they had the presumably novel experience of a picnic with hot dogs. That night the minister in attendance was party to a midnight conversation in which Roosevelt talked largely of the aid he would give Britain and Canada if war came, and King George observed that he would not wish to appoint Winston Churchill to any office, 'unless it was absolutely necessary in time of war.' Re-entering Canada on June 12, the King and Queen sailed from Halifax on the 15th, stopping briefly in Newfoundland en route home to threatened London.[29]

Wherever they had gone in Canada the welcome had been tremendous. All the traditional regard for the 'British connection' was in it, all the warmer because the connection was so personally represented, and somewhat also perhaps because the visitors came now as the King and Queen of Canada. One suspects that at that moment in history the country, and one might say the continent, saw in these two modest and unaffected people a striking and heartening contrast with the posturing dictators who threatened the world's peace. Queen Elizabeth's charm was all-conquering (a couple of years later, the present writer, following the King and Queen as they inspected Canadian troops in England, heard an officer murmur, 'Boy, does she mow 'em down'). There was little in Canadian newspapers that May and June except the King and Queen.[30] Even the dour *Devoir* produced on May 19 the streamer headline, 'La foule montréalaise acclame et admire les souverains du Canada.'

How much did these events have to do with what happened in Canada in the following September? The answer seems to be, something, but probably not a very great deal. As we have seen, the stage had been pretty fully set for intervention by the events of March. But the royal tour strengthened the influence on the situation of human and personal elements that were and are beyond the power of calculation. On the eve of war Mackenzie King told the Governor General that he thought 'the

ARCADIAN INTERLUDE, 1939
In the course of their North American tour on the very eve of war, King
George VI and Queen Elizabeth visit the Canadian pavilion at the New
York World's Fair.

King's visit had helped immensely re uniting Canada for this crisis';[31] and he was certainly an acute observer.

THE FINAL CRISIS

The scare early in 1939 led Mackenzie King to make a personal approach to Hitler. Hearing that Erich Windels, the German consul general in Ottawa, was going home on leave, he entrusted to him a letter to the Führer recalling their interview in 1937.[32] The squire of Kingsmere told the squire of Berchtesgaden he had been comforted to read of his being at his mountain retreat, 'knowing, as I do, how greatly the quiet and companionship of Nature helps to restore to the mind its largest and clearest vision':

> The purpose ... of this letter, is just to recall to your memory the conversation we had together, and to express anew the hope that regardless of what others may wish, or say, or do, you will, above all else, hold firm to the resolve not to let anything imperil or destroy what you have already accomplished, particularly for those whose lives are lived in humble circumstances. If you would not think it too presumptuous on my part, I should like even more to say how much I hope that you will think not only of the good you can do for those of your own country, but that you will remember, as well, the good that you can do to the entire world.
>
> You will, I know, accept this letter in the spirit in which it is written – an expression of the faith I have in the purpose you have at heart, and of the friendship with yourself which you have been so kind as to permit me to share.*

There was no immediate reply (it has been alleged that Hitler had observed that King had sent him no New Year's greeting),[33] but on July 21 (noted by King in his diary as 'a day *of Destiny*') Windels came to Laurier House and delivered a verbal message supported by a memorandum: Hitler invited a dozen Canadians, six students and six army officers, to visit Germany as his guests at his expense. King's regard for Hitler, which seems to have been shaken by the events of the previous September, came flooding back; he accepted at once, and said he would like to go himself, 'that I would like to head the party.' To his diary he confided:

---

* *The Prism of Unity* is mistaken in asserting that in this letter King repeated his warning of 1937 that if Britain went to war Canada would inevitably be involved.

... it seemed to me Canada was being used as a screen to let friendly relations develop in a manner that would 'save face' as between Germany & Britain: that it was a sincere gesture based on mutual faith in each other on the part of Hitler & myself, – above all I felt that 'forces unseen' – loved ones in the beyond, – were working out these plans, that there were no accidents, or chances in this but all part of a plan in which God was using man to effect his Will in answer to prayer, the Mediums being those in the beyond who were working for peace on earth ... I felt elections were relatively unimportant* – but I recognized that great care would be needed in each step & the utmost secrecy preserved, that no one could be trusted (except absolutely sworn to secrecy). I felt I must communicate with Chamberlain, but that to do so through diplomatic channels would be dangerous. I did not mind the King knowing, but I wanted him the only one (in Eng. at present) if that could be. I felt I wanted Joan [Patteson] to know all, as it is a part of the plan for which we are chosen as instruments & which has been told to us.[34]

Mrs Patteson suggested the letter to Chamberlain might go 'by *aeroplane*'; King thought this 'a good suggestion to avoid coding & others knowing.' But she also suggested that Hitler might be trying to get Canada's goodwill – to 'draw her away' in case of war. King rejected this idea but seems to have been more receptive to another – 'that Canada might resent any action towards Germany just now & that it might injure myself & the party politically to take a step before an election.' King duly got his letter off to Chamberlain – probably by the Pan-American Airways flying-boat service to Southampton, which had lately been inaugurated; good sense had asserted itself and he did not suggest making the trip himself. On August 10 he received a reply recommending that the invitation be accepted, and next day he saw Windels and said he would like the party to go to Germany early in November if the election was over by that time. During this conversation he revived the idea of going himself. He had already told the great secret to Skelton (though apparently not until the letter to Chamberlain had gone); now he told Lapointe and Pickersgill, very confidentially.[35] Of course, neither the election nor the visit took place as planned; war supervened.

Whatever one may conjecture about Hitler's motives in this bizarre incident, it reinforces the conviction that King's whole curious relationship with Hitler can only be understood as an episode in the Prime Minister's mystical life. Joan of Arc (above, page 213) comes into his diary here

* Nearly four years had passed since the last general election, and King's thoughts were much on the date of the next one.

again (in connection with a gift of lobster from the mother superior of the Joan of Arc Institute in Ottawa!); this, says King, 'had the direct mystical association': 'Hitler being a mystic, [and] I certainly am becoming increasingly such.'[36]

By the time this affair was resolved, the final crisis with Germany was close at hand.

German pressure on Poland began in connection with Danzig, the German-speaking 'free city' set up by the 1919 peace settlement at the end of the corridor to the Baltic which that settlement handed over to Poland. Frontier incidents added to the tension. The Anglo-French political discussions with Russia went on. On August 11 a military mission from the two western countries arrived in Moscow with a view, supposedly, to making plans for co-operation against Germany. But so far as the Russians were concerned this was all a false front. Since the beginning of August Germany and the Soviet Union (two countries which for years had hurled unmeasured abuse at each other) had been moving towards an agreement behind the backs of Britain and France. On August 22 it was announced that Hitler's foreign minister, Ribbentrop, was flying to Moscow to sign a non-aggression pact. It was signed the following day. The news struck the West like a thunderbolt. The British intelligence service had known nothing about these developments.* The track was now clear for Hitler's attack on Poland. The Russo-German agreement, surely one of the most cynical documents of modern times, contained a secret article setting up a demarcation line through Poland, a boundary between German and Russian zones in the event of the two countries undertaking a new partition of Poland.

For the second time in six months, Neville Chamberlain's policy lay in ruins. In Ottawa, O.D. Skelton wrote to King on August 22:

The press news this morning of the decision of Germany and Soviet Russia to conclude a non-aggression pact means the collapse of the Anglo-French house of cards in Eastern Europe.

* The Americans had known, thanks perhaps to leaks from the German embassy staff in Washington; but they gave the British only hints. When they finally told the British what was going on, Sir Ronald Lindsay's cable giving the information lay undeciphered in the Foreign Office in London for four days. The presence in the Foreign Office's communications staff of a Soviet agent, who was shortly uncovered, may be the explanation of this.[37]

It is not wholly unexpected (you had feared some such deal all along), but it is still almost incredible that it could have happened without any knowledge or anticipation on the part of London or Paris.

It is a crushing condemnation of the handling of British foreign policy. Not only Chamberlain and his government, but even more so, Churchill and Eden and the Liberal leaders who have been egging the Government on, must share the responsibility for the greatest fiasco in British history ...

This week's news will, I think, finish all United States idea of intervention in Europe on the side of the 'democracies.'[38]

Skelton hated Chamberlain and all his works. Laurier's biographer had sought to warn Laurier's successor against Joe Chamberlain's son.[39] Perhaps this was not unnatural. But the note of satisfaction in this memorandum has, it must be said, an unpleasant ring.

Chamberlain's reaction to the appalling news from Moscow was to stand firm on the guarantee to Poland. On the evening of the day on which the first information was published he telegraphed to Hitler through the British Embassy in Berlin a letter which the cabinet had approved.[40] Some quarters in Berlin, he wrote, apparently considered that the new development indicated that British intervention on behalf of Poland need no longer be reckoned with:

No greater mistake could be made. Whatever may prove to be the nature of the German-Soviet Agreement, it cannot alter Great Britain's obligation to Poland, which His Majesty's Government have stated in public repeatedly and plainly, and which they are determined to fulfil.

It has been alleged that, if His Majesty's Government had made their position more clear in 1914, the great catastrophe would have been avoided. Whether or not there is any force in that allegation, His Majesty's Government are resolved that on this occasion there shall be no such tragic misunderstanding. If the need should arise, they are resolved and prepared to employ without delay all the forces at their command, and it is impossible to foresee the end of hostilities once engaged. It would be a dangerous delusion to think that, if war once starts, it will come to an early end, even if a success on any one of the several fronts on which it will be engaged should have been secured.

Such a warning might have impressed the government of imperial Germany in 1914. On Hitler it had less effect. It is true that he suspended for a week the movement against Poland which had been planned for August

26, in the hope of 'eliminating British intervention'; but when the British remained obdurate he launched his invasion. Early in the morning of September 1 the guns of the old German battleship *Schleswig-Holstein*, firing on a Polish position near Danzig, announced the beginning of the Second World War. The German Air Force bombed Polish cities, the German armoured divisions rolled across the frontier. The Poles offered brave but increasingly ineffective resistance, which was finally nullified when on September 17 Soviet Russia, intent on seizing her agreed portion of the spoils, invaded the country from the east.

On the afternoon of September 1, when there was no doubt whatever that Germany was making war on Poland, the British government dispatched to Berlin what was called a warning rather than an ultimatum – there was no time limit – to the effect that unless Germany suspended all aggressive action against Poland and withdrew her forces, the British 'will without hesitation fulfil their obligations to Poland.'[41] There followed a short period when Chamberlain was torn between two forces – the French, who wanted more time to complete their mobilization, and the men of action in his cabinet and the House of Commons, who wanted no further delay.[42] Then, at 5:00 a.m. on September 3, the ultimatum went to the German Foreign Minister: since the German attacks on Poland had been continued and intensified: 'I have ... the honour to inform you that unless not later than 11 a.m. British Summer Time, today September 3, satisfactory assurances have been given by the German Government and have reached His Majesty's Government in London, a state of war will exist between the two countries as from that hour.'[43] No reply came; and at 11:15 Chamberlain, the man of peace, sadly broadcast to the nation that Britain was at war. That evening – it was Sunday – King George spoke to Britain and the Commonwealth. Canadians, to whom the King was now a rather less distant figure than he had been, heard him – if they lived in the central part of the country – at one o'clock.* Britain had been 'forced into a conflict,' he said, to meet the challenge of 'the principle which permits a State, in the selfish pursuit of power, to disregard its treaties and its solemn pledges; which sanctions the use of force, or threat of force, against the Sovereignty and independence of other States.' This principle amounted to 'the mere primitive doctrine that Might is Right':

* My wife and I (we were on our honeymoon) heard the broadcast in the dining-room of the La Salle Hotel in Montreal. I do not recall any expression of emotion among the respectable people present. There was silence; grim resignation; and, I suspect, considerable grim resolution.

It is to this high purpose that I now call my people at home and my peoples across the Seas, who will make our cause their own. I ask them to stand calm and firm and united in this time of trial. The task will be hard. There may be dark days ahead, and war can no longer be confined to the battlefield. But we can only do the right as we see the right, and reverently commit our cause to God. If one and all we keep resolutely faithful to it, ready for whatever service or sacrifice it may demand, then, with God's help, we shall prevail.

May He bless and keep us all.[44]

CANADA GOES TO WAR

As in 1938, Canadians, from the Prime Minister down, were mere spectators in this crisis. The British government kept the government of Canada fully informed of developments; but it did not ask for comment or advice, and Ottawa, though it could have offered them, did not choose to do so. The public at large read the newspapers, listened avidly to the news broadcasts, and waited tensely for what might come.

Mackenzie King, at Kingsmere, got the first news of the German-Soviet agreement from Mrs Patteson, who had heard a radio bulletin. His first reactions were confused. There was relief ('I have never trusted the Russians'). He assumed that Britain and France would now 'have to withdraw' from their undertakings to Poland, though he recognized that this would mean that Britain would again become 'perfidious Albion' in the eyes of Europe (he might have added, in the eyes of the United States as well). He comforted himself with the thought, 'anything is better than war at present, with still a chance to work out peace even at considerable sacrifice.'[45] There was no abuse of Chamberlain in the Skelton manner. The following day (August 23), when it was clear that war was a more immediate threat than ever, Kind decided (against Skelton's advice) to issue a statement informing the public that with the War Measures Act, 1914, still on the statute book the government was armed with ample powers to meet an emergency, but that in case of war in Europe Parliament would be called at once. This action, he thought, 'would help to show a certain sympathy' between the British and Canadian governments and might head off demands from the press 'to come out and say where we stood.'[46]

Where we stood. The time had come, King resolved, when the cabinet must decide on Canada's course. On the main point – participation – there could now be little doubt; but it was desirable to make the implicit explicit, and to face the question of procedure. This was done on August

24. That morning the Prime Minister read to the cabinet the latest dispatches, including one 'which indicated that in all probability the zero-hour might come tonight'; this, we have seen, had actually been very close to Hitler's intention. They recessed until the afternoon. King then raised the question of policy, precisely as he had done in the crisis eleven months before (above, page 216). He wrote in his diary:

> At the Council table, I said that while we were all still in a calm frame of mind, it was advisable we should decide upon our policy in the event of war breaking out. That I had a clear idea in my own mind as to what it should be, but would like my colleagues to express their views first of all.
>
> I then began going around the Council table ...

The result was very similar to that of September 23, 1938. King addressed himself first to Lapointe, who said he too would prefer to hear what others had to say first. Next was Michaud, whose view was 'that there should not be participation outside of Canada; that we should stand by the statement I had made in Parliament.* Abide by that, at all events, until we see what the situation further might demand.' Norman Rogers took a very different line: 'Rogers thought that we should take all measures to meet the situation, as it develops, from hour to hour, and to be prepared to meet every eventuality. That, if Britain became involved, there was no question as to what our position would be. All our resources, man power, etc., should immediately be brought to assist Britain. He agreed that the important thing was to keep the country united meanwhile. Personally, he would like an announcement made immediately, that Canada was prepared to give support to Britain in every effort she was making for peace; that, if these efforts were not effective, we would immediately go into the war on Britain's behalf.' Power 'was not prepared to go as far as Rogers in issuing a blank cheque to Britain.' Agreeing that Canada would 'have to go into the war,' he opposed saying so before Parliament met. Cardin agreed with Power; 'we should prepare, above everything else, for the safety of our own people and not enlarge on the declaration of yesterday.' J.L. Ilsley stood with Rogers, and spoke even more strongly. He 'did not see how we could avoid a statement of our policy as to what we would do if war were declared; that we would stand with Great Britain. Would like to see a statement issued at once that

---

* Michaud was presumably thinking primarily of King's speech of March 30 (above, page 243), and generally of the repeated statements that Parliament would decide.

Canada would participate at once if Great Britain found it necessary to go to war with [sic] Poland. He thought it was apparent that, under those circumstances, there could be only one policy and that was to participate in the defence of Europe in the name of decency, etc. That the people wanted the government to say now what the country would do.'

'Mackenzie said he agreed with Ilsley, that Democracy was at stake, and that there should be an immediate declaration of policy. It was not the fact of participation that there could be any question about, but the extent of participation.' This the government and Parliament would have to decide. As Defence Minister, he thought steps should be taken at once, on a voluntary basis, to safeguard 'vulnerable points' in Canada.

Ilsley's strong words brought Lapointe out of his tent. He broke in and said that he 'saw no purpose in making any preliminary statement as to our participation in the event of war.' W.D. Euler said he agreed with that but proceeded to go a great deal further. 'He would be prepared to do anything for the defence of Canada. Did not feel it was our business to be too much concerned about what was taking place in Europe. He honestly held that view. He thought we should make clear there would be no conscription; that he detested war. Thought Danzig was a bad issue and that if there was no greater issue he would oppose sacrificing life for that purpose.' Norman McLarty, an Ontario man who had entered the cabinet as Postmaster General early in 1939, 'was of the view that we were going to participate' but opposed an immediate statement, while C.D. Howe, though clear that in case of war Canada should support Britain and France 'to the limit of our resources,' felt that 'we' should say and do nothing to divide the country in the meantime; this presumably meant that he opposed an immediate statement.

Mackenzie King then summed up. He was, he said, 'immensely relieved to find that on the all-important matter of Canada's participation in the event of Britain being drawn into war, we were of one mind and united.' Where there was a difference of view was on the question of whether to announce this now or to await developments. King proceeded: 'I have been criticized for saying that Parliament would decide, impression having gained ground that I meant by that we would leave it to a sort of general discussion in Parliament when Parliament was assembled, to see what the majority felt. That I had not meant anything of the kind, as they knew;* that I thought the position to take lay between these two extremes and it was that we would not wait until Parliament assembled to announce our policy, but would, when summoning Parliament, let the

---

* One wonders whether they really did know.

country know what the policy was on the matter of participation, leaving to Parliament to decide the details of nature, extent of, etc., etc. [sic]. Our views on these would be given to Parliament immediately it assembled and the government would stand or fall by its policy as stated.' King proceeded to record, 'I got general agreement and unanimity on this position.'[47]

The familiar division had appeared in the cabinet, but as King thankfully noted it was not fundamental. Nobody had proposed neutrality. The two who came closest were Michaud and Euler, who believed that Canada should do nothing beyond defending her own soil, a position for which Cardin also showed some partiality. Euler's position may have been useful in a sense, in that it blurred the division between the French and the rest.* The demand for immediate action had come from ministers from Ontario, the Maritime provinces, and British Columbia. It is interesting that King did not record those from the prairie provinces as saying anything. On the basis of his record, indeed, they had been generally silent during the cabinet's important discussions on external questions going back to 1935.

King had hit on a successful compromise. Faced with the pressing demand by Rogers, Ilsley, and others for an immediate statement of support for Britain, and Lapointe's firm opposition to this, he had sidetracked the problem by proposing that such a declaration should be made, not now, but at the moment when Parliament was called. The cabinet would then declare its interventionist views, and would ask Parliament to support them. The statement that Parliament would 'decide details' clearly did not mean very much. It was for the government to propose policies, large or small, and for Parliament to approve them if it chose. It would certainly do so, in the light of the government's large majority and the state of public opinion in the country. And, whether King fully realized it at this moment or not, Parliament would certainly have to go through the motions of 'deciding' the basic question of peace or war. From the moment the decision of August 24 was made, it was pretty clear that there would have to be a Canadian declaration of war separate from

* As we have noted, Euler's background was German. He had been mayor of Berlin (afterwards Kitchener), Ontario, in 1913-14, and was first elected to Parliament, as 'a fervent anti-conscriptionist,' in 1917, after a very bitter campaign. He did not long remain in the government after the outbreak of war; King, who clearly did not like his fellow-townsman, retired him to the Senate in May 1940, remarking in his diary, 'I think it is just as well for him and for all of us with his German nature and manner that he is out of the Cabinet.'[48]

that of the United Kingdom, though nothing was said of this in the cabinet and it is even possible that King's thinking had not yet gone so far as this. One's impression is that he was feeling his way, not working to a long-term plan.

The cabinet did something else on August 24, though King did not get around to noting it in his diary until the following day. It did in fact do a good deal in the direction of 'deciding details.' O.D. Skelton had put before the Prime Minister a paper entitled 'Canadian War Policy,'[49] and King in turn put it before his colleagues. It made an attempt at prescribing 'forms and objectives' for the Canadian effort in the event of participation being decided on. It began by assuming that there would be 'immediate consultation with the United Kingdom and France, and equally important, discreet consultation with Washington.' Under 'Military Action,' it proclaimed, 'The defence of Canada should be put in the foreground.' The Pacific could not be ignored. 'There is a big job in defending our coasts.' Aid to Newfoundland and the West Indies should be considered within 'the measure of our capacity.' And Skelton was quite prepared to give advice on military policy: 'If any military action is to be taken overseas, it should, in the first instance, be in the air service rather than by military contingents. An announcement of an immediate and intensified programme of building planes and training men for air service in Canada and for a Canadian air force operating in France, would be effective from the standpoint both of military value and of consolidation of public opinion.' Passing on to 'Economic Effort,' Skelton remarked that while economic effort without military activity 'would not be a satisfying or satisfactory means of participation,' it was in the economic field that Canada could give aid 'most effective to our allies and most consistent with Canadian interests.' Attention should be concentrated on providing 'munitions, raw materials and foodstuffs.' Finally, Skelton briefly noted that there should be 'Closer touch with Washington' and a 'Statement of War Aims.'

King wrote on this paper: 'Read to Council. Met with general approval.' We know no more of the discussion, if there was any. It would be strange if some of the cabinet did not have at least mental reservations about Skelton's programme. It was, of course, a blueprint for limited war. The government (and the opposition) had already committed themselves to limited war in the previous March, when they declared against overseas conscription. Since war is essentially not an activity susceptible of limitation, these decisions were unrealistic, and this would become apparent in due time. But in 1939 the concept of limited liability certainly contributed to the maintenance of unity in Canada.

When evening fell on August 24, King could have reflected that he had obtained from his colleagues precisely the decisions he had been working towards for months: decisions forecast in his conversation with Norman Rogers in September 1938 (above, page 236) – 'that Canada should regard herself as part of the British Empire, one of the nations of the sisterhood of nations, which should cooperate lending every assistance possible, in no way asserting neutrality, but carefully defining in what ways and how far she would participate.'

At this point King made one more attempt at exploiting the relationship which his fantasy told him he had established with Adolf Hitler in 1937. The fact that Mrs Patteson also had the idea of sending a message to Hitler led King 'to feel that the thought was being inspired.' On August 25 he set to work to draft a communication, to go to both Hitler and Mussolini. Encountering difficulty, he talked to Skelton, who 'seemed somewhat hesitant.' King then telephoned his principal secretary, Arnold Heeney, and told him 'to get Pickersgill at work' on it. In the existing circumstances, King clearly felt he must consult the cabinet. He found them 'not too responsive.' 'Rogers was inclined to question the wisdom of sending anything, thinking that people might regard it as another effort at appeasement – time for which had passed.' Ilsley was 'almost violently outspoken' against the idea; the people, he thought, 'would resent anything that looked like having anything at all to do with Hitler.' But Lapointe made an 'almost passionate' plea for sending the message, and Mackenzie also favoured it. King decided the cabinet was 'sufficiently agreed' to justify him in going ahead. He called in the German consul general and the acting Italian consul general (he had in fact arranged this earlier) and gave them the messages, which were brief straightforward appeals to the two dictators to use their great power and influence in favour of peaceful settlement.[50] Windels suggested that the message to Hitler should also go to the President of Poland, and King agreed to this.

In the interviews with the German and the Italian King asked both men to send personal messages to their governments warning them, in effect, that in case of war Canada would stand with Britain. He records that he said to Windels: 'I thought perhaps he ought to let Herr Hitler know that there was no doubt in my mind as to what we would do. That we had had a meeting of the Cabinet and were all of one mind as to what the nation's attitude was certain to be.' Windels suggested that he might send this as the answer to a direct question from himself as to whether he was right in believing that 'Canada would be at the side of Britain and France if war were declared'; King was glad to assent. It seems evident that, without making a direct statement, he left no doubt in his hearers' minds about Canada's position. His caution may have been due in part to Power's having questioned in cabinet the desirability of making such statements, 'as committing us in advance before Parliament met, and getting us into a dangerous position later on with Quebec.'[51]

Somebody else had to be told. It would hardly do to give this information to Berlin and Rome and not give it to London. Sir Gerald Campbell called on the Prime Minister on the morning of August 25 to give him the latest intelligence, and King told him about the communications he was sending to Hitler and Mussolini (this was before the cabinet meeting) and also told him what he proposed to tell the consuls general: 'that our Cabinet was united in the matter of policy, and that it would be well for the leaders of each of their countries to know just exactly where Canada would be in the event of any active aggression which involved England and France in war. That we would certainly be at their side immediately.' King felt it desirable to make a further remark: 'I said that we would take this stand on our own, not in any colonial attitude of mind, simply following the lead from England but standing on our own as to policy, etc. I made clear that we were not issuing any blank cheque; that whatever was done would depend on exactly what transpired meanwhile, if the condition continued to be as we viewed it at the moment.' It would be interesting to have Sir Gerald's comments on this. Unfortunately, his memoirs do not help.[52]

The cabinet meeting on the 24th had sanctioned emergency expenditures of nearly $9 million, chiefly for purchase of aircraft in the United States, but also for work on coast defences; since there was no parliamentary appropriation, these would be authorized by Governor General's Warrant. The meeting of the 25th went further; it approved the recommendation of the military authorities to call out, on a voluntary basis, units of the Non-Permanent Active Militia to man the coast defences and guard vulnerable points – roughly 10,000 men in all. That night, instructions to this effect went out to the military districts, prefaced by the warning, 'Reference Defence Scheme Number Three. Adopt Precautionary Stage against Germany.'[53]

Sunday the 27th was a quiet day at Kingsmere. Mackenzie King reflected on Wagner and Hitler: 'Wagner's music has possessed Germany, – his philosophy with it. Hitler loves his music to the exclusion of much else, & doubtless has imbibed his philosophy. Is a mystic, a spiritualist, believes I am sure in reincarnation – and thus his life becomes intelligible. It is that which makes [t]his appeal to his good, his spiritual side, so important.' King's final appeal to Hitler's spiritual side was unsuccessful. Mussolini and the Polish President sent polite replies to his messages;

Windels merely brought on August 29 a verbal message that 'the German Chancellor wished the Prime Minister to know that his communication had been received personally by him.'[54] King never again addressed himself to the Führer.

The last days of peace slipped by. The people of Canada read the increasingly alarming dispatches from abroad. The militiamen guarded the bridges and canals and familiarized themselves with the armament of the forts; air squadrons flew to war stations on the east coast; two of the four destroyers that had been on the Pacific made their way to the Atlantic.[55]

At 6:30 in the morning of September 1 the Prime Minister, at Kingsmere, was awakened by a telephone call from Arnold Heeney, who told him it was reported that Poland had been invaded. King instructed him to call the cabinet for nine o'clock, and himself hastened in to Ottawa. The first business before the ministers was an order-in-council calling Parliament for Thursday, September 7. The 8th had been thought of, but King decided that the 7th should be possible. 'Besides,' wrote the superstitious Prime Minister, 'I like the "7".' Other orders were passed, proclaiming a situation of apprehended war under the War Measures Act, placing the forces on active service, and instituting censorship. The cabinet then took up the question of the statement to be issued to the press; and after very careful consideration of this, with every member present, King gave it out at 1:15 p.m. Noting that Parliament had been summoned, he proceeded: 'In the event of the United Kingdom becoming engaged in war in the effort to resist aggression, the Government of Canada have unanimously decided, as soon as Parliament meets, to seek its authority for effective co-operation by Canada at the side of Britain.'[56] Thus he carried out the arrangement agreed on August 24. The phrasing was not strong, but it must be remembered that Britain was not yet at war. With the guns firing, but with Britain not yet a party to the conflict, the Canadian government had at last committed itself.

When Britain declared war the status of Canada at once became a matter of question. It could not be finally settled until Parliament met. In the meantime, would German forces treat Canadian soil and property as those of an enemy? Immediately after the news of the British declaration arrived, the cabinet authorized a message to the commanders of the coastal military districts: 'Take all necessary defence measures which would be required in a state of war.' It added, however, that this order was to be kept severely secret.[57] On September 5 the question of Canada's position was raised from Washington. Secretary of State Hull telephoned, with President Roosevelt listening in, to ask the Prime Minister whether

Canada was at war. The United States was about to issue proclamations under the neutrality laws. King told them that Parliament was meeting to decide the question, and they then told him that no proclamation affecting Canada would be issued for the present. This technical neutrality had a practical advantage; while it lasted (until September 10) the aircraft purchased in the United States were being brought across the border. Once Canada became a belligerent this source of supply was, for the present, cut off.[58]

On the same day on which Britain declared war a German submarine sank without warning the liner *Athenia*, carrying over 1300 passengers bound from the Clyde and Liverpool for Montreal; 112 persons lost their lives, including a dozen Canadians. The submarine commander's action was contrary to Hitler's current policy, which was politic restraint in the west combined with bloody massacre in the east; the dictator still hoped that when Poland was crushed Britain and France would withdraw from the war. The officer claimed he had mistaken the ship for an armed merchant cruiser.[59] It would have been difficult to invent an incident much better calculated to bring the fact of war home to Canadians, or to convince them that the Nazi regime was in fact the brutal and bloody thing it was reputed to be.

Parliament, meeting on September 7, 'decided' on the evening of the 9th.[60] King had belatedly announced that morning that an affirmative vote on the Address in reply to the Speech from the Throne would be taken as approval for a declaration of war. The result was a foregone conclusion. No party in the House of Commons opposed the Address, but the leader of the socialist Co-operative Commonwealth Federation, J.S. Woodsworth, a lifelong pacifist, deserted by his followers, raised a lonely voice against it.* Three French-Canadian nationalists, two of whom put forward an amendment opposing 'war outside of Canada,' were the only other vocal dissidents. There was no recorded vote. On this, as on other matters, the government had had no plan in readiness. The Prime Mini-

---

* The national council of the CCF had met on September 6 and decided by a majority vote not to oppose the declaration of war. Among the minority supporting Woodsworth were the academic isolationists Underhill and Scott (above, page 232). It is evident that the more politically-minded members of the party realized that opposing war with Hitler would lose votes. The council nevertheless declared that Canada's share in the war should be 'limited to economic aid' and that there should be no expeditionary force. The party progressively abandoned this attitude during the years that followed; by 1942 it was marching under the slogan, 'Victory and Reconstruction.'[61]

ster was actually in the government lobby arguing with Arthur Cardin as to whether a recorded vote should be taken at the moment when the Speaker declared the amendment negatived (without a vote) and the Address passed (by a voice vote). Somebody (probably Woodsworth) was heard to say 'On division,' and after a conference between ministers and the Speaker and his officials the phrase was recorded in Hansard.[62]

If this parliamentary occasion had a hero, it was, by common consent, Ernest Lapointe. In his speech on September 9 the Minister of Justice took his text from the King's broadcast: 'Our King, Mr. Speaker, is at war, and this parliament is sitting to decide whether we shall make his cause our own.' He said, as he had said in March, that neutrality for Canada was utterly impossible. 'They say – and the hon. member who preceded me [Maxime Raymond] said it – 'for the sake of unity let us be neutral.' I am telling the hon. member where I differ from him. I know, and I believe he should know, that for the sake of unity we cannot be neutral in Canada.' Conscription for overseas service was equally impossible. 'I am authorized by my colleagues in the cabinet from the province of Quebec ... to say that we will never agree to conscription and will never be members or supporters of a government that will try to enforce it. Is that clear enough?' Lapointe was prepared to support an expeditionary force of volunteers if public opinion called for it: 'no government could stay in office if it refused to do what the large majority of Canadians wanted it to do.' He ended by recalling the Queen's final words of blessing to Canada, spoken in French, and said: 'Yes, God bless Canada. God save Canada. God save Canada's honour, Canada's soul, Canada's dignity, Canada's conscience.' The Toronto Globe and Mail's reporter, deeply moved, wrote that with this appeal 'the expected French-Canadian rebellion vanished.'[63] Such a revolt within the Liberal party had not been very likely, but Lapointe made it even less so.

Mackenzie King's own speech on September 8 was not one of his best. It lasted nearly four hours (Tommy Church compared this adversely with Chamberlain's sixteen minutes on the radio and the King's six), and it ended with fourteen interminable stanzas of a poem by James Russell Lowell, which King thought would make a favourable impression on the United States. The British High Commissioner reported that as King droned through this 'a buzz of conversation broke out around him.'[64] Nevertheless as the debate ended King had every reason to be abundantly pleased with himself. The unheroic policy of 'parliament will decide' and 'no commitments,' which he had clung to in the face of so much abuse over so many months, had been more than justified by the event. The country had gone to war, and it had gone to war united. It had not come apart; there had been no civil war. Two years before people would not have believed it. And as the present writer recalls, people at the time were not disposed to withhold a meed of praise from the Prime Minister. I remember one academic saying: 'I've never been a great admirer of Mackenzie King, but I have to give him credit for a remarkable accomplishment.' The unity attained was incomplete and to some extent artificial; it was to fray badly as the war proceeded; yet the parliamentary and national decision arrived at in September 1939 was the greatest achievement of Mackenzie King's career. It should be added, however, that some credit is also due to Adolf Hitler.

The act of declaring war required the approval of the King, and it was clear to the cabinet that his signature, and not merely that of the Governor General acting for him, was required, and that the proclamation of the declaration should be issued by the Governor General in the King's name.[65] The text of a submission to the King requesting his authority to issue such a proclamation was telegraphed to the High Commissioner in London, and Mr Massey visited the King and obtained his signed approval soon after 1:00 p.m. London time on September 10. (Subsequently, to satisfy constitutional proprieties, a more formal copy bearing the Prime Minister's signature was forwarded and likewise signed by the King.)* The proclamation was issued at Ottawa as an extra of the *Canada Gazette* published at 12:40 p.m., local time, on September 10; and Canada was at war with Germany by decision of her Parliament, having been technically neutral for one week after the declaration by the United Kingdom.[66]

Until that moment constitutional experts had continued to debate the question whether or not Canada possessed the legal right to remain neutral in a British war. W.P.M. Kennedy, in a new edition of *The Constitution of Canada* published in 1938, affirmed that she clearly did not; in effect, he said that Laurier's 'If England is at war' statement was still good law. To this question the Parliament of Canada had now given an answer. Parliament had authorized a declaration of war. If it had not authorized it, the country would presumably have remained neutral. The question was highly theoretical, and nobody was much interested in theoretical questions in September 1939. The separate declaration of war, in spite of all its large implications, encountered comparatively little adverse comment in

---

* L.B. Pearson in his memoirs tells the story of a draft 'declaration of war' (presumably a proclamation of the sort issued on September 10) which was put before the King for approval or comment during the week of neutrality, and which the King proceeded to sign. Whether this draft became the basis of the proclamation finally issued is not clear, but it seems unlikely.

Parliament or elsewhere. Not surprisingly, the most forthright criticism came from Arthur Meighen, speaking in the Senate on September 9: 'I have never felt that it has been within the competence of Canada to decide whether we are at war or not. I do not feel so now. Either we are part of the British Empire or we are not; and we know that we are a part. We cannot be at peace while the head of this Empire is at war. The pronouncement of Laurier stands, and will ever stand.' R.J. Manion, the leader of Meighen's party, was not quite so firm in the House of Commons, though he too declared his agreement with Laurier. Tommy Church criticized what was being done, but he was regarded as an eccentric. Even the *Globe and Mail*, thought of as the organ of what King called the Toronto jingoes, seemed to take the procedure that was followed as a matter of course; it was interested in the result, not in the way it was arrived at.[67]

WHY DID CANADA GO TO WAR?

The motives that moved Canadians in September 1939 are sure to be of interest to later generations, and however impossible it is to arrive at certainty in the matter we should at least discuss it.

It is interesting that during and after the Czechoslovak crisis of September 1938 several people in the Department of External Affairs thought it worth while to speculate on the forces that would have moved Canada to intervene (they all assumed she would have intervened). One of these was O.D. Skelton, who wrote to the Prime Minister on September 24:[68] 'If war breaks out between Germany & Czechoslovakia, if France goes in, and Britain to help France, and we go in then, it will be to help Britain – as L'Evenement said the other day, "Is there one interventionist in Canada, however much he dislikes Hitler, who would be an interventionist if Great Britain were not in the war?" There is (a) dislike of Hitler increasingly, but it would be (b) sympathy for Britain that would be the determining force if we went in. Of course both factors are present, but (b) would work without (a) conceivably but not (a) without (b).' Hume Wrong had replaced W.A. Riddell at Geneva, where presumably he had comparatively little to do; and on December 7, 1938, he sent to Skelton a very long memorandum called 'The Canadian Position in the Light of the September Crisis.'[69] It was clear to Wrong that if war had come Canada would have been involved at once, and on a large scale. He was deeply disturbed by the implications: 'in the present state of Canadian opinion no Canadian Government is likely to be able to keep Canada out of a great war in which the United Kingdom is engaged.' 'Canadian self-government,' he wrote, 'obviously is incomplete so long as the most vital decision which can arise in the life of a nation is not taken in fact as well as in form by the leaders of the Canadian people.'

Here Wrong was in accord with other advanced nationalist thinkers such as F.R. Scott[70] and Loring Christie,[71] and with the prevailing tone in the Department of External Affairs. (Forty years on, these people's belief in the ability of a nation of eleven million people to exercise absolute control of its own destiny seems a trifle naïve; but this was 1938.) Wrong wanted to see the situation changed: 'The means should be both the education of the Canadian people to think boldly about Canada's place as a nation in the world, and the orientation of Canadian policy and the machinery for its conduct so as to make the most productive use of existing sentiments and loyalties towards attaining the eventual object.' The patronizing reference to educating the Canadian people certainly reflects a prevailing attitude in External. As for machinery, Wrong went on to argue for a much enlarged Canadian foreign service: Canada, he thought, was far too dependent, 'for the day-to-day conduct of Canadian business abroad, on officials who are appointed by and responsible to the Government of the United Kingdom.'* His comment on the recent crisis is interesting for our purpose:

The post-war policy of Canada, reflecting her geographical remoteness from the danger points of the world, leads logically towards isolation. Isolation certainly has many advantages, but I need not debate them here because the events of last September seem to show that Canadian opinion is far from ready to accept it. The sympathies and loyalties of large sections of the Canadian people are too deeply involved. A positive Canadian policy cannot therefore pursue the will o' the wisp of isolation here and now, but must start from acceptance of the present state of Canadian opinion and must seek to combine effectively the strains which go to make it up – loyalty to the British Commonwealth and Crown, concern for the welfare of the United Kingdom, anxiety for the preservation of democracy and freedom, economic self-interest, and so on.

What Wrong seems to be saying is that isolation is probably the ideal policy for Canada, but that the uneducated state of Canadian opinion makes it impracticable at the present time.

* When Wrong wrote Canada actually possessed only the three legations abroad she had had in 1928. Early in 1939 two more were opened, in Belgium and the Netherlands, with a single Minister accredited to both countries.[72]

Skelton naturally agreed with Wrong. In a reply which he sent in due course,[73] he wrote that he felt as Wrong did on the matter of 'the education of the Canadian people to think boldly,' and said:

I think your assumption is correct that if war had come Canada would have been involved as a belligerent, technically from the start and actually after Parliament had met. There would have been a good deal of dissension and bitter feeling but I have myself not much doubt of what the immediate outcome would have been.

That is certainly not a satisfactory situation to anyone who believes in self-government and its implications ...

... The plain fact is that if we go into any European war it will be simply and solely on the grounds of racial sympathy with the United Kingdom. Why obscure this fact or try to dress it up with talk about saving democracy or our League obligations?

It must be added that another member of the Department of External Affairs expressed an opinion quite different from Skelton's and Wrong's. This was the Secretary of State. Mackenzie King wrote in his diary on September 28, 1938, at the height of the crisis: 'I do not agree with S[kelton]'s view that it would be sympathy for Britain that would be the determining factor for Canada going into war. I believe the determining factor would be the determination not to permit the fear of Force to dominate in the affairs of men and nations.'

A year passed between the crisis that called forth these opinions and the actual outbreak of war. During that year Canadian public opinion moved on, as it had moved in the year before. We have seen (above, page 218) that the cabinet was less united in 1938 than it was in 1939; and this certainly reflected opinion in the country at large. Canadians, like the people of Britain in these years, were passing through a process of education, though not perhaps of quite the sort Skelton and Wrong had in mind; they were being educated by Adolf Hitler. In both countries a population that in 1933 was predominantly isolationist, pacifist, and sympathetic to Germany was converted by 1939, as it watched the Nazi excesses, into one that would accept war with Germany. Skelton noted in September 1938 that 'dislike' of Hitler was increasing. It had undoubtedly increased considerably a year later.

Nevertheless, with all due respect to Mackenzie King's opinion, one may question whether hostility to Hitler and devotion to the ideals of freedom and decency which his regime certainly threatened would in themselves have been enough to make Canadians go to war. It is worth while to look at the situation in the adjoining country. During these pre-war years the writer was living and teaching in the United States. It would have been hard to imagine a more violent hostility than that which developed there against Nazi Germany. The American press was full of it. I remember a young German post-doctoral fellow at Princeton, not a Nazi, I imagine, but a patriotic German, who was so deeply disturbed by the New York and Philadelphia newspapers that he seemed to spend most of his time reading them and complaining to anyone who would listen of the picture of Germany that they presented and their comments upon it. He was quite sure that the atrocities they reported had never happened or were grossly exaggerated. The American people had clearly taken sides. Two students of the period write very truly, 'By the autumn of 1937 hardly a trace of intellectual or spiritual neutrality remained.'[74] Yet along with this commitment to the opposition to Hitler went a fixed determination to keep out of the threatened war. And the United States did keep out of the war until its own forces and territories were actually attacked. If the American people's deep antipathy to Hitlerism was not enough to take it into the war, would similar feelings have been enough to lead Canada to fight if other circumstances had not been present? Each country, one suspects, was in its own way moved by its own history, and the two heritages pushed in opposite directions.

One would give a good deal for a 'scientific' sampling of Canadian public opinion in those pre-war days, but Dr George Gallup's activities were not extended to Canada until 1941. Looking at what evidence we have, it seems hard to avoid the conclusion that Dr Skelton was close to the truth: that the inherited feelings and preferences of the Canadian people (which Skelton and Wrong hoped to educate them out of) played the most vital part, and that the hostility of a democratic people for a cruel, tyrannical, and aggressive regime was secondary. That is not to say that the hostility was unimportant. It undoubtedly had a good deal to do with the comparative unanimity with which the country went to war. In 1939 there was not the 'good deal of dissension and bitter feeling' that Skelton had expected the year before; and this was probably mainly due to the increasing dislike of Hitler which he had also noted.

Obviously, French Canada was more reluctant than the predominantly 'Anglo-Saxon' parts of the country. The most that can be said is that it accepted the declaration of war without enthusiasm. It is significant that King, discussing with Cardin the possible merits of a recorded vote on the matter at that moment when the Speaker was actually calling the vote, suggested (on the basis of representations to him by a French member) that a recorded vote would make it 'very difficult for many of the French members who felt that, at the present stage in their constituency [sic], they might be strongly criticized for not having voted with the few who were opposing participation in the war.'[75] The fact that, at the last moment, the godless regime in Russia had thrown in its lot with the Nazis undoubtedly did something to reconcile godly Quebec to the situation; but a more important element in the reconciliation was without doubt the pledge against overseas conscription, first suggested publicly by the leader of the Conservative opposition.

Although Skelton had complained that Canadians had yet to learn to apply to their situation the criterion of 'their own interest and safety' (above, page 235), in fact the decision of September 9, 1939, was completely in accord with the fundamental national interests of Canada. Canada's situation in 1939 was on the whole remarkably comfortable and favourable, in terms of both economic and military strategy. As long as Britain and France had secure control of western Europe and the north Atlantic, Canada's safety and prosperity were assured. Her wheat and other products moved freely across a free sea to open markets abroad, particularly in the United Kingdom (she exported $153 million worth of wheat to Britain in 1937). While these liberal nations protected Canada's interests on the European flank, she was in the happy position of having a very satisfactory relationship with another great liberal community, the United States, on her continental border. Her greatest North American export, newsprint, had crossed that border free since 1913; and since 1935, under the Roosevelt regime, other lucrative export trades had been improving their status. Protected by British sea power and the French Army and by her established friendship with the United States, for generations Canada had been in the fortunate position of being able to avoid large expenditures on defence; and she enjoyed a democratic form of government under which civil liberty was essentially secure.

The rise of Hitler threatened all this. If Nazi Germany had conquered Britain and France, Canada's secure overseas markets would have vanished and her protecting ocean would have been protective no longer. Canada would have become entirely dependent upon the United States. North America would have had to be converted into a fortress, a garrison community, devoting its resources primarily to defence, with consequences for democratic liberties which might have been serious. Canada would probably shortly have been absorbed into the United States, and in the circumstances would have welcomed the absorption. Few people thought of these possibilities in 1939. It is doubtful whether Skelton, or Wrong, or for that matter most Canadians, thought of the defeat of Britain and France as a really likely development. The following year, after the collapse of France, almost everyone was suddenly aware of the danger of complete catastrophe. At the moment of the outbreak of war the person who showed most perception was probably Arthur Meighen, who, in the speech of September 9 in the Senate which we have already quoted, said that in the event of a German victory the British and French Atlantic islands would inevitably pass into German possession: 'Therefore ... imagine, if you will, the day when the forces of Germany crush to the ground the forces of Britain and of France: then, not in twenty-five years, nor in twenty-four hours, but at once the battle must be taken up by the arms of this continent ...'

Knowing what we do today, few people would deny that Canada did right when, alone among the free nations of the Americas, she went to war in 1939 against the Hitlerite tyranny. If mere detestation of that tyranny was not her chief motive, and she was moved primarily by concern for Great Britain, she was nevertheless acting, whether her people thought of it in those terms or not, in accordance with her own national interests. The prosperity and security of Canada were closely linked with the prosperity and security of Britain. It made very good sense for Canada to fight in defence of a strategic situation so favourable to her interests as the North Atlantic situation of 1939. The people whose lack of sophistication Wrong and Skelton deplored arrived by mere instinct at a conclusion sounder than that of the isolationist intelligentsia (to use Mackenzie King's word) in the Department of External Affairs. King himself, as the reader knows, was much closer to the views of the despised populace than to those of the ex-academics on his staff. One can imagine Skelton's circle whispering among themselves that the Prime Minister too could have done with a little education in bold thinking.

CHAPTER EIGHT

THE SECOND WORLD WAR: 1939-41

SKETCH OF A WAR EFFORT

In September 1939 Canada went to war with Germany for the second time in a generation. In 1914 she had been a self-governing colony, automatically committed to the conflict by the action of the mother country. In 1939, after twenty-five years of constitutional evolution, she was an independent state within the British Commonwealth, capable, as she demonstrated in the crisis, of making a separate declaration of war, but nevertheless still following the lead of Britain. The next six years would put to the test the genuineness of the 'nationhood' she had acquired, and show just how significant 'constitutional progress' was when weighed in the power balance of world war.

We cannot tell in this and the following chapter the whole story of Canadian war policy. That has been told, with moderate completeness, elsewhere.[1] And it is certainly not our business to tell of battles and campaigns. We must limit ourselves to external policy strictly so called, the relations of Canada with other states as they were affected by the exigencies of the war.

As we have seen, the King government had consistently refused to engage in any military consultation with London, since this might be held to involve commitments. But on the afternoon of September 1, after Parliament was called, the Prime Minister himself initiated consultation, though still with characteristic caution. He wrote in his diary,

I ... went to call on Sir Gerald Campbell. He had left to come ... to see me. I met him at the East Block door and told him in a few words I understood that Britain wished us to get on with what we could to help. Britain was not concerned in the matter of expeditionary force, if we did not wish to send an expeditionary force. He said he had already noticed the statements made in Parliament last year, and had made the British Government acquainted with them, but would communicate further and indicate what he thought himself would best meet our situation, in the hope of getting word back which would be helpful before Parliament met. I told him I was anxious to avoid direct communications that might prove embarrassing.

It seems clear that King said rather more than he set down in his dictated diary. Campbell hastened back to his office and cabled London. King, he said, had told him that he was most gratified by the 'absolute unanimity' of the cabinet during the day's meetings; 'he feels that his policy during these critical months is justified now by the fact of a united Canada ready and willing to help Great Britain to the utmost of its power and resources':

He plans to telegraph direct to the Prime Minister shortly but in the meantime he asks me to enquire from the United Kingdom Government informally and to communicate to him unofficially before Parliament meets on 7th September what assistance they actually desire from Canada. He has no hesitation in saying that Canada will assume responsibility for the protection of her Atlantic coastline and her commerce and will also assist in the protection of Newfoundland ... but he must present to Parliament some definite programme of participation including as he suggests food supplies, raw materials, munitions and aviation pilots of which last named a considerable number should be ready to come according to an opinion expressed by the Minister of National Defence in council meeting to-day.

Campbell went on to say that King then raised the question of an expeditionary force, mention of which in Parliament would almost certainly bring on 'acrimonious debate.' The High Commissioner told him that the British government knew that Canada might be unwilling to send such a force, but he thought there would be many volunteers eager to enlist 'for service in Great Britain' and the British government would welcome them if Canada did not think it necessary to keep them for home defence. King 'neither agreed nor disagreed' but asked Campbell to ascertain his government's views 'for his own private information'. Campbell wrote further: 'My personal impression is that while he wants a perfectly frank statement of your desires, he would prefer that no great account should be made [sic] at this point upon the despatch of an expeditionary force as he is eager to present the world with an almost unanimous vote when Parliament meets. May I suggest however that advantage be taken of this opportunity to profound [? present] financial requirements in an attempt to relieve strain on the exchange occasioned by purchase of large supplies of food and materials.'

Campbell's message was passed to the British Chiefs of Staff, who produced on September 4 a statement of the aid they would welcome from Canada. By that time King had sent (on September 3) his formal telegram to the British Prime Minister. It was less forthcoming than his verbal approach to Campbell; its tentative sketch of a Canadian war effort clearly reflected Skelton's paper of August 24 (above, page 257), emphasizing economic effort. It said: 'As to further military cooperation we should be glad to receive your appreciation of the probable theatre and character of main British and Allied military operations, in order that we may consider the policy to be adopted by Canada.' The British reply (September 6) was entirely based on the Chiefs of Staff paper in reply to the High Commissioner's message of September 1. It was tactfully phrased, particularly with respect to the Army. There was a long list of naval measures, beginning with 'The six destroyers of the Royal Canadian Navy to be placed under Admiralty orders.' On the Air Force, the most important suggestion was 'the rapid expansion of present training facilities using civil aerodromes with the aim of 2,000 pilots a year.' As for the Army, this is the way the matter was put: 'While it is hoped that Canada would exert her full national effort as in last war, even to the extent of the eventual despatch of an expeditionary force, it is realised that no statement of policy on these lines is likely to be possible at the moment. Would it be possible, however, to consider as an immediate programme (a) the despatch of a small Canadian unit which would take its place along side the United Kingdom troops ...' The message went on to ask for technical units for attachment to British formations, and technical personnel for enlistment in British units.*

Mackenzie King had approached the final crisis that issued in the outbreak of war without any specific plan of his own for a Canadian war effort. Skelton's paper which the cabinet approved was a highly general plan for a very limited effort. The Chiefs of Staff produced a much more detailed military plan to which the cabinet gave a rather frosty reception. The Chiefs' scheme assumed the desirability of a considerable expeditionary force; Skelton's assumed the reverse. This was the main question the

---

* Examination of British records has enabled me to present here a fuller version of these events than that contained in my book *Arms, Men and Governments: The War Policies of Canada, 1939-1945* (Ottawa 1974).

Canadian government had to settle, and it was rendered more urgent by the British request for an immediate token force. Mainly undoubtedly as a result of the hostility to an expeditionary force expressed by Quebec representatives during the special session, the cabinet chose not to grasp this nettle until after Parliament was sent home on September 13. On September 15 it appointed a sub-committee to draft both a war programme and an announcement of it to the nation. The committee was headed by the new Minister of Finance, Colonel J.L. Ralston, a distinguished soldier of the First War and a veteran minister, much respected in the Liberal party and the country. He had not stood for election in 1935, but his sense of duty had now brought him back into the government. The committee insisted on greatly reducing the expenditures proposed by the Chiefs of Staff. The government's programme was announced in a long statement on September 19. Inevitably, it was a compromise reflecting the various pressures that had borne upon the cabinet: isolationist influence from Skelton and the French MPs, the tactful pressure from the British government, urgings from English Canada in favour of the sort of effort exerted in the First War – typified by the fact that King wrote in his diary on September 7: 'Found Council more favourable to an expeditionary force than I had imagined they would be, and growing feeling that it might become inevitable.' The statement announced that the programme endeavoured 'to put first things first and to co-ordinate Canada's effort with that of the United Kingdom in the most effective way.' The British telegram had said, 'perhaps the most valuable immediate assistance which Canada could give in this field [that of supplies] would be any steps which are possible to assist us in the financing of desired purchases'; and the first item in the published Canadian programme was 'facilitating the purchase by the United Kingdom of essential supplies in this country.' This would involve 'repatriation of Canadian securities held in London.'* The very last item was the intention 'to organize and train a division to be available as an expeditionary force, if and when required,' and to keep a second division 'under arms as a further measure of preparedness.' (These divisions already existed, having been mobilized on September 1.) Though the expeditionary force stood last on the list, everybody knew that it would be very far from least in importance. And the response to the British request for a 'small Canadian unit' had certainly been not ungenerous.[2]

---

* Thus began the painful process of 'disinvestment' which by the end of the war had greatly reduced the British financial stake in Canada.

A week after this carefully-drafted programme was unveiled, a cable from the British Prime Minister suggested something new and far-reaching: what came to be called the British Commonwealth Air Training Plan. The British government, we have seen, had originally asked for an air training scheme to produce 2,000 pilots a year; and 'a plan of intensified air training' was promised in the statement of September 19. Now, however, Neville Chamberlain made a much larger proposal. The fact is that Vincent Massey and Stanley Bruce, respectively the Canadian and Australian High Commissioners in London, had been pressing for a very big training scheme centring in Canada, and this is what Chamberlain proposed to Mackenzie King, in 'a special personal appeal,' on September 26. There was an anticipated annual requirement, he wrote, of 'not less than 20,000 pilots and 30,000 [other] personnel of air crews,' and this was more than twice the training capacity of the United Kingdom. What was needed was 'say fifty flying training schools' and some subsidiary schools. Could Canada undertake to provide them?[3]

The Canadian government received this proposition with mixed feelings.* In many ways it precisely suited their views. Their pre-war military program had given priority to the air, and the British scheme would mean that a large part of the Canadian air effort would be exerted in Canada and not overseas; at the same time, it clearly represented a major contribution to winning the war. On the other hand, it meant also a large increase in expenditure, over and above that envisaged in the programme of September 19, which had been carefully tailored to fall within conservative estimates of national capacity made by the Department of Finance. An entry in Mackenzie King's diary strongly suggests that if Chamberlain's proposal had been made ten days earlier, no Army expeditionary force would have gone overseas in 1939; an attempt would have been made to represent the Air Training Plan as an effective substitute.[5] Even as it was, however, the cabinet had no difficulty in accepting the idea; and on September 28 King cabled Chamberlain agreeing to his suggestion in principle.[6]

---

* Massey was vastly proud of his share in originating the plan, and in fact later obtained a letter from Anthony Eden (who was Dominions Secretary at the time) testifying to it.[4] He said nothing of the fact that he did the whole thing behind Mackenzie King's back. Since the project materially changed the balance of the Canadian war effort, it was a more than doubtful proceeding. King apparently never discovered what Massey had done.

CANADA AND HER ALLIES

When Canada declared war on September 10, 1939, she joined an existing coalition of powers formed to resist Hitler's Germany. The core of this coalition was the Anglo-French alliance. Britain and France agreed in the beginning that their war efforts should be co-ordinated by a Supreme War Council (such as had been set up in the First World War only in 1917). 'France and the United Kingdom should each be represented by the Prime Minister and one other Minister, and other Allied Powers, perhaps, by their Ambassadors.'[7]

With this organization Canada had no connection, and there is no indication that her government ever considered claiming any. It is true that the policy records for the early days of the war are exiguous. There are no cabinet minutes until February 1944; the Cabinet War Committee, which did keep valuable minutes, did not meet regularly until May 1940; and we are driven back on the files of the Department of External Affairs and on Mackenzie King's diary. Nothing has been found in either of these sources to suggest that Canada sought to have her Minister in Paris or her High Commissioner in London admitted to the Supreme War Council, or asked for any other form of representation. Had she chosen to stand on her national dignity, citing her status under the Covenant of the League of Nations or the Statute of Westminster, she might or might not have gained admission. As it was, she simply remained silent, tacitly accepting the practical fact that so far as she had a relationship to the Allied direction of the war it was through the British government and the result of her membership in the British Commonwealth of Nations.

The reasons for the quiet acceptance of this position by the autonomist government of Mackenzie King can be only a matter of speculation. Clearly, however, we are up against the hard facts of power. Canada was a partner in the Allied war effort, but she was a very junior one at best. Moreover, by her government's deliberate choice she was making only a limited contribution to the war. Sir Robert Borden in 1914-18 had claimed national status for his country on the basis of her great contribution; Mackenzie King in 1939 could scarcely claim a share in the direction of the new war while consciously pursuing a policy of limiting his country's liability. It is worth remarking also that neither King nor his adviser Skelton had any interest in or knowledge of the conduct of war. They would have understood those Chinese intellectuals who, we are told, regard soldiers as an inferior race of beings whose proceedings deserve only the contempt of civilized men. Skelton's programme of

August 24, it will be remembered, emphasized the desirability of a 'Statement of War Aims' but said nothing about a share in the direction of the war.

Proposals for the restoration of peace, however, were a different matter; and it was clear from the beginning that Hitler, when he had destroyed Poland, was going to talk peace. It was also clear that Britain and France, having screwed their courage up to the point of making war on the aggressor, had no intention of making peace with him because he had won a local victory. Chamberlain, indeed, had specifically warned him of this in his telegram of August 22 (above, page 251). Vincent Massey, after a conversation with Chamberlain and other ministers on September 28, reported to King, 'It is Chamberlain's unshakable view that Hitler can never be trusted again.'[8] Hitler duly launched his peace offensive, after a couple of preliminary gestures, in a speech to the Reichstag on October 6. The British government issued the same day a statement observing that though his proposals contained 'no suggestion of reparation for the wrongs done by Germany to other peoples' they would nevertheless be carefully examined 'in consultation with the Governments of the Dominions and the French Republic.'[9]

There is nothing in Mackenzie King's diary at this point to indicate that anything survived of his old regard for Hitler. He clearly hoped, however, that Hitler's initiative could be used to end the war. He at once sent off to Chamberlain a suggestion that if the German overture were rejected France and Britain should put forward 'their own positive programme of the basis upon which the war could be terminated.' Sunday, October 8, was a national day of prayer; and King, not unsuitably, devoted part of his time in church to roughing out a peace programme of his own, which he cabled to Chamberlain that evening. Both these messages were marked 'Personal,' and they had not been discussed with King's colleagues, though he had invoked the aid of Skelton. Nobody need be surprised that the Prime Minister's plan was, as he put it in his diary, 'all in the lines of our Industrial Disputes Act and also of L[eague] of N[ations] procedure, the theory being that it is a form of compulsory consideration not arbitration, permitting opportunity for public opinion to be brought to bear.' What he suggested was 'Investigation and report on methods of adjusting the European situation by a committee of neutral powers'; the committee might, he said, consist of the President of the United States, the King of Italy and the King of the Belgians. Their report would be conveyed to the belligerents 'for acceptance, rejection or modification after conference.' In the meantime there would be 'an unconditional truce ... pending investigation report and conference.'[10]

King did not really expect anything to come of his suggestion. He wrote in his diary: 'I have not much hope of the proposal made being accepted by Britain or France. I feel they are in the fight and are determined to see it through. On the other hand, I feel this effort may be so largely suicidal that almost anything which will save unparalleled destruction of human life and partially of civilization itself is worth attempting. Moreover, the stronger the case that can be made against Germany by her refusal to accept an obviously fair method of adjustment, the more likely are neutral nations and the U.S. in particular to lend their aid to Britain and France. What I put forward is what I have striven for all my life, and even if I should be alone in making the proposal, I feel I owe it to my conscience and to my fellow men to put the proposal forward.'[11] The polite reply from Chamberlain was what King had expected. Whitehall had undoubtedly regarded his scheme as the height of naïveté, as indeed it was. To speak of stopping Hitler by the mobilization of public opinion, in October 1939, was enough to take any practical person's breath away. The British Prime Minister remarked that all the evidence went to show that 'Hitler's present move is merely a tactical one couched in vague and unsatisfactory terms and intended to weaken our position.' Nevertheless, he wrote, King's suggestions had been 'considered most carefully.' 'But we have felt there would be little prospect at this stage that a Neutral Committee of Investigation, such as you suggest, would be acceptable either to neutral countries themselves or to other belligerents.'[12]

The consultation promised in the British statement of October 6 took the form of inviting Dominion comment on a draft of the statement Chamberlain proposed to make in the House of Commons in reply to Hitler. The Canadian cabinet discussed this and agreed, doubtless on King's suggestion, that it was not positive enough (Skelton had given King a memorandum to this effect). King then suggested to Chamberlain that it might be well to make 'a more positive statement of war aims and of the conditions or procedure upon which the Government of the United Kingdom consider that the war might now be terminated'; however, no very great change was made and Chamberlain's statement on October 12, as was probably inevitable, came close to being a declaration that it was impossible to negotiate with 'the present German Government.'[13] King reflected that the world might soon be 'questioning very seriously the wisdom of blank refusal of what the world will construe as peace overtures, and the failure, on Britain's part to make a definite proposal on her own.' He saw no virtue in 'consultation' as practised in this case, telling Lord Tweedsmuir: 'At most it was comment, and that to be accepted only if it suited the purpose ... It is a practice which should be stopped.'[14]

The discussion was resumed shortly when the French government suggested an exchange of views with Britain on the problem of Allied war aims and London invited the Dominion governments to comment. This called forth from King an enormously long memorandum addressed to Skelton, in which he paraded his whole stable of personal hobbyhorses.[15] He said that Canada was fighting for freedom, and that she believed in organizing international public opinion for the protection of freedom. He criticized the League of Nations for identifying collective security 'with coercion, sanctions, etc.' instead of relying on 'impartial investigation of existing wrongs' as provided in the Canadian Industrial Disputes Investigation Act. 'Canada,' he wrote, 'is in a strong position to make her voice heard and her views, if sound, prevail. We have gone into this war voluntarily. We are in it at great cost while our powerful neighbour is out of it at great material advantage, though I regret to say at equally great loss of moral power and prestige.' He quoted the Tennysonian line that he had placed on the memorial to his dead friend Bert Harper: 'If I lose myself, I save myself.' This, he said, was the spirit in which Canada had gone to war, a spirit quite different from that of Ireland, South Africa, and the United States, neutrals or near-neutrals – a spirit 'which I believe not only to be infinitely more chivalrous but also fundamentally more sound.' Perhaps on the whole it was as well that this discussion petered out. A long statement did go to London in which the Prime Minister's views were put forward in somewhat more sophisticated terms;[16] but the British government finally decided to send the French only an interim reply in which Ottawa had no difficulty in concurring.[17]

In November 1939 the Queen of the Netherlands and the King of the Belgians, alarmed about the possibility of German attack on their own countries, offered their services as mediators in an attempt to end the war. Again the British government invited Dominion comments on a draft reply, to the effect that if the two sovereigns could communicate any proposals from Germany which could hold out the hope of redeeming Europe from the recurring fear of German aggression King George's governments would give them most earnest consideration. Canada suggested a change in wording intended to broaden the meaning beyond Europe, and the United Kingdom and the other Dominions accepted the suggestion.[18]

Immediately after the outbreak of war in the west, Soviet Russia forced the Baltic states of Estonia, Latvia, and Lithuania to accept Russian garrisons on their territory – a move which proved to be merely a preliminary to the absorption of the three states into the Soviet Union. Similar demands on Finland were refused by the Finnish government, and at the end of November 1939 Russian invaded Finland – 'a ghastly bit of ruthless aggression,' in Mackenzie King's phrase.[19] The Finns met their gigantic antagonist with a combination of courage and skill that has few parallels in modern history, and which commanded the sympathy and admiration of the free world. The first Russian attacks were defeated at almost every point. The Assembly of the League of Nations passed (December 14) a resolution expelling Russia from the League and calling upon member states to give humanitarian and material aid to Finland.*

The Canadian government, pressed by public opinion to do something for Finland, considered its position. One possible obstacle was the Foreign Enlistment Act passed during the Spanish Civil War (above, page 197), the more so as J.S. Woodsworth had managed to eliminate from it a provision which would have enabled the government to make exceptions. After due consideration the view was taken that it would be proper to allow the enlistment of Finnish volunteers in Canada; the question of whether Canadians might be permitted to volunteer was not so simple, and the matter was still being discussed when the Russians launched their final, and successful, offensive against Finland. O.D. Skelton wrote that the governing principle should be to avoid going farther in this direction than the British and French governments did. The only actual aid the Canadian government gave was modest: the provision on January 18 of $100,000 'for the purchase and transport of Canadian foodstuffs for the relief of the people of Finland.' On March 11, however, Mackenzie King brought himself to sign a recommendation to the cabinet that passports should be provided free for Canadians enlisting for service in Finland. No volunteers went; the Finns capitulated the following day.[21]

Britain and France had had worse problems. Were they to send military aid to Finland, as many people in the two countries were demanding? Their resources were already stretched by the war with Germany. To reach Finland their forces would have to pass through Norway and Sweden, and it was more than doubtful whether those nations would consent. The prospect of war with Russia while still engaged with Germany was daunting – though contemporaries in London and Paris seem, surprisingly, to have been less alarmed by it than hindsight suggests they

---

* Mackenzie King's instruction to the Canadian Permanent Delegate was to support the expulsion resolution if the United Kingdom supported it. The vote was in fact almost unanimous.[20]

should have been. At the same time, Britain and France were anxious to cut the marine line of communication through Norwegian territorial waters by which iron ore from Norway was reaching Germany, an object which would have been served by the occupation of Norwegian ports. These possibilities were argued over for weeks and months. Sweden and Norway were too frightened of Germany to co-operate, and in the end the Finns, convinced that the British and French could not give them enough help to save them, made the best terms they could with Russia.[22] A moment of very grave peril for the Allies had passed.

Late in February, when the affairs of Finland were entering their final crisis, the British government sent to Ottawa a draft of a statement on the question of Norwegian territorial waters which they proposed to make. Comments were urgently requested – Mackenzie King's personal comments if those of the cabinet at large were not available. King was campaigning in Manitoba, but the papers were sent to him and he made his observations by telephone to Skelton:

The Prime Minister said that the following points should be made to Sir Gerald Campbell:

(1) That the Prime Minister was not in a position to make any comments or observations. Previous communications had been said to be for his personal information without any indication of a desire to have the Canadian Government express an opinion.

(2) If an opinion were required on a subject of this importance, he would consider it necessary to consult his colleagues, which would not be feasible or in some respects advisable under present circumstances.

(3) This would specially be the case if there were any likelihood of a desire arising subsequently in connection with a public announcement of any policy which might be decided upon by the United Kingdom to state that it represented the views of the Dominion Governments as well as the Government of the United Kingdom.[23]

It may be well to place beside this the passage from King's diary (February 27) describing how this result was arrived at. Lapointe and Crerar were with him in Winnipeg, and he read them the papers: 'The British Government anxious evidently to be able to say that the Dominions had been consulted and agreed with their views. We all took view that we should not make any observations, to make it clear that it would be necessary to have Cabinet as a whole to consult with before expressing an opinion; also, that we are in a campaign and it would be inadvisable to have anything said about the Dominion attitude at this time which could be avoided, to save raising an issue. Moreover, though we did not put this into the despatch, we all felt that, while Canada was at the side of Britain and France with our war effort and, particularly, as the matter referred to was distinctly a European one, it should be kept as between France and Britain themselves.' The British memorandum made no reference to Finland. King, however, discussed with his two colleagues what should be done if war were declared against Russia. 'Lapointe saw no objection to the distribution of our Forces in Europe in any direction that might be desired. I pointed out that I thought we ought to hold to Parliament deciding on Canada being at war with Russia; to get along, meanwhile, by using the League of Nations affiliation for whatever might be done.'

King's hastily-dictated diary is often ill-expressed, and these passages are a good example. It is pretty clear, however, that he was thinking of Canada's war as limited in more ways than one. She had committed herself to Britain and France, and made their interests her own; but she had made no commitments to other European countries and it is evident that King thought she should be backward about doing so. At a later stage of the war he would be noticeably cool towards the concept of 'the liberation of Europe.'

As for 'consultation,' if his views had not been clear before, they were clear now. He did not want to be consulted, particularly when the consultation took the form of a request for comment on a proposed British statement; and he certainly did not want to be asked to commit himself to a perhaps controversial policy in the midst of a political campaign. He very definitely refused to identify himself with any British policy on Norway, and he presumably would have made a similar refusal on Finland.

The late John Read, who in 1940 was still a senior official in External Affairs, told the present writer, and other people,[24] long afterwards, a story representing King as having saved the Allies and the Commonwealth from disaster in the Finnish affair. According to this, the British government sent to Ottawa a proposal for active military intervention on the side of Finland – a possibility which, we have seen, was certainly definitely considered in London and Paris. There was a request for King's comments. Read said that King saw clearly the appalling consequences of war with Germany and Russian simultaneously, but was also painfully aware of the popularity in Canada of the idea of intervening on behalf of Finland. He therefore simply refrained from answering London's question. 'Hasteners' continued to arrive from England asking for a reply, but King remained silent. He thus contrived to defer Allied action until the Finnish collapse ended the danger. Prolonged search has failed to elicit any documentary evidence for this tale. There is nothing in King's diary to support it, though the Prime Minister, if he had achieved such a *coup*, could hardly have failed to record it. Read apparently convinced himself, over a period of years, that something happened which never took place at all. The origin of the story is probably the episode just narrated. It may perhaps be assumed, incidentally, that after that episode, a fortnight before the Finnish capitulation, the British government would not have attempted to 'consult' Mackenzie King again, at any rate until after some lapse of time.

In the spring of 1940 two Canadian foreign service officers abroad raised the question of the Canadian relationship to the Allied direction of the war which no one seems to have raised in Ottawa.

One of these people was L.B. Pearson, Official Secretary at Canada House, London. In April the Minister of National Defence, Norman Rogers, was in London, and at his request Pearson gave him a memorandum entitled 'War-time Intergovernmental Consultation and Communication.' It complained ('too strongly and rather peevishly,' Pearson wrote long afterwards in his memoirs) that the Canadian authorities were not kept sufficiently informed: 'We are told what has happened; very seldom, what will happen or may happen.' It went on to say, 'so far as policy and planning ... are concerned, our status is little better than that of a colony': 'We have practically no influence on decisions and little prior information concerning them. We have no Service representatives on Planning and Operations Boards; we have no representatives on the War Cabinet or on Cabinet Secretariats, for the purpose of securing firsthand information. The Allied War Council meets with Norwegian and Polish representatives; but not Canadian. A very important meeting of that Council took place last Saturday but we have not yet received any information as to what took place at that meeting; neither has North Borneo ... But we do not seem to have been concerned at our exclusion from the Councils of our Allies in a war in which our whole future is at stake.' Canada's role, Pearson went on, seemed to be merely to supply soldiers and airmen who would fight 'as a result of deliberations in which we have had no part.' 'Personally,' he wrote, 'I dislike this role of unpaid Hessians.' He proposed specific remedies:

What steps can be taken to improve this situation during the war?

(1) Canada should be informed of all the deliberations of the War Cabinet.

This could be done through the Dominions Office, or, preferably, through the Cabinet Secretariat via Canada House. A Canadian official should be brought into touch with this Secretariat.

(2) Should not a Canadian representative have the right to attend the War Cabinet when questions which concern Canadian participation are under consideration so that the Government in Canada can be informed *at once* by its own representative?

(3) Certainly Canada should have the right to attend meetings of the allied War Council either in London or Paris.

(4) Should not Canadian Staff Officers be attached to the Secretariat of the Chiefs of Staff Committee or to the Military Secretary of the War Cabinet? This might, in fact, be the most effective way of securing advance information on strategic proposals which may involve the use of Canadian troops or Canadian airmen.

The above suggestions may or may not be practicable or desirable. It cannot be denied, however, that the machinery for intergovernmental contact and communication which may have been satisfactory in peace-time, may well prove dangerously inadequate in war-time. That machinery should therefore be re-examined in the light of war conditions.[25]

Almost simultaneously the Canadian Minister to France, Lt.-Col. G.P. Vanier, was raising the question of Canada's relationship to the war from another angle. The time was approaching when the 1st Canadian Division would move from England to France and take its place in the Allied order of battle. In a dispatch to the Department of External Affairs (which he also communicated to Mr Rogers) Vanier inquired what its position would be. Things had changed, he remarked, since the last war; the Statute of Westminster had been passed, and the division was therefore 'part of the armed forces of a sovereign state.' It might be necessary for this relatively small dominion force to be incorporated 'for tactical and administrative purposes' in the British Expeditionary Force whose organization and training were similar, but questions arose. In particular, 'Doubtless the Canadian Government will wish the Canadian Force to be under the command of General Gamelin in the same way as the B.E.F.'; and Vanier added, 'I assume that as a matter of principle the Commander of the Canadian Force will have direct access to the Allied Commander-in-Chief.' If this was not the case, then 'consideration might be given to the question of remedying a situation which the French Authorities would find difficult to conciliate [sic] with the normal prerogatives of a Sovereign State.'[26]

These two initiatives were taken at a most unfavourable moment. Before Norman Rogers reached Ottawa on his return journey, the Germans had launched their *Blitzkrieg* in the west. France was shortly tottering to her fall, and people were no longer talking comfortably about war aims and national dignity; they were thinking about mere survival. No evidence has been found that Pearson's memorandum was seriously considered in Ottawa; perhaps Rogers did not put it forward. The Department of External Affairs sent an answer to Vanier's dispatch, explaining possibly a trifle lamely that the Canadian force would be serving under a British commander by virtue of the Visiting Forces Acts (below, page 289); its commander would not have direct access to the Allied Commander-in-Chief. Vanier was, however, to approach the French government, 'informing them that to facilitate unity and effectiveness of Defence Measures, it was not proposed that Canadian Forces should be placed directly under the command of the French Commander-in-Chief, but that Viscount Gort was the Commander operating under and by virtue of the Canadian Statute Law, as the Commander of the Combined British Forces.'[27] This message was sent on May 29, 1940, at a moment when Lord Gort's men were scrambling on to the evacuation craft at Dunkirk. Vanier probably received it, but since the abandonment of Paris to the Germans was already being discussed before it was sent, it seems unlikely that he troubled the French government with its contents. In the midst of the crisis, Neville Chamberlain fell from power in Britain and was replaced as Prime Minister by Winston Churchill, who was much less likely to be sympathetic to arguments about the constitutional position of Canada, and in any case had many other things to think about. If Canada's constitutional rights were to be discussed, the time to discuss them would have been the quiet early months of the conflict, labelled by Joseph P. Kennedy the phony war. But the phony war was over.

COMMONWEALTH AT WAR

In one respect only, the outbreak of war was followed by an active extension of Commonwealth organization. The Canadian government used the opportunity to initiate an exchange of High Commissioners with other Dominions.

It will be remembered that this form of 'personal contact' had received cautious approval from the Imperial Conference of 1926, and that the United Kingdom appointed a High Commissioner to Ottawa in 1928. The Dominions divided on this question along the lines that had been apparent at the conference. The conservative Pacific Dominions viewed the innovation with suspicion, as being tarred with the brush of nationalism. R.B. Bennett in 1935 suggested to Australia an exchange of High Commissioners; the Australian Prime Minister (Joseph A. Lyons) briefly replied that the time was 'inopportune.'[28] But by the outbreak of war South Africa and Ireland both had representatives in Ottawa, and the

Canadian government had declared its intention of reciprocating. On September 3, 1939, it renewed its suggestion to Australia and made a similar approach to New Zealand. This time Australia warmly concurred. New Zealand, always clubby, replied that it would be 'most happy' to receive a Canadian representative, but did not commit itself to sending one to Ottawa immediately. (In June 1941 New Zealand finally broke down and decided to send High Commissioners to Ottawa and Canberra, at the same time appointing a Minister to Washington.) On September 11, 1939, the Canadian government announced that it would be appointing High Commissioners to Australia, New Zealand, South Africa, and Ireland.* A Canadian High Commissioner to Newfoundland was appointed in July 1941.[29]

These were relatively peripheral matters. For the Canadian government and the Canadian people relations with Britain were what mattered, particularly with Britain in the front line of the war. And neither Canada nor Britain had fundamental changes in the machinery of communication to suggest at the beginning of the war. In the beginning the British government considered the question of liaison with the Dominions and decided that 'the time was not propitious' for inviting Dominion ministers to the Supreme War Council or for proposing an Imperial War Cabinet on the model of 1917-18. It was thought desirable, however, that Dominion High Commissioners should have occasional meetings with members of the British War Cabinet, and that Dominion ministers and their technical advisers should be encouraged to visit the United Kingdom.[30] Canada, we have seen, made no suggestion at all, and it is evident that if the British had suggested an Imperial War Cabinet King would have rejected it at once.

What Chamberlain did suggest to the Dominion Prime Ministers on September 21, 1939, was that each of them might designate one of his cabinet colleagues to make a brief visit to London and discuss the situation with the British government 'and if possible with Ministers from other Dominions also.' It was also suggested that the ministers should be accompanied by senior military and air officers who might remain in London (the British Admiralty evidently felt no need for improved liaison with the Dominions). King made no difficulty about accepting the invitation, and asked T.A. Crerar, the Minister of Mines and Resources and the senior Privy Councillor after King himself and Senator Dandu-

---

* Neutral Eire, moving towards leaving the Commonwealth, would have preferred some other term such as Minister, but for the present accepted High Commissioner.

rand, to undertake the mission. In other respects he showed a certain lukewarmness. He remarked that it might be difficult to arrange for all the Commonwealth representatives to be in London at the same time, and that this should therefore not be an essential feature of the arrangement; and he also remarked that he was doubtful about the military representatives remaining indefinitely in London (nevertheless, Brigadier H.D.G. Crerar, who accompanied his namesake, did remain to set up Canadian Military Headquarters, the Canadian Army's static establishment there). When the English press speculated that the mission might indicate an intention of setting up an Imperial War Cabinet as in the previous war, King promptly and publicly denied that there was any such intention.[31]

The meetings in London in November were a sort of little Imperial Conference, Australia, New Zealand, South Africa, and India being represented as well as Britain and Canada. The strategic situation was reviewed. It is evident, however, that the Canadian government's main interest in these conversations was economic. Chamberlain had suggested that it might be desirable to consider special liaison arrangements concerning 'equipment, munitions and supply including food and raw materials'; and Mr Crerar was accompanied by representatives of the Departments of Trade and Commerce and Agriculture and of the Canadian Wheat Board. Subsequently the delegation was reinforced by Graham Towers, Governor of the Bank of Canada. (It is perhaps symptomatic of the lack of war-mindedness among the Ottawa bureaucracy that Towers' departure on this rather urgent mission was delayed by the need for getting a second seat on the Clipper aircraft to Lisbon – for Mrs Towers.) The fact is that the Canadians were looking for business, and this became very evident in the bilateral Anglo-Canadian discussions that followed the main conference. Crerar, as befitted a representative of the prairie west, went to London mainly to sell wheat; and the terms he proposed were not acceptable to the British. He suggested a long-term wheat-purchase agreement at a price of 93½ cents a bushel, at a time when the spot price at Winnipeg was 73 cents. When the British demurred, he argued that 73 cents was not a price at which a Canadian farmer could make a living, and that the price he had suggested was the lowest at which the farmer could survive without subsidy. The British responded that that price would add three halfpence to the cost of the Englishman's loaf of bread.

A recent Canadian writer describes this British statement, a bit surprisingly, as 'emotional blackmail.'[32] The British might have used at least equally hard words about a cable Mackenzie King sent to Chamberlain on

November 3. Hard bargaining was going on in Ottawa about the financing of the Air Training Plan; and King now said in so many words that a favourable decision on the Plan depended upon a wheat agreement: 'In our opinion the questions of military and economic participation in the war effort are inextricably intertwined and cannot be dealt with separately.'[33] The British Minister of Food offered to buy not less than 1,500,000 tons of wheat during the winter at 82½ cents a bushel; the Canadian Minister of Trade and Commerce (still Euler) refused, preferring the alternative of the British buying from time to time at the market price. Crerar went home without a wheat agreement, and the Canadians quietly forgot about the threat, no wheat agreement, no air training plan. And in May 1940 Canada accepted a British offer to buy 50,000,000 bushels during the summer at 82½ cents, the price rejected five months before. It was still above the market price, and an External Affairs officer in Ottawa commented that the deal 'should in all the circumstances be regarded as favourable from every Canadian viewpoint.'[34]

In April 1940, as already mentioned, Norman Rogers, the Minister of National Defence, visited England. This visit too was concerned in great part with economic matters, and particularly with the British authorities' apparent reluctance to place equipment orders with Canadian industry. While Rogers was in London, Chamberlain proposed a conference of Commonwealth Prime Ministers to be held during the coming summer. Mackenzie King, whose reluctance to use traditional Commonwealth machinery is evident, asked Rogers to call on Chamberlain and discourage the project. The arguments used were the uncertain duration of the Canadian parliamentary session, the Prime Minister's special responsibility for maintaining 'an unbroken front and a united sentiment' behind the Canadian war effort, and the importance of King's 'being available in Canada in the event of a situation arising in which he might be called upon to assist in maintaining the most friendly relations between Great Britain and the United States.' King was not the only Dominion Prime Minister who found the project untimely, and it was abandoned for the moment.[35]

THE MILITARY RELATIONSHIP WITH BRITAIN

Something must be said about the relationship of the Canadian fighting forces to those of Britain, with which they were very closely linked throughout the war.

The reader may remember that at the outset of the earlier war Canada's rudimentary naval force was placed 'at the disposal of His Majesty, for general service in the Royal Navy' as permitted by the Naval Service Act of 1910 (Volume I, pages 134 and 175). This statute was still in effect in 1939, but history did not precisely repeat itself. The British government did request, in the memorandum on war measures sent to Canada on September 6 (above, page 272), that the six Canadian destroyers should be placed under Admiralty orders, and the Canadian Chief of the Naval Staff (Rear Admiral Percy W. Nelles) recommended that this should be done. Obviously Canada's tiny force could not conduct a naval war against Germany on its own, and Nelles pointed out that it was desirable that naval operations in the western Atlantic should be directed by a single commander and staff, and that the most suitable commander was the Commander-in-Chief of the Royal Navy's America and West Indies Station, who had, with the Canadian government's concurrence, moved two 8-inch-gun cruisers into Halifax harbour even before Canada declared war. The cabinet on September 14 decided that, while the Canadian ships would not be placed 'at disposal,' they would 'cooperate to the fullest extent with the forces of the Royal Navy.' Co-operation was not defined, but it was interpreted in practice to mean that when British and Canadian ships were working together the senior officer present took command, whether he was Canadian or British. The practical effect in most cases was that a British officer was in command. Canadian ships throughout the war normally acted under higher British command. The cabinet decision of 1939, however, had an important effect. Canadian ships could not be moved out of Canadian waters, or from one theatre to another, without their own government's approval. Such approval was sought and given in May 1940 before Canadian destroyers crossed the Atlantic to join the hard-pressed Royal Navy in the struggle around the British Isles. The same thing happened in 1942 when sixteen escort vessels were sent to take part in the North African landing operations, and again in 1944 when the same number of minesweepers was authorized by the Cabinet War Committee for the Normandy landings, in which many other Canadian vessels took part. Later that year the War Committee, on Mackenzie King's insistence, greatly reduced the naval contribution to the Pacific War which the British Admiralty and the Canadian Chiefs of Staff had envisaged.[36]

On the Atlantic coast in the early days of the war the situation was this. Convoy was the great task; and the convoys to Britain were organized under the direction of a Canadian officer, the Commanding Officer Atlantic Coast, who had, however, the assistance of two trained officers provided by the Admiralty. The ocean escort forces were under a British officer of flag rank, the Rear Admiral Third Battle Squadron, whose command included the old British 'R' class battleships (*Revenge*, etc.); he in turn was under the Commander-in-Chief America and West Indies Station. The Canadian destroyers at Halifax took part in convoy escort to the limits of their range, taking their orders under the 'co-operation' instruction from the senior officers of convoys and the Rear Admiral Third Battle Squadron. It is interesting to note that though it might have been sensible for the latter officer to have his headquarters ashore at Halifax, in fact he flew his flag in a yacht in Halifax harbour. The reason, Norman Rogers explained to King, was the 'Canada would have to control her own naval establishments and could not permit its [sic] position in that regard to be usurped by a superior authority controlling the Canadian end.'[37] Although the constitutional position was thus formally protected, it is evident that the effective authority was being exercised by the power that provided the major forces.[38] The situation was symbolic.

The new constitutional situation as it affected the Army was reflected in the Visiting Forces (British Commonwealth) Acts,[39] passed reciprocally by the British and Canadian Parliaments in 1933.* These statutes, considered necessary consequences of the Statute of Westminster, provided a legal basis for the relations of Canadian and British forces serving in association. They made provision for two types of relationship: 'serving together' and 'in combination.' The former implied equality and no subordination; under the latter, however, the commander of one force was given powers of command over the other. In general, Canadian forces in the United Kingdom were considered to be 'serving together' with British forces, and were completely independent of them; but a Canadian force given a specific task in defence of the country was placed 'in combination' and came under the operational command of a British general. Thus when the 1st Canadian Corps was given a section of the Sussex coast to defend in 1941, it was placed 'in combination' with the British South Eastern Command, and General Crerar, the Corps Commander, came under the orders of the Commander-in-Chief, South Eastern Command, who shortly was General Montgomery. The same procedure was followed when a Canadian formation went to a theatre of operations to fight as part of a larger British force; in 1944-5 the First Canadian Army was in combination with the British 21st Army Group, and General Crerar again served under General Montgomery. The relationship was established in each case by an 'order of detail' under the Visiting Forces

* The other Dominions' parallel legislation reflected their differing views of the Statute of Westminster. South Africa's Act was passed as early as 1932, Australia's and New Zealand's only in 1939 – the latter after the outbreak of war.

CONFERENCE OF THE POWERS, 1941
Lt-Gen. A.G.L. McNaughton and the British Prime Minister, Winston Churchill, photographed during a visit by Mr Churchill to Canadian Corps Headquarters near Leatherhead, Surrey

Act issued by the senior Canadian field commander. General A.G.L. McNaughton, a strong nationalist who was largely responsible for the procedure followed, began in 1940 to include in these orders the phrase 'until I shall otherwise direct,' indicating that in an extreme case the Canadian commander had the right to withdraw the force from British command.[40]

The general principles governing the relation of the Canadian Army Overseas with the British Army were laid down in a memorandum given to General McNaughton, then commanding the 1st Canadian Division, by the Chief of the General Staff, Major-General T.V. Anderson, when the division went overseas in 1939.[41] The most vital paragraph ran: 'All matters concerning military operations and discipline in the Field, being the direct responsibility of the Commander-in-Chief of the British Army in the theatre of operations, will be dealt with by the General Officer Commanding, Canadian Forces in the Field, through the Commander-in-Chief, whose powers in this regard are exercisable within the limitations laid down in the Visiting Forces Acts (Canada and United Kingdom).' These principles are clearly recognizable as those worked out during the First World War, when it was agreed that while operational command was a matter for the British Commander-in-Chief in the field, organization and administration remained in Canadian hands. General Anderson's directive went on to make it clear that 'training and administration of personnel, including such matters as all questions relating to commissions, promotions, appointments, transfers, exchanges, recalls and demands for officers' were for Canadian authorities to deal with. It was made clear to the British army command in the beginning that training policy was a Canadian matter. Nevertheless, training was always on British lines, and the Canadian Army Overseas made great use of British facilities and establishments, which were very freely made available. This was all in line with the immemorial practice of maintaining uniformity with the British Army in matters of organization, armament, training, etc. When the time came to take the field against the enemy, Canadian Army formations were able to function within the framework of the British forces with smooth efficiency.

In one respect there was an advance beyond the practices of the First World War. In spite of Anderson's initial directive, 'discipline in the Field' did not remain within the purview of the British Commander-in-Chief. In 1914-18 a considerable number of Canadian soldiers were executed (for cowardice or desertion) by the sentence of courts martial confirmed by the British Commander-in-Chief. There was no such case in 1939-45. (Indeed, there was only one execution by sentence of a court martial in the Canadian Army; the offence was murder; and the sentence was confirmed by the Governor-in-Council in Ottawa.) The process by which control of discipline was firmly established in Canadian hands need not be reviewed in detail here.[42]

In the first weeks of the war the assumption in Canada was that the Royal Canadian Air Force would place in the field overseas an expeditionary formation that would be an all-Canadian national force parallel in its own way to the Canadian Corps of the last war or the new expeditionary force that the Army was now preparing. On September 12, 1939, the Prime Minister wrote the United Kingdom High Commissioner about air co-operation, describing the plans that were being made for expanded training facilities and remarking that Canada could lend some Air Force personnel to the RAF shortly. He wrote, however: 'It is the desire of this Government that Canadian Air Force units be formed as soon as sufficient trained personnel are available overseas for this purpose, such squadrons to be manned by and maintained with Canadian personnel at the expense of the Canadian Government.' Only three days later, however, when information was received that the British government was likely soon to request a very large further increase of training facilities in Canada, the Chief of the Air Staff told the cabinet's Emergency Council* that with this effort in prospect he opposed sending any RCAF personnel overseas in the near future.[43] Before the end of the month Neville Chamberlain proposed the British Commonwealth Air Training Plan; and this project in the form in which it was approved destroyed all hope of Canada's being able to place a genuinely national air force in the field for years to come.

When Massey and Bruce took it on themselves to interfere in the planning of air training they did not appreciate the possible consequences of their scheme for their national Air Forces. They proposed in fact that the men trained in Canada should 'be sent to the front as distinctive Canadian, Australian and New Zealand air forces.'[44] The agreement signed in Ottawa on December 17, 1939, which set up the BCATP, made any such result impossible. This was not merely because so many of the RCAF's resources had to be poured into setting up and operating the Plan in Canada that little was left available, for many months, for action overseas. The agreement provided for producing great numbers of partially trained aircrew; it had nothing to say about ground crew, who would also be required in large numbers if complete Canadian squadrons were to be

* Shortly, when the cabinet's committees were reorganized, the Emergency Council became the Cabinet War Committee.

formed. It also laid down that, apart from a small proportion of aircrew required for RCAF home defence units, Canadians completing their training would be 'placed at the disposal of the Government of the United Kingdom,' provided that government carried out the following arrangement, which was the result of difficult and acrimonious negotiation:

15. The United Kingdom Government undertakes that pupils of Canada, Australia and New Zealand shall, after training is completed, be identified with their respective Dominions, either by the method of organizing Dominion units and formations or in some other way, such methods to be agreed upon with the respective Dominion Governments concerned ...

The United Kingdom mission that came to Ottawa to work out arrangements for the Air Training Plan had in fact been instructed to try to arrange that graduating Dominion trainees should be *enlisted* in the Royal Air Force. This proposition the Dominions unanimously rejected; the Australians and New Zealanders had the particular objection that it would have made their men subject to the death penalty, which these Dominions' military law did not recognize. The mission also planned to propose that the training organization should be directed and controlled, not by the Royal Canadian Air Force, which they thought too small and inexperienced for the job, but 'by a Director General who would be an experienced officer of the Royal Air Force of high rank.' They soon found that this was not practicable, and the agreement provided that the administration of the Plan should be entrusted to the RCAF, subject to close consultation with a strong liaison staff in Ottawa to watch over the interests of the other partners. Lord Riverdale, the chairman of the mission, noted nevertheless, 'our misgivings were not entirely removed.'[45] In fact, something very like the mission's original plan came to pass. Fortunately, a highly qualified Canadian was available in the RAF. Early in 1940 Air Commodore Robert Leckie, a Scottish-born Canadian who had been a member of the old Canadian Air Board in 1919-22 and the RAF's Director of Training in 1935-8, came to Canada with other RAF personnel to help set up the Plan. He shortly became Air Member for Training in the Canadian Air Council and played a leading part in directing the scheme. In 1942 he transferred to the RCAF, and in 1944 he became Chief of the Canadian Air Staff.

The discussions with the mission turned, so far as Canada was concerned, largely on money. Britain was already short of dollar exchange; while King and his colleagues had been told by the Department of Finance that Canada was close to the end of her immediate resources. As we have seen, the suggestion for the Plan arrived after the government had completed its careful financial calculations for the first year of the war, and this additional commitment was regarded with alarm. The keynote was struck in the meeting of the Emergency Council with the British mission on October 31. British estimates of cost shook the Canadians. Captain Harold Balfour, the British Parliamentary Under Secretary of State for Air, speaking of the tremendous future cost of the British air effort, remarked, 'How these large expenditures could be financed, he could not say, but was content to leave that problem to the Chancellor of the Exchequer.' This fiscal frivolity deeply shocked Mackenzie King, who is recorded as replying: 'Canada, in her war effort, could not go beyond her resources, and would proceed under the advice of the Minister of Finance. Unlike Captain Balfour, he was unable to ignore the problem of where the money was to be found.' The Minister of Finance (Ralston) himself greeted the estimates of cost put forward by Lord Riverdale with the interjection that Canada could not come 'within shooting distance' of them. This so upset Riverdale that he referred to the British contribution in kind to the Plan as 'a free gift to you.' This in turn nettled King to the point where he made the very unfortunate remark, 'This is not our war.' What he seems to have meant was that it was not *exclusively* Canada's war – the British were contributing to a common cause. But the visitors were appalled. The tone of the negotiations never fully recovered from this disastrous first session. When it was all over Sir Gerald Campbell sent the Dominions Office a bitter dispatch asserting that, unlike the other delegations, 'The Canadian Government saw everything in terms of the advantage which might be secured for Canada and for themselves.' Anthony Eden sent this on to Chamberlain with the lofty comment that while it might be overdrawn, 'enough remains to show that we are not going to have a very easy job in keeping the present Canadian Government in line and in good heart.'[46]

There had been a growing realization among the Canadian ministers that what they were faced with was essentially a recruiting scheme for the Royal Air Force. In the circumstances as presented to them, they felt that they would have done their duty if they paid a large share of the cost of the training in Canada, without attempting to pay for maintaining the Canadian graduates of the scheme as a national Air Force in the field. The result was acceptance of the principle that the Canadian graduates should be handed over to the RAF and paid by the RAF; the only qualification being that Canada would pay them the difference between Canadian and British rates – precisely as had been done with the Canadian contingents in the South African War (1899-1902). In due course it was agreed (January 7, 1941) that up to twenty-five Royal Canadian Air Force squadrons should be formed overseas from RCAF men trained under the Plan; but these men continued to be paid by Britain. As the squadrons gradually came into existence it became evident that they were Canadian only in name. The only Canadian thing about them in the beginning was a proportion of the aircrew (and completing them with Canadian aircrew turned out to be a very slow process); the ground crews were almost entirely British; the British government provided the aircraft and other equipment; and the only part of the cost that Canada paid was the difference between Canadian and British rates of pay for the Canadian aircrew. As long as the original financial arrangement stood, Canada was in a very weak moral position in arguing for an improvement in this situation. Gradually, however, the financial situation changed; and at last, as of April 1, 1943, Canada assumed the whole cost of the Royal Canadian Air Force Overseas. Canadian expenditure under this heading leaped up from $23,666,000 in 1942-3 to $383,888,000 in 1943-4.[47]

The Canadian position was now very much stronger, and not so much passive resistance was encountered henceforth in RAF quarters to Canadian aspirations in the direction of something more resembling an independent national Air Force. The all-Canadian group (No 6) in the RAF Bomber Command, which began functioning on January 1, 1943, was an important forward step. This, however, was the only air vice-marshal's operational command – equivalent to an army division – available to an RCAF officer overseas. Apart from it there was no Canadian air formation higher than the two 'sectors,' commanded by group captains and controlling between them five RCAF wings, which took part in the North-West Europe campaign of 1944-5. By 1945 a total of forty-eight RCAF squadrons was overseas; and they were genuinely Canadian, except in a few cases completely or virtually completely manned with Canadian flying and ground personnel. In February 1944 a new agreement between the two governments recognized that in effect control of all RCAF personnel overseas rested with the RCAF Overseas Headquarters in London. The fact was also accepted that for the expected final phase of the war against Japan (which was forestalled by the Japanese surrender) Canada insisted on having, and was to have, 'a fully integrated Canadian Air Force available for service wherever the Canadian Government may decide that it may be most usefully employed in the interests of Canada, of the Commonwealth and of the United Nations.' This implied a status parallel to that of the First Canadian Army in North-West Europe. But it must be said that the RCAF never actually achieved such a status during the Second World War.[48]

Mackenzie King and his colleagues did not really know what they were doing when they signed the BCATP agreement in 1939. The Plan was a considerable contribution to winning the war – after all, it did produce 131,000 flying personnel, of whom 72,000 were Canadians – but in the form in which it was implemented it condemned the Royal Canadian Air Force to colonial status. The government's belief that it had to be guided by the conservative calculations of the Department of Finance resulted in Canada's airmen overseas being removed from Canadian control and scattered around the globe. (The astute O.D. Skelton pointed out at the time that the person who paid the piper was going to call the tune: 'there will be real difficulty in insisting on the one hand on our right to organize trainees in Royal Canadian Air Force units and on the other on the United Kingdom meeting the costs of the maintenance.'[49] But this was one occasion when he was not listened to.) One other point may be made. The butcher's bill was heavier than the government can have anticipated when it made the facile decision to concentrate its war effort so heavily in the air. In spite of the fact that a very high proportion of its personnel stayed in Canada, operating the Air Training Plan and the squadrons based in North America, the RCAF had heavier casualties in proportion to its total strength than either of the other services. Its large commitment to the RAF Bomber Command was especially lethal: of its 17,000 dead, almost exactly 10,000 lost their lives in that command.[50] The bomber offensive against Germany brought destruction to attacker and attacked alike.*

THE DESPERATE SUMMER, 1940

In April 1940 the Germans broke into Denmark and Norway; and the unsuccessful Norwegian campaign that followed brought down Neville Chamberlain. On May 10 Hitler launched his *Blitzkrieg* in the west; and

---

* Not all RAF officers appreciated the assistance which the service got from the Dominions. Sir Arthur ('Bomber') Harris, the Commander-in-Chief Bomber Command, wrote to the Air Ministry in August 1942 and again in January 1943, protesting against 'the growing tendency to increase the number of Foreign and Dominion elements within the Royal Air Force.' He wrote on the latter occasion, 'Over half of the aircrew personnel in the operational Squadrons of this Command are already of non-U.K. identity.' Sir Charles Portal and Sir Archibald Sinclair smoothed Harris down. Neither pointed out to him that without the 'Foreign and Dominion elements' the RAF could not have maintained its status as a major Allied Air Force.[51]

MARSHALLING LANCASTERS AGAINST STUTTGART
This painting by Carl Schaefer shows aircraft of Nos 408 and 426 Squadrons RCAF preparing to take off from Linton-on-Ouse, Yorkshire, October 1943. A high proportion of the RCAF's effort was devoted to the strategic air offensive against Germany, and nearly 10,000 Canadians lost their lives while serving with the RAF Bomber Command.

on the same day Winston Churchill became Prime Minister of Great Britain.

As the reader knows, Mackenzie King had entertained, since the conference of 1937, a deep respect for Chamberlain, and for a much longer time a deep mistrust of Churchill. In the war crisis of 1914, hoping for peace, he had written in his diary, as already mentioned, 'Winston Churchill is the one dangerous factor.' On the eve of war in 1939 he wrote, 'I think Churchill is one of [the] most dangerous men I have ever known.' A few weeks later, however, he was expressing envious admiration of one of Churchill's broadcasts as First Lord of the Admiralty.[52] His lack of enthusiasm for the change in Downing Street found rather comical expression in the telegrams he sent to the fallen leader and the new one. To Chamberlain he wrote: 'I was proud to be at your side the day you assumed office as Prime Minister.* I am equally proud, though separated by an ocean, to be again at your side this afternoon as you lay down the burdens of office ...' He assured Churchill of the 'whole-hearted co-operation and strong support of my colleagues and myself,' and went on to say, 'May you be given the vision and the endurance so necessary to the duties of your high office and never more needed in the guidance of public affairs than at this critical hour.'[53] Nevertheless, like some millions of other people, King soon began to realize that at that moment Churchill was indubitably the right man in the right place. After his first broadcast as Prime Minister on May 19 ('Arm yourselves, and be ye men of valour') he cabled him, with obvious sincerity, that he had heard it 'with feelings deeply stirred and with profound admiration and pride.' It was the beginning of a reluctant regard, which would reach its final point far on in 1947, when King would confide to his diary that, meeting Churchill again while on a visit to London, 'I felt that perhaps in more respects than one, he was the greatest man of our times.'[54]

All Churchill's leadership was needed. The weeks after his elevation witnessed the Allied *débâcle* in France and Flanders, the Dunkirk evacuation, the collapse of France and her withdrawal from the war. Before the end of June the Commonwealth stood alone. The British Empire had not been used to contemplating defeat. Now, however, it looked into the pit. The effect on the Canadian war effort was electric. Limited liability was forgotten (except for the one matter of manpower policy). A writer in *Maclean's* (July 1, 1940) said of Ottawa: 'The "quietest war capital in Christendom" has become a cauldron of excitement; disillusioned, shocked from its complacency. Day by day, as the shadow of the Swastika length-

---

* See above, page 204.

ens across the English Channel, old shibboleths, old comfortable delusions, go overboard. Where once reigned smugness, self-satisfaction, there is now a wholesome fear; with it, fortunately, more of war stir and vigor.' The change was in evidence as early as May 17, one week after the German onslaught began, when it was already clear that there was going to be a disaster. That day Mackenzie King is recorded in the minutes of the Cabinet War Committee as saying, 'The Empire was in extremis and we must say now what further steps we were prepared to take to help the common cause.' The steps came rapidly: dispatch of the 2nd Division to England, authority to form a Canadian Corps overseas, mobilization of a third division (and almost immediately the main elements of a fourth). On British request, troops were provided for garrison duty in Iceland and the West Indies. It is interesting that these measures were taken without any mention of money in the War Committee; the dollar sign had suddenly come off the Canadian effort. On May 23, with invasion becoming a possibility, the British government asked for destroyers. At that moment Canada had four in condition to go, and they were dispatched at once. Mackenzie King wrote grimly in his diary on May 24: 'One wonders if [the] Canadian destroyers will come back. We may find our own coasts left bare in giving our last possible aid to the Mother country. That, however, to my mind is right. We owe to her such freedom as we have. It is right we should strike with her the last blow for the preservation of freedom.' It was a new note for King, but men's perspectives were changing under the impact of terrible events. On the same day he made a note about his associate Skelton: 'It amuses me a little to see how completely some men swing to opposite extremes. No one could have been more strongly for everything being done for Canada, as against Britain, than Skelton was up to a very short time ago. Yesterday, in our discussion, he naturally [?actually] did not want me to suggest any help for Canada, but rather the need for Britain. He now sees that the real place to defend our land is from across the seas. He did not want the Americans to undertake the protection of our coasts, lest they might not do as much for Britain.' It was clearly better to defend Canada on the beaches of Britain than in the suburbs of Halifax.[55]

The collapse of the third French Republic in June 1940 presented the Canadian government with special problems. Under the terms of the armistice signed on June 22 the Germans occupied northern and western France. The new French government, headed by the aged Marshal Henri-Philippe Pétain, established itself at Vichy; its dubious relations with Britain were rendered much worse on July 3 when the British, fearful of the French fleet passing into German hands, made a damaging attack on it in the harbour of Oran. In London General Charles de Gaulle established a Free French movement dedicated to carrying on the war against Germany. No informed person could expect the French-speaking people of the province of Quebec, on which the power of Mackenzie King's government so greatly depended, to be very powerfully moved by the fate of the French republic; but they were certain to have some interest in the matter, and it was just possible that some French Canadians who had had little use for a *République française* whose motto was *Liberté, égalité, fraternité* might develop a degree of regard for an *Etat français* which inscribed on its coinage *Travail, famille, patrie*. Canadian relations with France – with the two Frances that existed from June 1940 onward – would clearly have to be handled with care.

Just how unpleasant things could get was suggested in the very beginning by the affair of the *Emile Bertin*. In the dying moments of the republic this French cruiser was freighted with gold (said to be worth £100 million) belonging to the Bank of France, which she was to carry to Canada to be added to the deposit already held in trust by the Bank of Canada. But by the time she reached Halifax the Pétain government had been installed and her captain was ordered not to land the gold in Canada but to take it to Martinique. The Bank of Canada informed the Bank of England, with the result that the British government instructed their High Commissioner in Ottawa to ask the Canadian authorities to take 'any action however strong' to prevent the *Emile Bertin* from leaving Halifax. For a moment there seemed to be a possibility of a sanguinary mess in Halifax harbour. Mackenzie King pressed the French Minister in Ottawa, René Ristelhueber, to have the ship stopped, but when this failed he was not prepared to use force to detain her, in spite of some contrary opinion in the cabinet. She sailed on June 21, the British authorities being informed so they could intercept her if they chose.* King recorded his reasons in his diary: to have fired on the ship would have created 'no end of trouble throughout Canada'; 'Also how the Americans would feel in seeing Canada firing on a French ship and what it would lead to in American feeling against entering the war.'[56] Worry over contending opinions within Canada, and particularly in Quebec, and the difficulty of reconciling British and American attitudes, would bedevil Canadian policy towards the French problem for years to come. Later in the summer

* King states in his diary that the War Committee 'finally decided' not to use force. There was no recorded meeting of the committee on June 21; this must have been an informal and unrecorded meeting.

the British Treasury tried to get King to release to it the French gold, and a French credit in American dollars, deposited in Ottawa. King refused, telling the British emissary 'that I did not propose to allow my name, or the name of this country, to go down in history as a party to any betrayal of trust at a time when we were fighting forces of evil.'[57] These French assets stayed in Ottawa.

When the Pétain government signed the armistice with Germany, Colonel Vanier withdrew from France with his staff, along with the British Ambassador. The ship that evacuated them was one of the Canadian destroyers now serving in European waters. This was the beginning of a long twilight period in the diplomatic relations of Canada with France. In spite of the carnage at Oran (and a reprisal by French aircraft against Gibraltar), it was evident that neither the British government nor the government at Vichy desired a complete break between their countries; while Mackenzie King and his colleagues were desperately anxious to avoid any such development. King wrote to the High Commissioner in London in August 1940, 'While such a break would be serious for the United Kingdom it would be disastrous for Canada.'[58] In consequence Georges Vanier continued to hold the title of Minister to France while a refugee in London and even after he had returned to military duty in Canada. Only in May 1941 did the old soldier, who loved France but strongly disliked the government at Vichy, insist on being relieved of this distinction; and even then the Cabinet War Committee was reluctant. M. Ristelhueber remained in Ottawa and remained French Minister, even though the government he represented was under the thumb of a country with which Canada was at war, and his continued presence was a constant source of adverse comment by critics of the King administration.[59]

Information out of Vichy was what the British government craved; and at the beginning of November 1940 the Foreign Secretary, Lord Halifax, asked Vincent Massey whether his chiefs would consent to a visit to the Pétain capital by Pierre Dupuy, a former member of the Canadian legation staff in Paris who now, in London, bore the imposing title of 'Chargé d'Affaires in France, Belgium and the Netherlands.' Mackenzie King agreed; and between that time and September 1941 Dupuy made three visits to Vichy. He had conversations with Marshal Pétain and reported that the marshal was essentially friendly to the British cause. Churchill was delighted, writing to King after the first visit, 'The Canadian channel is invaluable and indeed at the moment our only line.' When he came to Ottawa in December 1941, at a time when increasing doubts were current there about keeping up diplomatic relations with Vichy, he told the Cabinet War Committee that those relations might still turn out to be useful; it was, he said, 'good to have a window on that courtyard.'[60] In April 1942, however, the British War Cabinet expressed the opinion that Canada's maintaining relations with Vichy no longer served a useful purpose; and when, in spite of this, relations continued, and Dupuy announced in July that he was making another trip to Vichy, there were rude comments inside the Foreign Office. Only after the Allied landings in French North Africa in November 1942 was the French legation in Ottawa finally closed; the Vichy resistance to the landings and the German occupation of southern France made continuance of the relationship impossible.[61]

In the meantime, quiet hostilities had been in progress in Canada, and particularly of course in Quebec, between supporters of Vichy and adherents of General de Gaulle. The King government was embarrassed. In the beginning Ernest Lapointe advised his colleagues against giving any official countenance to de Gaulle: 'nothing would be more dangerous than to start a controversy in Quebec as between Pétain and de Gaulle.' The Cabinet War Committee decided in October 1940 that the government would 'neither assist nor interfere with' any collection of funds for de Gaulle's movement.[62] Only gradually did the official attitude towards Free France warm up, as English Canada became more and more hostile to Vichy and Quebec opinion seemed more and more disposed to accept de Gaulle. The staff of the Department of External Affairs became increasingly dubious of allowing the Vichy representation to continue, and more friendly to the Free French. In August 1941 Norman Robertson, now Under Secretary of State for External Affairs, wrote to King about French 'consular officers who, acting under Vichy instructions, have done their unsuccessful best to discredit the Free French Movement in Canada.'[63] However, the government did not decide to close the consulates until May 1942.[64]

The question was complicated by the government's anxiety to keep in step with the United States. The Roosevelt administration – neutral, it must be remembered, until December 1941 – maintained an embassy at Vichy and thought it could exert important influence there on behalf of the Allies.[65] Moreover, it had very little use for General de Gaulle. Here there was disagreement with Britain. The British, knowing only too well how difficult and arrogant de Gaulle was, knew also that he was fighting on their side and might some day inherit France. Washington, and particularly Secretary of State Hull, saw in him no such potential.

These difficulties were particularly evident in connection with the question of St Pierre and Miquelon. This minuscule French colony off the south shore of Newfoundland was ruled by an administrator loyal to Vichy. Though not of great strategic importance, it was inevitably an object of interest. During 1940 Canada and the Newfoundland commission government, working in association, managed to obtain a solution of issues that were causing apprehension – the presence at St Pierre of French fishing trawlers and of an old naval sloop, the *Ville d'Ys*, which was finally withdrawn to Martinique.[66] But the islands continued to cause some apprehension, particularly after the presence of a powerful wireless transmitter came to knowledge. After all, the trans-Atlantic convoy routes were only about one hundred miles away. As early as September 1940 the British government was making no secret of the fact that it considered the best solution was for the colony to 'change over to Free France without violence.'[67] This was mere common sense, but Secretary Hull did not see it in that light, and Britain, and still more Canada, did not wish to proceed without American concurrence. O.D. Skelton passed a copy of the British suggestion to the Canadian legation in Washington with the cold comment, 'You will see that we are being pressed to take action which would be contrary to our understanding with the United States* and would be contrary also to the ordinary rules governing the intercourse of two states that are mutually at peace.'[68]

It is necessary to make a long story short (which is what we are doing throughout this book). In September 1941 a Canadian Acting Consul was appointed to watch the situation in St Pierre.[69] Early in December it was suggested that Canada might assume supervision of the wireless station, using a landing party from a naval vessel to make this policy effective if necessary. On December 3 the Cabinet War Committee approved of laying this suggestion before the United Kingdom and the United States. But the two great powers could not agree. Britain still thought it the best solution to have the Free French 'rally' the islands; and the Americans were as hostile to this as ever. On December 19 Mackenzie King argued strongly in the War Committee that no action should be taken until the governments of the United Kingdom and the United States could agree. Decision was deferred; and there the matter rested until the Free French themselves cut the Gordian knot a few days later.[70]

In July 1941 the United Kingdom High Commission informed the Canadian government that Free French sloops were shortly to be detailed

---

* The reference is presumably to a phrase in a memorandum passed to the State Department by the Canadian Legation in Washington on July 20: 'There is, of course, no intention on the part of the Canadian Government to interfere with the sovereignty of the islands.'

for convoy duty in the western Atlantic and based at Newfoundland, and that Vice-Admiral E.-H. Muselier, naval commander at de Gaulle's head-quarters, had suggested that one of these vessels might call at St Pierre and Miquelon and rally the colony. Robertson did not like the idea, fear-ing that such action might encourage the Germans to put new pressure on the French North African colonies, and the Vichy men to yield to it; and King agreed.[71] The ultimate result was the Canadian suggestion about taking over the wireless station. On November 13, 1941, the British Admiralty signalled the Commander-in-Chief Western Approaches [to the British Isles], the Naval Officer-in-Charge Iceland, and the Commo-dore Commanding Newfoundland Force (L.W. Murray, RCN),* inform-ing them of a forthcoming visit by Admiral Muselier and 'requesting' that he be given facilities for seeing Free French ships in convoy work and for contact with Free French naval representatives at Halifax and St John's. The ships were working under Murray. He handed three French corvettes over to Muselier and the French admiral went to sea with them from St John's 'for exercises and passage to Halifax.'[72] From Halifax Muselier flew to Ottawa. There he had discussions with Canadian naval authorities and External Affairs officers and with the United States Minister (Jay Pierre-pont Moffat), and argued strongly for his being allowed to take over St Pierre and Miquelon. Moffat consulted Washington and was told that the President opposed this and preferred that any necessary action should be taken by Canada. The Canadian Cabinet War Committee made a decision to the same effect on December 16. Muselier agreed not to proceed with his plan for occupation.

Now, however, General de Gaulle himself took a hand. The news of the plan for the wireless station seems to have enraged him, and he decided that the colony must be saved from the predatory Canadians.†
On December 18 he sent a firm order to Muselier to take over St Pierre and Miquelon 'without saying anything to the foreigners.' He wrote, 'Je prends l'entière responsabilité de cette opération devenue indispensable pour conserver à la France ses possessions.' Muselier decided that this

---

* The chain of command was curious. Murray considered himself responsible to the Admiralty for the French ships. On the other hand, the Newfoundland Force had been formally under the 'coordinating supervision' of the U.S. Navy's Task Force 4 since September 1941. Neither the Admiralty nor Murray told the U.S. authorities about the arrangements for Muselier's visit.

† One wonders whether this affair perhaps left a mark on de Gaulle's mind which might have influenced his decision to make his 'Québec libre' declara-tion in 1967.

order had to be carried out, regardless of the promises he had given in Ottawa. On Christmas morning the world learned that on December 24 he had descended on St Pierre with his ships and seized the colony in a bloodless *coup*. An immediate plebiscite was held, and 98 per cent of the people voting favoured General de Gaulle.

Now it was Hull's turn to fly into a rage. He seems to have convinced himself that the Canadian government was responsible for what had happened, the ships having been under Canadian command. He telephoned Moffat and told him to present what Mackenzie King called in his diary an ultimatum, requiring Canada to take immediate steps to evict Muselier. Then, disregarding Moffat's attempts at protest and declining to wait to see King, who was about to visit Washington for discussions with Roosevelt and Churchill (the United States now being in the war), he issued a public statement which became notorious:

Our preliminary reports show that the action by three so-called Free French ships at St. Pierre-Miquelon was an arbitrary action contrary to the agreement of all parties concerned and certainly without the prior knowledge or consent in any sense of the United States Government.

This Government has inquired of the Canadian Government as to the steps that Government is prepared to take to restore the *status quo* of these islands.

The phrase 'so-called Free French' blew up in Hull's face; many Americans were offended by what seemed a gratuitous insult to the Frenchmen who were fighting Hitler. The Secretary of State explains in his memoirs that the words meant 'three ships supposedly of the Free French.' Pretty clearly they implied, 'but actually Canadian.' In Washington on December 26 Roosevelt asked King where Muselier got the ships; the Prime Minister recorded, 'Evidently there had been some thought that in some way the ships had been supplied by Canada or Newfoundland.'

King himself had been, he wrote, 'terribly annoyed as well as distressed' by Muselier's exploit. But he and his colleagues had no intention of getting involved in an operation to evict him, particularly since, in the words of the *New York Times'* correspondent, Canadians all across the country had received the news with 'pleased satisfaction.' Along with J.L. Ralston and Angus Macdonald, the Naval Minister, King drafted a firm reply to Hull: 'Canada is in no way responsible for the Free French occupation of St. Pierre. We have kept in close touch with both the United Kingdom and the United States on this question and have always been ready to cooperate in carrying out an agreed policy. We decline to commit ourselves to any action or to take any action pending such agreement. In the circumstances and until we have had an opportunity to consider action with the President and Mr. Churchill, the Canadian Government cannot take the steps requested to expel the Free French and restore the *status quo* in the islands.' There was no possibility of Britain and the United States agreeing on the matter. There is no reason to believe that the British authorities had any direct responsibility for the Free French action; but they had always openly favoured such action, and as we have seen they had set the stage for it by arranging Muselier's visit. There is something mildly comic about two decisions taken by the British War Cabinet on December 26, 1941. On the one hand, it invited the Lord President of the Council 'to send for General de Gaulle and inform him that his conduct in this matter could not be tolerated and had placed us in a position of great embarrassment'; on the other hand, it decided to ask the Canadian government 'to take no action in regard to any proposal to restore the *status quo* in the islands.' Mr Hull continued to fuss and fume, but the Free French remained in control of St Pierre, and the colony's threat to the convoy routes was at an end.[73]

In June 1940 the Commonwealth not only lost an ally but gained an enemy. With France defeated it seemed to the Italian dictator Mussolini safe to come down off his fence and declare war on France and Britain. He announced his decision on June 10. It had been long expected, and the necessary measures to counter it had been discussed between Britain and Canada. On June 2 the Canadian High Commissioner in London was instructed to begin preparing another submission to the King authorizing a proclamation of a state of war. Not quite the same form was followed, however, as in the case of Germany. On inquiry Massey found that the Palace did not desire a written submission, since without a minister's signature such a document would not be valid (perhaps the King's staff remembered that it had taken Ottawa a good many weeks to provide the formal signed paper after the German declaration);[74] verbal approval of a verbal submission would meet the case for the moment. Again Parliament decided, and it took little time to do so; on June 10, the same day on which Mussolini made his announcement, the House of Commons and the Senate passed a resolution approving a declaration of war. The Cabinet War Committee (not the full cabinet), 'acting for the purpose as "The Committee of the Privy Council,"' approved the Prime Minister's action in signing an order-in-council authorizing the submission to the King. It was too late for Massey to be received by the King that night, but the following morning (June 11) George VI gave his verbal approval, and a proclamation of war with Italy as of June 10 was issued in Ottawa that afternoon.[75]

AMERICAN NEUTRALITY AGAIN

In 1939-41, as in 1914-17, a belligerent Canada lived alongside a neutral United States. The situation, however, was quite different. Franklin Roosevelt was a very different President from Woodrow Wilson; and the American people in 1939 were in a quite different mood from that of 1914. Americans wanted the Allies to win (see above, page 267). The present writer, visiting a newsreel theatre in New York in September 1939, was astonished when a dull shot of troops mobilizing in Canada drew warm applause from the audience (I have never known any other American audience to show the slightest interest in Canada before or since). But Americans had no intention of getting into the war themselves. The *New Yorker* put it succinctly at the moment of the outbreak: 'Our people dislike Hitler and they want him soundly beaten by a couple of other fellows.' Mackenzie King, extraordinary to relate, wrote in his diary on September 1, 1939, 'I was terribly shocked and surprised when I learned that Roosevelt had told the press this morning that the U.S. ought to be able to keep out of the European war.' A man who knew the United States as well as King had no business to be surprised. It was a momentary lapse. King settled down to the task of maintaining good relations with the neutral neighbour and – within the very narrow limits that tact and common sense indicated – encouraging movement towards co-operation and participation.

War caused in the first instance a temporary interruption of the relation between King and Roosevelt that had been developing so auspiciously. The telephone conversation of September 5 about the Neutrality Act (above, page 260) was the last for months. Congress amended the Act to enable belligerents to purchase American goods on a 'cash and carry' basis – a change favourable only to the Allies, who had command of the seas. A new American minister, James Cromwell, arrived in Ottawa; King met him at the station and received 'very cordial and affectionate messages from the President to myself.' King sent a birthday message to the President, and got a telegram in return. On February 25, 1940, King ventured to telephone Secretary Hull to congratulate him on Congress having authorized a three-year extension of the trade-treaty programme. That was about all until April, when the German attack on Denmark and Norway ended the 'phony war.' A few days before the attack King told Cromwell that he was going to take a holiday in the United States, and would see the President 'if possible.' On reaching New York he received a message from Roosevelt saying he was anxious to see him.[76] The two men met at the President's southern retreat in Warm Springs, Georgia, on April 23-24, and again in Washington on the 29th.

King's long memorandum of the Warm Springs visit[77] notes that the President 'certainly gave up all his time to me and took the greater part of both days as a complete holiday for a real chance to share a sense of genuine companionship.' The Prime Minister sat by and listened (on the President's insistence) while Roosevelt transacted business on the telephone. King wrote, 'He did not say a single word about the U.S. going into the war though he did say that invasion of Norway and Sweden [sic] had changed the sentiment particularly in the middle west very much ... When speaking of the British and French being hard pressed, he said he might find it desirable to send some destroyers and cruisers across the Atlantic to assist the Allies.' In this connection Roosevelt, a student of naval history, recalled the undeclared 'quasi-war' which the U.S. had conducted with France in 1795. This is King's record of what seems to have been his one cautious essay at influencing the President: 'I said to him two or three times that I wondered if Britain and France were going to be able to carry the load they had taken on. That it might become too heavy for them to bear. He said that people, thus far, had not begun to think of anything being possible other than the Allies winning. That if the situation changed, he thought sympathies would grow stronger with the Allies. It was in this connection that he spoke of possibly finding it necessary to send destroyers and cruisers to assist the British.'

One problem discussed was that of Greenland. The occupation of Denmark by Germany had caused apprehension for the safety of this Danish dependency, particularly as Greenland was the world's main source of cryolite, important to the production of aluminium, so vital to the aircraft industry. The Canadian government had been urged both by the Aluminum Company of Canada and the British authorities to take steps to secure the cryolite mine at Ivigtut. It was felt that such action by Canada was less likely to arouse opposition in Washington than a move by Britain. This idea proved ill-founded. When Canada informed the State Department that it was considering sending a small force to Greenland for the duration of the war, to act 'as trustee for a restored and independent Danish Government,' Loring Christie (who had been Canadian Minister in Washington since September 1939) was firmly told that it would be 'highly inadvisable' for Canada to take such action. This was on April 19, a few days before King arrived at Warm Springs. The President now reinforced the effect in his conversations with him, though he does not seem to have been especially emphatic. King recorded, 'The Americans were anxious that Canada should not undertake anything in particular.' King was quite prepared to go along with them. In Washington a few days later he wrote that he was 'astonished' to find that Christie had been instructed to say that Canada would prepare a force for Greenland: 'Clearly our people had been a little over-zealous in preparing for a little war on Canada's own account.'[78] King told his colleagues that preparations for military action in Greenland should be stopped. Without going into further details, it is enough to say that the United States consistently made it clear that it did not want either Canadian action or Canadian co-operation there. An unsatisfactory feature of the situation was that Washington, while so hostile to protective action by other people, was slow to take any effective action itself. Finally, in April 1941 an agreement with the Danish Minister in Washington virtually turned the big island into an American protectorate for the duration of the war. American forces moved in, and the U.S. Air Force is still there.[79]

The Allied disaster in North-West Europe in May and June of 1940 had important consequences in North America. Americans suddenly perceived that a European system very favourable to the interests of the United States was on the verge of total collapse. General Pershing, the venerated leader of the American Expeditionary Force of 1917-18, told his countrymen: 'The Allies are fighting a war for civilization. They are holding our front line, and we have a vital concern in the outcome.'[80] The republic plunged into what I called at the time 'one of those great emotional and intellectual upsets which help to make its history fascinating and its foreign policy totally unpredictable.'[81] Congress rapidly passed astronomical defence appropriations; and the most striking evidence of the impact of the crisis was the sweeping draft law which reached the statute book in September. The administration began forwarding to Britain great quantities of reserve war material. In Canada, we have already seen, the shock was at least equally great, and the emotion keener; not only because of her links with Britain, but because she had soldiers, sailors, and airmen sharing the perils of the moment overseas. Both countries were very badly frightened. Those 'ties of common funk' of which Kipling once wrote were about to come into play. The stage was set for great changes of policy.

The wheels began to move when the Canadian destroyers were ordered to Europe on May 23. Rejecting the good advice of Skelton to do nothing that might lead the United States to use on the local defence of Canada forces that might better be devoted to strengthening Britain (above, page 299), Mackenzie King decided to send a personal message to the President telling him that the Canadian coasts were left bare. But before the message went King heard from Hull that the President desired that someone King implicitly trusted should come to Washington for conversations with him. King sent H.L. Keenleyside of External Affairs, who had already served as a messenger to the President to ask for aircraft for the Air Training Plan (which he didn't get) and had brought back a message to the effect that Roosevelt would like to see King privately. Keenleyside now made two more trips, seeing Hull and Roosevelt on May 25 and 29. The Dunkirk evacuation was just beginning, and it is clear that Washington was taking a very pessimistic view of Britain's chance of survival. What Roosevelt wanted was an assurance that the British fleet would not fall into German hands, and he hoped that King would get the other Dominion prime ministers to join him in representations to Churchill on this point. King was embarrassed; this business of being the linch-pin between the United States and Britain was not all it was cracked up to be. He did not approach the other prime ministers, but he sent to Churchill a message making Roosevelt's point about the fleet (without explaining just how the information had come to him). On June 4 Churchill made a famous speech in the British House of Commons, which was obviously written with King's message before him: '... we shall fight on the beaches, we shall fight on the landing-grounds, we shall fight in the fields and in the streets, we shall fight in the hills; we shall never surrender, and even if, which I do not for a moment believe, this island or a large part of it were subjugated and starving, then our Empire beyond the seas, armed and guarded by the British Fleet, would carry on the struggle, until, in God's good time, the New World, with all its power and might, steps forth to the rescue and the liberation of the old.' When Keenleyside made another trip to Washington on June 7, he found Roosevelt delighted with this speech. He was not nearly so delighted by a memorandum from King quoting part (but not all) of Churchill's reply to him, including the sentence: 'But if America continued neutral and we were overwhelmed, I cannot tell what policy might be adopted by a pro-German administration such as would undoubtedly be set up.'[82]

The Canadian government was now anxious for staff consultations with the American military authorities on the defence of North America, and also for aircraft and other war material from the U.S. In mid-June the matter was taken up through diplomatic channels. At first the Americans were not particularly friendly to the idea, but on July 3 the President authorized secret and informal staff conversations, on the basis of no commitments being made. The talks took place in Washington a week later. Much information was exchanged. Incidentally, the Canadian officers made it clear that they considered the United Kingdom North America's first line of defence; and they requested that no material earmarked for Britain should be diverted to Canada.[83]

The Royal Navy was in desperate need of destroyers, and Britain was pressing Washington to release some of its vessels of 1917-18 vintage. Canada had comparatively little to do with this question, but it opened the way for moving the Canadian-American relationship into a new phase. On August 10 Loring Christie reported a story he had heard that Roosevelt had expressed disappointment that Canada had expressed no opinion in the matter. King then instructed Christie to tell the President that he was well aware of the importance of destroyers, and to add that he hoped that when there was discussion of the destroyer question the state of naval defence in the western Atlantic could also be considered. Christie saw the President on the 15th, and Roosevelt told him he would be speaking to King shortly. There was no suggestion of a personal meeting; but it seems that on the following day the President received a letter written by the United States Minister in Ottawa two days before. Moffat reported growing public demand in Canada for 'some form of joint defence understanding with the United States.' This was being heard, he said, even from 'elements which in the past have been least well disposed towards us, such as the Toronto public and the English-speaking sections of Montreal ... The old fear that cooperation with the United States would tend to weaken Canada's ties with Great Britain has almost entirely disappeared. Instead, Canada believes that such cooperation would tend to bring Britain and the United States closer together, rather than to force Britain and Canada apart.'

It seems likely that this letter, coming at that moment, produced one of Roosevelt's characteristically impulsive acts. At noon on the 16th he held a press conference and announced that the United States was discussing with Britain the acquisition of naval and air bases for hemisphere defence; he added that separate conversations on hemisphere defence were going on with Canada. At that precise moment this was at least an exaggeration; but after the conference the President telephoned Mackenzie King, told him what he had said, and invited him to meet him on the following evening at Ogdensburg, NY, where he would be inspecting troops. King accepted with the greatest pleasure. He had reason for satisfaction. Something very desirable in terms of Canadian policy and Canadian public opinion had happened as a result of Roosevelt's own initiative, and without any suggestion from Ottawa.[84]

It would have been tactful of King to send a line to Churchill before he went off to the Ogdensburg meeting. He did not do so. Nor, it may be added, did he consult any of his own cabinet colleagues, let alone the Canadian Chiefs of Staff. Roosevelt himself seems to have taken no military advice whatever before making this defence arrangement with Canada. This was strictly the Franklin-Mackenzie axis at work. After dinner in the presidential train it was Roosevelt, it seems clear, who suggested the creation of a joint board of members from both countries, both civil and military, to discuss plans for the defence of 'the Northern Half of the Western Hemisphere.' Henry L. Stimson, the American Secretary of War, who was present, recorded that King was 'perfectly delighted'; and on August 18 the President and the Prime Minister issued a joint statement the core of which was the sentence, 'It has been agreed that a Permanent Joint Board on Defence shall be set up at once by the two countries.' No agreement was signed. This accord, which can be seen in retrospect as the beginning of a new era in the relations of Canada with the United States, had no basis more formal than a press release.[85]

The timing of the arrangement was perfect. The press in Canada and Britain was quite unanimous in praising it. In the United States there was almost equal unanimity, though some isolationist editors had lingering doubts. But there were reservations in Whitehall. Winston Churchill, to whom King sent a long account of the meeting once it was over, shocked him by remarking that there might be 'two opinions' about what had been done. Some months later Lord Cranborne, the Secretary of State for the Dominions, wrote Churchill saying he thought Britain should 'resist the whole principle of hemisphere defence' and citing as one unfortunate example the Ogdensburg arrangement, 'which constituted an agreement between a foreign country and a Dominion for the defence of North America, without any reference to or consultation with us.' These developments, he thought, might ultimately 'drive a wedge between us and Canada.' Perhaps Churchill might think of making a personal communication to Roosevelt or Harry Hopkins, and to Mackenzie King?[86] It was not a very practical suggestion, and there is no indication that Churchill acted on it. Nobody drove any wedges. But, as we said in connection with the 1935 trade agreement, the ancient ties with Britain gradually became less important to Canada, and the developing relationship with the United States became more and more dominant. And if one had to indicate a moment from which these tendencies became fully evident, it would have to be August 1940.

The Permanent Joint Board on Defence (which King emphasized was a purely advisory body) was set up at once and went to work. Its proceedings cannot be described in detail here. It made a series of recommendations to the two governments, virtually all of which were approved and most of which were implemented. The recommendation (August 27, 1940) that the service members of the Board proceed with preparation of

FIRST MEETING OF THE CANADIAN-AMERICAN
PERMANENT JOINT BOARD ON DEFENCE,
OTTAWA, AUGUST 1940

The United States still being neutral, the American officers, except one attaché, are in mufti. Front row, left to right: Lt-Gen. S.D. Embick, USA; Col. O.M. Biggar, Canadian Chairman; J.P. Moffat, U.S. Minister to Canada; Mackenzie King; Fiorello LaGuardia, U.S. Chairman; Col. J.L. Ralston, Canadian Minister of National Defence; Capt. H.W. Hill, USN. The four men at left in the back row are, left to right, H.L. Keenleyside, Canadian Secretary; John D. Hickerson, U.S. Secretary; Brig. Kenneth Stuart; and Capt. L.W. Murray, RCN a detailed plan for the joint defence of the two countries led in the end to considerable controversy. Two plans were prepared: one to meet the emergency situation that would arise if Britain were overrun, the other for use in the event of the United States entering the war and becoming a partner in offensive operations against the Axis powers. What caused difficulty was the question of command. The Americans, as the much more powerful partner, naturally and inevitably assumed that command would vest in them in all circumstances. The Canadian service representatives, and their government, were prepared to concede 'strategic direction' to the Americans in the case of the emergency plan, subject to consultation with the Canadian Chiefs of Staff. Nothing else would have made much sense. However, in the case of the second plan, which was really not a plan for the defence of North America, the Canadians considered this concession unnecessary. Unfortunately, the two plans were under discussion at the same period in 1941, and O.M. Biggar, the elderly Ottawa patent lawyer whom King had made chairman of the Board's Canadian section, did not make the distinction clear to the American members. In the end it was agreed that in the second plan ('ABC-22') co-ordination should be 'effected by mutual cooperation.' The American service members hated this; but there was nothing they could do about it.[87]

The Ogdensburg arrangement was followed by an Anglo-American deal by which Britain got fifty much-needed obsolete destroyers in exchange for leasing to the United States for ninety-nine years naval and air bases in a number of British island colonies in the Western Hemisphere.* One of these colonies was Newfoundland, an area of vast strategic interest to Canada. Britain consulted Canada when the transfers were first mentioned, and it is interesting that the Minister of National Defence (Ralston) gave the Prime Minister an opinion favourable to the cession without seeking the professional advice of the Chiefs of Staff. The Chiefs subsequently emphasized Newfoundland's great military importance, and the Canadian government made an attempt to ensure that Newfoundland should be made the subject of a negotiation with the United States separate from those relating to the other islands. This was unsuccessful, but a special protocol was signed by Canada, the United States, and Britain recognizing, for what it might be worth, Canada's 'special concern' in the defence of Newfoundland and providing that Canada would have the right to participate in any consultations concerning Newfoundland arising out of the agreement on island bases.[88]

* The rights to bases in Newfoundland and Bermuda were described as gifts, whereas the other bases were conceded in exchange for destroyers.

During the months following Ogdensburg, when a basis was laid for military co-operation with the United States, the problems of wartime economic co-operation with the Americans caused constant concern in Ottawa.

By way of simplifying an extremely complex matter, it may be said that Canada's difficulty was, as so often, a result of the interplay of her relations with Britain on one side and the United States on the other. Canada was now manufacturing for Britain a great variety of war material which Britain could not possibly pay for in Canadian dollars; Canada therefore had to finance these purchases. At the same time, Canada's 'unfavourable' balance of trade with the United States was growing steadily worse; as Norman Robertson wrote to the Prime Minister: 'Our merchandise exports to the United States are keeping up quite satisfactorily, but they do not come close to paying for the great expansion of imports from the United States required by our war industries.' These imports were in great part components for the material being manufactured for Britain. Canada's situation was only further complicated when in March 1941 the American Congress passed the Lend-Lease law permitting the President to furnish military equipment to Britain without payment. Apprehensive that this might lead Britain to divert orders from Canada to the United States, the Canadian government undertook, on conditions, to finance the whole British deficit in Canada; and on this basis the British government undertook to divert no orders.[89] But the Canadian balance-of-payments problem with the United States was growing steadily worse.

Readers of Volume I of this book may recall that in 1918 Canada was faced with a very similar problem, and that Sir Robert Borden solved it by going to Washington and negotiating with President Wilson an arrangement by which the United States purchased from Canada enough war material to redress the balance. History now repeated itself. But there is no evidence that Mackenzie King or his advisers had any knowledge of the proceedings of 1918. It might have been useful if they had.

What happened in 1941 is well known. On April 20 King met President Roosevelt at the President's Hyde Park estate and put before him a piece of paper which he accepted with no important change. This paper, since famous as the Hyde Park Declaration, laid down the principle that 'each country should provide the other with defence articles which it is best able to produce, and above all, produce quickly, and that production programmes should be coordinated to this end.' It also provided that components purchased in the United States for material produced in Canada for Britain might be obtained and forwarded by Britain under the Lend-Lease Act. This opened the way for large American purchases of war material in Canada, and very largely solved Canada's problem of obtaining American dollars.[90]

The background of this fortunate happening deserves a moment's examination. The person who was carrying the main burden of Canada's high economic policy was Dr W.C. Clark, the Deputy Minister of Finance. Clifford Clark was, like Skelton, an ex-member of the faculty of Queen's University at Kingston. He had been hired for the public service by R.B. Bennett, who said in retrospect that in his time Clark virtually *was* the Department of Finance. He was not less important under King.[91] Before the Prime Minister left Ottawa to see the President in April 1941, Clark gave him a series of memoranda emphasizing the importance of getting help with the exchange problem. These mentioned the desirability of the United States allowing Britain to 'lease-lend the United States component of British purchases in Canada,' but said nothing of the possibility of the United States itself purchasing war material in Canada. About the same time, however, the Minister of Munitions and Supply, C.D. Howe, who approached the problems of his department in the spirit of a manufacturer who wants to sell his product, pointed out to the Prime Minister that the U.S. could 'save the situation' for Canada by purchasing war material in production north of the border and paying for it with American dollars.[92] Thus briefed, King set out for Washington. Before discussing the question with anybody else, he saw Henry Morgenthau, Jr, Roosevelt's Secretary of the Treasury, and put before him the suggestion Howe had made. Morgenthau was most receptive, and King arranged for him to talk with Clark the following day (April 18).[93] It seems likely that Morgenthau had already had in mind the possibility of purchasing war goods in Canada, for a memorandum of the next day's meeting, written by James Coyne, financial attaché to the Canadian legation, who was present along with Clark, runs in part as follows:

Morgenthau said that he had told the Prime Minister of his suggestion that the exchange position could be helped through the United States buying munitions in Canada. He had told this idea to the President, who liked it. (It was quite evident that the whole idea had come up, perhaps in very general terms, at a cabinet meeting.) Morgenthau said that last September he had suggested to Howe and the Prime Minister that Canada should produce at least one kind of every munition of war, and that they had approved the idea. Morgenthau said the United States could give Canada very sizeable orders if there was any available capacity. This was especially true with regard to ships ...

Clark said that Howe had told him that it would be easy to build an additional 50 corvettes and minesweepers during the present year ...

Morgenthau said he wanted to find some way to give additional dollars to Canada, so that Canada could pay for its orders in the United States.

Morgenthau added, 'now is the time to rush this through,' and said that it should be put before the President during the Prime Minister's visit.[94]

The result of this discussion was that a 'draft press statement' was drawn up by Coyne, in consultation with Clark and Hume Wrong, now counsellor at the Legation; this statement, Wrong later wrote, 'was in fact issued on April 20th by the President and the Prime Minister with scarcely any alterations.'[95] Such were the immediate origins of the Hyde Park Declaration. In a letter to Howe, Clark called Morgenthau 'the real originator of the program.'[96] How far was it really an American plan that King put before Roosevelt on that 'grand Sunday' at Hyde Park? In so far as it was, the Prime Minister's powers of salesmanship were the less needed. Where Morgenthau may have got the idea is a matter of speculation. It is not impossible that it was implanted in his mind by C.D. Howe.

THE COMMONWEALTH ALONE

Though the Americans were now co-operating with Canada in organizing the defence of North America, and were sending great quantities of military supplies to sustain Britain in her battle, they were still not in the war; nor were they until they were blown into it by Japanese bombs. In the meantime, until Hitler attacked Russia in June 1941, the countries of the Commonwealth carried on the fight alone, and Canada was actually Britain's strongest single ally.

No new constitutional machinery was improvised to co-ordinate the Commonwealth effort. It is true that Robert Menzies, the Australian Prime Minister, visiting London early in 1941, argued strongly for an Imperial War Cabinet of the sort that had found such favour with Sir Robert Borden in 1917-18. But Mackenzie King was not Borden, and when Menzies called in at Ottawa on his way home he wholly failed to sell King on this device, which the Canadian told him would bring the Dominions merely 'responsibility without power.'* King preferred to dwell upon the virtues of modern communications – cable, wireless, and

* It's worthwhile to recall Lapointe's fierce attack on the Imperial War Cabinet in 1919 (Volume I, page 291).

transatlantic telephone – and the presence in the various Commonwealth capitals of representatives of the other countries of the group. This, he said in the House of Commons on February 17, 1941, made possible a 'real but invisible imperial council,' always in session, and with each Prime Minister able to express not only his own view – as would be the case in a meeting in London – but the view of the cabinet 'in the light of its responsibility to parliament.' As for Churchill, though he declared himself willing to consider the formation of an Imperial War Cabinet, he clearly was not fond of the idea, and he emphasized that he was not prepared to have any Dominion minister other than a Prime Minister sit with the British War Cabinet. Since no Prime Minister could leave his own country for more than a limited time, this meant that any idea of an Imperial War Cabinet permanently in session was ruled out. The fact was that Churchill had no intention of sharing his power if he could avoid it. His notion of ideal machinery for directing the war was clearly the British Prime Minister (who was also Minister of Defence) supported by an able and submissive Chiefs of Staff Committee. And, apart from the fortunate fact that the Chiefs were not submissive, that, it may be said, was increasingly the actual machinery the United Kingdom used. The British War Cabinet had little to do with strategic direction.[97]

We have seen King discouraging the idea of a Prime Ministers' Conference when Neville Chamberlain proposed one shortly before his fall (above, page 287). Possibly as a sop to Menzies, Churchill made a similar proposal for the summer of 1941. King's reaction was the same. He explained at great length why it was impossible for him to leave his post in Canada, and Ernest Lapointe asked Massey to tell Churchill for him 'that King is one national leader who cannot must not leave own country.' Churchill abandoned the conference proposal for the moment. It is curious that two months after protesting that such a trip was utterly out of the question, King flew to England, not for a conference, but for discussions with the British government and contacts with Canadian troops (who, sad to say, booed him). His change of heart was apparently due mainly to what he heard while on a trip to Western Canada, where opinions were different from those held in Quebec.[98] In his discussions with Churchill it appeared the two men were completely agreed in their ideas on Commonwealth organization. King attended several meetings of the British War Cabinet, and gave them good advice on American relations. Roosevelt, he said, drew support both from people who wanted the United States in the war and people who wanted it to stay out: 'It would therefore be very rash for us to attempt action in order to force American public opinion.'[99]

The High Commissions in London and Ottawa were playing useful parts, in spite of King's prejudice against using them in important negotiations. Massey and the other Dominion High Commissioners met regularly with the Dominions Secretary – an improvement on pre-war conditions, when King refused to allow the Canadian to join in the general meetings, and a busy minister was obliged to meet with him separately to say over again what he had already said to the others collectively. These meetings yielded the overseas representatives a good deal of information for their governments, but this varied with the Secretary; Massey records that Attlee was particularly close-mouthed. (Churchill himself, it may be said, had difficulty getting out of the nineteenth century; he prints in his memoirs bullying minutes he sent to the Dominions Office complaining of secrets being told to the Dominion governments.) [100] From April 1941 Ottawa was blessed with a particularly admirable British High Commissioner in Malcolm MacDonald. He had the prestige of an ex-Minister and a Prime Minister's son; and it was certainly a recommendation in Mackenzie King's eyes that he was not a Tory. He established an excellent relationship with King and in general may be said to have sympathized with his attitudes; and not the least virtue of the able and eloquent dispatches that he sent back to London was their understanding portrayal and interpretation of that curious and complex personality. He saw at once that King was the reverse of anti-British, and he was impressed by his determination to see the war carried through to victory. 'I feel,' he wrote, 'that many people in Britain, and some of those who have reported on him from here in the past, have not appreciated his true strength.'[101]

The face of the war was changed on June 22, 1941, when Hitler, with Britain still confronting him undefeated, launched his armies against Soviet Russia. Hasty reappraisals followed. Since the notorious Russo-German agreement of August 1939 that cleared the way for Hitler's war, the USSR had been regarded as a quasi-enemy country; when it tried to buy wheat, in January 1940, the Canadian government passed an order-in-council requiring permits for exports to neutral states contiguous to territories under enemy control, and refused the necessary permit to Russia.[102] On the day of Hitler's attack the veteran anti-Communist Churchill announced that Britain would give all possible help to the Soviets ('Any man or State who fights against Nazidom will have our aid'). The British government explained to the Dominions that the matter had been too urgent to permit of consulting them in advance. Canada made no complaint, and King at once echoed Churchill with a statement of his own ('Everyone who engages our enemy advances our cause') though, perhaps with an eye on anti-Communist Quebec, he said nothing of aid to Russia.[103] In due course a good deal of aid would go to the USSR from Canada.

The Russian alliance brought in its train changed relations with other countries of eastern Europe. Notably, on December 7, 1941, in conjunction with Britain and the other Commonwealth countries, Canada declared war on Finland, Romania, and Hungary. All three of these countries were waging war on Russia, and Russia naturally insisted that her allies should go to war with them. None of the three yielded to British requests to make peace. In the light of the sympathy felt for Finland after the Russian attack upon her in 1939, there was no enthusiasm for war with that country; and in Canada, once the proper action had been taken to indicate support for the Russian ally, unoffending Finnish nationals were in practice not treated as enemy aliens under the Defence of Canada Regulations.[104] Another country was a special case. Bulgaria declared war on the United Kingdom and the United States on December 13, 1941. Britain had broken diplomatic relations with Bulgaria in March, and at that time Canada, by order-in-council, made Bulgaria proscribed territory, 'which means that all transactions with Bulgaria will be subjected to the regime of the Trading with the Enemy Regulations.' There were no Bulgarian consulates in Canada, no Canadian representatives in Bulgaria, and the matter went no further; Canada never formally declared war on Bulgaria, but the omission made little difference in practice.[105]

On December 7, 1941, Mackenzie King, making the final arrangements for going to war with Finland, Romania, and Hungary, was a little troubled by the fact that Parliament was not in session and would therefore be unable to 'decide' the issue. He comforted himself by reflecting that these declarations were 'all part of the same war' in which Parliament had authorized participation in September 1939. The same afternoon he had a much greater problem, when news arrived of the Japanese attack on the United States fleet at Pearl Harbor.

There was no doubt what had to be done. (Apart from all other considerations, Canadian troops were under Japanese fire at Hong Kong, which was attacked soon after dawn, about six hours after Pearl Harbor.) The Canadian government had been maintaining close touch with both London and Washington as relations with Japan grew worse. King, who, like Churchill, was full of the fear that the Japanese might be intelligent enough to attack the British and the Dutch while leaving the Americans alone,* had cabled Churchill on November 30, 'I cannot express too strongly my view that so long as there is any uncertainty about the degree and immediacy of United States support it would be a terrible mistake to permit any course of action which might result in war between Japan and the British Commonwealth of Nations.' At the moment when the Japanese blow fell, the British nations were preparing to deliver a joint warning to Japan that a move by her into Thailand, which seemed to be about to happen, would have grave consequences; and a characteristic argument was in progress. London strongly desired that the warning should be delivered by the British Ambassador on behalf of the whole Commonwealth, though he might be accompanied by the Canadian and Australian *chargés d'affaires.* Canada preferred that the Canadian should accompany the Ambassador and deliver a separate note 'associating Canada completely with United Kingdom representations.' The discussion between London and Ottawa was still in progress when the bombs went down on Pearl Harbor.[107] King was maintaining his determination to maintain the forms of independence and avoid using Commonwealth machinery. Yet the fact is that Canada was joining the rest of the Commonwealth in what was a definite threat of war if Japan persisted in her course.

War existed by the act of Japan, but there were formalities to go through. Parliament would have been applied to had it been in session. As it was, King telephoned the leaders of the other parties at their homes, and they agreed that there was no need of assembling it. The affair reminds one that the power of making peace or war is a prerogative of the Crown, exercised on the advice of Ministers. That Parliament should be consulted may be a political requirement, but is not a legal one. The cabinet met early in the evening of the 7th. The draft order-in-council it had before it, prepared by External Affairs, referred to Japanese attacks on British territory. King thought there should also be a reference to the attacks on United States territories, 'for historical reasons; and also for reasons of high policy.' The final text recited that Japan had 'wantonly and treacherously attacked British territory and British forces, and also United States territory and United States forces.' It noted that 'in accord-

---

* In the summer of 1940, before Ogdensburg and when the government was painfully aware of the unprotected state of Canada's Pacific coast, King actually gave tentative and theoretical thought to the question whether, in the event of U.S. neutrality in an Anglo-Japanese war, Canada should not, for a time at least, try to be neutral too, while cutting off strategic materials to Japan.[106] It was an unsatisfactory solution to an utterly insoluble problem.

ance with the decision of the Parliament of Canada for effective co-operation by Canada at the side of Britain to resist aggression,' Canada was associated with Britain in hostilities. The implication was that only that association sanctioned by Parliament in September 1939 made Canada a party to the new conflict. There was no reference to the Crown, and only an incidental one to the Commonwealth. Again, the forms of independence. The order recommended that the King be moved to authorize declaring a state of war with Japan. King George VI gave his oral approval at 1:10 p.m., London time, on December 8, declaring war on behalf of Canada for the fourth time in two days. Since the British government, perhaps remembering Mackenzie King's advice of a week or so before, had decided to withhold their own declaration so that it could immediately follow the American one, and since the joint resolution of Congress in Washington was approved at 4:10 p.m., local time, Canada formally declared war on Japan some hours before either Britain or the United States.[108] The point is hardly of more than academic interest.

END OF AN ERA

After sixteen years, the guard changed in the Department of External Affairs when O.D. Skelton, the Under Secretary of State, died at the wheel of his car in Ottawa on January 28, 1941. For better or for worse, Skelton had largely made the Department what it was. King recorded that this was 'the most serious loss thus far sustained in my public life and work.' He added: 'However, there must be a purpose and, as I see it, it may be meant to cause me to rely more completely on my own judgment in making decisions ....'[109] We have seen his increasing rebellion against Skelton's doctrinaire isolationism as the Second World War drew on; it should be added, we have also seen Skelton showing signs of a different attitude in the critical days of 1940. Events were breaking in upon the comfortable little world of the East Block, and the department would never again be what it had been in Skelton's day.

For reasons which remain uncertain, King appointed as Skelton's successor Norman Robertson. Robertson was an extremely able man, but he was junior in the service to a number of other people, including Pearson and Wrong, who certainly did not appreciate his being promoted over their heads. It is possible that King thought Robertson likely to be more pliable than either of the other two. Mr Pickersgill's informed comment on the results of the appointment is: 'No one ever completely took Skelton's place, although Norman Robertson ... quickly gained and retained a greater measure of Mackenzie King's confidence than any other adviser of the closing years of his life.'[110]

Only a few weeks after Skelton, on April 8, 1941, another figure destined to be legendary passed from the scene. The reader is well acquainted with Loring Christie, who had left his mark on Canadian history as the adviser and confidant of Sir Robert Borden during and after the First World War, when a new status was being carved out for Canada as one of the 'autonomous nations of an Imperial Commonwealth.' When the onetime imperial federationist returned to the service as an advanced nationalist and bitter isolationist, it was to a lower estate than he had held before: not the confidential associate of the Prime Minister, but that associate's henchman. His opinions made him a somewhat strange appointee to the office of Minister at Washington in September 1939. Viscount Bennett, watching from abroad, called the appointment 'a very great insult to the British people,' but recorded that Lord Tweedsmuir suggested that the responsibilities of office had somewhat lessened Christie's antipathies.[111] His death, closing one of the most extraordinary odysseys of opinion in Canadian annals, appears in retrospect another indication that an era was ending.

CHAPTER NINE

THE SECOND WORLD WAR: 1942-45

CHURCHILL, ROOSEVELT, AND KING

Winston Churchill and Franklin Roosevelt dominated the war effort of the western Allies after Pearl Harbor; and to a very considerable extent Canada's official relations with Britain and the United States, and with what Churchill loved to call the Grand Alliance, centred in the relationship of Mackenzie King with these two great men. That relationship, then, is worth examining.

Both Churchill and Roosevelt, it is important to note, enjoyed enormous personal popularity among Canadians. The President was something of a hero in Canada from the days of the New Deal in 1933. Churchill's heroic status was clear from the time of his first speeches defying Hitler in the grim summer of 1940. Radio brought these great orators into almost every Canadian home. With their popular impact Mackenzie King could not compete, oratorically or otherwise.* Malcolm MacDonald summed it up in a letter to J.M. Keynes commenting on a report by Keynes on a visit to Ottawa in 1944. Keynes, he said, had used one wrong word about King: 'You are quite right in saying his prestige is unrivalled. But his popularity is certainly not unrivalled unless you mean it in the reverse sense! In fact, the position is paradoxical. It would be true to say that "his prestige and unpopularity are unrivalled." It is an extraordinary

---

* In September 1946 the Canadian Institute of Public Opinion asked Canadians, 'What person living in any part of the world today do you admire most?' Churchill headed the poll by a large margin, with 28 per cent. Had Roosevelt still been alive, he probably would have been next. As it was, Mackenzie King was a bad second, with 8 per cent. Third was the Pope (Pius XII), for whom 6 per cent voted. Presumably most of the Pope's votes came from Quebec.

case of a national leader whose authority and power are, by the repeated consent of the voters, immense, and who is yet definitely disliked by, probably, a great majority of these same people. The reasons for this make one of the most interesting studies in politicians that I have ever come up against. It would need a small volume to analyse them. But I am damned if I am going to write that particular volume.'[1] King was well aware of the situation, and nothing made him angrier than the regrettable tendency of Canadians to speak of 'our leaders, Churchill and Roosevelt.'[2] But that consummate politician had an answer. If he could not compete with these two overpowering personalities, he could identify with them. And he made it his business to appear before Canadians on every possible occasion as the friend and close associate of the British Prime Minister and the American President.

How genuinely close was King to his two senior partners? Neither Churchill nor Roosevelt kept a diary, so the evidence is slim. In the case of Roosevelt, it was always difficult to determine what really went on behind that affable, enigmatic facade. But he probably had some degree of personal regard for King, buttressed by that rather special consciousness of Canada that we have remarked as so unusual in an American President (above, page 230). The consideration he showed King in those two days at Warm Springs in April 1940 is striking. As for Churchill, his whole background and approach to life were so different from King's that it would be difficult to imagine his having any really warm feeling for his Canadian colleague. King could be useful to him, and therefore he was polite to him; but that surely was as far as it went. One remembers Churchill's unwillingness to take King into his confidence on the date of the Normandy D Day;[3] this seems symptomatic. Mike Pearson was sure that Churchill and Roosevelt flattered King to keep him happy,[4] and I have seen no evidence to refute his opinion.

Occasionally one gets a glimpse of hard fact. In 1942 the Canadian government proposed an air training conference in Ottawa. Its origin was an idea of co-ordinating the air training programmes in Canada and the United States; but, pretty evidently because there was a desire in Ottawa to stage an international conference which would lend a certain prestige to Canada (and King),* it developed until fourteen nations took part. (Even the Russians were invited; but those tough realists had better things to do with their time.) The one really important part of the confer-

---

* The Governor General, Lord Athlone, assumed that, as the Sovereign's representative in Canada, he would have the task of formally opening the conference. King disagreed. He opened the conference himself.

ence came after most of the fourteen had gone home; the Commonwealth countries then got down to making a new air training agreement to replace that of 1939.[5] King had broached the idea of a conference to Roosevelt in April, and the President sent Churchill a revealing cable:

Mackenzie King has been at the White House for two days and he was very anxious to have something to show for his Washington visit and proposed a conference in Ottawa early in May to discuss the greatly expanded Air Training Programme and the renewal of your Empire Training Plan on an overall basis for the United Nations. I see no harm, and a good deal of probable good in such a conference.

I talked with your Embassy about an immediate [press] release to synchronize with King's departure and they say [saw?] no reason to bother you with it beforehand.

I hope you will let someone come over from England for it, in addition to your top people over here.[6]

The note of patronage and indulgence is very audible, and it must be said that the proposal for an unnecessary conference goes far to justify it.

For Canada the practical value of these personal relationships was no doubt considerable; but it had its limits. Mackenzie failed to prevail on Franklin to intervene effectively on more than one Canadian-American issue which the Canadian government considered exceptionally important. One such, we shall see, was the question of the establishment of a Canadian military mission in Washington. After failing to get satisfaction on this through all other channels, King took it to the President; but though Roosevelt appeared to assent nothing was accomplished for a long time thereafter. The same thing happened with respect to Canada's desire for a seat on the Munitions Assignment Board.[7] In spite of King's belief that it was easier for Canada to get what she wanted from the Americans than from the British (below, page 341), he certainly had better luck with his applications to Churchill.

DIRECTION OF THE WAR

Immediately after Pearl Harbor, Churchill went to Washington for the conference with Roosevelt and his advisers that went by the name 'Arcadia.' From this meeting new machinery emerged for the direction of the war effort of the western Allies.

The strategic direction of the war thereafter was the business of the powerful military committee known as the Combined Chiefs of Staff. With its seat in Washington, this consisted effectively of the Joint Chiefs of Staff (as the American Chiefs of Staff came to be known) plus representatives of the British Chiefs of Staff. The Combined Chiefs' most important decisions were taken in a series of strategic conferences, chiefly held in places other than Washington, which were usually attended by the British Chiefs of Staff themselves and by Churchill and Roosevelt. The Combined Chiefs of Staff was a purely Anglo-American committee. It included no representatives of Russia or China, or of the British Dominions or the European governments in exile.

At 'Arcadia' Roosevelt and Churchill also set up a Munitions Assignment Board, to operate under the Combined Chiefs of Staff. This had the task of co-ordinating the assignment of newly-produced weapons and equipment to various theatres of operations as the needs of strategy dictated. It consisted of a Washington committee and a London committee, the latter being subordinate in that, while assigning all United Kingdom production, it distributed to Dominions and European allies what the Washington committee assigned to it from United States production. 'Arcadia' set up two other 'combined boards,' both civilian: the Combined Shipping Adjustment Board and the Combined Raw Materials Board. In June 1942 the British and Americans instituted two more, the Combined Food Board and the Combined Production and Resources Board. All these bodies were composed exclusively of representatives of the British and United States governments.[8]

In the process of establishing this machinery to direct the Allied effort, Canada (and the other Dominions of the Commonwealth) were not consulted in any way. Late in January 1942 Canada was formally told (by circular telegrams from London going also to the other Dominions) that the Munitions Assignment Board and the two civilian boards had been established. It is an extraordinary fact that, although it is evident that it was expected that Canada's forces should be put at the disposal of the Combined Chiefs of Staff, and the lives of her soldiers, sailors, and airmen hazarded in accordance with their decisions, the Canadian government never received so much as an official notification that the Combined Chiefs of Staff had been set up. It got the information from the newspapers.*

Here there was a serious failure of British policy. Malcolm MacDonald, writing from the perspective of 1943, blamed it in part for a deterioration in relations with the Dominions which he thought had taken place since the exalted and critical days of 1940-1. Australian confidence, he recalled, was shaken by the events which ended in the fall of Singapore:

* When I told this to a British official historian he refused to believe it. However, after searching the records he had to admit that no notification could be found.

The Canadians ... remained much steadier, and avoided recrimination even when their troops in Hong Kong were lost to a man. But other developments began to shake their high confidence in Britain. The first cause of this was the establishment in Washington of a series of important Combined Boards, on which Great Britain and the United States alone were represented, to direct various aspects of the war on behalf of the United Nations – without any prior consultation with the Dominions. In some cases they were given only meagre or even no prior information on the subject. Responsible Canadians resented this. It was not only that they regarded the failure to inform them properly as a gross discourtesy. They felt that non-consultation in matters which might be of great concern to them was a breach of the constitution of the British Commonwealth of Nations. All the trouble which arose afterwards could have been avoided if Canada (and the other Dominions) had been taken into our confidence beforehand.[9]

These strictures need one qualification. The feeling MacDonald reports existed, but it was largely limited to the official circles in Ottawa with which he was in touch. The matters we have described, and particularly the failure to consult, were confidential, and ordinary Canadians had little knowledge of them while the war lasted. If they had realized the cavalier manner in which their country had been treated, there would have been some bitter comment.

The responsibility for the failure was certainly largely Churchill's. He had many other worries, and the Dominions were never in the front of his mind. Nevertheless, their problems were specifically put before him in the midst of the 'Arcadia' conference when he made a visit to Ottawa. On December 29, 1941, he met with the Canadian Cabinet War Committee, and Mackenzie King made a mild complaint. It seems to have centred chiefly on the difficulty of getting a Canadian military mission in Washington, but King wrote in his diary: 'Said quite openly to him the problem we faced was that while we had been in [the war] during two and a quarter years, things would be so arranged that the U.S. and Britain would settle everything between themselves, and that our services, Chiefs of Staff, etc., would not have any say in what was to be done.' The minutes of the meeting record,

Mr. Churchill expressed the view that, where Canadian interests were concerned, Canada should certainly be consulted, and should be represented on any body devised for the conduct of strategy in theatres of Canadian interest.

At the same time, the U.K. government were anxious to keep the United States to the fore, and avoid anything in the nature of partisanship. As far as joint U.K.-Canadian matters were concerned, it was his responsibility to see that the Canadian government were fully informed.

The fact is that in the strategic discussions during the war Churchill assumed that he was entitled to represent the Dominions, and to give them as much or as little information about events as he chose. No one had authorized him to speak for Canada; on the other hand, the Canadian ministers were too polite ever to point this out to him. It is a notable fact that during this meeting in Ottawa he gave them no indication of the nature of the machinery for directing the war which was then in preparation. At that date, of course, the plans were still incomplete.

By mid-January 1942, when the 'Arcadia' conference was ending, what had happened was fairly clear, and the Cabinet War Committee agreed that the Canadian Minister in Washington should inquire 'as to the form of joint machinery likely to be proposed.'[10] This produced no result (nobody intended to make a proposal to Canada); and on February 4 the War Committee again faced the question. It was reported that there had been no consultation whatever. 'The information received through Sir John Dill* and other British officers, and through the Legation in Washington, had been wholly informal.' King's statement on the matter is thus recorded in the minutes:

The Prime Minister said that he had informed Sir John Dill that, while Canada realized the practical necessity of limiting representation upon combined bodies for the efficient conduct of the war, and would not seek to complicate the situation by unreasonable requests, at the same time Canada had been in the war for more than two years and Canadians would expect that their interests would not be ignored in any of these fields.

The present position was unsatisfactory but there was, at present, no useful initiative that Canada could take.

On February 12 there was further discussion in the Committee. Ralston, Minister of National Defence since June 1940, pointed out that the government had made no representations about its exclusion from the combined bodies, and that it was apparently being assumed in Washington that Canadian production and requirements would be dealt with through the Anglo-American assignments machinery. It was agreed that a tele-

* Field-Marshal Sir John Dill had been Chief of the Imperial General Staff, and was now to represent Churchill on the Combined Chiefs of Staff in Washington. He had lately visited Ottawa.

gram should be drafted, for the approval of the Prime Minister and interested ministers, making it clear to Britain and the United States that Canada had not been consulted concerning participation in the work of the combined bodies and therefore was not included in arrangements made by them for allocation of munitions and raw materials. But no record has been found of such a telegram being sent. The fact is that Canada never made a formal protest about her exclusion from the combined organizations or about the lack of consultation before they were set up. The reason, undoubtedly, was the reluctance of the Prime Minister to take such action, in spite of pressure from Ralston and perhaps other ministers.

The government's policy as it developed was to attempt to gain membership on certain of the organizations but not others. Canada never sought admission to the charmed circle of the Combined Chiefs of Staff; that was clearly the preserve of the very big battalions. The Munitions Assignment Board, however, was another matter. Canada was a relatively large producer of munitions, standing in this matter third (a rather poor third, it must be said) among the western Allies. The government made a determined but unsuccessful effort to obtain a seat on the MAB. Without rehearsing all the detail, it may be said that in the spring of 1942 formal application was made, and, as we have mentioned, Mackenzie King took the matter up with President Roosevelt personally. After some hesitation the British government supported the application subject to certain reservations. But Harry Hopkins, who was very powerful in Washington at this stage of the war, was unalterably opposed. An offer was made for partial membership, 'when Canadian production and Canadian North American requirements are under discussion'; but there was disagreement between Ralston and C.D. Howe, Ministers respectively of National Defence and Munitions and Supply. The latter, a civil department, was not anxious to see Canadian military procurement in Washington transferred to military hands, which would have happened if it had been handled through the MAB. After long wrangling in the War Committee the offer was not accepted. Canadian production was never formally pooled in Washington, but was allocated in Ottawa by a Canadian Munitions Assignment Committee (Army), on which representatives of the British Army Staff, Washington, and the United States War Department sat as full members.[11]

When the creation of the Combined Production and Resources Board and the Combined Food Board was announced in June 1942, without consultation with Canada, the Canadian government was again faced

with a question of policy. C.D. Howe thought that he could work satisfactorily through Donald Nelson, chairman of the War Production Board
in the United States, who was the American member of the CPRB; but J.L.
Ilsley, the Minister of Finance, was doubtful about 'accepting silently a
position of exclusion.' It was decided to ask for representation on the
Combined Food Board.[12] Applications were made to both London and
Washington accordingly. Success was long delayed, and Canada became a
member of the Combined Production and Resources Board (November
1942) long before she attained the Food Board (October 1943). Shortly
after the formation of these two boards was announced the waters were
further muddied by the appearance of another project – that of the body
which ultimately became the United Nations Relief and Rehabilitation
Administration [UNRRA]. This time there was some gesture in the direction of consultation. Sir Frederick Leith-Ross, a British Treasury official
who had been involved in planning the organization, came to Ottawa to
explain the scheme, which unfortunately struck the Canadians he talked
to as thoroughly bad. The idea was that the body should be managed by a
Policy Committee composed of representatives of the United States, the
United Kingdom, Russia, and China.

MacDonald took Leith-Ross to see the Prime Minister, and King gave
him an earful. (He was always readier to speak frankly to British officials
than to ministers, and readier to be tough in conversation than on paper.)
MacDonald reported him as saying, '... those proposals would not be
acceptable to the Canadian Parliament and people. He realised that in all
the circumstances Russia and China must have places on the proposed
Policy Committee. But there would be strong criticism of that, if Canada
were left off. Those two countries would contribute little or nothing to
post-war relief and rehabilitation; they would be large receivers of help.
Canada on the other hand would be a contributor on a considerable scale.
The Policy Committee would have a great measure of control of her productions [sic]. In that case the people of Canada would certainly want a
proper say in the deliberations of the Committee, and the Cabinet did not
think it enough that a Canadian representative should only be called in,
not as a full member, at meetings of the Committee when Canada's interests were directly affected.' In the matter of the Food Board, Canada had
been 'treated as though she did not exist.' King feared that 'unless the
situation were remedied this would have a permanent effect on relations
between Canada and Britain after the war.'[13] Leith-Ross also got strong
words from Norman Robertson and from Clifford Clark. Due note was
taken of the remark of the Deputy Minister of Finance that if Canada's

special position was not recognized there might be 'great difficulties' in renewing the 'billion dollar gift,' the Dominion's contribution to financing British purchases in Canada (below, page 357).[14]

There is little doubt that the apprehension of financial consequences influenced the subsequent British decision to make concessions to Canada. Some weeks after these conversations in Ottawa a meeting of representatives from eight British government departments took place at the Dominions Office in London. A paper written in the Dominions Office which seems to have been before it described Canada's situation and remarked: 'The Canadian Government's feeling in the matter has now become so strong that it is beginning to colour their attitude in regard to other aspects of their relations with us, and especially in regard to financial assistance.' The meeting agreed to recommend 'that, as it was desirable on grounds of technical efficiency, the Canadian Government ought to be offered full membership of the Combined Production and Resources Board.'[15] The British government seems to have acted in this sense even before the meeting; American concurrence was obtained, and as we have seen Canada became a member of the CPRB in November.[16]

The application to join the Food Board had been allowed to lapse, but since the situation was considered to have changed it was renewed in April 1943. By September Britain and the United States were agreed in accepting it, and as noted above Canada joined the Board the following month.[17] Although the Dominion had thus been admitted to two of the four civilian boards, and was the only country except Britain and the United States to achieve such membership, it was a rather empty honour. The fact is that these boards were not very powerful or important in practice.[18] If they had been, Canada might have had more difficulty in obtaining membership. She never did achieve her ambition of sitting on the Munitions Assignment Board, a genuinely significant body. The UNRRA story was not much better. The Cabinet War Committee was told on January 21, 1943, that Russia was opposed to the enlargement of the committee, for which the United Kingdom was pressing. The United States and China were disposed to side with the USSR, which was arguing that UNRRA would be a pattern for other postwar international organizations. Britain had contended for a seven-power committee, to include both France and Canada. It was all no use. Canada finally made the UNRRA committee only in September 1945.[19]

A principle had been emerging from Canada's contentions. She had argued that she deserved a seat on the Munitions Assignment Board because she was a large producer of munitions; that she belonged on the Food Board and on UNRRA because she was a large producer of food. It was Hume Wrong who reduced her practice to a theory: 'functionalism.' As early as January 1942 he wrote to Norman Robertson: 'The principle, I think, is that each member of the grand alliance should have a voice ... proportionate to its contribution to the general war effort. A subsidiary principle is that the influence of the various countries should be greatest in connection with those matters with which they are most directly concerned.'[20] Mackenzie King enunciated the idea to the House of Commons on July 9, 1943, as an answer to the problems of the 'middle powers,' like Canada, in connection with postwar international organization:

The time is approaching ... when even before victory is won the concept of the united nations will have to be embodied in some form of international organization. On the one hand, authority in international affairs must not be concentrated exclusively in the largest powers. On the other, authority cannot be divided equally among all the thirty or more sovereign states that comprise the united nations, or all effective authority will disappear. A number of new international institutions are likely to be set up as a result of the war. In the view of the government, effective representation on these bodies should neither be restricted to the largest states nor necessarily extended to all states. Representation should be determined on a functional basis which will admit to full membership those countries, large or small, which have the greatest contribution to make to the particular object in question. In the world there are over sixty sovereign states. If they all have a nominally equal voice in international decisions, no effective decisions are likely to be taken. Some compromise must be found between the theoretical equality of states and the practical necessity of limiting representation on international bodies to a workable number. That compromise can be discovered, especially in economic matters, by the adoption of the functional principle of representation.

Functionalism was a sensible as well as an ingenious idea; but Canada was not going to have much more luck in applying it to international politics in peacetime than she had had during the war.

We mentioned the great strategic conferences in which Churchill and Roosevelt and the Combined Chiefs of Staff made the basic decisions that won the war. These conferences, like the Combined Chiefs committee itself, were strictly Anglo-American, except for the rare occasions when it was considered politic for the western leaders to meet with the leaders of Russia and China. The lesser allies, including all the Dominions, were on the outside, not even looking in. Churchill considered it his responsibility to keep the Dominions informed, up to a point. After each conference he normally sent a message to the Dominion Prime Ministers telling them in at least general terms what had occurred. Thus after the Casablanca meeting (January 1943) telegrams from him and from the Deputy Prime Minister (C.R. Attlee) reported the decisions in considerable detail. They did not, however, report the decision to invade Sicily, merely forecasting 'in due course further amphibious offensive operations on a large scale.'[21] A strong military case could be made, of course, for maintaining such secrecy about important future operations.

Two of the conferences, 'Quadrant' in August 1943 and 'Octagon' in September 1944, were held on Canadian soil, at Quebec City. Even to these Canada was not a party. When the first Quebec conference was in prospect, Mackenzie King was urged, by both Norman Robertson and Malcolm MacDonald in concert, to insist on a dignified position in it for himself as Prime Minister of Canada; King reports Robertson as saying that he should be with Churchill and Roosevelt 'as an equal.' King himself recorded, 'I saw the force of this but felt embarrassment in the matter.' He drafted a cable mildly asserting that his position as Prime Minister would 'have to be considered'; subsequently, however, he deleted this passage. Nevertheless, Churchill felt it necessary to give some recognition to Canada in the circumstances; and he suggested that King and the Canadian Chiefs of Staff should be admitted to *plenary* sessions of the conference, the British and American representatives still being able to retire into private session at will. Roosevelt vetoed this suggestion instantly, using an argument that Canadian heard many times during the war: if Canada were admitted, Brazil, China, Mexico, and the other Dominions would clamour to be admitted too. King made not the slightest complaint; the suggestion, he said, had been Churchill's, not his. As long as Churchill and Roosevelt came to Quebec, and he could be seen with them there, he was well satisfied. He wrote: 'My own feeling is that Churchill and Roosevelt being at Quebec, and myself acting as host, will be quite sufficient to make clear that all three are in conference together and will not only satisfy but will please the Canadian feeling, and really be very helpful to me personally.' Here we get a hint of one probable reason for King's reluctance to press for a more active role for Canada in the direction of the war; he did not care to risk disturbing the relationship with the President and the British Prime Minister which he considered so valuable to him politically. At the two Quebec conferences Canada played merely the part of host, providing the whisky and soda, and was not admitted to the strategic discussions. But King was amply photographed with Churchill and Roosevelt, and few Canadians realized the true facts.[22]

A HOST AND TWO GUESTS, QUEBEC, 1943
Mackenzie King (host to the conference, but not a member of it) meets
the press with President Roosevelt and Mr Churchill during the First
Quebec Conference. Left rear, left to right, Anthony Eden, Brendan
Bracken, Harry Hopkins

Between conferences Canadian officers maintained what contact they could with the Combined Chiefs of Staff organization in Washington. Major-General Maurice Pope was sent there in March 1942 primarily for that purpose, and after the Canadian Joint Staff was finally set up he became its head. One of his main tasks was picking up as much information as possible around the Combined Chiefs (mainly in practice from the British representatives). The Canadian staff maintained touch with the Combined Chiefs' various committees, where most of the actual work was done. Only on one occasion, it seems, did General Pope actually appear before the great men in formal session.[23]

Just how unsatisfactory the whole situation was from the Canadian point of view is obvious. Early in 1944, as the invasion of North-West Europe, in which Canadian forces would play an important part, drew near, the group of senior civil servants around the Prime Minister took action in an effort to 'clarify the formal character of the relationship of the Canadian armed forces to our allies.' A paper which Norman Robertson sent to Mackenzie King on March 1 compared the recent retirement of General McNaughton as commander of the First Canadian Army (below, pages 350-2) with the procedures followed in the appointment of the Supreme Commander for the coming campaign (General Eisenhower) and the British ground commander for it (General Montgomery). In the former case there was 'the fullest and most receptive consultation of competent United Kingdom opinion by the responsible Canadian authorities.' In the latter cases Churchill and Roosevelt had not chosen even to inform the Canadian government of the appointment of the officers under whom their troops were to fight; King and his colleagues got the news from the press. There was a contrast here with practice in the Pacific, where General Douglas MacArthur's formal appointment as Supreme Commander in the South-West Pacific was made by the United States, Britain, Australia, and New Zealand in combination, and the directives for MacArthur and Admiral Chester W. Nimitz as theatre commanders were issued in the names of the same four countries.

Although something had been accomplished on the economic side, in the matter of the combined boards, Canada had no formal relationship to the strategic high command. Robertson suggested that King might consider formally delegating to the Combined Chiefs of Staff 'those duties and powers in respect of Canadian forces which they have, in fact, been exercising without ever having received any formal assignment of these duties and powers from the Government of Canada.' He also suggested that a Canadian Joint Staff Mission of senior officers be set up in London, separate from the Canadian field commands but 'capable of ensuring suitable Canadian association at a high level with the strategic conduct of the invasion operations.' The Canadian Chiefs of Staff had doubts about the workability of the scheme, but the War Committee approved it. Messages were accordingly sent to Churchill and Roosevelt requesting that the Supreme Commanders in North-West Europe and the Mediterranean be informed that their authority over Canadian forces under them derived from the government of Canada, and advising that the government was considering setting up a Joint Staff Mission in London which would serve as a channel of communication between the Canadian Chiefs of Staff and these two supreme commands. The immediate result was a brusque rejection of the second part of the plan by the American Joint Chiefs of Staff supported by the President. Should the Joint Staff Mission be established, the JCS said, 'the appropriate channel of communications between the Canadian Chiefs of Staff and the Supreme Commands must be through the Combined Chiefs of Staff and not directly through the Mission, to the Supreme Commands.' This effectively wrecked the project of liaison with the Supreme Commanders, even though Churchill had taken no exception to it. In due course, however, the Combined Chiefs did inform Generals Eisenhower and Wilson, the two Supreme Commanders concerned, that they had been asked by the Canadian government to notify them that they exercised command over the Canadian forces in their theatres 'with the full authority of the Canadian Government.' Thus some formal legal basis was established for their right to command Canadians.[24]

Enough has been said to make it quite clear that the Canadian government had no effective share in the higher direction of the war. In the beginning it sought no share; and when in the later stages it made some attempt at achieving influence, the attempt was limited, half-hearted, and largely ineffective. So far as purely strategic control was concerned, the situation was summarized in the statement made by Mackenzie King at the meeting of the Canadian Cabinet War Committee on August 11, 1943, during the first Quebec Conference, which was attended by two members of the British War Cabinet (Churchill and Sir John Anderson) and was grandiloquently styled a 'Joint Meeting' with that cabinet. The minutes record King as saying: 'The Canadian government had accepted the position that the higher strategic direction of the war was exercised by the British Prime Minister and the President of the United States, with the Combined Chiefs of Staff. It was recognized that the participation of the Canadian military heads, in meetings of the Combined Chiefs of Staff, might give rise to difficulties with the United Nations. It had been agreed that opportunities would be made [during the present conference] for consultation between the British and Canadian Chiefs of Staff.' Churchill replied that arrangements had already been made for a meeting between the British and Canadian Chiefs. Further meetings could be held as required, and their conclusions could be reviewed later by the two Prime Ministers. The War Committee formally agreed 'that the position as described by Mr. King and Mr. Churchill was satisfactory.'[25]

It is easy to criticize the Canadian government, and particularly King, with whom the chief responsibility rested; but the problem was enormously difficult.[26] In a war waged by a coalition made up of countries of different scales of power there is bound to be constant competition between the claims of military efficiency and those of national sovereignty. Victories are won by concentrated power. In a war directed by a committee – as coalition wars usually are – the effectiveness of the committee is in inverse ratio to its size; the larger the number of interests it has to reconcile within itself, the less efficient its leadership will be. It is stupid to insist on national sovereignty being respected if the cost is defeat. On the other hand, the fact remains that the great powers dominating a coalition may sometimes think of their own interests rather than those of the alliance. They will not take much account of the interests of their junior partners, or perhaps even know what those interests are. They may use the argument of military efficiency merely as a convenient means of keeping power in their own hands.

In these circumstances the position of a power of middle strength like Canada is bound to be difficult, and its policy is almost certain to be a succession of compromises. If it takes a genuinely responsible attitude, it must be prepared to make large concessions to the leadership of the great powers on its side; but it must also be ready to raise its voice to assert its own interests and must seek to influence its great associates to take account of them. And yet it can do this only to the extent that it can be done without injury to the common cause. Broadly speaking, this was the sort of policy which the government of Canada sought to pursue in the Second World War.

Mackenzie King certainly cannot be faulted for interfering with the directors of Allied strategy, for he never showed any tendency to do so. Abstention was the easier as neither King himself nor any member of his government had any training or experience fitting them for the direction of war. Canada had no Churchill or Smuts. If King is to be criticized it is for erring in the opposite direction, for allowing his concern for maintaining his pleasant personal relationship with Churchill and Roosevelt – if my interpretation is correct – to prevent him from asserting his country's interests at moments when he might have done so. In King's favour it must be said that a more assertive policy would probably not have got

Canada a great deal. Australia made much more noise than Canada* and got few practical concessions. What a more active policy might have achieved was more respect for the forms, rather than the substance, of Canadian sovereignty. Australia did get something here; we have seen that Australia and New Zealand were at least formally consulted in the appointment of Allied commanders in the Pacific, and were formal parties to their directives, and we have noted the painful contrast with the situation concerning the North-West Europe campaign, in which over a quarter of a million Canadians fought without Canada having any part or recognition in the Allied command. A more assertive government could have accomplished something in such matters. And it is just possible that it might have got Canada on to the Munitions Assignment Board.

A particular problem which troubled the Canadian government, Parliament, and people alike throughout the war was that of 'recognition.' Canadians, French as well as English it is probably fair to say, were proud of the steadily increasing part their country was playing in the struggle, were avid for information about it, and were disturbed when they thought the Canadian contribution was receiving less public recognition than it deserved by comparison with those of other countries. The matter was important to the King government because when the recognition seemed to be inadequate the government was blamed. It was a constant problem in relations with Britain because the three Canadian services all fought under higher British command and closely integrated with British forces; and the British had four Dominions and various other communities to think of in addition to their own people at home. The business of assigning public credit as between all these was such as to make one sympathize with London.

One particularly difficult case may be mentioned as indicating the nature of the problem: the announcement of the participation of the 1st Canadian Division in the invasion of Sicily (July 10, 1943). It was especially important to the Canadian Government and public, because after years of garrison duty in England a large Canadian Army force was being committed for the first time to a major campaign. And the affair unfortunately developed in a way that gave Mackenzie King the impression that Canadians were being discriminated against and that the British authori-

---

* The minutes of the Cabinet War Committee for December 29, 1941, record Churchill as saying with respect to Hong Kong: 'In spite of the tragic circumstances, there had been no "whimper" from Canada; none of the bitter and harmful criticism which had come from Australia.'

ties were responsible. Both these impressions were mistaken, but it was impossible to eradicate them from the Prime Minister's mind.

To describe the Sicilian 'crisis' briefly is difficult, for the affair was complicated. It should be explained that it is a concern of every Intelligence staff in the field to gain as much and as early information as possible about the enemy's 'order of battle' – the composition of his force, and particularly the movement of formations from one theatre to another. The staff of General Eisenhower, the Allied commander in the Mediterranean, were therefore anxious to avoid giving the Germans 'on a platter' early information of the arrival of Canadians in the theatre, or details of what Canadians they were. The Canadian government on their side were anxious for the earliest possible announcement. It is worth emphasizing that every objection to such an announcement originated in Eisenhower's headquarters. Mackenzie King never understood this.

On July 2 the Chief of the General Staff in Ottawa called the attention of the Canadian military authorities in London to the desirability of the Canadian government being able to give as much information as possible as soon as possible. On July 7 Ottawa received the texts of the announcements of the operation proposed by Eisenhower. They were three: a communiqué for general release; an *avis* to the French people; and a proclamation to the Italian people, first planned as coming from Eisenhower, but later changed into a statement by Churchill and Roosevelt. None made any mention of Canadians; the phrases used were 'Allied forces' and 'Anglo-American forces.' This was quite unacceptable to Ottawa, and on July 8 representations were made to London and Washington. The following day Eisenhower agreed that the Canadian Prime Minister might make a reference to the presence of 'a Canadian force' in Sicily twenty-four hours after the first landing. A message from Massey, the High Commissioner in London, received on the 8th, referring to 'military reasons' making it difficult to meet the Canadian views, unfortunately implanted in King's mind the notion that it was the British who were making the trouble, and made him 'quite indignant.' In addition to replying strongly to Massey, King that evening telephoned the White House in Washington, got Harry Hopkins who was at dinner with the President, and arranged with him for the President to see the Minister-Counsellor at the Canadian Legation (L.B. Pearson) at once. (The Minister, Leighton McCarthy, was on leave.) Pearson obtained from the President an assurance that Canadians would be duly mentioned. From London following Massey's representations the War Office telegraphed Eisenhower's headquarters informing him that the British Chiefs of Staff had arranged for the Canadians to be mentioned in the Churchill-Roosevelt proclamation and that it was assumed there would be similar mention in the *avis* to the French.

What actually happened was this. Eisenhower, having made the concession of authorizing the delayed statement by King, remained obdurate. His communiqué and the *avis* were issued in the form originally planned, referring respectively to 'Allied forces' and 'Anglo-American forces.' To the astonishment of everyone in Ottawa, however, the War Department in Washington issued an announcement, ten minutes after Eisenhower's communiqué, that 'British, American and Canadian troops' were landing in Sicily. King naturally considered that this left him free to act, and issued his own statement.[27]

Most regrettably, King was left with the impression that only his intervention in Washington had saved the day (it must certainly have been responsible for the War Department statement) and that the British had been obstructionist. He wrote in his diary that he could not help remarking 'how different the attitude of the Americans was from the British. Was it any wonder that our people ... were antagonized at the English, and were beginning to be more and more friendly with the Americans? There could be no more striking example than this, that, after our men had been defending Britain for nearly four years, we were told by the British authorities that, for reasons of security, no mention can even be made of Canada's participation ...' If he had limited his remarks to the diary no great harm would have been done, but unfortunately on July 15, after being needled by the Opposition in the House of Commons which asked why more information about the Canadian share in the operations was not available, he boiled over in public, saying that only the intervention of Roosevelt had brought Canada the news of her troops' participation, and that 'the military authorities in Great Britain' had tried to prevent its publication. When he declared that he would see to it that Canada's soldiers received equal recognition with those of other countries, he was 'loudly cheered in every part of the House of Commons.'[28]

One place where King's statement caused consternation, as the present writer well remembers, was Canadian Military Headquarters, London. The staff there considered that the British War Office had given full and generous co-operation, making every effort on our behalf to get Eisenhower to relax his position. In these circumstances, to have the Canadian Prime Minister make this attack on the 'military authorities in Great Britain' was embarrassing and humiliating. Churchill was naturally disturbed. On July 25 he sent through Malcolm MacDonald a message to King saying that he was being asked a parliamentary question on the matter, that (to use MacDonald's words) 'he obviously could not accept the situation as created by Mr. Mackenzie King's statement, and that equally obviously he wished to give an answer which was helpful to everyone concerned'; he asked for suggestions. The sequel is best described by quoting MacDonald's subsequent dispatch to the Dominions Office:

When I delivered the message to Mr. Mackenzie King that evening he asked what Mr. Churchill meant when he said that he could not accept the situation created by his statement. I said that this statement left the impression that, whilst the American authorities had agreed to the request for references to Canadian troops in the announcements of the Sicilian landings, the British authorities had resisted. Mr. Churchill could not accept the suggestion that the British had adopted any such attitude.

At that Mr. Mackenzie King became angry. He told me that I could reply to Mr. Churchill that if he made any answer to his Parliamentary Question which reflected on the truth of his (Mr. Mackenzie King's) statement, he (Mr. Mackenzie King) would seek a dissolution of Parliament and appeal to the country on that issue. Nor would he fight the Election on this single incident. He would appeal against the treatment of Canada by the British Government on many occasions during the last two years. The Government in London frequently forgot that Canada was a Dominion. They treated her as a colony. He and his colleagues fully recognized that in war the normal processes of peacetime government were inapplicable. The urgency of many situations required a concentration of the power to take decisions in two or three Allied Governments. The Canadian Cabinet had readily accepted that decisions on the strategy of the war should belong primarily to Britain and the United States ... But the Government in London had gone much further than the emergency warranted. On matters where the Canadian Government could and should be consulted they dispensed with that consultation and ignored Canada's rights as a free member of the British Commonwealth. He mentioned the failure to consult Canada about the Combined Boards, about the shackling of prisoners,* and about such an important political statement of United Nations policy as was contained in the President's and Prime Minister's proposed

* Here King had a very well-grounded complaint. After some British and Canadian prisoners taken in the Dieppe raid were shackled in Germany, Churchill announced reprisals against German prisoners without any reference to Canada, in spite of the fact that most of the Dieppe prisoners were Canadians, and most of the German prisoners were in Canada and it would fall to Canada to carry out the reprisals. The Canadian government, moreover, for excellent reasons, disagreed with the reprisal policy. They nevertheless co-operated in it in order to avoid encouraging the enemy by a public controversy with Britain.[29]

proclamation to the Italian people. On these and other occasions he and his cabinet had felt strong resentment. Some of his colleagues were so angry that they wished public protests to be made, so that the Canadian people as a whole might learn of Canada's treatment. But he had so far prevailed on them to remain quiet ... He had sometimes permitted himself to be ignored in a way that no Canadian Prime Minister should be ... But he was prepared to put up with that in the interests of good relations amongst those responsible for conducting the war efforts of the United Nations. He was not prepared, however, to remain quiet when Canadian soldiers were put in a position of inferiority to those of Britain and America. The time had come for him to speak out. If necessary he would fight an Election on the whole issue, and the vast majority of his countrymen would support him.

He strode angrily up and down the room whilst saying these things. At this point I interrupted to say that by his permission I had read his copies of the relevant documents about the publication of the Canadian troops' presence in Sicily, including communications to and from Mr. Massey in London and Mr. Pearson in Washington. After reading his statement to Parliament I had expected that I would have to send a telegram to my Government saying that someone in London had blundered. But instead I found that London's attitude had been as unexceptionable as Washington's. The attitudes of the two Governments were precisely the same, and they had actually co-operated in sending instructions to Allied Headquarters in North Africa to carry out the Canadian requests. He had misunderstood the British authorities' attitude, and had been unfair to them.

He was surprised at this and vigorously contested my opinion ...

The argument went on. King brought up other complaints. Churchill and other British ministers in speeches and conversations paid little heed to the part the Dominions were playing. 'They always spoke of British and American troops, and of the R.A.F. and the American Air Force. They rarely mentioned the Royal Canadian Air Force, although its part alone in the offensive against Europe was bigger than that of the American Air Force.' (At that moment, this was probably true.) MacDonald urged that in the Sicily incident the apparent slowness of answers coming from London was due to the six hours' difference in time (King's call to Washington on the 8th having been made in ample time for action to be taken that evening, whereas his message to Massey in London arrived in the small hours).* It is pretty evident that the trouble would not have happened if Ottawa had been as close to London as it was to Washington, and

* In fact, Massey's diary indicates that the difference in times did not make difficulty for him.

if telephone communication between the two had been equally easy. Finally King grudgingly agreed to consider making a conciliatory reply to Churchill; but it took two more meetings the next day to settle the matter. MacDonald reported to the Dominions Secretary: 'The incident ended with the amicable exchange of messages between him and Mr. Churchill of which you are aware. When I asked him whether he still wished me to tell Mr. Churchill that if he gave an unsatisfactory Parliamentary reply at Westminster there would be a General Election in Canada, he answered in the negative.'[30]

Here we have a picture of Mackenzie King almost at his worst, throwing one of the childish temper tantrums of which a fair number are on record. Moreover, he was clearly in the wrong, and his outburst in Parliament certainly did at least momentary harm to the Anglo-Canadian relationship, a relationship which was undoubtedly dear to his heart. MacDonald charitably pointed out that at the moment of the Sicilian crisis King was much harassed in the House of Commons, fighting his departmental estimates through and with his henchmen Robertson and Heeney on the floor of the House with him. In these circumstances the incoming messages were presumably read with less than the usual care. But MacDonald used the occasion to drive home to his masters in London the same lesson he had read them a few months before in connection with the combined boards. He recalled that affair now, and mentioned several others, notably the shackling case, to indicate that Canada had genuine grievances. The Canadian ministers, he wrote, 'have pursued a conciliatory policy which would reduce difficulties to a minimum':

For example, they felt most bitterly about the shackling of prisoners and disagreed whole-heartedly with the United Kingdom Government's policy. If they had even hinted at that disagreement in Parliament they would have received overwhelming support from public opinion. But in order not to embarrass the United Kingdom Government they chose to carry out a policy which they strongly disapproved and which involved them in widespread criticism from their own people ... They have supported us magnificently and unswervingly. Let us treat them in the same comradely spirit. Their readiness to be conciliatory ought not to make us respect their standpoint any the less. And certainly it ought not to make us blind to the fact that the resentment which they feel is not dissipated, but will be stored up until it bursts the bounds of their patience and good will again, as it did over the Sicilian incident.

MacDonald's dispatch noted a very curious feature of the Anglo-Canadian war situation.

United Kingdom Ministers who visit Canada get an incomplete impression of Canada's sentiments towards Britain. You all exert a hypnotic effect upon your Canadian hosts. The magnificent genius of the Prime Minister and the prestige surrounding you, Sir,* and the Foreign Secretary over-awe Canadian Ministers when they find themselves momentarily in your presence. This is one of the last survivals of that period of Colonial tutelage to Britain out of which Canada has passed, and which these Ministers themselves are amongst the first to relegate to the irrevocable past. They do not feel the same respect for a High Commissioner. When you have left Ottawa, believing that all is for the best in the best of all possible Canadas, they turn round and tell me exactly what they feel about Britain. Their sentiments are a mixture of affection, admiration, gratitude and annoyance.

If this seems overdrawn, it should be recalled that Vincent Massey, the Canadian High Commissioner in London, gives precisely the same picture as the British High Commissioner in Ottawa. Canadian ministers visiting the British capital, he recorded, 'were generally too inhibited in speaking their minds'; even C.D. Howe was 'reluctant to talk as I hoped he would about the problem of our relation to the direction of the war effort.' 'They won't stand up to their opposite numbers here and state their views firmly and candidly. When this does happen, as in the case of St. Laurent [during a visit of Anthony Eden to Ottawa] the reaction on the British side is always favourable.'[31] MacDonald was undoubtedly right; this too-respectful approach to British statesmen was a colonial survival. Doubtless a French Canadian like Louis St Laurent was less affected by it.

PROBLEMS OF THE CANADIAN FORCES

We have been dealing with Canada's wartime external relations on the level of international politics. We must now look at those relations as they affected the fighting forces in the latter part of the war. These were almost entirely a matter of relations with Britain – as matters on the higher political level to a large extent also were. Much of the story is to be found elsewhere,[32] and here we shall tell it as briefly as possible.

Unlike the Canadian Expeditionary Force of 1914-18, the Canadian Army of 1939-45 had a long period of idleness in England, following the expulsion of British forces from the Continent in 1940. The greater part of one division had one day's bloody fighting in the unsuccessful raid on Dieppe on August 19, 1942. Only in July 1943, with the invasion of

---

* The dispatch was addressed to C.R. Attlee, Secretary of State for the Dominions. The Foreign Secretary was Anthony Eden.

CANADIAN SOLDIERS AND SAILORS TOGETHER ON D DAY
Landing craft of the Royal Canadian Navy putting men of the reserve brigade of the 3rd Canadian Infantry Division ashore in Normandy, June 6, 1944

Sicily, was part of the force committed to a protracted campaign; and the whole five divisions got into action only after the North-West Europe campaign was launched when the Allies landed in Normandy on June 6, 1944. In the meantime the force was gradually built up to full strength and trained hard in the south of England, playing a large part in the defence of the country as long as invasion was a threat. All this meant that an enormous number of Canadians (well over a quarter of a million in the Army alone) lived in Britain for periods of up to five years and sometimes longer. This was a unique episode in the social history of the Common-wealth; and its importance consists in the fact that the evidence is overwhelming that the Canadians established as time passed an extraordi-narily good relationship with their British hosts. It began badly in the days of the 'phony war,' with the 1st Canadian Division occupying what they thought very uncomfortable barracks in Aldershot in the coldest winter in years. After reading a batch of their letters, a postal censor wrote, 'The recent bad weather has made them dislike this country considerably.' They viewed the British people with somewhat jaundiced eyes. But when the bombs began to fall things changed; the English under bom-bardment looked rather different, and the Canadians warmed to them. Friendships burgeoned; many a Canadian found himself a second home in a British household. In April 1944, four and a half years after the first Canadians arrived, the postal censors read some 12,000 Canadian letters and reported: 'The relations between British civilians and Canadian troops continue to be very cordial, and no one adverse comment has been seen.' This was surely very remarkable. There were troubles to mar the relationship, of course – the patient British police could testify to that – but that it was basically excellent is very clear. When hostilities ended, over 43,000 'war brides' of Canadian servicemen came to Canada; the vast majority of them were British.[33] These things are part of the story of Can-ada's external relations, though hardly of her external policies; and they form an episode which most of those who were involved in it remember with pleasure.

Turning to the official external relations of the Army, we have already noted that the basic principles followed were those that had gradually been worked out in 1914-18. Where a Canadian force was serving with and as part of a larger British force (and this was always the case in the major campaigns), Canada recognized that operational command was the business of the senior British commander. From him the senior Canadian commander took his orders about fighting the battle. On the other hand, organization, administration, and discipline were purely Canadian concerns. The British commander's operational powers over Canadians were subject to certain limitations. He operated within the framework of the Visiting Forces Acts of 1933 (above, page 289). We have noted that orders issued under these Acts gave the Canadian Army Commander the power to withdraw his forces from the state of being 'in combination' with the British in certain circumstances. His directive from the Canadian government also gave him the right of reference to that government when he considered it necessary; normally he was not to exercise this right except when the 'remedial or other action' he deemed necessary had been refused by the 'Officer Commanding the Combined Force.' Similar powers were accorded the senior Canadian commander in Italy. These emergency powers were modelled on those accorded a British commander serving under higher foreign command. It may be said at once that they were never used. Even so, their known existence may have served a useful purpose.[34]

Except in the rather improbable case of a Canadian commander being faced with a military task so perilous that he might exercise the right of appeal to his government, the Canadian authorities had no means of influencing the course of a campaign to which a Canadian force had been committed; nor had they any source of official information on the course of planning for such a campaign as it proceeded. The American veto on the proposed liaison between the Canadian Joint Staff Mission in London and the Supreme Commanders had the effect of depriving them of this information beyond such as they might receive in reports from the Canadian Army Commander in North-West Europe and the Canadian Corps Commander in Italy – and those two commanders had no more knowledge of high-level future planning than any other army or corps commander, and that was not a great deal. One can sympathize with the obvious desire of the American Chiefs of Staff to prevent the government of a minor power from interfering with the course of operations. Nevertheless, even minor powers have a legitimate interest in the safety and welfare of their forces; and interference could only take the form of representation at a high level, and such representation can always be refused if they are not well founded.

There were aspects of the relations of the British and Canadian armies that did not depend on statutes or written agreements. They were controlled by custom, tradition, and the tricks of chance and personality. The time-honoured arrangements by which uniformity of training methods, organization, and equipment was maintained throughout the Commonwealth had great influence. Brilliant passages in the history of the British Army chronicled its work in Canada; and the Canadian Militia in its beginnings was merely an auxiliary to the regular forces of the Crown and looked to them, not in vain, for inspiration and leadership as well as for a pattern of organization. Though national feeling had flowered in the Canadian Corps of the First World War, these older loyalties and instincts were not extinguished. If Canadian ministers of the Second War found themselves hypnotized by their British opposite numbers, it was also true that Canadian soldiers (and Canadian politicians too) had a tendency to defer to British generals. And the British generals on their side had a tendency to regard Dominion forces in colonial terms. (The fact is that the British Army's political science was perhaps a little bit in arrears.)

The problems of relations between the two armies during the years in England centred around the striking figure of Andrew George Latta McNaughton. General McNaughton, commanding successively the 1st Canadian Division, the (1st) Canadian Corps, and the First Canadian Army, was the senior Canadian army officer overseas until he relinquished the Army command at the end of 1943. He was a man of distinguished intellect, and the most vivid personality involved in Canada's war. He was also, as we have said, a strong nationalist, a product of the old Corps, who had startled his fellow students at the Imperial Defence College in 1926-7 by suggesting that in a future war the position of the Canadian commander in a Commonwealth force would approximate to that of Sir John French vis-à-vis General Joffre in 1914-15, and that, like Lord Haig when operationally subordinated to Marshal Foch in 1918, he would still be accountable to his own government for the safety of his troops.[35] He said to the present writer in 1941, 'The acid test of sovereignty is the control of the armed forces.' These views were likely to grate on British traditionalists.

The British military authorities exercised considerable influence over Canadian appointments overseas. The Canadian Army had a serious problem affecting its senior commands, the lack of battle experience resulting from the years of idleness in England. Had the army been fighting in the years 1939-43, it would have developed its own group of experienced commanders as the Corps of 1915-18 did. As it was, officers went up the ladder of promotion and became brigade, division, and even corps commanders without having smelled powder since the earlier war. The British, who made a particular fetish of battle experience, exalting it even beyond its very real importance,* did not allow this to be forgotten. They

* I once heard General Eisenhower, who perhaps had some personal feeling in the matter, comment on this British tendency. The way he put it was: 'They say, "You're no good if you weren't in the Battle of the Sangro."'

would not have thought of throwing it up to the Americans that General Dwight D. Eisenhower had never smelled powder in either war before becoming commander-in-chief of the Allied force that landed in North Africa in November 1942 (though they took the precaution of insisting on inserting experienced British leaders between him and the forces he was officially commanding). They did not hesitate to talk about it to the Canadians, whose colonial status was more recent.

The supreme example of British influence on appointments was the case of McNaughton himself. The War Office did not directly use the argument of lack of battle experience when they set about unseating McNaughton, though it was certainly in some minds. They argued that he was not suited to command the First Canadian Army in the coming great invasion of North-West Europe. The fact that British troops would be fighting under the Canadian headquarters gave them a good excuse for interfering. The Chief of the Imperial General Staff, Sir Alan Brooke, launched a backstairs campaign against McNaughton in May 1943, in Washington, when he told his Canadian opposite number, General Kenneth Stuart, and the Canadian Minister of National Defence that he had doubts about the Army Commander's fitness. He repeated the opinion to Stuart and separately to Vincent Massey in London in July. He told Massey he was doubtful about raising the matter with Colonel Ralston (though he had already done so). Massey, who may have been tired of running second to the much more charismatic McNaughton as Canada's leading representative in British eyes, encouraged Brooke. At the end of the month Ralston was in England, and Brooke repeated his criticisms of McNaughton.[36]

At this moment, as Brooke knew, McNaughton was involved in a very serious controversy with his own government. Certain people in Ottawa, most notably Ralston and Stuart, had become convinced that it was vital to end the Canadian overseas army's long period of idleness and get at least part of it into action. There had been increasing public criticism of its 'home guard' role in England. Even the Department of External Affairs had joined in; Hume Wrong, now Assistant Under Secretary of State, had sent a paper to the Prime Minister arguing that Canada's influence at the peace table would be lessened if her troops did not fight.[37] (That influence was sure to be rather limited in any case, and it is interesting to speculate how many Canadian lives it would have been worth while to sacrifice to effect a small increase in it.) I remember General Stuart, on one of his visits to England, remarking, 'It seems an awful thing to say, but the people of Canada are calling out for blood.' McNaughton favoured resisting this call. He was opposed to breaking up the army in order to send a detachment to fight in the Mediterranean. He maintained that the morale of the force in England was equal to surviving a further waiting period, and that the proper role of the First Canadian Army was to fight as a national unit in the great final invasion of the Continent. Here he was following in an old and sound tradition of Canadian policy, going back through Sir Arthur Currie's resistance to breaking up the Canadian Corps in 1918 to Lord Minto's insistence in 1899 that the contingent sent to South Africa should be a unit under a senior Canadian officer, not little packets scattered through the British Army (Volume I, pages 57-69, 194-8). Not only did Canadians maintain that they fought most effectively concentrated under their own officers, but it is evident that, in circumstances like Canada's, national control of the country's forces could best be ensured by keeping them together.

McNaughton had accepted without enthusiasm his government's intervention with London to obtain a share in the Sicilian campaign; as a result of this political initiative, essentially undertaken over McNaughton's head, a Canadian division had at a late date been substituted for a British one in the attacking force. McNaughton had hoped, optimistically, that the division could be brought back to the main body in England after acquiring valuable battle experience in Sicily. But Ralston and Stuart immediately began pressing for sending another division out to join it and the creation of a Canadian Corps in the Mediterranean theatre. This brought on a crisis with McNaughton. Mackenzie King had watched these developments with anxiety. At first his obsessive concern with avoiding overseas conscription led him to support McNaughton; while the army remained in England there would be no battle casualties. Later, the same concern led him, doubtfully, to accept the Ralston-Stuart position. Churchill's talk of the heavy losses to be expected in an attack across the Channel seems to have influenced him; and he reflected that if more Canadians were sent to Italy fewer would be involved in this probable blood-bath. The government persisted with the project over McNaughton's strong and bitter opposition.[38]

The conjunction of War Office hostility and the quarrel with his own government was fatal to McNaughton. When the British views about him were finally revealed to him by Ralston and Stuart in November 1943 he jumped to the conclusion that they themselves had poisoned the minds of the British against him (there is no reason at all to believe this). He proceeded to appeal to King in a letter of resignation which abused Ralston. He presumably thought King might support him. King tried to avoid choosing between McNaughton and Ralston; but when forced to act he inevitably sided with the Minister rather than the General. Nevertheless, by a masterpiece of personal diplomacy he contrived to effect McNaughton's departure while retaining his goodwill towards himself. Thus he kept available a possible alternative Minister of National Defence against the future day when Ralston might leave the government. McNaughton was in due course succeeded as Army Commander by Lieutenant-General H.D.G. Crerar, who was acceptable to Brooke. There had been a momentary possibility that since the new arrangements left only one Canadian corps (three divisions) under the First Canadian Army in England, and British troops would have to take the place under its command of the Canadians who had gone to Italy, a British officer might be put in command at the army headquarters.* It seems that Stuart was ready to pay even this price to get rid of McNaughton; but Ralston refused to consider it.[39]

One can speculate endlessly about Alan Brooke's motives in this affair. He claimed to be a loyal personal friend of McNaughton's who was driven by duty to do what he did. McNaughton's later interpretation was that Brooke was in fact satisfying a personal grudge dating back to Vimy Ridge in 1917. There is little doubt that Brooke and other senior British officers resented and disliked McNaughton's insistence on being treated as a national commander, and on the Canadian Army being treated as a national army rather than just one more British formation. This insistence had been much in evidence during the preliminaries of the Sicilian enterprise.[40] Yet whatever Brooke's motives, he may have been right about McNaughton's fitness. The Army Commander had been working under heavy strain for years, and was tired; he might not have been able to withstand the further strain of high command in a great campaign. His interests had centred in technical rather than tactical matters, and many people had felt that he had not applied himself strongly enough to training his army. Crerar's qualities were in many ways more ordinary, but perhaps they were what was needed in 1944.[41]

On the question of policy, however, McNaughton was clearly right and the Canadian government wrong. The government's pressure for the acceptance of a Canadian corps in Italy is a particularly deplorable example of political interference in military arrangements in war. The Allied Mediterranean command did not want another corps headquarters

---

* There was the alternative possibility that the Canadian headquarters might be dissolved, and a British one organized to take its place; but time was short, and there would certainly have been an outcry in Canada.

or another armoured division;* Eisenhower, still in charge there, wrote: 'While the arrival of these troops at this time is likely to cause us considerable embarrassment, General [Sir Harold] Alexander advises me, and I agree, that, appreciating the political considerations which may be involved, we accept the Canadian Corps Headquarters, Armoured Division and non-divisional troops ...'[42] That the British government should have sponsored such arrangements is evidence, all the Canadian government's complaints about British action or inaction to the contrary, that Churchill and his colleagues were prepared to go a very long way to meet Ottawa's views.

In terms of Canadian national policy, as we have said, what was done was even worse. Dividing the country's relatively small military force between two theatres meant some additional administrative overhead, but it also meant that maintaining national control was more difficult. With only three Canadian divisions under his command, Crerar's arm was weakened. This was one of the great aberrations of Canadian war policy. And the measure of it was the fact that the same government that had demanded the dispatch of the Corps to the Mediterranean was asking for its return before it had fought a real battle.[43] It was not surprising that this time its views were not met until the strategic situation made it convenient, early in 1945. At that time First Canadian Army was finally reunited under Crerar's command in the North-West Europe theatre.

From the inherited disposition of Canadian politicians to defer to British ministers when face to face with them Mackenzie King was not exempt; nor was he free from exaggerated respect for famous British generals. Sir Bernard Montgomery was already a world figure when King met him in England shortly before the Normandy invasion; and King's account of the conversation is rather embarrassing. Montgomery talked patronizingly about Crerar and Lieutenant-General G.G. Simonds, the Canadian Army Commander and Corps Commander who were to fight under him, particularly emphasizing Crerar's lack of experience. King should have made it clear that they were national commanders who would have his support, but he did not. When Montgomery talked about Crerar being too much interested in 'keeping all the Canadian formations together in the fighting, and, at all times, having Canadians commanded by Canadian officers as against British officers,' King reacted very mildly.

* The Canadian authorities insisted on sending the 5th Canadian Armoured Division because sending another infantry division would have left in England two armoured and one infantry divisions, an impossible balance for a corps.

Montgomery said, King reports, that 'emergency in the field might lead to separation and amalgamation, all of which had to be done very quickly,' and he asked King for an assurance of support. King replied, he says: 'I will give you the assurance that the Government of Canada will not put any pressure on you for political reasons, or ask that any such pressure be placed upon you where there are military considerations involved.' It looks very much as if Montgomery sought to undermine the Canadian commander with his own government, and to ensure against the sort of pressure in favour of a united national army that Currie and Borden exerted in 1918; and he must have been very well pleased with the result.[44] There were colonial survivals in the attitudes of both men: Montgomery assuming proprietorial airs towards the Canadians which he would never have ventured upon in connection with United States forces; and King deferring to the British general in a way that he would never have used with a Canadian officer.

The basic facts about Royal Canadian Air Force relations with the RAF have been stated in the preceding chapter in connection with the British Commonwealth Air Training Plan. The contention over 'Canadianiza-tion' of the RCAF overseas went through its most unpleasant phase early in 1943, when two needling signals from Ottawa, one asking why the total Canadian aircrew in three RCAF squadrons was less than 60 per cent, the other asking why four recently-formed RCAF bomber squadrons were commanded by RAF officers, led the senior officer at the RCAF head-quarters in London, Air Marshal H. ('Gus') Edwards, to boil over and assail the British Air Ministry in unmeasured terms for failing to make more progress in such matters. The affair was adjusted (and after some lapse of time Edwards was recalled to Canada); perhaps the ultimate result was to clear the air. And as we have already seen, the contempora-neous decision in Ottawa to pay the whole cost of the RCAF overseas put Canada in a very much stronger position. But the country had paid a heavy price for the colonial-spirited arrangements made in 1939.

Although steady progress was made towards what one may call 'nation-alizing' Canada's overseas Air Force, it cannot be said that a completely satisfactory result had been achieved by the end of the German war. We have seen that there were very few really high commands available to Canadian airmen. The most unfortunate situation was that in the North-West Europe campaign of 1944-5. Here there were fifteen RCAF squad-rons, all serving under Headquarters No 83 Group RAF, which at the beginning of the campaign had twenty-nine squadrons in all. But there were virtually no Canadians in that headquarters – a contrast with the situation in the army, where it was agreed that, since British troops would be fighting under First Canadian Army, up to 50 per cent of the Army Headquarters staff might be British officers (the actual total was only about 15 per cent). And No 83 Group supported the Second British Army, while First Canadian Army was supported by No 84 Group, which did not contain a single Canadian unit. Reasons could be adduced for this arrangement, but it was really not a good one, and many Canadians in both services regretted it. It is safe to bet that it would never have been accepted if General McNaughton had remained in command of the Army.

Operational control remained throughout completely in British hands. Thus, although the Canadian bomber group and Canadians in RAF units dropped a large proportion of the bombs that implemented the Allied policy (much criticized then and since) of the area bombing of German cities, the Canadian government was never consulted about this policy. What Ottawa did expect to be consulted about was the movement of RCAF units from one theatre to another, and this was punctiliously done. No Air Ministry request for such a transfer was ever refused, and it seems evident that the Canadian government was chiefly concerned that the constitutional niceties should be observed. And it is worth noting that in spite of the progress of 'Canadianization,' the majority of Canadian aircrew overseas remained in Royal Air Force units to the end. As late as August 1944 there were over 17,000 in the RAF as against about 10,000 in RCAF units and formations.[45]

The facts concerning Canadian naval policy have also been stated in the previous chapter. The Royal Canadian Navy expanded vastly during the war. In many ways it was the most British of the services. In it, nevertheless, one meets the same urge as in the Army and the Air Force, in the direction of the concentration of units under Canadian authority. This appeared notably in 1941, when ten Canadian destroyers were operating from the United Kingdom. The British Admiralty decided that the antisubmarine war required a new escort base at St John's, Newfoundland; and the Canadian Naval Service Headquarters offered to take charge of the escort operation in that area, using the destroyers and about twenty corvettes, under higher direction of the Admiralty. The British agreed, and the result was to concentrate the main Canadian naval fighting force under Canadian command, on a task directly related to the security of Canada. Very shortly, however, there was a change. During the meeting between Churchill and Roosevelt at Argentia, Newfoundland, in August 1941, the President undertook, in spite of the fact that the United States was still neutral, to assume the burden of convoy operations in the western Atlantic. There seems to have been no consultation with Canada (Mackenzie King was not at Argentia, and was very angry that this meeting so close to Canada was held not only without his being invited, but without his receiving any prior notice of it);[46] but the result was to place the country's Newfoundland Escort Force under (neutral) U.S. command.

This situation continued even after the United States entered the war, which resulted in the bulk of U.S. naval forces being withdrawn from the Atlantic. With the United Kingdom and Canada contributing almost the whole of the Atlantic convoy escorts (it was estimated, 50 and 48 per cent respectively) this seemed absurd; moreover, there were occasional difficulties when the American naval commander at Newfoundland interfered with the allocation of Canadian ships to the various forces and commands, which was not his business. After considerable Canadian pressure, an Atlantic Convoy Conference was held at Washington in March 1943; and it set up the Canadian Northwest Atlantic Command under a Canadian officer with headquarters at Halifax. Subject to the U.S. Navy's general strategic control of the Western Atlantic, the new command was responsible for protection of convoys to and from the British Isles north of New York City and west of the 47th meridian. The Royal Canadian Navy thus acquired command responsibilities more commensurate with the share it was taking in the Battle of the Atlantic.[47]

INDUSTRY AND FINANCE

During the war a great feat of industrial organization was performed in Canada, when a country that had had virtually no munitions industry created within a year or so the plant to produce a large variety of weapons and other military equipment.[48] In 1914-18 Canadian industry's contribution, though considerable, was largely limited to shells, ships, and aircraft. No weapons were made except Ross rifles. In the second war, shells, ships, and aircraft were produced, all in great numbers; but in addition there was a great miscellany of weapons, including guns up to 4-inch, and much technical equipment. Production of military vehicles was enormous.

All this is highly relevant to our theme, for only about one-third of Canadian war production went to the Canadian forces. The rest went to Canada's allies, and primarily to Great Britain, which took more than half of the total; it was computed, '60 per cent. of the tanks, 67 per cent. of the artillery, 70 per cent. of the rifles and 53 per cent. of the combat aircraft.'[49] Not much was done towards the production of army equipment in Canada before the spring of 1940; but after Dunkirk enormous British orders flowed in. Canada, unlike the United States, was willing to produce weapons of British types (which were of course used by her own forces). The great expansion now began. Late in 1941 a British 'Management and Labour Delegation' visiting the United States were induced to extend their tour to Canada. They were clearly astonished by what they saw: great new armament plants working where nothing had stood before, and factories that had made only the household necessities of peace now engaged in turning out the weapons of war. They reported: 'In the opinion of the Delegation, it is regrettable that the impressive effort, to which reference is made in the aforegoing, is not more widely appreciated.'[50]

How was Britain to pay the enormous bill for the material Canada produced for her? We have already glanced at this problem in connection with the Hyde Park Agreement (above, pages 215-17). Britain simply did not have the dollar exchange to meet these obligations; and from the beginning of the war Canada had been financing her purchases in the Dominion. We have seen that the exchange position was troubling the British government even before Canada declared war (above, pages 271 and 273). In the early months the United Kingdom contrived to meet its obligations largely by selling gold and liquidating Canadian securities held in England, but as time passed large 'sterling balances' incapable of being converted into dollars began to accumulate to Canada's credit in London. As munition production in Canada grew, the situation worsened, and by the end of 1941 heroic measures seemed required. On January 2, 1942, the Canadian government decided to make to Britain a 'billion-dollar gift' to finance British purchases in Canada during the coming year. At the same time the sterling balances were converted into an interest-free loan of $700 million.[51]

These measures were not universally popular in Canada, and they were particularly unpopular in Quebec. When in February 1942 the Canadian Institute of Public Opinion asked whether Canada should send 'war materials and food supplies to Britain free, instead of charging the British for these shipments,' 60 per cent of the English-speaking respondents approved and 28 per cent disapproved; in the French-speaking community, only 33 per cent approved and 56 per cent disapproved.[52] By June, the billion-dollar gift was already rapidly being exhausted, and Chubby Power told Harold Balfour, who was in Ottawa for the air training conference, that there might be 'considerable political difficulty in repeating anything of the same sort.'[53] As so often in Canada, 'political difficulty' meant Quebec. A somewhat different expedient was now produced to meet the British financial problem: 'Mutual Aid.' Again the Canadian

Parliament appropriated one billion dollars, but this time it was for aid not to Britain only but to all the United Nations associated in the common effort; and instead of paying money Canada would purchase the goods and ship them. The difference was largely one of form; Britain continued to be by far the largest beneficiary of the programme. At the same time other means were found for easing the British exchange position. It was now that Canada undertook the cost of equipping and maintaining all the RCAF squadrons overseas, as well as that for pay, clothing, etc., for Canadian aircrew serving with the RAF. Moreover, Canada purchased the United Kingdom's interest in Canadian war plants which the British government had financed, the cost being about $200 million, and took over certain lesser expenses which Britain had borne, including costs for camps for prisoners of war and internees whom Canada had accepted at Britain's request.[54]

The British government do not seem to have been unduly impressed by the original billion-dollar gift,[55] but by the time Mutual Aid was proposed they realized that they were getting important help from Canada. In February 1943 the Secretary of State for Dominion Affairs and the Chancellor of the Exchequer circulated to their cabinet colleagues a memorandum describing what was proposed and making this comment:

We should like to emphasise how large this Canadian assistance is. Canada has a relatively small population only about 11½ millions as against over 130 millions in the United States. Nevertheless, her free assistance to us has been running at a rate equivalent to more than a quarter of the lend-lease aid given to us by the United States; per head of the population, therefore, it has been more than three times as great. She is giving away goods to the value of nearly one quarter of her budget expenditure, whereas lend-lease assistance by the United States to all countries has been running recently at about one-eighth of *her* budget expenditure ... The new proposals will place a tremendous burden upon the Canadian taxpayer. Direct taxation in Canada is now, generally speaking, as high as in this country: it may have to go higher. The broad position is that Canada is not only devoting as large a proportion of her national income to defence expenditure as any other country, but that the proportion of the defence expenditure which is given away in the form of free supplies is higher in Canada than in any other country.[56]

The memorandum went on to remark that it should not be taken for granted that the Canadian legislation embodying the new gift would be passed without difficulty, and added that British government departments should remember what Canada was doing, and take the utmost care to avoid any action which might be embarrassing to the Canadian government.

The legislation in fact did not pass without some noisy protest from Quebec. On the second reading of the Mutual Aid bill the most intransigent of the French-Canadian nationalist members of the House of Commons made a fierce attack, J.-F. Pouliot saying: 'I am opposed to granting one cent to England, because England is much richer than we are,' and Liguori Lacombe describing the measure as 'steeped in colonialism.' The group twice divided the House, being defeated 10 to 135 and 10 to 127.[57] But their voices undoubtedly found many echoes in Quebec.

In 1944 the British financial problem still existed. This year the Canadian Parliament appropriated $800,000,000 for Mutual Aid and for the United Nations Relief and Rehabilitation Administration.[58] This did not meet the full need, but Canada was still not paying the full cost of her overseas forces: she now undertook the additional burden of paying for advanced training for her airmen in Britain until they reached the point of joining operational squadrons, this amounting to $120 million per annum. In addition, she agreed to pay for stores held in Britain for the RCAF, worth between $200 and $300 million, plus similar provision for the Canadian Army, and to increase the daily capitation rate per man paid to the British government to cover the goods and services it provided for the Canadian Army Overseas, which it was agreed was now unrealistically low with most of the troops in active theatres of war. Thus the British authorities obtained additional Canadian dollars. It was explained that the Canadian government found these arrangements 'politically easier to assume than to make available additional Mutual Aid appropriations.'[59] (It should be emphasized that throughout the war the British continued to pay cash for many of the goods obtained from Canada. Mutual Aid in its various forms covered only the deficit between British 'earnings' of Canadian dollars through exports to Canada and services to Canadian overseas forces, and the cost of the materials supplied by Canada to Britain.)

In the early spring of 1945 it was apparent that the war with Germany was almost over. In these circumstances the Canadian government put through Parliament a single appropriation act[60] providing $2,000,000,000 for all war purposes, including Mutual Aid, during the coming fiscal year. Mutual Aid came to a very abrupt end with the Japanese surrender; it is evident that 'political' considerations were important here too.[61] The British Treasury calculated that, lumping the 'billion dollar gift' and Mutual Aid together, Britain had received from Canada during the war financial assistance amounting to $3,043,000,000.[62] It was a tidy sum, and as a support to the British war effort a material contribution to the winning of the war.

SOME PROBLEMS WITH THE UNITED STATES

We have already dealt fairly fully with Canadian relations with Britain during the war, and to a considerable extent with relations with the United States. Some threads of the latter subject remain to be knitted into the pattern.

We mentioned in passing the difficulty over Canadian military representation in Washington. This began in June 1941. Early in that year Anglo-American staff conversation in Washington to which Canada was not a party produced a report called ABC-1 which was intended to provide a basis for co-operation between Britain and the United States in case the latter entered the war. The report assumed that Canada would be represented in Washington through the British Joint Staff Mission there. In view of the special military relationship Canada had already built up through the Permanent Joint Board on Defence, neither the Canadian Chiefs of Staff nor the government considered this adequate; Canada accordingly asked for a Canadian Military Mission of her own in Washington. It appears that the American State Department was agreeable, but the War and Navy Departments opposed; the usual argument was invoked – if Canada had a military mission, other British Dominions and South American republics would want one too. It is possible that American officers felt that the refusal of a mission might be used to press Canada to accept U.S. 'strategic direction' under Basic Defence Plan No 2 (above, page 314). Mackenzie King took the matter up himself, first through the United States Minister and subsequently direct with the President; but these efforts were unsuccessful. Not until long after the United States entered the war did Canada win her point; and it is worth noting that her representative body when she at last obtained it was called the Canadian Joint Staff – the word 'Mission' was never used. It may be remarked in passing that in November 1943 the Canadian and United States legations in Washington and Ottawa were reciprocally raised to the rank of embassies.[63]

Canadian and American forces serving abroad had little contact with each other. The regions where the two countries' military interests may be said to have competed were the outpost areas of North America.

One of the most important of these areas was Newfoundland. It will be remembered that the United States obtained bases there as a result of the 'destroyer deal' of September 1940. It is a fair assumption that this would not have happened had Newfoundland been part of Canada at the time, for Mackenzie King always made it clear that he was opposed to selling or leasing sites in Canada: 'facilities,' yes, but leases, no.[64] American troops began to arrive in Newfoundland in January 1941. Canadian forces were already there; RCAF aircraft were given the use of Newfoundland airfields a few days before Canada declared war in 1939, and both air and ground units moved in, by arrangement with the Newfoundland government, in June 1940. In the following August, under the shadow of the Allied disaster in Europe, C.G. Power visited St John's and made on behalf of Canada an informal but firm agreement with the colonial government by which Newfoundland's forces were placed under Canadian command and Newfoundland and Labrador were incorporated within the boundaries of the Canadian Army's Atlantic Command.[65]

Mackenzie King was fully seized of the strategic importance of Newfoundland to Canada. Speaking of Power's agreement in the Cabinet War Committee, he said, 'The defence of Newfoundland would always be a primary Canadian interest.'[66] This awareness is reflected in the actions of the government, and particularly in its evident determination not to let Newfoundland drift into the American orbit. Canada maintained considerable forces in Newfoundland throughout the war, and it is clear that they had two distinct functions: to protect Newfoundland against the Germans, in co-operation with the United States forces; and to ensure by their presence that United States influence did not become paramount there. This appears with particular clarity in October 1944, when the forces in the island were being reduced. The Cabinet War Committee then approved a recommendation of the Chiefs of Staff that withdrawals should be co-ordinated so that the strength of the Canadian Army garrison should never fall below that of the American.[67]

We noted in Chapter Four that a highway across Canadian territory connecting the United States with its territory of Alaska had been much discussed before the war, but that nothing was accomplished beyond the appointment of two national commissions. The matter was considered further after the outbreak of war in Europe, but in the first instance the Permanent Joint Board on Defence, the U.S. War Department, and the Canadian Chiefs of Staff all agreed that its military value would be slight. After the United States entered the war, however, Americans became much more friendly to the idea, and Canada agreed to it, on condition that the U.S. should pay the whole cost of building the road and maintaining it during the war; while at the end of the war it would become part of

Canada's highway system. The road was built accordingly, with great speed and efficiency, by American engineer troops; and as forecast it proved to have very little military importance. (By the autumn of 1943, by which time the military importance of Alaska was waning, only 54 tons of supplies had gone over it to Alaska.) It *was* important, however, as support for the chain of airfields between Edmonton and Alaska, which already existed, in a very rudimentary form, before Pearl Harbor, and was greatly developed afterwards. Large numbers of aircraft for the Soviet Union were flown over this route. Another important route to Alaska was the combined rail and sea one by way of Prince Rupert, BC, where the Americans undertook a large construction programme.[68]

A project that brought many Americans into the Canadian Northwest was 'Canol,' launched in the spring of 1942. The object of this was to produce oil from the field at Norman Wells to meet American requirements in the Northwest Territories and Alaska. The Americans rushed into this without worrying too much about getting Canadian consent; the main contract seems to have been signed the same day on which they requested Canadian approval, and long before they received it. As American activities in the Northwest multiplied, the authorities in Ottawa were troubled. On March 31, 1943, Mackenzie King invited Malcolm MacDonald to give the Cabinet War Committee his impressions of a visit he had recently made to the region. (This is striking evidence of the position this British High Commissioner had made for himself.) MacDonald, the minutes state, 'expressed concern as to the result of immense U.S. construction and activity in this area':

The extensive nature of the programme of development being carried on by Americans and under American auspices could not be appreciated without actual experience. It was quite evident that these vast undertakings were being planned and carried out with a view to the postwar situation. Canadian representatives in the area were few and quite unable to keep control or even in touch with day to day developments.

The Canadian government might well despatch a special official to the northwest to review the position and report.

Shortly afterwards the War Committee agreed to appoint a Special Commissioner for Defence Projects in the Northwest, Major-General W.W. Foster, who would have his headquarters at Edmonton. His task was to ensure that all United States requests to launch new projects or expand existing ones were properly referred to the Canadian government; and his instructions specified: 'The Canadian Government desires to ensure that the natural resources of the area shall be utilized to provide the maximum benefit for the Canadian people and to ensure that no commitments are made and no situation allowed to develop as a result of which the full Canadian control of the area would be in any way prejudiced or endangered.'[69] It seems evident that Foster's appointment established rather more effective Canadian control; at the same time it was agreeable to the Americans, who were glad to have a responsible Canadian authority available on the spot.

In the light of Mackenzie King's pride in his relationship with President Roosevelt, and his ill-founded conviction that it was easier for Canada to get what she wanted from the United States than from Britain, it is curious that as the war proceeded he became suspicious of the United States' long-term intentions towards Canada. He became, in fact, increasingly convinced that it was American policy to absorb Canada.

On December 30, 1942, the War Committee discussed a project for joint study with the United States of the territory traversed by the Alaska Highway. King opposed this, speaking of 'the efforts that would be made by the Americans to control developments in our country after the war, and to bring Canada out of the orbit of the British Commonwealth of Nations into their own orbit.' He added: 'I am strongly opposed to anything of the kind. I want to see Canada continue to develop as a nation, to be, in time, as our country certainly will, the greatest of nations of the British Commonwealth.' When Canol was being examined in 1944, King recorded that he held strongly to the view 'that we ought to get the Americans out of the further development there, and keep complete control in our own hands ... With the United States so powerful and her investments becoming greater in Canada, we will have a great difficulty to hold our own against pressure from the United States.' Such comments recur for the rest of King's life, indicating his genuine belief that Canadian independence was in danger, not merely from American cultural and economic pressure, of whose existence there is no doubt, but from American government policy, for which there is much less evidence.[70] One recalls that King was a child of the nineteenth century, a product of Victorian Ontario, and wonders whether the annexation bogey of those days was stirring deep down within him.

LOOKING FORWARD

Once defeat had been staved off, and victory glimmered on the horizon, both British and Canadian statesmen began to think of their countries' positions in the postwar world. A curious episode of January 1944, the repercussions of Lord Halifax's speech in Toronto, suggests what was happening.

On January 24, Halifax, British Ambassador in Washington and formerly Foreign Secretary, addressed the Toronto Board of Trade. His speech amounted to a plea for unified Commonwealth action after the war. The passage that attracted most attention was: 'Not Great Britain only, but the British Commonwealth and Empire must be the fourth power in that group upon which, under Providence, the peace of the world will henceforth depend.' (The other powers of the moment were the United States, Russia, and China.) The Statute of Westminster, Halifax said, had left some problems unsolved. 'The right of each member to determine its own external affairs ... is an immeasurable gain if on vital issues we can achieve a common foreign policy, expressed not by a single voice but by the unison of many.' The response of the Dominions in 1939 was 'not ... too late to save the cause ... but there is a real sense in which it was too late to save peace.'[71]

This utterance threw Mackenzie King into something very like a fit – another temper tantrum like that at the time of the Sicily affair. He wrote in his diary that it looked like 'a conspiracy on the part of Imperialists'; he went on writing about it for days. He told the Governor General that but for the war, 'I would this evening be asking him for a dissolution of Parliament to appeal to the people on this issue.' He told Malcolm MacDonald that he thought it part of a deliberate design by the British government and some Dominion statesmen 'to revive an imperialism which left the Dominions something less than national sovereignty.' He also thought that the speech amounted to 'an attack on his personal position' (he did not know until MacDonald told him that it had in fact included a personal tribute to him).[72]

News of King's violent reaction caused some disturbance in London. The text of Halifax's speech had been cabled in advance through a Ministry of Information channel, but no one had 'vetted' it. Now Churchill suggested that the government should be consulted before such statements were made; and Anthony Eden wrote to Halifax: 'I know how troubling all this is. But if in future you could let us know rather more in advance what you propose to say, so that we could, if necessary, send you our comments, it would greatly help all of us here, including your humble servant.' The Minister of Information at a press conference said that Halifax's statement was his own idea, and was not in any way an expression of government policy.[73] It is quite clear nevertheless that it echoed an idea which was very widespread in official circles in Britain.

MacDonald himself had contributed to propagating it by a paper of February 1943 entitled 'The Post-War Position of the British Commonwealth of Nations.' This was the paper in which he had so seriously criticized Britain's attitude towards the Dominions in the matter of the combined organizations (above, page 327). His argument was that this sort of failure to consult was inimical to the post-war relationship that was desirable. Essentially, he took the same view as Halifax: 'If Britain stands alone after the war, she will gradually sink to the position of a second-class Power in world affairs. But there is a means by which she can retain a position of equal authority with America and Russia. That is if she makes herself the central member of a group of nations who are collectively as important as each of those two others. Such a group already exists. It is the British Commonwealth of Nations.'[74] The Secretary of State for the Dominions, Clement Attlee, adopted the idea in a paper written in the following June: 'If we are to carry our full weight in the post-war world with the United States and U.S.S.R., it can only be as a united British Commonwealth. At the same time, it will be necessary to satisfy the legitimate claim of each of the Dominions to rank in the world as an independent nation.'[75] In March 1944 the Vice-Chiefs of Staff wrote: 'We regard it ... as of great importance that the British Commonwealth should be in a position to speak with a united voice, and to throw its whole weight into the scale when vital issues are at stake.'[76]

The reason why Mackenzie King took the Halifax speech so hard is evident. He saw in it an attempt at reviving an old idea which he had fiercely opposed and believed he had scotched: the idea of a uniform Commonwealth foreign policy. The reader is familiar with all this. King had no intention of allowing what he considered an important part of his life-work to be destroyed.[77]

In May 1944 the first and only Prime Ministers' Conference held during the war took place in London. It was not a full-dress Imperial Conference of the traditional sort (the 1937 conference, it turned out, was the last of that breed); only the Prime Minister attended from each Dominion – though, as King complained to his diary, there were six British ministers in addition to Churchill (there are seven in the official photograph).[78] In the light of the documents we have quoted, it was to be expected that the British government should seek to take the opportunity of putting forward some measure of Commonwealth consolidation. In doing so they must have been somewhat embarrassed by Halifax's speech and the adverse reaction it had produced in Canada. Nevertheless the attempt was made, and it was essentially defeated by Mackenzie King, who played much the same part that he had played in 1937. Talk by Churchill of annual conferences accompanied by meetings of some sort of defence committee (presumably a version of the old CID, to be attended by Dominion delegates) he met with a firm negative, warning his hosts against 'any kind of new machinery' or anything that would 'only raise suspicion as to commitments.' He continued to talk, as he had in 1941, of the 'continuing conference of Cabinets' which actually existed thanks to modern communications, and the general adequacy of the existing arrangements.[79]

Serious questions arose when the conference discussed post-war international security arrangements. A paper which King read to the meeting of May 11[80] put forward the case for the 'middle powers': 'Just as we are prepared to recognise the great difference in power and responsibility between Canada and the Soviet Union, for example, we should expect some recognition of the considerable difference between Canada and Panama.' It also firmly rejected an idea of Churchill's that the central Peace Council of great powers which he conceived of as carrying the main responsibility for maintaining peace should have the Commonwealth and Empire as one of its members:

> Frankly I do not think representation on the world Peace Council for the 'British Commonwealth and Empire' as such is feasible or really desirable. Representation of the United Kingdom, on the other hand, is indispensable. The United Kingdom is indisputably a Great Power in its own right ... The foreign policy of the United Kingdom should be firm and decisive. Can it be firm and decisive if every issue must be decided on the majority vote of countries, some of which are not directly in touch with the affairs of all parts of the world at once?

The prestige of the Commonwealth, King said, had never been higher than it was today, particularly in the United States. 'This prestige is based upon a belief that in the British Commonwealth there has been evolved a unique alliance of a peculiarly tough and enduring kind whose members act together, unlike so many allies bound by explicit treaties, not because they are compelled to act together, but because they have the will to act together. What is more, our friends have discovered that the primary objects for which the members of the Commonwealth act together are objects which can be shared by other countries of goodwill. They have realised that the Commonwealth is not a Power *bloc* exploiting its own selfish interests, but a group of like-minded nations whose close association has in the past and may in the future form the most reliable element within the framework of the world order. We must be very cautious, therefore, about moving in directions which might rouse old suspicions.' King continued: 'It has been suggested that Great Britain is not properly a Great Power unless she always speaks with the united voice of a great Empire. But Great Britain's strength has always been in her "alliance potential" – as Mr. Eden has said ... Her most faithful allies in the past two wars have been the other nations of the Commonwealth, and no nation who wishes to attack Great Britain can dare to ignore the lessons of 1914 and 1939 ... None of us can defend ourselves by ourselves, and we shall all seek so to co-ordinate our policies that we can count on support in times of crisis ...'

Later the same day King had an opportunity to present these ideas publicly, when by invitation he addressed the two Houses of the British Parliament. The speech, like so many of King's, would have been more successful had it been shorter. It made no reference to Halifax, but was in fact a temperate reply to him.[81] Like Sir Wilfrid Laurier at London conferences long ago, King was defending the status quo against would-be centralizers. He summed his argument up by recalling a famous epitaph: 'I was well; I wanted to be better; and here I am.'

In the last stages of the conference the British government made an attempt to obtain agreement on a future defence programme involving what King called an Imperial Joint Board for Defence. King politely declined to commit himself; he was, he said, not the Canadian Cabinet but only one member of it, and had no power to accept such arrangements.[82] The Prime Ministers went home without any agreement having been made on 'new machinery.'

One of the striking things about Mackenzie King is how little his ideas or his policies changed in the course of his long career. We said that in 1944 he was acting much as he had in 1937; it could equally well be said that he was following precisely the same line as in 1923. The policy which the British government was wistfully adumbrating in 1944 was essentially the policy that had attracted Sir Robert Borden: a uniform Commonwealth foreign policy arrived at by consultation between Britain and the Dominions. It is interesting that by 1943 the Foreign Office in London was lecturing its staff on the importance of consultation (it may not be wholly fanciful to suggest that Malcolm MacDonald's missionary work was having some effect). An office circular signed by Sir Alexander Cadogan states: 'As a broad principle it may be laid down that Dominion Governments and, *a fortiori* Dominion Prime Ministers should be informed on matters of political importance either before or simulta-

'THE SPEECH WOULD HAVE BEEN MORE SUCCESSFUL
HAD IT BEEN SHORTER'

Mackenzie King addressing the two houses of the British Parliament during the Prime Ministers' Conference in London, May 1944. Churchill presides; facing the camera at the extreme right is Clement Attlee. Identifiable in the front row are Anthony Eden, Field-Marshal Smuts, and Mr and Mrs Vincent Massey.

neously with the United States and Soviet Governments but never later than those Governments except in very exceptional circumstances ... A situation should never be allowed to arise in which Dominion Prime Ministers receive their first intimation of important decisions of policy from the British Broadcasting Corporation or from their own newspapers.'[83] (One thinks back to Chanak; not to mention the much more recent occasions when Vincent Massey complained of getting from London taxi-drivers information that he should have had from British ministers.)[84] Back in 1923 Mackenzie King, tearing down the Borden policy, received, we saw, unknown to himself, support from the Foreign Office under Curzon and Crowe, who had no use for consultation. It was Curzon who had said that he would have 'no time for daily or frequent conferences with a British Empire Delegation' at Lausanne (above, page 36). The Foreign Office's conversion now was too late to affect events.

It seems evident that there was little likelihood in 1944 of convincing anything like a majority of Canadian public opinion of the desirability of the sort of Commonwealth policy that the Churchill government hoped for. The Commonwealth was popular, at least in English-speaking Canada; Churchill's Britain commanded vast admiration and affection; but that did not mean that it was practicable to revive the Borden policies. (And even Sir Robert Borden had firmly declined to discuss a new system of imperial naval defence in 1918.) The *New York Times* correspondent in Ottawa, commenting on the discussion aroused by the Halifax speech ('a livelier debate than this country has known for some time'), wrote: 'The discussion ... has revealed very emphatically that opinion, in general, is opposed to any centralization of the British Commonwealth that might even remotely commit Canada to a course of action that could, in her opinion, be contrary to her interest, and position on this continent or to the wider interests of international peace ... the belief appears still to be strong that peace can be obtained without the organization of power, or, at least, it is evident that a large, and probably majority, opinion wishes and intends to avoid being involved in any power group.'[85] Whether this rather high-flown analysis was sound or not, there had been general acceptance in Canada of the facts of nationhood; the separate declaration of war in 1939 had passed, I think, into the national consciousness as a symbol of an established situation; the second war, like the first, had produced heightened national feeling, especially in the forces; and there would certainly have been strong criticism of any proposal interpreted as derogating from the national status purchased by the sacrifices of the two great conflicts. In March 1944, clearly as a result of the Halifax affair, the Canadian Institute of Public Opinion asked a selection of Canadians which they would prefer after the war: for Canada to decide for herself how to deal with other countries, or to 'join with the other dominions and Britain' in concerting one foreign policy for the whole empire. The result was almost a dead heat: 47 per cent of those responding favoured the independent policy, 46 per cent the empire policy. In Quebec, however, to which the Liberal party was bound to listen with special attention, 70 per cent favoured the independent line, and only 21 per cent the Empire foreign policy.[86] There was no mandate here for Canada to adopt the Churchill government's line.

There was consciousness too of a shift in the balance of power. In 1918 the victorious British Empire had still contrived to dominate the scene. In 1944 the vast war effort of the friendly United States (so much greater than in 1917-18) and of the gigantic Soviet ally, which many Canadians (though not Mackenzie King)* managed to think of as benevolent, were obvious to everyone who could read a newspaper. It is probably true that ordinary Canadians thought vaguely of peace as being secured for the future by some international body in which these powers (and Britain) would be active and in which Canada could play a part as an independent entity.

THE SECOND WAR AND THE NATION

Germany surrendered in May 1945 and Japan in September. Canada had played a considerable part in defeating them. (Canadians have spent a good deal of time since in reading books about the war by Englishmen and Americans and wondering how it happens that their country is never mentioned.) After its long period of waiting in England, the Canadian Army had its full share of bloody fighting in Italy and in the victory campaign in North-West Europe. Falaise, the Scheldt, the Rhineland are among its battle honours. The Royal Canadian Air Force fought on many battlefronts, but most notably in the bombing of Germany. The men of the Royal Canadian Navy, some of whom had never seen the sea before they joined the service, carried much of the burden of the Battle of the Atlantic. Over one million men and women saw full-time service in the forces; over 42,000 lost their lives. We have spoken of the new factories and the old farms, and the financial aid to Britain that enabled her to profit by their efforts.

* In his survey of foreign policy given to the Prime Ministers' Conference he said 'he trusted that we would view with great circumspection all that came from that source.'[87]

The shaky unity between English and French Canada, so severely strained in 1914-18, was strained again in 1939-45, but somewhat less extremely. The national government now came from a party largely dependent on Quebec and determined to avoid giving offence to French Canada. Mackenzie King's foremost interest throughout the war was the maintenance of his pre-war pledge against conscription for overseas service. He stood his ground until late in 1944, when his hand was forced by the threat of mass resignations of English-speaking ministers from his cabinet. That was his limit; he would not stick to his anti-conscription principles if the cost was the fall of his government. So the conscripts went overseas – and King remained in power. French Canada grumbled, but it was clear that King had fought hard for her cause, and he was a far lesser evil in her eyes than the traditionally conscriptionist Conservatives, who after blowing hot and cold on the question had finally gone all out for conscription after the Normandy invasion.

In Volume I we sought to illustrate the reactions of the regions of Canada to the First World War by the statistics of voluntary enlistments in the various provinces (page 235). Here are the parallel statistics for 1939-45, compiled as far as possible on the same basis:[88]

	Population 1941	Voluntary enlistments* (three services)	Percentage
Prince Edward Island	95,047	8,939	9.40
Nova Scotia	577,962	56,797	9.82
New Brunswick	457,401	41,516	9.07
Quebec	3,331,882	131,618	3.95
Ontario	3,787,655	374,486	9.88
Manitoba	729,744	70,529	9.66
Saskatchewan	985,992	72,512	8.09
Alberta	796,169	71,634	8.99
British Columbia	817,861	85,350	10.43

These figures are crude, and subject to many obvious qualifications; but like those in the previous volume they offer a general indication of the different Canadian regions' response in this second great crisis of the

* The women's services (which did not exist in the earlier war) are not included. Figures for the Territories are included under Saskatchewan and British Columbia, whose totals are inflated to that small extent. Population figures are those for the census of 1941. Officer appointments are included.

Age of Conflict. It is interesting that the percentages for the Maritime provinces are roughly twice as high as in the first war; this change in proportion is certainly due at least in part to the absence in 1939-45 of the great mass of recent British immigrants who in 1914-18 contributed half of all the Canadian volunteers, and who were numerous in Ontario and the West but almost non-existent in the Maritimes. (Note that whereas in the first war the Canadian Army was only 51.3 per cent Canadian-born, the figure rose in 1939-45 to 84.6 per cent.)[89] It is interesting too that Saskatchewan, far below the average in enlistments in 1914-18, had in 1939-45 been almost assimilated to the English-speaking norm. Outside Quebec there was less variation between the provinces than in the earlier war; though the leading position of British Columbia is rather striking.

Quebec remains. That the percentage of 2.4 in 1914-18 has risen to 3.95 in 1939-45 does not necessarily mean a great deal; for all the provincial percentages were higher in the six-year war than in the four-year one. The fact is that (even including the large English-speaking minority) only about four Quebecers in every hundred of the population volunteered, whereas in the rest of the country the figure was closer to ten. A crisis which moved English-speaking Canada to great sacrifices moved French Canada only slightly. The French, roughly one-third of the Canadian population, still viewed Canada's external problems and connections in a quite different light from the other two-thirds, as they had from the beginning.

In a sense, perhaps, the French and the 'English' had come closer together. The stronger national spirit which the second war (like the first) had tended to produce in English-speaking Canadians might have made them sympathize with the traditional nationalism of Quebec. Differences persisted, however. English-Canadian nationalism was less fiercely isolationist than its French counterpart. My belief and recollection are that the national feeling of the Canadian forces of 1945 was not an echo of the aridly rejectionist doctrine of the pre-war academic isolationists who believed that Canada could and should merely withdraw into her shell. It continued, I think, the tradition that goes back at least to the South African War – the desire that Canada should play an active and distinctive part in world affairs. Most French Canadians would have preferred to see no Canadian forces in Europe; English-Canadian nationalists would have liked to see them under more exclusively Canadian control and playing a more visibly national role. But it is well to add that there were still many varieties of opinion and that old preferences died hard. It is worth remembering that in that poll of March 1944 nearly half of all Canadians – and 55 per cent of non-French Canadians – were ready to accept the Halifax prescription of one foreign policy for the whole empire. Of course, at that moment the war was far from over, and the Churchill magic was still strong. A year or two later the figures might have been somewhat different.

Perhaps in one respect, however, French and English had drawn closer. In January 1945 the pollsters asked whether Canada should join if a world organization were formed after the war to try to keep the peace. Ninety per cent of all Canadians – and 79 per cent of Quebecers – thought she should. Racial differences appeared more strongly, however, when the matter was pursued further. Seventy-six per cent of all Canadians thought Canada should be prepared to contribute men to an international armed force to keep the peace; only 51 per cent of Quebecers approved. And to the question whether Canada should be ready to send men to fight in this force even if the matter arose at a time when Canada was not a member of the international organization's controlling council, only 25 per cent of Quebecers said yes, whereas in the rest of Canada the figure was 65 per cent.[90] The hostility which the League of Nations idea had encountered in Quebec in 1919 was perhaps declining, but apparently it was not extinct. These questions had to be faced in the immediate future.

CHAPTER TEN

FACING A NEW ERA, 1945-48

'THE OLD LEADER ...'

Between Germany's defeat and Japan's surrender there was a general election in Canada (June 11,1945). Mackenzie King, announcing that this was his last election, said, 'It is as the leader of a government pledged to the promotion of world security and world prosperity in the international arena and to policies of full employment and social security in our country that I am seeking once more an expression of confidence of the people of Canada.' He reminded the voters of the 'intimate and far-reaching associations' that had been formed between the members of the governments of the wartime alliance, and begged them not to reject his administration in favour of new leaders who lacked these established connections with Canada's friends abroad.[1]

The electorate apparently listened, for King's Liberal government remained in power, though with its parliamentary strength somewhat reduced. It obtained a comfortable plurality of seats over the Conservatives (now termed the Progressive Conservatives), while the socialist Co-operative Commonwealth Federation, which at one time had appeared to be a serious threat, remained in the event a minor party. Quebec, for all its resentment over conscription, continued to prefer the Liberals to the Conservatives. So King was securely in the saddle for the last three years of his remarkable political career, which ended only with his retirement in November 1948.

Fifty-seven years earlier the most nearly comparable Canadian career had drawn to a close when Sir John A. Macdonald died in office, like King 'not out.' Macdonald had fought his last election with the slogan, 'The Old Leader, The Old Flag, The Old Policy.' The parallel with King is closer than might meet the eye. Certainly the 'Old Leader' was to the fore in 1945. King had never inspired the affection that had accumulated around Sir John, but his followers knew him for the greatest vote-getter in the country's history and the reputed close friend of Roosevelt and Churchill. (Roosevelt was dead before the election, but Churchill was, for the moment, still in office.) Even the flag is not wholly irrelevant. Although Canada's official flag was still the Union Jack, there had long been calls for a 'distinctive' Canadian emblem. In 1924 King's government had authorized the use of the Red Ensign with the Jack in the hoist and the arms of Canada in the fly – a flag used unofficially in Canada for generations – on Canadian buildings abroad. In 1944 the government ordered that it was to be flown by units of the Canadian Army serving with other countries' forces, and next year, in the aftermath of victory, an order-in-council directed that the Ensign should be flown on federal buildings in Canada 'until such time as action is taken by Parliament for the formal adoption of a national flag.'[2] There is no doubt that King favoured the Red Ensign in some form as that flag – he told the present writer so in 1946 – but the matter was controversial, French Canada was unfriendly to a flag incorporating the Union Jack, and King never nerved himself to take action. When a national flag was at last adopted in 1964, the Jack was not in it. The whole affair reflects the changes that were coming over Canada. As for policy, we shall see that King did indeed to a great extent cling to his own 'old policy' to the time of his retirement, maintaining the consistency that had been his hallmark from the beginning.

New and strange problems, however, were swirling around the old statesman in his last years. Typifying them was the terrifying riddle of atomic energy, suddenly revealed to the world when the Americans dropped atomic bombs on Hiroshima and Nagasaki in August 1945. As in so many other matters, Canada had been a junior partner in the top secret Allied atomic project, chiefly because she possessed accessible supplies of uranium. Now, in consequence, she had a small share in the problem of how, if at all, this awful power was to be controlled.

The world that confronted this question was much changed from that of 1939. Germany and Japan had, for the moment, been swept from the power map. Britain, it gradually became evident, had been greatly and permanently weakened. The war had brought her glory and admiration, but very little else. The wealth built up through centuries of prosperity, already much reduced, had been further dissipated in her tremendous effort against Hitler, and her population and natural resources were not equal to maintaining a contest with countries more richly endowed. Two super-powers now dominated the scene, the communist Soviet Union and the capitalist United States of America. Both had exerted themselves vastly in the war without exhausting their strength, and the two late allies regarded each other with mutual distrust. In the background was China, torn by civil strife but potentially also a super-power. Canadians noted with disquiet that in the new age of long-range bombers and atomic weapons the Russians and the Americans faced each other across the top of the world – and across Canada. There was a new balance of power. The comparatively comfortable international situation of 1939 was gone, and the new one was going to be less agreeable. The world of 1945 was a much better world than it would have been if Hitler had won, but it was to be an awkward place for a respectable 'middle power.'

Tempora mutantur, et nos mutamur in illis. Canadian policy had changed, and was changing, with the times. We have seen (above, page 299) Mackenzie King noting with amusement in May 1940 how the crisis in Europe was altering the views of O.D. Skelton: 'He now sees that the real place to defend our land is from across the seas.'[3] The facts of war changed Skelton's opinions, and the opinions of his staff – among which his successors were to be found – and in some degree those of King himself. Undoubtedly they also affected the opinions of the population at large; though as we have said (above, page 269), the public, and also the Prime Minister, had begun to move away from isolation before such a movement was visible among the civil servants in the East Block.

Just what a second world war within a quarter of a century had done to Canadians' opinions was to be strikingly reflected at the beginning of 1947 in the Gray Lecture on 'The Foundations of Canadian Policy in World Affairs' delivered at the University of Toronto by Louis St Laurent, who had then become Secretary of State for External Affairs.[4] This exposition, which seems to have excited no serious dissent in any quarter, began in the best King manner by affirming that the first concern of Canadian external policy should be to avoid disturbing the country's internal unity. It went on, however, to declare as a principle 'the acceptance of international responsibility in keeping with our conception of our role in world affairs.' 'If there is one conclusion that our common experience has led us to accept,' said St Laurent, 'it is that security for this country lies in the development of a firm structure of international organization.' He went on to describe the active part that Canada had been playing since the war in international organizations and conferences, and particularly those under the aegis of the new United Nations. It would have been premature, in January 1947, to say that 'no commitments' as a Canadian policy was entirely obsolete, for Mackenzie King was still Prime Minister, and there were decided limits to his internationalism. If he had been ahead of his staff in readiness to accept responsibility in 1939, it would probably be true to say that now his colleagues and his staff were ahead of him; but the country as a whole was moving towards a readiness to accept very large commitments to likeminded states in the interest of purchasing security.*

One other general comment on the new situation is in order. In the more complex age that was dawning the professional diplomatists were coming fully into their own. Long gone were the days when King could be a one-man foreign office in addition to being Prime Minister, or Skelton could run External Affairs by himself under King's direction. With Canadian missions proliferating around the globe and Canada becoming involved in an increasing variety of international organizations and affairs, only a large staff of trained specialists could keep abreast of the business. It was fortunate that the nucleus of such a staff had been created in the Skelton period, and that its members in general were so highly competent.

As early as July 1943 the War Committee of the cabinet, faced with inquiries from London concerning Canada's views on certain post-war European problems, took steps to set up mechanism to formulate some basis for future Canadian policy. Ultimately there were two committees of officers and officials, drawn mainly from the Departments of External Affairs and National Defence – an Advisory Committee on Post-Hostilities Problems, composed of people on the Deputy Ministers/Chiefs of Staff level, whose business it was to make recommendations to the War Committee, and a Working Committee of more junior people to do the 'donkey work' for the Advisory Committee. Both committees included able people – Hume Wrong was chairman of the Working Committee and Norman Robertson of the Advisory Committee – and during the next two years they produced many able papers.[5] Their influence is difficult to evaluate; probably their chief importance was to crystallize official thinking rather than to produce original ideas. One of their major productions was a paper on 'Post-War Canadian Defence Relationships with the United States' which the War Committee approved on February 28,

* Volume 1 of John Holmes' valuable book, *The Shaping of Peace: Canada and the Search for World Order, 1943-1957* (Toronto 1979), was published after the present book had been completed. It gives a much more detailed account of the post-war years than is possible here.

1945. Its basic conclusion was 'that the defences of Canada should be closely co-ordinated with those of the United States after the war.'[6] This, in 1945, was hardly more than a glimpse of the obvious.

One signpost to the future may be briefly noticed here. On January 23, 1945, Mackenzie King raised in the cabinet 'the desirability of making provision for the establishment of a status of "Canadian Citizenship," with particular reference to first and second generation Canadians who were naturally desirous of being associated in this formal way with the country of their allegiance.' The matter was actively pursued by the Secretary of State (Paul Martin), with the result that the Canadian Citizenship Act became law in June 1946. Until that time the concept of a 'Canadian citizen' had been almost, though not quite, unknown to the law; Canadians had been 'British subjects,' in common with other subjects of the King around the globe. The new statute, it is true, proclaimed, 'A Canadian citizen is a British subject'; but by providing that henceforth a British subject not born in Canada or resident in the country for five years before the Act came into force could acquire the new status and privileges of a Canadian citizen only by establishing eligibility and being granted a certificate it destroyed the idea of common nationality throughout the Commonwealth and obliged the other countries of the Commonwealth to pass parallel legislation, which they did. These matters were criticized in Parliament; nevertheless, it seems likely that in 1946 Canadians generally agreed with Mr Martin that it was desirable 'to establish clearly a basic and definite Canadian citizenship which will be the fundamental status upon which the rights and privileges of Canadians will depend.'[7]

A NEW LEAGUE OF NATIONS

During the First World War, it may be recalled, idealists in many countries had called for the creation of an international organization that would make such another war impossible. The result was the League of Nations. Hamstrung from the beginning by the withdrawal of the United States, and successfully defied by one powerful nation after another, the League was reduced to impotence and failed to prevent a second holocaust. It went without saying that demands were heard from the belligerent peoples that this time things should be done better: that an organization should be set up which would avoid the weaknesses of the League and provide genuine security for peace.

This became one of the Allies' proclaimed war aims. A 'permanent system of general security' was promised in the Atlantic Charter, issued by Churchill and Roosevelt during their Newfoundland meeting in August 1941. There was Anglo-American discussion of the question during the Quebec Conference of August 1943, and in the following October a meeting of the British, American, and Soviet foreign ministers at Moscow issued a declaration, in which China joined, calling for 'a general international organization, based on the principle of the sovereign equality of all peace-loving states, large and small, for the maintenance of international peace and security.' Canada was not represented at Moscow – any more than she had been at Quebec! – but her government was given an opportunity, through the British channel, to comment on the terms of the declaration in advance; and Mackenzie King issued a statement associating Canada with the four-power declaration.

As we have seen (above, page 366), the proposed international organization was discussed during the Commonwealth Prime Ministers' conference in London in the spring of 1944. King not only made clear his conviction that it was out of the question for the Commonwealth as such to be a member of the organization, he also threw his weight against the conception of the organization favoured by Winston Churchill. The British Prime Minister was arguing for a world council (apparently of the three great Allied powers) and three regional councils (for North America, Europe, and Asia), whereas Anthony Eden and the Foreign Office had put forward a paper favouring a single global organization. The Churchill idea seemed to foreshadow complete great power domination, and the possibility of encouraging a United States return to isolation. King politely observed that the Foreign Office paper seemed in general 'a sound basis on which to work'; 'The emphasis ... ought to be very much on the World Council,' and anything done on regional councils ought to emanate from the world council. Churchill was displeased, but this meeting seems to have ended his regional council conception.[8]

In the late summer of 1944 representatives of the United Kingdom, the United States, Russia, and China met at Dumbarton Oaks outside Washington to make a plan for the new organization. The British Dominions were kept informed of the progress of the discussions by the British representative, and Canada attempted, without much success, to exercise some influence on them through him. The aspect that most alarmed the Canadians was reports that the powers were proposing to give themselves individually an absolute veto on the proceedings of the Security Council, the body that was to take the place of the Council of the old League.[9] The Dumbarton Oaks plan was published in October, though with the rules governing voting in the Security Council omitted for further consideration. It envisaged machinery much like the League's – an Assembly representing all the member states, and a Security Council in which the great powers would have permanent seats and various lesser states would be elected to temporary seats. After studying the scheme with care, the Canadian government on January 12, 1945, sent a reasoned commentary on it to the four 'sponsoring states' and also to France.[10]

This document made two main points. First, it pointed out that, although the primary responsibility of the great powers for the maintenance of peace was recognized, there was no recognition of the variety of strength among the lesser states, 'despite the fact that their power and their capacity to use it for the maintenance of peace range from almost zero upwards to a point not very far behind the great powers.' Could not means be devised 'of associating more effectively with the work of the Security Council states of the order of international importance of Canada'? It might be ensured that 'such states were chosen to fill elected seats on the Council more frequently (or possibly for longer periods) than states with less to contribute to the maintenance of security.' Canada, in other words, was suggesting applying the functional principle. The other point related to the position of states not members of the Security Council if called upon by the Council to provide military forces for use against an aggressor state. We have noted (above, page 373) the doubts of French-Canadian public opinion on this question at this moment. The Canadian government suggested that Security Council decisions 'should be made binding, in the first instance, only on states which are members of the Council,' while states not on the Council should be required to take positive action 'only when the decision has been endorsed by a two-thirds majority of the Assembly (when it would become binding on all members), or when the country or countries concerned have by special invitation participated on the same footing as elected members in the Council's proceedings, or when they have individually agreed with the Council to join in a particular task of enforcement.'

This paper may be considered the 1945 equivalent of the careful memorandum of 1919 in which Sir Robert Borden and his colleagues at Paris commented on the draft Covenant of the League of Nations and took exception to Article 10 (Volume 1, pages 263-5). And it had, if possible, even less effect. Much further pressure was required to make any impression on the great powers.

In February 1945 Churchill, Roosevelt, and Josef Stalin held the last of their tripartite conferences, at Yalta in the Crimea. They agreed on the form of the great powers' veto in the Security Council: it would not apply on 'procedural matters,' but would on all other matters.[11] In April, on the motion of the British government, the Commonwealth countries met in

London to discuss the new organization in advance of the general meeting which was now proposed of the nations opposing the Axis. King explained that political commitments in Canada made it impossible for him to attend or to send a minister; Hume Wrong, now Associate Under Secretary, represented Canada in co-operation with Vincent Massey.[12] The reasons for the Prime Minister's evident doubts about this meeting are illustrated by President Roosevelt's rather snide remark about it to the Governor General, Lord Athlone, who was visiting him: 'a united front was being arranged.'[13] In point of fact, however, the Commonwealth was far from united in this conference; to mention only one example, Canada's view that countries expected to provide forces should be allowed to take part in the Security Council proceedings was opposed by the United Kingdom, Australia, and India, the argument being that this would unduly reduce the Council's authority. On this and various other matters the conferees could do no more than discuss the various points of view in an amicable family manner and agree to differ.[14]

In March 1945 the Canadian House of Commons, on King's motion, endorsed almost unanimously the government's action in accepting the invitation which had been received to attend the conference proposed at San Francisco to organize the new league. In doing so it also approved the four great powers' proposals as 'a satisfactory general basis for a discussion of the charter of the proposed international organization.' The vote on March 28 was 202-5; all the five dissenters came from Quebec.

On April 25, 1945, the founding conference met at San Francisco. Procedures different from those of 1919 were being followed. Then, the Covenant of the League of Nations had been part of the Treaty of Versailles. Now the international organization was to be set up by the Allies before the war ended. The fifty countries attending the conference were those that had declared war on Germany and Japan, including some very late arrivals – notably Argentina, a state with a pro-Nazi record, which scrambled on to the band-wagon less than a month before the conference met. The Canadian delegation, headed by Mackenzie King, included the leaders of the major opposition parties in Parliament.* But with an election in prospect at home the politicians did not stay long, and Canadian interests were left to the professional diplomatists, an able group headed

---

* The Conservative representative was Gordon Graydon, the party's leader in the House of Commons. King refused to appoint the titular party leader, John Bracken, who had not yet ventured to seek a seat in the House. Another Conservative, John Diefenbaker, appeared at San Francisco quite unofficially. King wrote in his diary, 'why Diefenbaker is here I cannot think.'[15]

by Robertson, Pearson, and Wrong. The chairman of the conference was Edward R. Stettinius, Cordell Hull's unimpressive successor as American Secretary of State. Its most distinguished figure was Field-Marshal Smuts, the only survivor present of the hopeful idealists of 1919. The Commonwealth's noisiest representative was the leader of the Australian delegation, Dr Herbert Evatt, whom Pearson described as 'an arrogant and aggressive fellow, but intelligent and well informed.'[16]

The task of the conference was to produce the Charter of the United Nations, the new organization's equivalent of the League Covenant. (The term 'United Nations,' coined at the beginning of 1942 as a term for the Grand Alliance acceptable to American susceptibilities, was now taken over by the new league, which in due course was to become universal in its membership.) In essentials, the Charter was the document produced by the great powers at Dumbarton Oaks and Yalta; but it was modified in some particulars as a result of the San Francisco discussions.[17] We cannot describe the conference in detail, and must limit ourselves to the part played by Canada.

The Canadian delegates' main object is not in doubt. They considered that the future of the world depended on the successful establishment of an international organization with both the Soviet Union and the United States as members. For this they were prepared to make and to counsel sacrifices. They did not like the veto which the Yalta plan conferred upon the permanent members of the Security Council; but they were willing to accept it as the price of achieving the great object. Evatt was the leader of the attack on the veto and the vociferous spokesman of the interests of the smaller powers; at one point he and Fraser of New Zealand became involved in an undignified public wrangle with the delegates of the United Kingdom. However much they might agree with Evatt in theory, the Canadians regarded his campaign with some alarm. On June 10 Robertson reported to Ottawa that he and Pearson were going to see Evatt in the hope of ascertaining 'just what object he hopes to achieve by the tactics he is pursuing.' The Canadians considered that there was danger of the Russians refusing to join the organization. 'Our view,' wrote Robertson, 'is that it is better to take the Organization that we can get and, having come to that decision, to refrain from further efforts to pry apart the difficult unity which the Great Powers have attained.' It was best to eschew the 'luxury of making any more perfectionist speeches.'[18] Mackenzie King fully approved this.[19] A few days later Robertson reported: 'We should, of course, not cast our vote for any proposal which would endanger ratification of Charter by United States.'[20] Canada's influence was limited, but it was exerted on behalf of sane and sound aims.

CANADA AT SAN FRANCISCO

L.B. Pearson (then Canadian Ambassador in Washington) speaking in a committee meeting during the founding conference of the United Nations, 1945

At the same time the Canadians fought quietly and consistently for the changes in the Charter which had been defined in Canada's paper of January 12. They did achieve something. They failed to gain for the 'middle powers' the special position among the non-permanent members of the Security Council that they had sought; but Article 23 of the Charter as signed provided that in the election of the six non-permanent members 'due regard' should be specially paid 'in the first instance to the contribution of Members of the United Nations to the maintenance of international peace and security and to the other purposes of the Organization, and also to equitable geographical distribution.' The other basic point that Canada had pursued, that of gaining a voice in the Council for states not represented on it if they were being asked for forces to enforce the Council's decisions, caused considerable concern. It was discussed more than once within the United States delegation, and after meeting initial hostility was taken more seriously when it was reported that Mackenzie King had said that without concessions on this matter it would be difficult to get the Charter through the Canadian Parliament. King himself had played a rather limited part in the negotiations, but he made an effective contribution on this point the day he left San Francisco (May 14). In an interview with Stettinius, who was accompanied by John Hickerson, the State Department official who had had much to do with Canadian relations, he made so strong a case that Stettinius accepted it. The 'Big Five' (the United States, the United Kingdom, Russia, China, and France) subsequently agreed, Russia insisting that Canada should withdraw other amendments she had offered concerning temporary membership on the Security Council. The result was Article 44 of the Charter:

When the Security Council has decided to use force it shall, before calling upon a Member not represented on it to provide armed forces in fulfillment of the obligations assumed under Article 43 [requiring all members to provide forces, etc., on the call of the Council], invite that Member, if the Member so desires, to participate in the decisions of the Security Council concerning the employment of contingents of that Member's armed forces.

Thus Canada achieved the essence of what was probably her chief special desire in connection with the Charter. It did not prove to be particularly important in the later history of the United Nations. Down to the time of writing, Article 44 had never been invoked.[21]

It had, perhaps, more importance in Canada, and may have been responsible for the fact that the Canadian House of Commons approved the United Nations Charter on October 19, 1945 without a division. Much was made of Article 44 during the debate, and just before it ended the Acting Secretary of State for External Affairs (Louis S. St Laurent made a rather surprising commitment: 'The agreement to be entered into between Canada and the security council as to the kind and quota of the forces to be provided will be submitted to parliament for approval before Canada will become bound by it.' Nothing like that had been said at San Francisco, and if it had been it is possible that Article 44 would never have appeared in the Charter.

Fresh from his electoral victory, Mackenzie King returned to San Francisco to sign the Charter on behalf of Canada on June 26. Things were not quite the same as in 1919. Then, the treaty enshrining the League Covenant had been signed by the British Empire as a group, the United Kingdom signing first (though not under that designation) followed by Canada and the rest. Now the Commonwealth countries signed mingled with the other nations in alphabetical order, Canada coming between the Byelo-Russian Soviet Socialist Republic* and Chile. There were, however, two alphabets. The five permanent members of the Security Council signed first, followed by the lesser states. No one was left in any doubt that, although all nations might be theoretically equal, the Great Powers were considerably more equal than the others.

Long before San Francisco much had been done towards organizing the post-war world in its economic aspects. The story cannot be told in detail here. As early as May 1943, on President Roosevelt's initiative, a conference was held at Hot Springs, Virginia, to discuss world questions of food and agriculture. L.B. Pearson was one of the Canadian representatives, and when an interim commission to plan a permanent body was set up he was made its chairman. The permanent body finally emerged at a meeting in Quebec City in October 1945, as the United Nations Food and Agriculture Organization, again with Pearson as its first chairman.[22] In July 1944 Canadian representatives attended, and played a valuable part in, a conference of the Allied nations at Bretton Woods, New

* At Yalta Roosevelt and Churchill had felt constrained to give Russia three seats in the Assembly, agreeing that apart from Russia proper two of the sixteen Soviet Republics, Byelo-Russia and the Ukraine, might be founding members of the United Nations. This led to revived talk, as in 1919, of the 'six British votes'; and Roosevelt talked briefly at the end of March 1945 of seeking three votes for the United States, a suggestion which was almost immediately withdrawn.

Hampshire, from which emerged agreements to set up an International Monetary Fund and an International Bank for Reconstruction and Development (which became known as the 'World Bank'). In 1945 Parliament approved Canadian participation in these two organizations intended to ensure a degree of international financial and monetary stability in the difficult post-war years.[23] The great wartime development of flying, and Canada's geographical position, made the regulation of post-war civil aviation a matter of urgent national interest, and Canada was very actively involved in the international conference at Chicago in 1944 out of which grew the International Civil Aviation Organization, which set up its headquarters in Montreal.[24] At San Francisco the Canadian delegation had a good deal to do with framing Chapter X of the Charter, relating to the United Nations Economic and Social Council; and Canada was elected to the Council at the first meeting of the UN Assembly. And it should be noted that the International Labour Organization, founded in connection with the League of Nations, continued its work under the new body.

MAKING PEACE – AFTER A FASHION

If the Great Allied Powers showed themselves determined to maintain firm control in and over the United Nations, they were no less decided in their attitude towards the process of making peace. In July 1945 the Big Three – Stalin; Harry S. Truman, the new president of the United States; and the British Prime Minister, who was Churchill until July 28 and Clement Attlee thereafter – met at Potsdam. They decided, without consulting any of the other countries that had helped them win the war, that the task of drafting treaties of peace should be confided to a Council of Foreign Ministers representing the United States, Britain, Russia, France, and China.[25] The first meeting of the Council was held in London in September. Attlee proceeded to cable the Dominion prime ministers suggesting that they or their personal representatives should meet in London at that time; he proposed to seek admission for the Dominion representatives to Council meetings when issues of interest to the Dominions were under discussion, but could not guarantee this in advance. Mackenzie King declined the invitation, the fact that the Canadian Parliament was called to meet on September 6 providing a convenient excuse. Shortly he told the House of Commons:

It is important that Canada should not merely be consulted, but that there should be clear recognition of Canada's right to effective participation in the great decisions where questions affecting the general ordering of the future peace of the world are under consideration. During the war, for military reasons, it was necessary to acquiesce in the operation of war-time arrangements under which responsibility for major decisions on the direction of the allied war effort was concentrated in a very few hands. The continued use of methods such as were improvised to meet the urgent strain and hazards of war, whereby private settlements are arrived between the great powers on issues of general interest might well become a source of difficulty and even of danger. Every possible precaution should, therefore, be taken to see that in this particular the war-time pattern is not perpetuated in the framing of the peace settlement and in the united nations organization.[26]

All this of course made good sense, but the Great Powers went on behaving much as they had during the war. Britain was necessarily aware of the Dominions and made an effort to keep their interests in view, but the Americans and the Russians had no such concern. The growing tension between the Soviets and their former allies was a constant complication. In the summer of 1946, however, the powers went so far as to assemble at Paris a peace conference in which the lesser countries that had fought would have an opportunity to comment on the treaties which the Council of Foreign Ministers had drafted for Italy, Romania, Bulgaria, Hungary, and Finland. Canada sent a delegation headed by the Prime Minister, who was accompanied by Brooke Claxton, the Minister of Health and Welfare, and the usual competent team of senior civil servants. The conference was largely an exercise in frustration; all it could do was pass recommendations for later consideration by the Council of Foreign Ministers. Canada and King in particular had little interest in the territorial or other detail of the treaties but were interested in general principles and the maintenance of international security. The Canadians therefore tried to avoid any action that might further exacerbate relations between Russia and the West. Their attitude is well summarized in remarks made by King in a meeting of the Commonwealth delegations: 'If the effect of an effort to obtain amendments was a breakdown of the settlement, they would be defeating their own object ... It was preferable to accept an imperfect solution in order to make some progress.'[27] The fact that King was old and tired* no doubt contributed to the Canadians' keeping a low profile.

* When I was called over from London to arrange and guide a tour of the Normandy battlefields for the Prime Minister, Claxton and Arnold Heeney told me to explain this to the local authorities in Normandy by way of discourag-

'THE CONFERENCE WAS LARGELY AN EXERCISE IN FRUSTRATION'
Canadians at the Paris Peace Conference, 1946. Left to right, Norman
Robertson, Mackenzie King, Brooke Claxton, Arnold Heeney

On behalf of Australia the remarkable Dr Evatt took a quite different line, again making himself the spokesman of the small countries, enraging the Russians and demanding innumerable alterations in the drafts. He put forward no fewer than seventy-three amendments. (Canada put forward just one.) In the end a considerable number of the recommendations made by the conference were accepted by the Council of Foreign Ministers, thanks mainly to some relaxation of attitude on the part of Russia. The treaties were signed in Paris on February 10, 1947, General Georges Vanier, the Ambassador to France, signing those with Italy, Hungary, Romania, and Finland on behalf of Canada. As the reader knows, Canada had not been at war with Bulgaria (above, page 320). The treaties were laid before Parliament with the explanation that they were the best that could be obtained in the circumstances. There was some Opposition criticism of the limited role Canada had played, but the treaties were approved and in due course ratified.[28]

Canadians at large were certainly more interested in the settlement with Germany than in that with Italy and the lesser German satellites. Canada's effort in two great wars had been directed mainly against Germany, the country that seemed historically to have presented the chief threat to the peace of Europe and the world in the twentieth century. In the innumerable homes across Canada that those wars had darkened in one way or another, the possibility of preventing a revival of the German threat was a matter of real and personal concern. Since in the end there was no German settlement, the matter is perhaps not one to detain us long. Nevertheless, the official Canadian attitudes towards the German problem should be noticed. The great Allied powers were as little desirous of advice from their smaller partners on this as on other matters; the most Canada achieved was a brusque invitation to make a submission to the deputies of the Council of Foreign Ministers who were charged with preparing a German treaty. Louis St Laurent told Parliament that the government saw no advantage in 'a Canadian representative making a formal appearance before the deputies, presenting his submission without the privilege of discussion, and then withdrawing.' What the government did was to put before the deputies a careful written document expressing its 'preliminary views on the principles that should, in its opinion, underlie

---

ing too numerous ceremonies. But King made a liar out of me. He got a great reception from the people of the ruined towns and villages where the Canadian Army had fought two years before, the sort of reception he never got in Canada; and under the influence of the cheers of the populace he grew younger mile by mile. The more ceremonies there were the better he liked it.

the German peace settlement,' and present the document to the House of Commons the same day.[29]

The paper recalled Canada's part in winning the Allied victory, and claimed for her 'an opportunity to contribute to the negotiation of peace on the same basis of honourable partnership that characterized her contribution to the war.' Since at present there was no German government to sign a treaty, it suggested that the best immediate plan might be to prepare 'an international statute' constituting a new German state and governing its relations with the outside world until this could be replaced with a permanent treaty. It opposed the dismemberment of Germany, but argued that the German state should be federal and not unitary. It advocated a 'measure of international control' of German industry, and argued that Germany should be disarmed, to the extent of being left 'with only a police force for purposes of domestic security.' Finally, it asserted that the problem of preventing further aggression by Germany could 'only be solved as part of the wider problem of the prevention of aggression by any state': the United Nations must be built 'into an effective instrument for the preservation of peace.'

Fine words, and it all went no further. The Council of Foreign Ministers utterly failed to agree on procedure for producing a German settlement, one point of contention being participation by the smaller Allies, to which Britain and the United States were somewhat more friendly than the Soviet Union and France. The basic problem, however, was the Soviets' determination to hold what they had in Eastern Europe. The Russians had been difficult allies, and as the end of the war came in sight they became even more difficult. The first great issue was Poland, fought out mainly with Britain, which had gone to war on behalf of Poland in 1939. It gradually became grimly apparent that the only government Russia would tolerate in Poland was a Communist puppet administration manipulated by herself.[30] As for Germany, wartime agreements between the Allies had divided the country into occupation zones, Russian, British, American and (a late adjustment) French. The city of Berlin was similarly divided. The Russians came into possession of the whole of East Germany. Here too in due course a Communist puppet government was set up; and Germany remained a divided country, as it remains to the time of writing. In 1949 Canada, in common with her allies, recognized the new Federal Republic of Germany, the democratic western state with its capital at Bonn. In 1951 a Canadian royal proclamation, following the pattern of action by the other western powers, unilaterally ended the state of war between Canada and Germany.[31] There has never been a treaty of peace.

Disagreements between Russia and the West long delayed a peace settlement with Japan. A Far Eastern Advisory Commission representing all the powers that had signed the Japanese surrender terms (including Canada) was set up, but Russia refused to take part until promised that the Great Power veto would apply to its operations as in the Security Council. In 1947 the United States proposed a peace conference, to be attended by all countries represented on the Commission; Russia insisted that the treaty should be drafted by the Great Powers alone, and the scheme collapsed. After the outbreak of the Korean War in 1950, the United States itself drafted a treaty on which allied states including Canada were given an opportunity to comment. This was signed at a conference at San Francisco in 1951. Canada attended and signed. The Soviet Union and its satellites attended but did not sign. There was no Chinese participation (by this time mainland China was under a Communist government, which was actually fighting the United States in Korea).[32] But these matters are beyond the scope of the present volume.

It used to be traditional to abuse the peacemakers of 1919, and no doubt their weaknesses were great. But at least they did a job that was 'neater and completer' than that done by their successors after 1945.

The relationship of Canada to the two settlements makes one think. Sir Robert Borden and his colleagues in 1919 used the occasion to seek to ensure that Canada should possess in future both the status of a sovereign nation and a share in the councils and influence of the still-powerful British Empire-Commonwealth. Their Liberal successors after 1921 concentrated on the first of these objects and rejected the second. At San Francisco, and before and after, Mackenzie King and his associates tried to enforce respect for the sovereign status won on old battlefields and to see to it that independent Canada's sacrifices in a second war would secure for her a respectable share in shaping the new state system. They had small success. What they discovered once more was the hard facts of power: that the theoretical equality of sovereign nations was a theory only, and that a country of twelve, or twenty, millions of people did not carry much weight in the councils of the world. A so-called 'middle power' might make a loud noise, like Herbert Evatt's Australia, or take the line of quiet diplomacy, like Mackenzie King's Canada; it came in the end to the same thing, and that was very little.

THE DIPLOMATIC FRONT WIDENS

One result of the war was to multiply Canada's official contacts with foreign states. At the outbreak of war the total of foreign missions, including those just established in Belgium and the Netherlands (above, page 265n), was still only five. We have noted the opening of new high commissions in Commonwealth countries early in the war. The governments-in-exile of the countries overrun by Hitler were eager for recognition, and after some hesitation Canada agreed that they should have legations in Ottawa. Late in 1942 General Vanier was appointed a sort of portmanteau Minister to the governments in London of Belgium, the Netherlands, Czechoslovakia, Greece, Norway, Poland, and Yugoslavia; perhaps more important, the Vichy French representative in Canada having finally been given his walking papers, Vanier was to 'act in consultation with' General de Gaulle's French National Committee, not yet recognized as a government.[33] About the same time, direct relations were established with two important powers at war with Canada's enemies when Ministers were appointed in China and the Union of Soviet Socialist Republics. The Minister to the USSR was Dana Wilgress, who will be remembered as Trade Commissioner at Omsk in 1916 (Volume 1, page 278). Mr Wilgress gave up the appointment of Deputy Minister of Trade and Commerce to come over to External Affairs and become Canada's first diplomatic representative in Russia, as he had been one of her first commercial representatives there.[34]

Simultaneously, eyes were turning southward – far southward. Canada's loss of European markets after the outbreak of war in 1939 made people in Ottawa wonder whether substitutes might be found in Latin America. During 1940 both Argentina and Brazil made approaches looking to diplomatic representation, and the most important Canadian business interest in South America, the Brazilian Traction, Light and Power Company, used its influence in favour of the idea. Mackenzie King was inclined to wait, but O.D. Skelton favoured a forward policy, and by October King was convinced and King George VI's approval was obtained. The exchange of ministers with the two countries took place in 1941; and after representations from Chile (incidentally supported by the United States) that state was included, the Canadian Minister to Argentina being also thriftily accredited to Chile in the first instance.[35]

James MacKinnon, who succeeded W.D. Euler as Minister of Trade and Commerce, is said to have been anxious to make a mark in the annals of the department, and his method was to lead a trade mission to South America. (This was not entirely a new idea; Canada had tried it as early as 1866, and again in 1930.)[36] MacKinnon's first attempt, in 1940, was ruined when he fell ill, but he set out again in August 1941, fortified with full powers to negotiate trade agreements with Ecuador, Peru, Chile, and Argentina, to which Brazil was later added.[37] The mission received quite a warm reception, and most-favoured-nation trade agreements were duly concluded with Argentina, Brazil, and Chile, while an exchange of notes was effected 'constituting a commercial "modus vivendi"' with Ecuador, and Peru and Canada signed a declaration signifying their intention to work towards a trade agreement. Another tour by MacKinnon in 1946 produced agreements with Mexico and Colombia.[38]

A by-product of the MacKinnon mission of 1941 was an actual bid by Canada to join the Pan-American Union (later called the Organization of American States). This question had been discussed off and on for years; the United States had been cool to Canadian membership, and Canadians were divided, many feeling that to join would merely present the country with unnecessary problems, since Canada would be expected to take sides when, as often happened, the United States found itself at odds with the other American republics.[39] The members of MacKinnon's mission seem to have come back convinced joiners, and Escott Reid, who had represented External Affairs on the trip, wrote a strong memorandum urging adhering to the Union; H.L. Keenleyside took the same line.* King was sufficiently convinced that on December 16, 1941 – nine days after Pearl Harbor – a message went to the Canadian Minister in Brazil authorizing him to tell the Brazilian authorities confidentially that 'Canada would be prepared to accept an invitation to join the Pan American Union.' The United States Minister was informed of this action, though the Americans had not been previously consulted. Immediately Washington imposed a total veto: it was 'absolutely impossible for any government to be represented at the forthcoming conference [at Rio de Janeiro], other than the American republics.' Apparently it was feared that the British Commonwealth was infiltrating the Pan-American Union. King promptly abandoned the scheme.[40] It is interesting to speculate what the reaction of the Canadian public would have been had it been proceeded with.

Within a few years the American attitude had changed. In April 1947 Senator Arthur H. Vandenberg, Chairman of the Foreign Relations Committee of the United States Senate, publicly suggested that Canada should join the Union. But Mackenzie King's memory was not short. Visiting President Truman later that month, he gave the idea its quietus: 'The Prime Minister ... referred to Senator Vandenberg's recent speech advocating that Canada join the Pan American Union. Mr. King declared this to be a fine gesture but hoped that the subject would not be pressed at this time. He said that to do so would certainly give rise to misunderstanding in the rest of the British Commonwealth if nowhere else, and that the inference would be drawn that Canada was giving up its ties with the

---

* That the External staff were not all of the same opinion is indicated by a couple of rather sharp minutes which L.B. Pearson wrote on the Reid paper.

Commonwealth for the sake of its neighbors in the Western Hemisphere. The President agreed that Canada had an important role to play in both the British Commonwealth and the Americas and said that he understood the Prime Minister's position.' The Vandenberg initiative led to considerable discussion and controversy in Canada, but, King's attitude being what it was, there was no action.[41] A generation later, there has still been no action.

Pressure from foreign states anxious to exchange representatives with Canada continued, and though considerations of expense and shortage of personnel made the Department of External Affairs hold back, the missions multiplied. By 1944 there were twenty-five Canadian posts abroad; by 1947 the number had risen to thirty-six. Inevitably the cost rose also, from less than one million dollars in 1942 to over five million in 1947.[42] It was still a very small proportion of the national budget. The expansion of the Ottawa diplomatic corps had some unexpected consequences. One of these was the Gouzenko Affair of 1945.

On September 2 of that year the Japanese formally surrendered to General MacArthur in Tokyo Bay. Four days later, it is hardly too much to say, Canada's own section of what came to be called the Cold War with Russia broke out in Ottawa. A cipher clerk named Igor Gouzenko 'defected' from the Russian Embassy (by now most legations had become embassies) and, after great difficulty in getting anyone to listen to him, made over to the Canadian authorities a bundle of files which proved beyond doubt that the Embassy was the base for a very active 'spy ring.' Its tentacles were found to extend into the cipher section of the Department of External Affairs, the National Research Council, the Wartime Information Board, the British High Commission, the group of scientists from Britain who were pursuing atomic research in Montreal, and the House of Commons (the country's one Communist MP was in due course sentenced to a term of imprisonment for espionage). Mackenzie King, in spite of his long-standing distrust of Russia, was at first unwilling to believe Gouzenko's story and only gradually came to admit that Canada's ally had been carrying on these activities against her during the war.[43] That such things should happen in Ottawa! The quasi-colonial capital of 1939 was losing its innocence.

With the arrest of the suspects in February 1946 the affair became public. The Russians poured abuse on Canada and King, but they withdrew the members of their mission who were implicated when it was suggested they do so. Although King felt that a breach of diplomatic relations was inevitable, and would probably be initiated by Russia,[44] no formal break took place. The Russian Ambassador had left Canada before the revelations were made, and did not return. In Moscow Wilgress, who had once felt himself 'at the very top in Soviet esteem,' fell to the bottom. At the Paris Peace Conference, when Wilgress moved Canada's lone amendment (above, page 389), Andrei Vyshinsky of the Soviet Foreign Office made a violent personal attack upon him. Mackenzie King, always the conciliator, had actually briefly considered using the occasion of the conference to make a trip to Moscow, but Wilgress discouraged the idea in the strongest possible terms. With the Soviets, he wrote, 'it is not good policy to turn the other cheek after being the recipient of an insult.'[45] The plan died a quick death. When Wilgress was withdrawn from Moscow no ambassador was appointed to replace him. For some years the Russian Embassy in Ottawa and the Canadian Embassy in Moscow were headed by *chargés d'affaires*. Only after Josef Stalin's death in 1953 were ambassadors again exchanged.[46]

The episode seems to have had a considerable effect upon the Canadian public's view of the Soviet Union. During the Prime Ministers' Conference of 1944, King, while expressing his own mistrust, remarked that Canadians were very sympathetic to Russia.[47] This sympathy, firmly rooted in regard for the enormous Russian contribution to the war,* certainly helped to facilitate the Soviet espionage operation. But it does not appear to have survived the Gouzenko revelations. A month after they were made, the Canadian Institute of Public Opinion asked Canadians whether they believed that any nation wanted to dominate the world; 58 per cent did so. Asked which nation, 50 per cent of the 58 said Russia. Parallel questioning in the United States, France, and Australia showed that only 25, 26, and 33 per cent, respectively, feared Russian domination; it is interesting that in France 25 per cent of the respondents saw American domination as a menace, and in Canada only 3 per cent.[49] It is arguable that Comrade Gouzenko had made Canada, for the moment, an anti-Soviet state.

DEFENCE AFTER THE WAR

One of the curious aspects of Canadian history after the First World War, the reader may recall, is the fact that that tremendous military experience had virtually no effect at all on the country's military policy. After 1918 Canada returned to maintaining the tiny and inefficient forces inherited

* It is worth while to recall that 82 per cent of all the German Army's casualties between June 1941 and March 1945 were suffered on the Eastern Front.[48]

396 / CANADA AND THE AGE OF CONFLICT, 1921-48

from her colonial past. At a time when Canadian policy was mainly concerned with establishing and maintaining national status, no attention was paid to the apparatus of national defence which most countries have found a necessary complement to independence. In the happy circumstances of those days Canada was able to do this and survive. Only under the immediate threat of another war did the government take belated and inadequate steps towards improving her defences. When the outbreak came in 1939 the country's professional army was little larger than it had been in 1914 – some 4,000 men.

After 1945 things were rather different. The experience of the second war had clearly had some effect on the thinking of both government and people; the former was ready to propose, and the latter to accept, larger forces and heavier military expenditures than the country had ever before known in peacetime. Nevertheless, we shall see, all was not changed. The old Canadian antipathy to military preparation was not extinct. Above all, it was not extinct in the bosom of Mackenzie King; and as long as he was Prime Minister the armed forces would continue to be viewed with a hostile and suspicious eye.

Interim decisions on the strength of the forces were rapidly made in the summer and autumn of 1945. The Chiefs of Staff naturally asked for forces which, though tiny by comparison with those that had fought the war, were still considerable: for the Navy, 20,000 men, with a force of two aircraft carriers, four cruisers, and two destroyer flotillas; for the Air Force, 30,000 men in the regular force; for the Army, 55,000 regulars and a system of universal compulsory training which would produce a large reserve. This programme was dealt with in September by a new Cabinet Defence Committee presided over by the Prime Minister and roughly equivalent to the old War Committee. The result cannot have surprised the more experienced of the service officers. The Navy was told to plan in terms of 10,000 men; the Air Force, 15,000 to 20,000 regulars; the Army, 20,000 to 25,000; compulsory service was rejected. The services' proposed budget of $290,000,000 was reduced to $172,000,000.[50]

The establishment thus sketched became, in essentials, that of the early post-war forces. (The Navy, it may be noted, never actually had in operation more than one carrier, or more than two cruisers; these large ships were not popular with the government, and in due course they vanished from the scene.) Obviously, the forces were tiny by comparison with those of the great powers. Yet it is worth while to make the point that by Canadian standards there had been a revolution. Normal Canadian defence expenditure before the war, after 'rearmament' had begun, had run around $33,000,000 annually. After the war it never fell below

$195,000,000. The total of regular personnel in the three services, under 8,000 in 1939, was never less than 35,000 after the demobilization at the end of the war.[51]

Mackenzie King viewed these developments sourly; and by the autumn of 1946 he was ready to make an attack on them. Something unprecedented happened on November 14 and 15, when the cabinet devoted two full days to a discussion of defence policy. The main and most urgent question was defence relations with the United States, a matter to be dealt with below; but the whole field was examined and the current state of the forces reported on. The Prime Minister remarked: 'Expenditures for defence would have to be considered carefully in relation to the whole national budget and in particular to the government's social security programme. Large expenditures upon defence would inevitably entail reductions in the amounts available for social purposes.' It was agreed that the Army and Navy programmes should be re-examined (King, as before the war, was inclined to think, the minutes report him as saying, 'that the defence responsibilities of Canada would involve a very high proportion of air strength') and the defence estimates looked at with care. One decision (which had in fact already been announced) was that henceforth one Minister should be responsible for all three services (in wartime each service had its own; in 1946 one Minister was responsible for the Air Force, and one for both the Army and the Navy).[52]

Soon after these meetings King appointed Brooke Claxton, an able, brash, and energetic junior member of the cabinet, Minister of National Defence with a mandate to cut costs. King told the cabinet on January 3, 1947: 'What we needed now was to get back to the old Liberal principles of economy, reduction of taxation, anti-militarism, etc.'.[53] Claxton laid about him with a will, as the present writer has reason to remember (one of the projects this 'scholar in politics' sought to eliminate was the Army's history of the late war); but even for Claxton there were limits. Faced with a demand from the Minister of Finance and his powerful Deputy, Clifford Clark, to cut his estimates to about $150 million, he refused; however, the cabinet forced him down to $200 million.[54] This was the forces' post-war nadir. During 1948 the Cold War, we shall see, got colder; late in that year Mackenzie King retired; and with the advent of the North Atlantic Treaty (1949) and the outbreak of the Korean War (1950) a new era of military expansion began.

One question dealt with at the November meetings was military liaison in London. King had made this a matter of special difficulty before the war,[55] and he seemed disposed to do the same now. However, he was not hostile to 'liaison' as such; what he would not countenance was the maintenance of a military 'mission' in the British capital or any participation in joint planning. On December 19 the cabinet approved instructions submitted by the Prime Minister under which the Joint Staff Mission set up in London early in 1945 (above, page 336) disappeared, and each armed service and the Defence Research Board would have a liaison officer attached to the staff of the High Commissioner in London. King remarked, 'The functions of the Service representatives were to be confined to liaison and would not include participation in planning of any kind.' Claxton observed that the liaison officers would need staffs, but assured the Prime Minister that these would be kept to a minimum.[56] In fact, very considerable Canadian service liaison establishments shortly came into existence in London, a marked contrast with the situation before 1939. Similar British staffs existed in Ottawa.[57] It is also worth noting that, again in contrast with pre-war practice, service attachés were now appointed to many Canadian missions abroad.[58] Canada thus acquired the means of gathering intelligence of and forming independent appreciations concerning military situations in distant parts of the world.

THE POST-WAR COMMONWEALTH

We have noted the desire of many British statesmen that Britain should face the post-war world as the leader of a unified Commonwealth, and the fact that Mackenzie King and his colleagues prevented any movement in the direction of setting up 'new machinery.' It remains to see how the old machinery functioned in the early days of peace.

The first thing that had to be done as between Canada and Britain was to achieve a financial settlement to liquidate outstanding wartime obligations and, Canadians hoped, clear the way for a resumption of the large and mutually advantageous trade of peacetime. The two countries' positions were very different. Britain's economic situation, we have seen, had greatly deteriorated as a result of her efforts in the war. Of Canada, on the other hand, it might have been said again, as after 1918, 'She gave greatly to the war and in turn the war gave much to her' (above, page 14). It is true that her national debt had more than quadrupled since 1939,[59] but her national income had considerably more than doubled,[60] her industry was more diversified, and her general industrial capacity had much increased. Nevertheless, to be prosperous she still needed to sell her wheat and other staple products abroad.

The Canadian government opened the ball before the German war was over, sending to London on February 23, 1945, three carefully-drafted telegrams on post-war trade policy. In one of these King told Churchill that he hoped Britain would be willing to take part in a 'co-operative effort to remove obstacles to expanding world trade generally.' Another suggested that Canada might make a large loan to Britain on 'realistic and flexible' terms. The result was a Canadian economic mission to Britain whose members were entertained by Lord Keynes on behalf of the British Treasury at King's College, Cambridge, and treated to a brilliant exposition of the country's problems (May 1945).[61] The final stage was reached when a British financial delegation visited Ottawa in February 1946. The negotiations were not easy. The British asked for an interest-free loan, and Graham Towers, the Governor of the Bank of Canada, and other senior civil servants supported the request; after all, a primary purpose of the loan was to enable Britain to make purchases from Canada. But the British had lately signed an agreement for an American loan bearing 2 per cent interest, and Canadian politicians did not venture to grant more generous terms. The main reason, undoubtedly, was that they feared the hostility of Quebec. The person who was toughest with the British negotiators was Louis St Laurent, the Minister of Justice. Here is part of the British High Commissioner's report:

At the Tuesday morning meeting St. Laurent ... said that he was speaking on his own account and in no way making proposals. He spoke of his familiar difficulties in persuading Quebec to give further aid to United Kingdom or in expecting Canadian taxpayers to pay the interest on a loan while we paid none and also continued to receive dividend income from Canadian securities. His idea therefore was that we should pledge all our Canadian securities to cover the total of outstanding liabilities (about 1 billion dollars) and a further credit of 5 hundred million dollars to see us through until the American loan is out of the way ... All the dividend receipts from our Canadian securities were to go as interest on the one and a half billion dollars mentioned ...

The British reply was that they were 'really shocked.'[62] How shocked is suggested by a brief provided for the Chancellor of the Exchequer when he visited Ottawa six months later: 'The French-Canadian element is suspicious of the investment holdings which we still retain. Mr. St. Laurent, the Minister of Justice and a possible next Prime Minister of Canada, spoke of them in terms of Canada paying "tribute" to Great Britain. This is a sensitive topic which is best avoided, but if it is brought up in such a way that it is impossible to avoid comment, it may be helpful to point out that what is happening is that, while British investments in Canada are dwindling, American investments in Canada are rapidly increasing. There will be no point in artificially reducing the volume of tribute to Great

Britain only to see an increasing volume of tribute going to the United States.'[63]

It was an undeniably good point. The estimated value of British capital invested in Canada declined, under Canadian government pressure (above, page 273), from $2,682.8 million in 1939 to $1,668 million in 1946; while in the same period United States capital so invested increased from $4,491.7 million to $5,157 million.[64] It continued to increase thereafter.

The Canadian attitude in the negotiations was summarized by King in the cabinet: he 'emphasized the necessity of finding some method for providing assistance to the United Kingdom which could be understood by the Canadian people on the ground of direct and prompt benefit to Canada.'[65] Many Canadians would have been glad to make a gesture of appreciation for what Britain had done in the fight against Hitler, but clearly this was not considered politic. The agreement finally signed[66] provided for a loan of $1,250 million, to bear interest at 2 per cent and to be repaid in fifty annual instalments beginning in 1951. The interest-free loan made in 1942 (above, page 357) would continue interest-free until 1951. The balance of $425 million owed by the United Kingdom to Canada under the British Commonwealth Air Training Plan agreements was cancelled. The effect of this act of generosity is somewhat reduced by the fact that it was extorted from the Canadian negotiators only by British insistence. The cabinet on February 21 approved proposals which did not include it; and the decision to put it in the package was made on the 25th when it was clear that agreement was not possible on the earlier terms.[67] It may be worth while to quote the terms of the agreement on the purpose of the loan: 'The purpose of the credit is to facilitate purchases by the United Kingdom of goods and services in Canada and to assist in making it possible for the United Kingdom to meet transitional post-war deficits in its current balance of payments, to maintain adequate reserves of gold and dollars and to assume the obligations of multilateral trade.' Since the American loan was for $3,750 million, in proportion to population the Canadian one was much larger.

The loan had in one sense a rough passage through the Canadian Parliament. The group of French-Canadian nationalists who had fought all the wartime measures for financial aid to Britain opposed it tooth and nail, J.-F. Pouliot making speech after speech. They divided the House of Commons on the third reading. The vote against them was 167 to six; but as always there was the feeling of much sympathy for them in the Quebec background. The British High Commission reported that though the

MALCOLM MacDONALD SIGNING THE ANGLO-CANADIAN
FINANCIAL AGREEMENT, 1946
Behind the British High Commissioner are, left to right, Clifford Clark,
Canadian Deputy Minister of Finance; Gordon Munro, British Treasury;
J.L. Ilsley, Canadian Minister of Finance; Mackenzie King

English-language press was 'completely unanimous' in supporting the loan, the French press was less favourable, the clerical and nationalist papers all being hostile, 'largely on the grounds that these amounts, which are unlikely to be repaid are in reality subventions wrung from a poor and industrious Canadian people to support a tottering and degenerating British Empire.' Predictably, the Saint-Jean Baptiste Society made itself heard along the same lines.[68]

Winston Churchill had said he did not become the King's first minister to preside over the dissolution of the British Empire. That dissolution, nevertheless, was about to take place, and the process had begun before Mackenzie King ceased to be Prime Minister of Canada. The last Commonwealth meeting he travelled to England to attend (he did not actually attend it, because his health broke down), that of 1948, had as members the prime ministers of three new Dominions, India, Pakistan, and Ceylon. The Indian Empire had become independent, and been partitioned, the previous year. That was the beginning of a process by which a long succession of British dependencies, great and small, became independent states within the Commonwealth, or, in some cases, outside it.

We have remarked that the gathering of 1937 was the last of the old Imperial Conferences. The new official formula was 'Meetings of Prime Ministers.' The first post-war meeting was in 1946, and it misfired rather badly. Other commitments on both sides of the ocean – the meeting of Parliament and a Dominion-Provincial Conference, in Canada, and the uncertain date of the Paris Peace Conference in Europe – made things difficult. Mackenzie King was not anxious for a Commonwealth meeting in the circumstances, and in finally informing the British Prime Minister of his travel plans he told him that he was not prepared to engage in serious discussion of defence or commercial policy without his Ministers of Defence and Finance to support him.[69] It turned out that the conference broke down into three series of meetings, the Prime Minister of Australia being present for only the first and second, the Prime Minister of South Africa for the second and third, and the Prime Minister of Canada only for the third.[70]

In spite of King's warning, the British ministers laid before the conference the question whether, without suggesting 'contributions to a common pool, nor ... any modification of the present freedom of action of the different members of the Commonwealth,' some means could be found of relieving the United Kingdom of part of her 'defence burden.' Joseph Chamberlain had said something like this forty-four years before. Laurier had offered little comfort then, and King had little to offer now. He said again that he could not discuss this matter in detail at the moment, but he made a general remark:

... in his view, the surest way to win the support of the Dominions was to trust them to accept the obligations which they believed to be natural and right. The experience of the war had proved the wisdom of this course. If there had been a highly centralized policy there might have been a very different response from the Dominions. But if every liberty was at stake, they could be trusted to respond wholeheartedly to the call.

Mr. Mackenzie King believed in the closest co-ordination and closest understanding which could be achieved, but he was not in favour of reversing the tendencies of the last 20 years.

King also pointed out, truly enough, that 'Canada's own obligations were already very much greater than they had been before the war'; everyone understood, presumably, that he was speaking of her delicate relationship with the United States in connection with the joint defence of North America.[71]

We have mentioned that Mackenzie King, though present in London, was unable to attend the Meeting of the Prime Ministers held in October 1948. He remained in his sickbed at the Dorchester Hotel, receiving visitors from the King and Winston Churchill down, and incidentally enjoying *séances* with his favourite English mediums.[72] Louis St Laurent, already chosen as his successor as Liberal leader and hence Prime Minister, was hastily summoned from Canada to take his place. In the conference St Laurent took the traditional Canadian and Liberal line; but it was notable that in a discussion of foreign and military policy, in which Clement Attlee, the British Prime Minister, remarked grimly, 'The Soviet Union had a vested interest in chaos,' he made it clear that Canada was prepared to take part in 'an Atlantic scheme of defence.' (He also said, however, 'Agreement on defence policy and general strategy by all the Commonwealth Governments was not in his view a prerequisite for regional planning.')[73] In a session on Commonwealth consultation St Laurent said he was anxious that it should not appear that co-operation in defence matters was confined to Commonwealth countries: 'It would be quite unrealistic for Canada to agree to any arrangement which precluded her from concerting defence measures with the United States, and the same applied also in the economic sphere. This point found general acceptance ...'.[74] In a communication to the Canadian High Commissioner in Britain in 1946, King had said of the phrase 'Imperial defence': 'This is a phrase that we should like to see dropped from the current vocabulary as it leads to unnecessary misunderstandings and irritations and has little value in relation to the strategic realities of to-day.'[75] The concept of imperial defence was one which, in practice, had had little relevance for Canadian governments as far back as John A. Macdonald's. Now it was definitely obsolete. But in defence generally Canada was now more interested than she had ever been before in time of peace.

TRADE AND DOLLARS

The anxiety with which Canadian planners had looked ahead at the post-war world economy was only too well founded. Six years of war had done such damage that very drastic measures were required to restore a degree of prosperity in Europe; and the British market, so vital to Canada in pre-war days, never did revive in the manner for which Canadian economists had hoped.

'Multilateralism' and 'bilateralism' were words much used in these years. King's telegram to Churchill of February 23, 1945 (above, page 398) had voiced some apprehension lest Britain should go in for 'bilateral deals, and a form of sterling area isolationism,' allowing the shortage of Canadian dollars to influence her away from Canada as a trading partner. The loan negotiated a year later was intended, we have seen, to make it easier for Britain to buy in Canada 'and to assume the obligations of multilateral trade.' Thus Canada formally declared her allegiance to the international trading system that had been associated with the name of Cordell Hull. Nevertheless, in this same year 1946 she herself made an important bilateral agreement – a wheat agreement with the United Kingdom covering the next four years, under which the British government undertook to purchase large quantities of wheat (160 million bushels a year for the first two years, 140 million for the next two) at prices declining from $1.55 per bushel in the first two years to $1.00 per bushel in the final year. This agreement was controversial: the Department of Agriculture, and particularly its Minister, 'Jimmy' Gardiner, were for it, the Department of External Affairs and the Canadian Wheat Board disliked it; the United States also disliked it, and the signing was held up while the matter was discussed with Washington.[76] Other special agreements on supply of foodstuffs to Britain were also made in 1946.[77]

The structure erected in 1946 threatened to collapse in 1947. Britain was using up the American and Canadian loans with unexpected rapidity. Canadians, starved for consumer goods during the war, rushed to buy American manufactures. Canada ran short of United States dollars; and on November 17 the Minister of Finance was forced to announce serious restraints. Pleasure travel to the United States was rationed, restrictions on imports were imposed (they fell mainly on American goods), and a loan of $300 million was obtained from the Export-Import Bank in Washington. These measures were effective, the United States government was understanding, and the restrictions were soon relaxed.[78]

American aid to ruined Europe gave indirect assistance to Canada. In June 1947 General George C. Marshall, the United States Secretary of State, announced the European Recovery Program, the 'Marshall Plan.' Great sums of American money were to be expended in loans and grants to enable European nations to obtain the means of subsistence and to rebuild their economies. This opened up the possibility of some of this money being spent in countries other than the U.S. ('offshore purchases'); if such purchases could be made in Canada it would go far to solve Canada's American dollar problem. But would the United States Congress agree? Ultimately Congress did agree, largely because some commodities, including grain, turned out to be in short supply in the U.S. After Congress acted, in April 1948, the immediate Canadian situation was considerably eased.[79]

During the same months negotiations important to the future of multilateral trade were going on at Geneva. These issued in October 1947 in the General Agreement on Tariffs and Trade, 'authenticated' in the first instance by twenty-three nations. This comprehensive multilateral trade agreement laid down general principles for the conduct of international trade, but it also incorporated 'more than one hundred separate and distinct agreements' worked out between the countries represented at Geneva. These included new Canadian agreements with both Britain and the United States. In the case of the United States, while the new arrangement superseded the trade agreement of 1938, that agreement would come back into force if both nations abandoned GATT The new agreement provided for numerous concessions in duty on Canadian goods entering the United States, from which much was hoped. Canada's preferential arrangements with Britain, long a subject of American hostility, survived the GATT negotiations and were incorporated in a special section of the agreement. The life of the General Agreement was to be three years, but it would continue in force thereafter subject to member nations giving six months' notice of termination. In fact, a generation later GATT continues to exist, though considerably modified. By 1976 its membership had increased to eighty-three nations.[80] It seems evident that the General Agreement, which may be considered a monument to the Roosevelt-Hull concept of international trade, has been found to be a general boon.

In 1948 there was a curious episode when for a moment Canada and the United States seemed to be on the verge of negotiating something like a customs union. This affair is dealt with below (pages 419-25).

DEFENCE OF NORTH AMERICA

At Ogdensburg in 1940 Canada and the United States had drawn together in an unprecedented defence arrangement because of common fear of Germany. Beginning in 1945 they were propelled into joint defence measures from fear of Soviet Russia. This introduced a new complication into Canadian-American relations.

We have seen the Advisory Committee on Post-Hostilities Problems and the Cabinet War Committee agreeing in February 1945 that 'the defence of Canada should be closely co-ordinated with those of the United States after the war,' and have observed that this was in fact a pretty obvious proposition (above, page 378). Co-ordinating the defences in practice was not always easy. The major and the middle power were seldom in full agreement on military measures, partly because they were not in full agreement concerning Russia's probable intentions. Speaking very broadly, Canadian ministers, officials, and officers (and, perhaps, the public) were probably somewhat less disposed than their American opposite numbers to believe that the USSR intended to attack the West; they were rather more inclined to the opinion that Russian truculence was the result of fear, that Soviet policy was basically defensive rather than offensive.[81] On these matters there were, of course, wide differences of opinion among Canadians as among Americans, and gusts of apprehension sometimes shook Ottawa; discussions with Ernest Bevin, the British Foreign Secretary, in November 1947 left Mackenzie King feeling there might be another world war within weeks. This, however, would have happened not because either side had planned it, but as the result of more or less accidental acts resulting from Russian interference with Allied access to Berlin.[82]

The nature of the practical problem with which Canada was likely to be faced in planning joint defence with the U.S. was indicated in June 1945, when at a meeting of the Permanent Joint Board on Defence Major-General Guy V. Henry, the U.S. Army member, presented a statement on the 'continental defence value of the Canadian Northwest,' and on post-war collaboration generally, which indicated that Washington might 'in future decide to request Canada to undertake defence responsibilities, chiefly with respect to the Northwest Staging Route and related weather and communication facilities.' The Canadian conclusion from

Henry's remarks was that the United States might be 'expected to take an active interest in Canadian defence preparations in the future and may indeed exert pressure.'[83] At the next meeting of the Board, in September, the Canadians politely responded, remarking among other things that post-war military collaboration appeared to present no special difficulty, that the Board, being 'Permanent,' would presumably have an important part to play, and that at the moment the Canadian services had no information as to the views of the U.S. Army and Navy on the basic assumptions that must underlie joint planning. In November the Board met again, and the United States members now presented official communications from the Secretary of War and the Secretary of the Navy proposing that steps be taken to revise the joint defence plan ABC-22 (above, page 314) 'in the light of changed world conditions.'[84]

The Cabinet Defence Committee and subsequently the cabinet accepted this proposal, allotting the responsibility for Canadian participation to the Chiefs of Staff 'with the addition of appropriate civilian officials.' These officials emerged in due course as the Secretaries of the Permanent Joint Board and the Cabinet Defence Committee; and the cabinet took the view that arrangements for joint planning should be made through the Permanent Joint Board.[85] The sequel cannot be described in detail here.[86] After an episode in which the Permanent Joint Board on Defence, of which General McNaughton was now chairman of the Canadian section, seemed to show some signs of usurping the functions of the Chiefs of Staff,[87] matters settled down to a more normal routine which produced two important documents: a draft 35th Recommendation of the PJBD, and an 'Appreciation of the Requirements for Canadian-U.S. Security' approved by an international staff committee constituted in accordance with the views of the Canadian cabinet.[88] At these the Canadian civil authorities looked with care. It is evident that they had two main concerns: to ensure that Canada was not committed to a military programme larger than the situation really called for or more expensive than the country could afford; and to ensure that vital decisions remained under political, not military, control.

The 35th Recommendation, in the form it had reached in October 1946, specified the desirability of 'close co-operation' between the two countries' forces in such matters as interchange of personnel, common designs and standards 'as far as practicable' in equipment, organization, training, etc., exchange of observers in exercises and tests of material, reciprocal provision of military, naval, and air facilities, and some other matters. The 'Appreciation' recognized that major invasion of Canada and the United States was impossible for 'at least several years,' but added that 'limited invasion in the north with a view to further operations was possible. 'An effective air defense system' was one fundamental requirement. A new 'Basic Security Plan' replacing ABC-22 was attached to the Appreciation. In July 1946 the Canadian Chiefs of Staff recommended to the Cabinet Defence Committee that the Appreciation and Plan be approved.[89] While the matter remained in abeyance Mackenzie King visited President Truman in Washington on October 28 and they had a general discussion on defence matters, the only special point made by the President being the desire of the U.S. (which had already been made clear) to maintain considerable air forces at Goose Bay, Labrador. King mentioned that Goose Bay was in Newfoundland territory and also took occasion to speak of the need for Canada safeguarding her sovereignty.[90] Subsequently the President sent King, through the U.S. Ambassador in Ottawa, a long document curiously termed an 'oral message'* which went into much more detail.[91] It suggested that the two governments might concur in the 'Appreciation,' and that the Canadian government should give 'further' endorsement of 'joint planning now in progress,' approve the 35th Recommendation, and permit the stationing of 'certain United States Army Air Force units' at Canada's leased base at Goose Bay.

It is worth noting that at this moment of decision Lester Pearson, who had just left the Embassy in Washington to succeed Norman Robertson as Under Secretary of State for External Affairs, presented to King a memorandum of advice[92] which may perhaps reflect the heated atmosphere of the capital where he had lately been working. He wrote in part: 'My own view, for what it may be worth, is that without some fundamental change in the Soviet state system and in the policies and views of its leaders, the U.S.S.R. is ultimately bound to come into open conflict with western democracy. This, of course, does not mean that war is inevitable, because changes and collapse do take place. But without them – and there are few convincing signs of them in Russia – the end must be conflict. The Russian leaders themselves insist on this. We should not make the mistake we made with Hitler, of refusing to take seriously the words those leaders utter for home consumption.' Pearson went on to say that the world situation dictated close co-operation with both Britain and the United States in working out sound combined plans. It was necessary to organize Canada's national strength in 'combination and co-operation with others, primarily, I think, with the United States of America.' His last word was: 'We should examine, with the greatest possible care, our defence plans, to

---

* Apparently Truman had been supposed to hand this to King, but he either forgot it or thought it more tactful not to deliver it.

make sure that they fit into our proper place in this combined effort and are not dictated by merely traditional and possibly outworn concepts.' One is left wondering whether the new Under Secretary of State had not been pretty fully indoctrinated in Washington, and whether he was not delicately suggesting to the Prime Minister that the old unwritten military alliance with Britain was now wholly irrelevant. However, Pearson was not in a position to control the situation. In Ottawa the hand on the lever was still Mackenzie King's.

The day after Pearson wrote this paper the Cabinet Defence Committee met to consider the situation.[93] It heard the Chief of the Air Staff, Air Marshal Leckie, express serious doubts about the way it was developing. He had had a preliminary look at the air defence scheme which the international planning team (with Canadians participating, as usual and inevitably, as junior partners) were producing; and he was troubled by the scale of the planned undertakings and dubious of the strategic concept on which they were based: '... The military view in Washington was that, in any future war, an aggressor would attempt to neutralize the war potential of this continent before embarking on a programme of expansion elsewhere. He did not altogether share this view, and felt that any attacks which might develop would be of a diversionary nature which would not warrant the establishment of an elaborate defence scheme employing our resources in a static role. With this in mind, and, in view of the immense financial outlays involved, it might be more appropriate to adopt measures of more modest proportions.' The committee referred the problem to the full cabinet, which on the two following days held the unprecedented meetings on defence problems already mentioned (above, page 397).

In these meetings[94] Leckie again expressed his doubts, and Brooke Claxton (Minister of Health and Welfare, shortly to be Minister of Defence), who had clearly been impressed by the Air Marshal's argument, urged that a halt should be called before the country was deeply committed. The new Secretary of State for External Affairs, Louis St Laurent, recalled that the British Foreign Secretary, Ernest Bevin, had lately suggested that so far as possible the development of airfields should be carried on on a civilian basis.* The cabinet decided that a 35th Recommendation 'along the lines of the draft submitted' would be favourably considered; but it also agreed that while 'general endorsement could be

---

* The External Affairs portfolio had now been separated from the office of Prime Minister (below, page 414). Bevin had in fact urged the Canadian government to go slow with northern defence measures lest they provoke 'Soviet reactions which would tend to divide the world into two armed camps.'[95]

given to the principle of joint defence planning with the United States,' it could not concur in the draft Appreciation pending discussions between the two governments 'on the diplomatic level'; no decision could be taken about Goose Bay pending those discussions, and discussions with the United Kingdom and Newfoundland; joint defence planning with the U.S. 'should not proceed beyond the present stage' pending the coming discussions and agreement between the governments; and the Canadian Chiefs of Staff should be directed to prepare forthwith a Canadian defence programme taking account of the course of joint planning with the U.S. as well as local defence, Commonwealth relationships, and possible United Nations obligations.

From this point things ran more smoothly. On December 16 and 17 the discussion on the 'diplomatic level' took place in Ottawa, between two national groups of senior officers and officials, including on the U.S. side the Ambassador, Ray Atherton; George Kennan from the State Department, a Russian expert of moderate opinions; and General Henry. Canada was represented by Pearson, Heeney, Air Vice-Marshal W.A. Curtis, and others. Pearson reported to the Prime Minister, 'The most frank and cordial atmosphere prevailed throughout.' General Henry said that in any war within five or six years the threat to North America would be so slight that few of Canada's forces would be required to meet it; after that the threat would in his opinion grow greater. Kennan expressed the view that the Soviet Union could be contained 'by non-provocative defence measures' and firm and fair diplomacy. The Americans urged early action to permit stationing a Very Heavy Bombardment Group of aircraft at Goose Bay shortly, and it was agreed that the matter should be discussed with the United Kingdom High Commissioner in Ottawa at once. On this the Americans got what they wanted. The question of publicity for the 35th Recommendation caused some discussion, the Canadians feeling that since there had been sensational press reports about U.S. involvement in defence projects in the north, a public statement was vital. It was finally agreed that a joint statement should be made containing the substance of the Recommendation and making reference to the Ogdensburg Declaration and obligations under the United Nations.[96]

During 1946 there had also been discussions with the United States about other northern projects, notably weather stations. These stations, and the basis on which they could be maintained to the satisfaction of the United States and without damage to Canadian sovereignty, were the subject of an agreement early in 1947 covering that year and the next; the matter continued to give the diplomats employment.[97]

The joint statement deriving from the 35th Recommendation of the Permanent Joint Board on Defence was finally issued in Ottawa and Washington on February 12, 1947.[98] It was very cautiously phrased, doubtless to the displeasure of the American services. One point is worthy of special comment. Perhaps the most important section of the 35th Recommendation had run, 'adoption, as far as practicable, of common designs and standards in arms, equipment, organization, methods of training and new developments to be encouraged, due recognition being given by each country to the special circumstances prevailing therein.' In spite of the qualifications, this came close to being a precise repudiation of the one written military agreement between Canada and Britain – that relating to uniformity throughout the forces of the Empire which resulted from the Defence Conference of 1909 (Volume 1, page 132). The statement now issued introduced a more definite qualification: 'Encouragement of common designs and standards in arms, equipment, organization, methods of training and new developments. As certain United Kingdom standards have long been in use in Canada, no radical change is contemplated or practicable and the application of this principle will be gradual.' A new 'principle' also made its appearance: 'As an underlying principle all cooperative arrangements will be without impairment of the control of either country over all activities in its territory.'

The statement should be quoted at somewhat greater length. It began:

Announcement was made in Ottawa and Washington today of the result of discussions which have taken place in the Permanent Joint Board on Defence on the extent to which the wartime cooperation between the armed forces of the two countries should be maintained in this postwar period. In the interest of efficiency and economy, each Government had decided that its national defence establishment shall, to the extent authorized by law, continue to collaborate for peacetime joint security purposes. The collaboration will necessarily be limited and will be based on the following principles:

The principles were 'interchange of selected individuals,' 'general cooperation and exchange of observers' in connection with excercises and tests, mutual and reciprocal availability of military, naval, and air facilities in each country, and those just mentioned. '... No treaty, executive agreement or contractual obligation has been entered into. Each country will determine the extent of its practical collaboration in respect of each and all of the foregoing principles. Either country may at any time discontinue collaboration on any or all of them. Neither country will take any action inconsistent with the Charter of the United Nations. The Charter remains the cornerstone of the foreign policy of each.' It was noted that each government had sent a copy of the statement to the Secretary General of the United Nations for circulation to all members.

It would be hard to imagine a document with more saving clauses. It bore the clear hallmark of Mackenzie King. No commitments; or, if commitments had to be made, let them be as few and as limited as possible.

There is no space here to tell in detail the story of Canada's comparatively small involvement in the more-than-epoch-making international drama of atomic energy.*

Her possession of a uranium mine brought Canada into the picture in 1942. In the same year the British-sponsored scientific team which had been working in Cambridge, England, towards the production of an atomic weapon was brought to Montreal. During the Quebec Conference of 1943 Churchill and Roosevelt made an agreement providing for improved collaboration between their countries on the atomic project (at that moment collaboration had virtually ceased). To this Quebec Agreement Canada was not a party; but it set up a Combined Policy Committee of six members, one of whom was to be a Canadian (it is apparent that in effect the plan was for equal representation, and the British chose to give one of their seats to Canada). In the spring of 1944 the Combined Policy Committee decided to undertake the construction of a 'heterogeneous heavy water pilot pile' in Canada as a joint project. This gave employment to the Montreal group, which was reinforced from other sources, particularly Britain. The chosen site was at Chalk River on the Ottawa, and the establishment there may be said to have launched both Britain and Canada into the atomic age. It had, however, no part in the production of the bombs that were dropped on Japan. The main pile at Chalk River did not 'go critical' until July 1947. By that time the senior British scientific personnel had been withdrawn from the Canadian plant in order to get on with establishing one in England – a development which surprised and displeased C.D. Howe, the Minister who had been responsible for the Canadian development from the beginning.[99]

The Combined Policy Committee continued to meet at intervals, grappling with difficult questions of supplies of raw material and exchange of information, chiefly between the British and Americans. In 1948 a tripar-

* It is told in part in James Eayrs' *In Defence of Canada*, Vol. 3: *Peacemaking and Deterrence* (Toronto 1972), chapter 5, and the present writer's *Arms, Men and Governments: The War Policies of Canada, 1939-1945* (Ottawa 1970), Part 8.

tite agreement was made, replacing that concluded at Quebec, which had been so secret that the U.S. Congress first heard of it only in 1947; it provided for a continuation of the CPC, which operated for some years longer.[100]

Not many words need be wasted on the attempt to control atomic energy through the United Nations. This was one of the early UN dreams that faded. Canada favoured international control and joined with Britain and the United States in an initiative pointed that way. And although she had failed of election to the first UN Security Council, the UN General Assembly decreed that the United Nations Atomic Energy Commission should consist of the members of the Security Council plus Canada, because she was at least a potential atomic power. In the commission General McNaughton, the Canadian representative, worked hard for an accommodation between the United States and Russia. In the end, King and St Laurent in Ottawa decided that Canada must support the American position. There was complete deadlock between the two super-powers, and by the end of 1947 it was evident that there would be no international control of atomic energy.[101] The United States monopoly of the bomb ended in 1949 with the first Soviet atomic explosion. Now there was international atomic anarchy, and henceforth the security of the world would depend on the balance of terror.

A word should be said of the fortunes of the St Lawrence Waterway project in the last years of the King era.

In the spring of 1938 the United States put forward a draft treaty intended to take the place of the one defeated by the U.S. Senate in 1934. The King government considered that provincial attitudes made action impossible at that time; but immediately after the outbreak of war the following year Ontario became more friendly to the scheme, with the result that a new international agreement for construction of the water-way was signed in March 1941. But progress in the U.S. Congress was slow, and in 1942 President Roosevelt felt obliged to admit that shorter-term projects were more important to winning the war. Supporters of the seaway kept the issue alive in Congress, but without achieving a success-ful issue. Not until five years after Mackenzie King's retirement was a basis found for the construction of a waterway that would open the Great Lakes to ocean shipping.[102]

WORLD POLITICS AND CANADIAN PERSONALITIES

When the war ended Mackenzie King was nearly seventy-one, and the vitality that had seemed inexhaustible was showing signs of ebbing. His health was not what it had been and he tired easily. He had never been an easy man for his colleagues and subordinates to work with; now they found him increasingly difficult and unpredictable.[103]

Weakening health certainly had something to do with King's decision to separate, at long last, the office of Prime Minister from that of Secretary of State for External Affairs. The necessary legislation was passed early in 1946, and King finally vacated the Secretaryship in September. Louis St Laurent was his choice to head the External Affairs department.[104] The change was overdue, for there had long been more than enough External business to warrant the appointment of a separate minister to handle it. It was inevitable, however, that the Prime Minister – any Prime Minister – should continue to take a close interest in the country's foreign policy, and when the Prime Minister was King there was a definite possibility that the interest would be so close as to make difficulty with the person holding the External portfolio. The change had one consequence which may not have been expected: it certainly contributed to the decline of the general importance of the Department of External Affairs in Ottawa. External's dominance in the government machine had been established in the days of O.D. Skelton. It was due partly to Skelton's own abilities and his personal relationship to Mackenzie King; but it also owed something, as we have said (above, page 10) to the fact that the permanent head of External had immediate and automatic access to the Prime Minister as the political head of his own department. This made the Under Secretary of State for External Affairs the most influential civil servant in Canada. After 1946 this situation no longer existed.

The difficulties the new arrangement could create in the cabinet were painfully illustrated in December 1947. King returned from England to find that in his absence some of his colleagues had agreed to Canada's serving on a 'United Nations Temporary Commission on Korea' which had been set up on American initiative. An agreement that United States troops should take the surrender of Japanese forces in south Korea, and Russian forces perform this function in the north, had resulted in the country being divided at the 38th parallel. The Temporary Commission was supposed to supervise elections throughout the country with a view to setting up a united and independent state from which both occupying powers could then withdraw. The Americans, apparently without consulting the Canadian delegation, nominated Canada as a member, and the delegation, headed by J.L. Ilsley, though not enthusiastic, agreed to act. The Secretary of State for External Affairs, St Laurent, who was also Acting Prime Minister in King's absence, concurred.[105] Nobody thought the matter particularly important. But on December 18, when an order-in-council appointing a Canadian representative to the commission came before the cabinet, King blew up. It seems evident that his old isolationist prejudices had combined with personal pique at not having been consulted.

The Prime Minister said he 'felt a great mistake was being made by Canada being brought into situations in Asia and Europe of which she knew nothing whatever, of interfering with Great Powers without realizing what consequences might be ... We knew nothing about the situation and should keep out of it.' He had now become as hostile to the United Nations as he had once been to the old League; it served, he said, 'mostly the purpose of the Russians who used it for propaganda purposes and the like.' He demanded that the Canadian acceptance of membership on the Commission should be withdrawn. St Laurent and Ilsley politely but firmly opposed him. If these two senior members of the cabinet were repudiated on the insistence of the Prime Minister they would have no course but resignation, but it is not clear from King's diary that he fully realized this in the beginning. The matter dragged on until January 7, when St Laurent made a definite threat of resignation on behalf of both Ilsley and himself. At the same time he suggested that the Commission was authorized to supervise elections in both the northern and southern zones of Korea or not at all; since the Soviets would almost certainly not agree to this, the Commission would have little to do. King grasped at this as a pretext for abandoning his opposition to Canadian representation, and the crisis ended.[106] But it had become pretty clear that it was time for the old Prime Minister to retire.

Tension with Russia had grown steadily. Repeated Soviet use of the veto in the Security Council had largely stultified the operations of the United Nations. Then in February 1948, by a bloodless *coup*, the Communists took over Czechoslovakia. The shock to the West was profound. In the spring the Russians began to interfere with communication through their zone with the Allied sectors of Berlin; in June all rail traffic was halted. War seemed possible unless the Allies abandoned West Berlin. This they would not do; instead, they organized a mass airlift to supply the city, which went on for months. The Russians did not venture to try to stop it, and in time the crisis passed. Canada played no part in the airlift. Her small occupation force in Germany had been withdrawn in the face of British protests. Reports in the British press that she had been asked to provide planes for the lift enraged King and led him on June 30 to tell the cabinet yet once more the story of Chanak. Nevertheless, he recorded: 'I said I felt it was quite certain that if war broke out, between the three great powers and Russia, Canada would wish to come in instantly. The Cabinet agreed with that. They felt that there could be no two views on that score. They were, however, pretty chary about how far they were prepared to go at this time.' King told Parliament that no request for aircraft had been received from Britain, while admitting that there had been some informal conversations. Parliament and the country were not told that after the meeting on June 30 a message had been sent to the High Commissioner in London telling him to let the British know that it would be 'a great embarrassment to us if any request were made for transport planes.'[107] Such was the disorganized state of Canadian policy less than a year before the country signed a treaty of alliance committing it to military action in case of Soviet attack.

The North Atlantic Treaty was not signed until after Mackenzie King had retired, but during the last two years of his administration the country was steadily moving towards participation in some such security arrangement. The hopes – exaggerated they now seem – that had been built on the United Nations had been disappointed, and the western countries turned increasingly to the idea of a regional mutual defence pact among themselves which would serve as a deterrent against Russian attack and ensure that none of them would stand alone if attack came. As early as August 1947 Escott Reid, now a senior officer in the Department of External Affairs, made with his superiors' approval a public speech in which he suggested that 'the peoples of the western world' could create if they chose an international security organization of their own, 'with teeth,' without conflict with the United Nations Charter. The same idea was mentioned officially in a speech by Louis St Laurent to the United Nations General Assembly the following month; and it began to appear in Britain and the United States. In March 1948 the Treaty of Brussels united Britain, France, Belgium, the Netherlands, and Luxembourg in a defensive alliance which became the model for the North Atlantic Treaty Organization. The same month, with the Czechoslovak *coup* under their eyes, the British government proposed to the United States and Canada that the three countries should have their officials meet at once to discuss a mutual assistance pact. Mackenzie King agreed; indeed, when issuing a statement on March 17 welcoming the Brussels treaty, he went so far as to say, 'The peoples of all free countries may be assured that Canada will play her full part in every movement to give substance to the conception of an effective system of collective security by the development of regional pacts under the Charter of the United Nations.'[108]

Nevertheless, when the suggestion was made that the meetings to discuss the pact should be held in Canada, King's old misgivings asserted themselves again. He did not want Canada to seem to be taking the lead;

it might produce awkward 'discussion in Quebec, throughout Canada generally,' perhaps with mention of conscription; Pearson did not 'see that the Big Powers are using us.' It was better that the meetings should be held in the United States.[109] They were; and a year passed before they issued in the North Atlantic Treaty. In the meantime Louis St Laurent was engaged in what he called a 'crusade' to ensure public support for such a treaty. He argued that if war came involving Britain and the United States, Canada would inevitably be involved also, and an alliance would make the defence more effective. It was interesting to see a French-Canadian statesman taking this line, the more so as he felt not wholly certain of support from Mackenzie King.[110] St Laurent's task was eased however by the fact that in his native province of Quebec hostility to Communism in 1948 was more universal than hostility to Nazism had been in 1939; in the cabinet there seems to have been none of the hesitation that had been evident among the French members as the Second World War approached.[111]

The treaty that ultimately emerged bound, in the first instance, twelve nations – Britain, the United States, France, Canada, Belgium, the Netherlands, Luxembourg, Norway, Denmark, Italy, Portugal, and Iceland – to prepare to resist attack, and to consider an armed attack against any of them an attack against them all, to be met by such action as might be necessary, 'including the use of armed force.' (These slightly weasel words were inserted to ensure approval by the United States Senate, which in fact ratified the treaty by a comfortable majority.) The Canadians insisted on putting in an article on non-military co-operation by which the twelve parties undertook, among other things, to 'seek to eliminate conflict in their international economic policies and ... encourage economic collaboration between any or all of them.' This has had little practical significance.[112]

The most notable thing about the treaty was the fact that it represented a remarkable abandonment of traditional isolationist positions by several of the signers. Britain had already renounced her old reluctance to accept binding continental commitments in the Treaty of Dunkirk with France (1947) as well as the Treaty of Brussels; but for the United States the North Atlantic Treaty was a new departure which those who remembered 1919 and the inter-war years found vastly heartening. What of Canada? 'No commitments' was a very old Canadian song. The King government had consistently refused peacetime commitments to Britain – though it had subsequently gone to war by her side and fought beside her through six gruelling years; and more recently it had shown itself very cautious about making commitments to the United States even for the local defence of North America. No one can be fully certain what Mackenzie King would have done had he still been in office when the North Atlantic Treaty finally presented itself for approval; as we have seen, he had become the essence of unpredictability. Nevertheless, it seems very probable that King would have accepted this treaty. He had, we have seen, actually committed himself to its basic principle quite early. And from the Canadian point of view it had special features to commend it. Commitments might be intrinsically undesirable, but these particular commitments were undertaken not to any single country but to a very respectable group of countries including the three with which Canada had her strongest traditional ties. There would still have been hostility – particularly in Quebec – to a defence pact with Britain; there would still have been opposition to an unlimited military alliance with the United States alone; but a general commitment to a group including both these countries, whose object was security against a menace which even French Canada recognized as such, was a different matter.

The North Atlantic Treaty, signed on April 4, 1949, was warmly approved by all parties in the Canadian Parliament, and the irreconcilable isolationists from Quebec mustered only two votes to oppose it. The final approval, indeed, was unanimous.[113] It is perhaps not too much to say that this treaty, to which Canadian statesmanship had made a contribution, marked the coming of age of Canadian foreign policy, and is therefore a suitable place for this account to end.

It remains to pick up a couple of loose ends and to note the final departure from the scene of the man who had dominated Canadian policy for a generation.

Confederation with Newfoundland was not achieved until after Mackenzie King's retirement, but the basis for it was laid while he was still Prime Minister. It was an object which he pursued with characteristic caution but with a good deal of determination. On July 12, 1943, he said in Parliament: 'If the people of Newfoundland should ever decide that they wish to enter the Canadian federation and should make that decision clear beyond all possibility of misunderstanding, Canada would give most sympathetic consideration to the proposal.' The following year instructions prepared for a new Canadian High Commissioner to Newfoundland stated that the first object of Canadian policy there was, 'to overcome the traditional suspicion of Canada in the minds of the people of Newfoundland and to substitute therefor an attitude of confidence and friendship.'[114] Canada, it appeared, was ready for union, but it was vital that the decision should be freely made by the Newfoundlanders. The National

Convention elected in Newfoundland in 1946 to settle the island's future sent delegates to Ottawa in 1947 to discuss a basis of union, and an agreed set of proposals was arrived at. In the second of two referenda in which the people of Newfoundland voted on the possibilities before the colony, in July 1948, 52.34 per cent of the voters supported confederation with Canada as against the alternative – Newfoundland going it alone with responsible government. It was perhaps hardly a decision 'clear beyond all possibility of misunderstanding,' but King decided it was good enough, and negotiations for a final agreement were undertaken at once. At the end of March 1949 Newfoundland became Canada's tenth province, an arrangement which made very good sense in terms both of geography and strategy.[115]

One final incident. The dollar crisis of the autumn of 1947 (above, page 404) led officials of the Canadian Department of Finance to try to produce a long-term scheme to eliminate such troubles. Late in October Hector McKinnon, the veteran negotiator who was Chairman of the Tariff Board, and John Deutsch, Director of the International Economic Relations Division of the Finance Department, approached the State Department in Washington with a proposal for very extensive trade reciprocity – 'a comprehensive agreement involving, wherever possible, the complete elimination of duties.' The American record of the discussion on October 29 states that McKinnon said that the approach had been authorized by the Canadian cabinet.[116] This was clearly an error. The two Canadian officials were fresh from Geneva, where they had conducted the complicated GATT negotiations on behalf of Canada, and from long sessions in Ottawa where they had reported to the Prime Minister and the cabinet (and had been treated by King more or less as returning heroes) and further cabinet discussions on the deepening exchange crisis. It is possible that during these sessions someone suggested to them that, while visiting Washington to discuss measures to meet that crisis, they might make an exploratory approach on a comprehensive trade agreement; but there was certainly no cabinet authority, and the Prime Minister made no mention of the matter in his diary.[117] The official in the State Department with whom they conferred promised to take the matter up with his superiors.

By the end of the year the discussion had reached the point where Woodbury Willoughby, Director of the Commercial Policy Division of the State Department, had become enthusiastic about the project and produced a scheme for a 'modified customs union' which he put before Deutsch. Shortly the Minister of Finance, Douglas C. Abbott, became directly involved. On January 13, 1948, he called on King and told him (King recorded) that

on his last visit to Washington, where he had met [Averill] Harriman, [Robert A.] Lovett, and several others, the Americans themselves had brought up the question of [a] complete reciprocity treaty with Canada. He and the officials of his Department, Clark and Deutsch, had been working on the extension of the present treaties ... The question of a commercial union had come up. I do not know by whom. At all events, it was discounted at once, certainly in Abbott's mind, and I told him would be equally so in mine. That the word 'commercial' would soon be dropped in political discussions and the campaign be on the question of union with the States. However, if a treaty of complete reciprocity, such as in Sir Wilfrid's day, was before the country, [it] would, I told him ... meet with a different kind of reception. The country had learned they had made a mistake in not accepting the treaty in Sir Wilfrid's day. What we had since achieved in reciprocity would have prepared the public mind for a complete reciprocity.

Abbott asked King if he would agree to a discussion 'on the official level on complete reciprocity' going ahead. Such discussion had already been in progress for two and a half months without King, apparently, being aware of it. He now told Abbott to 'lose no time' in pushing it on. 'What Abbott emphasized,' he wrote, 'was that the proposal was not his, but had come from the Americans themselves ... Abbott himself pointed out that this would be the answer to all our present restrictions. If we could get complete reciprocity, he felt we would no longer be dependent on uncertain markets of Europe, which are bound to be uncertain for some time, and that this would give what was needed to maintain, as far as could be maintained, the prosperity of our country.' There would be opposition from manufacturers, especially in Ontario; King 'said he need not mind that.' The Prime Minister summed up in his diary:

The real points were:
(1) The matter having been suggested by the United States;
(2) his own discussion with leading men in finance;
and
(3) strong feeling in Finance Department – Clark, Towers and Deutsch, who were all favourable;
(4) approval of proceedings on official level. My own approval strongly given. It is clear to me that the Americans are losing no opportunity to make their relations as close as possible with our country.[118]

It is clear, of course, that the idea in fact did not originate with the Americans, but was suggested to them by Deutsch and McKinnon. It seems improbable, though it is not quite impossible, that the Americans on higher levels whom Abbott had met had thought of it themselves quite separately.

By March 1948 the negotiators had worked out a detailed plan, the important points of which were 'Immediate removal of all duties by both countries' and 'Prohibition of all quantitative restrictions on imports after 5 years' subject to certain exceptions. In Washington the scheme (marked 'Top Secret') now went up to the Under Secretary of State (Robert Lovett) with a warm recommendation, which suggested that it would 'result in immediate elimination of all Empire preferences granted by Canada, with important political and economic implications for the United States,' while Canada would be able 'simultaneously to make similar offer of free trade to the UK which would lessen likelihood of British opposition to proposal.' There was another argument: 'Postponement would incur a serious risk that conditions would so change that we would lose a unique opportunity to knit the two countries together – an objective of United States policy even since the founding of the Republic.' A detailed plan was suggested for obtaining approval within the administration and by Congress; in Canada, there would probably have to be a general election.[119]

Early in February Mackenzie King had another talk with Abbott, who asked him whether it would be 'all right' for the United States to push on, with the possibility of a treaty reaching Congress before the summer. King wrote: 'I told him he could say that he and I were agreed, that our Government would be prepared to ask Parliament to support a Treaty of the kind, should it be negotiated before mid-summer.' King first showed signs of second thoughts on the subject on March 16, when he told Abbott to read an article on commercial union in the American magazine *Life*. He was 'relieved,' he recorded, when Abbott assured him that what they two had agreed to 'was not any immediate complete free trade but rather trade so arranged as to make possible the gradual integrating of our systems along lines of the Hyde Park Agreement.' On the 22nd King met with two cabinet ministers, St Laurent and Howe, as well as Clark, the Deputy Minister of Finance, and Deutsch and McKinnon. Deutsch explained what was proposed, and King seems to have commented at length, chiefly by way of expressing doubts about the scheme. Timing, he said, would be enormously important. He dwelt on the opposition that might be expected from the Conservatives: 'The cry would be raised at once that it was commercial union that we were after,' and the government would be accused of wanting to separate from Britain. He also wondered about the scheme's possible relationship to the North Atlantic Treaty project, still highly secret. He worried over his own fatigued state, which made him doubt his capacity to carry on an important negotiation: 'I found myself much too cautious and conservative in international matters to feel my views were shared by some of the younger men around me.' And his suspicions of American intentions came flooding back: 'I said I thought I ought to say that I believed the Americans in their attitude were carrying out what I felt was really their policy and had been for many years, of seeking to make this Continent one. That I thought they had long seen that a conflict likely to come would be between Russia and themselves, and that they had felt that their position would be strengthened if they controlled all of North America ... That personally I would rather have Canada kept within the orbit of the British Commonwealth of Nations than to come within that of the United States. That all my efforts had been in that direction.' One wonders what King would have said had he seen that document in which Woodbury Willoughby spoke of 'knitting the two countries together' as 'an objective of United States policy ever since the founding of the Republic.'

Those who listened to King that day must have realized that the free trade scheme's chances of ever passing into law were now slim indeed. It seems evident that the Prime Minister was harking back to the defeat of reciprocity in 1911, which had driven him into the political wilderness for eight years, and that he was no longer confident that the public reaction would be different now. His mind was doubtless essentially made up, but two days later his decision was confirmed in a characteristic manner described in his diary:

I now want to record a quite extraordinary experience which I took to be a perfect evidence of guidance from Beyond. This morning, apropos of nothing but feeling I ought to look at some book, I drew out from my shelves a volume entitled 'Studies in Colonial Nationalism' by [Richard] Jebb.* A book I have not looked at in twenty years ... I found myself looking with interest to the last chapter of all which was entitled 'The Soul of Empire.' Was amazed to see how completely the views there expressed accorded with my own. The desire for fuller independence of the Commonwealth, at the same time preserving the unity of the Empire, etc. ... A true picture.

When I had read them, I had felt they were significant in reference to the proposals being made to me to support the programme of complete freedom

* London 1905

of trade between the United States and Canada which I have felt to be extremely dangerous, specially at this time, as calculated to raise an issue that would be very serious ...

Later in the day King had some discussion on the scheme with his confidential secretary Pickersgill, who, he found, already knew something about it. 'He volunteered the statement that he knew Clark of the Department of Finance felt it was the only way we could come to balance our accounts with the States and was pressing very strongly for something of the kind. He used the expression that we would absolutely be selling the soul of the people, meaning the whole relationship with Britain and the Commonwealth. The use of that word brought at once the title of the chapter I had read in the morning.' Reading that chapter, he concluded, 'was no matter of chance,' and he wrote in his diary: 'I would no more think of, at my time of life and at this stage of my career, attempting any movement of the kind than I would of flying to the South Pole.'[120]

On March 30 King was in Washington and made his position clear to the Ambassador, Hume Wrong. They talked mainly, he recorded, about the impossibility of carrying such an arrangement as was proposed through in a short space of time. But King said that what was at stake was the future of Canada – was it to be part of the Commonwealth or part of the United States? 'I said I felt sure that the long objective of the Americans was to control this Continent. They would want to get Canada under their aegis.' It seemed to King that Wrong was 'a little disappointed that matters were not likely to be proceeded with. I had the same feeling in talking with Pearson. I am afraid most of External Affairs have become imbued with the attention they have received from the Americans and the place the Americans have allowed them to take in the foreground of international affairs.' The following day Wrong wrote the State Department that the ministers concerned in Ottawa had decided that the government was 'not in a position to take immediately a favourable decision' on the trade proposals, and that 'the official talks should be suspended for the time being.' He was at pains, however, to explain that this was not necessarily the end of the matter. The fullest development of trade with the United States might be 'the only firm foundation for Canadian economic stability and prosperity.' The signing of the North Atlantic treaty might be the opportunity for continuing the discussions, and perhaps it might be possible to bring the United Kingdom into them, thereby removing a political obstacle.[121]

This was not, in fact, quite the end. A month later C.D. Howe (Minister of Trade and Commerce) was in Washington, and Wrong took him to see

Lovett. The free trade scheme was evidently still alive in Howe's mind, and he suggested: 'The Prime Minister would be retiring in August [not until November, it turned out] and there would be an election in the spring of 1949.' The procedure would be to put a free-trade plank in the party platform – one including the United Kingdom; then all would be well. Lovett thought this time-table 'would fit in quite well' with the American situation.[122] But Wrong felt obliged to report the matter, Pearson felt obliged to forward Wrong's letter to King, and King spiked Howe's plan very neatly. Confronted with Wrong's letter, Howe claimed that the whole idea was Wrong's, and that he (Howe) had made no suggestion of Canada being ready to make an agreement at any time. (This is not the impression given by the American report of the conversation.) King then told Pearson firmly that the American government should be advised at once of the true position: 'I told Pearson that while I might miss to be the head of the Government, I would never cease to be a Liberal or a British citizen and if I thought there was a danger of Canada being placed at the mercy of powerful financial interests in the United States, and if that was being done by my own party, I would get out and oppose them openly. It is only too clear that Clark with McKinnon and Deutsch and Towers of the Bank of Canada have all got it into their heads that this is the only way to balance trade with the United states.'[123] This, needless to say, was the absolute and final end. King had found a way to extend his power beyond his impending departure. No Liberal was prepared to face the prospect of William Lyon Mackenzie King emerging from retirement to oppose the party in a general election. Free trade was, for the nonce, forgotten; and the country survived.

The reader will note that following his change of heart King, within a few months of retiring, scotched the free-trade plan single-handed. In the cabinet, Abbott, Howe, perhaps in lesser degree St Laurent, his successor as Prime Minister; in External Affairs, Pearson and Wrong; in Finance, Clark, McKinnon, Deutsch, all favoured the scheme; and King beat them all. Such is the power of a Prime Minister; such was the obstinacy of Mackenzie King. The reader may also have noticed the Macdonaldian touch. Sir John had said in 1891, in his last campaign, *à propos* of unrestricted reciprocity. 'As for myself, my course is clear. A British subject I was born – a British subject I will die ...' King's 'British citizen' may have been a conscious or unconscious echo of those famous words. The old autonomist went down with the Union Jack – or, at any rate, the Red Ensign – flying. Some might have thought this incongruous; no such idea would have occurred to Mackenzie King. As for King's belief that he had been guided from the Beyond, it is pretty evident that his mind was made up before he took down Jebb's old book. He had got his guidance where many people get it – from the past, and specifically from his own painful experience in Laurier's day, when the member for North Waterloo lost his seat fighting for reciprocity. (Perhaps, too, he thought of that earlier party misfortune in 1891.) The past was very much with the old man in these last days of his power, and he cherished the British symbols at a time when the British Empire he had known was in fact coming to an end.

No one has yet achieved an adequate estimate of Mackenzie King, and this book is scarcely the place to attempt one. Nevertheless, it would hardly be proper to end a survey of Canadian external policies in his time without looking back at the man and his influence.

It is interesting that no serious student of King's career, and virtually no Canadian of any sort, has ventured to call him a great man. Norman Robertson, a highly intelligent person who worked closely with King for many years, is recorded as saying, when he heard of his death in 1950, 'I never saw a touch of greatness in him.'[124] Yet King was Prime Minister for twenty-one years; during that period Canada made remarkable advances; and he can hardly be denied some share of the credit. He was not the creator of Canadian 'nationhood.' The foundations for that had been well and truly laid by the Canadian Corps of the First World War and by the Borden government; but King presided over the process by which a British Dominion with uncertain and shaky international status came to be recognized, and to recognize itself, as an undoubted independent nation – in a modest way, a power in its own right. The gradual process that transformed the self-governing colony of 1914 into the relatively confident nation-state that emerged from the Second World War was never ratified by a referendum or submitted to the voters in a general election; but there is no doubt that the overwhelming majority of Canadians came to approve of it. French Canada of course was glad to see the ties with Britain slackening; the rest of the country, while in general always friendly to the British connection, thought the transition from colony to nation natural and inevitable. Within the span of a lifetime there was a remarkable change of outlook. Canadians of 1914, outside of Quebec, thought of themselves as citizens of the Empire, at least as much as citizens of Canada. A generation later Mackenzie King's Canadian Citizenship Act of 1946 seemed quite sensible legislation; and a little after King's time, in 1964, the new flag without the Union Jack, after some noise in Parliament, won general acceptance with remarkably little difficulty. This long development was in accordance with King's philosophy (though it will be remembered that in the matter of the flag he preferred the Red Ensign); and while it cannot be said that he was wholly or even mainly responsible for it, he certainly did much to encourage it. His policies were the policies which the Canadian people as a whole were, in the long run, disposed to make their own.

The ancient problem of national unity was always before King's eyes. In his own time people in English Canada sometimes grew a little bored with his endless talk about it. Today, with the problem in a grimly acute phase, they are perhaps readier to take it seriously and to do justice, in retrospect, to King's relative success in dealing with it. We have suggested that taking the country into the Second World War united was the greatest achievement of his life. Bringing the country through the war, one cannot say without serious 'racial' difficulties, but at least without troubles as bad as those of 1917-18, was also no small achievement; though he made many enemies while about it.

With another man, or perhaps in another country, this sort of record might be accepted as the credentials of greatness. That Canadians have denied greatness to King has perhaps been the result of his personality and his style rather than of his policies. His staff, including Robertson, were exposed daily to the man's innumerable pettinesses and his vast ego; they were unlikely to think him a hero. The public were only too well acquainted with his painful lack of colour, his appalling verbosity, his embarrassing failure to rise to occasions (his war speech of September 8, 1939, is a sad example). His obfuscations and circumlocutions are remembered ('Not necessarily conscription, but conscription if necessary' was perhaps the most famous).* His prose style was as undistinguished as his person. His greatest triumphs were won, not by bold initiatives and dashing leadership, but by the tactics of caution and delay. (Those tactics were also used by John A. Macdonald, who is generally remembered as a 'great' Canadian; but Macdonald had a different personality.)

Research in his extraordinary diaries has not helped King's reputation. That he has been shown to have patronized prostitutes in his youth has probably done him no harm – on the contrary, it has made him a little more human than before; some very eminent people have been spiritualists; but who can impute greatness to a man who sang hymns to his terrier as it expired, or who visited teacup-readers in earnest search for revelation? It seems very unlikely that King's historical image will ever overcome these handicaps to the point where his countrymen will see him as cast in a heroic mould; but it will be surprising if as time passes his smallnesses and eccentricities do not become less prominent in the public mind than his solid achievements.

* House of Commons, June 10, 1942; almost always misquoted.

EPILOGUE

The story of Canadian external relations after 1948 can better be written by some other historian when the records are all open. It will be very different from that related in this volume and its predecessor.

It cannot, unfortunately, be said that the Age of Conflict is over. The years since the Second World War have witnessed constant violence and bloodshed in many parts of the world. At least, however, there has been no Third World War – yet. The nuclear balance of terror has so far operated to prevent it; one hopes that the common sense of most will be powerful enough to continue to prevent it. Since 1948 Canadian armed forces have fought in one actual war, under the United Nations flag in Korea in 1950-3; they have also been involved in 'peacekeeping' operations in various troubled countries, and have contributed to maintaining the defensive shield of the Western alliance. Canadian diplomatic influence was probably at its peak in the days – now long past – when the F-86 Sabre was the best fighter aircraft in the world, and Canada had an air division of twelve squadrons of Sabres deployed under the North Atlantic Treaty Organization in Europe. A strange contrast this with the 'no commitments' policy associated with the name of Mackenzie King!

The Empire-Commonwealth, which plays so great a part in these volumes, has changed and declined. The Empire is no more; the Commonwealth is still with us, but even the most crusted British Tory has finally abandoned any idea of using it as an instrument of international power. The days of the old Imperial Conferences, when the small group of heads of governments was photographed decorously arranged by seniority, with the United Kingdom always in the Number One position and Canada always Number Two, are gone; when the leaders assemble nowadays the front row is full of happy black and brown faces, the Prime Minister of the United Kingdom is somewhere in the rear. (This was notably the case in 1961, when however the Canadian Prime Minister of the day somehow managed to make the front rank near the Queen.)[1] The modern Commonwealth is a multi-racial community whose chief political function seems to be that of reconciling differences between and within its African and Asian members, a valuable role but one of rather secondary importance to Canada. The British armed forces, on which Canada's modelled themselves so long, have shrunk to the point where they are scarcely important in the world balance of power. The once-splendid Royal Navy is puny by comparison with the naval forces of the superpowers.

Relations with what our grandfathers called the great republic to the south dominate the Canadian scene even more than they did in Mackenzie King's day. Canada now has dozens of missions in capitals around the globe, but the posts that matter most to her are the Canadian Embassy in Washington and the United States Embassy in Ottawa. In the period 1867 to 1948 Canada had two great 'trading partners,' the United Kingdom and the United States. Today Britain has fallen into the third position, Japan, the enemy of 1941-5, having moved ahead of her. (Indeed, in exports to Canada she ranks fourth – behind Venezuela, which sends oil.) But Japan, and Britain, and Venezuela, and all the other countries of the world together, account for only about one-third of Canada's trade; the other two-thirds are with the United States.[2] It is hardly too much to say that Canada now trades with one country. She sells great quantities of wheat to China and Russia as the state of the market dictates; but even these huge transactions, a comparatively recent phenomenon, are small by comparison with the normal tides of commerce that roll north and south across the undefended border. And the growing figures of American investment in Canada, once contemplated by Canadians with complacent satisfaction, have lately become a source of acute apprehension.

The emergence of the United States from its ancient isolation, and its decision to play an active part as a world power, were applauded by Canadians, but have created complications for them. One of the secondary effects of the long Vietnam war, which caused so many miseries, was to help to poison the wells of Canadian-American relations. The violent attacks on United States policy made by Americans themselves were echoed in Canada and added to the hostility engendered by economic complaints. (Nowadays, we import even our anti-Americanism from the United States.) Cultural pressures from south of the border, powerful for many generations, are even stronger in the age of television. Mackenzie King near the end of his career, contemplating the whole situation, wondered whether absorption was Canada's fate: 'It might be inevitable for us to have to submit to it – being so few in numbers and no longer able to look to Britain for protection.'[3] But he did not like the idea, and it seems that few of his countrymen today like it either; although it seems also that the great majority of them remain friendly to the great, floundering, usually amiable colossus alongside. The decline of the British Empire, however, has been, on balance, no blessing for Canada. For her the days of the Pax Britannica were a comfortable time. As the reader of this book knows, Canada could usually, in the end, get what she wanted out of London. In the last quarter of the twentieth century Canadian influence in Washington is a rather more uncertain commodity.

A constant theme in this book has been the effect of Canada's 'bicultural' character upon her external policies. (There are far more cultures than two in Canada today; but politically the country remains divided between English and French – or would it be truer to say, between the French and the rest?) We have remarked that during our period the 'English' view of Canadian policy has come steadily closer to the 'French' view: the English-speaking part of the country has come to hold in these matters more 'distinctively Canadian' opinions than it held when the British Empire was in flower. One might have expected this to result in a more united country. So far, however, this has not been the case. In Canada as in other places, particularistic nationalism has lately flared up in extreme forms. A separatist movement in Quebec threatens to disrupt the nation that French and English Canadians created in 1867, and in which they have since lived together in a fair degree of amity. Even in the West separatist talk is heard. Canadian diplomats abroad find themselves being asked politely whether, or when, Canada is going to break up; and Americans wonder what their country's attitude should be to this curiously uncharacteristic development in the adjoining peaceable kingdom. Mackenzie King was fond of saying that a statesman's highest achievement was often found not in the things he accomplished but in those he prevented. Whether Canadian statesmanship, and Canadian common sense, are equal to preventing the destruction of Canada, is the greatest question that confronts the country today.

CANADIAN EXTERNAL TRADE:
STATISTICS OF IMPORTS AND EXPORTS, 1921-48

Canadian exports to the United Kingdom, the United States, and other countries

Year	Exports to United Kingdom	Per cent Can. exports to U.K. to total Can. exports	Exports to United States
	$'000		$'000
1921	312,845	26.3	542,323
1922	299,361	40.4	292,588
1923	379,067	40.7	369,080
1924	360,057	34.4	430,707
1925	395,843	37.0	417,417
1926	508,237	38.5	480,199
1927	446,872	35.6	468,434
1928	410,691	33.3	483,700
1929	429,730	31.4	504,161
1930	281,745	25.1	515,049
1931	219,246	27.4	349,660
1932	174,043	29.0	257,770
1933	184,361	34.9	197,424
1934	288,582	43.3	220,072
1935	290,885	38.4	304,721
1936	321,556	37.9	360,302
1937	407,996	38.4	435,014
1938	409,411	38.3	423,131
1939	325,465	36.0	375,939
1940	508,095	43.0	442,984
1941	658,228	40.6	599,713
1942	741,717	31.4	885,523
1943	1,032,647	34.8	1,149,232
1944	1,235,030	35.9	1,301,322
1945	963,238	29.9	1,196,977
1946	597,506	25.8	887,941
1947	751,198	27.1	1,034,226
1948	686,914	22.3	1,500,987

(Source: *Canada Year Book*, 1940, 1942, and 1950)

Per cent Can. exports to U.S. to total Can. exports	Exports to other countries	Total exports	Year
	$'000	$'000	
45.6	333,995	1,189,163	1921
39.5	148,290	740,240	1922
39.6	183,303	931,451	1923
41.2	254,585	1,045,351	1924
39.0	255,806	1,069,067	1925
36.4	332,130	1,320,568	1926
37.3	338,861	1,254,168	1927
39.2	339,512	1,233,903	1928
36.8	434,367	1,368,259	1929
46.0	323,462	1,120,258	1930
43.7	230,835	799,742	1931
42.9	168,217	600,031	1932
37.4	146,278	528,064	1933
33.0	157,298	665,954	1934
40.3	161,019	756,625	1935
42.4	167,171	849,030	1936
41.0	218,170	1,061,181	1937
39.5	237,685	1,070,228	1938
39.9	225,557	926,962	1939
37.5	227,874	1,178,953	1940
37.0	363,062	1,621,003	1941
37.5	736,533	2,363,773	1942
38.7	789,596	2,971,475	1943
37.8	903,601	3,439,953	1944
37.2	1,058,116	3,218,331	1945
38.4	826,769	2,312,216	1946
37.3	989,478	2,774,902	1947
48.8	887,537	3,075,438	1948

Canadian imports from the United Kingdom,
the United States, and other countries

Year	Imports from United Kingdom	Per cent imports from U.K. to total imports	Imports from United States
	$'000		$'000
1921	213,973	17.3	856,176
1922	117,135	15.7	515,958
1923	141,330	17.6	540,989
1924	153,586	17.2	601,256
1925	151,083	19.0	509,780
1926	163,731	17.6	608,618
1927	163,939	15.9	687,022
1928	186,435	16.7	718,896
1929	194,041	15.3	868,012
1930	189,179	15.2	847,442
1931	149,497	16.5	584,407
1932	106,371	18.4	351,686
1933	86,466	21.3	232,548
1934	105,100	24.2	238,187
1935	111,682	21.4	303,639
1936	117,874	20.9	319,479
1937	129,507	19.3	393,720
1938	145,008	18.1	487,279
1939	115,636	17.6	412,476
1940	161,216	14.9	744,231
1941	219,419	15.1	1,004,498
1942	161,113	9.8	1,304,680
1943	134,965	7.7	1,423,672
1944	110,599	6.3	1,447,226
1945	140,517	8.9	1,202,418
1946	201,433	10.4	1,405,297
1947	189,370	7.4	1,974,679
1948	299,502	11.4	1,805,763

Per cent imports from U.S. to total imports	Imports from other countries	Total imports	Year
	$'000	$'000	
69.0	170,008	1,240,158	1921
69.0	114,710	747,804	1922
67.4	120,259	802,579	1923
67.3	138,523	893,366	1924
64.0	136,068	796,932	1925
65.6	154,978	927,328	1926
66.6	179,930	1,030,892	1927
64.9	203,624	1,108,956	1928
68.6	203,625	1,265,679	1929
67.9	211,651	1,248,273	1930
64.5	172,708	906,612	1931
60.8	120,445	578,503	1932
57.2	87,369	406,383	1933
54.9	90,510	433,798	1934
58.1	107,108	522,431	1935
56.8	125,364	562,719	1936
58.6	148,647	671,875	1937
61.0	166,781	799,069	1938
62.7	130,115	658,228	1939
68.7	176,502	1,081,949	1940
69.4	224,874	1,448,791	1941
79.3	178,450	1,644,243	1942
82.1	176,439	1,735,076	1943
82.3	201,073	1,758,898	1944
75.8	242,840	1,585,775	1945
72.0	320,549	1,927,279	1946
76.7	409,895	2,573,944	1947
68.5	531,681	2,636,946	1948

EXPORTS FROM CANADA TO THE UNITED KINGDOM AND THE UNITED STATES: SELECTED IMPORTANT COMMODITIES, 1928-48

This table continues the similar one in Volume I, with modifications to meet changing conditions. The years chosen reflect the situation on the eve of the Depression, on the eve of the Second World War, and at the end of the period. The general course of trade throughout the period is illustrated in Appendix A, where the great temporary expansion of the war years, not shown here, is observable. Manufactured articles missing from this table were prominent in the war years; notable among them were automobiles, which were negligible among Canadian exports in peacetime at this period. The dominance of the great staples, particularly wheat and newsprint, continues to be marked; and the positive and negative influence of successive United States tariffs is evident.

Selected Canadian exports to the United Kingdom and the United States, 1928-48 (values in Canadian dollars)

	1928		1938		1948	
	U.K.	U.S.	U.K.	U.S.	U.K.	U.S.
Fishery products	5,418,787	13,973,579	6,074,628	12,930,414	1,811,893	57,697,742
Cattle	130,140	12,843,917	1,590,153	12,090,329		61,563,904
Furs	9,185,200	14,335,751	9,328,888	4,627,579	7,965,968	15,615,058
Cheese	17,827,648	2,444,452	11,862,240	558,199	11,085,099	47,796
Bacon and hams	10,241,395	1,481,300	36,622,079	551,926	67,844,842	2,497
Planks and boards	7,460,920	42,519,884	23,106,201	14,178,502	43,888,185	127,947,843
Pulpwood		15,182,842	33,315	11,817,955	279,438	42,237,021
Newsprint	2,889,786	118,404,904	4,709,966	99,588,555	5,319,660	340,334,045
Wheat	244,816,036	9,503,662	89,793,196	1,182,452	196,533,828	6,608,490
Wheat flour	20,247,022	46,357	13,517,262	175,244	61,640,100	4,696
Whisky	123,796	18,380,070	117,835	18,500,716	550,261	23,254,341
Nickel	5,784,572	7,132,350	29,605,514	19,057,109	12,626,831	56,318,271
Precious metals*	73,033	13,912,332	10,976,585	100,460,845	11,276,570	13,795,573

* Includes gold for 1928 and 1938, but not in 1948.
(Source: *Canada Year Book*, 1930, 1940, 1950)

ABBREVIATIONS

BT	Board of Trade
CAB	Cabinet
CAR	*Canadian Annual Review of Public Affairs*
CHA	Canadian Historical Association
CHR	*Canadian Historical Review*
CID	Committee of Imperial Defence
CO	Colonial Office
CYB	*Canada Year Book*
DCER	*Documents on Canadian External Relations*
FO	Foreign Office
FRUS	*Foreign Relations of the United States*
GATT	General Agreement on Tariffs and Trade
IJC	International Joint Commission
MG	Manuscript Group
PAC	Public Archives of Canada
PC	Privy Council (used in numbering orders-in-council)
PJBD	Permanent Joint Board on Defence
PRO	Public Record Office (London)
RG	Record Group
T	Treasury
UNRRA	United Nations Relief and Rehabilitation Administration
USSR	Union of Soviet Socialist Republics
WO	War Office

REFERENCES

CHAPTER 1: MACKENZIE KING AND THE REVERSAL OF POLICY

1 R. MacGregor Dawson, *William Lyon Mackenzie King: A Political Biography*, Vol. 1: *1874-1923* (Toronto 1958), p. 113
2 C.P. Stacey, ed., *Historical Documents of Canada*, Vol. 5: *The Arts of War and Peace* (Toronto 1972), pp. 36-43
3 J.W. Pickersgill and D.F. Forster, *The Mackenzie King Record*, Vol. 2: *1944-45* (Toronto 1968), p. 87
4 December 4, 1921, Stacey, ed., *The Arts of War and Peace*, pp. 76-7
5 October 4, 1921, ibid., pp. 72-6
6 J. Murray Beck, *Pendulum of Power: Canada's Federal Elections* (Scarborough, Ont. 1968), p. 155
7 Ibid., pp. 157-61
8 Stacey, ed., *The Arts of War and Peace*, pp. 32-6. See W.L. Morton, *The Progressive Party in Canada* (Toronto 1950).
9 C.P. Stacey, *Mackenzie King and the Atlantic Triangle* (Toronto 1976), pp. 16-19, 31-2
10 King Diary, Public Archives of Canada [PAC], January 1-14, 1919. See C.P. Stacey, *A Very Double Life: The Private World of Mackenzie King* (Toronto 1976), pp. 118
11 King Diary, particularly December 2, 1921. Stacey, *A Very Double Life*, pp. 118-38. H. Blair Neatby, *William Lyon Mackenzie King*, Vol. 2: *The Lonely Heights, 1923-1932* (Toronto 1963), pp. 198-9
12 Maurice Pope, ed., *Public Servant: The Memoirs of Sir Joseph Pope* (Toronto 1960), pp. 290-1
13 R.S. Bothwell, 'Loring Christie: The Failure of Bureaucratic Imperialism' (Ph.D. thesis, Harvard University, 1972), pp. 324-34
14 Borden Papers, PAC, folio 148398
15 Borden Diary, May 12, 1922, quoted in Bothwell, 'Loring Christie,' pp. 327-8

16 Crerar to King, February 17, 1923, King to Crerar, February 23, 1923, T.A. Crerar Papers, Queen's University. I owe this reference to Donald M. Page.

17 Christie to Borden, March 13, 1923, Borden Papers, folios 148073-4

18 Christie to Rowell, May 29, 1923, Christie Papers, PAC, MG 30, E 15, vol. 3

19 King Diary, September 14, 1939

20 See the correspondence between Skelton and Laurier, 1918-19, in Laurier Papers, PAC, vols. 696-729. On Skelton generally, see Norman Hillmer, 'O.D. Skelton: the scholar who set a future pattern,' *International Perspectives*, September-October 1973.

21 Skelton to King, September 24, 1911, King Papers, PAC, J 1, vol. 19. Correspondence re prices report in same volume.

22 *Canadian Bookman*, April 1919. Ramsay Cook kindly called this reference to my attention.

23 *The Canadian Club Year Book, 1921-1922* (Ottawa 1922), pp. 58-69

24 W.A. Mackintosh, 'O.D. Skelton,' in R.L. McDougall, ed., *Canada's Past and Present, A Dialogue* (Toronto 1967), p. 69

25 King Diary, August 27, 1924

26 J.W. O'Brien, Public Records Section, PAC, to the author, June 27, 1974. PC 105, approved January 18, 1924

27 Pope, ed., *Public Servant*, p. 292. Telegram, King to Skelton, July 7, 1923, King Papers, J 1, vol. 95

28 J.W. Pickersgill, *The Mackenzie King Record*, Vol. 1: *1939-44* (Toronto 1960), 6

29 King Diary, September 11, 1923, August 27, 1924

30 Skelton to King, October 13, 1922, King Papers, J 4, vol. 60. This passage was first called to my attention by J.P. Sellers.

31 King Diary, e.g., July 18, 1895, February 6, 1917

32 Ibid., December 17, 1934

33 Ibid., January 25, 1944

34 Ibid., December 30, 1942

35 Information from Norman Hillmer, who has examined the records in the India Office Library, London.

36 To Adam Shortt, March 1, 1902, Adam Shortt Papers, Queen's University Archives. I owe this reference also to Mr Hillmer.

37 Vincent Massey, *What's Past is Prologue: The Memoirs of the Right Honourable Vincent Massey, C.H.* (Toronto 1963), p. 135

38 November 14, 1938

39 *Canadian Club Year Book, 1921-1922*, pp. 112-27. King Diary, April 8, 1922

40 Sir Charles Lucas, ed., *The Empire at War*, 5 vols. (London 1921-6), 2:294. The words are Lucas's own.

41 *Canada Year Book* [CYB], 1920, p. 345

42 M.C. Urquhart and K.A.H. Buckley, eds., *Historical Statistics of Canada* (Cambridge 1965), p. 463

43 Ibid., p. 14. These figures are on the basis of the definition of 'rural' and 'urban' adopted in 1956.

44 W.T. Easterbrook and Hugh G.J. Aitken, *Canadian Economic History* (Toronto 1958), pp. 519-20
45 A.W. Currie, *The Grand Trunk Railway of Canada* (Toronto 1957). Stacey, ed., *The Arts of War and Peace*, pp. 237-40
40 Stacey, ed., *The Arts of War and Peace*, pp. 227-8, 244-5
47 *Canadian Annual Review* [CAR], 1923, pp. 83-84
48 CYB, 1938, pp. xxxiv-xxxv
49 A.J.P. Taylor, *English History, 1914-1945* (Oxford 1965), pp. 206-8
50 King Diary, September 27, 1920
51 James Eayrs, *In Defence of Canada*, Vol. 1: *From the Great War to the Great Depression* (Toronto [1964]), pp. 168-72. Gilbert Tucker, *The Naval Service of Canada*, 2 vols. (Ottawa 1952), 1:327-8
52 12-13 George V, c. 34; Stacey, ed., *The Arts of War and Peace*, p. 524
53 Stacey, ed., *The Arts of War and Peace*, p. 523
54 *Canadian Club Year Book, 1921-1922*, p. 126
55 Notably, David Walder, *The Chanak Affair* (London 1969); Lord Beaverbrook, *The Decline and Fall of Lloyd George* (London 1963); Harold Nicolson, *Curzon: The Last Phase, 1919-1925* (London 1934); and Martin Gilbert, *Winston S. Churchill*, Vol. 4: *1916-1922* (London 1975). On Canadian aspects, Dawson, *King*, pp. 407-23, and G.P. de T. Glazebrook, *History of Canadian External Relations*, 2 vols., rev. ed. (Toronto 1966), 2:63-9. Documents in Stacey, ed., *The Arts of War and Peace*, pp. 418-23, and Lovell C. Clark, ed., *Documents on Canadian External Relations*, Vol. 3: *1919-1925* (Ottawa 1970) [DCER, 3] 74-84.
56 Summary, G.M. Gathorne-Hardy, *A Short History of International Affairs, 1920 to 1934* (London 1934), pp. 108-15; Bernard Lewis, *The Emergence of Modern Turkey* (London 1961), chapter 8
57 Conclusions of cabinet 49 (22), September 15, 1922, 4 p.m., PRO, CAB 23/31 (PAC, microfilm reel B-3850)
58 Secretary of State for Colonies to Governor General, King Papers, MG 26, J 1, vol. 81. On timing, Secretary of State for Colonies to Governor General, January 27, 1923, ibid., MG 26, J 4, vol. 60
59 *The Times Weekly Edition* (London), November 16, 1922
60 Secretary of State for Colonies to Governor General, January 27, 1923, King Papers, MG 26, J 4, vol. 60
61 It is to be found in *The Times* (London), September 18, 1922, and in Winston S. Churchill, *The Aftermath* (New York, 1929), pp. 452-4.
62 *The Times Weekly Edition*, November 16, 1922
63 Beaverbrook, *Decline and Fall of Lloyd George*, pp. 101-2
64 King Diary, May 19, 1944
65 Conclusions of Cabinet 49 (22), September 15, 1922, 4 p.m., PRO, CAB 23/31. Official statement, *The Times*, September 20, 1922. Stephen W. Roskill, *Hankey: Man of Secrets*, 3 vols. (London 1970-4), 2:284. Conferences, CAB 23/39 (PAC, reel B-2851)

66 Nicolson, *Curzon*, pp. 270-7. C.L. Mowat, *Britain between the Wars, 1918-1940* (London 1956), pp. 116-19. Cf Gathorne-Hardy, *Short History*, p. 114

67 King Diary, 'Imperial and Economic Conference 1923,' October 20, 1923

68 Memos, F.A. McGregor to [King], n.d., and F.L.C. Pereira to Sladen, January 23, 1923, both in King Papers, J 4, vol. 60 (folios C 46238 and unnumbered). King Diary, September 17, 1922

69 King Diary, September 16 and 17, 1922

70 Ibid., September 17, 1922

71 Governor General to Secretary of State for Colonies, September 17, 1922, King Papers, J 1, vol. 81

72 September 17, 1922

73 King Diary, September 18, 1922

74 DCER, 3: 76-8

75 Ibid. King Diary, September 18, 1922

76 Governor General to Secretary of State for Colonies, Prime Minister to Prime Minister, September 18, 1922, King Papers, J 1, vol. 81. DCER, 3:78

77 DCER, 3:78

78 Dawson, *King*, p. 411. Nicholas Mansergh, *The Commonwealth Experience* (London 1969), pp. 218-19. On Squires, *The Times* (London), September 19, 1922. On Smuts, King in *Debates*, House of Commons, June 9, 1924 (p. 2975). There seems to be no reference to Chanak in W.K. Hancock, *Smuts: The Fields of Force, 1919-1950* (Cambridge, 1968).

79 Conference of Ministers, 11:30 a.m., September 29, 1922, CAB 23/31

80 Text of Mudania agreement, *The Times* (London), October 14, 1922

81 Text of Baldwin's speech, G.M. Young, *Stanley Baldwin* (London 1952), pp. 40-2

82 Conclusions of cabinet 48 (22), September 7, 1922, PRO, CAB 23/31

83 Roskill, *Hankey*, 2:283-5

84 King Diary, October 24, 1922

85 Sifton to Dafoe, December 14, 1922, Ramsay Cook, ed., *The Dafoe-Sifton Correspondence, 1919-1927* (Altona, Man. 1966), pp. 126-30

86 King Diary, September 26, 1922

87 Ibid., January 5, 1922

88 CAR, 1922, pp. 181-4. For *Le Droit*, see the survey of opinion in *The Times*, September 20, 1922.

89 King Diary, September 23, 1922

90 CAR, 1922, p. 184

91 Sifton to Dafoe, September 18 and October 4, 1922, Cook, ed., *Dafoe-Sifton Correspondence*, pp. 121-4

92 King Diary, September 22, 1922

93 Their cables to King are printed in Glazebrook, *History of Canadian External Relations*, 2:65-6.

94 CAR, 1922, p. 184

95 *Mail and Empire* (Toronto), September 23, 1922 (in Stacey, ed., *The Arts of War and Peace*, p. 423)

96 Roger Graham, *Arthur Meighen: A Biography*, Vol. 2: *And Fortune Fled* (Toronto 1963), chapter 8

97 12-13 George V, c. 49, June 28, 1922. See *Debates*, House of Commons, June 24, 1922.

98 CAR, 1922, p. 185, and King Diary, September 23, 1922. The *Review* is of course in error in stating that the statement was made in Parliament (which was not in session).

99 See, for example, King Diary, March 7, 1925.

100 *Globe* (Toronto), July 13, 1922. Pope memo, September 25, 1920, DCER, 3:898

101 *Globe*, July 13, 1922, and *Mail and Empire*, same date. Documents on the trip, King Papers, J 4, vol. 58, file 370

102 *Mail and Empire*, July 13 and 14, 1922

103 Stacey, *Mackenzie King and the Atlantic Triangle*, pp. 39-45

104 Canadian confidential print, King Papers, J 4, vol. 58, file 370: Governor General to Secretary of State for Colonies (Prime Minister to Prime Minister), August 8, 1922; Secretary of State for Colonies to Governor General (Prime Minister to Prime Minister), October 19, 1922. Colonial Office minute by E.J.H. Hardinge, August 10, 1922, PRO, CO 42/1041 (PAC, microfilm reel B-3368)

105 DCER, 3:905-15

CHAPTER 2: THE REVERSAL COMPLETED, 1922-25

1 W.N. Medlicott, Douglas Dakin, and M.E. Lambert, eds., *Documents on British Foreign Policy, 1919-1939*, First Series, 18 (London 1972), Hardinge to Crowe, from Curzon for the cabinet, September 23, 1922, pp. 96-7; cf draft, pp. 84-5

2 Ibid., pp. 198-201, 203-6, Curzon to Poincaré, October 18 and 20, 1922. Philip G. Wigley, *Canada and the Transition to Commonwealth: British-Canadian Relations, 1917-1926* (Cambridge 1977), pp. 83-4, 168. Crowe's minute should presumably be dated 1922, not 1923. PRO, CAB 23/31, cabinet meeting 49 (22), September 15, 1922; I owe this point to T.F. Rahilly.

3 PRO, CAB 23/31 and 23/32 (PAC, microfilm reel B-3850)

4 Lovell C. Clark, ed., *Documents on Canadian External Relations* Vol. 3: *1919-1925* (Ottawa 1970) [DCER, 3], p. 84

5 King Diary, PAC, October 28, 1922

6 Ibid., October 29, 1922

7 Ibid., October 31, 1922. Colonial Secretary to Governor General, October 27, 1922, DCER, 3:85

8 DCER, 3:85-6

9 Conclusions, cabinet 67/22, November 16, 1922; cf DCER, 3:86

10 King Diary, November 24, 1922. Governor General to Colonial Secretary, November 25, 1922, DCER, 3:87-8

11 Colonial Secretary to Governor General, December 8, 1922, DCER, 3:88-9

12 King Diary, December 30, 1922

13 Governor General to Colonial Secretary, December 31, 1922, DCER, 3:89-90

14 Ibid., pp. 90-1 (December 31, 1922)

15 Colonial Secretary to Governor General, January 27, 1923, ibid., p. 91

16 *Documents on British Foreign Policy, 1919-1939*, First Series, 18, pp. 972-3 (Rumbold to Curzon from Lausanne, July 24, 1923). *British and Foreign State Papers*, vol. 117 (1923, Part I), pp. 543-91

17 King Diary, March 24, 1924. Governor General to Colonial Secretary, March 24, 1924, DCER, 3:94

18 *Parliamentary Debates*, House of Commons, United Kingdom, April 1, 1924

19 Governor General to Colonial Secretary (Prime Minister to Prime Minister), April 3, 1924; Colonial Secretary to Governor General, private and personal, April 7, 1924; Governor General to Colonial Secretary, private and personal, same date, DCER, 3:94-7

20 Ibid., pp. 97-111

21 Canada, Sessional Papers, 1924, no 232

22 H.B. Neatby, *William Lyon Mackenzie King*, Vol. 2: *The Lonely Heights, 1924-1932* (Toronto 1963), p. 35. The memorandum is in King Papers, PAC, J 1, vol. 109.

23 King Diary, October 30, 1922

24 Ibid., November 17, 1922

25 Ibid., April 13, 1923. See also Fielding's memorandum of April 24, 1924, DCER, 3:41-3.

26 King Diary, April 14, 1923

27 Election Manifesto, October 4, 1921: C.P. Stacey, ed., *Historical Documents of Canada*, Vol. 5: *The Arts of War and Peace* (Toronto 1972), pp. 72-6

28 F.W. Taussig, *The Tariff History of the United States*, 8th ed., rev. (New York 1964), pp. 452-3

29 *Canada Year Book* [CYB], 1924, pp. 462 ff; ibid., 1925, pp. 466 ff; ibid., 1938, p. 532

30 Election Manifesto, October 4, 1921, note 27, above

31 Stacey, ed., *The Arts of War and Peace*, pp. 32-6

32 Neatby, *The Lonely Heights*, pp. 17-21. R.M. Dawson, *William Lyon Mackenzie King: A Political Biography*, Vol. 1: *1874-1923* (Toronto 1958), pp. 391-3

33 Stacey, ed., *The Arts of War and Peace*, pp. 182-3

34 Documents in DCER, 3:942-66

35 Ibid., p. 945

36 Ibid., pp. 967-70. Text of this convention in *Treaties and Agreements Affecting Canada in force between His Majesty and the United States of America ... 1814-1925* (Ottawa 1927), pp. 509-11

37 DCER, 3:971-5

38 Ibid., pp. 979-83. Text, *Treaties and Agreements affecting Canada*, pp. 511-13
39 Neatby, *The Lonely Heights*, pp. 286-9, 313-14. C.P. Stacey, *A Very Double Life: The Private World of Mackenzie King* (Toronto 1976), pp. 74-5
40 Governor General to Ambassador in U.S., April 15, 1921, DCER, 3:851-2
41 Ibid., pp. 852-70
42 DCER, 4:399-400, 452, 458; ibid., 5:203, 215
43 Ibid., 3:620-3. Wigley, *Canada and the Transition to Commonwealth*, p. 175
44 DCER, 3:621-50
45 Ibid., pp. 793-4
46 The correspondence with the British government and the Ambassador in Washington concerning the Halibut Treaty was published contemporaneously as Sessional Paper No 111a, Canada, 1923. See also DCER, 3:650-4, and Stacey, ed., *The Arts of War and Peace*, pp. 424-8.
47 DCER, 3:650-1
48 Ibid., pp. 652-3
49 Ibid., pp. 653-4 (February 28 and March 1, 1923). Full telegram, Devonshire to Byng, March 1, PRO, CO 532/235
50 Dawson, *King*, p. 434
51 *Globe* (Toronto), March 2, 1923. Text of treaty, *Treaties and Agreements affecting Canada*, pp. 505-7
52 Wigley, *Transition to Commonwealth*, pp. 176-7
53 Ibid., p. 177. And see Byng to Devonshire, February 20, 1923, PRO, CO 532/235
54 King Diary, March 2, 1923
55 Sessional Paper No 111a, 1923
56 DCER, 3:655-663. Wigley, *Transition to Commonwealth*, p. 179
57 Ibid. King Diary, March 20, 1923
58 *Congressional Record*, Senate, March 4, 1923, p. 5611; May 31, 1924, p. 10014. DCER, 3:653-70. Wigley, *Transition to Commonwealth*, pp. 181-2
59 *Debates*, House of Commons, June 27, 1923 (extract, Stacey, ed., *The Arts of War and Peace*, pp. 430-1)
60 *Debates*, House of Commons, May 2, 1923
61 DCER, 3:446-9 (July 20, 1922)
62 *Report of the Canadian Delegates to the Third Assembly of the League of Nations, September 3 to 20, 1922* (Sessional Paper No 36, 1923)
63 *Report of the Canadian Delegates to the Fourth Assembly of the League of Nations, September 3 to 29, 1923* (Sessional Paper No 35, 1924). Richard Veatch, *Canada and the League of Nations* (Toronto and Buffalo 1975), pp. 84-9
64 Ibid., pp. 91-100
65 *Report of the Canadian Delegates to the Fourth Assembly*
66 F.P. Walters, *A History of the League of Nations* (London 1967), pp. 225-6
67 DCER, 3:533-5
68 Ibid., pp. 535-9. Walters, *League of Nations*, pp. 226-7
69 Walters, *League of Nations*, pp. 272-4

70 October 2, 1924: Walter A. Riddell, ed., *Documents on Canadian Foreign Policy, 1937-1939* (Toronto 1962), pp. 462-5

71 King Diary, February 2, 1925. Marcel Hamelin, ed., *Les Mémoires du Sénateur Raoul Dandurand (1861-1942)* (Quebec, 1967), pp. 273-4

72 DCER, 3:542-50

73 Ibid., pp. 538-9 (June 12, 1924)

74 King Diary, November 19, 1924

75 G.P. deT. Glazebrook, *A History of Canadian External Relations*, 2 vols., rev. ed. (Toronto 1966), 2:85-6

76 DCER, 3:540-2

77 Ibid., pp. 551-2

78 Ibid., p. 552

79 Governor General to Colonial Secretary, March 8, 1925, ibid., pp. 551-2

80 King Diary, November 19, 1924

81 DCER, 4:639-65. Veatch, *Canada and the League of Nations*, pp. 58-60

82 Veatch, *Canada and the League of Nations*, pp. 167-8. Cf James Eayrs, 'A Low Dishonest Decade,' in H.L. Keenleyside, *et al.*, *The Growth of Canadian Policies in External Affairs* (Durham, NC 1960)

83 DCER, 3:433-4

84 Alex. I. Inglis, ed., *Documents on Canadian External Relations*, Vol. 4: *1926-30* (Ottawa 1971) [DCER, 4], pp. 612-24

85 Skelton to King, July 13, 1927, ibid., p. 622

86 Dandurand, *Mémoires*, p. 298. King Diary, September 4, 1927

87 Skelton to King, September 17, 1927, DCER, 4:624-8

88 King Diary, September 9, 1923

89 King Papers, J 4, vol. 81, folios C-62245-69; extracts, Stacey, ed., *The Arts of War and Peace*, pp. 431-4, 438-40

90 C.P. Stacey, 'From Meighen to King: The Reversal of Canadian External Policies, 1921-1923,' *Transactions of the Royal Society of Canada*, 1969

91 King's Conference Diary, October 5, 1923

92 Ibid., October 8, 1923. The official 'stenographic notes' of the conference are in King Papers, PAC, MG 26, J 4, vol. 82. Canadian speeches and other papers, DCER, 3:224-84

93 Ramsay Cook, 'J.W. Dafoe at the Imperial Conference, 1923,' *Canadian Historical Review*, March 1960

94 King's Conference Diary, November 5 and 7, 1923

95 Ibid., October 25, 1923

96 Wigley, *Transition to Commonwealth*, pp. 86-9, 184-5

97 DCER, 3:282-4

98 King's Conference Diary, October 25, 1923

99 Wigley, *Transition to Commonwealth*, pp. 183-5, 192-5

100 Ibid., pp. 195-9. Cf Philip G. Wigley, 'Whitehall and the 1923 Imperial Conference,' *Journal of Imperial and Commonwealth History*, January 1923

101 DCER, 3:278-80

102 Documents on Imperial Economic Conference, Maurice Ollivier, ed., *The Colonial and Imperial Conferences from 1887 to 1937*, 3 vols. (Ottawa 1954), 3:43-134. Wigley, *Transition to Commonwealth*, pp. 199-205
103 King's Conference Diary, October 20, 1923
104 Ibid. Wigley, *Transition to Commonwealth*, pp. 200-1

CHAPTER 3: THE LATER TWENTIES: PROSPERITY AND PROBLEMS

1 Meighen's opening speech, September 9, 1924; King's opening speech, September 5, 1925, C.P. Stacey, ed., *Historical Documents of Canada*, Vol. 5: *The Arts of War and Peace* (Toronto 1972), pp. 84-8, 78-83
2 H. Blair Neatby, *William Lyon Mackenzie King*, Vol. 2: *The Lonely Heights, 1924-1932* (Toronto 1963), p. 73. Cf Roger Graham, *Arthur Meighen: A Biography*, Vol. 2: *And Fortune Fled* (Toronto 1963), chapter 12
3 J. Murray Beck, *Pendulum of Power: Canada's Federal Elections* (Scarborough, Ont. 1968), pp. 174-5
4 King Diary, PAC, October 30-November 2, 1926. Neatby, *The Lonely Heights*, chapter 6
5 Graham, *And Fortune Fled*, p. 356
6 Ibid., chapter 13
7 King Diary, November 10, 1924
8 Neatby, *The Lonely Heights*, chapter 8. Graham, *And Fortune Fled*, chapter 15. E.A. Forsey, *The Royal Power of Dissolution of Parliament in the British Commonwealth* (Toronto 1943)
9 Byng to Amery, June 30, 1926: Amery to Byng, July 3, 1926; Amery to Byng, July 1, 1926, Stacey, ed., *The Arts of War and Peace*, pp. 4-6; Alex. I. Inglis, ed., *Documents on Canadian External Relations*, Vol. 4: *1926-30* (Ottawa 1971) [DCER, 4], p. 11. Many other documents, Roger Graham, ed., *The King-Byng Affair, 1926: A Question of Responsible Government* (Toronto 1967)
10 Graham, *And Fortune Fled*, chapter 16. Neatby, *The Lonely Heights*, chapter 9. Beck, *Pendulum of Power*, pp. 188-9. Speeches of leaders, Stacey, ed., *The Arts of War and Peace*, pp. 91-8
11 Beck, *Pendulum of Power*, pp. 188-9. Neatby, *The Lonely Heights*, pp. 122-4. Personal recollection
12 Text of main treaty, *British and Foreign State Papers*, 121, pp. 923-6. Harold Nicolson, *King George the Fifth, His Life and Reign* (London 1952), p. 409
13 Philip G. Wigley, *Canada and the Transition to Commonwealth: British-Canadian Relations, 1917-1926* (Cambridge 1977), pp. 241-4. The numerous cables advising Ottawa of the progress of the Locarno negotiations are collected in 'The Locarno Treaties and their Negotiation,' PAC, RG 25, D1, vol. 753, file 230.
14 Lovell C. Clark, ed., *Documents on Canadian External Relations*, Vol. 3: *1919-1925* (Ottawa 1970) [DCER, 3], pp. 556-7 (November 18, 1925)
15 King Diary, January 6, 1926

16 Undated and unsigned memo, undoubtedly by Skelton, King papers, PAC, J
1, vol. 139; another copy in PAC, RG 25, D1, vol. 753, file 230. Memorandum,
January 1, 1926, King Papers, J 4, vol. 92. Wigley, *Transition to Commonwealth*, pp. 245-6. Neatby, *The Lonely Heights*, p. 179

17 Governor General to Dominions Secretary (Prime Minister to Prime Minister), January 8, 1926, DCER, 4:679-81; extracts, Stacey, ed., *The Arts of War
and Peace*, pp. 451-4

18 King Diary, January 25, February 23, 1926

19 DCER, 4:134-7

20 Ibid., p. 137

21 Ibid., pp. 613-15

22 W. Stewart Wallace, *The Memoirs of the Rt. Hon. Sir George Foster* (Toronto
1933), p. 216. Marcel Hamelin, ed., *Les Mémoires du Sénateur Raoul Dandurand
(1861-1942)* (Quebec 1967), p. 297

23 Christie to Borden, February 25, 1926, Borden Papers, PAC, vol. 264. C.P.
Stacey, 'Nationality: The Experience of Canada,' CHA *Historical Papers*, 1967.
R.S. Bothwell, 'Loring Christie: The Failure of Bureaucratic Imperialism'
(Ph.D thesis, Harvard University, 1972), chapter 8

24 Wigley, *Transition to Commonwealth*, p. 245. Borden to Chamberlain (incomplete copy), January 30, 1926, Borden Papers, vol. 264

25 Vincent Massey, *What's Past is Prologue: The Memoirs of the Right Honourable
Vincent Massey, C.H.* (Toronto 1963), p. 112

26 King Diary, October 25, 1926

27 Both the printed 'stenographic notes' of the conference and the mimeo-
graphed minutes of the Committee on Inter-Imperial Relations are in King
Papers, J 4, vol. 84. Items of special Canadian interest, DCER, 4:85-170. The
published proceedings of the conference are in British Parliamentary Papers,
Cmd. 2768, 1926. See also Maurice Ollivier, ed., *The Colonial and Imperial
Conferences from 1887 to 1937*, 3 vols. (Ottawa 1954), Vol. 3, and extracts in
Stacey, ed., *The Arts of War and Peace*, pp. 455-67.

28 October 28, 1926: King Papers, J 4, vol. 84, folio C 63956

29 King Diary, October 27, 1926; see Neatby, *The Lonely Heights*, p. 184

30 Wigley, *Transition to Commonwealth*, pp. 269-70

31 Ramsay Cook, ed., 'A Canadian Account of the 1926 Imperial Conference,'
Journal of Commonwealth Political Studies, March 1965; extract, Stacey, ed., *The
Arts of War and Peace*, pp. 454-5

32 Ibid. Cf DCER, 4:166-7

33 Wigley, *Transition to Commonwealth*, p. 283

34 Ibid., p. 278

35 *Globe* (Toronto), November 12, 1928. King Diary, November 10, 1928

36 Neatby, *The Lonely Heights*, p. 192. Balfour Committee report (Stacey, ed.,
The Arts of War and Peace, pp. 463-4). D.W. Harkness, *The Restless Dominion:
The Irish Free State and the British Commonwealth of Nations, 1921-1931* (London
1969), pp. 63-7

37 Massey, *What's Past is Prologue*, pp. 109-10. King Diary, September 25, 1926
38 DCER, 4:13-14. Massey, *What's Past is Prologue*, pp. 121-3
39 Neatby, *The Lonely Heights*, p. 119
40 DCER, 4:30-47
41 Ibid., pp. 30-76. Neatby, *The Lonely Heights*, p. 193. Charles Ritchie, *The Siren Years: A Canadian Diplomat Abroad, 1937-1945* (Toronto 1974), pp. 13-16. Massey, *What's Past is Prologue*, p. 137
42 DCER, 4:17-25
43 Ibid., pp. 14-15
44 Ibid., p. 42
45 King Diary, August 23, 26, 27, 1928
46 DCER, 4:43
47 October 10, 1928: ibid., pp. 47-8
48 Memorandum of Chamberlain interview, King Diary, November 12, 1928. Ibid., March 18, 1929. G.N. Hillmer, 'Anglo-Canadian Relations 1926-1937' (Ph.D. thesis, Cambridge University, 1974), pp. 117-20
49 DCER, 4:52-80. Ibid., 5:2-11
50 King Diary, February 25, 1926
51 Norman Hillmer, 'A British High Commissioner for Canada, 1927-28,' *Journal of Imperial and Commonwealth History*, May 1973. [Norman Reddaway], *Earnscliffe* (London, Commonwealth Relations Office, 1955)
52 Massey, *What's Past is Prologue*, pp. 138-9
53 Documents of 1938 on file M-2 −45, RG 25, D3, vol. 835, PAC, McCloskey Papers
54 Lester B. Pearson, *Mike: The Memoirs of the Right Honourable Lester B. Pearson*, 3 vols. (Toronto 1972-5), 1:58-60
55 Ibid., p. 71. Dates of appointment, list sent to Civil Service Commission, August 2, 1935, McCloskey Papers, vol. 835, file 0-1-B Pt. II-53. Douglas LePan, 'The Spare Deputy: A Portrait of Norman Robertson,' *International Perspectives*, July/August 1978
56 LePan, 'The Spare Deputy.' Max Wershof, 'A Salute to John Erskine Read,' *International Perspectives*, May/June 1974. On abolition of post of Legal Adviser see King statement, House of Commons, *Debates*, June 9, 1924, p. 2990
57 King Diary, August 7, 1929
58 *British and Foreign State Papers*, Vol. 128, pp. 447-9. *Annual Register*, 1928, Public Documents, pp. 77-9
59 *Annual Register*, 1928, pp.77-9. Samuel Flagg Bemis, *A Diplomatic History of the United States* (New York 1936), pp. 723-5
60 W.C. Sellar and R.J. Yeatman, *1066 and All That* (London 1930), p. 111
61 May 6, 1928: DCER, 4:694-5
62 King Diary, May 11, 1928
63 May 11, 1928: DCER, 4:695-6
64 Ibid., pp. 696-7
65 Ibid., p. 698

66 King Diary, May 22, 1928
67 DCER, 4:701-6
68 Ibid., pp. 712-17
69 King Diary, August 27, 1928
70 *Annual Register*, 1928, Public Documents, pp. 77-9
71 *Debates*, House of Commons, February 19 and 22, 1928
72 *Canada Year Book*, 1938, p. 848
73 Massey, *What's Past is Prologue*, pp. 144-7. *New York Times*, December 7, 8, 9, 1927. Correspondence between Willingdon and the Palace, RG 7, G 26, vol. 108
74 Massey College, Massey Diary, October 28, December 8, 1927 (by permission of the Master and Fellows)
75 King Diary, November 23, 24, 1927
76 Ibid., January 11, February 3, 1928. Skelton to Massey, February 14, 1928, PAC, RG 25, D1, vol. 741, file 147. I have not found the President's letter.
77 Massey, *What's Past is Prologue*, pp. 128-9
78 Captain Jack Randell, *I'm Alone* (London, n.d.). *New York Times*, March 23-27, 1929
79 DCER, 4:495-7 (March 26, 1929)
80 *The I'M ALONE Incident: Correspondence between the Governments of Canada and the United States, 1929* (Ottawa 1929)
81 DCER, 4:503-31
82 *Claim of British Ship 'I'm Alone': Documents* (Ottawa 1935). This contains Canadian and U.S. briefs, statements by both sides, and the Commissioners' reports. See also Alex. I. Inglis, ed., *Documents on Canadian External Relations*, Vol. 5: *1931-35* (Ottawa 1973) [DCER, 5], pp. 124-44.
83 DCER, 5:144 (January 19, 1935)
84 Ralph Flenley, ed., *A History of Montreal, 1640-1672, from the French of Dollier de Casson* ... (London and Toronto 1928), p. 32
85 D.G. Creighton, *The Commercial Empire of the St. Lawrence, 1760-1850* (Toronto and New Haven 1937). *The Canals of Canada under the Jurisdiction of the Department of Transport, 1946* (Ottawa 1946)
86 The standard account is William R. Willoughby, *The St. Lawrence Waterway: A Study in Politics and Diplomacy* (Madison, Wis. 1961).
87 Ibid., chapter 7. DCER, 3:917-24
88 DCER, 3:922-5
89 Ibid., pp. 125-42. Willoughby, *St. Lawrence Waterway*, chapter 8
90 Massey to Secretary of State, January 31, 1928, DCER, 4:421-6
91 March 12, 1928, ibid., pp. 430-3
92 Minister in U.S. to Secretary of State, April 5, 1928, ibid., pp. 433-5
93 King Diary, November 23 and 24, 1927
94 Willoughby, *St. Lawrence Waterway*, chapter 9. DCER, 4:435-59. Neatby, *The Lonely Heights*, pp. 284-6, 273-7. King Diary, November 17, 1928, April 4, 1929

95 November 17, 1928, DCER, 4:176-7
96 Stenographic Notes of 1st Meeting, Conference on the Operation of Dominion Legislation and Merchant Shipping Legislation, October 8, 1929, PAC, RG 25, Accession 74-5/46, file S2/205/1. Extracts of material of special Canadian interest in this series of notes are reproduced in DCER, 4:177-213. O.D. Skelton's valuable undated 'Notes on Conference on Operation of Dominion Legislation and Merchant Shipping' are in King Papers, J 4, vol. 134, file 1059, folios C97519-49. There is an excellent account of this conference in Hillmer, 'Anglo-Canadian Relations 1926-1937.'
97 Stenographic Notes of 1st Meeting, above, note 95
98 Ibid., 9th Meeting, October 22, 1929
99 Ibid., 12th Meeting, October 25, 1929. *Report of the Conference on the Operation of Dominion Legislation and Merchant Shipping Legislation, 1929*, British Parliamentary Paper, Cmd. 3479, 1930, paras. 95-109, especially 100. Extracts from the Report (not including portions on merchant shipping), Stacey, ed., *The Arts of War and Peace*, pp. 474-7
100 Stenographic Notes, 12th Meeting, October 25, 1929
101 *Report of the Conference*, above, note 99
102 Stenographic Notes, 5th Meeting, October 15, 1929
103 *Report*, para. 50. The Colonial Laws Validity Act (28 & 29 Vict., c. 63) is conveniently available in Appendix I to F.C. Wheare, *The Constitutional Structure of the Commonwealth* (Oxford 1960).
104 Skelton 'Notes,' note 96 above. Hillmer, 'Anglo-Canadian Relations, 1926-1937,' pp. 160-2
105 Stenographic Notes, 5th Meeting, October 15, 1929
106 Stacey, ed., *The Arts of War and Peace*, pp. 100-6
107 Statute 15-16 George V, c. 30, June 27, 1925. Cf Neatby, *The Lonely Heights*, pp. 57-8
108 Stacey, ed., *The Arts of War and Peace*, p. 102
109 *Globe*, November 13, 1928
110 *Canadian Annual Review*, 1929-30, pp. 195-6
111 Beck, *Pendulum of Power*, pp. 191-203
112 March 1, 1927: *Times Law Reports*, vol. 43, 1926-7. Extracts, Stacey, ed., *The Arts of War and Peace*, pp. 514-21

CHAPTER 4: DEPRESSION DIPLOMACY

1 Ernest Watkins, *R.B. Bennett, A Biography* (Toronto 1963) is comparatively slight, and Lord Beaverbrook's own *Friends: Sixty Years of Intimate Personal Relations with Richard Bedford Bennett* (London 1959) has the limitations the title suggests. Richard Wilbur has written several valuable scholarly articles, notably *The Bennett Administration, 1930-1935* (CHA Historical Booklet No 24, Ottawa 1969).

2 L.M. Grayson and Michael Bliss, eds., *The Wretched of Canada: Letters to R.B. Bennett 1930-1935* (Toronto 1971)

3 Sir Alan Lascelles to Baldwin, November 22, 1932, Robert Bothwell and Norman Hillmer, eds., *The In-Between Time: Canadian External Policy in the 1930s* (Toronto 1975), pp. 86-7

4 Interview with Read, Read Papers, PAC, MG 30, E 148, vol. 10. (This interview should be used with great reserve.)

5 Bennett to Grote Stirling, 15 April 1941: Bennett Papers, PAC, reel M-3172, folios 593759-64. I was led to this and a number of other references by Donald Clarke Story, 'Canada's Covenant: The Bennett Government, The League of Nations and Collective Security' (Ph.D. thesis, University of Toronto, 1976). This thesis, based on a wide range of sources, deals to a considerable extent with Bennett's external policies generally.

6 H. Gordon Skilling, *Canadian Representation Abroad: From Agency to Embassy* (Toronto 1945), p. 115. Vincent Massey, *What's Past is Prologue: The Memoirs of the Right Honourable Vincent Massey, C.H.* (Toronto 1963), prints Massey's memoranda of his conversations with Bennett, pp. 171-8. Peter Oliver, *G. Howard Ferguson, Ontario Tory* (Toronto 1977), p. 379. See the Arch Dale cartoon in Bothwell and Hillmer, eds., *The In-Between Time*, p. 80.

7 C.P. Stacey, *A Very Double Life: The Private World of Mackenzie King* (Toronto 1976), pp. 86-105. King Diary, PAC, April 7, 1926

8 *Canadian Annual Review* [CAR], 1930-1, p. 357. Story, 'Canada's Covenant,' pp. 65-9. Evidence of O.D. Skelton, King Diary, October 25, 1935

9 W. Stewart Wallace, ed., *The Macmillan Dictionary of Canadian Biography*, 3rd ed. (Toronto 1963), p. 497. Cf Alex I. Inglis, ed., *Documents on Canadian External Relations*, Vol. 5: *1931-35* (Ottawa 1973) [DCER, 5], pp. 716, 738

10 Charles A. and Mary R. Beard, *America in Midpassage* (Toronto 1939), pp. 41-2

11 Hoover statement, *New York Times*, June 16, 1930. Detail of tariff schedules, and comparison with previous rates, ibid., June 15, 1930

12 'The United States Tariff and Canadian Trade Since 1911,' PAC, RG 25, D 1, vol. 744, file 161. Ibid., Governor General to Ambassador, January 21, 1921

13 Skelton to Massey, February 27, 1929 and April 6, 1929, PAC, RG 25, D 1, vol. 744, file 160

14 Peter Kasurak, 'American foreign policy officials and Canada, 1927-1941: a look through bureaucratic glasses,' *International Journal*, summer 1977

15 Budget speech by C.A. Dunning, House of Commons, May 1, 1930

16 21 George V, c. 3, September 22, 1930

17 21-22 George V, c. 30, August 3, 1931

18 *Canada Year Book*, [CYB], 1938, pp. 532, 769. Cf Statistics Canada, *National Income and Expenditure Accounts*, Vol. I: *The Annual Estimates 1926-1974* (Ottawa 1976), pp. 94-5

19 *New York Times*, May 5, 1930

20 *Imperial Conference, 1930: Summary of Proceedings* (British Parliamentary Paper, Cmd. 3717, 1930), pp. 5-9

21 Cabinet conclusion, September 30, 1930, G.N. Hillmer, 'Anglo-Canadian Relations 1926-1937' (Ph.D. thesis, Cambridge University, 1974), pp. 163-5
22 Hadow to Passfield, May 31, 1930, quoted in ibid., p. 166
23 Remark by Read in 10th meeting of Committee on Inter-Imperial Relations, October 27, 1930, Bennett Papers, PAC, reel M-993, folios 98942. Cf Bennett's remark in meeting of Prime Ministers and Heads of Delegations, October 31, 1930 (Appendix to minutes, p. 6), and his statement in House of Commons, June 30, 1931, p. 3197
24 The minutes of 'Meetings of Prime Ministers and Heads of Delegations' are in Bennett Papers, University of New Brunswick, and microfilms in PAC, MG 26, K, vol. 149.
25 Minutes of meetings of Prime Ministers and Heads of Delegations, November 4, Appendix III, p. 5, and November 5, Appendix, p. 11
26 Ferguson to Bennett, and attached memorandum, September 10, 1930, PAC, RG 25, D 1, vol. 759, file 254, and see Bennett's statement in House of Commons, September 20, 1930
27 Summary of Proceedings, pp. 17-19
28 British statute, 22 George V, c. 4 (December 11, 1931); text conveniently available in F.C. Wheare, *The Constitutional Structure of the Commonwealth* (Oxford 1960), Appendix II, and in C.P. Stacey, ed., *Historical Documents of Canada*, Vol. 5: *The Arts of War and Peace* (Toronto 1972), pp. 485-8
29 *Debates*, House of Commons, June 30 and July 8, 1931, especially statement by Bennett, June 30
30 *Imperial Conference 1926. Appendices to the Summary of Proceedings* (Sessional Paper No 10a, Ottawa 1927), pp. 123-7
31 Minutes of Committee of Imperial Defence, 1923-33, PRO, CAB 2/4 and 2/5 (PAC, microfilm reel B-3821): especially 217th meeting (November 11, 1926), 250th meeting (September 29, 1930), 251st meeting (November 28, 1930). Bennett to Hankey, December 2, 1930, Bennett Papers, folio 103978
32 C.P. Stacey, *Arms, Men and Governments: The War Policies of Canada, 1939-1945* (Ottawa 1970), pp. 90-1
33 Skelton's 'Notes' on the 1929 Conference, King Papers, J 4, vol. 134, file 1059
34 Statute of Westminster, Sec. 10. Nicholas Mansergh, *The Commonwealth Experience* (London 1969), pp. 236-8. Stacey, ed., *The Arts of War and Peace*, pp. 296-301
35 W.P.M. Kennedy, *The Constitution of Canada, 1534-1937: An Introduction to its Development Law and Custom*, 2d ed. (London 1938), p. 538
36 'Defense and External Obligations: A Canadian View,' *Conference on Canadian-American Affairs Held at The St. Lawrence University, Canton, New York, June 19-22, 1939* (Boston 1939), p. 193
37 CAR, 1932, p. 28
38 A.J.P. Taylor, *Beaverbrook* (London 1972), chapters 11 and 12
39 Text in Stacey, ed., *The Arts of War and Peace*, pp. 482-4

40 Minutes of Meetings of Prime Ministers and Heads of Delegations, Bennett Papers, PAC, MG 26, K, vol. 149: Appendix II to minutes of October 9, 1932. I am grateful to Arthur Bousfield for the use of his graduate paper, 'R.B. Bennett's External Policies, 1930-1935: The Empire.'

41 Letter dated October 13, 1932, Appendix III to Minutes of meeting of Prime Ministers and Heads of Delegations, October 14

42 Ian M. Drummond, *Imperial Economic Policy, 1917-1939: Studies in Expansion and Protection* (Toronto 1974), chapter 4

43 Maurice Ollivier, ed., *The Colonial and Imperial Conferences from 1887 to 1937*, 3 vols. (Ottawa 1954), 3:340-1

44 A.J.P. Taylor, *English History, 1914-1945* (Oxford 1965), pp. 288-97, 321-31. Charles Loch Mowat, *Britain between the Wars, 1918-1940* (London 1956), pp. 379-416

45 Drummond, *Imperial Economic Policy*, chapter 5. Dominions Secretary to Secretary of State for External Affairs, May 9, 1932, DCER, 5:43-4. This cable, and Sir William Clark's account of its reception in Ottawa (May 22, 1932), are in Bothwell and Hillmer, eds., *The In-Between Time*, pp. 52-5.

46 Ferguson to Bennett, March 3, 1932, Bennett Papers, vol. 970. See Oliver, *G. Howard Ferguson*, pp. 394-6.

47 See particularly 'Manifesto on Intra-Imperial Trade,' *Globe* (Toronto), July 18, 1932; and cf *Gazette* (Montreal), July 19 and 22.

48 Judith Robinson, July 25

49 *Globe*, August 2 and 3. Personal recollection

50 *Imperial Economic Conference 1932: Minutes of Meetings of Heads of Delegations and Meetings of the Conference other than the Opening and Closing Sessions*, Bennett Papers, vol. 167; another copy, PAC, RG 7, G 21, vol. 667. (Published in part in DCER, 5:45 ff, where some committee minutes are also to be found.) The conference *Report*, with some omissions, is in Ollivier, *Colonial and Imperial Conferences*, 3:349-424.

51 Ollivier, *Colonial and Imperial Conferences*, 3:393

52 Keith Feiling, *The Life of Neville Chamberlain* (London 1946), p. 215

53 Ibid., p. 213. Runciman memorandum of August 5, 1932, Drummond, *Imperial Economic Policy*, pp. 296-9

54 Runciman memorandum of August 5, 1932

55 Ibid. Dana Wilgress, *Memoirs* (Toronto 1967), p. 96

56 British delegation's telegram to London, August 15, 1932, Drummond, *Imperial Economic Policy*, pp. 290-5. For an example of Bennett on Russia, see minutes of second meeting of Committee on Trade Promotion, July 25, 1932, DCER, 5:51-3.

57 Drummond, *Imperial Economic Policy*, pp. 238-42

58 The agreement forms a schedule to Canadian statute 23-24 George V, c. 2, November 25, 1932, which approved it; printed in part in Stacey, ed., *The Arts of War and Peace*, pp. 209-12. See also Chapters 3, 4, and 5 of the same date, respectively approving agreements with South Africa, the Irish Free State, and Southern Rhodesia.

59 21-22 George V, c. 55, August 3, 1931
60 Telegram of August 15, above, note 56
61 Ollivier, *Colonial and Imperial Conferences*, 3:361
62 CYB, 1938, pp. 532-3. *Economist*, 'Dominion of Canada Special Review,' January 18, 1936. A.E. Safarian, *The Canadian Economy in the Great Depression* (Toronto 1970), pp. 220-1
63 Above, note 3
64 Stacey, ed., *The Arts of War and Peace*, p. 101. CAR, 1929-30, p. 107 (Tilbury, Ont., July 24)
65 Alex I. Inglis, ed., *Documents on Canadian External Relations*, Vol. 4: *1926-30* (Ottawa 1971), [DCER, 4], pp. 466-7 (September 2 and 10, 1932)
66 *New York Times*, January 31, February 2, February 6, 1932. CAR, 1930-1, p. 30. William R. Willoughby, *The St. Lawrence Waterway: A Study in Politics and Diplomacy* (Madison, Wis. 1961), p. 134 (no precise source given)
67 There is virtually nothing in DCER, 5, reflecting the poverty of the official files.
68 PAC, RG 25, D 1, vol. 734, file 116, vol. 3: memo for Skelton, January 25, 1933
69 Willoughby, *St. Lawrence Waterway*, p. 134
70 MacNider to Stimson, October 6, 1931, and Bennett to MacNider, September 12, 1931, *Foreign Relations of the United States* [FRUS], 1931, 1:892-3
71 Ibid., pp. 893-4
72 FRUS, 1932, 1:63-9
73 Statutes of Canada, 1932-3, Prefix, pp. xii-xvii
74 Ibid., pp. v-xi. Also in FRUS, 1932, 1:69-78, and in *New York Times*, July 19, 1932
75 *New York Times*, July 19, 1932
76 *The Canals of Canada under the Jurisdiction of the Department of Transport, 1946* (Ottawa 1946), p. 23
77 *New York Times*, July 19, 1932
78 Willoughby, *St. Lawrence Waterway*, pp. 141-4, 148-9. *New York Times* (editorial), March 15, 1934
79 *New York Times*, July 19, 1932
80 Willoughby, *St. Lawrence Waterway*, p. 155
81 Ibid., pp. 153-9. *New York Times*, March 13, 14, 15, 1934
82 'St. Lawrence Waterway (Washington, December 10-11th)' [1934], memo by Skelton, PAC, RG 25, D 1, vol. 734, file 116, vol. 3
83 Willoughby, *St. Lawrence Waterway*, pp. 160-5
84 DCER, 5:117-24, 126-7, 152-4; cf FRUS, 1932, 2:78 ff
85 DCER, 5:136-8 (Wrong to Secretary of State External, December 5, 1933)
86 FRUS, 1931, 1:894-8
87 DCER, 4:575-6 (July 9, 1928). There are brief authentic summaries of the background in the decisions of the Trail Smelter Tribunal, 1938 and 1941.
88 *New York Times*, March 6, 1931. *Report of the International Joint Commission, Signed at Toronto, 28th February, 1931*, is Appendix A3 to *Trail Smelter Question. Reference of Certain Complaints ... Documents, Series A* (Ottawa 1936)

89 DCER, 5:224-7
90 FRUS, 1934, 1:874-97 (January 27, 1934)
91 DCER, 5:228-9 (February 13, 1934)
92 Skelton to Herridge, February 2, 1934: DCER, 5:227-8
93 Bennett to Robbins, February 17, 1934: FRUS, 1934, 1:898-910
94 Ibid., pp. 925-55, 965
95 Phillips to Roosevelt, March 15, 1935: FRUS, 1935, 2:32-3
96 Canada Treaty Series, 1935, No 20
97 CAR, 1937 and 1938, p. 143. *New York Times*, March 13, 1941. 'Decision
    Reported on April 16, 1938 to the Government of the United States of
    America and to the Government of the Dominion of Canada by the Trail
    Smelter Arbitral Tribunal ...' PAC, RG 25, G 1, vol. 1692, file 103 – XI (FP).
    *Trail Smelter Question. Decision reported on March 11, 1941, to the Government of
    the United States of America and to the Government of the Dominion of Canada by
    the Trail Smelter Arbitral Tribunal ...* (Ottawa 1941)
98 DCER, 5:243-6; also 261-4
99 Ibid., pp. 256-60, especially Roosevelt to Representative John J. McSwain,
    April 19, 1935. *New York Herald Tribune*, April 28, 1935. *Gazette* (Mont-
    real), May 2, 1935. C.P. Stacey, *The Military Problems of Canada* (Toronto
    1940), pp. 30-2
100 DCER, 5:263, 268. *New York Times*, September 29, 1938
101 DCER, 5:264-7 (August 24, September 6, September 14, 1935). Stacey, *Mili-
    tary Problems of Canada*, pp. 36-8
102 C.P. Stacey, *Six Years of War* (Official History of the Canadian Army in the
    Second World War, Vol. 1) (Ottawa 1955), pp. 29-30
103 James Eayrs, *In Defence of Canada*, Vol. 1: *From the Great War to the Great
    Depression* (Toronto 1964), pp. 70-8. Charles Taylor, 'Brigadier James Suther-
    land Brown' in *Six Journeys: A Canadian Pattern* (Toronto 1977). Richard A.
    Preston, *The Defence of the Undefended Border: Planning for War in North
    America, 1867-1939* (Montreal and London 1977), chapter 8
104 Extracts, Eayrs, *Great War to the Great Depression*, Document 1. Defence
    Scheme No 1 is now in PAC, RG 24, vols. 2926 and 2927.
105 Preston, *Defence of the Undefended Border*, pp. 217-27
106 Ray S. Cline, Washington Command Post: The Operations Division (United
    States Army in World War II) (Washington 1951), p. 35 (quoted in Preston,
    Defence of the Undefended Border, p. 219)
107 Stacey, *Arms, Men and Governments*, p. 95n. Cf Preston, *Defence of the
    Undefended Border*, pp. 216-17
108 Stacey, *Six Years of War*, p. 30 (January 29, 1931)
109 Eayrs, *Great War to the Great Depression*, pp. 77-8
110 *Globe and Mail* (Toronto), December 9, 1933
111 Roberts to Bennett, December 21, 1933; Bennett to Roberts, December 21,
    1933: Bennett Papers, Vol. 429. The letters are in Bothwell and Hillmer,
    eds., *The In-Between Time*, pp. 108-12.

112 J.W. Pickersgill, *The Mackenzie King Record*, 4 vols. (Toronto 1960-70), 1:683 (King's record of conversation with Churchill, May 13, 1944)
113 Finlayson Papers, PAC, Memoirs, p. 302
114 Story, 'Canada's Covenant'
115 See, e.g., the reference to 'British Group' meeting in Riddell to Skelton, September 25, 1933, PAC, RG 25, D 1, vol. 762, file 279 (III-13). On Dandurand's phrase, DCER, 4:626
116 DCER, 4:719-44. See G.M. Gathorne-Hardy, *A Short History of International Affairs, 1920 to 1934* (Oxford 1934), pp. 179-82
117 To Skelton, February 15, 1932, DCER, 5:466-7
118 May 2, 1932: ibid., pp. 468-9
119 Ibid., p. 515. L.B. Pearson, *Mike: The Memoirs of the Right Honourable Lester B. Pearson*, 3 vols. (Toronto 1972-5), 1:89-92
120 Gathorne-Hardy, *Short History*, pp. 284-92. Cahan's instructions, December 2, 1932, DCER, 5:313-15
121 Documents in DCER, 5:317-28. Text of Cahan speech, Bennett Papers, PAC, reel M-1094, folios 272799-809. Story, 'Canada's Covenant,' chapter V. Richard Veatch, *Canada and the League of Nations* (Toronto and Buffalo 1975), chapter 9. Extracts from an essay written for me by Alan Mason on Canadian-Japanese relations are published in Bothwell and Hillmer, eds., *The In-Between Time*, pp. 113-19.
122 Instructions to Riddell, February 19, 1933, DCER, 5:333-4. *Debates*, House of Commons, February 24, 1933. F.P. Walters, *A History of the League of Nations* (London 1967), chapter 40. M.S. Donnelly, *Dafoe of the Free Press* (Toronto 1968), p. 146

CHAPTER 5: TURNING-POINTS IN NORTH AMERICA AND AFRICA

1 *Debates*, Senate, 1934: April 17, 24; May 1, 2, 8, 15, 16, 22, 29, 30, 31; House of Commons, March 27. Richard Veatch, *Canada and the League of Nations* (Toronto and Buffalo 1975), chapter 9. Extracts from essay by Alan Mason, in Robert Bothwell and Norman Hillmer, eds., *The In-Between Time: Canadian External Policy in the 1930s* (Toronto 1975), pp. 119-21
2 'Impressions of Canada, December, 1934' (PRO, CAB 63/81): J.L. Granatstein, ed., 'The "Man of Secrets" in Canada, 1934,' *Dalhousie Review*, Vol. 51, No 4
3 Donald Page, 'The Institute's "popular arm": the League of Nations Society in Canada,' *International Journal*, winter 1977-8
4 Veatch, *League of Nations*, p. 127. 'Delegates and Substitute Delegates to League of Nations Assemblies' [1920-33], PAC, RG 25, D 1, vol. 765, file 297.
5 Veatch, *League of Nations*, pp. 134-5. Alex. I. Inglis, ed., *Documents on Canadian External Relations*, Vol. 5: *1931-35* (Ottawa 1973) [DCER, 5] pp. 291-3
6 J. Murray Beck, *Pendulum of Power: Canada's Federal Elections* (Scarborough, Ont. 1968), pp. 206-22. Richard Wilbur, *The Bennett Administration, 1930-*

1935 (CHA Historical Booklet No 24, Ottawa 1969), pp. 14-18. C.P. Stacey, ed., *Historical Documents of Canada*, Vol. 5: *The Arts of War and Peace* (Toronto 1972), pp. 107-14. C.P. Stacey, *A Very Double Life: The Private World of Mackenzie King* (Toronto 1976), p. 184 and illustration 21

7 King Diary, PAC, October 25, 1935

8 Ibid., October 17, 1935

9 Ibid., October 18, 1935. Cf Ramsay Cook, *The Politics of John W. Dafoe and the Free Press* (Toronto 1963), p. 211

10 P. de L. Boal to Under Secretary of State, April 14, 1933, *Foreign Relations of the United States* [FRUS], 1933, 2:44-9; reprinted in Bothwell and Hillmer, eds., *The In-Between Time*, pp. 61-5

11 Richard N. Kottman, *Reciprocity and the North Atlantic Triangle, 1932-1938* (Ithaca, NY 1968), pp. 85-6 (note the quotations from letters of R.J. Manion)

12 *New York Times*, April 30, 1933. Cf ibid., April 26, 27, 28, and 29, 1935. Bennett Papers, PAC, reel M-1025, folios 184864-5, 'Tentative Program' of visit to Washington

13 Kottman, *Reciprocity*, p. 90

14 Ibid., p. 91n. Herridge to Hull (No 157), November 14, 1934, PAC, RG 25, D 1, vol. 811/622; printed in DCER, 5:176-83

15 Hull to Herridge, December 27, 1934, DCER, 5:184-5. Cf Kottman, *Reciprocity*, pp. 92-6

16 Kottman, *Reciprocity*, pp. 82-3n, 96

17 Herridge to Bennett, May 25, 1935, DCER, 5:190. Herridge to Skelton, June 22, 1935, PAC, RG 25, D 1, vol. 811/622

18 Herridge to Skelton, July 8, 1935, DCER, 5:190-1

19 Dana Wilgress, *Memoirs* (Toronto 1967), p. 101. Memorandum by James C.H. Bonbright of conversations with Armour, August 14, 1955; and Hickerson to Secretary of State, August 28, 1935, FRUS, 1935, 2:19-22. Cf Kottman, *Reciprocity*, p. 122

20 Bennett to Herridge, September 7, 1935, DCER, 5:192-3

21 Kottman, *Reciprocity*, p. 104n (quoting Phillips diary)

22 Unsigned memo, 'Negotiations with the United States: Summary of Discussions on October 2 and 3,' PAC, RG 25, vol. 745, file 167/1. Herridge to Skelton, September 21, 1935, PAC, RG 25, D 1, vol. 811/622

23 King Diary, October 24, 1935

24 Armour to Secretary of State, October 25, 1935, and enclosed memo dated October 24, FRUS, 1935, 2:27-30

25 Kottman, *Reciprocity*, p. 109, quoting Phillips to Roosevelt, November 7, 1935

26 King Diary, November 8, 1935. Cf H. Blair Neatby, *William Lyon Mackenzie King*, Vol. 3: *The Prism of Unity, 1932-1939* (Toronto 1976), pp. 144-5

27 *New York Times*, November 12, 16, 1935

28 Memorandum by Armour, September 21, 1935, FRUS, 1935, 2:23-4

29 Text, Schedule to 1 Edward VIII, c. 3, April 8, 1936: The Canada-United States of America Trade Agreement Act, 1936. Also in *New York Times*, November 18, 1935.

30 *New York Times*, November 18, 1935
31 Wilgress, *Memoirs*, pp. 102-3. O. Mary Hill, *Canada's Salesman to the World: The Department of Trade and Commerce, 1892-1939* (Ottawa 1977), p. 545
32 *Canada Year Book* [CYB], 1940, pp. 534-5
33 Kottman, *Reciprocity*, p. 106
34 Stacey, *A Very Double Life*, pp. 181-2, 183-4. C.P. Stacey, *Mackenzie King and the Atlantic Triangle* (Toronto 1976), pp. 12-22
35 Notably, James Eayrs, *In Defence of Canada*, Vol. 2: *Appeasement and Rearmament* (Toronto 1965), chapter 1. Robert Bothwell and John English, '"Dirty Work at the Crossroads": New Perspectives on the Riddell Incident,' CHA *Historical Papers*, 1972. Peter Oliver, *G. Howard Ferguson, Ontario Tory* (Toronto and Buffalo 1977), chapter 18. Personal accounts are W.A. Riddell, *World Security by Conference* (Toronto 1947) and L.B. Pearson, *Mike: The Memoirs of the Right Honourable L.B. Pearson*, 3 vols. (Toronto and Buffalo 1972-5), 1:92-101. A useful summary is in Veatch, *League of Nations*, chapter 11. Many of the important documents are reproduced in DCER, 5:357-430.
36 Stacey, ed., *The Arts of War and Peace*, pp. 110-12. On the military precautions, Denis Richards, *Portal of Hungerford: The Life of Marshal of the Royal Air Force Viscount Portal of Hungerford ...* (London 1977), chapter 12, and Kenneth Edwards, *The Grey Diplomatists* (London 1938)
37 Bennett to Ferguson, August 15, 1935, DCER, 5:379
38 Ibid., p. 383. Veatch, *League of Nations*, pp. 146-7 and Appendix B (Christie's notes of the discussions with Bennett on September 13)
39 Ibid., pp. 148-50. DCER, 5:386-90
40 Skelton's notes of conversation, October 10, 1935, DCER, 5:391-2
41 Ibid., pp. 392-3. Mary C. McGeachy to Dafoe, October 15, 1935, Veatch, *League of Nations*, p. 152
42 DCER, 5:393-403
43 'Canada and the Italo-Ethiopian Conflict. Summary' ('memorandum prepared by Dr. Skelton, January 1936'), King Papers, PAC. This is an instance where I cannot give a more precise reference because I obtained a copy of the document before the present organization of the papers was adopted.
44 DCER, 5:403-5
45 Riddell to Skelton, December 3, 1935 (a very full account of events in the Committee of Eighteen): King Papers
46 King to Riddell, November 7, 1935, DCER, 5:408
47 'Canada and the Italo-Ethiopian Conflict,' above, note 43
48 Skelton to Beaudry, November 27, 1935, DCER, 5:410-11
49 Ibid., pp. 411-12
50 King Diary, November 29, 1935. Skelton to Beaudry, same date, DCER, 6:413
51 *Documents relating to the Italo-Ethiopian Conflict* (External Affairs, Ottawa 1936); extract, Stacey, ed., *The Arts of War and Peace*, pp. 512-13
52 Neatby, *The Prism of Unity*, p. 141
53 December 4, 1935
54 *Le Devoir* (Montreal), December 9, 1935 (*Telegram* (Toronto), December 4)

55 Riddell, *World Security by Conference*, pp. 128-9
56 *Winnipeg Free Press*, October 1, 1936; see Eayrs, *Appeasement and Rearmament*, p. 40.
57 Eayrs, *Appeasement and Rearmament*, pp. 37, 40
58 'Summary of expressions of opinion about Canadian statement on oil embargo,' attached to 'Canada and the Italo-Ethiopian Conflict', above, note 43. *New York Times*, December 4, 1935
59 Riddell, *World Security by Conference*, p. 115
60 Ibid.
61 Ibid. Veatch, *League of Nations*, p. 167
62 King Diary, October 19 and 25, 1935
63 Ibid., October 29, 1935
64 Herridge to Finlayson, October 8, 1935: Bennett Papers, PAC, reel M-1025. Cf Eayrs, *Appeasement and Disarmament*, p. 4. My attention was first called to this letter by F.W.J. Major.
65 King Diary, October 25, 1935
66 CYB, 1938, pp. 578-80
67 The Japanese Treaty Act, 3-4 George V, c. 27, April 10, 1913. Cf Vol. I of this book, p. 83, and Hill, *Canada's Salesman*, p. 148
68 DCER, 5:715-56
69 Minister in Japan to External, May 20, 1935, ibid., pp. 719-20
70 Ibid., pp. 732-9
71 July 23, 1935: ibid., pp. 738-9
72 King Diary, October 24, 1935
73 DCER, 5:750-2
74 *New York Times*, November 15, 1935
75 DCER, 5:754-6
76 1 Edward VIII, c. 19, June 2, 1936, and c. 31, June 23, 1936
77 King in House of Commons, January 25, 1937. John A. Munro, ed., *Documents on Canadian External Relations*, Vol. 6: *1936-1939* (Ottawa 1972), pp. 775-89. The account of the trade negotiations in Hill, *Canada's Salesman*, pp. 550-2, is incomplete; that in Aloysius Balawyder, *Canadian-Soviet Relations Between the World Wars* (Toronto 1972), pp. 217-9, seems to imply that a trade agreement was made in 1936.

CHAPTER 6: TOWARDS A NEW CATASTROPHE

1 The text of the speech is in R.A. Mackay and E.B. Rogers, *Canada Looks Abroad* (Toronto 1938), pp. 363-9.
2 Winston S. Churchill, *The Second World War: The Gathering Storm* (Toronto 1948), pp. 192-7
3 *Debates*, House of Commons, March 23, 1936
4 Victor Hoar, with Mac Reynolds, *The Mackenzie-Papineau Battalion: Canadian Participation in the Spanish Civil War* (Toronto 1969), p. x

5 1 George VI c. 32, April 10, 1937. Order-in-Council, PC 1837, July 30, 1937, John A. Munro, ed., *Documents on Canadian External Relations*, Vol. 6: *1936-1939* (Ottawa 1972) [DCER, 6], pp. 976-7

6 To Sir George Perley, June 5, 1933 (*L'Action nationale*, Montreal, September 1933), in C.P. Stacey, ed., *Historical Documents of Canada*, Vol. 5: *The Arts of War and Peace* (Toronto 1972), p. 195

7 *Canada Year Book* [CYB], 1940, p. 152; ibid., 1941, p. 114. F.C. Blair to W.R. Little, June 6, 1938, DCER, 6:796-800

8 H. Blair Neatby, *William Lyon Mackenzie King*, Vol. 3: *The Prism of Unity, 1932-1939* (Toronto 1976), pp. 304-5

9 *Globe and Mail* (Toronto), December 15, 1938

10 CYB, 1941, p. 114

11 Churchill, *The Gathering Storm*, pp. 114-15. *The Memoirs of General the Lord Ismay* (London 1960), pp. 73-4

12 C.P. Stacey, *Six Years of War* (Official History of the Canadian Army in the Second World War, Vol. 1) (Ottawa 1955), pp. 6-8. C.P. Stacey, *The Military Problems of Canada* (Toronto 1940), pp. 97-8, and Appendix C

13 March 26, 1936: Neatby, *The Prism of Unity*, p. 181

14 Ibid. Stacey, *Six Years of War*, pp. 9-10

15 King Diary (original copy), notes of *séances*, Kingsmere, August 22, 1936. Cf C.P. Stacey, *A Very Double Life: The Private World of Mackenzie King* (Toronto 1976), pp. 185-6

16 Neatby, *The Prism of Unity*, pp. 182-3 (King Diary, October 23, 1936)

17 Stacey, *The Military Problems of Canada*, p. 104 (March 24, 1938)

18 Stacey, *Six Years of War*, pp. 10-13. Neatby, *The Prism of Unity*, p. 183. Stacey, *The Military Problems of Canada*, p. 102 (speech by Mackenzie, February 15, 1937)

19 Ibid., pp. 105-10

20 *Imperial Conference, 1937: Review of Imperial Defence by the Chiefs of Staff Sub-Committee of the Committee of Imperial Defence: Naval Appendix*, p. 19 (King Papers, PAC). The specific reference here is to the 'naval seaward defences' of the ports, not the batteries.

21 Stacey, *Six Years of War*, p. 14 (January 20, 1937)

22 *Debates*, House of Commons, February 15, 16, 18, and 19, 1937. See Neatby, *The Prism of Unity*, pp. 193-4.

23 C.P. Stacey, *Mackenzie King and the Atlantic Triangle* (Toronto 1976), p. 37

24 The United Kingdom Trade Agreement Act, 1937 (1 George VI, c. 17, March 31, 1937). O. Mary Hill, *Canada's Salesman to the World: The Department of Trade and Commerce, 1892-1939* (Ottawa 1977), pp. 547-50. Douglas R. Annett, *British Preference in Canadian Commercial Policy* (Toronto 1948), pp. 82-3. Ian M. Drummond, *Imperial Economic Policy, 1917-1939: Studies in Expansion and Protection* (Toronto 1974), pp. 378-85. DCER, 6:324-62

25 Hill, *Canada's Salesman*, pp. 554-7. DCER, 6:326-88

26 Neatby, *The Prism of Unity*, pp. 210-11

27 See, e.g., minutes of 11th meeting of Principal Delegates, June 2, 1937
28 The conference is described in Neatby, *Prism of Unity*, chapter 12, and in James Eayrs, *In Defence of Canada*. Vol. 2: *Appeasement and Rearmament* (Toronto 1965), pp. 53-61, 81-91; also in chapter 8 of G.N. Hillmer, 'Anglo-Canadian Relations 1926-1937' (Ph.D. thesis, Cambridge University, 1974). The secret printed minutes of the meetings of Principal Delegates are in King Papers, PAC, where a good many other relevant items are also to be found. There is a considerable selection of documents in DCER, 6:117-72 and 180-203.
29 Minutes, 13th meeting of Principal Delegates, June 4
30 Minutes, 3rd meeting. Extracts, Stacey, ed., *The Arts of War and Peace*, pp. 488-91
31 Minutes, 10th meeting, June 1
32 'Notes on the Australian Draft Resolution respecting "Co-operation in Imperial Defence" – Paper E(37)27,' May 31, 1937
33 Minutes, 17th meeting, June 10
34 *Imperial Conference, 1937. Summary of Proceedings* (Ottawa 1937), pp. 19-20. This document was published both in London and Ottawa.
35 Eayrs, *Appeasement and Rearmament*, pp. 87-91
36 C.P. Stacey, *Arms, Men and Governments: The War Policies of Canada, 1939-1945* (Ottawa 1970), p. 89
37 Minutes, 16th meeting, June 9
38 *Summary of Proceedings*, pp. 51-2. Minutes, 8th meeting, May 27
39 Hillmer, 'Anglo-Canadian Relations 1926-1937,' Appendix D (PRO, FO 372/3202/T9371)
40 Correlli Barnett, *The Collapse of British Power* (London 1972), p. 227
41 Alice R. Stewart, 'Sir John A. Macdonald and the Imperial Defence Commission of 1879,' *Canadian Historical Review*, June 1954
42 *A Very Double Life*, pp. 183-4. Violet Markham, *Return Passage: The Autobiography of Violet R. Markham, C.H.* (London 1953), p. 82
43 King Diary, PAC, October 23 and December 26, 1936
44 Eayrs, *Appeasement and Rearmament*, pp. 44-5. Neatby, *Prism of Unity*, pp. 222-3
45 Hillmer, 'Anglo-Canadian Relations 1926-1937,' Appendix D
46 King Diary, June 27, 1937. On King's visit to Berlin I have had the advantage of reading an essay on King and Hitler written by Andrei Grushman for my colleague Michael Bliss. I have commented on King's relations with Hitler generally in 'The Divine Mission: Mackenzie King and Hitler,' *Canadian Historical Review*, LXI, 4, 1980.
47 King Diary, June 29 and 30, 1937
48 Eayrs, *Appeasement and Rearmament*, p. 46n
49 The memorandum is printed in ibid., Document 3.
50 King Diary, October 1, 1936
51 Minute of July 25, 1937, Robert Bothwell and Norman Hillmer, eds., *The In-Between Time: Canadian External Policy in the 1930s* (Toronto 1975), p. 163

52 King Diary, December 25, 1937
53 Ibid., March 27, 1938 (*A Very Double Life*, p. 187)
54 *A Very Double Life*, p. 193
55 Churchill, *The Gathering Storm*, p. 272. Charles Loch Mowat, *Britain between the Wars, 1918-1940* (London 1955), pp. 594-601
56 Chronology of the crisis, '29 World-Shaking Days,' *New York Times*, October 16, 1938
57 Ibid. Mowat, *Britain between the Wars*, pp. 604-19. Churchill, *The Gathering Storm*, chapters 16 and 17. See also J.W. Wheeler-Bennett, *Munich: Prologue to Tragedy* (London 1963); Keith Robbins, *Munich 1938* (London 1968); and Telford Taylor, *Munich: The Price of Peace* (New York 1979).
58 Eayrs, *Appeasement and Rearmament*, chapter 3
59 DCER, 6:1090-4
60 *Globe and Mail* (Toronto), September 30, 1938. Vincent Massey, *What's Past is Prologue: The Memoirs of the Right Honourable Vincent Massey, C.H.* (Toronto 1963), pp. 258-62. Minutes of High Commissioners' meetings, PRO, DO 114/94, secret print Dominions no 186
61 Text of message, September 24, 1938, Eayrs, *Appeasement and Rearmament*, p. 48
62 Keith Feiling, *The Life of Neville Chamberlain* (London 1970), p. 372
63 King Diary, September 27 and 28, 1938. Text of statement, DCER, 6:1097
64 Stacey, *Arms, Men and Governments*, p. 7 (August 26, 1939)
65 Ibid. (August 31, 1938)
66 King Diary, September 24, 1938
67 Stacey, *The Military Problems of Canada*, Appendix C
68 Stacey, *Six Years of War*, p. 17
69 King Diary, December 16, 1938
70 Stacey, *Six Years of War*, pp. 13, 17
71 Stacey, *Arms, Men and Governments*, p. 106. Stacey, *The Military Problems of Canada*, pp. 116-19, 121-5
72 *Debates*, House of Commons, April 26 and May 12, 13, 15, and 18, 1939
73 Stacey, *The Military Problems of Canada*, pp. 128-36. *Report of the Royal Commission on the Bren Machine Gun Contract. Hon. Henry Hague Davis, Commissioner* (Ottawa 1939)
74 Stacey, *Arms, Men and Governments*, pp. 81-9; Eayrs, *Appeasement and Rearmament*, pp. 91-103
75 Stacey, *Arms, Men and Governments*, pp. 82-3
76 Chiefs of Staff to the Minister, May 6, 1937, King Papers. King Diary, May 5, 1937, Stacey, *Arms, Men and Governments*, p. 83
77 Stacey, *Arms, Men and Armaments*, pp. 83-5. Eayrs, *Appeasement and Rearmament*, pp. 92-6
78 Stacey, *Arms, Men and Governments*, pp. 81-2
79 Ibid., p. 85. Christie's paper, 'The Imperial-Flying-School-in-Canada Idea,' June 19, 1938, is in DCER, 6:209-10.

80 Stacey, *Arms, Men and Governments*, p. 86
81 Ibid., p. 87 (October 4, 1938)
82 Ibid., pp. 86-9
83 King Diary, July 31, 1936
84 Ibid. Cf *New York Times*, August 1, 1936. CYB, 1936, p. 1093. DCER, 6:36-42
85 King Diary, May 9, 1927
86 Stacey, *Arms, Men and Governments*, pp. 96-7
87 Ibid., pp. 97-8. Stacey, *The Military Problems of Canada*, pp. 29-35
88 Much of the detail is found in Richard N. Kottman, *Reciprocity and the North Atlantic Triangle, 1932-1938* (Ithaca, NY, 1968), chapters 4-7.
89 Memorandum by Assistant Secretary of State, September 21, 1937, FRUS, 1937, 2:68
90 Memorandum by [King], 'Memorandum re U.K.-U.S. Agreement,' of events July 26-30, 1937, King Papers, J4, vol. 216
91 Minister in Canada to Secretary of State, October 14, 1937, FRUS, 1937, 2:164
92 Dana Wilgress, *Memoirs* (Toronto 1967), p. 108
93 Hull to Kennedy (two messages), November 3, 1938, FRUS, 1938, 2:69-71. *New York Times*, November 18, 1938
94 The Canadian-American agreement is a schedule to the Canada-United States of America Trade Agreement Act, 3 George VI, c. 29, May 19, 1939. For the Anglo-American agreement, see *New York Times*, November 18, 1938. Various reports and comments, *New York Times*, November 18, and 19, 1938. CYB, 1939, p. 461. Wilgress, *Memoirs*, pp. 108-10. Hill, *Canada's Salesman*, pp. 558-63
95 Kottman, *Reciprocity*, pp. 267-71
96 Editorial, November 18, 1938
97 King Diary, November 8, 1935; Stacey, *Mackenzie King and the Atlantic Triangle*, p. 55. J.W. Pickersgill, ed., *The Mackenzie King Record*, Vol. 1: *1939-1944* (Toronto 1960), p. 436
98 *New York Times*, August 1, 1936. Stacey, *The Military Problems of Canada*, p. 29
99 Forrest C. Pogue, *George C. Marshall: Education of a General* (New York 1963), pp. 338-42
100 *New York Times*, August 1, 1936
101 From a Canadian Institute of International Affairs paper of 1935: see MacKay and Rogers, *Canada Looks Abroad*, p. 269.
102 Ibid. This book is the best survey of Canadian opinion for the period. On the isolationists, see particularly chapter 18, 'Non-Intervention.' The bibliography has a useful list of articles, pp. 392-3. See also F.R. Scott, *Canada Today: A Study of Her National Interests and National Policy* (Toronto 1938); bibliography, pp. 153-6
103 This point emerges strongly from an essay written for me by Charles Spencer on the Canadian academic community and the threat of war, 1931-9.

104 'Canadian Foreign Policy,' in Reginald G. Trotter, Albert B. Corey, and Walter W. McLaren, eds., *Conference on Canadian-American Affairs Held at Queen's University, Kingston, Ontario, June 14-18, 1937* (Boston 1937), pp. 220-31
105 King Diary, September 11, 1929
106 On King's views at this period, and the conflict with Skelton, see J.L. Granatstein and Robert Bothwell, '"A Self-Evident National Duty": Canadian Foreign Policy, 1935-1939,' *Journal of Imperial and Commonwealth History*, January 1975
107 This paper, 'Central European Situation,' September 11, 1938, has become divided into two parts, the first being in PAC, RG 25, D 1, vol. 724, file 66, vol. 2, and the second, dealing with Canada, in ibid., vol. 726, file 74, vol. 7. It is unsigned, but Skelton's authorship is clearly established by King Diary, September 12, 1938.
108 King Diary, September 12, 1938
109 Ibid., January 27, 1939. On Pickersgill, ibid., January 20, 1939

CHAPTER 7: 1939: THE OUTBREAK

1 On Laurier's remark, see Volume I of this book, pp. 134-5.
2 *Debates*, House of Commons, March 30, 1939, pp. 2423-4
3 King Diary, PAC, January 14, 1940
4 Ibid., January 26, 1939. Dominions Office to External, for Prime Minister, January 25, 1939, John A. Munro, ed., *Documents on Canadian External Relations*, Vol. 6: *1936-1939* (Ottawa 1972) [DCER, 6], pp. 1117-19. For the background, see Sidney Aster, *1939: The Making of the Second World War* (London 1973), pp. 43-50, where however the message is not mentioned, and David Dilks, ed., *The Diaries of Sir Alexander Cadogan, O.M., 1938-1945* (London 1971), pp. 139-44, which publishes the message as sent to Washington.
5 King Diary, January 27, 1939
6 Ibid., January 30, 1939
7 DCER, 6:1134-6
8 Aster, *1939*, chapter 1. C.L. Mowat, *Britain between the Wars, 1918-1940* (London 1955), pp. 636-8
9 Simon Newman, *March 1939: The British Guarantee to Poland* (Oxford 1976), argues that in fact it was not a new policy, but a continuation of the policy of stemming German expansion in eastern Europe 'by any means short of war but in the last resort by war itself.'
10 Mowat, *Britain between the Wars*, pp. 638-41. Dilks, ed., *Cadogan*, pp. 158-68. The course of negotiations with Russia in described, undoubtedly on the basis of communications from London, in Loring Christie's memorandum of July 19, 1939, DCER, 6:1205-21.
11 Aster, *1939*, pp. 91-5

12 Memorandum for the Prime Minister, August 25, 1939, DCER, 6:1247-52
13 Ibid., pp. 1162-4 (memorandum of April 12, 1939)
14 King Diary, March 20, 1939. H. Blair Neatby, *William Lyon Mackenzie King: The Prism of Unity, 1932-1939* (Toronto 1976), pp. 298-9
15 King Diary, March 19, 1939
16 Ibid., April 27, 1939
17 Ibid., March 24, 1939
18 Ibid., April 25, 1939
19 Night edition: see C.P. Stacey, ed., *Historical Documents of Canada*, Vol. 5: *The Arts of War and Peace* (Toronto 1972), pp. 494-6
20 James Eayrs, *In Defence of Canada*, Vol. 2: *Appeasement and Rearmament* (Toronto 1965), pp. 75-6 (L.A. Taschereau to King, April 1, 1939)
21 King Diary, March 31, 1939. Neatby, *Prism of Unity*, pp. 300-3
22 King Diary, January 27, 1939. Cf Janet Adam Smith, *John Buchan: A Biography* (London 1965), pp. 450-1
23 King Diary, April 26, 1939. John W. Wheeler-Bennett, *King George VI: His Life and Reign* (London 1958), pp. 376-7. The Earl of Halifax, *Fulness of Days* (London 1957), pp. 203-4
24 King Diary, November 17, 1938
25 Ibid., February 28, 1939
26 Ibid., March 20, 1939
27 Ibid., March 14, 1939. Wheeler-Bennett, *King George VI*, pp. 374-5
28 E.g., King Diary, February 28, 1939
29 Wheeler-Bennett, *King George VI*, pp. 377-94. Gustave Lanctot, *The Royal Tour of King George VI and Queen Elizabeth in Canada and the United States of America* (Toronto 1964). Neatby, *The Prism of Unity*, pp. 310-14. C.P. Stacey, *Arms, Men and Governments: The War Policies of Canada, 1939-1945* (Ottawa 1970), pp. 98-9. *Canada Year Book*, 1939, pp. 1155-60
30 See, e.g., *Winnipeg Free Press*, May-June 1939, *passim*.
31 Stacey, *Arms, Men and Governments*, p. 7 (August 26, 1939)
32 King to Hitler, 'Personlich,' February 1, 1939, DCER, 6:1122-3
33 Eayrs, *Appeasement and Rearmament*, p. 77. King's diary does not mention whether or not a New Year's greeting was sent to Hitler.
34 King Diary (handwritten), July 21, 1939. Windels' memorandum is in DCER, 6:1221-2.
35 King Diary, handwritten notes re events July 25-August 11 added to text for July 21, 1939; also handwritten diary for July 25, and entries for August 10 and 11. Neatby, *The Prism of Unity*, pp. 315-16. Eayrs, *Appeasement and Rearmament*. pp. 76-8
36 King Diary, July 21, 1939
37 Aster, *1939*, pp. 314-19; Dilks, ed., *Cadogan*, pp. 199n, 207-8
38 DCER, 6:1233
39 E.g., Neatby, *The Prism of Unity*, pp. 297-8

40 E.L. Woodward and Rohan Butler, eds., *Documents on British Foreign Policy, 1919-1939*, Third series, Vol. 7 (London 1954), pp. 127-8 (Halifax to Henderson, August 22, 1939). Also in Winston S. Churchill, *The Second World War: The Gathering Storm* (Toronto 1948), p. 396, and cf Dilks, ed., *Cadogan*, pp. 200-1. British cabinet minute 41 (39), August 22, 1939 (PRO, CAB 23/100; PAC, reel B-3895)

41 Woodward and Butler, eds., *Documents on British Foreign Policy*, III:7:488

42 Aster, *1939*, pp. 373-88. Dilks, ed., *Cadogan*, pp. 210-13. See British cabinet minute 49 (39), September 2, 1939 (11:30 p.m.) (PRO, CAB 23/100; PAC, reel B-3895).

43 Woodward and Butler, eds., *Documents on British Foreign Policy*, III:7:535

44 Wheeler-Bennett, *King George VI*, pp. 406-7

45 King Diary, August 22, 1939

46 Ibid., August 23, 1939

47 Ibid., August 24, 1939

48 Barbara M. Wilson, ed., *Ontario and the First World War, 1914-1918* (Toronto 1977), p. lxxxiv. King Diary, May 10, 1940

49 King Papers; when I examined it it was in a binder entitled 'Military Co-Operation with United Kingdom: General.' See Stacey, *Arms, Men and Governments*, p. 9, and Stacey, ed., *The Arts of War and Peace*, pp. 595-6.

50 King Diary, August 25, 1939

51 Ibid.

52 Ibid. Sir Gerald Campbell, *Of True Experience* (New York 1947)

53 C.P. Stacey, *Six Years of War* (Official History of the Canadian Army in the Second World War, Vol. 1) (Ottawa 1955), pp. 40-1

54 King Diary, August 27, 1939. King in House of Commons, September 8, 1939 (*Debates*, pp. 29-30)

55 Stacey, *Six Years of War*, pp. 41-2

56 King Diary, September 1, 1939. *Globe and Mail* (Toronto), September 1, 1939

57 Stacey, *Six Years of War*, p. 46

58 J.W. Pickersgill, ed., *The Mackenzie King Record*. Vol. 1: *1939-44* (Toronto 1960), pp. 30-1

59 J. Rohwer and G. Hummelchen, *Chronology of the War at Sea, 1939-1945*, trans. Derek Masters, 2 vols. (London 1972-4), 1:2. S.W. Roskill, *The War at Sea, 1939-1945*, Vol. 1 (London 1954), p. 103. *Globe and Mail*, September 4, 1939. It is difficult to determine exactly how many Canadians lost their lives, because the Donaldson Line's list of missing did not distinguish between Canadians and other British subjects; see *The Times* (London), October 10, 1939, and *Globe and Mail*, October 10 and 16, 1939.

60 *Debates*, House of Commons, 'Fifth (Special War) Session – Eighteenth Parliament, September 7-September 13, 1939'

61 Walter D. Young, *The Anatomy of a Party: The National CCF, 1932-61* (Toronto 1969), pp. 92-3, 106

62 King Diary, September 9, 1939
63 *Globe and Mail*, September 11, 1939
64 King Diary, September 8, 1939
65 Ibid., September 9, 1939
66 Jbid., September 9, 10, 11, 1939. King statement in House of Commons, September 11, 1939. Vincent Massey, *What's Past is Prologue: The Memoirs of the Right Honourable Vincent Massey, C.H.* (Toronto 1963), pp. 278-80. Lester B. Pearson, *Mike: The Memoirs of the Right Honourable Lester B. Pearson*, 3 vols. (Toronto 1972-5), 1:137-40
67 *Globe and Mail*, September 11, 1939. W.P.M. Kennedy, *The Constitution of Canada, 1534-1937* ... (Oxford 1938), pp. 540-1
68 'Memorandum for the Prime Minister,' King Papers, MG 26, J 4, vol. 165. The final portion, here quoted, is in longhand.
69 DCER, 6:1104-10
70 See Scott's impassioned declaration of June 22, 1939, in Albert B. Corey, Reginald G. Trotter, and Walter W. McLaren, eds., *Conference on Canadian-American Affairs Held at The St. Lawrence University, Canton, New York, June 19-22, 1939* (Boston 1939), pp. 214-15
71 See Christie's paper of December 1938, 'The Canadian Dilemma,' Christie Papers, PAC
72 H. Gordon Skilling, *Canadian Representation Abroad: From Agency to Embassy* (Toronto 1945), pp. 247-8. On the circumstances in which these legations were opened, see DCER, 6:48-63.
73 Ibid., pp. 1129-31 (March 2, 1939)
74 William L. Langer and S. Everett Gleason, *The Challenge to Isolation, 1937-1940* (New York 1952), p. 12
75 King Diary, September 9, 1939

CHAPTER 8: THE SECOND WORLD WAR: 1939-41

1 C.P. Stacey, *Arms, Men and Governments: The War Policies of Canada, 1939-1945* (reprint, corrected, Ottawa 1974)
2 The British communications of September 6, 1939, are in ibid., Appendix 'C.' British Chiefs of Staff paper, September 4, 1939, with Campbell's message of September 1 attached, PRO, CAB 66/1. See also John A. Munro, ed., *Documents on Canadian External Relations*, Vol. 6: *1936-1939* (Ottawa 1972) [DCER, 6], 6:1301-5. The Government's policy statement is in *Ottawa Journal*, September 20, 1939.
3 Prime Minister to Prime Minister, September 26, 1939: David R. Murray, ed., *Documents on Canadian External Relations*, Vol. 7, *1939-1941*, Part 1 (Ottawa 1974) [DCER, 7], pp. 549-52
4 Vincent Massey, *What's Past is Prologue: The Memoirs of the Right Honourable Vincent Massey, C.H.* (Toronto 1963), pp. 303-6

5 J.W. Pickersgill, *The Mackenzie King Record*, Vol. 1: *1939-1944* (Toronto 1960), pp. 40-1
6 DCER, 7:556-7. On the matter in general, Stacey, *Arms, Men and Governments*, pp. 17-20, and cf James Eayrs, *In Defence of Canada*, Vol. 2: *Appeasement and Rearmament* (Toronto 1965), pp. 103-14
7 J.R.M. Butler, *Grand Strategy*, 2 (*History of the Second World War, United Kingdom Military Series*) (London 1957), p. 9
8 September 29, 1939: DCER, 7:167-8
9 Ibid., pp. 168-9
10 King to Chamberlain, October 6 and 8, 1939, ibid., pp. 169-71. King Diary, same dates.
11 Ibid., October 8, 1939
12 Chamberlain to King, Most Secret and Personal, October 10, 1939, DCER 7:176
13 Ibid., pp. 171-84
14 King Diary, October 11, 1939
15 DCER, 7:187-93 (November 2, 1939). Also in Eayrs, *Appeasement and Rearmament*, Document 4, but with several paragraphs omitted
16 DCER, 7:200-4 (November 25, 1939)
17 Ibid., pp. 207-8
18 Ibid., pp. 284-52
19 King Diary, PAC, November 30, 1939
20 DCER, 7:1080-88
21 David R. Murray, ed., *Documents on Canadian External Relations*, Vol. 8: *1939-1941*, Part II (Ottawa 1976), [DCER, 8], pp. 1046-62. King Diary, March 11, 1940
22 Sir Llewellyn Woodward, *British Foreign Policy in the Second World War*, 5 vols. (London 1970), 1:39-99. David Dilks, ed., *The Diaries of Sir Alexander Cadogan, O.M., 1938-1945* (London 1971), pp. 235-63. Winston S. Churchill, *The Second World War: The Gathering Storm* (Toronto 1948), pp. 538-74
23 Memo by Skelton, February 27, 1940, DCER, 8:1066-7
24 Read Papers, PAC, MG 30, E 148, vol. 10 (interview)
25 Stacey, *Arms, Men and Governments*, pp. 141-2. Lester B. Pearson, *Mike: The Memoirs of the Right Honourable Lester B. Pearson*, 3 vols. (Toronto 1972-5), 1:170-1
26 DCER, 7:757-8 (April 20, 1940)
27 Ibid., pp. 773-4
28 DCER, 5:30 (January 11/February 13, 1935)
29 DCER, 7:1-18
30 Butler, *Grand Strategy*, 2:9
31 DCER, 7:375-80. Stacey, *Arms, Men and Governments*, pp. 143-5
32 J.L. Granatstein, *Canada's War: The Politics of the Mackenzie King Government, 1939-1945* (Toronto 1975), p. 64
33 DCER, 7:597-9

34 DCER, 7:473-5, 478-83. On the Crerar mission generally, ibid., pp. 375-408; Stacey, *Arms, Men and Governments*, pp. 11, 21-2, 143-5; Granatstein, *Canada's War*, pp. 63-5

35 Stacey, *Arms, Men and Governments*, p. 145. DCER, 7:408-14

36 Stacey, *Arms, Men and Governments*, pp. 308, 320-2, 57-60

37 King Diary, December 15, 1939

38 Stacey, *Arms, Men and Governments*, pp. 16, 310

39 The Canadian Act is 23-24 George V c. 21, April 12, 1933. Extract in C.P. Stacey, ed., *Historical Documents of Canada*, Vol. 5: *The Arts of War and Peace* (Toronto 1972), pp. 524-6

40 Stacey, *Arms, Men and Governments*, pp. 211-13, 218, 248-9 and Appendix 'G.' C.P. Stacey, *Six Years of War* (Official History of the Canadian Army in the Second World War, Vol. 1), 3d printing (Ottawa 1957), pp. 255-6

41 December 7, 1939, Stacey, *Arms, Men and Governments*, Appendix 'H.' Also in DCER, 7:734-6

42 Stacey, *Six Years of War*, chapter 8. Stacey, *Arms, Men and Governments*, pp. 247-52

43 Stacey, *Arms, Men and Governments*, p. 18. DCER, 7:855-6

44 Massey, *What's Past is Prologue*, p. 304

45 Agreement, Stacey, *Arms, Men and Governments*, Appendix 'D.' Riverdale's undated general report, PRO, Air 8/280/1P3/574

46 Minutes, Cabinet War Committee, DCER, 7:586-91. Riverdale to Sir Kingsley Wood, November 6, 1939, PRO, Air 20/338/IIIc/3/14. Campbell to Eden, December 19, 1939, and Eden to Chamberlain, January 16, 1940, PRO, Premier 1/397. Skelton to King, November 1, 1939, External Affairs file II-B-84, Pt 2. For the negotiations generally, see DCER, 7:578-671; Stacey, *Arms, Men and Governments*, pp. 17-30; Pickersgill, *Mackenzie King Record*, 1, chapter 3; Eayrs, *Appeasement and Rearmament*, pp. 103-14

47 Stacey, *Arms, Men and Governments*, pp. 252-88, and Appendices 'B' (Table 3) and 'I'

48 Ibid., pp. 288-303, and Appendices 'L' and 'M'

49 Ibid., p. 26 (December 13, 1939)

50 Ibid., pp. 66, 305

51 Harris to Secretary of State for Air, August 13, 1942, and to Under Secretary, January 19, 1942 [1943]; [Sinclair] to Harris, September 2, 1942, and Portal to Harris, February 7, 1943, all on PRO, Air 20/3798/1D6/53/2

52 C.P. Stacey, *Mackenzie King and the Atlantic Triangle* (Toronto 1976), pp. 18, 52-3

53 May 10, 1940, King Papers, PAC. At the time I did most of my work on the wartime King Papers they had not been arranged and many of them, like these two cables, were simply loose sheets.

54 May 20, 1940: Stacey, *Mackenzie King and the Atlantic Triangle*, p. 53. November 25, 1947, ibid.

55 Stacey, *Arms, Men and Governments*, pp. 31-7

56 DCER, 8:519-34. Pickersgill, *Mackenzie King Record*, 1:98-9. Figure of £100 million, undated 'Note for the Chancellor of the Exchequer,' [August 1940?], PRO, T 160/1045

57 Pickersgill, *Mackenzie King Record*, 1:180-3. DCER, 8:668-722

58 DCER, 8:560-1

59 Ibid., pp. 534-91, particularly pp. 569-70

60 Minutes, Cabinet War Committee, December 29, 1941. DCER, 8:631-66, particularly p. 645, Churchill to King, December 29, 1940. Woodward, *British Foreign Policy*, 1:427-30. Minutes of May and July 1942 on FO 371/31957 (PRO)

61 Pickersgill, *Mackenzie King Record*, 1:422-9. J.F. Hilliker, 'The Canadian Government and the Free French: Perceptions and Restraints, 1940-1944,' in *Canadian Committee for the History of the Second World War: The first conference at Collège Militaire Royal de Saint-Jean, 20-22 Oct 1977* (mimeographed) [1978]. Minutes, PRO, FO 371/31957, May-July 1942

62 Lapointe to Ralston, September 30, 1940, Hilliker, 'The Canadian Government and the Free French.' DCER, 8:602 (minutes, Cabinet War Committee, October 1, 1940)

63 DCER, 8:580-1 (August 13, 1941)

64 Hilliker, 'The Canadian Government and the Free French.' Pickersgill, *Mackenzie King Record*, 1:424

65 William L. Langer, *Our Vichy Gamble* (New York 1947; new ed., Hamden, Conn. 1965)

66 DCER, 8:723-802

67 Foreign Secretary to Ambassador in US, October 19, 1940, ibid., pp. 787-8, and cf pp. 770-86

68 Ibid., p. 788 (October 19, 1940). Legation in Washington to Department of State, July 20, 1940, ibid., p. 751

69 Ibid., pp. 838-9

70 Minutes, Cabinet War Committee, December 3 and 19, 1941

71 DCER 8:828-39

72 Stacey, *Arms, Men and Governments*, 1974 reprint, p. 373n

73 Ibid., pp. 372-3. Pickersgill, *Mackenzie King Record*, 1:318-24. E.-H. Muselier, *De Gaulle contre le Gaullisme* (Paris 1946), pp. 247-64. Charles de Gaulle, *War Memoirs*, 1 (London 1955), p. 128, and accompanying *Documents*, 1, pp. 38-9 and 239. Nancy Harvison Hooker, ed., *The Moffat Papers: Selections from the Diplomatic Journals of Jay Pierrepont Moffat, 1919-1943* (Cambridge, Mass. 1956), pp. 357-73. Cordell Hull, *The Memoirs of Cordell Hull*, 2 vols. (New York 1948), pp. 1128-38. *New York Times*, December 25-31, 1941. FRUS, 1941, 2:540 ff. Conclusions, British War Cabinet, 136 (41), December 26, 1941, PRO, CAB 65/20. On the episode generally, Douglas G. Anglin, *The St. Pierre and Miquelon AFFAIRE of 1941* (Toronto 1966)

74 Pearson, *Mike*, 1:139. This episode is not covered in DCER.

75 DCER, 7:324-37. Minutes, Cabinet War Committee, June 10, 1940. Stacey, *Arms, Men and Governments*, p. 119n

76 Ibid., p. 328. King Diary, January 23, February 7, 25, April 5, 13, 1940
77 'Memorandum re Conversations with the President, Warm Springs, Georgia, April 23 and 24, 1940,' ibid.
78 Ibid., April 28, 1940
79 Stacey, *Arms, Men and Governments*, pp. 367-70
80 *New York Times*, June 9, 1940
81 'The War: The Desperate Grapple,' *University of Toronto Quarterly*, July 1940
82 Stacey, *Arms, Men and Governments*, pp. 328-32. Keenleyside's reports and related documents are in DCER, 8:65-97.
83 Stacey, *Arms, Men and Governments*, pp. 332-6
84 The account in ibid., pp. 336-8, is fully documented. Moffat's letter to Sumner Welles, August 14, 1940, which Welles passed on to the President on August 16, is in FRUS, 1940, 3:144-5.
85 Stacey, *Arms, Men and Governments*, pp. 338-9. On Roosevelt's failure to take military advice, Stanley W. Dziuban, *Military Relations between the United States and Canada, 1939-1945* (Washington 1959), p. 29. DCER, 8:134-40
86 Stacey, *Arms, Men and Governments*, pp. 340-2. Cranborne to Churchill, March 6, 1941, PRO, Premier 11/43A/12
87 Stacey, *Arms, Men and Governments*, pp. 343-54
88 Ibid., pp. 129, 357-60. C.P. Stacey, *The Military Problems of Canada* (Toronto 1940), pp. 40-5
89 April 7, 1941, DCER, 8:303-7. Stacey, *Arms, Men and Governments*, p. 49
90 Stacey, *Arms, Men and Governments*, p. 489. Text of declaration, Canada, *Treaty Series*, 1941, no 14, in Stacey, ed., *The Arts of War and Peace*, pp. 651-2. R.D. Cuff and J.L. Granatstein, 'The Hyde Park Declaration, 1941: Origins and Significance,' in the same authors' *Ties That Bind: Canadian-American Relations in Wartime from the Great War to the Cold War* (Toronto 1977)
91 For a British view of Clark, Gordon Munro to S.D. Waley, November 17, 1942, PRO, T 160/1252
92 Clark to King, April 9, 1941, covering three memos; Howe to King, April 8, 1941; DCER, 8:307-21
93 Pickersgill, *Mackenzie King Record*, 1:191-2
94 DCER, 8:321-3. John Morton Blum, *From the Morgenthau Diaries: Years of Urgency, 1938-1941* (Boston 1965), pp. 248-9, is very little help.
95 DCER, 8:329-32 (April 25, 1941)
96 Ibid., pp. 327-9 (April 23, 1941)
97 Stacey, *Arms, Men and Governments*, pp. 146-8
98 Ibid., pp. 147-51
99 Ibid., p. 151. British War Cabinet Conclusions, August 25, 1941, PRO, CAB 65/19
100 Stacey, *Arms, Men and Governments*, pp. 154-5. Massey, *What's Past is Prologue*, pp. 297-302. Winston S. Churchill, *The Second World War: Their Finest Hour* (1949), pp. 693, 707; *The Grand Alliance* (1950), p. 751; *The Hinge of Fate* (1951), p. 847

101 Note for Cranborne, August 8, 1941, enclosed in Cranborne to Churchill, August 20, 1941, PRO, Premier 4/44/7. Cf undated and untitled note by [MacDonald] [spring 1941?], PRO, Premier 4/44/10 END, and dispatch February 3, 1942, CAB 66/22. On King's relationship with MacDonald, Pickersgill, *Mackenzie King Record*, 1:178-9

102 DCER, 8:1093-4 (January 22, 1940)

103 Ibid., pp. 1099-1102

104 Ibid., 7:349-73

105 *Chronology of the Second World War* (London 1947), p. 94. DCER, 7:340-2 (Memo by Legal Adviser, March 5, 1941). Documents in PRO, FO 371/48132

106 British Ambassador, Tokyo, to Foreign Office, July 6, 1940 (PRO, FO 371/24725); Secretary of State External to Chargé in Japan, June 20 and October 28, 1940, DCER, 8: 1270-1 and 1335-7; British High Commissioner, Ottawa, to Dominions Office, August 15, 1940, PRO, WO 106/4900; King Diary, August 15, 1940. I owe these references to Alan Mason.

107 Pickersgill, *Mackenzie King Record*, 1:296-7. DCER, 8:1530-1, 1546-50

108 Ibid., pp. 1552-61 (order-in-council, PC 9592, p. 1554). *Mackenzie King Record*, 1:297-300. FRUS, 'Japan, 1931-1941,' 2 vols. (Washington 1943), 2:795. Cf ibid., 1941, 4:732-5

109 Pickersgill, *Mackenzie King Record*, 1:166

110 Ibid., p. 167. Pearson, *Mike*, 1:192-4. Order-in-council appointing Robertson, PC 4645, June 24, 1941

111 Bennett to Stirling, April 15, 1941, Bennett Papers, PAC, reel M-3172

CHAPTER 9: THE SECOND WORLD WAR: 1942-45

1 August 28, 1944: PRO, T 247/126

2 C.P. Stacey, *Mackenzie King and the Atlantic Triangle* (Toronto 1976), p. 54

3 C.P. Stacey, *Arms, Men and Governments: The War Policies of Canada, 1939-1945* (Ottawa 1970), p. 154

4 Lester B. Pearson, *Mike: The Memoirs of the Right Honourable Lester B. Pearson*, 3 vols. (Toronto 1972-5), 1:215

5 Stacey, *Arms, Men and Governments*, pp. 278-83

6 No 136, received April 18, 1942: PRO, Air 19/339/1D/5/72

7 Stacey, *Arms, Men and Governments*, pp. 356, 168

8 Ibid., pp. 161-2

9 MacDonald's 'The Post-War Position of the British Commonwealth of Nations,' February 23, 1943, PRO, FO 371/36603

10 Minutes of Cabinet War Committee, 136th meeting, January 14, 1942

11 Stacey, *Arms, Men and Governments*, pp. 167-74

12 Minutes of Cabinet War Committee, 170th meeting, June 11, 1942

13 Memo by MacDonald, July 30, 1942, of conversation same day, PRO, T 188/252

14 Memo by [Leith-Ross], July 30, 1942, of conversation previous day, ibid.

15 'Some Thoughts on Provision for Dominion Representation in the Machinery for the Higher Direction of the War,' September 5, 1942, PRO, FO 371/31543. Memo by N.B. Ronald, September 16, 1942, of meeting September 14, 1942, ibid.

16 Documents in ibid., September 9-11, 1942

17 Minutes of Cabinet War Committee, 229th meeting, April 7, 1943. Memo by Robertson, April 13, 1943, PRO, DO 35/1221, and later documents, ibid.

18 S. McK. Rosen, *The Combined Boards of the Second World War* (New York 1951), pp. 258-9

19 Minutes of Cabinet War Committee, 216th meeting, January 21, 1943. Retrospective memo by W.J. Hasler, April 7, 1945, PRO, FO 371/51365. External file 2295-AR-40 (2)

20 January 20, 1942: External file 3265-A-40. I owe this reference to the Historical Division, Department of External Affairs.

21 Stacey, *Arms, Men and Governments*, p. 180 and Appendix 'F'

22 Ibid., pp. 181-4. Stacey, *Mackenzie King and the Atlantic Triangle*, pp. 56-9. J.W. Pickersgill, *The Mackenzie King Record*, Vol. 1: *1939-1944* (Toronto 1960), pp. 527-60. For the conversation with Robertson and MacDonald, King Diary, July 19, 1943

23 Stacey, *Arms, Men and Governments*, pp. 165-7

24 Ibid., pp. 184-93

25 Minutes of Cabinet War Committee, 254th meeting, August 11, 1943

26 The passage that follows is condensed, and to some extent quoted, from the discussion in my *Arms, Men and Governments*, pp. 137-8.

27 G.W.L. Nicholson, *The Canadians in Italy, 1943-1945* (Ottawa 1956), pp. 73-5. Pickersgill, *Mackenzie King Record*, 1:520-6. Pearson, *Mike*, 1:240-3

28 Pickersgill, *Mackenzie King Record*, 1:521. Malcolm MacDonald to Attlee, August 6, 1943, PRO, CAB 66/40

29 Stacey, *Arms, Men and Governments*, pp. 152-3

30 MacDonald to Attlee, August 6, 1943, note 28 above

31 Vincent Massey, *What's Past is Prologue: The Memoirs of the Right Honourable Vincent Massey, C.H.* (Toronto 1963), pp. 310-11

32 In Stacey, *Arms, Men and Governments*, Part 5

33 C.P. Stacey, *Six Years of War* (Official History of the Canadian Army in the Second World War, Vol. 1) (Ottawa 1955), pp. 419-25

34 Stacey, *Arms, Men and Governments*, pp. 210-13. General Crerar's directive, C.P. Stacey, *The Victory Campaign* (Ottawa 1960), Appendix 'A'

35 Stacey, *Arms, Men and Governments*, pp. 210-11. On McNaughton, John Swettenham, *McNaughton*, 3 vols. (Toronto 1968-9), and Douglas LePan, *Bright Glass of Memory* (Toronto 1979)

36 Stacey, *Arms, Men and Governments*, pp. 230-3. Massey Diary, Massey College, Toronto, July 14, 1943

37 Nicholson, *The Canadians in Italy*, pp. 20-2

38 Stacey, *Arms, Men and Governments*, pp. 231-7
39 Ibid., pp. 236-46
40 Ibid., pp. 223, 226-8
41 Ibid., p. 229
42 Ibid.
43 Ibid. Crerar's directive, May 11/24, 1944, note 34 above
44 Stacey, *Arms, Men and Governments*, pp. 220-1. Pickersgill, *Mackenzie King Record*, 1:690-3 (May 18, 1944)
45 Stacey, *Arms, Men and Governments*, pp. 261, 291, 301
46 Ibid., pp. 149-51
47 Ibid., pp. 310-14
48 Ibid., Part VIII. J. de N. Kennedy, *History of the Department of Munitions and Supply*, 2 vols. (Ottawa 1952). H. Duncan Hall, *North American Supply* ('History of the Second World War, United Kingdom Civil Series') (London 1955)
49 H. Duncan Hall and C.C. Wrigley, *Studies of Overseas Supply* ('History of the Second World War, United Kingdom Civil Series') (London 1956), p. 46
50 Report, November 3, 1941, PRO, FO 414/278
51 Pickersgill, *Mackenzie King Record*, 1:333-4. Stacey, *Arms, Men and Governments*, p. 49
52 Wilfrid Sanders, *Jack & Jacques* (Toronto n.d.), p. 21
53 PRO, T 160/1252: Balfour to MacDonald, June 3, 1942
54 Minutes, Cabinet War Committee, January 13 and 21, 1943. Pickersgill, *Mackenzie King Record*, 1:483-4. War Appropriation (United Nations Mutual Aid) Act, 7 George VI, c. 17, May 20, 1943
55 Draft Memo by Chancellor of Exchequer, early 1942, PRO, T 160/1252
56 February 5, 1943: PRO, FO 371/35519
57 *Debates*, House of Commons, May 10, 1943
58 War Appropriation (United Nations Mutual Aid) Act, 1944, 8 George VI, c. 15, June 23, 1944
59 Memo by R.H. Brand (covering letter October 18, 1944), PRO, T 160/1376
60 9 George VI, c. 3, April 16, 1945
61 High Commissioner, Ottawa, to Dominions Office, August 4, 1945, PRO, BT 11/2785
62 'Financial Relations with Canada,' brief for the Chancellor of the Exchequer, August 30, 1946, PRO, DO 35-1220
63 Stacey, *Arms, Men and Governments*, pp. 354-7. *New York Times*, November 12, 1943
64 Stacey, *Arms, Men and Governments*, p. 339
65 Ibid., p. 135. Paul Bridle, ed., *Documents on Relations between Canada and Newfoundland*, 1: *1935-1949* (Ottawa 1974), pp. 159-62
66 Minutes, Cabinet War Committee, 31st meeting, September 5, 1940
67 Ibid., 317th meeting, October 5, 1944
68 Stacey, *Arms, Men and Governments*, pp. 382-4

69 Ibid., pp. 384-7. Minutes, Cabinet War Committee, 228th, 231st, and 237th meetings, March 31, April 16, and May 19, 1943

70 Pickersgill, *Mackenzie King Record*, 1:436, 644. Stacey, *Mackenzie King and the Atlantic Triangle*, pp. 60-2, 67-8

71 Greater part of text, *Times* (London), January 25, 1944

72 Pickersgill, *Mackenzie King Record*, 1:636-41. MacDonald to Dominions Office, January 27, 1944, PRO, CAB 66/46

73 Eden to Halifax, February 10, 1944, PRO, FO 371/38553. Notes of press conference, January 27, 1944, PRO, DO 35-1204

74 Above, note 9

75 June 15, 1943, PRO, CAB 66/37

76 March 30, 1944, PRO, Air 8/97/1D3/2228B

77 C.P. Stacey, 'From Meighen to King: The Reversal of Canadian External Policies, 1921-1923,' *Transactions*, Royal Society of Canada, 1969

78 Stacey, *Arms, Men and Governments*, pp. 155-6. Photo, Nicholas Mansergh, *The Commonwealth Experience* (London 1969), fig. 68

79 The greater part of King's diary of the conference is in Pickersgill, *Mackenzie King Record*, 1:663-88.

80 Appendix I to PMM (44) 12th Meeting, PRO, Premier 4/42/5

81 Text, *Times*, May 12, 1944

82 Pickersgill, *Mackenzie King Record*, 1:686-7

83 Office Circular No 14, May 31, 1943, PRO, FO 371/50373

84 Massey, *What's Past is Prologue*, p. 302

85 Dispatch from P.J. Philip, *New York Times*, January 30, 1944

86 *Public Opinion Quarterly*, summer 1944

87 PMM (44) 7th Meeting, PRO, Premier 4/42/5

88 Enlistment figures from Appendix 'R,' *Arms, Men and Governments*, adapted by subtracting totals for NRMA (conscripts) from total intake

89 C.P. Stacey, *The Canadian Army, 1939-1945: An Offical Historical Summary* (Ottawa 1948), p. 309

90 *Public Opinion Quarterly*, spring 1945

CHAPTER 10: FACING A NEW ERA, 1945-48

1 *Gazette*, (Montreal), May 17, 1945 (extract in C.P. Stacey, ed., *The Arts of War and Peace* (Toronto 1972), pp. 121-2)

2 On 'The Old Leader,' see *Toronto Mail*, February 18, 1891 (motto hung at the Academy of Music, Toronto, for a Macdonald rally). Order-in-council PC 1341, January 26, 1924; Canadian Army Routine Order, January 22, 1944; Order-in-council PC 5888, September 5, 1945, Stacey, ed., *The Arts of War and Peace*, pp. 27-9

3 C.P. Stacey, *Arms, Men and Governments: The War Policies of Canada, 1939-1945* (Ottawa 1970), p. 37 (King Diary, PAC, May 24, 1940)

4 January 13, 1947: conveniently available in R.A. MacKay, ed., *Canadian Foreign Policy, 1945-1954: Selected Speeches and Documents* (Toronto 1971), pp. 388-99

5 James Eayrs, *In Defence of Canada*, Vol. 3: *Peacemaking and Deterrence* (Toronto 1972), pp. 142-7. Don Munton and Don Page, 'Planning in the East Block: the Post-Hostilities Problems Committees in Canada 1943-5,' *International Journal*, autumn 1977

6 'Post-War Canadian Defence Relationships with the United States: General Considerations,' n.d., External file 52-C(s). Cabinet War Committee minutes, February 28, 1945

7 Cabinet Conclusions, January 23, 1945 (PAC, RG 2, 16, Vol. 2). The Canadian Citizenship Act, 10 George VI, c. 15, June 27, 1946. *Debates*, House of Commons, April 2-May 16, 1946 (Martin speech, April 2). Robert A. Spencer, *Canada in World Affairs: From UN to NATO, 1946-1949* (Toronto 1959), pp. 374-9. Nicholas Mansergh, *Survey of British Commonwealth Affairs: Problems of Wartime Co-operation and Post-War Change, 1939-1952* (London 1958), pp. 382-7

8 *The Memoirs of Cordell Hull*, 2 vols. (New York 1948), 2, chapters 89 and 92. Eayrs, *Peacemaking and Deterrence*, pp. 137, 141-2. Volume 1 of this book, pp. 254, 269n. PMM (44), 9th Meeting, May 9, 1944, King Papers, PAC, J 4, vol. 322, F3407, *Full Record of Meetings and Memoranda*. PMM (44), 12th Meeting, May 11, 1944, Appendix I, ibid.

9 Eayrs, *Peacemaking and Deterrence*, pp. 151-7

10 The document is published in *External Affairs*, February 1965, and in MacKay, ed., *Canadian Foreign Policy 1945-1954*, pp. 7-10; the greater part of it is in Stacey, *The Arts of War and Peace*, pp. 536-8.

11 Winston S. Churchill, *The Second World War: Triumph and Tragedy* (Toronto 1953), pp. 354-8

12 Secretary of State External to Secretary of State Dominions, February 26, 1945, External file 7-V(s)-6, top secret docket

13 Wrong to Under Secretary of State External, March 26, 1945, External file 7-V(s)

14 Wrong's reports from London, April 1945, ibid., and 7-V(s)-7; Massey's long letter to Robertson, April 23, 1945, 7-V(s)-7

15 J.W. Pickersgill and D.F. Forster, *The Mackenzie King Record*, Vol. 2: *1944-45* (Toronto 1968), p. 378

16 Lester B. Pearson, *Mike: The Memoirs of the Right Honourable Lester B. Pearson*, 3 vols. (Toronto 1972-5), 1:273

17 Text of the Charter, *Canada, Treaty Series, 1945*, No 7. Extracts, Stacey, ed., *The Arts of War and Peace*, pp. 538-46

18 Under Secretary External (San Francisco) to Secretary of State, Ottawa (Read from Robertson), June 10, 1945, External file 7-V(s)-8 (top secret docket)

19 Secretary of State to Under Secretary (San Francisco), June 12, 1945, External file 7-V(s)

20 Under Secretary External (San Francisco) to Secretary of State, Ottawa, June 16, 1945, External file 7-V(s)-8

21 FRUS, 1945, 1:711-12, 727-9, 799-800, 806-7, 966. Pickersgill and Forster, *Mackenzie King Record*, 2:386-9. Under Secretary External (San Francisco) to Secretary of State, Ottawa, June 3, 1945, External file 7-V(s)-8. Eayrs, *Peacemaking and Deterrence*, pp. 159-61

22 Pearson, *Mike*, 1:246-9

23 Press release by Minister of Finance, July 26, 1945, External file 6000-F-40(2). The Bretton Woods Agreements Act, 9-10 George VI, c. 11, December 18, 1945. A.F.W. Plumptre, *Three Decades of Decision: Canada and the World Monetary System, 1944-75* (Toronto 1977)

24 F.H. Soward, *Canada in World Affairs: From Normandy to Paris, 1944-1946* (Toronto 1950), pp. 181-9; Spencer, *From UN to NATO*, pp. 178-81

25 *Annual Register*, 1945, p. 54

26 Cabinet Conclusions, August 29, 1945. *Debates*, House of Commons, September 27, 1945 (extract in MacKay, ed., *Canadian Foreign Policy 1945-1954*, p. 26). Eayrs, *Peacemaking and Deterrence*, pp. 174-6

27 Donald M. Page, ed., *Documents on Canadian External Relations*, Vol. 12: *1946* (Ottawa 1977) [DCER, 12], p. 112 (July 30, 1946)

28 Ibid., pp. 67-148. Soward, *From Normandy to Paris*, chapter 7. Spencer, *From UN to NATO*, pp. 14-20. Eayrs, *Peacemaking and Deterrence*, pp. 174-6. FRUS, 1946: Vol. 3 is *Proceedings of the Paris Conference*, Vol. 4 is *Documents* concerning it (see 3:288-9 for one Australian-Russian altercation, and 4:655-9 for details of amendments). Text of the four treaties signed by Canada in *Canada, Treaty Series, 1947*, Nos 4-7. *Debates*, House of Commons, June 30, 1947

29 *Debates*, House of Commons, January 30, 1947; printed in MacKay, ed., *Canadian Foreign Policy 1945-1954*, pp. 30-42. Eayrs, *Peacemaking and Deterrence*, pp. 195-6. Spencer, *From UN to NATO*, pp. 26-31

30 See Churchill, *Triumph and Tragedy*, Book Two, chapters 3, 6, 10, 15, 20

31 Ibid., particularly maps at pages 509, 607, 663. MacKay, ed., *Canadian Foreign Policy 1945-1954*, pp. 42-3. *Annual Register*, 1951, pp. 42, 356

32 MacKay, ed., *Canadian Foreign Policy 1945-1954*, pp. 276-86

33 *Report* of Secretary of State for External Affairs for 1942, p. 5. David R. Murray, ed., *Documents on Canadian External Relations*, Vol. 7: *1939-1941*, Part I (Ottawa 1974) [DCER, 7], pp. 22-45

34 Ibid., pp. 89-96. *Report* of Secretary of State for External Affairs for 1942, p. 5. Dana Wilgress, *Memoirs* (Toronto 1967), pp. 122-3

35 DCER, 7:45-89. *Report* of Secretary of State for External Affairs for 1941, p. 9

36 J.C.M. Ogelsby, *Gringos from the Far North: Essays in the History of Canadian-Latin American Relations, 1866-1968* (Toronto 1976), chapter 1.

37 Wilgress, *Memoirs*, pp. 116-21. David R. Murray, ed., *Documents on Canadian External Relations*, Vol. 8: *1939-1941*, Part II (Ottawa 1976), pp. 1032, 1035

38 Wilgress, *Memoirs*, pp. 117-21. *Report* of Secretary of State for External Affairs for 1941, pp. 12-13. Ogelsby, *Gringos*, pp. 24-5

39 Colonel Stanley W. Dziuban, *Military Relations between the United States and Canada, 1939-1945* (United States Army in World War II) (Washington 1959), p. 143. For a classic statement of Canadian opposition, see Massey's memorandum of July 23, 1930, in Vincent Massey, *What's Past is Prologue: The Memoirs of The Right Honourable Vincent Massey, C.H.* (Toronto 1963), pp. 165-6.

40 Ogelsby, *Gringos*, pp. 50-3. Dziuban, *Military Relations*, pp. 144-6. Nancy Harvison Hooker, ed., *The Moffat Papers: Selections from the Diplomatic Journals of Jay Pierrepont Moffat, 1919-1943* (Cambridge, Mass. 1956), p. 373. DCER, 7:1103-10 (including Reid and Keenleyside memos)

41 'Memorandum of Conversation, by the Chief of Protocol,' April 23, 1941, FRUS, 1947, 3:108-10. Spencer, *From UN to NATO*, pp. 330-5

42 Correspondence, DCER, 12:30-5. Table, ibid., p. xvii

43 J.W. Pickersgill and D.F. Forster, *The Mackenzie King Record*, Vol. 3: *1945-46* (Toronto 1970), chapter 2. *The Report of the Royal Commission Appointed to Investigate ... the Communication ... of Secret and Confidential Information to Agents of a Foreign Power* (Ottawa 1946). *People and Places: Random Reminiscences of the Rt. Hon. Malcolm MacDonald* (London 1969), pp. 182-200

44 DCER, 12:2058-60. Pickersgill and Forster, *Mackenzie King Record*, 3:144

45 Wilgress, *Memoirs*, pp. 147-9 (Wilgress' memory betrayed him on the precise terms of his amendment to article 71 of the draft treaty, article 82 of the final one; see Eayrs, *Peacemaking and Deterrence*, p. 182). Wilgress to Robertson, April 15, 1946, DCER, 12:2053-5

46 Eayrs, *Peacemaking and Deterrence*, p. 41. Spencer, *From UN to NATO*, pp. 416-17

47 PMM (44), 7th Meeting, Confidential Annex, King Papers, J 4, vol. 322, F3407

48 C.P. Stacey, *The Victory Campaign* (Ottawa 1960), p. 278n

49 *Public Opinion Quarterly*, spring 1946, p. 114

50 Eayrs, *Peacemaking and Deterrence*, pp. 84-6. This book (Introduction and chapter 1) is by far the best account available of the post-war forces.

51 *Report* of Department of National Defence for fiscal year ending March 31, 1950, Appendix 3

52 Cabinet Conclusions, November 14 and 15, 1946

53 J.W. Pickersgill and D.F. Forster, *The Mackenzie King Record*, Vol. 4: *1947-48* (Toronto 1970), p. 6

54 Eayrs, *Peacemaking and Deterrence*, pp. 92-3

55 Stacey, *Arms, Men and Governments*, pp. 76-8

56 Cabinet Conclusions, December 19, 1946

57 Personal recollection 58 DCER, 12:11-26 and chart of 'Representatives Abroad'

59 *Canada Year Book* [CYB], 1950, p. 1024

60 Ibid., 1948-9, p. 1089

61 The episode is strikingly described in Douglas LePan, *Bright Glass of Memory* (Toronto 1979), chapter 2. See documents in PRO, BT 11/2730 and BT 11/2765.

62 High Commissioner Ottawa (MacDonald) to Dominions Office, February 13, 1946, PRO, FO 371/53060

63 'Financial Relations with Canada,' August 30, 1946, PRO, DO 35/1220

64 CYB, 1950, p. 392

65 Cabinet Conclusions, February 13, 1946

66 Schedule to the United Kingdom Financial Agreement Act, 1946, 10 George VI, c. 12, May 28, 1946

67 Cabinet Conclusions, February 21 and 25, 1946

68 *Debates*, House of Commons, April 11, 12, 16; May 6 and 7, 1946. Holmes to Addison, Dominions Office, April 6, 1946, PRO, DO 35/1220. The Canadian record of the discussion with St. Laurent is somewhat different: see DCER, 12:1400-7. Pickersgill and Forster, *Mackenzie King Record*, 3:175.

69 DCER, 12:1235-60, particularly King to Attlee through British High Commissioner, May 10, 1946, pp. 1258-60

70 Description, Acting High Commissioner in Great Britain to Secretary of State External, June 3, 1946, ibid., pp. 1278-87

71 Ibid., pp. 1266-72 (Eighteenth Meeting, May 12, 1946)

72 C.P. Stacey, *A Very Double Life: The Private World of Mackenzie King* (Toronto 1976), pp. 212-14

73 PMM (48), 11th Meeting, October 20, 1948, Confidential Annex (King Papers, J 4, vol. 325, F3416)

74 PMM (48), 13th Meeting, October 21, 1948, ibid.

75 DCER, 12:1235-6 (March 23, 1946)

76 Ibid., pp. 1427-46. Pickersgill and Forster, *Mackenzie King Record*, 3:262-4. Cabinet Conclusions, June 20, 27, July 23, 1946

77 DCER, 12:1423-5, 1446-69

78 Robert Bothwell and John English, 'Canadian Trade Policy in the Age of American Dominance and British Decline, 1943-1947,' *Canadian Review of American Studies*, spring 1977. R.D. Cuff and J.L. Granatstein, *American Dollars – Canadian Prosperity: Canadian-American Economic Relations, 1945-1950* (Toronto 1978), pp. 54-63

79 Cuff and Granatstein, *American Dollars – Canadian Prosperity*, pp. 39-42, and chapter 4. Cf the same authors' 'Canada and the Marshall Plan, June-December 1947,' Canadian Historical Association, *Historical Papers*, 1977

80 CYB, 1948-9, pp. 873-7; ibid., 1978-9, pp. 738-45. MacKay, ed., *Canadian Foreign Policy 1945-1954*, pp. 79-83

81 See the various opinions quoted in Cuff and Granatstein, *American Dollars – Canadian Prosperity*, chapter 7

82 Pickersgill and Forster, *Mackenzie King Record*, 4:107-16

83 Journal of Permanent Joint Board on Defence, meetings of June 14-15, 1945, quoted in 'Memorandum for the Prime Minister,' June 18, 1945, External file 52-C(s)-1

84 'Note on General Henry's statements ... for use by Canadian Section ...' September 3, 1945, and PJBD Journal, September 4 and 5, 1945, King Papers, J 4, vol. 318. 'Memorandum for the Cabinet,' December 13, 1945, External file 52-C(s)
85 'Memorandum for the Cabinet,' December 13, 1945
86 It can be traced in DCER, 12:1598-1725.
87 Ibid., pp. 1598-1607
88 Ibid., pp. 1651-3 (version of October 21, 1946) and pp. 1617-27
89 Ibid., pp. 1638-40 (July 15, 1946)
90 Pickersgill and Forster, Mackenzie King Record, 3:360-4
91 DCER, 12:1663-6
92 Ibid., pp. 1670-2 (November 12, 1946)
93 Minutes, November 13, 1946, ibid., pp. 1673-7
94 Cabinet Conclusions, November 14 and 15, 1946; printed, DCER, 12: 1679-95. See also Eayrs, Peacemaking and Deterrence, pp. 341-4.
95 Aide-mémoire, 'United States Bases in Canada' [November 13, 1946], DCER, 12:1678-9
96 Canadian minutes of meeting, ibid., pp. 1712-20. Pearson report, December 23, 1946, ibid., pp. 1721-5. U.S. Minutes, FRUS, 1946, 5:68-75
97 DCER, 12:1541-76. FRUS, 1947, 3:135. Pickersgill and Forster, Mackenzie King Record, 4:25
98 Pickersgill and Forster, Mackenzie King Record, 4: pp. 24-5. FRUS, 1947, 3:104-5. New York Times, February 13, 1947
99 Eayrs, Peacemaking and Deterrence, pp. 301-5
100 Ibid., pp. 309-18. FRUS, 1948, 1:677-91
101 Eayrs, Peacemaking and Deterrence, pp. 274-95
102 DCER, 8:351-447. William R. Willoughby, The St. Lawrence Waterway: A Study in Politics and Diplomacy (Madison, Wis. 1961), chapters 13-14
103 Pickersgill and Forster, Mackenzie King Record, 3:3. Eayrs, Peacemaking and Deterrence, pp. 4-7
104 An Act to amend the Department of External Affairs Act, 10 George VI, c. 6, May 28, 1946. Pickersgill and Forster, Mackenzie King Record, 3:333-7. DCER, 12:4
105 Denis Stairs, The Diplomacy of Constraint: Canada, the Korean War, and the United States (Toronto 1974), pp. 5-8
106 Ibid., pp. 9-17. Pickersgill and Forster, Mackenzie King Record, 3:134-53. Eayrs, Peacemaking and Deterrence, p. 24
107 Pickersgill and Forster, Mackenzie King Record, 4:189-95. Annual Register, 1948, pp. 242-5, 270-1
108 Escott Reid, Time of Fear and Hope: The Making of the North Atlantic Treaty, 1947-1949 (Toronto 1977), pp. 30-48
109 Pickersgill and Forster, Mackenzie King Record, 4:176-7
110 Reid, Time of Fear and Hope, pp. 77-8. MacKay, ed., Canadian Foreign Policy 1945-1954, pp. 182-9. Spencer, From UN to NATO, pp. 268-70

111 Pickersgill and Forster, *Mackenzie King Record*, 4:192
112 Text of treaty, *Annual Register*, 1949, pp. 475-6, and in many other sources. Senate vote, ibid., p. 187. Spencer, *From UN to NATO*, pp. 268-70
113 Ibid., pp. 274-9. *Debates*, House of Commons, March 28 and April 29, 1949
114 Paul Bridle, ed., *Documents on Relations between Canada and Newfoundland*, Vol. 1: *1935-1949* (Ottawa 1974), pp. 211-15 (May 17, 1944)
115 Spencer, *From UN to NATO*, pp. 337-63
116 FRUS, 1947, 3:129-30
117 Pickersgill and Forster, *Mackenzie King Record*, 4:86-9
118 Ibid., pp. 260-1. Cuff and Granatstein, *American Dollars – Canadian Prosperity*, p. 70
119 Memo, Willoughby to Thorp, n.d., covered by Thorp to Lovett, March 8, 1948, FRUS, 1948, 9:406-9
120 Pickersgill and Forster, *Mackenzie King Record*, 4:261-8
121 Ibid., pp. 269-70. FRUS, 1948, 9:410-11
122 Memorandum of Conversation, by C. Tyler Wood, April 27, 1948, ibid., pp. 411-12
123 Pickersgill and Forster, *Mackenzie King Record*, 4:271-3. Robert Bothwell and William Kilbourn, *C.D. Howe: A Biography* (Toronto 1979), pp. 219-20
124 Douglas LePan, 'The Spare Deputy: Portrait of Norman Robertson,' *International Perspectives*, July/August 1978

EPILOGUE

1 See the photograph in Nicholas Mansergh, *The Commonwealth Experience* (London 1969), p. 99. See also fig. 113 (1964).
2 *Canada Year Book*, 1976-7, pp. 908-9, 913-16. Cf ibid., 1978-9, pp. 769-72
3 J.W. Pickersgill and D.F. Forster, *The Mackenzie King Record*, Vol. 3: *1945-46* (Toronto 1970), p. 219 (May 9, 1946)

INDEX

Abbott, Douglas C. 419-21, 424
Air Training Conference, 1942 325-6
Air training controversy, 1936 ff 220-4
Alaska Highway 155, 361-2
Amery, Leopold: King on 62; and King-Byng crisis 76; UK High Commission in Ottawa 95
'Arcadia' Conference 326, 329
Armour, Norman 171-4
Article 10 (League of Nations Covenant): Canadian campaign against it 56-9
Athenia, SS: sunk 261
Athlone, Lord 325n, 381
Atomic energy 375, 412-13
Attlee, Clement R. (later Earl) 319, 334, 365, 386, 403
Australia and direction of the war 317, 339

Baldwin, Stanley (later Earl): Chanak 21-2, 26; visit to Canada, and UK High Commission 95; advice to King on defence 200
Beaudry, Laurent 96
Bennett, R.B. (later Viscount): opposes Washington legation 91; as Prime Minister 122-3; tariff policy 127-8; at Imperial Conference, 1930 129-33; on Committee of Imperial Defence 132-3; clash with Snowden 137-8; Ottawa Conference 140-5; and League of Nations 159-63; at Geneva 166; visits to Washington 146, 169; Ethiopian crisis 180-2
Berlin airlift 415-16
Bessborough, Lord 142
'Billion dollar gift' 332, 357
Borden, Sir Robert: protest about Locarno 83
Bourassa, Henri: on Chanak 28; advice to King 80
Bracken, John 381n
Breadner, R.W. 143
Bren gun 'scandal' 220
Bretton Woods Conference 385-6
British Army: Canadian relations with 347-54
British Commonwealth Air Training Plan 292-5
British people: Canadian relations with 347
Brooke, General Sir Alan (later Field-Marshal Lord Alanbrooke) 350
Bulgaria: no declaration of war on 320
Byng, Lord: private messages to London 39-41, 54; Halibut Treaty 51-4; advice to King 74; crisis with King 75-7

Cahan, C.H.: on the Commonwealth 119; speech on Manchuria 162

Canadian Citizenship Act, 1946 378
Canadian Forum 232
Canadian Institute of International Affairs 165-6
Canadian Joint Staff, Washington 360
Canadian Joint Staff Mission, London 336-7
'Canol' 362
Chamberlain, Sir Austen 62, 65; Locarno 78; on 'Commonwealth' 88
Chamberlain, Neville, Prime Minister 204; appeasement 213-14; new policy of containment 239; warning to Hitler, August 1939 251; proposes Commonwealth Air Training Plan 274; fall from power 296-7; King's regard for 208, 298
Chanak Affair 17-27
Chicago water diversion 48-9
Christie, Loring C.: and King 6-8, 27; change of views 82; Rush-Bagot Agreement 33; return to External, and Ethiopian crisis 181; Imperial Conference, 1937 203n and 206n; Minister in Washington, and re Greenland 308; death 323
Church, T.L. 103, 262, 264
Churchill, Winston: and Chanak 18-27; Prime Minister 284; and Ogdensburg meeting 312; and Imperial War Cabinet 318; Dominions and secrets 319; relationship with King 324-6; failure to consult Dominions 328
Clark, Clifford 316, 331; reciprocity 420-4
Clark, Sir William 95
Claxton, Brooke 387; Defence Minister 397
Combined Boards (civilian) 327, 330-2
Combined Chiefs of Staff 326; Canada not told about it 327
Committee of Imperial Defence 132-3
Conferences, strategic 333-4

Coolidge, President Calvin: and Canada 104
Co-operative Commonwealth Federation 167, 374
Crerar, General H.D.G. 352-3
Crowe, Sir Eyre 36, 70, 78, 82
Currie, General Sir Arthur 44-5
Curzon, Lord: and Chanak 20; Lausanne Conference 35 ff; no time for Empire delegation 36; Imperial Conference of 1923 67-71
Cushendun, Lord 92

Dafoe, John W. 163; offers from King 168; on King at Geneva 186; classification of Canadian opinion, 1937 233-4
Dandurand, Senator Raoul: at Geneva 60; 'fire-proof house' 61; President of League Assembly 64
Defence policy, 1922 17; 1936 ff 199-202; acceleration of rearmament 219-20; after the war 395-8; defence of North America 406-12
Defence schemes 155 ff
Deference, Canadian, to British ministers 344-5
De Gaulle, General Charles 300, 302, 304, 306
Depression 128-9, Chap. Four passim.; international consequences 158-9; election of 1935 167
Deutsch, John 419-25
Devonshire, Duke of 36
Diefenbaker, John 381n
Dieppe raid 345; shackling incident 342, 342n, 348
Direction of the war: Canada and 275-6; suggestions by Pearson and Vanier 282-3; meeting of Dominion representatives in London, 1939 285-7; abortive suggestion re liaison with Supreme Commanders 336-7; King on the actual position 337-8
Dollar crisis, 1947 404-5
Dumbarton Oaks meeting 379-80
Dunkirk crisis: effect in Canada 296-9

Dupuy, Pierre: visits to France 301-2

Edward VIII, King 202-3
Eisenhower, General Dwight D.:
   Sicily 340-1, 349n
Elections: 1921 3-4; 1925 73-4;
   1926 76-7; 1930 119-21; 1935
   167; 1940 280; 1945 374
Elizabeth, Queen, consort of George
   VI 243-6, 262
Emile Bertin incident 300
Enlistments, by provinces 371
Ethiopian War 179 ff; divisions in
   Canada 185-6; in King's cabinet
   188-90
Euler, W.D. 193; in crisis of 1939
   255, 256
Evatt, Herbert 382, 389
Ewart, John S., and King 13-14, 40,
   42, 61; King on 'staunch Canadian-
   ism' 80; death 166
External Affairs, Department of:
   expansion 95-7; professionals come
   into their own 377; Prime Minister
   no longer Secretary of State 414

Falconer, Sir Robert 185, 187
Ferguson, G. Howard: on Seaway 112;
   High Commissioner in UK 125; on
   Statute of Westminster 131; resig-
   nation as High Commissioner 168;
   part in Ethiopian crisis 180-2
Fielding, W.S.: Chanak 29; opposition
   to representation in Washington
   44; at Geneva, 1922 57; on the
   tariff (1902) 136
Finnish War, 1939-40 279-82;
   Canada declares war on Finland
   320
First World War: economic effects
   14-16
Fordney-McCumber Tariff 45
Foster, Sir George: at Geneva 82; on
   'Commonwealth' 88
France: wartime relations with 299 ff;
   representation in 90
French Canada and the Second World
   War 372; and international organi-
   zation 373

'Functional' principle 332-3

Gallup poll 267
General Agreement on Tariffs and
   Trade 405, 419
General Motors 16
Geneva Protocol 60-4
George VI, King 203; visit to North
   America 243-8; speech to the
   Commonwealth, September 1939
   252-3; declarations of war 263,
   306, 322
Germany: lack of peace settlement
   with 340
Gouzenko affair 394-5
Greenland question 308-9
Greenwood, Lord 18, 21
Grey, Viscount, of Fallodon 81

Halibut Treaty 49-56
Halifax, Lord, 238n; accepts risk of
   war 240; speech in Toronto 364-5,
   367, 369
Hankey, Sir Maurice (later Lord):
   Chanak 21, 27; in Canada 165-6
Harding, President Warren G.: visit
   to Canada, 1923 16
Harper, Bert 278
Harris, Sir Arthur: hostility to 'For-
   eign and Dominion' elements in
   RAF 296n
Hawley-Smoot Tariff 113, 126-8
Hazen, Sir Douglas: fishery treaties 50
Herridge, William Duncan: career
   125; Imperial Conference, 1930
   129, 132; Minister to Washington
   147; advice to Bennett re 'New
   Deal' 167; and proposed trade
   treaty with US 170-2; resignation
   168; advice to Bennett re declaration against overseas conscription
   190
Hickerson, J.D.: reciprocity 171; San
   Francisco 384
High Commission, UK, in Ottawa
   94-5; other high commissioners
   appointed 284-5
Hitler, Adolf: seizure of power 159;
   receives King 209-13; destroys

Czechoslovakia 239; King's final approaches to 248-50
Hoare-Laval plan 186
Hoover, President Herbert 104; Seaway 110, 113; Hawley-Smoot Tariff 113, 126, 127
Hopkins, Harry: on tariff negotiations ('all baby stuff'), 171; Munitions Assignment Board 330
Howe, C.D. 316-17, 330, 331, 345; atomic energy 412; reciprocity 423-4
Hull, Cordell 152, 170, 174, 260; St Pierre and Miquelon 302-6
Hungary: Canada declares war on 320
Hyde Park Declaration 315-17

I'm Alone case 104-7
Imperial Conferences: 1923 66-72; 1926 83-9; 81-2; 1930 129-33; Ottawa, 1932 140-5; 1937 202-9
Industry and finance, war 356-60; war production 356-7; 'billion dollar gift' 357; 'Mutual Aid' 357-8; French-Canadian opposition 357-8
International Civil Aviation Conference 386
Isolationism in 1930s 231-6
Italy: declaration of war on 306

Japan: representation in 90; trade war with 191-2; declaration of war on 320-2; peace settlement with 391
Jewish refugees 197-8
Josephine K. 149

Keenleyside, H.L.: visits to Washington 309-310; Latin America 393
Kellogg Peace Pact 97-103
Keynes, J.M. (later Lord) 324, 399
King, W.L. Mackenzie: becomes Prime Minister 3; and parties 4-5; personal life 5-6; 'military fads' 17; Chanak 17-27; visit to Washington, 1922 31-3; and Lausanne Conference 36-44; Halibut Treaty 50-6; Geneva Protocol 61-4; on Canadian membership on League Council 65-6; Imperial Conference of

1923 66-72; on Canada and a great war 72, 81, 235; to Paris and Geneva, 1928 100-1; and US trade treaty, 1935 173-4; first visit to Roosevelt 174; view of the US 177-9; his *séances* 178-9; Ethiopian crisis 184-9; speech at Geneva, 1936 186, 195; 'no commitments' and 'Parliament will decide' 195-6; advice from the spirits 200; and speeches in French 202n; at Imperial Conference, 1937 203-9; visit to Hitler 209-13; relationship with Roosevelt 230; concerns as war approached 237-9; worried by approach to Russia 241; and royal tour 244-8; dealings with Hitler, 1939 248-50, 258-60; and outbreak of war 253-63; war speech 262; unity in 1939 his greatest achievement 262-3; reasons for Canada going to war 266; attitude to peace proposals 276-8; changing attitude towards Churchill 298; Dunkirk crisis 299; visit to Roosevelt at Warm Springs 307-9; relationship with Roosevelt and Churchill examined 324-6; unwillingness to protest about Canadian exclusion from direction of war 328-30, 334; functional principle 333; attitude on strategy 338-9; complaint re announcement of Canadians in Sicily 340-4; deference to Montgomery 353-4; suspicions of US intentions 363; reactions to Halifax speech 364-5, 367; at Prime Ministers' Conference, 1944 364-7; Paris conference, 1946 387; tour of Normandy 387-9; continued hostility to military preparation 396-7; in London, 1948 403; Korea crisis, 1947 414-15; rejects reciprocity 419-25; comment on his career 425-6
Korea: cabinet crisis, 1947 414-15

Lapointe, Ernest: Chanak 29; liquor treaty 47; Halibut Treaty 51-3;

Geneva Protocol 60n; Imperial Conference of 1926 81, 83; Conference on Operation of Dominion Legislation 113-18; on the Commonwealth 119; League of Nations Society 166; desire for External portfolio 168; on Ethiopian crisis 180, 184-5; rejects neutrality, 1939 243; hero of the war debate 262; on de Gaulle 302

Latin America, representation in 392-3

Lausanne Conference question, 1922 35 ff; treaty 39

League of Nations: Canada on Council 65-6; Manchurian crisis 161-3; Ethiopian crisis 179 ff; mortal blow 186; see also Article 10

League of Nations Society 165-6

Leckie, Air Marshal Robert 293, 409

Leith-Ross, Sir Frederick 331

Lloyd George, David (later Earl): Chanak 17-27; fall of government 26; criticism of Lausanne arrangements 43; signature of treaties 34

Locarno Treaties 77-83

MacDonald, J. Ramsay: and Lausanne 39-41

Macdonald, Sir John A. 28, 374-5

MacDonald, Malcolm: UK High Commissioner in Ottawa 319; criticizes British attitude towards Canada 327-8; urges King to assert himself 334; and the Sicily crisis 341-4; US operations in the North-West 362

McKinnon, Hector 143; reciprocity proposal, 1947-8 419-21

MacKinnon, James 392

McNaughton, General A.G.L. 129, 157, 291, 336; and relations with British Army 349-53; right and government wrong 352

Macphail, Agnes 103

McRae, Brig.-Gen. A.D. 164-5

McSwain, Representative John J.: Roosevelt letter to 154

Mahoney, Merchant 96

Manion, R.J.: at Geneva 166; Jewish refugees 198; urges commitment against overseas conscription 242-3; separate declaration of war 264

Marler, Sir Herbert 91, 125

Martin, Paul 378

Massey, Vincent 83-5; Minister to Washington 89-90, 103-6; Bennett refuses him London appointment 124-5; appointed to London 168; and Air Training Plan 274; declarations of war 263, 306

Meighen, Arthur: election, 1921 3-4, 45-6; Chanak ('Ready, aye ready') 30; Hamilton speech 74-5; election of 1925 73-4; of 1926 76-7; in Senate 164; air training question 223; on separate declaration of war 264; consequences of British and French defeat 269

'Middle' power: difficult position of 338

Military questions with US under Bennett 154-5; after the war 406-12

Military relationship with Britain 287-96

Moffat, J.P. 304-5

Montgomery, Field-Marshal Viscount 353-4

Motherwell, W.R. 37

Munich crisis 213-19

Munitions Assignment Board 326, 327, 330

Muselier, Vice-Admiral E.-H. 304-5

Mussolini, Benito 179

National Defence Act, 1922 17

National flag 140, 375, 425-6

Naval Defence Act, 1910 4

Neutrality Act, US 205n, 260, 307

New Zealand 68-9; exchange of high commissioners 285

Newfoundland: and Kellogg Pact 102n; boundary dispute 121; at conferences 134n; and Statute of Westminster 134; Canadian-US military relations 360-1; Confederation with 418-19

North Atlantic Treaty 416-18

Ogdensburg meeting 179, 311-12
Optional Clause 64

Pan-American Union: proposals to
join 393-4
Paris Peace Conference, 1946
387-9
Patteson, Joan (Mrs Godfroy B.) 5-6,
178; and Hitler 249, 258
Pearson, Lester Bowles: joins External
96; memo re League of Nations
166; Ethiopia 180; Imperial Con-
ference, 1937 203n; story about
declaration of war 263n; on Canada
and direction of war 282-3; on
King 325; Hot Springs Conference
385
Permanent Joint Board on Defence:
set up and early operations 312-14;
post-war 406-12
Pershing, General John J. 309
Phillips, William 91, 95
Pickersgill, J.W. 236, 249, 423
Poincaré, Raymond: and Lausanne
Conference 35, 43
Poland: British guarantee to 239;
German attack on 252
Pope, Sir Joseph 6, 27, 32; on Treaty
of Mutual Assistance 60n; retire-
ment 9
Pope, Major-General Maurice: role in
Washington 336
Post-Hostilities Problems, committees
on 377-8
Power, C.G. 164, 201, 216, 254
Prime Ministers' Conference, 1944
365-7; 1946 402; 1948 403
Prohibition problems 46-8, 104-7;
end of Prohibition 150

Quebec Conferences 334; first, Roosevelt vetoes Churchill suggestion re
Canadian participation 334; King
unwilling to protest 334

Radio broadcasting 178n
Ralston, Colonel J.L. 350-2
Read, John E. 9n; joins External 97;
on Bennett 124; story about King
and Finland 281

Reid, Escott 166, 393, 416
Representation abroad, increased 89
ff, 265n, 392, 394
Rhineland occupation 196, 198
Riddell, Walter A. 64; and Cahan
speech 162; Ethiopian crisis 180-8;
comment 188
Rinfret, Fernand 216, 218n
Ristelhueber, René 300-1
Robertson, Norman Alexander: joins
External 96; trade negotiations,
1935 171; on Free French 302;
succeeds Skelton 322-3; urges King
to assert himself 334; suggestion re
liaison with Supreme Commanders
336-7; at San Francisco 382
Rogers, Norman 236; overseas visit,
1940 282-4
Romania: Canada declares war on 320
Roosevelt, President Franklin D. 148;
Bennett visits 169; and trade nego-
tiations, 1935 172-4; state visit to
Quebec 224, 231; 'not stand idly
by' 225; relationship with Canada
230-1; and royal tour, 1939 244;
wartime relations with King
307-17, 360-3
Rowell, N.W. 94, 185
Roy, Philippe 90, 92
Royal Canadian Air Force: relations
with RAF 354-5
Royal Canadian Navy: relations with
RN 355-6
Runciman, Walter 140, 142-3
Rush-Bagot Agreement 27, 32-4, 54

St Laurent, Louis S. 345; Gray Lec-
ture 376; takes over External 414;
Korean crisis 414-15; North Atlan-
tic Treaty 417
St Lawrence Seaway 107-13; treaty,
1932 145-9; later history 413
St Pierre and Miquelon question
302-6
San Francisco Conference, 1945
381-5
Scott, F.R. 232, 236, 261n
Second World War, Chapters Seven-
Nine, passim. Outbreak 253 ff;
Why Canada went to war 264-9;

government war programme 273;
Canada's war effort 370
Senate, U.S.: and treaties 50, 55, 148,
148n
Sicily invasion: announcement of
Canadian participation 339-44
Sifton, Sir Clifford: advice to King
14, 28; speech April 1922 17-18;
Chanak 29; death 166
Six Nations Indians: at Geneva 58
Skelton, Oscar Douglas: career 8; joins
External 8-9; relationship with
King 9-13; Imperial Conference of
1923 66-72; expansion of External
96-7; Conference on Operation of
Dominion Legislation 113-18; rela-
tions with Bennett 123-4; Bennett
on 124; and Quebec 167; scuffle
with Bennett over Ethiopia 124,
181-2; Imperial Conference, 1937
203n; tension with King 235-6;
comment on Nazi-Soviet pact
250-1; Canadian reasons for going
to war 264, 266; his sketch of a war
effort 257, 272; and Air Training
Plan 296; changing views, 1940
299, 376; death 322
Smuts, Field-Marshal Jan C.: on
Locarno 83; at San Francisco 382
Snowden, Philip 136, 137
Soviet Russia: R.B. Bennett's dislike
of Russian trade practices 143-4;
trade war with Russia 193; Russia
admitted to League 166; expelled
279; German attack on 319; King's
suspicions of 370; tension with
415-16
Spanish Civil War 196-7
Statute of Westminster: origin 118;
discussions, 1930 129-32; enactment and significance 133-5

Stettinius, Edward R. 382, 384
Stuart, Lt.-Gen. Kenneth 350, 351

Tariff Board 143
Trade: post-1945 404-5, 428
Trade treaty with U.S., 1935 174-8;
agreements with U.S. and Britain,
1938 229
Trail Smelter case 150-4
Treaties, procedure in signing: King
suggestion re Rush-Bagot 34; Con-
ference, 1923 69
Truman, President Harry S. 386

Underhill, F.H. 232, 236, 261n
United Nations: origins 378-81;
Charter 382-5
United Nations Relief and Rehabili-
tation Administration 331-2

Vanier, Georges 283; withdrawal
from France 301; signs treaties 389;
minister to governments in exile
392
Visiting Forces (British Commonwealth) Acts, 1933-9 289-91, 348

Weir, J.G.: mission to Canada, 1938
221-2, 224
Wilgress, Dana 96n; trade negotiations in Washington, 1935 171
Willingdon, Lord 91; visit to
Washington 103-4
Woodsworth, J.S. 103, 195; outbreak
of war 261
Wrong, Humphrey Hume: joins
External 96; on Kellogg Pact 100;
at Geneva 264; Canadian reasons
for going to war 264-5; urges getting Canadians into action 350;
reciprocity 423-4